To Arch bishop
Weakla
with my
best wishes to you in
all you do!

Dm Pienkos

AEQUALIS OMNIBUS CARITAS

ARCHBISHOP
REMBERT G. WEAKLAND

PNA: A CENTENNIAL HISTORY OF
THE POLISH NATIONAL ALLIANCE OF THE
UNITED STATES OF NORTH AMERICA

DONALD E. PIENKOS

EAST EUROPEAN MONOGRAPHS, BOULDER
DISTRIBUTED BY COLUMBIA UNIVERSITY PRESS, NEW YORK

1984

EAST EUROPEAN MONOGRAPHS, NO. CLXVIII

Copyright © 1984 by Donald E. Pienkos
Library of Congress Card Catalog Number 84-80619
ISBN 0-88033-060-0

Printed in the United States of America

To John, Thomas, Paul and Mark

CONTENTS

PART III

Appendices

INTRODUCTION

This centennial history of the Polish National Alliance of the United States of North America (the PNA as it is usually known) is the product of several years of research. It is offered to readers so that PNA members and non-members alike may gain a better understanding of the Alliance's aims and the record of its activities since its founding in 1880. Today, with nearly 300,000 insured members and assets approaching $180 million, the Polish National Alliance is the eighth largest fraternal insurance association in the United States, the largest ethnically-based fraternal and the largest of the numerous fraternals serving Polish Americans.[1] How the PNA grew to such proportions from a tiny patriotic group of no more than a few dozen men and women and what its members accomplished over the years to merit mass support from within the Polish American population is certainly a story worth telling, especially on the occasion of its centennial.

But the PNA has always been more than an organization selling life insurance, important and socially beneficial as this activity is. The Alliance has also served as a mass movement uniting people behind a variety of causes in support of the economic, cultural and political advancement of Polish Americans, the preservation of ethnic consciousness and pride in their heritage among successive generations of Americans of Polish descent, and the realization of a free and independent Poland, today the ancestral homeland of twelve million Americans. If this work generates greater understanding of the PNA and leads individuals to become involved in its activities, I will have accomplished a good deal.

In point of fact, this is the fifth commissioned PNA history, although the first to appear in the English language. Earlier historians documented the origins and development of the Alliance and provided their readers with an insight into the workings of the fraternal of their day and a look at its leading personalities and major attainments. These works remain of value and interest and I have relied heavily upon them in developing my own approach to the movement. But the last substantial PNA history came out between 1957 and 1963 (and it covered only the period from 1905 to 1949); ensuing events, both in and outside the organization, made it highly appropriate that another study be published, not only to bring things up to date but also to reconsider the movement in light of changing conditions over the years.[2] To its credit the PNA, at its conventions in 1975 and 1979, authorized such a study to coincide with its other centennial commemorative celebrations. Further, the executive leadership of the Alliance determined that such a history be written in an objective and scholarly fashion and the author be permitted complete freedom to approach his task in the manner in which he believed to be most fitting. It was clearly their intention that the centennial history be taken seriously by its readers while providing them with a full picture of the organization. I hope this work merits the trust which was bestowed upon me.

My actual research began in February, 1980 and continued through the centennial year and into late 1983. Given this consideration, I decided to include into my study pertinent information for the years beyond the PNA centennial in order to provide readers with a picture of the fraternal that included significant developments affecting the Alliance in the last three years. In a real sense then, this work constitutes a history of the first 103 years of the Polish National Alliance, a history which has traditionally been characterized by a strong commitment of service to Poland, the United States and the Polish ethnic community in America.

While the intended audience for this study is primarily the members of the Alliance, I also offer this work to the growing number of scholarly students of American immigration and ethnic history in the hope that they too will benefit from its appearance. Since the early 1960s there has been a noteworthy surge in research into this entire field, one including a growing interest in the history of Polish immigration and settlement in the U.S. Unfortunately, scholarship on the Polish experience has neglected the history and development of the fraternal movement, despite its great impact upon the formation and cohesion of the ethnic population through the past century and the fact that vast numbers of people both took part in its activities and benefitted from its programs. Numerous monographs and scholarly articles on the Polish American past have appeared in recent years, but surprisingly few have focused upon the fraternals. Yet taken together, the fraternals have constituted the Polish community's most significant and durable mass membership associations in America. Formed essentially for national and social (as distinguished from religious) purposes, the fraternals have served as the engines driving the Polish ethnic population in its organized community activities, particularly during the past seventy-five years.

Scholarly neglect of the Polish fraternal movement is unfortunate for yet a second reason, one having to do with the leadership question in the Polish ethnic community. While it is true that clergymen and journalists played the major leadership roles within the immigrant population during its earliest years, it has been the fraternals that have produced the spokesmen of the organized ethnic community, or "Polonia," since the beginning of the twentieth century. To neglect the contributions of fraternal activists and their organizations, for whatever reasons, is to provide contemporary readers with an incomplete and thus inaccurate picture of Polonia's history.[3] Similarly no adequate description of present day strengths and weaknesses within the Polish ethnic community can proceed far, unless one appreciates the role of the fraternals in American Polonia. Perhaps there is no better place to begin to remedy these inadequacies than with the Polish National Alliance, whose members have been in the forefront of every cause animating the ethnic community for more than a century. (Indeed, even when the PNA experienced internal rifts which spawned other fraternals in Polonia, its influence remained significant. Hence a look at the constitutions of such organizations as the Polish Union of America, the Polish National Union, the Polish Falcons' Alliance, the Polish Women's Alliance, among others, demonstrates that despite their differences, each of these movements remained pledged to the same progressive goals maintained by the PNA.)

Given its size and financial condition plus its record of past achievement, one is led to ask how to explain the success enjoyed by the Polish National Alliance in its many areas of activity. In fact, I did ask a number of individuals whom I interviewed about this point; their most frequent reply emphasized the idea that the PNA traditionally tended to attract into its midst the "best" people in the Polish ethnic community. They recalled, for example, that the founders of the Alliance were nearly all educated men and many were successful businessmen in an era when the overwhelming majority of Polish immigrants were poorly educated at best and usually employed as unskilled laborers. Later on, as more Poles became better educated, the PNA continued to attract disproportionately large numbers of community activists into its ranks. In the opinion of many with whom I spoke, it was in the quality of its leadership that one found the best explanation for the PNA's consistent record of progressive and enlightened ethnic activity through the years, whether such activity focused upon patriotic work, educational and cultural matters, or the formation of a series of all-Polonia organizations culminating in the Polish American Congress and dedicated to the unification of the

Polish American population. One elderly past PNA leader put it bluntly when he told me, "We always had the very best people in our lodges and not only were they the best educated people either. We had the leaders, not the followers, and no one was about to tell us what to do, even the priests." Another PNA veteran emphasized the point that "PNA members were practically all deeply religious and devoted Catholics. But they were also thinking people. If a priest told them something on a religious matter that was one thing. But if he interfered in Alliance matters, they were willing to disagree and to stand firm."

But on second thought, explaining the PNA's success in terms of its leaders only seems to beg the question. Why would "quality" individuals become attracted to the organization in the first place, unless the Alliance possessed certain characteristics which made its activities worthwhile and important.?

A better answer may be found in reviewing the principles of the PNA itself and the organizational character of the fraternal. Ideologically, the Alliance espoused a set of aims that could hardly help but engender enthusiastic support. These mixed an idealistic commitment to Poland's rebirth and the cultural enlightenment of the immigrant with one's economic survival and advancement in America through participation in a fraternal insurance program. But added to its aims was another ingredient that proved crucial to the ultimate success of the Polish National Alliance, its democratic organizational structure.

From the very outset, the PNA was a public (not secret) organization open to every Polish immigrant, whether he was Catholic or not. Its leaders proudly affirmed the ideals of the Polish Constitution of May 3, 1791 and reached out to all whose ancestors had been members of the old Polish pre-partition state that had gone out of existence in 1795. This state had included Jews, Lithuanians and Ruthenians (or Ukrainians) and its historic constitution had embraced religious tolerance as the fundamental law of the land. In politics too, the PNA attempted to remain open to all; by 1895 its members, after years of debate, concluded that anyone, regardless of his political views, could belong to the fraternal, so long as he accepted its objectives. This formula excluded only anarchists committed to violence. In 1900, full membership rights were also extended to women, a decision which largely completed the process in which the fraternal was transformed into an open arena where all could compete to realize their vision for Polonia.

But not only was the PNA largely able to avoid the pitfalls of sectarianism, it also succeeded thanks to its continuing commitment to representative and democratic methods of self-governance and decision making. Every level of PNA organizational life was organized along democratic lines and the national structure of the fraternal was created in conscious imitation of the American federal system and the Polish constitution of 1791.

Given these considerations, there existed a strong impulse among those who belonged to the PNA to participate actively in the movement and to recruit into its ranks others who shared their views. As the Alliance came to be perceived as Polonia's most effective mass patriotic movement, this impulse was even further reinforced.

In the following pages, one will find the names of hundreds of individuals who made notable contributions to Polonia as members of the PNA. But, while I have attempted to include a wide variety of activists into this work, I am very well aware that there will be readers who will fault my failure to include still other individuals who in their opinion contributed significantly to the movement. To them let me say that a complete listing of everyone who served in some responsible fashion within the Alliance over the years would require a work of several hundred additional pages. In this connection, it would be well to recall that during its first one hundred and three years of service, the PNA enrolled more than 1.2 million people into its ranks. Were one to simply construct an appendix listing every individual who served as a lodge president during this period, one would come up with more than 40,000 names, with nearly as many on a second list of lodge financial secretaries. Perhaps as many as 3,000 men and women have held the office of president of a PNA council during the past seventy-five years. And, more than 3,500 people have at one time or other been elected a delegate to a national convention of the Alliance. Given these figures, I trust that readers will accept my apologies for having failed to include someone who merited mention. At the same time, I hope that they will regard as accurate my description of PNA goals and activities over the years. If this be the case, my work will constitute its own recognition of all those who dedicated themselves to the causes of the PNA between 1880 and 1983.[4]

All serious writing efforts depend upon the help and encouragement of many people and this work is certainly no exception. Many individuals connected with the PNA provided me with assistance and advice during my frequent visits to its Chicago home office and I would like to take this opportunity to thank them for their consideration. In particular I want to recognize the support, direction and counsel given me by PNA President Aloysius A. Mazewski, along with the many contributions made along the way by Mr. Joseph Wiewiora, Editor of *Zgoda,* and Dr. Edward Rozanski, Manager of Alliance Printers and Publishers and acting co-editor of *Zgoda* during Mr. Wiewiora's illness. While I take responsibility for any inaccuracies that appear in this book, all of these individuals fully deserve praise for their contributions to my telling the PNA story anew.

I cannot adequately express my appreciation to my wife, Angela, for all she has contributed to this project. Not only did she read and reread successive drafts of the manuscript and do her best to correct and improve my prose, she also was of invaluable help in commenting upon the themes I developed in interpreting the history of the Alliance and prodding me to think over my approach to my subject. All this in addition to managing a household including one husband and four other growing boys as well as achieving success and esteem in her professional work.

Mrs. Lois Kohlmetz and Ms. Wanda Wimes performed yeoman service in patiently deciphering my handwriting and cheerfully typing and retyping the manuscript on so many occasions. And last of all I'd like to thank my colleagues in the Political Science Department of the University of Wisconsin-Milwaukee for all the times they shared their knowledge so freely on topics about which I was unfamiliar. One can only feel a great sense of pride in being a member of such a faculty body.

A Note on Names

In a work of this type, a problem one must face deals with identifying individuals by their Polish or English language proper names. A great many of the people who appear in this history were born in Poland yet contributed greatly to the PNA and American Polonia and are frequently identified in printed sources by their English language proper names but at other times by their Polish equivalents. Even many American-born Polonians are often called by their Polish proper names, which can be a cause of inconsistency, and even confusion, for readers. To deal with this matter I have adopted what I hope will be a sensible approach to all proper names included in this study.

All Poles, that is, all individuals whose lives were spent primarily in Europe and not as participants in the Polish American community, are always referred to by their given Polish proper names. Thus, it is King Jan Sobieski who triumphed over the Turks at Vienna and Tadeusz Kosciuszko and Kazimierz Pulaski who fought for Poland's and America's freedom.

Individuals, whether born in Europe or America, whose public activities dealt primarily with PNA and Polonia matters, are provided with English language proper names whenever it is possible. Thus, references are always made to John Smulski, Julius Andrzejkowicz, Casimir Sypniewski, and so forth. Exceptions to this general rule do creep in whenever this author was unable to find an acceptable English language proper name to replace a Polish American's first name, e.g., Czeslawa, Wladyslaw or Wlodzimierz. A number of presently active PNA members also use their Polish surnames and in these cases I have tried to respect their preferences rather than to rename them simply for the sake of consistency.

I have also shortened a few proper names such as Val (for Walenty or Valentine) and Frank (for Franciszek or Francis) in the belief that these better convey the actual ethnic flavor of an individual's background while remaining easy to pronounce. Finally, there is the case of the name Stanislaw. I used "Stanislaw" for all Polish personalities, "Stanislas" for all Polonia activists involved in the community before 1939, and "Stanley" after 1939, the year the first American-born Polonian was elected president of the Alliance.

Though I do understand that this convention is hardly flawless, I hope that it does provide readers with a sense of the ethnic character of the people whose lives have been connected with the Alliance through the years while permitting readers unfamiliar with the Polish language a better opportunity to appreciate their contributions without stumbling too heavily over their proper names.

A NOTE ON SOURCES

In performing the research necessary for this study I was fortunate to have the opportunity to consult a wide array of sources containing information useful in describing and interpreting the history and development of the Polish National Alliance. A word about the most significant of these materials seems particularly appropriate at the beginning of my study, since it is my hope that future students of American Polonia will expand upon the work begun here in giving attention to specific aspects and periods of PNA history. For them to do so, it is imperative that they have a good knowledge of those sources which happen to be of greatest significance in the study of the Polish National Alliance. At the end of this work I have also included a more complete list of the printed materials used in researching this book.

The most valuable sources I found fall into five general categories; earlier published histories of the Alliance, other PNA publications, internal printed materials of the Alliance, interviews with PNA activists, and a variety of published and unpublished studies on American Polonia, Poland and the United States covering topics connected with PNA development.

Of particular interest to anyone seeking to gain an understanding of the early years of PNA history have been the earlier studies which the Alliance itself authorized at various intervals over the years. The first of these was Stefan Barszczewski's 1894 history, a short but informative chronological account of the founding of the Alliance published as part of the PNA's centennial observance of the Kosciuszko uprising. Emphasizing actions taken at the PNA's national conventions, Barszczewski's work set the standard for most of the later histories of not only the Alliance but other Polonia fraternals as well. Titled *Zwiazek Narodowy Polski w Stanach Zjednoczonych Ameryki Polnocnej: Jego Rozwoj, Dzialalnosc i Stan Obecny,* it was reprinted in 1980 by the PNA Educational Department as part of the Alliance's 100th anniversary celebration.[1]

In 1905, Stanislas Osada published a much larger and more detailed official PNA history, a study that was reprinted in 1957. In general format, Osada followed Barszczewski's approach fairly consistently although his study provides far more information and evaluation of the personalities who shaped the organization than the first Alliance history. Titled *Historia Zwiazku Narodowego Polskiego i Rozwoj Ruchu Narodowego Polskiego w Ameryce,*[2] the 1957 edition includes a large number of photographs of early PNA leaders and like Barszczewski's history provides a wealth of interesting data about PNA membership, conventions and lodges.

In 1940, Karol Piatkiewicz, editor-in-chief of the two Alliance newspapers, authored a third and somewhat abbreviated history on the occasion of the PNA's 60th anniversary.[3] Though chronological in design, Piatkiewicz's study departed somewhat from this approach by providing sketches of the activities of a number of PNA departments, including those concerned with women, education, youth, sports and the operation of the Alliance college. Benefitting from the perspective of 60 years, Piatkiewicz was the first PNA historian to attempt to analyze the fraternal's ideological position in American Polonia, one which stressed its place in the vital center of Polish American life as a progressive and patriotic ethnic movement.

Between 1957 and 1963, a fourth PNA history appeared written by Adam Olszewski who, like his predecessors, was a journalist employed by the Alliance. Olszewski's enormous work, covering the history of the PNA from 1905 to 1949 in five volumes (and titled *Historia Zwiazku Narodowego Polskiego),*[4] differed from Osada and Piatkiewicz's efforts in reporting in a rather slavish chronological fashion events in PNA, Polonia, Polish and American history with no noticeable effort at analysis. Moreover, since it was researched during a period of sharp internal factional conflict, Olszewski's "in house" work avoids discussion of dissident elements in the PNA during the years after 1905, a most unfortunate failing restricting the contemporary reader's understanding of its political development. Nonetheless, a good deal of useful information about the formative years of the Polish American Congress, formed in 1944, and many other topics can be gained from Olszewski's work.

Several short histories of the Polish National Alliance have also been used which provide additional information and insight into the fraternal's goals and accomplishments. One of these works is an unpublished manuscript written by Constance Krassowska Grodska in 1954 titled "An Historical Outline of the Polish National Alliance," a manuscript which the author graciously loaned to me in 1980. A second useful short overview of PNA history is *Zgoda* editor Joseph Wiewiora's 36 page brochure, *In the Mainstreams of American Life: A Centennial Outline of Polish National Alliance History,* most recently published in revised form in 1980. A third appeared in 1923 in the PNA *Almanac* written by Nikodem Zlotnicki, an associate editor of *Zgoda* at the time. This work is distinguished by its author's fervently nationalist interpretation of PNA history. Yet a fourth brief study was written by Casimir Midowicz in 1927.

A second major source for this study has been the mountain of publications which the Polish National Alliance itself has sponsored throughout its history. Included among these are *Zgoda,* the official organ of the PNA since 1881, *Dziennik Zwiazkowy,* the PNA's Chicago-based daily published since 1908, the *Kalendarz Zwiazkowy,* the Alliance's own "Poor Richard's Almanac," which first appeared in 1914, and *Promien,* the magazine of the PNA Youth and Sports Department appearing on a somewhat irregular basis since 1948. All of the publications can be found in the home office of the PNA in Chicago. Both *Zgoda* and *Dziennik Zwiazkowy* have been microfilmed through 1972 by the University of Chicago library. The only limitation connected with that effort concerns *Zgoda,* (a weekly until 1948 when it became a bi-weekly newspaper). No copies of *Zgoda* are to be found from 1881 through 1886. More unfortunate, when the paper was microfilmed, it was the women's edition rather than the general edition which was mistakenly used for a number of years between 1910 and 1920. Despite this error, much of the editorial content of the general edition of *Zgoda* was reprinted in the women's version, which is itself distinctive because of its concentration on women's activities in America and the world during the rise of the feminist movement in the World War I era.

Of special interest to the individual interested in early PNA history but not familiar with the Polish language are those issues of *Zgoda* and the *Dziennik Zwiazkowy* which were selected for translation by the Works Progress Administration in Chicago during the Great Depression. More than 16,000 articles in eight different Chicago-area Polonia newspapers appearing between 1887 and 1931 were translated, including articles appearing in *Zgoda* between 1887–1894 and 1897–1903 and *Dziennik Zwiazkowy* between 1908–1918. These translations have been preserved on microfilm and can be found in many university libraries under the general title of the Chicago Foreign Language Press Survey (CFLPS).

Over the years, the PNA has published scores of histories, political tracts, literary works and commemorative brochures in keeping with its historic educational mission to enlighten Polonia to its members' civic and patriotic responsibilities. Three of these works are particularly worth mentioning here. In 1911, Romuald Piatkowski, later the first rector of the PNA school in Cambridge Springs, Pennsylvania, compiled a massive, thorough and informative illustrated volume to commemorate the dedication of the Kosciuszko and Pulaski monuments in Washington, D.C. and the holding of the first world congress of Poles. Both of these major events took place under PNA sponsorship in May, 1910. In 1959, PNA/PAC President Charles Rozmarek authorized the printing of a collection of press clippings documenting his activities between 1955 and 1958 on behalf of Poland's liberation from communist rule. And in 1976, Joseph Wiewiora authored a revised edition of *Jamestown: Pioneers from Poland,* which recounted the story of the first Poles who came in 1608 to the Virginia colony established by John Smith a year earlier.

A wealth of information about PNA activities and policies can be garnered from a careful reading of the minutes of the national board of directors' meetings, which in recent years have been held four times a year but in the more distant past took place on a more frequent basis. Other major informational sources are the printed and official minutes of the PNA national conventions and the reports made by national officers to the delegates attending the conventions. These reports can be found in separate bound volumes for every PNA convention since 1901. Earlier convention proceedings are in *Zgoda.* All of these materials were made available to me by the PNA leadership and are housed in the Alliance's home office, either in its library or archives.

In order to add to the written record I interviewed a number of individuals who have been active in the Alliance over the years and were in a position to provide their own recollections and insights about particular events affecting the fraternal. These conversations ranged from thirty minutes to two and one-half hours in length and were extremely helpful to me. Among those who provided their time and assistance to this research were Censor Hilary Czaplicki, PNA Director of Public Relations Edward Dziewulski, Vice President Joseph Gajda, *Dziennik Zwiazkowy* Editor Jan Krawiec, Secretary Lottie Kubiak, Polish American Congress Vice President Kazimierz Lukomski, Polish National Alliance-Polish American Congress President Aloysius Mazewski, former PNA Director Bonaventure Migala, Helen Moll, Treasurer Edward Moskal, Director Mitchell Odrobina, Director of Fraternal Activities Anthony Piwowarczyk, former Commissioner Gladys Podkomorska, Manager of Alliance Printers Edward Rozanski, Wanda Rozmarek, PNA Librarian Josephine Rzewska, Director of Sales Frank Spula, former Censor Francis

Swietlik, Vice President Helen Szymanowicz, former Treasurer Adam Tomaszkiewicz, *Zgoda* Editor Joseph Wiewiora, and former Director Melanie Winiecki. Adding to my understanding of the history and development of Alliance College were College Librarian Stanley Kozaczka, Professor Walter Smietana, College Trustee Patricia Sikora, and President of the Alumni Association Helen Kostecki. In addition, I benefitted greatly from the opportunity to attend a number of major PNA-sponsored events during the course of my research effort and through these experiences gained something of a first-hand appreciation of the ways in which the fraternal has sought to carry out its mission as an ethnically-based movement. In September, 1980 I attended the regular meetings of the PNA Supervisory Council and the PNA School Commission which were held in Chicago at the time of the Alliance's centennial celebration under the chairmanship of Censor Czaplicki. I also attended the centennial banquet of the PNA on September 20, 1980 at which President Jimmy Carter, Illinois Governor James Thompson, Chicago Mayor Jane Byrne, PRCUA President Joseph Drobot, PWA President Helen Zielinski and Falcons' Alliance President Bernard Rogalski together with nearly three thousand PNA and Polonia activists honored the record of the Alliance by their presence. In October 1981, I attended a similar centennial banquet celebrating the establishment of *Zgoda* and there had the opportunity to speak at length with Arthur Waldo, one of Polonia's greatest historians, who provided me with a host of insightful comments that aided greatly in my research.

On May 1, 1982 I attended the annual Polish Constitution Day Parade in Chicago, an enormous, colorful and moving demonstration by thousands of people on behalf of Poland's right to political democracy and full national sovereignty. In June, 1982 I visited Alliance College in Cambridge Springs, Pennsylvania and while there attended the fourth quadrennial Youth Jamboree which brought together more than 600 Polish American youngsters belonging to dance and cultural groups sponsored by the PNA throughout the country. While there I attended a meeting of the School Commission at which plans for a fund raising campaign on behalf of the College were announced on the occasion of the school's 70th anniversary. And on April 30, 1982 I was privileged to attend a most informative and interesting regular meeting of the PNA Board of Directors in Chicago. All these activities, together with frequent conversations I was able to have with President Mazewski and every other member of the present executive leadership of the Alliance gave me a unique opportunity to become better informed on a personal level with the subject of my research, for which I am grateful.[5]

Besides Mr. Waldo, I was able to speak about the Polish National Alliance with several scholarly students interested in Polonia history during the past few years, including Professor Frank Renkiewicz, past editor of *Polish American Studies,* the journal of the Polish American Historical Association, Professor William Galush of the History Department of Loyola University of Chicago, and Professor Andrzej Brozek of the Jagiellonian University of Krakow. These individuals share a deep interest in Polish fraternalism and their observations about its past, present and future helped me a great deal in shaping my own understanding of the subject.

A final resource used heavily consisted of a large number of published and unpublished scholarly studies on Polish and Polish American history which touch on the origins, development and activities of the Polish National Alliance. Among the most useful of these works, which have been listed in complete fashion in the bibliographical section which follows, are two recent and excellent interpretive histories of the Polish experience, M. K. Dziewanowski's *Poland in the Twentieth Century* (1977) and Piotr Wandycz's *The United States and Poland* (1980). Both authors give great attention to the development of Polish nationalist thought and politics in the 19th and 20th centuries, a subject which crucially shaped the outlook of the PNA. The work of Joseph Wytrwal, Frank Renkiewicz and Andrzej Brozek on the place of fraternalism in the history of American Polonia proved to be extremely valuable. Brozek's monograph, *Polonia Amerykanska, 1854-1939* (Warsaw, 1977) is one work eminently deserving an English translation in the near future. Roman Korban's *Sport wsrod Polonii Amerykanskiej* (Warsaw, 1980) is an interesting effort to describe the efforts of Polonia fraternals in promoting youth and sports activities. Arthur Waldo's monumental history of the Polish Falcons' Alliance, in Polish, is yet another indispensable piece of work to the student of not only the Falcons but indeed American Polonia as an entity.

The most useful recent scholarly work on American Polonia during the Second World War is Richard Lukas' excellent study, *The Strange Allies: The United States and Poland, 1941-1945* (1978). Susan S. Lotarski's article, "The Communist Takeover in Poland," in Thomas Hammond's edition entitled *The Anatomy of Communist Takeovers* (1975) is an accurate, complete and dispassionate review and analysis of the Soviet-sponsored seizure of power by the Polish communist party after 1944. The finest memoir covering U.S. policy toward Poland during and after World War II is by Charles Bohlen, later the American Ambassador to Moscow, which is titled *Witness to History, 1929-1969.* I was also able to read a number of Ph.D. dissertations in connection with this research, several of which proved to be of enormous value. Much of the best research has since found its way into print, I am glad to report, primarily in the pages of three excellent scholarly journals, *Polish American Studies, The Polish Review,* sponsored by the Polish Institute of Arts and Sciences in America, and *Ethnicity,* issued by the University of Chicago. A comprehensive list of dissertations completed at American universities and dealing with the Polish American experience has been published, moreover, in Polish American Studies.[6]

In sum, it should be clear from these comments and from a perusal of the bibliography that follows that a good deal of solid research has been produced on the Polish ethnic experience. Still, several areas of Polish American studies remain which are deserving of scholarly interest. Greater attention needs to be focused upon the secular institutions of Polonia and the men and women who led them. Research dealing with the careers of such individuals as Smulski, Rozmarek, Zychlinski, Swietlik and Sypniewski, just to name a few luminaries of the past, would contribute considerably to our understanding of the evolution of Polish ethnic life in America. Only when these tasks have been performed will it be possible to have a more accurate and complete appreciation of this fascinating subject.

Part I

Chapter 1

THE PLACE OF THE FRATERNAL SOCIETY IN
POLISH AMERICAN LIFE

One of the great ironies about the Polish experience in America revolves about the historic development and significance of organizational life in the Polish ethnic community. While it is well known that the Polish immigrants gradually established an extensive, complex, satisfying, and enduring system of mass membership organization to meet their many needs—social, recreational, spiritual, economic, communications and political-relatively little attention has ever been paid to analyzing the organizational character of the Polish American community. Indeed, despite their great role in shaping the outlook and purposes of the immigrants and their offspring, the social structures and networks they formed in America have almost been taken for granted.

Instead, Polish Americans have directed their attentions to other aspects of their heritage. One object of interest has focused upon the Polish nation's heroic history and its struggle to win a secure place in the sun on the European continent. Throughout the nineteenth century and up to 1917, the causes which animated the Poles in America were those of working for the eventual restoration of Poland's independence and in the meantime preserving the national language and culture in the face of the foreign occupation. This was understandable since the rulers of partitioned Poland made serious and systematic attempts to destroy national consciousness, particularly in the zones under German and tsarist Russian control. In America, ethnic patriotic celebrations keyed upon Polish Constitution day[1] and the anniversaries of a succession of uprisings which occurred from 1794 onward. Only for a relatively brief period, from 1918 when Poland did achieve its independence up to 1939 when it was conquered and partitioned once again, were Polish American aspirations toward Poland temporarily realized. During this era the focus of the community turned inward, with priority given to domestic

3

concerns. Yet, Poland once again exploded as an issue of highest concern following the Nazi-Soviet invasion of September, 1939, which set off the Second World War. And ever since the War, Polish Americans have directed their concerns once more to the ancestral homeland.[2]

A second area of intense interest for Polish Americans had been in the exploits of heroic Poles, whose achievements have seemed to symbolize all that is worth preserving in the national heritage. Emphasis has been focused on individuals such as Tadeusz Kosciuszko, Kazimierz Pulaski, the author Henryk Sienkiewicz, the scientist Maria Sklodowska-Curie, King Jan Sobieski, Ignacy Jan Paderewski, Pope John Paul II, Frydryk Chopin, the actress Helena Modjeska, and Mikolaj Kopernik (known universally by his latinized name Copernicus), just to name a very few of Poland's more illustrious sons and daughters through the centuries.

Yet, the emphasis rightfully placed upon Poland and the exploits of famous Poles has somewhat obscured other significant aspects of the Polish experience and identity. One of these lies in the stories of the individuals who migrated to America in ever growing numbers in the years following the "November" insurrection of 1830–31. According to research Professor Helena Lopata has conducted on this subject, at least 1.8 million Poles settled in the United States over the ensuing 150 years.[3]

The stories of such individuals, astonishingly, have rarely been told despite the fact that their accomplishments were genuine enough. Indeed, they were

Table 1.   Summary Data on Permanent Immigration of Ethnic Poles to the United States, 1820–1980

Period	Designation by US Department of Immigration	Total number of immigrants
1820–1885	Persons identifying selves as Polish	33,489
1885–1898	Persons identifying Poland as the land of their birth	131,694
1899–1932	Persons identified as Polish by race or people	1,148,649
1932–1972	Persons identifying Poland as their land of birth	509,808
1973–1980	Persons admitted into the U.S. from Poland	33,603

made in the face of great disadvantages due to the immigrants' initial unfamiliarity with the English language and American culture and because so many brought to America no skills other than those they had learned as peasant farmers.

The question of American society's impact upon the immigrants has caused intense debate for decades and still generates emotion. Beginning with the publication of William Thomas and Florian Znaniecki's landmark sociological study, *The Polish Peasant in Europe and America* (1918–1920), one school of scholarly observers has emphasized the generally destructive effects of American conditions upon the pre World War I migration, whose entry coincided with the industrial revolution. Thomas and Znaniecki saw the Polish peasant population in America as confused and disoriented by its immersion into an alien society and they predicted that the ethnic communities they established would rapidly disintegrate in their collision with American institutions and values. This view, interestingly enough, continues to exert considerable influence within the Polish American community. One recent author, for example, has summarized the immigrants' experience in America in the following fashion:

> They (the Polish immigrants) were totally unequipped for the American experience. They had no skills, no superior qualities, no language that anyone could understand . . . (What they did possess) was a capacity for backbreaking labor, hardship and endurance that could rival that of the slaves of the old South.[4]

So harsh an evaluation of the Polish ethnic experience has some validity. But it fails to explain why the overwhelming majority of immigrants freely chose to remain in America, especially after Poland's independence was restored in 1918. Emphasizing the desperate conditions facing the immigrants indeed tends to ignore the sense of genuine achievement they felt when they forwarded money to their families in the homeland and the prestige they enjoyed in the "old country" when they did return.[5] One Polish writer of peasant origin, Stanislaw Pigon, discussed this subject in his autobiography, *Z Komborni w Swiat,* in which he recalled his youth in Austrian Galicia.

> The emigration, especially to America, played an immense role in lifting the level of village life in material as well as intellectual ways. Already those who had gone to Hungary and Bukovina came into brief contact with the world. They saw different ways, different manners, and were viewed as having experienced a better way of life. They also achieved some material improvements over their age-old poverty . . . . Among the 'Americans' all these developments occurred in an even more remarkable degree. After several years stay in more civilized

conditions, they returned with a few more social graces and were dressed abundantly like lords. These improvements they sought to maintain after their return. The home of the returned emigrant also differed sharply from those of his neighbors. It was supplied with a chimney, had larger windows, an entrance way, and the roof was often made of tin . . .[6]

In America itself, the immigrants energetically established a host of parish churches, schools, and meeting houses, while all along providing for the economic needs of their families. One turn of the century estimate of the total value of church property alone financed by Polish Americans, made by the early Polonia newspaper editor Michael Kruszka, placed the figure at more than $200 million.[7]

Furthermore, generational studies of Polish American social and economic mobility show that its members have made notable advances educationally, occupationally and in income. One sociologist, Andrew Greeley, termed the Polish Americans' rapid rise up the socio-economic status ladder since the late 1950s nothing less than an "ethnic miracle." He found that by the mid 1970s, several ethnic groups (of which the Poles were one) already exceeded white Anglo-Saxon Americans in terms of average annual income. Eugene Obidinski concurred with this conclusion after examining 1970 U.S. census data and comparing second generation Polish Americans with their immigrant parents. "Contrary to the blue collar working class stereotype," he wrote, "Polish Americans are found at all occupational levels." In her research Helena Lopata went further, comparing third generation Polish Americans with the immigrants and their offspring. Her work pointed out that the median level of schooling among Polish Americans between the ages of twenty-five and thirty-four was 12.7 years, second only to the "amazing sixteen plus median" attained by American Jews. She also found that the proportion of Polish Americans completing college was more than twice that of older Polish Americans and the proportion of young persons attending college was three times greater. In all areas, Lopata concluded, younger Polish Americans were moving rapidly up the socio-economic status ladder, entering white collar professions, relocating to the suburbs and into newer sections of their home towns, surpassing the enviable record of second generation Polish Americans, many of whom had themselves risen from work as manual laborers into high level blue collar jobs.[8]

What conclusions can we draw from these findings? It is clear that those who migrated to America came with few "readily marketable skills" but with an awesome commitment to the attainment of economic success they could not realize in Poland. There, the countryside was overpopulated, the typical farm tiny, and opportunities to find work or education in the cities minimal. Against great odds, they, their children and their later descendants made genuine successes of their lives in this country.

Yet, the history of the Poles in America cannot be understood only in terms of the lives of individuals. A second and equally neglected side of the Polish American story concerns the immigrants' building of enduring communal associations in their new homeland and the role these associations have continued to play in the ethnic community ever since their origins in the late 1860s. In recent years, scholars of Polish American history have begun to focus attention upon one important communal institution exerting great power over the immigrants, the Church. Yet, little attention has been given to the many types of secular associations that Poles established, even though literally millions of people have belonged to such voluntary groups during the past century. Most important among them have been the fraternal associations, which provided their members with a wide array of benefits, ranging from life insurance and sick and relief assistance to satisfaction gained from working together for commonly agreed upon goals. The fraternals also took the lead in attempting to unite the immigrant community on a national scale along ethnic and patriotic lines and as such, they have been p imarily responsible for stimulating and preserving a sense of heritage among hundreds of thousands of people who were themselves American-born. The largest, most significant, and one of the earliest of these organizations has been the Polish National Alliance, which in 1980 celebrated its centennial anniversary and whose history is the subject of this work. Yet to fully appreciate the role played by the PNA in the development of the Polish American community, one must first look at the community itself and the way in which it took shape in this country.

As large numbers of immigrants congregated in various American towns and cities after the American Civil War, they began to organize highly complex networks of associations and institutions to meet their communities' economic, cultural, social, political and recreational needs. This organizational network was known commonly as "Polonia" and developed in practically every town where large numbers of immigrants lived, enabling them to adapt more successfully to the conditions they found in America. Already by the 1870s, a number of thriving local Polonia communities were in existence with the largest settlements found in Chicago, Buffalo, Philadelphia, Milwaukee, New York, Detroit, and Cleveland. Later on, the term Polonia came to have a second meaning, one referring to the organization of Polish Americans on the national as well as the local level. Indeed, today one can speak of American Polonia, Canadian Polonia, or English Polonia, for example. But initially, and even to this day, the term also continues to refer to local organized activity.

Polonia was in every respect a highly complex social system serving a diverse set of needs, foremost of which dealt with religion. The Polish immigrants were deeply committed to Roman Catholicism and attempted to establish parishes presided over by Polish clergymen to direct and perpetuate the traditional religious customs and celebrations they had practiced in their homeland. In time, a variety of secular organizations also formed to satisfy the immigrants' desire for social contacts, recreation, information about developments at the community, national and international levels, economic security and political advancement. These included fraternal associations, singing societies, athletic and gymnastic clubs. Some established successful businesses and employed their fellow immigrants in them. The Poles' fascination with the value of the printed word and freedom of expression in their own language (due at least partly to the absence of this freedom in partitioned Poland) caused them to found a bewilderingly large number of publications which dealt with nearly every aspect of ethnic life. And, Poles organized politically and were receptive to industrial labor unions such as the United Mine Workers long before the coming of the New Deal.

Three observations about the institutional and organizational complexion of American Polonia over the years might be made. First, due to cultural and social differences between the Poles and other groups with which they came into contact, Polonia developed a defensive character whose purposes were to protect the immigration from the loss of its religion, language and national heritage. Polonia's defensive-mindedness reinforced its seeming self-sufficiency or "institutional completeness" and these factors all help to account for the capacity of its institutions to satisfy most of its members' needs for two generations. Some needs, of course, could not be fully met; perhaps no more than half of Polonia's children were trained in Polish parish schools and relatively few laborers were employed by their countrymen. Furthermore, it was relatively easy for Polish Americans to travel outside their communities, to receive information from the "outside," to participate in non-ethnic affairs and even to withdraw spiritually from Polish community life. One way to understand the relationship between Polonia and the wider non-Polish community in which it was imbedded is to imagine that between the two there existed a kind of translucent membrane which sheltered Poles from the outside while enveloping Polonia life and giving it meaning and attractiveness.

Second, though most immigrants originated from the Polish countryside, they congregated mainly in cities and mining towns, drawn to these areas by the promise of quick opportunities to earn and save money. But the immigrants readily adapted to differences in the style and substance of life in America which contrasted with the less frenetic pace they had known in Poland. Gradually, they accustomed themselves to the cacophony of life that was the American melting pot, while finding a measure of security within the culture and values embodied in their community. At the same time, the Polonia they created was a social system different from both the rural Poland from which so many immigrants had originated and the America to which they had arrived. As Thomas and Znaniecki noted, Polonia was neither completely Polish nor American; rather it existed as a distinctive hybrid combining elements of both societies.

Thirdly, Polonia life provided immigrants having no previous experience in self-government with opportunities to become leaders in their community affairs. From the 1880s through the first two decades of the twentieth century there were numerous manifestations of such behavior. Significant was the conflict in several Roman Catholic dioceses over the leadership and management of Polish parishes, which led to the formation of the Polish National Catholic Church in 1904 and the appointment of a Polish American bishop in 1908.[9] But no less important were the efforts to organize nationally to work for the independence of Poland. Such activities achieved their greatest success during the eras of the two world wars.

Historically, four types of organizations and institutions predominated in Polonia—the parishes, the press, the fraternals, and a wide array of diverse special interest associations appealing to young people, war veterans, cultural enthusiasts and professionals. From the years of the first large-scale Polish migration to America, the parish was traditionally the central religious, social and cultural institution; what is more, it continued to be the focus of ethnic life until after the Second World War. In 1870, there were but a few Polish Roman Catholic parishes serving the still tiny Polonia; by 1880 the number had risen to 75 and by 1900 there were 330 parishes in existence. In 1920, Polonia could claim 760 Polish Roman Catholic parishes and in 1935 there were 830 parishes. As recently as the mid 1950s, more than 850 Polish parishes with more than four million members were in operation, and nearly 600 of these operated their own primary schools. Though the number of Polish American parishes has since declined due to the migration of thousands of people into new neighborhoods, the Polish ethnic parish remained as one of the most visible mass membership institutions in the Polish American community.[10]

One reason for the parishes' importance in Polonia was their role in ministering to the spiritual and liturgical needs of the traditionally religious immigrants. But the churches, Catholic and National, were more than centers of worship; they provided the Poles with a sense of community and social interaction reminiscent of what they had left behind in the homeland.[11]

Moreover, the hundreds of priests who came to America to organize and direct the parish-centered communities formed Polonia's first leadership *corps* from its origins in the 1850s until after the First World War. Indeed, the early history of no local Polonia can be discussed without mentioning their activities. In Chicago, clergymen such as Vincent Barzynski, leader of the Resurrectionist order in the city and pastor of St. Stanislas Kostka parish (1873–1899) and Casimir Sztuczko, pastor of Holy Trinity parish (1893–1949) deserve special recognition along with Paul Rhode, the first Roman Catholic bishop of Polish heritage in America. In Milwaukee, Wenceslaus Kruszka, Boleslas Goral, Hyacinth Gulski and Bronislas Celichowski headed a long list of clerical leaders. The Franciscan missionary Leopold Moczygeba together with the Reverend Joseph Dabrowski were responsible for establishing a Polish seminary school in Orchard Lake, Michigan; John Pitass led the Polish community in Buffalo and Lucjan Bojnowski played a similar role in New Britain, Connecticut. In 1904 Francis Hodur became the founder of the Polish National Church headquartered in Scranton, Pennsylvania. And of course there were many others who helped to shape the early Polonia communities in America.

Writing about the early Polish priests in America, one Polonia historian described them as "confessors, teachers, counselors, social directors, alms givers, and even political leaders . . . . They gave voice to Polish hopes and aspirations and when they spoke on secular, as well as religious matters, it was with authority."[12] As important, though less recognized was the contribution made by members of the religious orders of Polish women in educating the youngsters who attended the parish schools. The Polish Felician sisterhood, founded in Warsaw in 1855, established its first convent in Polonia, Wisconsin in 1874 and by 1932 was organized in six territorial provinces throughout the country. A teaching order, the Felicians directed 8 schools in 1883, approximately 100 by 1909 and 204 grade schools and 13 high schools by 1939. Formed in 1875, the Polish sisters of the Holy Family of Nazareth were also active in teaching as were the Sisters of Saint Joseph, founded in 1901 and the Sisters of the Resurrection, founded in 1882. These orders together educated hundreds of thousands of youngsters in their religious and national heritage.[13]

A second institution was Polonia's press. The first Polish language paper, the New York-based *Echo z Polski,* dates back to the 1863 insurrection and was established to promote the independence cause. Though its existence was brief, it was followed by many other publications. One of the earliest was *Zgoda* (Harmony), established in 1881 as the official organ of the then one year old Polish National Alliance. The PNA example was in turn imitated by other fraternals; for example, the Polish Roman Catholic Union set up its own publication, *Narod Polski* (The Polish Nation), in 1886 and in 1900 the Polish Women's Alliance did the same, inaugurating *Glos Polek* (The Polish Women's Voice). In addition, a number of commercially-based Polish language dailies and weeklies were founded in the cities with large Polonia populations. By 1905 there were at least 24 major Polish papers in the United States and in 1920 this figure had more than trebled, to 76. After the War, the popularity of the Polish language press continued to rise, peaking in 1930, when 129 papers were in operation with a combined circulation of approximately 1.3 million.

But the precipitous decline in Polish immigration after the First World War together with the onset of the Great Depression inexorably reversed this growth pattern. By 1940, only 43 Polish papers remained, one-third the number in existence only a decade before. Still, new publications continued to appear, largely in response to the needs of the new migration of Poles entering the country after 1945 and to a lesser degree as an expression of ethnic pride within one segment of the American born Polish population. In 1960, 43 papers and magazines claimed 717,000 subscribers while in 1980 the Polonia press still reached more than 400,000 subscribers. By this time, the fraternal-sponsored publications claimed by far the greatest number of readers. The bi-weekly *Zgoda* possessed a circulation of more than 94,000 copies. *Narod Polski* published more than 38,000 issues. *Glos Polek* was similarly significant, distributing nearly 30,000 copies to its members each month. Other publications with large circulations included the monthly *Polish American Journal,* originating in Buffalo and having a circulation of 50,000, and the *Gwiazda Polarna* (Polar Star) of Stevens Point, Wisconsin, a weekly with a circulation of 30,000.[14]

The numbers and total circulation figures of Polish American periodicals are impressive; equally significant have been the many functions newspapers and periodicals performed over the years. Not restricted to providing "hard news" to their readers, these publications imparted ethnic awareness and patriotic feeling for Poland's cause among the masses of peasant immigrants who had come to America with little, if any, formal education about their homeland's history, culture or national aspirations. The foreign language press stimulated its readers' awareness of their religious heritage, defined in a plausible way the world in which they found themselves, helped them to understand the ties between Polonia, America and Poland, and gave Polish Americans a readily acceptable sense of social purpose to justify the time and energy they gave to Polonia activities. It helped parents train their children in the Polish language and folk culture, provided an outlet for literary creativity by publishing fiction and poetry written by Polish Americans, and popularized the current literature from Poland by individuals like Sienkiewicz, Stefan Zeromski and Eliza Orzeszkowa. The press also recorded events in local community life and publicized fund raising, patriotic events, business efforts and political office seekers. It also served as a forum for the conflicts that punctuated Polonia life, an important function that simultaneously helped stimulate readership. In all these ways, the Polonia press gave added meaning and enjoyment to the lives of its readers.

A third general type of Polonia organization with widespread appeal has included a diverse collection of voluntary associations reflecting their members' particular interests and experiences. Among the earliest of these were the choral societies which formed in various Polonia communities in the 1880s. In 1889, a national federation of these groups, the Polish Singers' Alliance was created to coordinate their activities. A second early Polonia association was the Falcons' youth movement, which stressed gymnastic and sports activities with the aim of generating ethnic pride. Imitating similar organizations formed in Czechoslovakia and Germany, and Polish Falcons' motto was "W zdrowym ciele, zdrowy duch" (A healthy spirit in a healthy body).[15]

In addition to the singers' and youth societies, a number of military-oriented formations sprouted throughout Polonia before 1900. With their colorful and history-inspired costumes, these groups of young Poles were prominent participants at Polonia patriotic events. One genuine military unit composed of Polish Americans was Milwaukee's "Company K" (for Kosciuszko), a division of the Wisconsin National Guard. Company K was formed in 1874 and saw action in the Spanish-American War of 1898, the U.S. expedition to Mexico in 1916 and World War I.

After the First World War, the amateur or "pseudo-military" societies were eclipsed by two new organizations. One, the Polish Army Veterans' Association *(Stowarzyszenie Weteranow Armii Polskiej, SWAP)* included members of the Polish army recruited in the United States who had later seen action under General Jozef Haller in Europe between 1918 and 1920. The other, the Polish Legion of American Veterans (PLAV) brought together the Polonians recruited into the American armed forces at the same time. Yet a third veterans' organization, the Polish Combatants' Association *(Stowarzyszenie Polskich Kombatantow, SPK)* was established in 1952 to unite the participants in various World War II military formations loyal to the Polish democratic government headquartered in London. These individuals had decided not to return to Poland once a communist-dominated government imposed by the Soviet Union had been established. All three veterans' organizations played a salient role in American Polonia life over the years and asserted the community's patriotic commitments to both countries.

A wide array of other voluntary associations also became visible in the Polish American community, among them professional associations such as the National Advocates' Society, a Polish American lawyers' association; the National Medical and Dental Association; and several scholarly organizations including the Polish Institute of Arts and Sciences in America, the Jozef Pilsudski Institute, and the Polish American Historical Association. Among groups specifically promoting greater appreciation of Poland's and Polonia's cultural heritage two organizations stand out, the Kosciuszko Foundation and the American Council of Polish Cultural Clubs (the latter a national federation of nearly forty locally-based community associations). In addition, there are many other smaller or local groups promoting Polish music, dance, literature or political concerns which have followings throughout the country. Most of these associations have been experiencing some modest growth by attracting into their rank members of the growing number of educated and ethnically conscious Polish Americans.

The fourth type of organizational unit in American Polonia has included its many fraternal insurance organizations. As of 1983, nineteen different fraternals were in operation with a combined insured membership of approximately 700,000 people and assets of more than $300 million. These organizations ranged in size from the Polish White Eagle fraternal headquartered in Minneapolis, which is active solely in the state of Minnesota, has a membership of 3,000 and assets of $1.2 million to the Polish National Alliance of the United States of North America, a nearly 300,000 member Chicago-based association with assets of $176 million which is licensed to do business in 38 states. The size and financial position of Polonia's fraternals make them the largest set of ethnically-based insurance associations in America and Polonia's most important system of secular group activity. Moreover, because the fraternals (unlike the Polish parishes) operated both in the local neighborhood and as countrywide organizations, their leaders were successful in gradually superceding the clergy as Polonia's chief spokesmen on ethnic and patriotic matters requiring unified national action.[16]

The earliest Polonia fraternals were in Chicago and came into being in the 1860s to provide immigrants with burial insurance and sick benefits based on the principle of mutual cooperation.[17] The first lasting national federation of local Polonia societies was the Polish Roman Catholic Union in America, founded in 1873. As is evident from its name, the PRCUA was organized purely for Catholics and operated under the general supervision of Polish Roman Catholic clergymen and laymen. The Polish National Alliance, formed in 1880, became Polonia's second national fraternal federation. Established initially as a primarily patriotic organization, the Alliance soon after set up its own insurance program and in fact predated the PRCUA in this respect. Though composed mainly of Roman Catholics and respectful toward the Church, the PNA differed from the PRCUA in that it was organized on a non-sectarian basis and led by laymen.

One reason helping to account for the Polish immigrants' early interest in fraternalism was their previous exposure to the idea of cooperation in the homeland. Most of the early immigrants came from the German ruled zone of the partitioned country where some had been active in the cooperatives permitted to operate there after 1865. One was the Central Economic Association *(Centralne Towarzystwo Gospodarcze),* founded by the land-owner Maximilan Jackowski, which promoted the spread of information about modern agriculture, cooperative activities among peasants and insurance programs. Stressing solidarity among landowners, peasants and clergy in the face of the German policy of ethnic repression, the Association soon attracted a sizeable membership and its principles were imitated in the other sections of partitioned Poland. In America, Polish interest in fraternalism was further reinforced by what they saw being accomplished by German and Czech immigrant brotherhoods in existence by the 1870s.

The concept underlying Polish fraternalism itself represented the product of a brilliant blending of diverse concerns which linked the individual's interest in providing his family with death benefit insurance with the immigrant community's commitment to group survival. In fraternalism material and idealistic objectives were united in the lodge, the basic community unit of the association, which met not only to collect insurance premiums from individual members but to enable them to keep in touch with one another regarding events both in their community and in "the old country." As such, the fraternal readily evolved into a social mechanism through which the immigrants could organize on behalf of local and nationwide needs.

Because of their patriotic and ethnic concerns, the fraternals were always more than insurance enterprises, although the collection and prudent invest-ment of increasingly large sums of money provided an excellent opportunity for lodge leaders to gain practical business experience in finance. At the same time, given their peculiar organizational structure, the fraternals differed markedly from typical American corporations and even possessed several characteristics making them similar to political organizations aspiring to be mass movements. At the grass roots was the lodge, whose executive officers were popularly chosen (usually each year) by an electorate made up of all insured adults. National officers were elected at conventions which brought together delegates representing the lodges. The convention was recognized as the highest representative and legislative body in all fraternals and guided by principles of majority rule, legitimate opposition and the secret ballot. As such, the fraternals proved to be excellent schools of political democracy for their members, few of whom had any experience of this type before.

As the fraternals grew in membership and spread out over the country, it became necessary for them to organize intermediate institutions to deal with a variety of administrative responsibilities too extensive for the central administration to handle directly. Thus were created the systems of councils (which grouped together the lodges in a particular territory) and districts (which were composed of groups of councils). Not only did these new institutional units serve important and definite purposes, equally notable, their very existence generated increased political interest in fraternal activities by providing ambitious lodge leaders with opportunities to become regional activists before trying their hand at running for national offices at the convention.

In yet one other respect, sheer durability, the fraternal concept proved to be remarkable. As far back as the 1830s Poles in America had organized societies of exiled patriots, but without a solid financial structure and mass membership base these groups soon disappeared as their members developed new interests. The fraternal, in contrast, was based not only upon ethnic solidarity; it also had an economic *raison d'etre* embodied in the insurance savings painstakingly accumulated by its members. Hence, even when a group became deeply divided, its members retained an incentive to stay with their lodge rather than secede and thereby forfeit their earlier contributions. Membership growth was also important and was stimulated by the fact that those who enrolled new members received bonuses or commissions for their efforts.

Thus, the fraternal movement was and remains important to the Polish American community for a variety of different yet interconnected reasons. As insurance societies they performed a valued service to the immigrants and their offspring. As patriotic associations striving to win a mass following on behalf of the cause of a restored and independent Poland, they helped to perpetuate a sense of national consciousness among several generations of Polish Americans that unified them in their adopted homeland and provided Polonia with a commitment to a highly attractive patriotic ideal. In realizing these goals, the fraternals became involved in a wide array of subsidiary activities that together further stimulated ethnic pride and cooperation. These included educating their people in the history of Poland and justifying its resurrection; recruiting people into positions of leadership within Polonia from which they could articulate the goals and needs of the ethnic community; providing mechanisms through which the immigrants could remain well informed about issues confronting Polonia such as their own lodges and their newspapers; representing the concerns of Polonia to the larger American community; and serving as mediating structures between their members and the great organizations of American society.[18]

Given their many attributes and characteristics, the Polish fraternals have been successful in playing significant and leading roles in Polonia for more than a century. Indeed, of all the organizations, secular and religious, which have appeared in Polonia, the fraternals were unique in bringing together large numbers of people to work effectively for specifically ethnic concerns. And, given their historic record of achievement and continuing significance, one might conclude that these organizations also retain the potential to lead the way in defining Polish America's future concerns.

Approaching PNA History

This study focuses upon one Polish American fraternal association, the Polish National Alliance of the United States of North America. Founded in 1880, the PNA has for the past ninety years been the largest Polish fraternal, both in terms of membership and financial assets. Moreover, thanks to its commitment to the independence of Poland, its expressions of loyalty to the United States and its concern for the well-being and advancement of the immigrants, the PNA has provided the most complete and satisfying set of aims ever to win mass support from Polonia. Though the Alliance was, historically, unable to unite everyone under its banner, its goals were eventually adopted in large part by other fraternal associations, including its early rival, the Polish Roman Catholic Union in America, as well as many smaller groups which came into existence in later years. Due to its programmatic appeal, the Polish National Alliance attracted the leading activists in American Polonia into its ranks from its earliest years. It was thus from the PNA that Polonia's major representatives continued to come, particularly after the movement assumed a mass membership character.

There are several ways to approach the history of the Polish National Alliance and the record of its contributions to America, Poland, and Polonia. One approach, taken by previous PNA historians, studies the development of the Alliance in a rigorously chronological fashion, giving major emphasis to events at its national conventions. While such an approach can be informative, provided that the historian's judgment is sound as to what events happen to be significant, it does not permit one to deal directly with the relationship between the organization and other American social forces with which it came into contact. Another approach places PNA history within the context of broader social developments occurring in the United States, Poland and American Polonia, the three larger cultural environments in which the Alliance has operated and at the same time sought to affect.

America's Impact on the PNA. Undoubtedly the Polish National Alliance has been heavily influenced by American society, its culture, values and political system during the past century. Indeed, much of the PNA's early success in propagandizing its message can be attributed to the fact that few restraints limited its activity. Probably the one serious problem which confronted the PNA was connected with communication and travel in a land as vast as the U.S. As the number of Polish immigrant communities in various sections of the country stretched from the Atlantic coast to Minnesota and Texas, it was not easy for ethnic activists to maintain contact with one another.

Three features of the American environment exerted their effects upon Polonia and the PNA. The first had to do with the positive feelings the immigrants harbored about their adopted land from the outset, attitudes that were subsequently reinforced by their success in finding employment in America and establishing their families and communities in this country. As a result, many were able to actually earn enough money to send back a sizeable portion of their incomes to family members left behind in the "old country" while at the same time they were busy building new lives in the new. While it would be inaccurate to suggest that the Poles in America went from rags to riches in Horatio Alger fashion in the course of a single generation, large numbers of immigrants apparently made substantial economic gains for themselves. In turn, their growing prosperity led most who stayed to regard their original decision to emigrate to have been a correct move. Reflecting this view was the growing surge of people from Poland which continued upwards in the last decade before the outbreak of World War I, peaking in 1913 when nearly 175 thousand people entered the United States. Moreover, optimism about their possibilities in America was well reported in the Polonia press of the day and in Poland as well.

A second environmental effect upon the immigrants was, ironically, associated with the indifference of U.S. government officials toward them and their communities. Indeed, once arrived at their destinations in this country, the Poles, as with other groups, retained little if any contact with American officialdom. This neglect was hardly benign in every respect, of course, and the immigrants were frequently objects of discrimination when they sought employment. In addition to their exposure to dangerous working conditions, immigrant housing was barely tolerable, proper sanitation often nonexistent and access to medical care extremely limited.[19] Still, left to fend for themselves in city tenement districts, the "prairies" or still unsettled sections of town, or out in the countryside, the Poles not only survived but went on to build churches and social organizations to supplement and preserve what they were achieving on an individual and family basis.

Third, there was the attraction of American politics, an activity open to all male citizens over the age of twenty-one which provided some rather tangible rewards to those who achieved a measure of skill in representing their compatriots. From the start, PNA leaders in particular recognized this and a constant theme of the Alliance press was to urge greater Polish involvement in the political process.

Poland's Impact. A second influence upon the PNA came from Poland itself. Unlike the impact of American society, however, which was pervasive and indirect, Poland was and remains even today an overt force in Alliance and Polonia affairs. One of the founding principles of the Polish National Alliance emphasized that its members fulfill their patriotic duties toward the homeland, for example, and throughout its history the movement has worked for national independence. One of the major mass demonstrations of Polish American concern for Poland has been the "Third of May" constitution observance begun by the PNA in 1891 and continued on an annual basis in many cities throughout the country since 1904. At this event Polonia leaders have never ceased extolling the ideals of the men who authored the second democratic constitution in modern world history, one which in 1791 guaranteed religious freedom to all and a representative form of government as well. In 1944, PNA concern for Poland led it to help establish the Polish American Congress, which has endured for nearly four decades as American Polonia's leading political action federation.

An extraordinarily significant influence upon the PNA emanated out of the political movements working for Polish independence and reunification, one which made an indelible mark upon the outlook of PNA leaders toward the homeland which remains to this very day. Already during the mid 1880s, the PNA had forged links with exiles from the 1863 insurrection who had established their headquarters in Rappersville, Switzerland. For their part, the exiles (one of whom was Agaton Giller, the spiritual father of the Alliance) promoted close ties with the embryonic fraternal in the belief that it could generate financial and moral support within the immigration for the independence cause. In the early 1890s, the Swiss-based exile movement was superceded, however, by a new nationalist group centered in Poland and headed by Roman Dmowski. Calling itself the National Democratic party, this group stressed solidarity across class lines in the struggle against foreign domination over the partitioned nation. Within a short time, Dmowski's movement also won enthusiastic backing from PNA leaders for its program and was able to maintain good relations with the Alliance for the next thirty years.

Yet another political influence upon the Alliance soon appeared in the form of the Polish Socialist Party headed by Jozef Pilsudski. Created at about the same time as the National Democrats, the socialists were from the start organized on behalf of the still small industrial working class. At first the party's anti-clerical orientation limited its appeal within American Polonia, which was primarily composed of deeply religious people from the countryside. Still, Pilsudski's commitment to fight for independence gradually enhanced its influence by rekindling memories of the insurrections of 1794, 1830 and 1863. When yet another revolt broke out in Poland during the Russian revolution of 1905, the socialists took the lead at a time when the National Democrats adopted a line opposed to violence. While the disturbances were soon quelled, it was Pilsudski whose prestige rose at Dmowski's expense in America.

It was during the decade between 1900 and 1910 too that a stream of Polish intellectuals from tsarist Poland entered the U.S. A number of these individuals became active in the Alliance, although Dmowski's partisans were generally able to maintain their command over the fraternal during the pre World War era. Nevertheless, while Dmowski and Pilsudski differed over many things, they shared a common nationalist commitment which profoundly shaped PNA thinking about Poland. That the Alliance became so important a battleground between the two sides was due largely to its growing size and influence in Polonia. Even as early as 1910, for example, the PNA already included more than seventy thousand members and possessed assets amounting to more than 1.1 million dollars, twice that of its chief rival, the Polish Roman Catholic Union. Further, thanks to its operation of two widely read newspapers, the PNA's impact extended outward to thousands of people who were themselves not members of the fraternal.

The PNA and Polonia. Yet a third influence upon the Alliance has been the people and institutions together constituting the Polish ethnic community in America, or Polonia. Not surprisingly, given their close proximity, their many shared goals and their frequently interlocking memberships, relations between the PNA and other Polonia organizations, secular and religious, have traditionally been highly salient and frequently stormy in character, particularly in the days when the Alliance sought to assert its leadership over the immigrant community. In 1886, for example, the delegates to the fifth PNA convention approved the idea of renaming the fledgling fraternal's central administration the "central government" of Polonia. Inherent in their reasoning was a conviction that the Alliance should provide the entire immigration with its leadership on a national level. This view was not appreciated by other groups in Polonia, especially the clergy, which sharply opposed the PNA on this score.

In the years between 1900 and 1912 the Alliance took a different tack and attempted to consolidate the ties it enjoyed with a number of other Polonia organizations having a progressive character, such as the Falcons' Alliance, the Singers and several smaller groups. In return for their cooperation, the PNA helped to underwrite the activities of the companionate groups and publicized their recruitment efforts in its newspapers. But these actions met resistance from elements within the Falcons' and Singers' movements which feared that such ties would inevitably lead to their complete absorption into the much larger PNA. By 1912, the PNA leadership itself had come to recognize the futility of its effort; thereafter, its attempts to unify the ethnic community have followed a third strategy, one which has put aside the Alliance's claims to lead Polonia in favor of cooperating with any and all who share its concerns. This approach has met with greater success over the years.

In 1912, the PNA took part in forming the Polish National Defense Committee *(Komitet Obrony Narodowej, KON)* and by 1914 had become a major supporter of another all-Polonia federation known as the Polish Central Relief Committee *(Polski Centralny Komitet Ratunkowy, PCKR)*. Still later during the World War I era, in 1916, the Alliance participated in yet a third all-Polonia federation, the Polish National Department *(Wydzial Narodowy)* and by its involvement in this organization made an enormous contribution to Poland's eventual restoration as an independent state. Once again in the World War II era the PNA followed the strategy of cooperation with great success, first through the Polish American Council *(Rada Polonii Amerykanskiej)*, a relief organization, and after 1944 through the Polish American Congress *(Kongres Polonii Amerykanskiej)*, a political action federation which has continued to the present day.

Yet it would be misleading to suggest that PNA relations with the rest of American Polonia have been solely defined in terms of adaptation by the Alliance to the ethnic community. Indeed, the PNA gradually won widespread support for its consistently moderate, and progressive approach to the issues of the day. While some early clerical leaders of Polonia criticized the Alliance for addressing itself too exclusively to Polish independence (they believed instead that the social, educational and religious needs of the emigration in America should be the top priority), by the First World War, the clergy and its allies in the Catholic fraternals had developed views on Poland that were very close to those traditionally held by the PNA. And, in spite of socialist criticism that its stress upon ethnic solidarity instead of class consciousness was misguided, it was the PNA position which was eventually adopted by Polish Americans, whatever their socio-economic position.

Periods of PNA Development

PNA history can be approached from still another perspective, one in which its development is divided into a series of periods or phases, each dominated by certain individuals, ideas, issues and events. While it would be foolhardy to expect complete agreement on either the characteristics or limits of such historical periods, dividing any lengthy era into a set of shorter time frames makes sense simply for the sake of analysis. For example, American history is better understood when divided into its pre Civil War and post Civil War periods and discussion of post Civil War era developments is further illuminated by distinguishing between what occurred before and since the great economic depression. So also, twentieth century Polish history can be sensibly subdivided into the period up to 1918, the interwar era, the years of wartime occupation (1939–1945), and Communist party rule (which itself can be subcategorized in terms of the policies and personalities of its leaders).

In this study I look at the century long history of the Polish National Alliance in terms of five successive periods and try to identify in each a set of dominant themes and personalities which define each and set it apart from what took place before and after. (Following this chronological account of PNA history, however, I also include a series of shorter topical chapters which focus upon activities of particular importance to the Alliance through its history including education, youth work, humanitarian service, the development of an effective press, and the unification of the Polish American community. One of these chapters deals with the role of women in the movement. Further, in the appendix of this work one can find statistical information on PNA membership and finances, the names of all PNA national officers, a set of brief biographical sketches of leading personalities associated with the Alliance, and a chronological chart whose function is to link events within the PNA with broader developments occurring in Poland, the United States and Polonia.)

Origins of the PNA and its 'Prehistory': 1830-1885. This period deals with the origins of American Polonia, the birth of the Alliance and the first five years of its existence. To better understand the formation of the PNA I treat its origins as a kind of culmination of the previous fifty years of Polish and immigration history in America, one which began with the collapse of the November, 1830 insurrection and the arrival of the first political exiles from Poland to our shores a few years later.

From the 1830s onward, political exiles in America were organizing patriotic societies aimed at keeping the flame of freedom alive from afar. By the 1850s they were being joined by the first waves of peasant and working class immigrants who were attracted to the United States for mainly economic reasons. A decade later, men and women from the two emigrations were beginning to build enduring ethnic communities centered around parishes but which also included fraternal and patriotic societies. In Chicago, which soon became the home of the largest Polish American settlement, two local groups were already in existence by 1866, the Saint Stanislas Kostka Society and the *Gmina Polska* club. Out of these rival associations eventually sprung Polonia's two largest and most influential fraternal movements, the Polish Roman Catholic Union in America (formed under priestly leadership in 1873) and the PNA, which was headed by secular leaders.

In the 1870s, several still-born efforts were made to create a nationwide federation of patriotic clubs that was based upon principles that had traditionally found acceptance among political exiles and which were later to become central to the Polish National Alliance. But these failed, largely because the still relatively small and widely scattered immigration was primarily occupied with the task of simply establishing itself in the new land. But as the number of immigrants grew, so did the number of ethnic associations they established in America. By the end of the 1870s, it was only a matter of time before another and more successful effort to unify the sprawling immigration would be attempted. In 1880 such an effort was in fact made and, despite the many problems it faced during its first formative years, the embryonic Polish National Alliance survived as a patriotic society devoted to the preservation of the ideal of Polish independence and the improvement of the peasant migration.[20] In a real sense, therefore, the entire era from 1830 and 1880 proved to be a "seed time" for the Polish National Alliance, and must be appreciated if the PNA and its later activities are to be properly understood.

During its first few years, the PNA remained a struggling and rather loosely coordinated group of local patriotic societies (later known as groups or lodges) bound together by a set of basic objectives agreed to by the handful of delegates who met at the Alliance's first convention in Chicago. It was not until later, in 1886, when the PNA succeeded in creating a viable national insurance program for all its members that organizational activities were centralized. Still, there were important forward steps during the early years of the Alliance. From the outset, the national convention (or *sejm*) was made the supreme legislative body, its delegates chosen from the local lodges by the membership in democratic fashion. A major function of the *sejm* was to elect the national officers of the Alliance who were responsible for directing its affairs in the intervals between conventions, which at first were held each year. The central administration *(zarzad centralny)* of the PNA was itself headed by the president, but the authors of the Alliance constitution in their collective wisdom also chose to create another supreme officer, known as the censor, to review the administration's decisions. This move created a perennial question of responsibility within the Alliance, one which could only be settled by political competition. Yet a last major development was the decision to create a PNA newspaper to serve as its official voice or "organ" within Polonia. Founded in 1881 this publication, *Zgoda,* quickly became an important force communicating the position of the Alliance on issues of the day along with its more prosaic task of reporting upon internal fraternal activities.

From 1885 to 1918. A second phase in PNA history represents one of the most stirring periods in its development. Its beginning occurred at a most inauspicious time, with the still tiny organization faced with imminent collapse. It ended thirty-three years later with the Alliance, by then a movement of more than one hundred thousand members, a witness to the restoration of an independent Polish state after 123 years of partition. Poland's rebirth came as a direct result of the events of the "First World War" and represented the realization of the highest item in the policy agenda of the Alliance. But the period was also distinctive in several other respects and it was during these years that the PNA took on the goals and most of the structural characteristics which continue to define its activities even to the present day.

During its second phase, the Alliance, which included fewer than three hundred members in 1885, successfully withstood a series of bitter attacks upon its activities from the clerical camp in Polonia. Headed by the Reverend Vincent Barzynski, the clerical camp opposed the PNA as an organization it considered to be anti-Catholic, largely because it was not led by clergymen. It was not until the late 1890s that friction with Barzynski and his supporters subsided but the conflict nevertheless greatly hampered the growth of the PNA; indeed at the time of Barzynski's death in 1899, its membership was still a rather modest 15,000 although the movement's very survival was no longer in jeopardy. Most significant, the PNA remained steadfast to its founding principles throughout these years while retaining its traditional regard for Catholic religious values, in spite of the criticisms it faced.

Following Barzynski's passing, tensions between the PNA and the clergy eased considerably, a development which significantly affected the remarkable expansion of the movement's membership to more than one hundred thousand participants by 1914. But parallel to its breakneck growth, the Alliance also was developing an institutional shape which would better meet its members' aims and needs. Already by 1895, for example, Chicago had become the permanent headquarters of the Alliance when it adopted a plan to build its own central office in the "windy city." In 1900, women were admitted to full membership in the organization for the first time, a decision which in one stroke nearly doubled the movement's ranks and permitted the expansion of its activities into educational and humanitarian affairs previously beyond its capabilities. In 1907, the fraternal significantly modernized its system of life insurance adopted in 1886; this action was a major factor in enabling the PNA to compete successfully with commercial insurance firms and continue to grow.

The second phase of PNA development also witnessed the establishment of an Alliance daily newspaper, *Dziennik Zwiazkowy,* to serve the informational needs of the massive Chicago Polonia. Founded in 1908, this paper joined with the Alliance weekly, *Zgoda,* to advance the work of the organization, a cause which both publications continue to the present. In addition, the PNA also initiated a separate women's edition of *Zgoda* in 1900 and later established a special Women's Department to respond to the interests and concerns of its growing female contingent. (The women's *Zgoda* was later merged into the general edition of the PNA weekly.)

Though PNA activists had expressed interest in educational matters affecting Polonia as early as 1880, it was not until the early 1890s that the organization established a central library and reading room in Chicago for Polonia and set up a special Educational Department *(Wydzial oswiaty)* to develop a systematic program aimed at promoting popular interest in learning. By the turn of the century this PNA agency had expanded its work to include the awarding of scholarships and student loans to children of its members. In 1912, PNA educational activity reached its culmination when the fraternal set up its own school located in the town of Cambridge Springs, Pennsylvania. Originally organized as a high school for boys, the Alliance "Kolegium" had evolved into a four year coeducational liberal arts college by 1948.

Structurally, the executive and legislative bodies created at the very first PNA convention were augmented in 1909 by the establishment of a third and separate judicial body. Named the Supervisory Council *(rada nadzorcza)*, this body was composed of all district commissioners and chaired by the censor. Another structural innovation was effected in 1911 when a system of local councils *(gminy)* coordinating the activities of lodges was set up. These changes, plus the adding of a preamble to the PNA constitution defining the fraternal's central aims in 1900, were among the major structural developments affecting the Alliance which by the time of the outbreak of the First World War had achieved an organizational character that has not significantly been altered in later years. The highest legislative institution of the PNA, its national convention, remained responsible for electing all executive officers of the fraternal including its president, vice president, treasurer, and secretary, along with the members of the national board of directors. It also elected the supreme judge of the organization, the censor. Until 1914, the editor of *Zgoda* was also elected by the national convention though it was not until 1963 that the position of chief medical examiner ceased to be elective. The national convention initially met once each year, usually in the autumn. From 1887, conventions were held every other year. After 1915, the convention was scheduled for every third year and beginning in 1935 it met every fourth year. The PNA constitution also permitted the calling of extraordinary conventions whenever the censor deemed them necessary. The first such convention was held in February, 1884 and a second was held in September, 1900. (In 1958 a third extraordinary convention was called but because not enough delegates from the previous regularly scheduled conclave were present to constitute the *quorum* necessary to conduct business, this affair had no official character.) Extraordinary conventions were envisioned as having a specific task to deal with as defined by the censor and did not have the power to elect officers. The first such conclave attempted to establish a workable insurance program for the PNA, although it failed to achieve this aim immediately. The 1900 convention was more successful and admitted women to full membership. The 1958 assembly was called to investigate the financial policies of the PNA.[21]

Until 1911, all delegates to the national convention were elected at meetings of the local lodges, the basic organizational unit of the PNA. Later, though delegates were elected to represent councils, the contests themselves continued to take place within the lodges. It was only after 1935 that the elections of delegates to the national convention were held at the council level, a sign of their growing importance as local organizational units.

The chief executive body of the PNA has always been its "central administration"[22] although the size and complexion of this body has changed appreciably over the years. Initially, the central administration was composed of six men, the president, one vice president, the treasurer, the secretary and one vice secretary, and a legal advisor. The first directors were elected in 1886, when three such positions were created. Between 1893 and 1897 two vice presidents were elected, although the Alliance reverted to the practice of electing only one vice president afterward until 1921, when a women's vice president was elected as second vice president of the organization. Since then, the structure and membership of the PNA central administration (now known as its board of directors) has remained virtually unchanged. Its fifteen members include the president, two vice presidents, the treasurer, the national secretary and ten directors. Together these individuals share the responsibility of managing the affairs of the Alliance between conventions and meet as a body every three months. In 1975, a resolution approved at the PNA convention in Milwaukee limited directors and commissioners to two consecutive terms in office.

Originally, the chief judicial authority within the PNA was its censor, who was elected at the national convention and whose major responsibilities included the calling of conventions, the supervision of the editorial policy of the PNA newspaper, *Zgoda,* and the moral leadership over the organization. Once the PNA developed its own insurance program, the censor supervised and reviewed the financial policies of the PNA administration, although state regulations requiring that all fraternals establish regular private audits of their activities and permit public audits as well made this task less significant by the 1930s. The name "censor" today is perhaps one of the least understood titles in American Polonia. When the founders of the Alliance created the office they were thinking of establishing a position harkening back to the ancient Roman Republic. Then the censor was the chief defender of public morals. Indeed they may also have considered the censor to be a kind of elected monarch with responsibilities similar to those of the Polish King under the May 3, 1791 constitution. Before the rise of strong presidents, the censor was the Alliance's most well known figure. The years after 1912, however, brought to the fore men such as Zychlinski, Romaszkiewicz, Rozmarek and Mazewski, and the gradual eclipse of the censor.[23]

Until 1909, the censor and his chief aide, the vice censor, alone were responsible for the review of PNA policies. Between 1900 and 1909, a growing number of vice censors were elected to oversee the activities of the burgeoning PNA around the country. In 1909, the regional vice censors were reorganized into a new body called the supervisory council and their titles changed to commissioners. The censor was made the chairman of this council, which served as a kind of court deciding on internal legal and jurisdictional disputes within the organization. After 1912, the censor also chaired the PNA school commission, composed of all commissioners and members of the board of directors, and was responsible for the overall direction of the Alliance school.

The supervisory council presently includes thirty-two members, two representing each of the sixteen supervisory districts *(okregi)* of the PNA. Each district has a male and a female commissioner, who are elected by the delegates from their district in attendance at the quadrennial national convention. In actuality commissioners are quasi-national officers. While they participate in two national PNA bodies (the supervisory council and the school commission), their primary function is to assist the lodges and councils in their supervisory districts in carrying out their various tasks. (One national responsibility of the commissioners as members of the supervisory council is significant. In the event of a vacancy in the offices of censor, vice censor, president, vice president, secretary or treasurer, it is the council which fills the post until the next convention.)

Initially, the lodges served as the sole local units within the PNA. However, the rapid growth in the number of lodges (known also as *grupy* or *towarzystwa*) led the Alliance in 1911 to establish a second layer of organizations to help coordinate its activities at the local level. These were the councils *(gminy)*, which brought together representatives of lodges located in particular geographical areas. In 1983, there were 210 *gminy* which included 1,123 lodges, for an average of 5.3 lodges per council. The largest councils in the PNA were council 19 in Buffalo with 22 lodges, councils 54 of Detroit and 622 in Chicopee, Massachusetts with 17 lodges apiece, council 13 of Wilkes-Barre, Pennsylvania (16 member lodges), council 120 of Chicago (15), councils 8 of Milwaukee, 122 of Hamtramck, Michigan and 67 of Utica, New York (14 each), council 88 of Chicago (13 lodges), council 15 of Detroit (12 lodges), and councils 58 of Hartford, Connecticut and 34 in Chicago (11 lodges apiece).

Ideologically, the Polish National Alliance had established its goals by 1900. At the fraternal's second extraordinary convention, which gathered in Chicago, a resolution was approved stating its aims as a kind of preamble to its constitution. This statement has remained practically unchanged ever since and asserts that the PNA's purpose is to develop the "moral, intellectual, economic and social position of the Polish immigration, perpetuating the Polish language and respect for Poland's customs and culture in the United States, and to work on behalf of the restoration and defense of Poland's independence."

It was in the PNA's "first generation and a half" that its leaders achieved a number of other ambitious aims connected with their effort to make the Alliance the leading Polonia association. Not only did the Alliance establish working ties with patriotic *emigre* groups in Western Europe and Poland; it raised thousands of dollars for Poland's cause through such instruments as the Polish National Fund *(Skarb Narodowy)* which it created in 1886.

It was during its formative years that the PNA promoted nationalist feeling within Polonia in a variety of imaginative ways. Throughout the 1890s the Alliance expressed its view about Polish independence to the heads of the American government and continued to do this in the decades that followed. The Alliance was largely responsible for realizing the idea of commemorating the exploits of Kosciuszko and Pulaski by leading the effort to have monuments in their honor built in Washington, D.C. The equestrian statue of Pulaski, built at government expense, was dedicated in 1910. This ceremony was complemented by a second one connected with the unveiling of an equally impressive monument to Kosciuszko. The statue of Kosciuszko was itself funded largely by the Alliance. (In 1979 at its thirty-eighth convention, held in Washington, D.C., the PNA organized a ceremony at the Kosciuszko monument in which the patriot's achievements were properly inscribed for the first time. The new and informative inscription etched into the monument read as follows: "Thaddeus Kosciuszko (1746–1817) Son of Poland, General and Military Engineer of the American Revolution, Fortified Saratoga and West Point/Hudson River Complex.")

Coinciding with the dedication of the two statues was an international congress held in the nation's capital under PNA sponsorship and bringing together for the first time representatives from Western Europe, Poland and Polonia for the purpose of bringing to world attention their demand for a resurrected Polish state. In 1912, the PNA reasserted its commitments to this goal by participating in the creation of the first truly all-Polonia federation committed to working for Poland, the Polish National Defense Committee (KON). Though the Alliance withdrew from this federation in 1914, its initial involvement made *KON* a viable ethnic movement of considerable importance in coordinating Polonia's early efforts on Poland's behalf.

World War I and Poland's Rebirth. The second phase in PNA history reached its climax with the First World War and the rebirth of an independent Poland following nearly five generations of foreign partition. Between 1914 and 1918, the PNA played a central role in every area of Polonia's efforts on behalf of Poland. Its leaders spearheaded the collection of funds and materials for relief and led the work to mobilize popular support for Poland's independence both within and outside the ethnic community. The PNA strongly supported the Polish National Department *(Wydzial Narodowy)* from its inception and helped make possible the formation of a Polish army in the United States which fought under Polish colors in Europe with the Western Allies. The PNA was a crucial element in realizing a series of Polonia congresses to rally the entire ethnic community behind the independence cause. The first of these Emigration Congresses *(Sejm wychodztwa)* was held in August, 1918, only a few weeks before independence was won.

The Interwar Era: 1918–1939. Poland's rebirth signalled the start of a third period of PNA history, one which came to an abrupt end in September, 1939 when the homeland was overrun and partitioned once more by Nazi Germany and Soviet Russia and World War II began. Ironically, developments between 1918 and 1939 proved to be a source of some disenchantment for Polonia and the PNA and hardly the unalloyed blessing that they had expected independence to be. That the era could only leave bittersweet memories was inevitable, however, since Polish independence required Polonia's members to begin to rethink their relationship to both the homeland and America in the light of reality. After 1918, most Poles made a fateful decision to remain in America rather than to return to the old country. But having done so, the question remained as to what Polonia's priorities should be in the years ahead. Some argued that with independence won, Polish Americans needed to focus their attention upon the purely domestic issues before the community, issues connected with the preservation of its institutions and native language. Others emphasized assimilation or at least the advancement of successful Polish Americans into professional and business pursuits heretofore reserved to native born "Yankees."[24] Still others continued to place their greatest emphasis upon efforts to promote the new Poland's interests in the United States, a perspective backed by the Polish government and its representatives in this country.

Within the PNA, two factions emerged in the 1920s with conflicting opinions about Poland and its proper relationship with the Alliance and Polonia. One group, the "old guard," was headed by the President of the PNA, Casimir Zychlinski and aligned itself with the conservative politics of Dmowski and Paderewski. A second faction came to be called the "left" or the "opposition." Its most prominent figure was Casimir Sypniewski, a Pittsburgh attorney elected PNA Censor in 1924. The "opposition" was enthusiastically inclined to Pilsudski and his politics even when they led to a controversial restriction of democratic liberties in Poland after 1926. For its part, Pilsudski's government became increasingly interested in developing closer relations with the PNA in order to build support within Polonia.

Factional conflict came to a head in September 1927, when approximately half the delegates to the Alliance's national convention bolted the meeting as it became clear that the left faction was about to gain control by using the tactic of rejecting the credentials of all contested delegates identified with the old guard. These delegates then staged a counterconvention at another hotel only a few blocks away. The internal fight over the fraternal eventually had to be settled in court; both factions were ordered to reschedule the convention and to try to solve their disagreement themselves. When this meeting was held in August 1928, the left faction won out, but its victory was short-lived. Three years later, an old guard leader, Francis X. Swietlik, defeated Sypniewski for the office of censor and his followers captured control of the board of directors. Under Swietlik, the PNA made a determined and successful effort to disentangle itself from internal Polish politics while taking pains to reaffirm its dedication to preserving the ethnic heritage in America. Indeed, Swietlik succeeded in redefining the PNA's and Polonia's relationship with Poland in his remarks at the 1934 world conference of Poles from abroad, which was held in Warsaw. There, speaking as the representative of American Polonia, Swietlik asserted the community's primary allegiance to the United States. Nonetheless, he assured his hosts that the Polish Americans possessed ties to their ancestral homeland which they wished to retain based on "feeling, tradition and culture."

Despite the intense infighting which so heavily colored PNA activities during the 1920s and 1930s, this period simultaneously witnessed an almost incredible expansion in membership. After the First World War, approximately 130 thousand people belonged to the PNA; by 1930 the total approached 290 thousand, a rate of growth that might have continued indefinitely had it not been reversed by the Great Depression. Assets also rose sharply to more than 20 million dollars, eleven times what they had been in 1913.

The Depression affected the Alliance in various ways aside from flattening out the rate of overall membership growth. Also threatened was the movement's appeal to young insurance policy holders, since many parents with insured children had to drop their coverage when they themselves lost their jobs.

This situation, however, led the PNA to redouble its efforts with the youth and simultaneously to address the problem of preserving its ethnic consciousness. As a result, the PNA organized the Polish scouting movement in America, or *Harcerstwo,* in 1931. At its zenith, *Harcerstwo* included more than fifty thousand youngsters. Though it passed from the scene after 1939, much of the vitality that the PNA demonstrated in later years was a product of those veterans of the scouting movement whose commitment to the PNA had first been kindled during the time they spent in *Harcerstwo* activities.

The Alliance, like many other insurance organizations, was buffeted by a sharp decline in its real estate investments caused by an epidemic of property foreclosures during the crisis. This experience led the PNA to restructure its investment portfolio to place less emphasis upon real estate and more upon government bonds, an action assuring a safer rate of growth in the future.

During this phase in its history, the PNA also evolved an enduring set of ties with other Polonia organizations. Prior to the First World War, competition was the word best describing relations between the Alliance and other Polonia organizations with PNA leaders at odds with both the Polish clergy in the Roman Catholic Church and their critics in the socialist movement and the Polish National Catholic church over matters connected with Polonia's priorities. After 1914, this situation changed dramatically. In the years that followed the Polish National Alliance succeeded in building firm bridges with the most significant clerical and moderate organizations in Polonia on the basis of their mutual commitment to the general well-being of Poland and Polonia. Best typifying the "era of good feelings" was the creation in 1936 of what became the Polish American Council, a joint effort of the PNA, the Polish Roman Catholic Union, the Polish Women's Alliance and other groups under Swietlik's leadership. Designed to provide humanitarian assistance to needy members of Polonia, the work of the Council focused upon Poland's relief following the outbreak of World War II.

The PNA under Rozmarek (1939–1967) and Mazewski (since 1967). Both the fourth and the fifth eras in PNA history are best understood in terms of the individuals who led the organization. Between 1939 and 1967, it was Charles Rozmarek who served as president; during this twenty-eight year span, Rozmarek, a Wilkes-Barre, Pennsylvania lawyer, placed his mark firmly upon the character of the PNA and indeed Polonia. Rozmarek was elected to lead the PNA just as Poland itself was being invaded by Germany. Not surprisingly the cause of Poland's independence, both during the war and in the years of communist rule after 1945, remained paramount throughout Rozmarek's long tenure in office.

Rozmarek's great achievement was in organizing and leading the Polish American Congress. Formed in 1944 this federation of ethnic fraternals, veterans' groups, churches and cultural organizations represented the fulfill-ment of the historic PNA goal of unifying Polonia on behalf of Polish independence. Nonetheless, the emphasis Rozmarek placed on Polish affairs meant insufficient attention to problems facing the PNA, whose membership began to drop in the late 1950s due to assimilation's impact upon Polonia.

It was during Rozmarek's long administration that the organized Polonia communities in cities such as Chicago, Buffalo and Detroit began to decline in size and vitality as their younger members moved away to new and non-Polish neighborhoods. This development also weakened the PNA since so many of its local lodges were located in aging neighborhoods that were inexorably losing their ethnic character. Instead of working to revitalize the existing lodges of the PNA Rozmarek placed emphasis upon the recruitment of foreign-born Poles from the post World War II emigration. Though sensible in many respects, this strategy accentuated the foreign character of the Alliance and lessened its attractiveness to young native-born Polonians reaching adulthood after the war.

The most recent era in PNA history began in 1967 when Aloysius Mazewski of Chicago defeated Rozmarek in his quest for an unprecedented eighth term as president and shortly thereafter was elected president of the Polish American Congress as well. The Mazewski era might be best characterized as a time of transition for an organization which needed to modernize its insurance and fraternal offerings in order to remain a vital force well into the next century. Since 1967 the fraternal's membership decline has been addressed more openly than was previously the case. While the PNA has been unable to identify and implement strategies to revitalize its local lodges (which remain its chief vehicle for the recuitment of new members), Mazewski's recognition of the problem of lodge inactivity was a welcome step forward. And, fortunately, the downward slide in membership has slowed recently, thanks partly to efforts originating in the Chicago home office to find new ways in which to recruit insurance holders.

Under Mazewski the greatest successes have come in the fields of the investment of PNA funds and in preserving the organization's historic commitment to Poland. Taking full advantage of the PNA's status as a tax-exempt enterprize, Mazewski directed the fraternal away from investment practices favored by Rozmarek and into the purchase of Federal securities. These actions combined a low degree of risk with an extraordinarily high rate of return, due largely to the inflationary conditions affecting the American economy during the 1970s. At the same time, the PNA remained firmly committed to its historic aims toward Poland under Mazewski. Efforts were made to revitalize the Polish American Congress, whose activities had noticeably diminished during the last years of Rozmarek's tenure. Hence, when Poland entered its most recent period of extended crisis in 1980, for example, the PAC was ready to play a constructive role in support of the country's political, economic and humanitarian needs.

Despite assimilation's corrosive effects upon Polonia and the PNA, Mazewski's policies helped preserve the fraternal as a significant mass membership organization which could continue to operate in the future. He also preserved the organization's ethnic identity in a period of great pressures to alter its traditional character in search of new policy holders. As its members look to the second century of PNA development, they have the opportunity to continue the work of an Alliance that has remained true to its historic aims.

Chapter 2

LAYING THE FOUNDATION: 1830-1885

The roots of the Polish National Alliance are to be found in the history of nineteenth century Poland and the events, social developments and political ideas which dominated Polish life in the years following the country's loss of independence in 1795. Most important were the series of insurrections against foreign rule and their impact upon popular thought, the difficult economic conditions inside the country which spurred increasingly large numbers of people to look abroad for work, and the persistence of nationalist feeling which by the 1890s had given rise to powerful political movements inside the country that reached out for support to the Polish migration and its organizations in America.

To most educated Poles throughout the nineteenth century, the central political cause animating their activities was nothing other than the restoration of Poland's independence. The Polish state dated back to the year 966, when one of its early princes, Mieszko, accepted Christianity from Rome and was recognized as king by the German emperor. For the next four centuries, the country's fortunes ebbed and flowed in relation to its leaders' ability to promote internal stability and to prevent foreign intrusions from permanently scarring its development.[1]

Perhaps its outstanding leader was King Kazimierz "Wielki" (the Great), who governed the country between 1333 to 1370. It was during the peaceful reign of this last member of the *Piast* dynasty, whose origins reached back to Mieszko, that a university was established in Krakow, the second such institution of learning in all of Eastern Europe. In 1386, Poland's development was decisively affected by the marriage between Jadwiga, Queen of Poland and a grand niece of Kazimierz, and the Grand Duke of Lithuania, Yagailo (known in Poland as Wladyslaw Jagiello I). Through this union, which remained in place after the Queen's death (though it was not made permanent until 1569), Poland was transformed into a vast kingdom whose territories

35

embraced present day Bielorussia, the Baltic states, much of the Ukraine and parts of western Russia. The Lithuanian-Polish domain achieved international recognition after Jagiello's triumph over the Teutonic Knights at the battle of Grunwald (Tannenberg) in 1410. During the following 160 years the kingdom not only reached its political apogee but also grew into a center of intellectual life best symbolized by the discoveries of the astronomer and mathematician, Nicolaus Copernicus.

In 1574, however, the king's death brought an end to the Jagiellonian dynasty. In its place the nobility established an elective monarchy. But this decision had disastrous consequences that led to the weakening of the central government at the very moment when strong authority was most needed to defend the vast Polish-Lithuanian kingdom from its powerful neighbors, tsarist Russia, Prussia and Austria. The ascendancy of the great nobility over the monarchy was further accentuated by its use of the notorious *liberum veto* to dissolve sessions of the national parliament (or *sejm*) to kill unwanted legislation. The debilitating effects of the constant border wars Poland had to fight to maintain its territorial integrity combined with the erosion of the power of the central government gradually brought about the country's complete ruin by the end of the eighteenth century.

In 1772, Russia, Prussia and Austria occupied one-third of Poland's territory and in 1793, Russia and Prussia took half of what remained. In 1795, after the failure of a massive revolt against the partitioning powers led by Tadeusz Kosciuszko, Russia, Prussia and Austria again divided the remnants of Poland and erased the state from the European map.

Many regarded the collapse of the Kosciuszko uprising as nothing less than the end of Poland, "finis Poloniae." But others persisted in believing that independence might be regained by force. Thus, between 1807 and 1815, Poles joined Napoleon in his wars against the rest of Europe in the hope that he would reward their service by restoring their country's independence. Though Napoleon's decision to create only a "Duchy of Warsaw" (carved out mainly from the territories taken by Prussia) disappointed the Poles, they continued to hope that France's ultimate triumph would bring about Poland's restoration. Napoleon's defeat meant the end of these expectations and continued partition for Poland.

In November 1830, a major revolt originated in Warsaw against the Russian ruled "congress kingdom" which had been created in Vienna in 1815 by the European powers. The revolt was crushed a year later; what few political freedoms the Poles had enjoyed under their own local constitution were removed and the "congress kingdom" dissolved. In 1846 and 1848 smaller revolts occurred against Austrian and Prussian rule but these too were quelled.

In January 1863, a massive uprising against Russian rule broke out, one which required the tsar's forces more than a year to suppress. With the crushing of the January insurrection, the romantic idea popularized by the poet Adam Mickewicz, that the justice of their cause required the Poles to fight to regain their freedom even against enormous military odds, was dealt a severe blow.

Though Poles continued to participate in the revolutions of other European peoples under the slogan, "For your freedom and ours," a new political outlook became preeminent in their homeland after 1864. This view was known variously as "positivism," "realism," and "organic work" and was at loggerheads with the Romantics' adherence to insurrection. Its partisans condemned romanticism and the idea of insurrection and instead emphasized that the nation's survival required a concerted effort to undertake social and educational policies aimed at uplifting the conditions of the peasants, the largest segment of the population but heretofore a passive element in the country's affairs, and bringing them into the mainstream of Polish life.

In fact, the origins of the organic work effort went back to the era following the first partition of 1772. Then, progressives such as Hugo Kollataj and Stanislaw Staszyc had led the struggle to bring about a systematic reform of Polish political and social life. The product of their efforts was a constitution promulgated on May 3, 1791. A "revolutionary document adopted in semi-revolutionary conditions" by the Polish *sejm,* the constitution enjoyed the full support of the king, Stanislaw August Poniatowski.

The "Third of May Constitution" introduced changes in the Polish government whose purpose was to end the anarchy that had increasingly typified political life after 1574. Through the constitution, the machinery of government was modernized and the *liberum veto* abolished, along with the system of elective monarchy. The constitution also included several democratic ideas considered radical at the time. One extended citizen rights until then enjoyed only by the nobility and the clergy to the townspeople, particularly the privilege of *neminem captivabimus,* or freedom from arbitrary arrest. Peasants were promised the protection of the law, although the problem of serfdom itself was not specifically considered. While Roman Catholicism was proclaimed the national religion, freedom of other religious faiths was assured. Furthermore, the rights of minorities such as the Jews were given constitutional guarantees, an action then without precedent.[2]

But, the proclamation of the 1791 constitution only caused Russia and Prussia to intervene militarily to prevent its implementation and Poland's revival. Following the second partition of 1793, the old system of misgovernment was reimposed on the Polish rump state. The Kosciuszko uprising of 1794 thus represented a last desperate effort to save Poland from dissolution. This revolt was noteworthy, however, in that Kosciuszko went beyond organizing the nobility in a quixotic crusade to save the old Polish kingdom; rather he promised citizen rights to every serf who joined the cause. Thousands of peasants took him seriously; armed only with scythes they fought bravely against the armies of Russia and Prussia. Although Kosciuszko was captured and his revolt put down, the 1794 insurrection advanced the social reform ideas initiated by Kollataj and Staszyc in recognizing the need to incorporate the peasants into national life and to deal with their problems.

Throughout the nineteenth century, a number of Polish leaders in the various partitioned zones attempted to develop policies to improve the conditions of the population. For example, between 1815–1830 in the Russian-ruled congress kingdom, Xavier Drucki-Lubecki and Adam Czartoryski took the lead in working to develop industry and education, although most of the political rights included in the kingdom's constitution were nullified after 1825 because of Tsar Nicholas I's opposition.

The defeat of the November, 1830 insurrection brought an end to these early reform efforts. Not until the rule of Tsar Alexander II, which began in 1855, was liberalization permitted once more in the Polish lands. By the early 1860s, improvements in political, cultural and economic conditions had been initiated by Aleksander Wielopolski and Andrzej Zamoyski. But their efforts generated pressure from nationalists for even greater liberalization, which Wielopolski unsuccessfully tried to repress. In January, 1863 the radical faction of the nationalist movement proclaimed a revolution; soon afterward it was joined by its more conservative rivals who together formed a "national government." Urging similar revolts in Lithuania and the Ukraine, the nationalists promised the serfs land and freedom in return for their support.

The disastrous failure of the January insurrection following upon the heels of smaller rebellions in the Prussian and Austrian zones turned the Poles more decisively than ever before away from romanticism and into the direction of political realism. Rejecting armed revolution as hopeless, "realists" stressed the need to develop industrial and agricultural life and to raise the population's standard of living. They placed new emphasis upon mass education, which included schooling about the Polish national heritage, but placed even greater stress upon technical training to assist the Poles in raising the partitioned country's economic standards. Realist intellectuals such as the University of Krakow historian Aleksander Swietochowski condemned the excesses of the romantic tradition and extolled the "heroism of a reasonable life." As he put it, "we wish to extend work and learning in society to discover new resources, to utilize existing ones and to concern ourselves with our own problems and not those of others," a direct slap at those who identified with Mickiewicz, who had written, "he who cares only about the interests of his own nation is an enemy of liberty."[3]

At first, the differences between the prescriptions of Poland's recovery offered by proponents of realist and idealist bent were starkly opposed to one another. Yet each orientation was at heart deeply nationalistic in spirit and this had become evident by the last years of the nineteenth century, when the most significant political movements in the country had come to embrace elements of each perspective. For example, a Marxian socialist party formed in 1892 and dedicated to the cause of the small but growing Polish working class asserted at the same time a call for "an independent, democratic and republican Poland" whose freedom would be brought about by armed insurrection. Another organization formed at about the same time and calling itself the National Democratic party took a different tactical position but agreed in principle with the socialists on the primacy of national independence. Headed by Roman Dmowski, the National Democrats opposed violence but stressed instead that Poles adopt a tough patriotic stance based upon ethnic, rather than class, solidarity. Dmowski urged his countrymen to imitate the spartan qualities of the hated Prussian nation, even as he unceasingly warned them of the threat Germany's forced assimilation policy posed over the Polish inhabitants under its dominion. Significantly, these two movements, one socialist the other nationalist, were to play decisive roles in shaping Poland's destiny just as their chief leaders, Jozef Pilsudski and Dmowski, would exert considerable influence upon the development of American Polonia and the Polish National Alliance.

Nineteenth century Polish conditions and political ideas also had their impact outside of Poland. This was due to the fact that an enormous number of people left Poland in increasing numbers especially after 1850 and settled primarily in the United States. This emigration was by no means monolithic or homogeneous in nature; on the contrary those who left their homeland were motivated by a wide variety of reasons for departing from Poland in favor of the uncertainties of a vast and alien society that was the United States. In appreciating the forces that together brought forth the PNA, however, it is important that these emigrations be analyzed in some detail.

The smallest emigration was made up of political exiles who trickled into this country following the failure of the insurrections. But while their numbers were few—in 1861, for example, only a thousand of the estimated 30,000 Poles then in the United States were considered "political exiles"—their influence was nonetheless considerable for it was out of their ranks that the first Polish patriotic societies and newspapers in America came. Moreover, the message of the most indefatigable of exile activists, that Poland's independence remained a cause worth working for, was ultimately adopted by practically all Polish organizations which possessed a mass membership by the turn of the twentieth century.

Far larger in numbers was the series of heavily peasant migrations out of Poland which began in the early 1850s and peaked during the years between 1890 and 1913. In all, more than three and one-half million people left Poland during this period with about two and one half million having the U.S. as their destination.[4]

The mass migrations occurred in response to worsening economic conditions in the three zones of partitioned Poland caused by a population explosion which saw the number of inhabitants more than double between 1850 and 1914.

What factors account for so massive a population movement? One had to do with the failure of Polish urbanization and industrialization to meet the needs of the ever growing rural population, although in the provinces under German and Russian rule there were some notable developments in both areas. In Russian Poland, for example, industrial output increased tenfold between 1860 and 1900; in 1914, one-fourth of all industrial production in the entire empire originated out of the Polish provinces, which accounted for only one-twelfth of the population. Another measure of development dealt with the expansion of cities and towns. In 1860, for example, Poland's ten largest cities possessed a combined total of 477 thousand

Table 1.   Population Growth in Partitioned Poland and Sources of Emigration, 1850–1914 (in Millions)

	1850	1860	1870	1890	1910	Total Emigration 1870–1914
Russian Zone	4.81	4.84	5.83	8.19	11.52	1.25
Austrian Zone	4.56	5.03	5.45	6.61	8.03	1.05
German Zone	3.45	3.81	4.21	4.74	6.01	1.21
Total Population	12.82	13.68	15.49	19.54	25.56	3.51

inhabitants, or 3.5 percent of the country's total population. By 1910, the ten largest cities had a combined population of 2.15 million, or 8.4 percent of the population. In 1860, Warsaw possessed 158 thousand inhabitants; in 1910 the number had grown to 781 thousand. Lodz, a minor town of 26,000 people in 1860 had risen to the rank of Poland's second city by 1910 with 408 thousand inhabitants. Wilno had expanded from 60 thousand to 181 thousand residents during the same period and Lwow and Krakow, the major centers in Austrian Poland, had risen to 196 thousand and 143 thousand inhabitants, respectively. Poznan, German Poland's leading industrial center, included 150 thousand inhabitants in 1910.[5]

Such dramatic developments could not, however, keep up with the rapidly expanding needs of the growing peasant population. In fact, economic conditions for the peasantry, which by 1863 had been liberated from serfdom in all three zones of the country, steadily deteriorated as the century wore on. In Austrian Poland, the trend in the countryside was toward pauperization. In 1859 two-thirds of all farms in Galicia were under ten acres in size; by 1900 four-fifths of all the parcels fell into this category. In Prussian Poland, the serf emancipation left many people without any land at all or with parcels too small to sustain them. Furthermore, German laws designed to drive the Poles off the land made it extremely difficult for them to purchase whatever acreage was for sale. By 1907, many Poles had already left the countryside in search of work in the cities or they had sunk to the status of farm laborers. Of the Polish farms that remained, 312 thousand of 575 thousand were less than three acres in size. In Russian Poland, it was once more the case of the population explosion negating the benefits of the tsar's emancipation decree of 1864 and the subsequent rise in industry. Between 1870 and 1891 alone, the number of landless peasant households grew from 226 thousand to 849 thousand.[6]

One response to the growing crisis came out of the programs of the realists, who propagandized the organizing of rural cooperative activities to assist the small peasant farmers in improving their crop yields and introducing modern farming practices into their work. Though progress in organizing such institutions was tortuously slow (as much due to peasant resistance to changes in their traditional farming practices as to the opposition of the ruling authorities), gradually the more enterprising villagers began to recognize the value of cooperative work in helping them achieve their individual interests.

The chief of these was the acquisition of land . . . the only investment that made sense to the peasant. The peasants turned also—guided at first by the intelligentsia and enlightened landlords and, later, on their own initiative—to economic and political cooperation. Their struggle for genuine independence took many forms—consumer cooperatives, savings and loan banks, agricultural associations (for the purchase of machinery, seed or breeding stock), the education of the young (to promote economic progress and prevent denationalization), and conservative populist parties.[7]

While cooperative activity took different form in each zone of partitioned Poland, what is significant is that by 1914 the movement was in full swing everywhere. One type of organizational form found in all sections of the country was the agricultural circle, a village level association dedicated to the modernization of farming practices and the sharing of information about planting and animal husbandry. The first agricultural circles had been formed in Prussian Poland in the 1860s under the auspices of several progressive large landowners but by 1914, the greatest number of circles was to be found in Austrian ruled "Galicia," the least politically repressive zone and the most agriculturally depressed as well. There, the movement included eighty-two thousand members in 2,081 villages. In the Russian zone, 1,051 village circles claimed fifty-two thousand members while in Prussian Poland fifteen thousand members belonged to 395 units. Moreover, by World War I, peasants had advanced to leadership roles in most of the circles in Galicia, at least, and held responsible posts in many other self-help cooperatives, savings associations and consumer groups.[8]

In spite of the salutory benefits of cooperative activity for the peasant population, the rate of modernization in agriculture was nowhere fast enough to nullify pressures brought on by population increases. Although their experience in participating in cooperative activities (including the chance to play leadership roles in their operations) must have made a positive impact upon those involved in the groups, there had to be another solution to the growing overpopulation problem facing the countryside. This was in emigration.

Originating in the 1850s, peasant migration out of Poland to America had assumed mass proportions by the late 1870s. Several of its characteristics deserve some comment. For one thing, emigration to the United States (and to Canada and Latin America as opposed to Germany) had a character that was permanent rather than seasonal, primarily because of the distances involved. While many emigrants to America planned to return home after a stay abroad a few years, most eventually remained in the United States and even brought over members of their families to join them as well. Eventually their numbers were sufficient to enable their formation of organized communities and institutions.

Some Poles did worry that mass emigration would deprive the homeland of its most energetic sons and daughters, to the detriment of its own development and future independence. They were convinced that those who left for the United States would also be rapidly assimilated within American society and lose touch with the homeland.[9] But others, such as the members of the Polish Emigration Society headquartered in Lwow were of a different opinion. After carefully reviewing the reports of visitors to America, the organization's leaders concluded that "the Poles in America have a very powerful national consciousness and they are much more enlightened than the generality in the mother country . . . America (has become) the school of our people . . . "[10] It was in America, indeed, that many of the immigrants became fully conscious for the first time that they were Poles. Commenting on this phenomenon was the author of the first history of the Polish National Alliance, Stefan Barszczewski. Writing in 1894, he noted that few Poles considered themselves Polish when they first entered the United States, although later they frequently did develop a solid national consciousness. "In answer to the question, 'where are you from?' our immigrants reply almost unanimously, 'from under the Prussians, the Austrians, or the Russians,' . . . Not surprisingly, American census officials report thousands of immigrants (from those countries) but few Poles, when the exact opposite is true!"[11]

Another side of the mass migration was its wave-like character and the subtle but real differences among the three population movements out of German, Austrian and Russian Poland. Initially, the German-ruled zone provided the greatest number of emigrants beginning in the 1850s and reaching peak levels in the 1880s and 1890s before sharply subsiding later on. For example, in the 1870s more than 90 percent of the more than 160 thousand Poles in America hailed from German-controlled provinces in Silesia, Poznania and Pomerania. By the 1890s only about 15 percent of the half million Poles coming to the United States were from this region and during the year between 1899 and 1913 the proportion dropped to only 4 percent out of 1.5 million in all.[12]

Though it is roughly correct to state that many of these people came to the United States "for bread," that is, for economic reasons, it seems clear that their decisions were greatly influenced by the repressive measures enacted by the German empire from the 1850s onward. In the German provinces, the less restrictive policies of the preceding decade were revoked following suppression of the 1848 uprising. Those enactments had permitted Karol Marcinkowski and others to set up vocational schools and businesses among the Polish inhabitants. From then onward until the outbreak of World War I, German policy remained unremittingly opposed to Polish aspirations.

Under Otto von Bismarck, Chancellor from 1867 to 1890, the official policy in Berlin was to fully integrate the Poles into the German nation. The position of the Polish nobility and landowners was the first to be attacked when laws were promulgated whose sole aim was to force them to sell their land to Junker purchasers. A *kulturkampf*, literally, a war on the status of the Roman Catholic Church throughout the empire was declared on the grounds that it was a "state within a state" and thus a threat to the regime. This action had particularly serious consequences for the Poles, who now became the target of cultural and religious as well as economic repression. German was also introduced as the official language in the Polish schools and in legal matters.

In 1885 and 1886, Bismarck's government supported the forcible expulsion of Poles from their own homes on the grounds that they were not legally citizens of Germany. Even more ominous, he established a government-supported colonization commission providing low interest loans to assist Germans in buying farmland in the Polish provinces, thereby helping to dilute their historic ethnic character. In the face of such relentless repression, however, Polish national consciousness did not wither but flourished. Movements such as the agricultural circle coops took an active role in shoring up the defenses of the embattled farmers. Awakened by the threat to its very existence posed by the *kulturkampf*, the Church became the champion of the rights of the people, thereby strengthening further the traditional ties between Polish nationality and religion. By the First World War, the position of the Poles in Poznania and Pomerania was stronger than it had been twenty years before. The Polish population was growing more rapidly than the German, Poles were holding onto their lands, and illiteracy was practically non-existent.[13] Politically, it was Dmowski's National Democratic party which became the most significant representative of Polish aspirations in this zone of the partitioned country.

The second emigration wave began in the 1880s and peaked in the 1890s before it was superceded during the years just prior to the War. Its origins were in the Austrian-controlled provinces which together were known as "Galicia." In the 1890s, approximately 60 percent of the Polish immigration to America came out of this zone, more than 300 thousand people in all. Between 1899 and 1913, even more came from Galicia, perhaps as many as 700 thousand, although by this time the greatest wave was arriving out of the Russian provinces.

Economically the most rural, backward and heavily overpopulated region of nineteenth century Poland, Galicia was, however, less burdened by political repression than the provinces under German and Russian rule; nor were the authorities particularly opposed to the use of the Polish language in the schools. Indeed, after 1867 Austria-Hungary permitted a measure of political participation in government by conservative and moderate Polish parties and enabled them to operate freely, run candidates for legislative office and become involved in parliamentary activities, both in Vienna and Lwow, the provincial capital. From 1889 onward, peasant deputies became permanent fixtures in these deliberative bodies; in 1895 the first mass-oriented peasant organization, the Polish People's Party, was formed. Its goals were progressive in character and included the further democratization of political life, the expansion of mass education opportunities at the village level, and a moderate redistribution of land aimed at advancing the interests of the small farmer. In contrast to German Poland, where the National Democratic movement was preeminent, activists belonging to the Galician peasant parties were increasingly visible in provincial politics.

The earliest populist leaders included the priest, Stanislaw Stojalowski, an individual who was also active in organizing newspapers and cooperatives promoting the ideas spelled out by Pope Leo XIII in his encyclical, *Rerum Novarum.* There, the Pope for the first time had placed the Church firmly on the side of social justice for all classes. A second Galician leader was Boleslaw Wyslouch, a newspaper publisher whose somewhat more liberal and secular periodical, *Przyjaciel ludu* (People's Friend) urged its readers to organize politically. Soon, however, Galician peasants themselves had supplanted Stojalowski and Wyslouch as populist leaders. One was Jakub Bojko, a prolific pamphleteer whose best known publication *Dwie Duszy* (Two Spirits) went through many editions. Bojko urged the peasants to reject their serf mentality of inferiority in favor of a new spirit of pride and self-reliance. The peasants, as much as the nobility and the clergy, were destined to play leading roles in building an independent and democratic future Poland, he asserted.

Jan Stapinski, a peasant like Bojko, became the chief populist leader between 1895 and 1913. Even more influential was another peasant named Wincenty Witos, who replaced Stapinski after an internal party fight just prior to the outbreak of the World War. During the 1920s Witos was elected prime minister of Poland on three separate occasions. Witos and his followers organized the *Piast* Peasant Party, which combined a commitment to moderate economic reform, a support for the rural cooperative movement, and a deep faith in parliamentary democracy. These ideas were pervasive among Galician immigrants to America as well.[14]

To the Prussian Polish sense of national solidarity in the face of foreign oppression and the Austrian Polish sense of political moderation and compromise, must be added the "Russian" Poles' commitment to revolution and their fascination with a form of socialism that was deeply nationalist in spirit and affected by the *Narodnik* movement. It was, after all, in the Russian-ruled provinces that the most bloody insurrections against foreign oppression had occurred—in 1794, in 1830-1, in 1863 and in 1905—and where the insurrectionist tradition remained strongest. Moreover, with the rapid growth of industrialization in Warsaw and Lodz, it was in Russian Poland where the socialist movement of Jozef Pilsudski gained its largest followings.

It was also in the Russian zone where the Poles faced their most complex task after 1864. There, Russification was imposed with a vengence, and this policy was never really moderated over the next fifty years. In Russian Poland, the tsar had imposed his own emancipation, turning class against class by posing as the peasants' true liberator while at the same time confiscating the insurrectionists' land and property. Because the Russian government resisted the formation of peasant self-help associations, however, the development of these institutions lagged behind what occurred in the other zones of partitioned Poland. But national feeling was stimulated among the Poles, largely through St. Petersburg's heavyhanded efforts to repress the Catholic Church and its prohibition on the use of Polish. Emigration out of the empire began to assume mass proportions only in the 1890s but afterward rose dramatically to peak of 113 thousand in 1913 alone. In all, Russian Poland provided the greatest number of emigrants to American Polonia. While the Polish community in the United States was already fairly well organized by the time the "Russians" began to make their presence felt, their contribution to Polonia was evident and consisted of a fierce hostility to the tsarist empire and an identification with the insurrectionist tradition.

It was thus out of these diverse movements of impoverished, little educated but courageous people that the mass membership of the Polish National Alliance would be derived. But the PNA itself was a product of a different emigration, the small but deeply nationalistic bands of politically conscious exiles in America which sought to mobilize the mass migration behind the ideal of a reborn Poland.

Roots of the Polish National Alliance

The first small wave of Polish exiles was in the United States as early as 1818, composed of refugees from Napoleon's Duchy of Warsaw who eventually settled in Alabama. The first Polish organization in the United

States was set up in New York city only later, however, after the failure of the November, 1830 uprising. Called the Polish Committee, it was made up of perhaps as many as two hundred *emigres* transported to America by the Austrian authorities, and its aim included winning U.S. approval of a Polish settlement in Illinois or Michigan. The plan failed and the Committee as well as its successor, the Polish National Committee, disappeared.

A more significant *emigre* organization, the Society of Poles in America, was established in 1842 in New York. Though not long in existence either, the Society included in its leadership an individual who was to play a vital role in Polish American matters for the next half-century, Henry Kalussowski.[15]

Kalussowski was born in Poland in 1806 and had taken part in the November insurrection. Arriving in America from Western Europe in 1842, he was already a trusted member of the Polish exile movement in Paris and rapidly assumed leadership of the newly-created Society of Poles. In 1848 Kalussowski returned to Poland to take part in the Poznan uprising only to return a second time to the United States, this time for good. From 1850 onward, Kalussowski played a pivotal role in the nascent American Polish community. Having secured a federal appointment in the Treasury department he became for all practical purposes the representative of the American Poles in Washington, D.C. and was later instrumental in winning military appointments for Polish officers during the Civil War.

In 1852 Kalussowski organized yet another *emigre* group, the Democratic Society of Polish Refugees in America, comprised of veterans of the 1830 revolution as well as newcomers from the 1848 rising. Founded on the principles of the May 3, 1791 constitution this society was open to all Poles regardless of their religious affiliation and was also committed to the emancipation of Negro slaves. This view later linked it with the newly established Republican party. Kalussowski's activities during the 1863 Polish insurrection were considerable, although less successful. Appointed the American representative of the Polish national revolutionary government and made responsible for generating public support for its cause, Kalussowski found American popular opinion unsympathetic to his efforts. This was largely because the Russian Empire was one of the few European states to openly support the Union cause, unlike the British and French governments which flirted with recognizing the Confederacy.

After the War Kalussowski became increasingly aware of the growth in the immigration and was one of the first Poles to perceive its potential significance in support of the independence cause. In 1878 he wrote to his old compatriot from the 1863 revolutionary days, Agaton Giller, urging his support of a patriotic movement of Poles in America. Kalussowski's letter was not the only one Giller received and acknowledged. Another was from Julian Lipinski, also a veteran of the 1863 insurrection who was living in Philadelphia. Still a third appeal came from the poet Teofila Samolinska, who had settled in Chicago in the late 1860s and become a proponent of both the *Gmina Polska* society and women's equality.[16] Already advanced in years, Kalussowski himself did not become active in the Polish National Alliance that came into existence through his initiative, but he remained a strong supporter of its work.[17]

Political groups such as those Kalussowski led were not the only organizations of Poles formed in America. The early migrations from Silesia to Texas, Wisconsin and Michigan were led by clergymen and once fledgling communities had been formed the first institution to be set up was the parish church. In Chicago, the still tiny Polish immigration was without any organizational character at all as late as 1864. At that point, its leaders were encouraged to form a fraternal aid society to meet its needs until it was large enough to establish a parish of its own. The inspiration for this idea apparently came from the Franciscan priest, Leopold Moczygeba, who in 1854 had organized the Polish settlement in Panna Maria in Texas and had travelled to Chicago to hear the Poles' Easter confessions. Under the leadership of two men, Peter Kiolbassa and Anthony Smarzewski (also known as Scherman), this group became the Saint Stanislas Kostka fraternal aid society, the first Polish benefit association in America.

Following Kiolbassa's return from Civil War military service, the Saint Stanislas Society was revived in 1866. Its goals were ambitious and ranged from raising money for its own church to creating an insurance program to cover burial expenses benefitting the families of deceased members. True to its name, the Saint Stanislas Society was clearly Catholic rather than nationalist in character. Not surprisingly, a more secular-minded group of Chicago Poles soon formed a second fraternal aid society in October, 1866 and named it "Gmina Polska" (The Polish Council). Created in the image of several already existing groups of Polish exiles in Europe, the *Gmina Polska* society was helped considerably by another leader of the 1863 uprising, Jozef Hauke.[18]

For the members of *Gmina Polska*, including such later PNA luminaries as Stanislas Kociemski, Michael Majewski, Max Kucera, Teofila Samolinska and Ignace Wendzinski, the central purpose of their society was definitely patriotic. This inevitably pitted the *Gmina* against the Saint Stanislas Kostka society over the issue of the very church that all agreed was necessary for the community. *Gmina* members wanted a stronghold of Polish patriotic feeling, an idea opposed by Kiolbassa and his associates. Because of this disagreement, the dedication of the first Polish parish in Chicago was delayed until 1869. Only when the parishioners at last accepted diocesan authority over their church were they allowed to invite a Polish religious order, the Resurrectionists, to take over its management.

The rapid growth of Polish immigration into the near northside neighborhood in which Saint Stanislas church was located caused a more serious crisis in 1872. A fund raising drive to build a second church in the neighborhood was taken over by *Gmina* supporters who formed their own committee to establish a church independent of Saint Stanislas parish, the Resurrectionists and the diocese. This conflict was heightened by an ideological dispute between the two factions which came to a head in 1873 at the annual observance of the November uprising. On this occasion the pastor of Saint Stanislas Kostka parish took issue with the slogan of the patriotic group, "The People will save Poland," and asserted that only through some sort of divine intervention, and not by human efforts, would Poland ever be free. His words epitomized the differences between the patriotic camp's idealism and the realism of its critics, who regarded independence as unattainable and therefore less important than work among the immigrants.[19]

The division further widened soon afterwards when another Resurrectionist priest, Vincent Barzynski, assumed the pastorate at Saint Stanislas Kostka parish. To Barzynski, though himself a participant in the 1863 revolution, the ideas of the *Gmina* group were bankrupt. Moreover, as a fervent but somewhat intolerant Catholic, he rejected the idea that Polish patriotism could be anything other than Catholic in character. This energetic cleric acted quickly to put his ideas into effect. Within a short time, he had become the chief representative of Catholic realism in the rapidly increasing immigrant community in Chicago and in later years, throughout the country.

Locally, Barzynski moved decisively to prevent the new parish of the Holy Trinity from operating under diocesan approval until it was restored to satellite status under Resurrectionist authority. As a result, the church remained closed for most of the next twenty years, since the supporters of the rebel parish were unable to find a Polish pastor in good standing with the diocese who was willing to risk Barzynski's wrath. Not until 1893 was the dispute settled, but only through direct intervention by a papal representative from Rome. Accordingly, Holy Trinity parish accepted diocesan authority but was placed under the supervision of the Polish Holy Cross priests headquartered in South Bend, Indiana and not Barzynski. The Holy Trinity parishioners, however, were bitter over their experience and remained

committed to the patriotic and religious sentiments which had inspired their
original effort. Under their first pastor, the Reverend Casimir Sztuczko (who
lived until 1949), the church became a bastion of nationalist feeling and
the religious center of its chief secular expression, the PNA.

Moreover, Reverend Barzynski was active in working to form a number
of Chicago Polish parishes outside of the immediate boundaries of his own
church. These he attempted to make dependent upon his personal leadership.
Of the fifteen Chicago Polish parishes founded between 1871 and 1898,
for example, nine were initially headed by Resurrectionist priests, and three
others received financial assistance from St. Stanislas Kostka. Only three
churches established during this period had no ties with him.[20] Nationally,
Barzynski was also visible: as early as 1875 he publicly called for the
appointment of a Polish bishop to serve the burgeoning Polish immigration,
which already included two-hundred thousand souls and forty-four parishes
around the country. Furthermore, he became the dominant force behind
the first national federation of Polish societies created among the migration,
the Polish Roman Catholic Union in America.

This idea did not originate with Vincent Barzynski, however. Indeed, the
founders of the patriotic *Gmina Polska* society in Chicago had aspired to
make their group the kernel of a national organization. (Karol Piatkiewicz,
author of the 1940 history of the Polish National Alliance goes so far as
to call *Gmina Polska* "the mother of all fraternals.") In 1870, another group
out of New York also proclaimed the formation of a Polish National Union
but its effort, like that of *Gmina Polska,* brought no results.

In mid 1873, however, a viable proposal to form a Polish federation
was made, this time by John Barzynski, Vincent Barzynski's younger brother
and the publisher of a weekly newspaper, *Pielgrzym,* operating out of
Missouri.[21] Barzynski, though a Catholic, called for the establishment of
an "Organization of Poles in America" that would be open to all, regardless
of their religious or social views. The initial response to his newspaper appeal
was enthusiastic; by October 1873 (when a temporary executive committee
for the OPA was formed with Barzynski as chairman and Kiolbassa as
vice chairman), 360 persons had applied for membership.

But at its founding meeting in Detroit (July, 1874), the Reverend Theodore
Gieryk persuaded Barzynski to limit membership to Catholics. There, the
OPA was also officially christened the Polish Roman Catholic Union in
America and defined its goals for the first time. These included the building
of Polish schools, loan associations, libraries, a hospital, a convent and a
theological seminary. Money was pledged to make Barzynski's *Pielgrzym*
(renamed the *Gazeta Katolicka*) the organ of the federation. The aims of

the new organization reflected the thinking in the realist camp in that they focused exclusively upon the needs of the immigrants rather than upon independence. Given the PRCUA's basis at the local parish level and the organization's failure to adopt a system to raise funds to help realize its ambitious goals, the activities of the new federation, not surprisingly, were slight in the following decade.

Gieryk was elected the first president of the PRCUA, Kiolbassa vice president and John Barzynski became its secretary. The question of membership eligibility, however, resurfaced again at the PRCUA's third convention in Milwaukee in June, 1875; this time it led to a serious split in the federation. At the meeting, the Reverend Dominik Majer (1838–1911) proposed that all Poles be permitted to join the organization in accord with the spirit of the original OPA. When Reverend Barzynski took issue with his motion, Majer and his supporters, including Gieryk withdrew from the PRCUA. From this time until his death in 1899 at the age of 61, Vincent Barzynski remained the unchallenged head of the PRCUA, although he held no executive office in the federation. Catholicism was reaffirmed as the basis of membership and it was Barzynski who led the charge against any competing group which included non-Catholics in its ranks. Not all of the Polish clergy, of course, particularly those outside of Barzynski's Resurrectionist order, went along with this notion and personality conflicts added fuel to the disagreement. Majer, for example, became an early supporter of the Polish National Alliance and attended its first *sejm* in September, 1880. He had by this time left his pastorate at Saint Adalbert parish on Chicago's west side and organized a new parish in Pine Creek, Wisconsin, only to move again to St. Paul, Minnesota in 1883.

The dramatic events occurring at the 1875 PRCUA convention had significant consequences for American Polonia. On the one hand, the victory of Reverend Barzynski's faction meant firm Catholic control of the one operating federation of Polish societies. The PRCUA meeting thus repeated his earlier triumph over the nationalists in his own near northside Chicago community. For the patriotic camp, whose members maintained that an organization to unite the immigration had to include Catholics and non-Catholics alike, it was clear that another federation would be needed to realize these aspirations. The PRCUA's inability to implement its goals provided the opportunity needed by the patriotic camp to do just that.

Once again a call went out to organize a federation of patriotic groups in America. Already in May, 1875 Wladyslaw Dyniewicz, editor of the *Gazeta Polska* in Chicago and a *Gmina Polska* leader, had circulated his own proposal for just such a federation. But his appeal fell on deaf ears;

only the Kosciuszko Society in Philadelphia and a Saint Stanislas Society located in Calumet, Michigan replied. Stanislas Osada, author of the 1905 history of the PNA put it bluntly when he said, "The best aims of the *Gmina* had come to nothing."

Yet the picture soon changed thanks to a stirring within the exile patriotic movement in Western Europe. In Switzerland, a number of exiles had organized a center of *emigre* political activity to preserve the spirit of resistance to partition. One of its leaders was Agaton Giller, a veteran of the 1863 insurrection and one who appreciated the potential significance of the migration in the struggle for independence. Giller's long letter came in response to Henry Kalussowski's appeal and was published in Lwow in 1879 as an essay titled "The Organization of Poles in America." Later reprinted in Polish papers in the United States, the letter was widely read and served to spark renewed interest in the need for a patriotic movement.

In his letter, Giller not only called upon the members of the growing emigration to unite for patriotic purposes. He prudently included a number of persuasive reasons why such organizational activity made sense as a way of helping the immigrant improve himself economically and socially in his adopted homeland. Giller was adamant in urging the immigrants to enter American society rather than to remain apart from the cultural mainstream; only through their full integration into American life would it be possible for them to advance socially and along the way to attain increased influence in promoting the Polish cause to non-Poles. Rejecting the notion that the immigrants should form secret societies or preach violence, Giller correctly gauged the moderate sentiments of his intended audience, which he hoped would be sympathetic to any patriotic organization that simultaneously promoted its own interests.

Because the Polish emigration in America constitutes an undeniably great force, it should be the task of those who are motivated by true patriotic feelings to direct this force, so that our Fatherland's cause will be presented to its best advantage (in America).

In what way can we best direct the realization of Poland's cause? Through organization, we reply, since it is only through organization that our scattered immigrants can be unified. Only organized work will enable us to channel their concerns so that individual efforts (on Poland's behalf) will not be wasted, but rather consolidated for the good of our Fatherland. . . .

Having become morally and patriotically uplifted by the fact that we have unified ourselves, the major task before a Polish organization must be to help our people attain a good standard of living in America. For, when the masses of Poles in America, simply by their very presence in the country, reflect the good name of Poland to all whom they meet, they will be providing an enormously important service to Poland. In time, this service will be even greater as Poles begin to exert influence upon the political life of the United States.[22]

The possibilities Giller outlined were little short of intoxicating to his readers. The simple key to the realization of his proposals, which mixed material and idealistic goals and linked patriotic aspirations with personal ambition to achieve a better life in America, was organization. Through such a unified, patriotic, moderate and public mass organization, one could fulfill one's destiny as Pole and American.[23]

There were other reasons why Giller's words were effective in 1880. For one thing, the number of Poles in America had by then significantly grown to perhaps 300,000; given the very size of the immigration alone, it could no longer be regarded lightly. The passage of time also allowed the patriotic movement's fortunes to revive after nearly two decades of demoralization following the crushing experience of the 1863 insurrection. Furthermore, the Polish Roman Catholic Union's failure to include a single nationalist aim into its own program plus its own inactivity had provided an open field to any group aggressively promoting the patriotic cause. Finally, by 1880 the very number of patriotic societies in America had risen. Although the combined membership of all these groups was probably less than two thousand men in no more than twenty different local groups, their existence provided individuals interested in organizing a national movement with a base from which to work for the first time. Too, by 1880 the Polish press in America was also beginning to operate on a more regular basis. Giller himself noted that in Chicago alone, three competing papers were already in existence, *Gazeta Polska, Gazeta Katolicka, and Przyjaciel ludu.*

Given these developments, only the occasion to initiate a federation along the lines Giller proposed was wanting but this need was satisfied when news arrived from Poland in November, 1879 about a severe famine in Silesia. By early 1880 a number of concerned people had initiated relief efforts in several Polish communities; in Philadelphia the fund drive included three men who were to play founding roles in the Polish National Alliance, Julian Lipinski, Julian Szajnert and John Popielinski. All had been active in the Tadeusz Kosciuszko society but had withdrawn from that group when it failed to commemorate the Polish Constitution day holiday in May 1879. Operating on an *ad hoc* basis Lipinski visited the business establishment of Andrejkovicz and Dunk, a local dye-making company, where he spoke with one of the proprietors, Julius Andrzejkowicz, about the plight of the Silesians and Giller's appeal. The fifty-eight year old Andrzejkowicz, who had left Poland in 1849 but remained well-informed about Polish matters, reacted enthusiastically to Lipinski's words and quickly agreed to do what he could to organize some of his friends behind the campaign. Together they decided to call a meeting, which was set for February 15, 1880 at Andrzejkowicz's office.[24]

That evening, Andrzejkowicz called upon those in attendance to support Giller's appeal for a nationwide federation of patriotic societies to work for Poland's independence. He compared the fate of Poland with that of Italy, which only recently had been united as a free nation under the inspiration of Giuseppi Mazzini and his Young Italy movement. What, Andrzejkowicz asked, prevented the Poles in America from creating their own Young Poland movement?

> What is the status of the Polish immigrant in America? Isn't America far safer than England? Aren't we strong and independent? Do we not have freedom of speech, press and assembly? Why then, couldn't we form a national organization with a strong central leadership endowed with unlimited confidence and power?[25]

Andrzejkowicz's proposal to call the new federation *Zwiazek Narodowy Polski,* or Polish National Alliance, carried. The proposed Alliance was to be a federation of local patriotic societies, with each member group retaining its identity and autonomy while gaining a voice in the election of national leaders and determining policy. Andrzejkowicz was elected the first president of the Alliance, John Szonert vice president, Szajnert its secretary and Lipinski its treasurer.[26]

The next two months proved to be a period of extraordinary activity for the little group. The Alliance met six times and accepted a large number of new members into its ranks. Within a few days of its founding meeting, Andrzejkowicz and Szajnert sent out an announcement which was published in a New York paper named *Ogniwo* (the Link) inviting all patriotic societies to unify and thereby bring together the immigrants. Only through their alliance could such unity be achieved, they asserted; otherwise the immigration would be as impotent as seeds scattered into the wind.[27]

Letters were also addressed to exile leaders in Europe and as early as April 22, 1880 Giller himself replied, praising the effort to unite Poles and Lithuanians in America, people thought to have been "lost to Poland." Another exile leader, Count Wladyslaw Plater, also wrote back and offered some prudent advice to Andrzejkowicz when he reminded him of the importance of remaining close to the Church and cooperating fully with its representatives, since the PNA's greatest potential lay in linking religion and patriotism.[28]

At the Alliance's fourth meeting, Andrzejkowicz brought up the group's need to raise funds to cover its expenses. A collection was taken which netted the grand total of $4.25. To this sum Andrzejkowicz and Szajnert each contributed a dollar, Lipinski and Popielinski fifty cents apiece, John Blachowski and Anthony Wojczynski a quarter each and Vincent Domanski seventy-five cents. Certainly the old saying about mighty oaks growing out of tiny acorns was never more appropriate than in characterizing the growth of the Polish National Alliance, which a century later possessed assets amounting to $176 million.[29]

On June 3, 1880 Dyniewicz's *Gazeta Polska* published the Philadelphia group's proposal for "a Society of Poles in the United States." The document asserted that the new Alliance would be considered duly formed on a provisional basis when five societies had agreed to its principles. By June 20, thirteen societies with 477 members had declared a readiness to join; within a month they had identified delegates whose first responsibility was to elect a censor, or moral leader of the provisional organization. On July 17, at Michael Majewski's tavern in Chicago, a popular meeting place of the *Gmina Polska* society, eleven delegates unanimously nominated Andrzejkowicz for the office of censor and called for a first convention, or *sejm* to be held in Chicago. On August 9, 1880 Andrzejkowicz was officially declared elected by mail ballot, 10-5. His initial act was to declare the Polish National Alliance formed and to call its constitutional convention. The day of his announcement, August 10, 1880, has usually been given as the Alliance's date of birth. Andrzejkowicz's brief appeal emphasized the need for resolute action to build a strong organization representing the Poles in America.

I urge all Polish units, regardless of their structure, and in the name of our national identity, to set aside all quarrels and disunity that bring us dishonor, and to address themselves directly to me with their declaration of joining the Alliance. . . . The power of solidarity will lift us above the heads of our enemies; for now, let us learn to be silent. Without wasting words, let us begin to act in earnest—one for all and all for one! Let this be the watchword of our Alliance.[30]

The Alliance's first convention, or *sejm* (the traditional name of the Polish parliament before the partitions) began on September 20, 1880. It was itself a modest affair, though no less historic because of that fact. To inaugurate the meeting a religious service was held at a Czech church, Saint Wenceslaus, located on Dekoven Street on Chicago's near North Side. Following the liturgy the delegates and a number of non-voting observers headed for the Palmer House, one of the city's leading hotels. There the main business of the convention was handled, which included the approval of a constitution and the election of the organization's first officers. In all, fourteen delegates took part in the *sejm,* ten of whom were from Chicago, along with Andrzejkowicz and Vincent Domanski, who travelled from Philadelphia to be present, Frank Borchardt, from Milwaukee's Kosciuszko Guard unit and Joseph Glowczynski from Grand Rapids, Michigan. Most of the Chicagoans belonged to the *Gmina Polska* society and they dominated the convention.[31] There are no records of this meeting, but it is believed that non-voting observers (that is, individuals not belonging to an organization themselves or representing groups that had not yet affiliated with the Alliance) outnumbered the voting delegates three to one. One of these was the Reverend Dominik Majer who had earlier tangled with Barzynski and later became a leader of clergymen who supported the PNA, the so-called "Alliance priests."

Most important among the actions taken by the convention was its adoption of a constitution. In this document were expressed the purposes of the Alliance. Five specific aims were stated:

1. To lay proper foundation for the construction of institutions dedicated to the material and moral advancement of the Polish immigration in America, by creating a permanent fund under the control of the Alliance. Institutions to be aided by the Alliance include Polish settlement houses, schools, educational training facilities, reading rooms, shelters for the sick, and industrial firms owned by Poles located in the areas of Polish immigrant settlement;
2. To care for the needs of the Polish immigration in America;
3. To strengthen the immigrants politically as American citizens by setting up a Polish newspaper and to make contacts with the American press in defense of Polish concerns;
4. To commemorate anniversaries that honor the Polish homeland;
5. To promote moderation in the consumption of alcohol.

Osada, in contrast to Barszczewski, lists a different fifth aim, that of providing insurance on a fraternal basis to the members. A resolution was adopted at the *sejm* to set up a burial insurance program and on December 9, 1880 three PNA officers, President Max Kucera, Secretary Edward Odrowaz and Treasurer Stanislas Kociemski made a formal application to the state of Illinois to do just that. In their letter, they proposed the formation of a "United Polish National Benevolent Society to preserve Polish national brotherhood for moral and intellectual improvement and also for reciprocal aid in sickness and misfortune." This Society was to be established on a not-for-profit basis. Nothing came of the insurance plan at first, however, and it was not until 1886 that the Alliance set up a nationally organized program, one that provided a $500 death benefit for male members and a $250 payment upon the death of a spouse.[32] In the constitution itself, the delegates declared their commitment to lead the Polish immigration in working to bring about independence for the homeland "by whatever peaceful means possible."

A rather intriguing question concerns the identity of the actual founders of the PNA. Just who might properly be accorded this honor? Interestingly, there is no consensus on the matter among the historians writing about the origins of the Alliance.

According to the minutes of the first meeting in Philadelphia, eleven men agreed to join the Alliance: Julius Andrzejkowicz, Julian Szajnert, John Szonert, Julian Lipinski, Rudolph Cyndel, Marcel Metelski, Marcel Gabryelewicz, Henry Pstrachowski, John Blachowski, John Popielinski, and a man whose surname was Lochowicz. But according to Stefan Barszczewski, the first PNA historian in 1894, nine men "enthusiastically applauded Andrzejkowicz's proposal" to form the Alliance and these individuals he identified as its founders. They were Lipinski, Szajnert, Popielinski, Blachowski, along with Vincent Domanski, John Bialynski, Anthony Wojczynski, Teofil Kucielski, Peter Beczkiewicz, and Andrzejkowicz.[33] All five individuals named by Barszczewski but not included in the February 15 minutes did join the Alliance soon afterwards. And two of them, Domanski and Beczkiewicz, were active in its work at the national level. But why they and not the others are included is not at all clear, particularly inasmuch as Gabryelewicz and Lochowicz were both active members in the original Philadelphia PNA group, which later became Lodge 1 of the national federation.[34]

Osada lists five founders, Andrzejkowicz, Szajnert, Popielinski, Lipinski, and Blachowski, and it is his enumeration which has most frequently been followed within the Alliance. Several portraits, including one hanging in the home office of the PNA, identifies the five as founders, a judgment reinforced by the fact that Lipinski, Szajnert, and Popielinski had long shared the goal of organizing a patriotic movement even before they created the PNA and in Andrzejkowicz found someone committed to leading the effort. Blachowski is another case; he was never active in the Alliance except at the local level, although he had chipped in to help in the PNA's first fund raiser.

Nevertheless, Osada also cites an opinion from Andrzejkowicz himself which adds still more confusion to the question. In replying to praise for his having founded the Polish National Alliance, Andrzejkowicz wrote a letter in which he generously asserted that "Szonert, Lipinski, Szajnert,

Odrowaz, Popielinski and several others in our circle" were equally deserving of the title. (Edward Odrowaz, a writer for the *Ogniwo* paper, had helped circulate the appeal to organize a nationwide PNA even though he was probably in New York, not Philadelphia, when the founding meeting took place.)[35]

Among the sixteen men included in the minutes of the first PNA meeting and in Barszczewski's history, only two actually played major roles in the Alliance. Andrzejkowicz who had become the Alliance's temporary president in February was elected its censor the following July and given the responsibility of calling the embryonic movement's first convention and chairing its proceedings. He was reelected to this post at the 1880 convention and in 1881 and 1882 as well. But in 1883 he declined the honor because of ill health.

Szajnert at first played no major role in the Alliance, although he became active in its affairs after having moved to Minneapolis around the turn of the century. From 1911 until 1918 and once again from 1924 to 1928, Szajnert was elected honorary PNA commissioner for all states, a position he held at the time of his death. For many years he was identified, incorrectly, as the last surviving PNA founder although both Domanski and Beczkiewicz outlived him.

Several other founders participated to a lesser extent in PNA affairs through the years. Vincent Domanski, a local banker, was a delegate to four early PNA conventions including the first *sejm* held in Chicago. After 1889 he apparently took no further part in Alliance activities but lived until 1935. Peter Beczkiewicz, who passed away in 1934, was also active and was elected a vice censor from 1901 to 1903. Lipinski attended five PNA *sejm* meetings and was voted a lifetime honorary membership in 1897. Popielinski also attended the 1897 *sejm,* which was held in Philadelphia. In comparison, Blachowski, Kucielski, Bialynski, Wojczynski and the others played no major part in any national activities of the organization they had helped to found.

The aims of the Polish National Alliance remained a subject of continuing debate throughout the movement's early years. In 1886, for example, due to pressure exerted by clergymen within the PNA, phraseology was introduced stressing its Catholic character. Thus its very first aim was restated to emphasize that the PNA was to concern itself with Polonia institutions "founded on the principles of the Roman Catholic Church." After Majer and his associates withdrew in 1889, the emphasis on Catholicism was downplayed although the debate over goals remained hot for years. It was only in 1900 that the aims of the organization were revised and set into a preamble of the constitution. As such these have remained, practically unaltered, ever since.

Accordingly, the movement committed itself to "form a more perfect union of the Polish people in America with the rest of the citizenry of the United States and to transmit this relationship to future generations; to insure to them a proper moral, intellectual, economic and social development; to foster and cherish the best traditions of the cultures of the United States and of Poland; to preserve the mother tongue, and to promote all legitimate means leading to the restoration and preservation of the independence of the Polish nation in Europe."

Already at the first *sejm*, the PNA's basic structure took shape as a national federation of autonomous local societies retaining control of their own treasuries, along with the power to initiate activities in their communities and to admit members into their ranks. In return for their agreement to abide by the national constitution and to pay the central office monthly dues of five cents per member along with an initiation fee for each new applicant, the local societies were entitled to send one delegate to the national *sejm* for every fifty members they possessed.

Two centers of authority existed from the very outset within the organization, the censor and the central committee (a name changed to central government in 1886 and central administration in 1897). The central committee was charged with the regular duties of administering the fraternal between conventions, a function which became increasingly important as the treasury and the institutions under its jurisdiction both expanded. The first central committee was made up of six men, and included a president, a vice president, a secretary, a deputy secretary, a treasurer and a legal advisor. The first president of the Alliance was Max Kucera of Chicago, a Polish-born tailor who had come to America in 1860 and had become a founder of the *Gmina Polska* society. Kucera served two successive one-year terms as president and one as treasurer in 1885. The second president was Stanislas Kociemski, another *Gmina Polska* organizer who had come to Chicago in 1854 and had been the proprietor of a picture frame factory. Kociemski had earlier served as the PNA's first treasurer and held the presidency from 1882 to 1886, then again between 1889 and 1891.[36]

The office of censor, a position unique to the Alliance, was its second center of authority. The censor's responsibilities were those of calling and then presiding over its convention activities. It was also his duty to make sure that the organization remained true to its constitution. After the PNA established its own newspaper, *Zgoda* in 1881, the censor was given the task of overseeing its editorial policy. The censor initially could veto central committee decisions which he deemed contrary to the bylaws or actions taken by the previous convention. Only a two-thirds majority of the delegates to the next *sejm* could override his veto.

Andrzejkowicz, the first censor, was succeeded by a Chicagoan, Frank Gryglaszewski, a thirty-year old *Gmina Polska* member who had come to America in 1872. Gryglaszewski, one of the most energetic Alliance leaders in its early years, had already been elected vice censor, an office that had been created in 1882. He was censor from 1883 to 1891.

The PNA central committee established its headquarters in Chicago and already by the end of 1880 had rented its own office space at 338 South Clark Street. The Clark Street office remained the home of the PNA until December, 1887 except for a year spent in Bay City, Michigan where the PNA headquarters were in a building located at 26 Washington Street. Once back in Chicago, the PNA again rented quarters at the Clark Street address, then in several buildings in the heart of the old Polish community on the city's near north side; 60 Noble Street (December, 1887); 112 West Division Street (October, 1888); and 547 Noble Street (April, 1892).

The PNA built its first permanent home office in 1896 at 1404 West Division Street after a last effort to move the Alliance headquarters to Buffalo failed at the 1895 convention by a vote of 63-53. Dedicated on November 26, 1896 in the presence of a large crowd which included representatives from Polish organizations from around the country and the patriotic movement in Europe, the edifice was proudly titled "the capital of Polonia" by one speaker. In the building were housed all the major activities of the Alliance, from the insurance departments to the editorial and printing offices of *Zgoda.*

A second and more spacious PNA home office was built in 1936, located at 1514-1520 West Division Street. In spite of its size and modern appearance, this building too proved to be inadequate by the late 1960s, a problem compounded by the economic decline of the neighborhood where it was located.

The search for a new PNA home office began in the early 1970s and ended with the decision to purchase an already existing building, one originally owned by the Federal Life Insurance Company and located at 6100 North Cicero Avenue on Chicago's rapidly growing and heavily Polish northwest side. The impressive and modern building's attractiveness was further enhanced by its placement on a 5.5 acre landscaped site. (The entire edifice and the sign "Polish National Alliance" are easily seen by the thousands of motorists who travel each day along the Edens Expressway into and out of the city.)

Purchased in late 1976 at a cost of $4.1 million, the third PNA Home Office was formally dedicated at ceremonies held on June 4, 1977 attended by the dignitaries of the Catholic and Polish National churches, the governor of the state of Illinois, James Thompson, the mayor of Chicago Michael

Bilandic, senators, congressmen, and representatives of the community and American Polonia. Chicago Auxiliary Bishop Alfred Abramowicz celebrated an open-air mass for all who were in attendance as part of the day's dedication ceremonies. President Aloysius Mazewski officiated at the dedication and called the new building a "showcase of Polonia" and "a dream come true," affirming to all the PNA's status, affluence and importance in the mainstream of American and Polonia life.

Like previous PNA home offices, the new edifice was not only a locus of business activity but a cultural center as well. The building housed the PNA library and museum and throughout its corridors are paintings, photographs, maps and statues which demonstrate the historic commitment of the Alliance to its ethnic heritage.

Chicago remained the location of the Alliance from 1880 onward, except for a one year interval following the sixth *sejm* in 1886, when Bay City, Michigan (the site of that year's convention) became its new headquarters and a local resident named Val Przybyszewski its president. A year later, Chicago was restored to its position and has remained the national head-quarters of the PNA ever since. Two obvious reasons account for the move from Philadelphia, the cradle of the Alliance, to Chicago. The "windy city's" rapid population growth after 1870 made it the most attractive destination for the work-seeking but largely unskilled Polish immigrants. Factory work, jobs in the foundries, steel mills and packing houses all were more plentiful in Chicago than in Eastern cities such as Philadelphia, where skilled workers were in demand.

Between 1870 and 1910 the population of Chicago rose from 298,000 to 2,185,000 inhabitants, a growth rate of 733 percent. During this time, Chicago became the second largest American city after New York. In contrast, Philadelphia, which in 1870 had been America's "second city," grew by 233 percent, from 694,000 to 1,549,000. A 1905 estimate placed the size of Chicago's Polish population at 250,000 people, ten times larger than the Polonia in Philadelphia. Indeed, even in the 1880s Chicago possessed the largest Polish immigrant population of any American city.

Equally important to the future significance of the Chicago Polish community in America was its organizational dominance. Many of the leading patriotic societies came to be clustered in Chicago, while the others were scattered throughout the rest of the country. It was thus not surprising that Chicago rapidly assumed preeminence in the new Alliance. During the founding year of 1880, twenty-three different Polish patriotic and fraternal societies belonged to the Alliance; of this number six were Chicago groups, compared to two from Philadelphia and five from New York (two of which dropped away during the first summer). Not surprisingly, four of the six officers elected at the first *sejm* were also Chicagoans.

Historically, a large proportion of PNA lodges have been in the Chicago metropolitan area: Of the 190 lodges Barszczewski identified in his 1894 history 46 were in Illinois, and most of these were in the Chicago area. Of 526 lodges identified by Osada in 1905, 124 were in Illinois. In the early 1920s, Illinois was again the state with the most lodges, with 423 of a total of 1657. In 1980, of 1205 lodges Illinois placed second to Pennsylvania with 227 lodges to 263, but Chicago retained a sizeable lead in lodges over other cities.

Chicago has also been the home town of the majority of PNA executive officers throughout its history. In all, of the eighty-one persons who have held the offices of censor, president, vice president, secretary and treasurer, fifty-five of these individuals have hailed from Chicago. Of the fifteen men who have been president of the Alliance, twelve represented Chicago lodges and councils. Only Przybyszewski (from Bay City, Michigan), John Romaszkewicz (from Boston) and Charles Rozmarek (from Wilkes Barre, Pennsylvania) came from other parts of the country. In contrast, sixteen men have served as censor, but only two, Gryglaszewski and Helinski were Chicagoans. Twenty-six of its thirty vice presidents, nine of fourteen secretaries and thirteen of fourteen treasurers have also been from Chicago over the years.

A problem looming like a dark cloud over the new federation was religion. The issue was serious for many reasons, not the least of which was the fact that a number of *Gmina Polska* members, who were among the most active proponents of the Alliance, had for years been antagonists of the Reverend Barzynski, head of the Polish Catholic faction. Other early Alliance members such as the Reverend Majer and the newspaper editors Ignace Wendzinski and Wladyslaw Dyniewicz were also harsh critics of Barzynski. Several patriotic groups had left Barzynski's PRCUA over the religious issue in 1875 when it had ruled that only Catholics could be members in good standing; the new PNA represented another challenge to the Resurrectionist leader. Significant too, perhaps, was the unwillingness of Alliance backers to readily defer to clerical leadership outside of church matters.[37] Indeed, many were successful in their own businesses and trades and were simply of no mind to take a back seat to clergymen in their own new patriotic federation.

Yet for the most part, the Alliance's leaders heeded Court Plater's advice not to antagonize the Church. Clearly, for the Alliance to become a mass movement, it had to attract the mostly peasant Polish emigration, which was deeply respectful of its religious leaders and would never join an anti-clerical group.[38] Thus it was a major blow to the fledgling Alliance when criticism apparently sparked by Barzynski appeared in the Catholic press decrying the proposed federation as masonic in spirit. In July 1880, the Bishop of Green Bay added more cold water by issuing a pastoral letter urging Catholic Poles to avoid what he termed the "liberal political alliance joining Poles together without regard for differences in religion." Already on the defensive before they had even formally organized, the delegates to the first *sejm* expressed their purposes as best they could. In Article III of their constitution they inserted two statements which they hoped would show the Alliance's true colors. "Since the Roman Catholic faith is the religion of the vast majority of people comprising the Polish nation," they emphasized, "we recognize it as our duty to show it respect, not wishing ever to interfere with any of its laws or doctrines. The Alliance will not be involved in religious matters, since these belong to the Apostolic See and to the Bishops."[39]

The first years following the formation of the Alliance saw its membership remain miniscule, partly because of concerns about the Green Bay bishop's criticism. Groups joined, only to drop away soon after, and the total number of societies in the Alliance hovered between nine and twelve between 1880 and 1885. The viability of a number of the local societies was also threatened when a larger than expected number of insured members died, leaving them insolvent and thus unable to pay their beneficiaries. By 1885, total membership in the Alliance had dropped to only 295; several insurance ideas had been proposed and tried, only to fail as various groups found the assessments too burdensome. It was not until the 1886 convention that a satisfactory national insurance program was at last effected.

Yet these years were productive in other respects. In 1881, the delegates to the second PNA *sejm* approved a weekly newspaper that would be its official publication. By the narrowest of margins, one vote, Frank Gryglaszewski's proposal to name the paper *Zgoda* (Harmony) prevailed over Andrzejkowicz who argued for *Niepodleglosc* (Independence). Edward Odrowaz, was elected its first editor. Gryglaszewski also pushed hard for a reasonable financial base for the newspaper venture and won from his colleagues $544 in pledges to go along with his own commitment of $150 to get *Zgoda* off the ground. On November 23, 1881 the first issue of the paper that would be thriving more than a century later appeared at an annual subscription price of two dollars. There were other accomplishments too, though perhaps Osada was right when he argued that the Alliance's greatest achievement in its early years was simply to survive.[40] Working with other

Table 2. Founding Elements of the Polish National Alliance in 1880

Name and location of Society	Date Society declared its intention to join Alliance	Participation in election of Andrzejkowicz as Censor (X=Yes), plus number of delegates (July-August, 1880)	Actual delegate at convention, September 21, 1880 (X=Yes)	Proxy named for Convention	No delegate or proxy	Withdrew prior to convention	Members
1. Polish National Alliance in Philadelphia	February 15, 1880	X(2)	X				52
2. Gmina Polska, Chicago	May 4, 1880	X(3)	X				145
3. Kosciuszko Society, Nanticoke, Pennsylvania	May 9, 1880	X(1)		X			42
4. Fraternal Aid Society, Grand Rapids, Michigan	May 9, 1880	X(1)	X				30
5. Kosciuszko Aid Society, Chicago	June 7, 1880	X(2)	X				175
6. Harmonia Singing Society, Chicago	June 9, 1880	X(1)	X				19
7. St. George Society Shenandoah, Pennsylvania	June 12, 1880	X(1)		X			40
8. Fraternal Aid Society, Berea, Ohio	June 20, 1880					X	22
9. Polish Union of N.Y.	June 20, 1880					X	7
10. Free Sharp Shooters of N.Y.	June 20, 1880					X	60
11. Polish Club of Chicago	June 26, 1880	X(1)	X				30
12. Kosciuszko Guard, Milwaukee	July 20, 1880		X				50
13. Polish Society in California	July 26, 1880	X(1)		X			30

No. / Society	Date						Members
15. Foundry Workers Society, Chicago	(just prior to convention)		X				Unknown
16. Poland Society of Brooklyn	August 18, 1880		X				27
17. Kosciuszko Society of Philadelphia	September 12, 1880		X				39
18. Warsaw Guard, Shenandoah, Pennsylvania	September 13, 1880	X(1)					32
19. *Lutnia* Society, N.Y.	June 11, 1880			X			53
20. Pulaski Guard, Northeim, Wisconsin	September 19, 1880		X				43
21. Polish National Society LaCrosse, Wisconsin	(just prior to convention)		X				Unknown
22. Poniatowski Society, Wisconsin	Not known					X	Unknown
23. Holy Cross Society, Chicago	June 20, 1880	X(1)				X	Unknown
23 Societies	June 20, 1880	X(1) 11(15)	14 (from 11 Societies)	6	— 1	X 5	Unknown

Source: Osada, pp. 129-154.

From this table one can clearly identify four levels of commitment to the new federation. The most intense and continuing support, measured by a society's participation in both the election of Andrzejkowicz and the founding convention, characterized the behavior of six different groups: 1, 2, 4, 5, 6, and 11. Four of these societies were based in Chicago and all told the six groups claimed a total of 451 members.

Five additional societies did not participate in Andrzejkowicz's election, in most cases because they had not as yet joined the Alliance at the time of his nomination. But all five groups were represented at the founding convention, 12, 14, 15, 20, 21. Their claimed membership totalled at least 144 individuals although two of the groups provided no information here, a good sign of their provisional or embryonic character.

Six lodges were represented by proxy at the founding convention, groups 3 and 7 (from Pennsylvania), 13 (California), 16 and 19 (New York) and 17 (Philadelphia). Their distance from Chicago seems in each case to be a sufficient explanation for their failure to send someone to represent their members. These societies claimed 231 members in all.

Six other groups either took no part in the convention or had withdrawn from the Alliance by September, 1880 after having earlier expressed an interest in joining the PNA. These were groups 8, 9, 10, 22, 23 and 18 with a combined membership of at least 121. Two of these groups had earlier participated in Andrzejkowicz's election (18 and 23) but withdrew, probably as a result of clerical criticisms.

Chicago groups, including the clerical faction, the PNA did take part in ceremonies commemorating the fiftieth anniversary of the November 1830 uprising and in the Spring of 1881, East Coast Alliance members inaugurated what became an annual event when they made a boat trip up the Hudson River to the Kosciuszko monument located at the West Point Military Academy.

Firm relations were established with the Polish exile movement from the start and reinforced in 1885 when Andrzejkowicz travelled to Switzerland. Efforts to develop cooperative ties with other Polonia groups on patriotic matters also marked the PNA from its earliest months of existence. At the 1881 *sejm*, for example, the delegates approved a resolution calling upon Polonia to unite on behalf of Polish independence. In 1883, the Alliance participated in a general Polonia-wide commemoration of the two hundredth anniversary of King Jan Sobieski's triumph over the Turks in Vienna. At the manifestation, which was headed by PRCUA leader Kiolbassa, PNA President Kucera spoke. In New York city, another early PNA member, General Wlodzimierz Krzyzanowski, addressed a large crowd in the English language for the historic occasion.[41]

Other gestures by the little group were of a more symbolic nature, partly because the Alliance was still too weak to carry them out. The idea of an immigrant settlement home in Philadelphia foundered for lack of funds. Gryglaszewski's idealistic scheme (similar to John Barzynski's proposal to the Polish Roman Catholic Union a decade before) to establish Polish agricultural homesteads with PNA assistance—this time in Wisconsin and Minnesota rather than Nebraska—seems never to have gotten very far at Alliance conventions.[42] Already in 1881 the delegates passed a resolution of condolence in response to the assassination of President Garfield and succeeded in having it published in the local American press. Even from this early date, the embryonic organization was attempting to make itself known in American society.

And a solid *cadre* of leadership, mainly composed of *Gmina Polska* activists such as Kucera, Kociemski, Gryglaszewski and others had become involved in the Alliance, thereby superceding the original Philadelphia-based founders. Morever, by the mid-1880s its members were beginning to slowly sort out the priorities of the Alliance so that a solid base for future action could be created. In a true sense, the next decade was to be critical if the organization was to attain its ambitious aim of leading Polonia and in the process become a mass movement.

Chapter 3

YEARS OF CRISIS AND GROWTH: 1885-1913

The fifth PNA *sejm*, held in LaCrosse, Wisconsin in February, 1885 was a sorry affair. Battered by a stream of clerical charges about its allegedly masonic and anti-Catholic character, the Alliance had also sunk deeply in debt. This was due to the costs of running *Zgoda* and the burden of paying an unusually large number of death benefits (six) during the previous year. Consequently, membership had fallen to only 210 and several societies had withdrawn completely from the federation. Former Censor Andrzejkowicz, for health and age reasons, was himself absent from the *sejm*. In his letter to the thirteen delegates, he urged them to remain faithful to the ideal of unifying Polonia. Once again no Polish priest could be found to officiate at religious services preceding the meeting.[1]

In retrospect a century later, it is difficult to appreciate the intense bitterness which some Polish clergymen felt toward the PNA. To men such as Barzynski a Polish organization not essentially Catholic had to be anti-Catholic in its outlook, regardless of its members' expressions of respect for the Church. Under the influence of Barzynski and the early criticism of the Alliance which had come from the Bishop of Green Bay, some priests actually refused to bury PNA members, christen their children, officiate at their marriages and urged their parishioners to have nothing to do with them socially. That the PNA survived such onslaughts was a testimony to the tenacity of its members' commitment to the cause of the movement.

Yet at the very moment when "the Alliance lay in ruins,"[2] it suddenly took on new vitality, thanks almost entirely to the efforts of three very different men who dedicated themselves to its revival.[3] One was its thirty-three year old Censor, Frank Gryglaszewski. In his job travelling through the Midwest as an inspector of U.S. government buildings, Gryglaszewski made the most of the opportunity to visit various Polish settlements where he preached the gospel of the Alliance. A kind of Johnny Appleseed and

67

St. Paul rolled into one vibrant force, the beefy and bearded Gryglaszewski organized scores of new lodges during the next year and one-half. (Morever, Gryglaszewski was the leading PNA advocate of "colonization," that is the purchase of farm lands for transfer to immigrants. On several occasions, he was able to purchase or receive *gratis* such lands from railroads in Wisconsin and Minnesota and worked to bring Poles to these areas. But the colonization scheme never caught on and by 1900 had given way to other ideas.)

A second renovator of the Alliance was the industrialist, Erasmus Jerzmanowski. Born in Kalisz, Poland in 1844, Jerzmanowski held the hereditary tital of Baron, a reward earned by his grandfather for distinguished military service during the Napoleonic wars. A student in Warsaw on the eve of the 1863 uprising, Jerzmanowski took part in the revolt and fled the country following its collapse. Arriving in Paris in 1864, he attended its Polytechnic Institute and earned degrees in engineering and chemistry. After distinguishing himself during the Franco-Prussian War of 1870, Jerzmanowski was employed by the Paris Public Gas Facility. In 1875 he was sent to the United States to study the New York public utilities system. Shortly after his arrival he obtained several patents for his invention of a gas burner device and several other mechanisms which made it practical to use natural gas for illuminating city streets.

In 1876, Jerzmanowski organized the Equitable Gas Company and became its executive director. The company aggressively established branches outside New York and made Jerzmanowski "the first financial giant among early Polish settlers in America." Between 1876 and 1886, he also patented seventeen different inventions in connection with the production of gas burners.

His fortune made, Jerzmanowski turned his attention to Poland and the immigrants. Already a member of the Polish National Alliance in 1880, he founded the Polish Central Welfare Committee in 1886 in cooperation with the PNA to provide shelter and aid to immigrants who were arriving in New York in steadily growing numbers and singlehandedly financed its operation. This agency was the forerunner of the Polish Immigration Home that the PNA purchased in 1909 and maintained for many years after. Jerzmanowski's philanthropies extended to his donating more than $75,000 to various charities on behalf of the immigrants. He was also entrusted with the responsibility of raising contributions on behalf of the Polish National Fund, headquartered in Rappersville, Switzerland and personally donated more than $13,000 to that cause.

His work with the Polish Central Welfare Committee led Jerzmanowski to aspire to lead the Polish National Alliance itself. To this end, he moved aggressively to establish PNA lodges throughout the East. Indeed, Osada credits him with bringing in twenty-four new lodges in time for the sixth Alliance convention, which was held in Bay City, Michigan in July, 1886. The combined energies of Gryglaszewski and Jerzmanowski helped to significantly strengthen the Alliance. At the 1886 convention, sixty delegates representing forty societies and more than two thousand members were in attendance. In only a year and one-half, the PNA had thus grown tenfold. At the *sejm,* the two men waged a hotly contested fight for the office of censor but in this battle, Jerzmanowski's ambitions were frustrated. Gryglaszewski was reelected by a 36-18 vote with six abstentions. Never again did Jerzmanowski seek an elective leadership post in the PNA. Less than a decade later, in 1894 he would become a leader in the Polish League, a new federation of Polonia groups dominated by Reverend Barzynski and the Polish Roman Catholic Union. The league failed because many PNA members considered its purposes to be the same as their own and aimed essentially at undermining the Alliance. They therefore refused to participate.[4]

Unable to win recognition for his efforts to lead American Polonia, Jerzmanowski retired in 1896 to live out his remaining years in Poland. There he gave his financial assistance to cultural and educational causes in all three zones of the partitioned country. At his death in 1909 he left the sum of one million Austrian crowns to the Jagiellonian University to support the development of what was later to become the Polish Academy of Sciences.[5]

A third influence in the Alliance's revitalization was none other than the Reverend Dominik Majer. An inveterate opponent of Barzynski, Majer organized a group of clergymen who agreed with his views in support of the PNA and rapidly became a major force in the movement. Already at the 1886 convention, he was able to achieve one of his central aims— that of revising the Alliance's constitution on its stance toward the Catholic Church. Originally the constitution had simply asserted the PNA's respect for the Church and its intention not to interfere in religious matters. This failed to satisfy Majer, who wanted the organization to be as Catholic as the PRCUA but with a stronger patriotic orientation. At the *sejm* he proposed additional language to the constitution committing the Alliance to assist in the building of parishes by providing them with loans. Majer also argued that, henceforth, the Alliance must prohibit individuals involved in anarchist and socialist groups from its ranks. He particularly condemned anarchist activities, no surprise in light of public reaction to violent labor demonstrations that had taken place at Haymarket Square in Chicago and the Bay View Rolling Mill in Milwaukee only a few months before the *sejm.* In both cities several Polish workers had been killed in confrontations with the authorities.

Majer, however, went further. He proposed another amendment to the Constitution, one transforming the Alliance into a kind of government directing the activities of Polonia in support of a free Poland. When the delegates unanimously approved this idea, Majer also issued a resolution in favor of Irish independence and a second condemning German and Russian repression of Poland. In all his actions, Majer's intent was clearly that of fashioning the PNA into a patriotic version of the PRCUA.

Majer's advocacy of close cooperation with the Church bore fruit at the seventh PNA *sejm*, which was held in his home diocese of St. Paul, Minnesota in September, 1887. With good reason, Barszczewski, the first PNA historian called the meeting "one of the Alliance's greatest triumphs." For one thing, the convention again registered impressive gains in membership and finances in the year since the sixth *sejm;* the Alliance could now claim 3,210 members in eighty-seven groups and assets of $7,300.

Even more impressive was the appearance of the Archbishop of St. Paul, John Ireland, and the praise he showered upon the PNA in his convention speech. Ireland's remarks were the first by a Catholic Church leader in support of the PNA's work among the immigrants. In rejecting the charges that the Alliance was anti-Catholic, Archbishop Ireland joined the Archbishop of New York and the Bishop of Newark who had already endorsed the PNA in writing in December, 1886 after reviewing copies of the organization's constitution Jerzmanowski had presented them.

In St. Paul, the delegates asserted their loyalty to Rome by approving a congratulatory message addressed to Pope Leo XIII on the fiftieth anniversary of his priestly ordination. Only a month later, a letter from Rome was received in which "the Holy Father blessed the Poles and their President (sic) Gryglaszewski."[6] Yet, attacks upon the Alliance continued to appear in print coupled with continuing harassment of PNA members in their own parishes. At last, the PNA took an unprecedented step in early 1888 and issued a public letter directed to Cardinal Mieczyslaw Ledochowski, the exiled Archbishop of Poznan and Prefect of the Propagation of the Faith in Rome. The letter was signed by 2,470 members and called upon Rome to intervene on behalf of the PNA to prevent any further unfair attacks upon its work by hostile Polish clergymen. The letter read as follows:

> We of the Polish National Alliance express through this letter our deep dissatisfaction with a certain element of the clergy which has gathered in Chicago from time to time and caused great disquiet among our members by refusing them the rites of our Church and Faith, Baptism and the sacraments. We as

Poles and as members of a patriotic society want to work for the good of our fatherland. We are doing so without interfering into matters pertaining to our Faith, which we hold sacred. Indeed our constitution (a copy of which we have enclosed), particularly its third paragraph, expressly forbids any meddling into Church affairs. That is entirely the province of the Holy See and the bishops, under whose spiritual authority we wish to live and direct our activities.

Thus far, our work has been quiet yet productive. For example, up to this time we have paid out death benefits amounting to more than $20,000 to widows and orphans of our members. We have also provided financial aid to our needy fatherland by creating a permanent fund raising drive. No one who is a member of any secret society condemned by the Church, whether it be socialistic or anarchistic in character, can belong to our Alliance. Our constitution again expressly forbids it. We long to fulfill our duties as Catholics, but at present there are clergymen who slander us and our Alliance, who criticize us for an absence of religious faith and even disobedience to the Church. They allege that we are masons and even refuse to offer Mass for us at the beginning of our conventions and so forth. They do this simply because we do not recognize and will not recognize their supremacy over our Alliance in political and patriotic matters. We have tolerated their actions for quite some time; we even remained silent when we learned that they had put out a secret memorandum dated March 2, 1887 in which they listed all the charges we have just noted. But once again, a number of clergymen met in Chicago on February 8, 1888 and publicly condemned us in the press. Not only were we publicly excluded from the Faith, the Polish people were also warned that they should be wary of us as unbelievers who had fallen away from the Church. Indeed, we were to be avoided like the plague!

When we continuously are subjected to such criticisms from the pulpit and when we are even refused absolution after confession we can no longer remain silent. By their actions, these clergymen have made it difficult for us to remain close to the sacraments. They have made light of what is sacred to us, the Faith and the Church itself. By their activities, these clergymen are also damaging the reputation of the entire Polish clergy in America, whom we have always regarded with respect. They shake and weaken the faith that the people place in their pastors by instigating unrest in many parishes. Worse still, they become symbols of shame which we as Poles must bear in the eyes of other nationalities.

We are saddened by these priests who publicly do such damage to us, to our Faith and our Fatherland. And we protest against everything we have had to suffer unjustly at their hands. We testify in God's name, in the name of the Catholic Church and the entire Polish nation, that we have not fallen away from our Faith, that we do not wish to do so, and that we trust that no one can ever shake our convictions. We will not be driven from our Faith by force. We similarly give witness that we will remain respectful of the Church in matters of faith and discipline.

In closing, we ask your Eminence to use your influence with those who have
harmed us in these matters of faith and religion to act in a gentle fashion to
bring about peace, quiet and love among the members of the Polish nation in
America.[7]

The petition to Ledochowski seems to have caused the clerical attacks
to subside. Moreover, Detroit's Archbishop, J. E. Foley, followed Archbishop
Ireland's lead and appeared at the 1891 PNA convention to congratulate
the delegates for their efforts. At the Detroit *sejm,* the PNA showed its
appreciation to the Archbishop by approving a special assessment or tax
upon the entire membership to assist in the financing of Saints Cyril and
Methodius Polish Seminary. This institution had been organized in 1886
by the Reverend Joseph Dabrowski in Orchard Lake, Michigan, a small
town near Detroit. The PNA contributed fifty cents per member for two
years and raised more than $3,500 for the Seminary, a considerable sum
given the fact that the Alliance's total net worth at the time was only $9,000.
This drive proved to be a major step forward in improving the Church's
view of the Alliance.[8]

The new spirit of activity had yet another source, aside from the considerable
personal efforts of Gryglaszewski, Jerzmanowski and Majer. In early 1886
Andrzejkowicz returned from a trip to Europe where he had visited the
headquarters of the exile movement in Rappersville, Switzerland. Back in
America, he called upon the PNA to organize a nationwide fund raising
appeal on behalf of the *emigre* patriotic movement. Following the 1886
sejm the newly elected PNA leadership, now renamed the "central government" of the Polish immigration, approved the plan; in March 1887 *Zgoda*
published an appeal throughout Polonia to create a Polish National Fund
(or *Skarb Narodowy*) under the PNA's auspices, with all contributions to
go to Rappersville. This decision was ratified later the same year by the
delegates to the seventh PNA convention.

The decisions to formally identify the PNA as Polonia's "central government" and to create the National Fund were controversial, although they
served to underscore its continued commitment to its original aims. In fact,
however, the name "central government" was regarded outside the PNA
as both presumptuous and offensive and it was dropped in 1897 in favor
of "central administration." Nor were the initial fund raising efforts particularly
successful, although the PNA continued to back the idea throughout the
next twenty-six years and in all raised more than $60,000 for the independence
cause.

Majer's Exit and the Crisis of 1889

PNA history has frequently been punctuated by stormy internal conflict; undoubtedly its earliest crisis of this type followed from events connected with its eighth *sejm* held in Buffalo in September, 1889. At this meeting the PNA suffered a major division in its ranks and not long afterward uncovered a serious scandal in its finances. Together, these developments threatened to reverse the successes achieved after 1885.

One reason for the turmoil surrounding the Buffalo convention was due to the intense personal rivalries that surfaced among rival leaders in the Alliance. But equally important was the existence of sharply opposing views about the nature of the PNA held by members of competing factions, each seeking to bend the organization to their will. One group was led by the Reverend Majer and included a number of his colleagues in the clergy; the other was made up of the supporters of Censor Frank Gryglaszewski.

Though he held no formal office, Majer had become influential in the Alliance from the outset. As chairman of the Polish Priests' Association, initially a group of a dozen clergymen from Minnesota and Wisconsin which he led *en masse* into the PNA, Majer became the spokesman for clerics who disagreed with Reverend Barzynski. (In opposition to Majer, Barzynski formed his own group, the "Society of Polish Roman Catholic Priests under the protection of the Sacred Heart of Jesus in Association with the Polish Roman Catholic Union in America." It's first public pronouncement included an attack upon the PNA labeling it "irreligious.")[9]

Majer had worked hard for the PNA and was in fact instrumental in winning Archbishop Ireland's endorsement of the fraternal at its 1886 convention. However, the chief "Alliance Priest" held a rather controversial set of ideas about the PNA which, if realized, would have divided the members of the movement. In his view the essential worth of the Polish National Alliance lie in its blending of patriotic concern for Poland with its solid support of the Church's missionary and pastoral work among the immigrants. Throughout his years with the Alliance he sought to shape the PNA into a patriotic version of the PRCUA (to which he had originally belonged) but minus Barzynski. This perspective gradually placed Majer at odds with secular activists who though respectful of the Church thought the PNA should remain open to all Poles regardless of their religious beliefs. Still, Majer's influence was such that in 1886 he succeeded in winning convention approval for changes in the by-laws; these amendments had converted the PNA into an essentially Catholic movement.

In Buffalo the lines of battle seem to have been firmly drawn between Majer's more conservative faction and the more liberal opposition. Sixty-nine delegates representing sixty societies were in attendance, a significant drop from the eighty-one delegates from seventy groups who had taken part in the previous *sejm*. (Osada explains the decline as resulting from the infighting that had gone on since 1887. Several groups, including Jerzmanowski's Central Welfare Committee of New York, were expelled and others had withdrawn for a variety of reasons.)

Majer characteristically established his patriotic credentials at the beginning of *sejm* deliberations by offering a constitutional amendment permitting Lithuanians and Ukrainians to join the Alliance. These two nationalities had belonged to the pre-partition Polish kingdom until the eighteenth century, and the idea of involving them in the Alliance had always been appealing. Indeed, the concept is still symbolized by the official PNA "logo," a shield divided into three sections and showing the Polish eagle, a Lithuanian prince on horseback and an angel with two swords representing the Ruthenian, or Ukrainian, nation. (In practice, few Lithuanian or Ukrainian immigrants ever joined the Alliance, largely because they tended to live separately from the Poles in America. By the end of the nineteenth century, each group was developing its own national consciousness and organizations which emphasized linguistic and cultural differences from the Poles, rather than its common historic heritage as a "little brother" in the old pre-partition Polish commonwealth. Nonetheless, several efforts were made to promote Lithuanian and Ukrainian participation in the PNA. In 1895, for example, Dr. Theodore Kodis, a Lithuanian socialist leader was elected a vice president of the Alliance. In 1901, Censor Leon Sadowski, President Frank Jablonski and *Zgoda* Editor Stefan Barszczewski met in Pittsburgh with a Lithuanian delegation headed by Jonas Sliupas to promote future cooperation between the two communities. At their gathering they forwarded an invitation to Ukrainian leaders to join in as well. But nothing substantial resulted from any of these efforts and they soon ceased.[10])

Majer's conservative faction held a small majority at the convention and defeated the liberals on two key issues. Both, not surprisingly, dealt with membership. One concerned the status of the New York-based *Ognisko* (the Forge) society, which included many socialists; this group was expelled at the convention. The second question dealt with a Detroit lodge which was also thrown out because of its backing of the "independent" Polish clergyman, Dominik Kolasinski.

These votes set the stage for a yet a third test of factional strength. An ally of Majer, the Reverend Konstanty Domagalski now proposed yet another membership restriction, which barred "notoriously irreligious persons and Jews" from the Alliance. His motion provoked a lengthy and heated debate that continued for several days. At first, the Domagalski-Majer position prevailed, 34-27, but the liberals would not accept defeat and unsuccessfully brought up the matter for reconsideration. Finally, with a number of delegates having already departed from the convention, the issue was brought up for a third vote. This time, Majer's group lost 31-8. Claiming foul tactics, the priests and their remaining supporters "ostentatiously exited the meeting hall" and asserted that they were withdrawing from the PNA. Shouts of "get out, the Poles will remain in the Alliance!" accompanied their departure.[11]

Soon afterward, Majer announced the formation of a new fraternal he named the Polish Union in America *(Unia Polska w Ameryce).* Centered in St. Paul, Minnesota, the Polish Union was designed to serve as a means of reuniting Polonia by emphasizing both the Catholic and patriotic concerns of the immigration. But Majer's new organization was rejected by both the PNA and the PRCUA as having divided, rather than united Polonia. The center of the Polish Union's strength soon shifted to the East and Buffalo became its headquarters after 1900. In 1908, the still small fraternal, itself the product of secession, suffered a permanent division when two organizations, one centered in Buffalo, the other in Wilkes-Barre, Pennsylvania came into being.

The withdrawal of Majer and his fellow clergymen was a serious blow but one that caused no permanent damage to the Alliance. In 1891, the PNA regained ground by providing financial support for the Polish seminary at Orchard Lake. And in 1893, the Reverend Casimir Sztuczko's appointment as pastor of the reopened Holy Trinity parish in Chicago afforded the Alliance with a new ally from the ranks of the clergy, one who remained so for more than a half-century. Equally fortunate, the PNA response to Majer's exit was not one of anticlericalism, an attitude that would have gravely weakened its appeal. Rather, by confirming the original aims of the Alliance, which combined respect for Catholicism and an abiding determination to preserve a genuine separation between church and secular concerns, the results of the 1889 *sejm* preserved the PNA as an organization open to Catholics and non-Catholics alike.[12]

In some ways, a more demoralizing blow to the PNA was the uncovering of the fraudulent handling of its funds by General Secretary Ignace Morgenstern. At the 1889 *sejm* considerable criticism surfaced against Morgenstern and a special committee was appointed to look into his financial records following the convention. Since Morgenstern happened to be Jewish (indeed, he was the one Jew who had attained national leadership status in the Alliance), his activities inevitably became connected with the floor fight over the exclusion of "notoriously irreligious persons and Jews" from the organization. The two issues fed upon one another and when Morgenstern's embezzlement became public knowledge, the liberal faction was placed on the defensive.

The PNA central administration was itself divided over the Morgenstern affair. Zbigniew Brodowski, then Editor of *Zgoda* and later President of the Alliance led those who favored an investigation, while Censor Gryglas-zewski stoutly defended his old Chicago associate. Gryglaszewski even called for Morgenstern's unanimous reelection, a suggestion the delegates ignored. Anthony Mallek defeated Morgenstern in a close vote, permitting a swift investigation of his activities following the *sejm's* adjournment. (Gryglaszewski himself, though reelected in 1889, was defeated in 1891 by former President Przybyszewski.)

Within a week's time, the special committee together with the central administration in Chicago had gathered sufficient evidence to prove that Morgenstern had used more than $2,000 in PNA funds for personal speculation. Though he readily admitted his guilt and promised to make restitution in full, the message of the scandal was obvious. Because the Alliance's financial activities were becoming increasingly significant, better methods of administering the organization's treasury were called for. Indeed, the assets of the Alliance which had amounted to less than $640 in 1885 stood at $9,295 only three years later. Death benefit payments had risen from $134 in 1885 to $19,500 in 1888. With membership, investments, claims and charitable activities all on the upswing, a new sense of business professionalism was needed to supplement reliance upon personal friendships.

(The Morgenstern affair unfortunately proved to be but the first of three scandals that occurred within the Alliance before World War I. In 1897 Treasurer Val Wleklinski was accused of having misused a large sum of money in his control. But this time there was no speedy investigation of the charges because the central administration remained badly split over the matter.

Censor Theodore Helinski led the fight to get the facts of the case but President Frank Jablonski defended the Treasurer in the face of mounting evidence that things were not in order. Wleklinski finally bowed out in 1899 but four more years passed before a satisfactory means of regaining the lost funds could be determined. Only in 1903 did the delegates at the fifteenth convention accept repayment of approximately $16,000, though nearly $19,000 had been lost.[13]

A third scandal uncovered in May, 1913 involved the misuse of PNA funds by General Secretary Simon Czechowicz, who then took his own life. For his failure to take prompt action in notifying the central administration of what he knew, Treasurer Michael Majewski was suspended from office, ending on a sour note his long career as a national officer and one of the earliest members of the organization.[14] In the Czechowicz affair, Censor Anthony Schreiber took aggressive action in gathering evidence. Moreover, on this occasion he served as a kind of chief justice in chairing the deliberative work of the PNA supervisory council *(rada nadzorcza)*. Created at the 1907 convention, the council was composed of the censor, the vice censor and all PNA district commissioners whose responsibilities were to support Alliance activities in the regions of the country where they resided. The supervisory council was established as a court of appeals with power to suspend elected officers in the Alliance, to investigate their conduct and to outline the general ideological orientation of the Alliance. The formation of the council was also sensible in providing district commissioners with some genuine national responsibilities.[15])

In the years that followed the 1889 *sejm,* even further liberalization in the area of membership took place within the Alliance. At the 1895 *sejm,* which was held in Cleveland, the PNA voted to drop its opposition to the admission of socialists and adopted a resolution encouraging acceptance of anyone who subscribed to its aims, regardless of his political or religious affiliation.[16] The decision to admit socialists was largely due to this movement's growing popularity, both in America and Poland. Indeed, by 1895 socialists active in the American labor movement were able to elect their candidate over Samuel Gompers for the presidency of the American Federation of Labor and several American socialist parties had established foreign language units to encourage Poles and other immigrants into their ranks. Even more important was the growing popularity of the Polish Socialist party, formed in 1892, among new immigrants. Due to its successful fusion of nationalist and traditional working class programmatic goals the Polish Socialist party had become a credible force in the PNA by 1900 under the leadership of Alexander Debski.

Another aspect of the membership question came to the fore during the 1890s and concerned the PNA's relationship toward disenchanted immigrants who had organized "independent" Catholic parishes in defiance of their non-Polish bishops. Most successful in leading and coordinating the various independent churches around the country was the Reverend Francis Hodur of Scranton, Pennsylvania. Between 1897 and 1904 Hodur even organized most of the secessionist groups into a new movement he named the Polish National Catholic Church. The rise of independentism was, of course, a source of sharp controversy in Polonia. Loyal Catholic Poles considered the dissidents nothing other than divisive renegades, especially after Hodur was able to have himself consecrated bishop in 1907. Particularly galling to Catholics, Hodur's elevation came at a time when no orthodox churchman had as yet been named to the hierarchy.

Its 1895 action symbolized the PNA's attempt to steer clear of the religious fight even as it opened its doors to both Roman Catholics and independents. But this stance produced few immediate dividends. Many Catholics, for example, were distressed by what they interpreted to be the Alliance's support for the dissidents. Indeed, not long after the 1895 convention had adjourned, one disenchanted former PNA vice-censor led several Ohio lodges out of the organization and organized his own fraternal, the Alliance of Poles in America, headquartered in Cleveland.[17] Similarly, PNA relations with the independents also remained tenuous. In 1908, the Reverend Paul Rhode became the first Polish auxiliary bishop of the archdiocese of Chicago. Upon receiving this news, the PNA Board of Directors issued a congratulatory telegram which reflected its long standing call for greater Church recognition of the Polish immigration. Nonetheless, Bishop Hodur took offense by this action which he interpreted to be a veiled attack upon his National Church movement. Soon afterward, twenty PNA lodges composed largely of Polish National Catholics withdrew in protest and organized their own fraternal, the Polish National Union in America *(Spojnia),* centered in Scranton and led by Hodur.[18]

Because of the Reverend Barzynski's intransigent opposition, relations with Roman Catholic institutions and clergymen remained the greatest problem facing the Alliance during its first twenty-five years. Perhaps the most widely cited interpretation of the magnitude and intensity of the conflict is that of Wenceslaus Kruszka, the first historian of Polonia.

> For a time neither Catholics nor Poles were to be found in America but only 'Unionists' (adherents of the Polish Roman Catholic Union) or 'Alliancers' (PNA advocates). He who did not belong to the Alliance was regarded as no Pole, while whoever was not of the PRCUA could not be accepted by the Unionists as a Catholic.[19]

Though certainly accurate in its description of the situation in the Chicago Polonia and several other Polish communities around the country, Father Kruszka's observation somewhat exaggerates the depth of animosity at the grass roots level in many of the Polish immigrant settlements. This is evident from a check of the official names chosen by members of particular lodges entering the PNA during the years of greatest discord, 1880–1905. When a local lodge was formed in a particular community and was approved by the Chicago-based board of directors as a unit belonging to the national organization, it was given a lodge number for easy identification purposes. The first lodge to join was numbered "1" and later groups were numbered consecutively, 2, 3, 4, and so on. At the same time, however, lodge organizers also gave their group a name which had, one must assume, some symbolic importance. An inspection of these popular lodge names would give a good indication of the sentiments valued by the early organizers and those who joined the local group as far as Poland, patriotism, religion and Polonia were concerned.

If Kruszka is correct, one would expect to see the local lodges of the PNA named strictly after secular and nationalistic symbols. In reality, this was not the case. For example, of the 189 Polish National Alliance lodges in existence in 1894, sixteen were named in honor of non-Polish Saints or strictly religious symbols, such as the Saint Joseph society or the society of Saint Michael the Archangel. Among the groups taking a Polish saint, Stanislas Kostka was most popular. Nine other lodges mixed religious and patriotic symbols, such as the Patriotic society of Saint Casimir of Bay City, Michigan and the Polish Catholic society of King Jan Sobieski. Still others chose rather neutral names for themselves such as the Progress society of Duluth, the Unity society of Lake, Illinois or the Dawn in the West society of Tacoma, Washington. Particularly popular among lodge organizers was the White Eagle and many chose some title emphasizing this traditional symbol. Other commonly used names possessed a martial character, with ten early lodges identifying themselves in this fashion. For example, one can mention the Pulaski guard of Pleasant Hill, Pennsylvania and the Ulans of St. Paul, a Chicago-based lodge.

Eleven early PNA lodges grouped individuals having a particular occupation or trade and these simply took a name for themselves underlining this fact. For example, lodge 5 of Chicago was composed of tailors, lodge 175 of Gniezno, Missouri of farmers, lodges 162 (Detroit) and 168 (Buffalo) of butchers and lodge 222 of Chicago of carpenters.

While 125 of the early PNA lodges chose patriotic symbols, what is most characteristic of the pre 1894 lodge names is their great diversity and non-partisanship. No less than seventeen lodges named their group after Tadeusz Kosciuszko and thirteen others identified with Sobieski, whose victory at Vienna in 1683 had only recently been commemorated in Polonia bicentennial observances. Yet lodge names were not restricted to only a few historic heroes but covered a wide range of popular personages from King Kazimierz the Great and King Stefan Batory to Prince Jozef Poniatowski, a hero of the independence struggle during the Napoleonic wars. Frequently too, lodges chose cultural figures such as the Renaissance era poet Jan Kochanowski, used by lodge 169 of Chicago, Henryk Sienkiewicz (207 of Buffalo) and Jan Matejko (233 of New Haven, Connecticut), among many others. Lodge 166 of Eureka, California was the first to name itself after Copernicus. On the other hand, a small number of groups did choose names firmly identified with the Alliance; lodge 1 became the "Polish National Alliance," and lodge 20 "*Gmina Polska* Number One." Lodge 44 became the "Third of May" society, lodge 111 honored Agaton Giller, the inspirational father of the PNA by adopting his name, and lodge 34 of La Crosse, Wisconsin became the Jerzmanowski society.

A similar picture can be drawn from a look over the names of lodges organized between 1894 and 1905, when the Alliance celebrated its silver jubilee. Of 374 groups established in this period, 85 emphasized the religious side of their members' heritage. Of 225 groups that took patriotic and secular names, 40 chose mixed symbols, such as the Defenders of the Faith and Fatherland society, lodge 271 of Syracuse, the Patriotic society under the protection of the Blessed Virgin of Czestochowa, lodge 635 of Beaver, Michigan, and the Polish Knights of St. Stanislas Kostka, lodge 652 of Steubenville, Ohio.

Table 1.   PNA Local Lodge Names, 1880-1905[20]

	1880-1894	1894-1905
Lodges with Secular Patriotic Names	125	225
Kosciuszko	16	23
Pulaski	8	8
Sobieski	13	17
Poniatowski	4	4
Polish Eagle	5	11
Military	19	40
Lodges composed of workers	11	19
Lodges named after Polish saints	10	22
Lodges named after non-Polish saints	16	63
Lodges with patriotic-religious mixed symbolism	9	15
Culturally-oriented lodge names	12	7
Groups with neutral names	6	23
Total Number of Lodges Identified	189	374

The rivalry between the PNA and Barzynski and his followers was keen in Chicago, however, and one expressed in a series of disputes. One centered around the long simmering argument over the opening of the Alliance-supported Holy Trinity church. This argument was settled in 1893 but only through Vatican intervention and under the auspices of the Holy Cross fathers, not Barzynski's Resurrectionist order. A second confrontation focused upon the manner in which the Poles of Chicago would unite to commemorate the centennial anniversary of the Third of May constitution. Barzynski and his followers, true to form, proposed that the Constitution day observance have a strictly Catholic character, a stance the Alliance representatives rejected as out of step with the document's premise of religious tolerance. In the end, two separate observances were held. On Saturday, May 2, 1891 the PNA sponsored a spirited parade through Chicago's near northside Polonia that culminated at the city's Central Music Hall. There, Zbigniew Brodowski, John Smulski, Frank Gryglaszewski and Casimir Zychlinski delivered remarks on behalf of the Alliance, Teofila Samolinska contributed a reading of her poetry and several patriotic choral groups provided musical entertainment. The event also included speeches by several local non-Polish politicians and civic leaders. They in turn praised the inextinguishable Polish spirit, compared the Poles' aspirations for independence with those of the Irish, and expressed the hope that by 1991 tyranny would be eliminated throughout the world. The event concluded with the showing of a series of blown-up slides "magically" projected onto the wall; the pictures depicted personages and events in Polish and American history. All in all, its planners considered the 1891 Constitution day observance a great success and in 1904 the event was repeated as an annual celebration, one which continues to this day under PNA sponsorship.

On Sunday, May 3, 1891 Barzynski and his followers initiated their own observances with a high mass celebrated in Saint Stanislas Kostka church. The activities went on for three full days, ending with another high mass followed by a meeting of the clergyman's supporters in the parish hall.[21]

A far more serious source of factional controversy occurred in 1894, one which for a time threatened to undermine the very existence of the Polish National Alliance as a patriotic movement. It involved Barzynski's attempt to organize a new Polonia federation bringing all existing institutions, clerical and secular, together for the primary purpose of raising funds for the betterment of the Polish community in America and Poland. This federation was named the Polish League. The League was significant not only because of its appeal to Polonia unity but also its pledge to more effectively generate funds for causes significant to the community. PNA members, of course, were committed to both aims; but because of their failure to win immediate and widespread support for the *Skarb Narodowy* many individuals were inclined to look favorably upon the League.

PNA experience with the *Skarb Narodowy* (or Polish National Fund) had indeed been a cause for disappointment. Originally the idea of setting up a fund raising campaign to support the exile movement headquartered in Rappersville, Switzerland had been raised by a group of Chicago Polish women activists. The idea had received a boost from Zygmunt Milkowski, a veteran of the 1863 insurrection and an exile leader of the *Liga Polska* movement. In his book, *On Active Resistance and the National Fund,* Milkowski (who was popularly known by his pseudonym, Teodor Tomasz Jez) argued for close collaboration between the Polish liberation movement and patriotic groups in America. For such collaboration to be productive, Milkowski argued, it was necessary for Polonia to provide a steady stream of financial assistance to the independence movement. In 1886, former Censor Andrzejkowicz had travelled to Switzerland where he discussed the idea with the *Liga Polska* leaders and agreed to put Milkowski's proposal into effect. Upon his return to the United States, Andrzejkowicz won enthusiastic PNA support for the plan to set up a *Skarb Narodowy* under its auspices. Indeed, the idea was so popular that the PNA actually incorporated its commitment directly into its constitution. Unfortunately, however, early efforts to raise funds were largely unsuccessful; in 1891, for example, the "central government" had to report that less than $2,300 had been collected over the previous four year period. To reinvigorate the fortunes of the *Skarb Narodowy* it voted to assess every PNA member 12 cents per year on behalf of the fund. Even then, problems continued to hamper the effort. Some PNA members objected to sending all proceeds directly to Europe; others argued that the exile movement should receive only the interest earned from the moneys collected. There were even heated disagreements over which bank should become the repository of *Skarb Narodowy* funds! Given these difficulties it is understandable that when Barzynski and his allies proposed that the new Polish League take over the fund raising task for Polonia-wide causes, they were able to take full advantage of a situation in which the PNA was open to criticism.

The first mass meeting of the new Polish League was scheduled to be held in Chicago in May, 1894 and Polonia leaders from around the country were invited to take part in the deliberations. Initially, a large number of PNA members expressed interest in at least participating in the meeting, which they understood to be preparatory in character. Among the strongest supporters of this strategy were Erasmus Jerzmanowski and Victor Bardonski, a vice president of the Alliance. But a majority in the central government remained cool; Censor Theodore Helinski expressed a number of its worries in a letter he addressed to the membership only a few weeks before the May meeting. Helinski's greatest concern focused upon the new federation's professed aims, which seemed identical to those traditionally proclaimed by the PNA. At the same time he criticized the League's general indifference to the Polish independence issue; aside from its intent to take over the *Skarb Narodowy,* the Polish League was silent about Poland.[22]

What most troubled Helinski was the possibility that the PNA might lose its own identity if it entered the Polish League, which he expected, correctly as things turned out, would be clergy-dominated. Jerzmanowski caused problems here when he imprudently asserted that with the formation of the Polish League to handle civic matters, the PNA could limit its future work to the sale of life insurance.

As the first scheduled meeting of the new League approached, the PNA central government voted to attend but to take no active role in its proceedings. Instead it gave Censor Helinski the responsibility of announcing that the question of PNA membership would have to be left to the delegates of the next national convention, which was set for September, 1895. At the meeting, Helinski presented his concerns to the 233 delegates in attendance and urged that no final action be taken to set up the Polish League until the PNA *sejm.* His proposal was rejected and at this point a number of Alliance members withdrew.[23] The Alliance's refusal to participate left the League still-born and it soon disappeared. Jerzmanowski himself resigned and instead accepted the post of North American Commissioner for the PNA-directed *Skarb Narodowy.* In 1896, frustrated over his continued failure to lead Polonia, he retired and returned to Poland, where he died in 1909.[24]

Occasionally during the 1890s, solidarity was achieved. On October 20, 1892 the PNA and most of the rest of Chicago's Polonia combined to participate in a grand celebration marking the 400th anniversary of Columbus' discovery of the new world. In all, more than 5,000 Poles marched in the day's parade. Over 500 PNA members took part in the extravaganza, which was viewed by a host of dignitaries including U.S. Vice President Levi Morton. For the occasion, the PNA even commissioned the Chevalier Antoine de Kontski to compose an original Polish National Alliance march.

On October 7, 1893 an even greater show of solidarity was in evidence at a special "Polish Day" celebration at the Chicago Columbian Exposition. For this occasion, approximately 25,000 Poles, many attired in martial or folk costumes glorifying Poland and America's histories, took part in a massive parade culminating at the city's Lake Front fair grounds. Perhaps even more significant, however, were the first all-Polonia efforts on the political front. In 1893, an ultimately unsuccessful attempt was made to rally the community in opposition to a proposed treaty between the United States and the hated tsarist Russian regime. In 1898, Polonia again coalesced, this time to issue a memorandum opposing restrictive immigration legislation sponsored by Senator Henry Cabot Lodge of Massachusetts.

As for the *Skarb Narodowy,* its fate remained a source of significant disagreement within the PNA for years afterward. For one thing, the original decision to establish the fund had flowed out of Andrzejkowicz's close association with the Swiss-based *Liga Polska* movement, which was dominated by the aging veterans of the 1863 uprising. But in 1893, Roman Dmowski, a twenty-nine year old activist who had organized a new secret movement operating inside Poland and calling itself the National League *(Liga Narodowa)* gained control over the Swiss-based *emigre* association. Dmowski's movement remained true to the ideal of independence but rejected Milkowski's emphasis upon armed insurrection. Instead, he stressed a program of educational and political work among the largest social class, the peasantry, to broaden patriotic feeling beyond the small aristocratic and landowning elements, which had traditionally been most responsive to the idea of insurrection. In Dmowski's view, it was essential that the National Democratic movement generate among the masses a feeling of unremitting, if passive, resistance to the three oppressor states. Only through such a policy would Poland's rulers gradually be convinced that Poland was more a burden than an asset and that its restoration as an independent state made sense. Dmowski also rejected the *Liga Polska* idea that the independent Poland of the future should include the ethnic minorities that had belonged to the pre-partition commonwealth. Instead, he embraced the nationalistic principle of a Poland for the Poles alone.

The leaders of the Polish National Alliance in America went along with these developments; throughout the 1890s they attempted to maintain close ties with both the National League and its *emigre* branch, the Alliance of the Polish Migration *(Zwiazek Wychodztwa Polskiego).* But within the PNA, individuals who were partial to the patriotic program of Dmowski's socialist rival, Jozef Pilsudski, opposed those ties and attempted to channel the fund raising work of the *Skarb Narodowy* away from Dmowski's movement. Pilsudski also won some popularity because of his ardent belief in the principle of armed insurrection, not passive resistance, as the means by which independence would be gained. Further, he continued to champion the restoration of a commonwealth including the Lithuanians and Ruthenians and fiercely opposed Russia as Poland's greatest enemy. Both of these ideas reflected the thinking of the 1863 revolutionaries.

Differences over both the purposes and the beneficiaries of the *Skarb Narodowy* continued to plague PNA efforts to generate money for the project up to the time of its dissolution in 1913. In 1895, representatives from the nationalist underground movement in Poland came to America with the expressed aim of transferring all *Skarb Narodowy* funds to Switzerland. At the PNA *sejm* held that year in Chicago, their appeal was rejected by the narrowest of margins, a 59-59 tie vote. Eventually, a compromise was worked out by the PNA leadership (which strongly favored transfer) and approximately $17,000 was sent to Europe.[25] By 1903, another $7,000 had been raised through the annual 12 cent assessment. By this time, however, the socialist faction led by Alexander Debski had become a major force at Alliance conventions and his group voiced heated opposition to continuing PNA backing of the National Democratic movement. To blunt Debski's proposal to direct PNA fund drives to Pilsudski, Censor Leon Sadowski made a special trip to Switzerland to learn for himself how funds were being used. Upon his return he published a powerful defense of the nationalist movement in the pages of *Zgoda,* but at the 1905 convention was defeated for reelection. Thereafter and until 1913, no significant further transfers of funds were made. Only in September of that year was the issue at last resolved. The decision was made at the twentieth *sejm* of the PNA. At this convention, a raucus affair attended by more than seven hundred delegates, it was agreed that the entire *Skarb Narodowy* (by then amounting to approximately $40,000) be turned over to the Pilsudski-led Provisional Committee of Confederated Parties for Polish independence, headquartered in Austrian Poland, for the purpose of establishing military detachments prepared to fight for the homeland's unity and freedom. Thus ended PNA involvement in the matter of the Polish National Fund, an activity inaugurated 27 years earlier in behalf of an entirely different nationalist movement.

If the fate of the *Skarb Narodowy* proved to be a source of persistent internal conflict, on several other matters there was far greater agreement. One of these concerned PNA efforts to work with like-minded Polonia organizations on behalf of the progressive programs it had developed. Another involved the success the PNA experienced in realizing a set of imaginative projects advancing its cultural, educational and patriotic aims. During the years preceding the outbreak of the First World War, PNA involvement in both of these areas was generally fruitful and filled with great achievement.

As far back as 1887, PNA members had helped form a new organization aimed at young people, the Polish Falcons' Alliance *(Zwiazek Sokolow Polskich).* Its purpose was that of working to generate patriotic feeling among the immigrant youth by offering them attractive physical educational programs (initially focusing upon gymnastics) together with information about Poland's history and culture. The Falcons' motto, "A healthy spirit in a healthy body" epitomized the movement's aims.

The list of prominent PNA activists who were simultaneously engaged in the Falcons' Alliance is a long and impressive one. The first president of the Falcons was Casimir Zychlinski, who later served as president of the PNA between 1912 and 1927. Marian Steczynski, another Falcons' leader, also presided over the PNA, from 1903 to 1912. Three chief editors of *Zgoda,* Zbigniew Brodowski, Thomas Siemiradzki, and Stefan Barszczewski, were active in the Falcons' Alliance, and Barszczewski served as editor of its official newspaper. John Smulski, the head of the Polish National Department during the First World War, belonged to both organizations.

Many PNA leaders envisioned the Falcons as having a kind of paramilitary character with gymnastics drills preparing young men for future service in a Polish army fighting for the liberation of the homeland. In fact, in the First World War, a large number of Falcons volunteered for service in the Polish army organized in the United States that eventually saw service in Europe. Clearly, the idea of military service on Poland's behalf was a powerful element in the ideology of the movement. Nevertheless, the Falcons' greatest contribution was in instilling national pride and awareness among thousands of young men and women who participated in its sports and social activities over the years.

"Special relationships" also arose between several other organizations and the PNA. In 1888, the Mallek brothers, Anthony and Konstanty, took the lead in creating the Polish Singers' Alliance *(Zwiazek Spiewakow Polskich).* The two had come to America in the 1870s from Prussian Poland where they had belonged to similar singing societies, whose choice of patriotic music made them "efficient tools in the struggle against enforced assimilation . . ."[26] In America, the choirs of the Singers' Alliance combined an interest in patriotic music with social activities designed to bring young people together. Between 1888 and 1903, the movement grew from four groups to thirty-five choirs which included more than a thousand members in all. Anthony Mallek also produced sheet music for its choirs, composed new music and published a magazine, *Ziarno,* filled with songs appropriate for use both at patriotic events in Polonia as well as PSA conventions (the latter featured spirited competitions among participating groups). Mallek, a church organist by profession, also found time to play a major role in the work of the Polish National Alliance. In 1889, he was elected its national secretary.

Close ties also developed between the PNA and the Polish Youth Alliance *(Zwiazek Mlodziezy Polskiej),* Polish Veterans' Alliance *(Zwiazek Weteranow)* and the Polish Women's Alliance. These successes in turn led to growing optimism that a kind of organic relationship could be fostered among these groups under the protection of its patron, the PNA.

In 1899, at the fourth national convention of the Polish Falcons' Alliance the idea of fusion took real form; a resolution was approved calling upon its members to join the PNA when they reached adulthood. At the same time, the Falcons also came up with another idea, that of bringing about a "federation of young Poland" (specifically the Falcons, Singers and Youth Alliances) with the PNA. The Polish National Alliance supported the project and at its 1905 *sejm* in Wilkes-Barre, Pennsylvania worked out a method in which the three groups could be admitted into the PNA without, however, losing their own identities or autonomy. According to this plan, the PNA agreed to create separate *Wydzialy* or departments for the Falcons, Singers, Veterans and Youth Alliances and to provide their activities with publicity and financial support, on the condition that their members buy insurance through the fraternal. The plan did not require individuals belonging to the companionate alliances to merge with existing PNA lodges. Rather, their local units were invited to enter as new PNA societies, thereby guaranteeing their continued autonomy.

However, this ambitious and rather sensible idea failed. Though many supporters of the plan could be found within each separate federation, there were just as many who feared that their identities would be lost if they established a formal association within the PNA, which after all, possessed eight times as many members as all the companionate Alliances combined.

The issue of formal involvement with the PNA was sufficiently controversial to help cause a split within the Polish Singers' Alliance in 1903, one not healed until 1912. And in 1906, shortly after the Falcons agreed to join the PNA, a large group of *Sokol* nests in the East seceded and organized their own movement headquartered in Bridgeport, Connecticut. Yet another division occurred in 1909, when opponents of the union with the PNA stormed out of the Falcons' national convention and held their own counter-convention as the "Independent Falcons' Alliance." Ironically, though the number of young people entering the Falcons' movement quadrupled during this hectic period, thanks in great measure to PNA support, the traditional good feeling had degenerated into bitter polemics.[27] Only in December 1912 was unity restored when representatives from the competing factions met at a special convention to iron out their differences. The convention proved a success when Zychlinski, an old Falcon and the new president of the Polish National Alliance, went along with a proposal that ended his organization's association with the pro-PNA Falcons.[28] By this time, PNA leaders had come to realize that the value of consolidating the progressive forces in Polonia was illusory at best; at worst it subjected the PNA to the charge of seeking to dominate smaller groups such as the Falcons and Singers. A more fruitful course was to encourage friendly relations with these movements but otherwise to stay out of their internal affairs. This approach, over the years, proved to be a wise and productive one.

If unifying the progressive nationalist camp in Polonia proved to be beyond the reach of the PNA, its members did achieve extraordinary success in a second area, that of realizing a set of projects of significance to the growing Polish population in America. One of its more dramatic achievements was to lead the way in creating fitting monuments to commemorate the exploits of Tadeusz Kosciuszko and Kazimierz Pulaski, the heroes of the eighteenth century independence struggles of Poland and America. Already in 1888, Chicago Poles had proposed a fund drive to cover the costs of an equestrian monument honoring Kosciuszko in Humboldt Park, a large public recreation area located in the heart of the north side Polonia community. But progress on the monument idea was initially disappointing because of difficulty in winning local government permission to put up the statue. However, in February, 1892 all the necessary permits at last had been granted and a Kosciuszko Monument Fund Association was duly established. By 1897, under Brodowski's chairmanship, the association had raised more than $8,000 and hired a Polish architect, Kazimierz Chodzinski (1861–1921) to work on a fitting monument. As Chodzinski's work neared completion, enthusiasm about the Chicago project spread and Kosciuszko monument committees were also formed in Cleveland and Milwaukee. On September 11, 1904, a crowd of more than one hundred thousand people was on hand in Chicago for the unveiling of the first Kosciuszko monument. On May 7 of the next year the Cleveland monument was unveiled before another enormous crowd and on June 18, 1905 fifty thousand persons witnessed the dedication of the Milwaukee statue.

Even more exciting a prospect was a Polonia-sponsored monument honoring Kosciuszko in Washington, D.C. This project developed in a circuitous fashion. In 1900, a Toledo-based group of Polish Americans headed by a Colonel Joseph Smolinski learned of a long-forgotten resolution of the American Continental Congress approved in 1779, one month after Pulaski's death at the battle of Savannah. In recognition of his services to this country, which included his organizing of cavalry regiments in the fight for independence, the Congress had pledged to fund a monument in his memory. Though nothing ever came of the original resolution, efforts began to win Federal funding of a monument to the fallen hero in the nation's capital.

This development prompted a meeting of Chicago Polonia activists on December 26, 1903 where a plan was discussed to raise funds for a Kosciuszko monument in Washington to complement the Pulaski memorial. Having agreed to present such a monument to the United States as a gift from the Polish people in America, the participants delegated Theodore Helinski, then the secretary of the PNA, to travel to Washington to present its plan to President Theodore Roosevelt. Helinski was able to meet the President on February 3, 1904 and soon afterwards Roosevelt authorized his director of monuments and public buildings to present Congress with a proposal in support of the construction of a Kosciuszko memorial. Already on April 2, 1904 a joint resolution approving the plan emerged from the Capitol and in Chicago Helinski was elected chairman of a fund raising committee embracing the major organizational units in Polonia.

Differences between Helinski and clerical leaders caused their withdrawal from the committee, leaving the PNA, the Polish Women's Alliance, the Falcons, the Singers and a few smaller groups as the only organizations involved in the project. To insure the fund appeal's success, the delegates to the 1905 PNA convention agreed to assess the membership 24 cents per year for the monument. Indeed, of the $76,837 that was eventually generated for the Kosciuszko monument, the PNA alone provided $75,089 of the amount, with the other organizations together accounting for $1,748.[29]

Both monuments were authorized at about the same time, since by 1905 the U.S. Congress had set aside $50,000 for the Pulaski statue and had hired Chodzinski to prepare an appropriate likeness. For its part, the PNA proposed that the artist of the Kosciuszko monument be selected on the basis of an international competition, but one open only to Poles. In all, eighteen designs were presented in December, 1906 at an exhibition in which Roosevelt's favorite was declared the winning entry. Chosen to create the memorial honoring Kosciuszko was Antoni Popiel (1865-1910), whose work included a 1904 monument in Krakow honoring Poland's greatest romantic poet, Adam Mickiewicz.

PNA influence was decisive in a number of other matters connected with the creation of the two monuments. Its leaders raised objections to the original plan for the Pulaski statue, which had the "father of the American cavalry" on foot. Having won approval of an equestrian likeness of Pulaski, the PNA then persuaded the monuments commission to have the memorial to Kosciuszko placed in Lafayette Square, across from the White House where the Pulaski statue had originally been set along with likenesses of Lafayette, Von Steuben and Rochambeau. Pulaski's statue instead was located on Pennsylvania Avenue.

Through the efforts of the Alliance, arrangements were made to dedicate both monuments in May, 1910. Because President William Howard Taft could not be in Washington on May 3, the dedication ceremonies were rescheduled for May 11. On that day, thousands of Poles from around the country, Europe and Poland attended a magnificant program in which two of Poland's greatest sons were recognized in the capital of the United States. Among the speakers were Bishop Paul Rhode of Chicago, PNA President Marian Steczynski, Censor Anthony Schreiber and President Taft. Sending his congratulations from Berlin was former President Theodore Roosevelt, whose telegram caused a minor diplomatic uproar in Germany. Roosevelt's note read: "Accept my best wishes for all Americans of Polish birth or heritage on the day of the dedication of monuments to two great Poles, Kosciuszko and Pulaski, whose names will always be immortalized in the pages of the history of America."[30]

Coinciding with the dedication of the monuments was a second major event sponsored by the PNA in Washington, a Polish National Congress which was held on May 11, 12 and 13, 1910. The idea for such a meeting, which brought together representatives from the Polish American organizations, the *emigre* movement in Western Europe and political parties in Poland, had been first broached in 1909 at the Milwaukee convention of the PNA. The purpose of what was expected to be the first world congress of Poles, one to be followed by regular conclaves in the future, was "to show the whole world that partitioned Poland—though in chains—possessed its own representatives." Just as important, however, was the PNA goal of demonstrating American Polonia's significance as "the fourth partition of Poland," and hence an integral and important element in the effort for independence.

Invitations went out to Europe and to every secular and religious organization in Polonia. But the congress failed to attract the type of response that its chief advocates, Censor Schreiber and President Steczynski, had hoped for. Most of the European guests were from the nationalist movement in Galicia or Austrian Poland. But several of the best known activists of the day, including Henryk Sienkiewicz and Ignacy Paderewski, were absent. Moreover, the clerical faction in Polonia, while present for the dedication ceremonies, boycotted the congress. With more than half of the delegates from the PNA, most of the rest represented such friendly groups such as the Falcons, Singers and the Polish Women's Alliance.

The Congress' agenda was divided into three concurrent sessions, dealing with emigration and economic matters, culture and scientific questions, and politics. At each of the sessions, speeches and discussion were followed by resolutions to be put into effect later. For example, at the Emigration-Economics session, a resolution was approved calling for better treatment of the immigrants and the creation of American commissions in the various Polonia settlements to assist them in adjusting to their new conditions.

The Scientific-Culture session approved resolutions demanding better educational facilities "free of partisan and religious dogmatism" which at the same time would emphasize instruction in Poland's language, history and culture. The Political session, not surprisingly, provoked the greatest controversy. One resolution called upon Polonia to rally for Poland under the PNA banner. Another appealed to the nations of the world to recognize Poland's right to independence, a proposal that some of the more cautious delegates considered "undiplomatic." Another source of disagreement arose between Thomas Siemiradzki and John Smulski, two of Polonia's leading lights. To Siemiradski, Editor of the Alliance newspapers and a major "fourth partition" advocate, the chief responsibility of the PNA and Polonia was the work for national liberation. For Smulski, however, a more practical priority faced Polonia's organizations—that of finding ways in which to assist Poles in "getting ahead" in their adopted homeland. Both men, of course, were correct since each man's thinking had traditionally been central to the purposes of the PNA and the patriotic camp. Indeed both ideas continued to be fundamental to the Alliance in the decades that followed the 1910 Congress.

In any event, the Congress was not repeated. The failure to unite PNA members with representatives of the other major wings in Polonia, the socialists and the Catholics, convinced its planners that a new strategy was called for, one that stressed cooperation rather than consolidation under PNA leadership. The history of interorganizational work on behalf of Polonia causes in the years since 1910 has shown this judgment to be correct.[31]

PNA leadership in Polonia affected the organizational work of Polish American organizations in many other areas as well. From 1886 onward, for example, the Alliance was involved in assisting immigrants entering New York in the difficult tasks of finding lodging and work. In 1909 the PNA Immigration Home was purchased at a cost of $47,000, one-tenth of the net worth of the organization. It remained a busy center of activity throughout the era of mass migration into the United States. In 1891 PNA delegates at the ninth *sejm* in Detroit accepted the library of Henry Kalussowski and in this fashion established the first of several hundred libraries and reading rooms operated under the fraternal's supervision around the country.[32] In 1895 the PNA also set up a special Educational Department or *Wydzial Oswiaty;* among its activities was the establishment of high school courses offering English language instruction along with training in American citizenship. Later on, courses in Poland's history and culture along with Polish language training were added to the programs of the Educational Department for the benefit of the children of the immigrants. The department sponsored hundreds of lectures and published scores of books and pamphlets to enlighten interested members of Polonia about their ancestral heritage and the salient characteristics of their new homeland.[33] One of the earliest and most important activities of the department was its student loan and scholarship program. Through more than ninety years, this program designed to assist the children of PNA members in attaining their educational goals has continued to function; in all more than $3 million has been invested in this field. All these activities, furthermore, stimulated other Polonia fraternals to develop similar programs of their own in education.

The commitment to leading Polonia caused PNA leaders to search for new ways in which to reach a larger audience with their message. Aside from the weekly *Zgoda,* the official organ of the Alliance whose readership consisted mainly of its own members, the PNA made efforts to establish a daily newspaper in Chicago. In 1897, the Alliance agreed to partially underwrite the publishing costs of the Chicago *Dziennik Narodowy,* but this arrangement broke down when differences arose over editorial policy. At the 1907 PNA Convention in Baltimore, a controversial motion to establish a daily newspaper owned and operated by the Alliance was approved, and on January 23, 1908, the first issue of the Chicago-based *Dziennik Zwiazkowy* went to press under the direction of former *Zgoda* editor and PNA President Frank Jablonski. In time, the "Polish Daily *Zgoda*" became the most widely read Polish language paper in America.[34]

Yet another PNA achievement was in establishing its very own school to further advance its commitment to education. Founding an Alliance school was approved in principle in 1905 when a special Educational and School committee was created by the delegates to the Wilkes-Barre convention. Counting the surplus yielded from the Kosciuszko monument fund drive along with its own money-raising activities, the Committee was able to collect more than $75,000 in the next few years. Soon after the 1911 PNA convention, Censor Schreiber won approval from the board of directors to establish a *Kolegium Zwiazkowy* in the town of Cambridge Springs, Pennsylvania, twenty miles from Erie. Originally a high school which included a program preparing youngsters to enter secondary school, the institution added a technical training program to its offerings in 1915. In the 1920s a junior college program was established followed in 1948 by the transforming of the school into a four year coeducational liberal arts college. The Alliance school, throughout the years of its operation, has represented the fulfillment of the dream of many in the PNA who wished to have their very own educational institution, one based upon the principles of the fraternal. And commitment to this dream has been kept in good times and bad for more than seventy years.

In insurance, too, the PNA made significant strides during its first decades in improving the quality of its program of benefits. Initially, the Alliance established a simple program of burial insurance in which each local PNA lodge provided a $500 death benefit to the family of a deceased member and $250 to a member if his wife passed away. This plan had one major drawback; were a society to lose even two or three insured members over a short period of time, its obligation could cause it to fall into bankruptcy. Hence, in the early years of the PNA, groups joined and left frequently to avoid the pitfalls of insurance. In 1886, the PNA reformed its insurance program by establishing a standardized program of assessment creating a centralized fund out of which death benefits could be paid. Accordingly, each new member joining the PNA paid an initiation fee and thereafter was required to pay one dollar each month to maintain his membership rights in both his local lodge and in the national organization. Part of these sums were forwarded to the central or home office to be used to cover death benefits to all eligible recipients throughout the country.

At first, only men between the ages of 18 and 45 could apply for membership in the PNA and every member paid the same amount to maintain his insurance. While a member's wife was indirectly insured through her husband, women could not attend lodge meetings, vote, or hold office in the organization. In 1895, the amount of insurance available to male members was raised to $900; spouses' policies were increased to $300.

The PNA position on female membership caused some friction from its inception, but opposition to full women's equality prevented a major change in policy before 1900. A common argument made against women's equality noted that as housewives, women possessed no means to pay their membership dues through outside work. But there were other reasons for the PNA stance, including the unwillingness of many men to have women attend their lodge meetings.

The question of women's equality came to a head in 1898 when several feminists in Chicago met to establish their own independent fraternal, which they named the Polish Women's Alliance, *Zwiazek Polek*. The significance of the new movement was not lost by other PNA leaders nor by the PRCUA. Within two years, both organizations acted to enable women to enter their ranks as equal voting members. For the Polish National Alliance, which held an extraordinary convention in 1900 to take up the issue, the decision to admit women was largely responsible for the great increase in its membership during the next decade. Between 1899 and 1900 alone, the PNA rose in size from 15,288 to 28,358 members!

Moreover, the issue of female attendance at the previously all-men's lodge meetings proved to be inconsequential. Women organized their own lodges and were happy to operate these groups independently of their husbands and fathers. And, the PNA women's movement was largely responsible for the successful effort to promote the education of children in the Polish spirit in the Polish American communities after 1900. In short, the decision to provide women with full PNA membership was one of the wisest it ever made. In addition, PNA relations with the *Zwiazek Polek* remained cordial. Throughout the history of the two movements, cooperation and collaboration have been the words which best describe their relationship.[35]

In 1907 another major step forward was achieved by the delegates attending the national convention in Baltimore. There, a program of variable premiums based on age was approved for the first time. This idea, basic to the appeal of commercial insurance firms, had been strongly opposed by many older Alliance members at previous *sejms* out of fear that it would mean a sharp increase in their dues. The compromise reached in Baltimore allowed current members to pay premiums without any changes and limited the table of variable premiums to future members. Thanks to this innovation, individuals over the age of 45 were able to join the PNA and younger people saw the cost of their insurance drop, enabling the PNA to remain competitive with other fraternals.

A final early innovation occurred in 1917 when children were made eligible for insurance for the first time. Juvenile members of the Alliance (those under the age of 16) were placed in a special department or division of the PNA with no right to vote or hold office in the organization until they reached maturity. Nor were such members counted in determinations of delegates for the conventions of the PNA. Nevertheless, the creation of the PNA Juvenile Department gave impetus to a new set of programs directed toward youth, including sports and scouting.

Thus, by the end of the First World War, the insurance program of the PNA was largely complete. Men and women of all ages had become eligible for membership and a variety of activities designed to meet their social needs in and outside of the lodges had been established. Simultaneously, in the home office of the PNA the rapid growth in membership had brought about increased professionalization, permitting the fraternal to process thousands of policies and claims each year.

Though the PNA decisions to admit socialists, religious dissenters and members of other ethnic groups had disappointing results upon its later growth, such actions reinforced the idea of an Alliance open to all who shared its general aims. Indeed it was as an open arena that the Alliance achieved its greatest success in attracting a variety of ethnic activists who joined out of the belief that through the PNA they could best reach and influence the millions of people of Polish origin and heritage in the United States. Within the Alliance, devout Catholics and non-Catholics coexisted with those who identified with Dmowski's nationalist cause as well as Pilsudski's social democratic movement. Businessmen and working people rubbed shoulders at the PNA national convention as did supporters of the Republican party and partisans of the Democratic camp.

Indeed, the Alliance's fraternal structure gave its members ample opportunity to compete with one another for influence in an orderly fashion. In an age before the advent of radio and television, the local lodge hall, often located in a tavern or church basement, was an important neighborhood social center where issues of the day were reported, discussed and, sometimes, hotly debated. Delegates elected by the lodge members to participate in regional meetings (called *Sejmiki*) or national conventions served the crucial function of communicating to one another the concerns of their constituents. Thus the structure of fraternalism supplemented *Zgoda* in keeping people informed about major developments facing Polonia. Equally important was the role of delegates in informing national officers about grass roots opinion at the conventions, which were themselves significant ethnic community events. Initially held each year, the PNA *sejm* became a semi-annual affair after 1887. After 1915, it was made into an event held every three years. Beginning in 1931, the *sejm* took place every four years.

At each *sejm,* elections were held for all national offices. Indeed, campaigns by competing candidates were important elements in the democratic process within the Alliance and considerably enlivened its activities. In recent years, individual office seekers have run on their own, with only informal support from friendly candidates for other offices. But in the past, there were periods in which well-defined parties or factions operated and organized entire slates of candidates to gain control over the movement. In the conflict over the Alliance, competition was as exciting and well-organized as at the national conventions of the major American political parties. While the greatest factional conflict took place between the two World Wars, when the "old guard" was challenged by the "opposition" or "lewica," this competition was distinctive primarily in terms of its intensity. Earlier, between 1900 and 1914, it had been the socialists who challenged the more conservative and nationalist PNA establishment for supremacy. And after the election of Charles Rozmarek to the presidency in 1939, the battle pitted his vaunted "machine" against a succession of rival groupings, which finally succeeded in unseating him in 1967.

PNA conventions were and remain similar to the gatherings of political parties or labor unions in a number of other ways. Reports by incumbent national officers on their past activities were followed by the elections of new leaders and a variety of resolutions defining the Alliance's political and business policies. Such activities consumed the greatest amount of time at the proceedings, especially after 1900, when the number of national officers was greatly increased with the creation of district commissioners responsible for directing the work of the movement at the state level. Another major activity involved the reports made to the delegates by the many committees, departments and commissions created to deal with concerns ranging from education, youth, emigration, women's activities, publications, assistance to members in need, libraries, colonization, and business, to special activities such as the Kosciuszko monument, the sponsorship of an international congress of Poles, the Alliance school, and the Polish National Fund. The convention was also responsible for approving the PNA's operating budget to cover the movement's activities and expenses for the period up to the next *sejm*. This obligation required the delegates to determine what special assessments were needed to enable the agencies of the fraternal to accomplish their goals. That so many delegates sat patiently through these lengthy sessions in halls lacking modern air conditioning and public address systems demonstrates their keen interest in the proceedings. It is also eloquent testimony to the PNA's role as a school for public activity.

A unique aspect of the PNA *sejm* was the delegates' right of "interpellation" of incumbent officers. After completing their reports, national officers were required to stand before the convention to answer questions from the floor as to their past stewardship. This extraordinarily democratic tradition made every official responsible before the membership in the most direct of ways. Even the mightiest leader could be placed on the defensive by the lowliest "back bencher" willing to raise a controversial issue before the assembly. The interpellation process made it difficult for national leaders to manipulate a passive convention unless they controlled an overwhelming majority of delegates and could rule certain questions out of order. The system also gave opposition leaders a forum to speak to the entire assembly and thereby broaden their base of support in the elections that followed the interpellation sessions. Though most questions were directed at minor issues or were personal in their criticisms, on occasion, the interpellation procedure played a significant role at the convention. For instance, in 1907 the president of the Alliance,

Marian Steczynski had to explain in detail the policies of the board of directors in placing large sums of money in a Chicago bank which had failed. In 1913, Censor Schreiber was sufficiently apprehensive about criticism of his involvement in the PNA decision to establish its school in Cambridge Springs, Pennsylvania that he initially refused even to attend the convention to submit his report!

Any review of the pre-World War I era of PNA history must conclude by noting the remarkable record of effort and achievements that characterized the "first generation and a half" within the Alliance. From a proverbial tiny acorn the PNA had grown into a mighty oak. At the fifth convention in 1885 the Alliance had included no more than 210 male members; at its twentieth *sejm* in Detroit in September 1913, more than 700 delegates representing 100,000 men and women were on hand for one of the most boisterous conventions in the history of the movement. (So large was the size of the convention that a resolution to change the procedure for selecting delegates to reduce their numbers was approved immediately before its final adjournment!)

Though it was unsuccessful in unifying Polonia under its banner, the PNA did establish enduring ties with other progressive Polish American organizations as well as the leading patriotic movements in Poland and Western Europe. Ideologically, the Alliance hued to the political center in Polonia. Respectful of the role of the Roman Catholic Church, it nevertheless refused to be led by priests in matters pertaining to secular issues and was not uncritical of certain Church policies. Similarly, while its leaders rejected the class conflict theories at the heart of the theories of Polish socialism which gained currency in the decade before the outbreak of the First World War, the Alliance was able to cooperate with the socialists on the issue of Poland's independence. Thus, when the socialists took a particularly militant stance against tsarist rule in its Polish provinces in 1905 the PNA outlook drew closer than it had in the past to the socialist cause. And in 1912 the PNA joined together with the socialists and the rest of Polonia in helping form the Polish National Defense Committee.

As a middle of the road movement, the PNA was sometimes torn by conflicting factions representing conservative and radical political outlooks. Taking the moderate and progressive course eventually yielded more roses than thorns, however, and helped the PNA to become the most attractive of Polonia fraternals. As a public and patriotic movement at once committed to both Polish independence and to central values of American society, the Alliance found itself squarely in the mainstream of Polish ethnic life. Further, thanks to its success in realizing a variety of activities connected with insurance, education, mass communication and patriotic work, the PNA

Table 2.   The PNA and PRCUA Compared, 1890-1915

	PNA	PRCUA	PNA	PRCUA
	Memberships		Net Worth	
1890	3,426	7,198	$5,145	$6,594
1895	7,515	8,782	28,183	4,051
1900	28,358	10,943	98,339	30,293
1905	45,271	19,854	321,931	154,264
1910	71,335	51,197	1,154,918	645,169
1915	110,331	85,208	2,936,607	1,704,564

was able to win widespread recognition as Polonia's most dynamic mass movement.

As it slowly retreated from the goal of consolidating Polonia under its sway, the PNA also found it increasingly possible to build friendly relations with the conservative clerical camp. Indeed, when no one followed in the Reverend Barzynski's footsteps in warring against the PNA, the way was cleared for a steady improvement in ties between the Alliance and the conservatives, something largely attained by 1914. Ironically, relations between the PNA and the largest Catholic fraternal, the PRCUA, improved at the same time that the Alliance had achieved its preeminence over its old rival, both in terms of membership and financial strength.

At the same time the popularity of the PNA's solidarity philosophy also attracted many liberal Poles away from more politically radical groups in Polonia. Even though a number of Alliance leaders flirted with some type of democratic socialism, their emphasis tended to be on its nationalist features as espoused by Pilsudski and Debski rather than its class warfare ideas, another tribute to the power of the PNA's message.

By 1914, the now 100,000 strong PNA whose membership averaged 35 years of age had compiled an impressive record of service that underscored far better than rhetoric its leadership of Polonia. During the war, the PNA continued to play a leading role in the ethnic community in cooperation with other Polish American groups. When a restored Poland was proclaimed after 123 years of foreign partition on November 11, 1918, much of the credit for this achievement could rightly be ascribed to the Alliance.

Chapter 4

WORLD WAR I, THE POLISH NATIONAL ALLIANCE
AND POLAND'S REBIRTH, 1914–1918

The outbreak of the general war in Europe in August, 1914 involving the three great powers that had partitioned Poland in the eighteenth century represented the greatest opportunity for independence since the Napoleonic conflict which had engulfed the continent a century before. And when the War ended in 1918 Poland was indeed restored, thanks in part to the efforts of American Polonia and its organizations. For the Polish National Alliance, the largest secular movement in the ethnic community, the resurrection of Poland symbolized nothing less than the culmination of its efforts to mobilize Polonia intellectually and politically behind the cause which had inspired its own creation in 1880.[1]

On the eve of the Great War, the PNA had in every respect become the leading force in Polonia. When its delegates gathered together at the Alliance's twentieth *sejm* in September, 1913, in Detroit, they learned that their movement included more than one hundred thousand members grouped together in 1,433 lodges and possessed financial assets of nearly $2 million. A movement open to both men and women, the PNA could look back with pride upon a record of enormous growth during the previous decade; only ten years before the fraternal had included thirty-six thousand members in 551 lodges and claimed assets totalling $240 thousand.

Not only had the PNA become far and away the leading Polish fraternal insurance association, it was increasingly involved in a wide variety of activities designed to meet its members' cultural and intellectual needs. The PNA published two newspapers and administered its own school, an immigration home, a museum and a central library. In addition, its local lodges directed a host of other activities which ranged from their own reading rooms to a thriving system of Saturday Polish schools. In 1899 the PNA established its first budget (amounting to $1,112) for cultural and educational work

99

sponsored by its *Wydzial Oswiaty*. In 1913, this commission's expenditures amounted to more than $600,000.[2]

The PNA's one failure had followed from its inability to unite Polonia under its banner behind the Polish independence cause. Not only did its sponsorship of the 1910 Polish National Congress prove disappointing, so also were its various attempts to consolidate the activities of other progressive organizations in support of its aims. A crucial element in realizing this second objective had been the Polish Falcons' Alliance. To many PNA members, a close association between the two movements was of paramount importance if the fraternal were to accomplish its patriotic goals. *Zgoda* Editor Siemiradzki well expressed this attitude in a 1911 editorial in which he described the PNA as Polonia's government and the Falcons as its fighting force.

But the close relationship established between the PNA and the Falcons after 1905 proved to be unproductive in the long run. Though the Falcons' movement grew considerably during this time, thanks to the support its activities received from the fraternal, a large number of dissatisfied *Sokoly* seceded from the organization out of fear that their groups' identity and aims would be lost due to their ties with the PNA. It was only in 1912 that the split within the Falcons' movement was healed when representatives of the feuding factions held an extraordinary convention and overwhelmingly approved a resolution not only to reunite but also to establish themselves in the future as independent from the PNA.

Though this action came as a great blow to the PNA, the circumstances surrounding the Falcons' unity convention rather unexpectedly provided a wholly new set of opportunities for the fraternal to once more play an active, if not dominating role in Polonia efforts on behalf of the Polish independence cause. Present at the unity convention were large numbers of representatives from all of the leading Polonia organizations. Once the Falcons' Alliance had reestablished itself as a united and independent movement, the opportunity existed for these representatives to meet together for the purpose of discussing ways in which they might cooperate effectively in behalf of Poland's independence. Although this question had caused nothing but discord in the past, their meeting proved to be highly constructive and led to the creation of the first true all-Polonia political action federation, the Polish National Defense Committee *(Komitet Obrony Narodowej,* or *KON).* Amazingly, *KON* included socialists, clergymen and pro-Catholic fraternals along with partisans of the nationalist movement, all of whom had been at loggerheads in the past on many issues. Much of the credit for the initial success of *KON* belonged to the Polish National Alliance, whose representatives enthusiastically accepted the new federation although it meant the likely end to their historic leadership ambitions.[3]

A second ingredient accounting for *KON's* initial success was the growing militancy of Polonia itself and rising sentiment in favor of using direct means to regain Polish independence, whose chief exponent in Poland was Jozef Pilsudski. During the 1905 Russian Revolution, Pilsudski's socialists had organized their own uprising against tsarist rule while Dmowski's National Democrats had opposed such a course. Though his revolt failed, Pilsudski's effort rekindled the romantic tradition of insurrection and gained him a wide following at Dmowski's expense. Many of those who opposed other elements of the Polish Socialist program nonetheless favored Pilsudski's militant stance, including large contingents in the Falcons and the PNA. The failure of the 1910 Polish National Congress was still another blow to the National Democrats and their supporters in Polonia, who were derisively dubbed the "political grandfathers" of the independence cause by their opponents.

In autumn, 1912 the militants' cause was further strengthened when the parties operating in the Austrian zone of the partitioned country temporarily buried their differences and agreed to fight for national independence in the event of war with Russia. The coalition, called the Provisional Commission of Confederated Independence Parties included both the socialists and nationalists; moreover, its leaders looked to American Polonia for financial support of their cause.

The coalition's militancy readily won it the backing of the Falcons, the PNA and the Polish Socialist Alliance. But crucial to its winning over the clergy and the Roman Catholic fraternals was its success in presenting a facade of unity linking together a number of traditionally rival parties in the homeland. So long as that coalition was preserved, *KON* would remain intact; but in fact, unity in both countries proved elusive and short lived.

Within Polonia, each of *KON's* major elements tended to have a different outlook about its priorities. For the Polish National Alliance, the Coalition's commitment to fighting for independence brought back memories of the time-honored insurrectionist traditions of 1794, 1830 and 1863. To the Falcons' movement, armed struggle for independence justified the transformation of its gymnastic societies into paramilitary training organizations which it expected would be sending volunteers to Poland in the near future. To the socialists, Polonia's primary responsibility was to give financial and political support to Pilsudski's forces being formed in Austrian Poland. To the Catholic clergy and its fraternal allies, in contrast, Polonia's chief obligation remained humanitarian in character and their political allegiance with the National Democrats.

Inevitably, differences among the Polish parties in Galicia led Dmowski's followers to oppose the Commission. Similarly, in America, antagonisms between the socialists and the conservative faction caused the clergy and its allies to leave *KON* in June, 1913 when the federation's national board of directors held its very first meeting. The cause of their walkout was ostensibly Polish National Catholic Bishop Hodur's demand to be included in the *KON* leadership. Even though a motion to add him to the board of directors failed, the progressive faction continued to press for Hodur's inclusion, which provoked the conservatives to leave and form their own patriotic group, the Polish National Council. An equally pertinent reason for the division within *KON,* however, had been Dmowski's growing hostility to the short lived coalition.[4]

Following the conservatives' withdrawal, the PNA found itself in a difficult and ambiguous position, one reflected by events taking place at it's *sejm* in Detroit in September, 1913. There, on the one hand, the nationalists retained a comfortable majority of 11-5 in the elections to the board of directors, with Casimir Zychlinski winning the presidency and Anthony Karabasz besting Siemiradzki for the office of censor. On the other side, the left faction also did surprisingly well. For example, Stanislas Mermel was elected a vice president and Stanislas Dangel became editor of *Zgoda.* Yet, while control over the PNA central administration eluded the left faction, Pilsudski's supporters pushed through a resolution turning over the money collected over the years for the National Fund to support the activities of his legions in Galicia. Through this action, the Alliance forwarded approximately, $40,000 to Poland and thereby terminated its twenty-seven year association with the Nationalist movement headquartered in Switzerland. Even the fiercely patriotic slogans and resolutions voiced at the convention had a distinctly proletarian ring, such as "Niech zyje niepodlegla Polska ludowa!" and "Niech zyje lud Polski!" (Long life to an independent people's Poland, Long life to the Polish masses).[5]

In retrospect, however, the Detroit convention proved to be the high water mark of socialist influence within the pre war Alliance. Only a few months after the *sejm,* the PNA withdrew from the Polish National Defense Committee to eventually coalesce with the conservative faction, although it remained committed to military action, "czyn zbrojny," on behalf of Poland.

The Detroit conclave was important in one other respect; at the meeting, several veteran PNA leaders who had helped shape the movement during its "first generation and a half" retired from further involvement in its leadership. One who had already stepped aside to become the business manager of the Alliance school was Marian Steczynski, President of the fraternal between 1903 and 1912. Another veteran activist who retired under less happy circumstances was Michael Majewski, one of the earliest supporters of the PNA in 1880 and a member of *Gmina Polska*. Majewski had been PNA national treasurer for all but four years after 1889. Held responsible in the Czechowicz scandal for failing to monitor PNA finances, Majewski was obliged to resign, his sorry end coming as a result of holding onto high office for too long a tenure. Siemiradzki, the most influential editor of the Alliance papers during the previous decade also left the scene at the convention, an unsuccessful candidate for the office of censor. Yet a fourth PNA leader to retire was Censor Anthony Schreiber, who had first won election in 1905. Schreiber, the proprietor of a Buffalo-based brewery, had been particularly energetic in organizing the 1910 Polish National Congress in Washington which had coincided with the dedication of the Kosciuszko and Pulaski monuments.

Controversy surrounded his handling of the purchase of the old Vanadium Hotel property in Cambridge Springs, Pennsylvania as the site of the Alliance school. Some delegates argued in favor of different locations, while others complained that the purchase price of the property, $175,000, had been excessive. Schreiber's ambition to expand the duties of the censor did not help him either. In his proclamation announcing the Detroit convention, Schreiber had proposed a clear division in responsibilities within the PNA in which ideological and political matters would be handled solely by the censor. In Schreiber's opinion, the board of directors' responsibilities would then be limited to managing the business affairs of the Alliance, a not particularly unpersuasive idea given the problems which surfaced in the Czechowicz scandal. At the convention, however, Schreiber's view was sharply criticized and in a fit of pique he withdrew from further PNA involvement.[6]

After the convention, the issue of its continuing participation in the Polish National Defense Committee was a source of growing tension within the factionalized PNA central administration. First to be affected was Dangel, who was informed by the board that his editorial responsibilities would be limited to *Zgoda* and that another man would be chosen to run the Alliance daily. Unsuccessful in appealing this decision to the supervisory council, the "supreme court" of the PNA, Dangel then resigned as *Zgoda* editor. In 1915, both he and Vice President Mermel were expelled from the Alliance for their outspoken criticisms of the board of directors, a dramatic sign of the bitterness of factional feeling at the time.[7]

Although its support of direct military action had placed the Alliance and the Falcons movement in agreement with the socialists, the PNA was increasingly uncomfortable with its remaining *KON* allies. The opportunity to withdraw from *KON* came in December, 1913 when Ignacy Paderewski gave an interview sharply critical of Pilsudski following a concert in Milwaukee. Paderewski's remarks were received enthusiastically by the conservative Polish National Council and caused PNA and Falcons leaders to request a conference with the great pianist to permit him to expand upon his published comments. Several days later, Paderewski met in Cleveland with a delegation from the two groups. While emphasizing that he was no politician and that his views on Pilsudski's political coalition were purely personal in nature, Paderewski nonetheless stood by his oblique but darted observations, which were aimed as much at *KON* as Pilsudski.[8]

The nationalist faction in the PNA seized this opportunity to call for a review of its involvement. In February, 1914 the supervisory council authorized Censor Karabasz and Vice Censor Adolf Rakoczy to visit Poland to gather some first-hand impressions about the political situation. Upon their return in May, the two gave a highly unfavorable report about Pilsudski's political coalition, prompting the PNA to withdraw from *KON*. But instead of immediately joining the Polish National Council, the Alliance organized its own "Independence Department" to raise funds for Poland. When the Falcons' Alliance also withdrew from *KON,* the fate of the Polish National Defense Committee was sealed. Though it remained in existence throughout the war, it now represented little more than the Polish Socialist Alliance. Moreover, following America's entry into the conflict in 1917, *KON's* support of the Central Powers caused U.S. officials to define its activities as subversive in nature. But *KON's* identification with Pilsudski, who in November, 1918 became one of the founders of the restored Polish state, revived the committee and enabled its members to play a visible role within Polonia through most of the interwar era.

In sum, on the eve of what became the First World War in July, 1914, American Polonia's organizations were once again divided. On the conservative side stood the Catholic clergy and its fraternal allies organized into the Polish National Council. Suspicious of violent efforts to bring about independence, the Council looked to Russia as a potential defender of the Polish nation against the German empire. The conservative faction also saw its role as primarily one of lending moral support to the independence cause; once war began it focused its activities upon providing charitable assistance to the people of Poland and looked to Dmowski and even more to Paderewski for leadership.

On the left were the Polish socialists, and for a time the Polish National Catholic Church, who backed Pilsudski, his legion, and the fight alongside

Austria-Hungary and Germany against Russia. In the center stood the PNA and the Falcons. Like the conservatives, they inclined toward the National Democratic cause but differed with them in favoring direct military action. However, instead of supporting Pilsudski's legion, PNA President Zychlinski and Falcons' President Starzynski continued to favor the concept of an army composed of Polish Americans trained by the Falcons and ready to travel to Poland itself to fight for its freedom. But once war was declared, the Alliance and the Falcons coalesced with the conservatives, an action that proved to be fortuitous. Through their efforts, which nearly united Polonia, three central objectives were eventually reached. These included the raising of substantial amounts of relief aid for Polish victims of the conflict, the mobilization of a genuine army of Poles recruited in America and carrying the national colors into battle alongside the western allies, and the forming of a political organization, the Polish National Department, to persuade the U.S. to recognize Poland's claim to statehood. In each of these activities, the Polish National Alliance contributed mightily, both as an organization and through the individual actions of its members.

    With the outbreak of hostilities, few observers could be optimistic about Poland's eventual reunification and independence, however. For this to occur, all three partitioning powers would have to suffer serious military defeat, a possibility that seemed highly remote since they were on opposing sides in the conflict. In addition, energetic and effective diplomatic pressure on behalf of Poland was called for by its representatives in Western Europe and the U.S., an effort that required the mobilization of public opinion throughout Polonia. This too was a task seemingly beyond the capabilities of the American Polish leaders in 1914.

    When war broke out, Polonia's worst apprehensions were realized. Thousands of young Poles were immediately mustered into the armies of the three warring empires and forced to do battle against one another and in their very homeland, which became the battleground between Russia, Germany and Austria-Hungary. Approximately 200,000 soldiers were to perish during the war with another 300,000 wounded. In addition, hundreds of thousands of civilians died of starvation and disease and far more were made homeless. When Poland's population was estimated in 1920, it was two million less than it had been in 1910.[9] Material losses were also devastating; food production dropped by 40-50 percent, and more than half the railway stations and bridges were destroyed and nearly as many locomotives. Eighteen percent of the country's buildings were ruined and much of its industry was levelled. For Poles living in America, a feeling of powerlessness in the face of the suffering of their families trapped in the conflict was made particularly vivid because so many were recent immigrants. In fact, more than 174,000 Poles had just entered the United States in 1913 and in the decade immediately preceding the war, more than a million persons had come to this country. Yet, uncertainty quickly gave way to concerted action as American Poles led by their organizations pulled together to aid their beleaguered countrymen.

Two men played particularly crucial roles in mobilizing American Polonia, Ignacy Paderewski and the banker John Smulski. Paderewski, who was already in the United States in the Fall of 1914 as an unofficial representative of Polish patriotic groups centered in Western Europe, quickly established contacts with both the conservative Polish National Council and the progressive camp headed by the PNA and Falcons. Later, when Dmowski's group in Paris organized itself into the Polish National Committee, a quasi-government in exile working for independence, Paderewski was named its American spokesman. Paderewski's fame throughout the United States made him admirably suited to promote the independence cause and gained him an extraordinary opportunity to meet many leading American businessmen and politicians of the day, even President Woodrow Wilson himself. Through these contacts he passionately pressed home Poland's cause.

Paderewski was also extremely successful in generating public support in favor of a cause about which few people were familiar prior to the war. Within Polonia too, Paderewski was particularly active. Moreover, in his contacts with Polish Americans he gradually altered his original views as to what their contribution should be. Earlier, Paderewski had looked upon Polonia's support as essentially financial. In opposing military involve-ment by Polonia he had agreed with Dmowski that Poles had already shed enough blood in their futile uprisings; henceforth, independence efforts should center on the diplomatic front. But the formation of Pilsudski's legion, the war itself together with the resolute stance of both the Falcons and the Polish National Alliance in favor of an army of American Poles committed to statehood caused a change in the great pianist-patriot's views. On September 22, 1914 Paderewski publicly called for the creation of such an army to fight alongside Great Britain and France, a proposal enthusiastically received in Polonia. Indeed, the PNA had already transformed the Alliance school into a training center for non-commissioned officers, the erstwhile future leaders of a Polish army formed in America, and 167 young men had applied, with 60 actually participating in the course. Due to America's neutrality, however, nothing came of these efforts. Active recruitment did not begin until after the United States' formal entry into the conflict on April 6, 1917.

Along with Paderewski, John Smulski deserves singular recognition for his outstanding service to the cause of Poland during the war. One of the greatest leaders ever produced by American Polonia, Smulski had previously been a success in every activity in which he had become involved. It is to the credit of the Polish National Alliance that as an active member of the PNA throughout his life, Smulski devoted so much of his energy to public affairs dealing with the Polish cause.

Born in the Prussian zone of Poland in 1867, Smulski came to America at the age of fourteen with his parents. His father became the proprietor of a publishing company in the burgeoning Chicago Polonia and was able to send young Smulski to one of America's leading educational institutions, Northwestern University. In 1890 he became the first Pole to graduate from its law school and from this time until his death in 1928 Smulski was a pivotal figure in the political, financial and ethnic affairs of the Chicago Polonia.

In 1893 Smulski was elected to the board of directors of the PNA at the age of twenty-six and soon became active in the larger field of Chicago and Illinois politics. First elected a city alderman, he became City Attorney in 1903 and in 1905 he was the first Polish American to win a statewide office when he became Treasurer of Illinois. At the same time, Smulski combined political achievement with business acumen. In 1905 he organized the windy city's first Polish-owned financial institution, the Northwestern Trust and Savings Bank of Chicago. Resigning in 1907 as state treasurer, Smulski never again held elective office although he campaigned for the Republican party mayoral nomination in 1911. A millionaire in 1914, Smulski next turned his energies entirely to the national independence cause. Active initially in Polonia relief work, in 1916 he organized the Polish National Department which directed the political activities of the ethnic community. In 1918, Smulski was responsible for organizing the first Polish National Emigration Congress *(sejm wychodztwa)*, a representative body including delegates from practically every Polonia organization, to manifest mass support for America's war effort and Polish independence.[10]

But the story of PNA organizational involvement in the patriotic cause is also impressive. Following Paderewski's call in September, the first all-Polonia action for Poland came in October, 1914 when the chief officers of the Polish National Alliance met in Chicago with leaders of the other major fraternals to form a unified charitable association, the Polish Central Relief Committee *(Polski Centralny Komitet Ratunkowy* or *PCKR)*. Elected President was PNA Censor Karabasz with Peter Rostenkowski, President of the Polish Roman Catholic Union, and Anna Neumann, President of the Polish Women's Alliance, chosen to be vice presidents. The *PCKR's* first major action was to organize a national "Polish Day" observance on January 24, 1915. This observance was a singular success and $250,000 was raised for humanitarian purposes. A second "Polish Day," held on January 1, 1916 with the support of the American government proved even more successful and nearly $1 million was collected. Throughout the conflict, the *PCKR* served as the major fund raising vehicle in Polonia for relief activities and in its work received extensive support from the Alliance. At the *PCKR's* founding meeting, for example, the PNA donated $15,000 to assist in its work and thereafter contributed generously to its activities throughout the war.

Within the Polish Central Relief Committee, the PNA played a leading role from the start. Among the most active in the work was President Zychlinski who delivered hundreds of talks at fund rallies and later, after America's entrance into the conflict, at Polish Army recruitment efforts. Other PNA leaders who extended themselves selflessly were Theodore Helinski, Adam Szwajkart, Casimir Sypniewski and Ignacy Werwinski. Magdalena Milewska and Mary Sakowska took the lead among PNA women in working for the committee. But their efforts represented but the tip of the iceberg, insofar as PNA involvement was concerned. Literally thousands of Polish National Alliance members throughout the country contributed to the cause.

Throughout the war, the PNA not only cooperated with the Polish Central Relief Committee; it continued its own separate fund raising effort through the Independence Department. Formed in July 1914, the Independence Department itself generated more than $170,000 for primarily humanitarian purposes, apart from the considerable activities of the Women's Division of the Alliance. In addition, there were PNA publicity campaigns in support of Paderewski, the Polish independence cause and, after 1917, the U.S. war effort, which were carried in the pages of the two Alliance newspapers. Through *Zgoda* and *Dziennik Zwiazkowy,* several hundred thousand readers were informed on a regular basis about Polonia's patriotic work.

As a leader of the Polish Central Relief Committee, Smulski was instrumental in formalizing links between the *PCKR* and Paderewski when the virtuoso visited New York in April, 1915 as a representative of Dmowski's Polish National Committee. Through Smulski, Paderewski in turn strengthened his contacts with the PNA. On May 3, 1915 the pianist-patriot spoke to more than fifty thousand people gathered in Chicago's Humboldt Park for the annual Polish Constitution Day observance. That September Paderewski spoke to the delegates at the PNA *sejm* at Schenectedy, New York and the following Spring he delivered the commencement address to the first graduating class at the Polish National Alliance school.[11]

Although the Polish Central Relief Committee was formally created to raise funds for humanitarian concerns, its leaders understood from the start that important political tasks also had to be performed outside Polonia to educate the population about the independence cause. And, because of their commitment to the "fourth partition" theory of Polonia, PNA and Falcons activists could hardly rest content in limiting their patriotic activities to fund raising within the 3.5 million member Polonia. As one writer in the Alliance daily put it, Polonia fully recognized its humanitarian responsibilities. But equally important was its concern that a postwar democratic Polish state be established, regardless of how many American Poles actually returned "home" after the war. In working for this cause, partisan differences needed to be subordinated to a single-minded commitment to Poland.[12] Smulski's efforts also extended beyond relief work and into the political realm. In August 1916, he played a key role in organizing a new political action subcommittee within the *PCKR*, called the National Department *(Wydzial Narodowy)*. Given responsibility for propagandizing the independence cause in Polonia and to the American people, this committee firmly backed Paderewski's efforts to publicize Poland's aims.

Although it was originally set up to be but a subcommittee of the *PCKR*, the National Department soon mushroomed into a major organization in its own right as the United States was drawn inexorably into the war. By the end of 1916, the National Department possessed more than five hundred local branches around the country and the English and Polish language editions of its publications, *Free Poland,* found wide distribution.[13]

Chairman of the Board of Directors of the National Department was Smulski; its president was Casimir Sypniewski, a Pittsburgh attorney active in the Falcons and the PNA. In November 1916, the National Department took its first major political action when it denounced the Central Powers' proposal to create a Polish kingdom under German and Austro-Hungarian auspices. Declaring that it alone represented American Polonia, the National Department firmly identified the future of an independent Poland with the cause of the Western Allies as defined by Dmowski and Paderewski. After the United States declared war, the relationship between Smulski's National Department and the Polish National Committee grew even closer. One of the first tasks of the National Department was to set up a press bureau in Washington, D.C. to coordinate the distribution of information throughout the country about the Polish cause in support of Dmowski's organization.

Paderewski's fame and charisma had helped win him an introduction to a large number of officials in President Wilson's administration, including

Secretary of War Josephus Daniels and Wilson's influential personal advisor, Colonel Edward M. House. In Colonel House, Paderewski found an individual who strongly supported the Western Allies in their war with the Central Powers although the U.S. was still neutral in the conflict. Furthermore, House agreed that Poland's independence "fit well with Wilson's developing championship of the small and oppressed nations of Europe." Sent to Paris and London as the President's special representative in December 1915, House brought up the Polish question, probably because of Paderewski's personal appeals. The President himself met Paderewski for the first time in the Spring of 1916 and the patriot-pianist was invited to his home on election day in November.

Wilson's first public statement in favor of Poland had come in May, 1916 when he expressed his support of the right of all nations to self-government. This idea was received enthusiastically by Polish Americans. The President's public posture continued to evolve in his "Peace without Victory" speech of January 22, 1917, which closed with his assertion that "I take it for granted statesmen everywhere are agreed that there shall be a united, independent and autonomous Poland" (after the war).[14] Following America's entry into the conflict, Wilson's commitment to Polish independence continued to evolve. His ultimate statement came on January 8, 1918 when he presented to Congress his fourteen point plan for world peace, which justified American participation in the conflict. The thirteenth point dealt specifically with Poland; "An independent Polish state should be erected which should include the territories inhabited by indisputably Polish population, which should be assured free and secure access to the sea, and whose political and economic independence and territorial integrity should be guaranteed by covenant."[15]

Paderewski's personal influence upon Wilson and House, however considerable, might have been insufficient without organized effort by Polonia. Here, the activities of Smulski's National Department counted a good deal. In past presidential elections, Polish Americans had tended to vote for Democratic candidates although the Polish National Alliance leadership favored the Republicans and had enjoyed friendly contacts with both Theodore Roosevelt and William Howard Taft. But in 1912, Wilson had lost the normally Democratic Polish vote and he was elected only because of a split in the Republican party between the "Bull Moose" progressive faction of Roosevelt and the party regulars who backed Taft.

In 1912, Woodrow Wilson had won surprisingly little backing from Polish voters. A little known Southerner then completing his first term as governor of New Jersey, he had, earlier in his career as a political scientist at Princeton

University, published a widely read history of the United States sharply critical of unrestricted immigration from Eastern and Southern Europe. Resurrected during the campaign, this book caused him no little embarrassment among immigrant groups traditionally loyal to the Democrats, and in Chicago he received less than one-third of the popular vote in a four-cornered contest led by Taft. In Milwaukee, the socialist candidate, Eugene Debs, actually carried the Polish wards over Wilson.[16]

In 1916, Wilson faced a reunited Republican party and needed solid Polish support in a number of hotly contested states to win reelection. During the campaign his stance in favor of Polish independence plus his opposition to immigration restriction helped patch up his poor past relations with the Polish community. But of equal importance was the Polish National Department formed in August, 1916. Throughout the campaign, the agency stressed Wilson's support for Poland and his friendly ties with Paderewski, although it did not explicitly endorse Wilson for reelection. In the close contest, Wilson needed all the help he could receive; his popular vote margin was only 51.7 percent and the electoral vote count 277-254.[17] Throughout Polonia, Wilson did extremely well; in Chicago, for example, he won more than 74 percent of the Polish vote and in Milwaukee's most heavily Polish ethnic wards he won a 75 percent majority over his Republican opponent, Charles Evans Hughes. Much of the credit for helping swing so large a segment of the Polish vote to the President must go to Paderewski and Smulski, who closely identified Polish independence with Wilson's leadership.

America's entry into the conflict intensified the Polish Americans' support of a war effort that was being waged, after all, not for one but two fatherlands. Polonia's backing of the war can be measured in various ways. Some 42,000 of the first 100,000 men to volunteer for American military service were Polish Americans; by the end of the conflict, as many as 300,000 Poles were in uniform. Indeed, while only about 3.5 percent of the American population was of Polish heritage, Poles composed 10 percent of the U.S. armed forces. Because Polish Americans inducted into the American military generally were grouped together with members of other ethnic groups it is difficult to measure the extent of their service during the war. One exception was Company K of the Wisconsin National Guard, which was comprised almost exclusively of Milwaukee Polish Americans. Retaining its ethnic character during the war, Company K distinguished itself in the bloody battles of Juvigny, Chateau Thierry and Argonne Forest.[18]

Polish Americans contributed heavily to Liberty bond drives organized to help finance the American war effort. By the end of the conflict, Smulski reported that at least $150 million in bonds had been purchased by Polish

Americans, an astounding amount in as much as there were probably no more than one million Polish American households and the average yearly worker's salary was less than $1,000. In many cities, Polish Americans were identified as the largest liberty bond purchasers and individual support of the drive was reinforced by the purchases arranged by fraternals. For example, the PNA bought more than one-half million dollars in Liberty bonds alone.[19]

Support for the war effort extended in other directions as well. The Polish Central Relief Committee's appeals in conjunction with the American Red Cross continued, eventually bringing in about $20 million in humanitarian assistance.[20] In February, 1918 a new organization, the Polish White Cross, was formed under the leadership of Madame Helena Paderewska and the female heads of the Polish fraternals, including, of course, the PNA. Along with its efforts to produce and send clothing and medical supplies to the War's victims, the White Cross trained nurses for the Polish army units being readied for service in France.[21]

A second activity revolved around the formation of a Polish army in America for service on the Western front. Its very existence gave added weight to the political and diplomatic efforts on behalf of Poland's freedom and also brought to a close Polonia's "Stand and Wait" position in force prior to America's entry into the conflict.

With the U.S. in the war, however, the situation changed dramatically. On June 4, 1917 the French government permitted the Polish National Committee to organize its own separate army composed of Poles living in Western Europe and the United States. In America, the National Department created a military commission to begin recruiting and training volunteers; the three member commission included former Censor Theodore Helinski, who was then the chairman of the Polish Central Relief Committee.

Though the United States agreed in principle to permit the formation of a separate American Polish army, it was not until October 6, 1917 that an agreement was reached to identify just who was eligible to serve from the ethnic population. Accordingly, only the foreign-born who had not yet taken out citizenship papers and who were not the heads of families could serve in the Polish army. American-born Poles, together with those who were either naturalized citizens or in the process of applying for their "papers" were restricted to service in the American armed forces. Many of these individuals were later rejected for military service because they were still listed as possessing Austrian or German citizen status, however.

Although the American government decisions considerably limited the manpower pool from which a Polish army could be created, the National Department's Military Commission was nonetheless able to place a significant and well trained force in the field. By November, 1917 forty-six recruiting centers in 18 states and Canada were in operation and training facilities at Fort Niagara-on-the-Lake, Ontario had been established. In December, 1917, a second training camp was established at Fort Niagara, New York and in February 1917 the first contingent including more than 6,000 men was transported to France. The PNA played a significant role in every aspect of the Polish army effort and several hundred members of the Alliance volunteered for service. In addition, in 1917–1918, more than five hundred Polish Americans and 220 non-Poles took officers' training courses at the Alliance school. PNA members such as Waclaw Gasiorowski (later the head of the Alliance School) and Frank Dziob played major roles in training the raw recruits.

By war's end, 22,395 men had been received into the Polish army out of a total of 38,108 who applied for induction.[22] The units from the United States contributed greatly to transforming the 100,000 man Polish army in France into a credible military presence.[23] Though the Polish army saw little active service in the war, this was only due to the decision of the beaten German state to request an armistice which ended the hostilities in October, 1918, just as the Poles were taking the field. Under General Jozef Haller, who took command in France just a week before the war's end, the Polish army was then transferred by Marshall Pilsudski's request to Poland to assist in its struggle for independence. Attired in distinctive blue uniforms, the Polish army (by then six divisions strong) played a significant role in a series of military actions which helped Poland regain its independence.

The "Blue Army" now became the Steppe Rifles Division and the Podhalan Division manning a front that extended from the Carpathian mountains through Lwow and northward up to Kowel. There, at various points the Poles faced well-equipped irregular German forces, the Bolshevik hordes, and the Ukrainians under Petlura.

The Army in blue was the shield behind which the regular Polish forces could regroup and rearm. Two divisions heroically bore the brunt of Budienny's Bolshevik cavalry charge at Lwow. (Later after the Bolshevik defeat at the battle of Warsaw) it was the Blue army that took the measure of the enemy at Komorowo and Zamosc and helped to drive the remnants of the retreating Red army from Polish territory.[24]

In retrospect, the "Blue Army" made a singular contribution to Poland's independence in World War I. Not only did it render considerable military service on Poland's behalf between 1918 and 1920, its very presence on the side of the Western Allies showed the Great Powers how serious the Poles were about independence and that the dream of a restored Poland did not merely reflect the musings of philosophers and diplomats. In this regard, the Polish army added muscle to the appeals of Dmowski and Paderewski. Though often minimized as a contributor to the independence cause, the Polish army units raised in the United States themselves represented an extraordinary expression of patriotism. One contemporary historian has put the matter in its proper perspective:

> If we remember that recruitment into Pilsudski's legions in Poland itself took in about 23,000 men, then the 24,000-25,000 American Poles who travelled willingly across the ocean to serve in France to achieve the ideal of an independent Poland must cause us to pay homage to their patriotic dedication, a commitment that characterized American Polonia throughout the First World War period.[25]

In yet one final area, American Polonia was particularly active on Poland's behalf after 1917 and this was in its successful effort to organize its resources on the national level. The work of the organization was largely under the direction of Smulski's National Department.

In cooperation with Paderewski, Smulski organized the first Polish emigrants' congress *(sejm wychodztwa)* in Detroit on August 26, 1918, to achieve this aim. The congress brought together nearly a thousand Polish American leaders from around the country and represented every element in Polonia except the socialists, who continued to support the Polish National Defense Committee. Alliance involvement in the Detroit meeting was heavy; more than 200 delegates were PNA members and a number of PNA leaders were elected to direct the Congress following its adjournment including Zychlinski, Smulski, Helinski and Joseph Magdziarz, the Treasurer of the Alliance.

Paderewski and Dmowski both spoke at Detroit, emphasizing the importance of the congress' solidarity with their cause. In addition, Paderewski's proposal to establish a ten million dollar fund drive to aid the future Polish state was enthusiastically approved. (The drive eventually collected more than 5.5 million dollars.) Emphasizing by resolution its status as the "central and chief organization of the entire Polish emigration in America for the matter of Polish independence," the Detroit convention achieved for the first time in history a soundly based coalition including practically every important element in American Polonia, including the fraternals, the Catholic clergy and the Polish National Catholic Church. Only *KON* remained outside the fold.

In retrospect, the Detroit congress sponsored by the National Department marked the high water mark of Polonia's involvement in the independence cause. On November 11, 1918, only ten weeks after its adjournment, Pilsudski declared Poland to be independent. Eventually, he and his rival Dmowski were able to work out a tortuous compromise whereby Paderewski returned to Warsaw as the country's first prime minister (as well as its foreign minister) in January, 1919. But Poland's complex problems, which included the stabilizing of its national boundaries and the enactment of a satisfactory land reform bill, proved to be too much for Paderewski to handle and he was forced to resign. Pilsudski's assumption of political leadership in Poland and his resulting war with the newly created Soviet Russian state in 1920 over the border issue brought to a climax Polonia's involvement in Polish affairs.

Recruitment into the "Blue Army" ended in January, 1919 and donations into the "ten million dollar fund" slowed considerably about the same time. Support for the National Department also considerably diminished although later emigration congresses were held at Buffalo in 1919, Pittsburgh in 1921 and in Cleveland in 1923. (In Cleveland, the organization was dissolved.)[26] With its primary goal, Poland's independence, achieved there simply was no consensus about the future. Some people worried about Smulski's ambitions. Far more significant was the fact that in Poland itself, the parties supporting Dmowski and Paderewski were out of power and the supporters of Pilsudski were on the rise. To many in Polonia, it was once again time to look after the ethnic community's domestic concerns now that independence was won. The old slogan, *Wychodztwo dla wychodztwa* (let the emigrant look after his own needs first) was, not surprisingly, resurrected.

Smulski had indeed wanted to make the National Department into a permanent fixture unifying the secular and clerical organizations within American Polonia in Poland's behalf. The new state clearly required a continuing influsion of financial aid from America; criticisms of Polish anti-semitism and propaganda attacks emanating from Germany served to weaken America's initial enthusiasm for Poland. Thus, a strong Polonia organization seemed essential to present Poland's case to the American people and to preserve Polonia's sense of solidarity with the resurrected homeland.

But a permanent National Department was not to be. In fact, it was the Polish National Alliance, once the most ardent supporter of the federation which helped deal a death blow to Smulski's plan. In September, 1921 at its national *sejm* in Toledo, a motion to withdraw from the National Department passed by a 321-106 vote, despite the opposition of Zychlinski and the board of directors. PNA historian Olszewski explains this decisive reversal by noting that 60 percent of the delegates to the Toledo convention were "new people" who presumably lacked an understanding of the historic significance of the National Department to the PNA. But there were other reasons for the delegates' action.

Within the PNA, support for Poland had indeed peaked in 1918 and 1919. In addition to the charitable activities of its Independence Department and Women's Division, the Alliance had opened its school to train officers for the Polish army and effectively propagandized the homeland's cause through its newspapers. The Alliance promoted the sale of Liberty Bonds within Polonia and Paderewski's 1918 appeal for the "ten million dollar fund." At its national *sejm* held a few weeks, later, the PNA authorized a $50,000 donation to this campaign. The Alliance also assisted Polish refugees interned in Canada during the war and helped in the resettlement of Polish children who had come to America via Siberia.

With American participation in the war a reality after 1917, the PNA showed its commitment to the effort in other telling ways. One decision was in honoring its insurance commitments to all young men called to military duty who held policies with the Alliance. This action was particularly significant inasmuch as it came at a time when no one knew just how many Polish American war casualties would occur and how the conflict would affect the fraternal's financial position.

Finally after the war, the PNA's support for the independence cause reached a climax with its own purchase of $50,000 in Polish bonds and decision to promote the sale of these securities to its members. During the election campaign held in the disputed coal mining region of Silesia, a territory claimed by both Warsaw and Berlin, the PNA also contributed more than $250,000 to get out the vote on behalf of reunification with the newly independent Poland. Summing up its overall contribution to Poland's independence struggle, Olszewski, the PNA chronicler of the time wrote:

> The Polish emigration, more than any other nationality in America, did its duty on behalf of the United States . . . It should be added that the Polish National Alliance with a membership of 130,000 did as much for Poland as all the rest of Polonia taken together . . .[27]

The demise of the National Department of 1923 brought to a close a glorious chapter in the history of both American Polonia and the Polish National Alliance. Through the confluence of numerous factors, the war itself, the Wilson-Paderewski tie, the collapse of tsarist Russia, the defeat of both Germany and Austria, and the Western Alliance's decision to support Polish independence, American Polonia's efforts had borne fruit in helping to reestablish an independent Polish state after 123 years of foreign partition. In this effort, the Polish National Alliance had contributed mightily and unselfishly. The results of its efforts were awesome—the Polish Central Relief Committee, the Polish White Cross and the $10 million fund drive in the humanitarian realm; the Polish National Council, the Polish National Defense Committee, the National Department and the Emigration Congresses in the political arena; and the Polish army in the military field. That so much could be done by organizations representing fewer than four million people, many of them lacking fluency in the language of a country of 100 million, is amazing.

In a letter to Smulski, Roman Dmowski summed up Polonia's war-time contribution by asserting that "Poland would not have gained what she possesses today if there had not been millions of Poles in the United States . . .

> Your substantial assistance made it possible for the National Committee in Paris to undertake its task especially in the early difficult beginnings when it had almost no financial means. Your voluntary enlistment in the Polish army in France made possible its creation, and thanks to its existence we were recognized as Allies and admitted to participate in the peace conference. Finally your strong support of the Polish delegation's positions at the conference greatly contributed to the fact that the President of the United States and the entire American delegation were on our side. This contribution of yours to the fatherland at its great historic moment will never be forgotten and every honest historian speaking about Poland's rebirth in the future will have to stress the role played in this occurrence by the Polish emigration in America and the services rendered by the National Department . . . .[28]

One leader who put his finger on the role of the Alliance in the restoration of Poland was Censor Michael Blenski. Speaking to the delegates at the 1918 PNA convention, he noted the support the Alliance had given to the Polish National Department in organizing the Detroit emigration congress, but he tied this involvement with the Alliance's historic commitment to Polish independence which went back to its origins in 1880.

> The Polish National Alliance, through its involvement in the National Department, has helped to crystalize the political consciousness of American Polonia and has brought about the unification of means and ends by supporting this federation. In this respect, one should recall the entire 38 year history of the PNA to realize that this idea, Poland's independence, has been one of the most impressive elements of the experience of the emigration of Poles to America. Our Alliance was founded upon the principle that Poland should be free and it was forever impressing this principle into the hearts of the Polish immigrants. The Alliance was always

in the forefront in rushing to the aid of Poland in its time of need. It was the Alliance which expressed Polonia's political goals with regard to Poland, which have turned out to be correct and which ultimately were approved by the overwhelming majority of our people living in this country. . . .

In the days of ideological conflict, when all Polonia was in disarray, it was the Alliance which withdrew from the Polish National Defense committee, but retained its commitment to the cause by forming its Independence Department . . . From then on, the Alliance worked for the unification of all Polonia under the slogan of independence for Poland. In uniting all Polonia organizations, the National Department represents a PNA achievement in that it not only brought us all together with the Polish clergy but recognized that all should work together for Poland's independence, the historic watchword. . .[29]

Chapter 5

STORMY TIMES—THE INTERWAR YEARS
AND THE POLISH NATIONAL ALLIANCE, 1918–1939

The story of the Polish National Alliance between the two World Wars is as interesting as it is little known. As with the general history of American Polonia between 1918 and 1939, it has received little attention, largely because the events and personalities of those years have been overshadowed by what occurred both before and later. The First World War years were indeed climactic, for they resulted in Polonia's successful effort to bring about Poland's resurrection. Similarly, the outbreak of World War II on September 1, 1939 with the Nazi German invasion of Poland once again focused Polonia's attention upon the homeland. The sacrifices Polish Americans made in the war years thus put far behind the memories of the interwar era. And, because Poland's independence was not fully regained after 1945 due to the Sovietization of the country, Polonia's attention remained riveted upon its fate and away from the experiences of the 1920s and 1930s.

One would err, however, in viewing the interwar period as but a twenty-year lull in Polonia and PNA life. In fact, these years were not only filled with activity on many levels but also represented a period in which Polish Americans gradually redefined their relationship to the ancestral homeland while they firmly established themselves in American society. In the process, they adapted their organizations to the changing concerns of their members without, however, disassociating themselves from their ethnic past. As a result, American Polonia, even in the 1980s, remains to a large degree the product of the interwar experience. Just as the community's formative years before 1914 witnessed the birth of the secular and religious institutions that still dominate Polish ethnic life, so too was Polonia's development enormously shaped by what occurred between 1918 and 1939.

For the Alliance, the first few years following Poland's rebirth climaxed the efforts by PNA members through two generations on behalf of the

119

independence cause. The PNA, together with the rest of organized Polonia, had accomplished much during the war years including the National Department, the Polish army in America, the Polish Central Relief Committee and the Polish White Cross. Further, the first Polish Emigration Congress had gathered in 1918 in dramatic demonstration of Polonia's nearly unanimous support for independence as represented by Dmowski and Paderewski, the chief spokesmen for the National Democratic party in the West. Donations and investments worth millions of dollars also poured in on behalf of humanitarian and political causes sponsored by Polonia.

Nevertheless, while Polonia enthusiastically backed independence for Poland, its people overwhelmingly demonstrated that their ultimate loyalties were, in fact, more with the United States. One sign was the high rate of volunteerism among Polish Americans for service in the U.S. armed forces. Another was their enormous financial commitment to the American war effort. In 1921, Smulski reported that Polish Americans had purchased approximately $150 million in Liberty Bonds, seven times what they had donated to specifically Polish causes. And after the War, relatively few Poles in America actually returned "home" when they at last had the opportunity to do so. Though a total of 96,237 men and women did reemigrate between 1919 and 1923, for example, they represented but a tiny fraction of the total Polish American population.[1]

Moreover, a variety of adverse post war developments in Poland served to undermine the initial enthusiasm Polonia felt for the new state. For one thing, there was the matter of Poland's political order. Polonia had largely absorbed the national democratic movement's ideology which stressed patriotic solidarity above partisan differences as the basis for a future Poland. But the new state's political system, modelled as it was after the French third republic, was riddled with parliamentary factionalism. Moreover, neither Dmowski nor Paderewski succeeded in playing leading roles in its affairs and the National People's Alliance, the party which best reflected their views, failed to achieve a dominant role in the nation's politics. In 1919 it did win 162 of 393 seats in the first parliamentary elections, but in 1922 it gained only 98 out of 444 seats. Instead, it was Jozef Pilsudski, hero of the small Polish National Defense Committee in America *(KON)*and leader of the Socialist party, who rose to prominence.

Disenchantment also marked Polonia's economic experience with the reborn state. At first there was widespread interest in the purchase of Polish government bonds and in 1920 alone, Polish Americans bought $18.5 million in these securities. But enthusiasm plummeted as rapidly as their market value. Individual investment activities were no more successful; one commentator of the time estimated that as much as $40 million was lost by Polish Americans in ill-fated business projects in the "old country." Such misadventures served to splash cold water on later efforts by Polish businessmen to generate capital in America. A typical response to such proposals was "Brother, button up your pocket book!"[2]

Disillusionment with Polish realities led many to call for greater emphasis upon American Polonia's domestic concerns, which had been put aside during the war years. Particularly important was the preservation of the Polish Roman Catholic parishes from the loss of their ethnic character, along with the elevation of Polish clergymen to the status of bishops in the hierarchy. Another concern dealt with the preservation of ethnic identity among the new generation of American-born youth. Back into vogue came the old slogan, "Wychodztwo dla Wychodztwa." Beyond slogans was the action by the delegates to the 1921 Polish National Alliance convention in Toledo. Surprising their own leaders, they voted 321-106 to withdraw the PNA from further formal participation in the Polish National Department. This move effectively shattered Smulski's dream of transforming the Department into a permanent representative of Poland's interests in the United States.

Changes within postwar American society also contributed to the trans-formation of Polish ethnic life, although the question of whether or not assimilationist pressures upon Polonia had a disintegrative impact remains a good subject for serious research. During World War I, U.S. authorities were concerned about the loyalty of the country's foreign-born peoples, but few Polish Americans were especially troubled by this matter.[3] After all, they enthusiastically backed the war effort in the hope that an American victory would also bring Poland its freedom. But after the War, Polish language instruction in public schools around the country, which had been suspended during the conflict, was not resumed. In 1920, the eighteenth amendment to the United States Constitution went into effect. This act prohibited the manufacture and sale of alcoholic drinks and was resented by Poles and other ethnics who saw nothing particularly evil in the moderate consumption of liquor. Far more distressful was the revival of the Ku Klux Klan, which for the first time became influential outside the states of the old Confederacy and whose targets included Catholics, Jews and Immigrants, along with Blacks. Though the Klan rapidly waned, the assimilationists made their message clear by their bitter reaction in 1928 to the Democratic party's presidential candidate, New York Governor Al Smith, who happened to be Catholic.[4]

But assimilationist feeling made its greatest impact in 1921 and 1924, when the U.S. Congress enacted legislation that significantly restricted immigration from Eastern and Southern Europe for the first time in history. Restriction had long been sought for economic reasons and by those who believed that open immigration would lead to the "mongrelization" of the Anglo-Saxon Protestant and Nordic cultural character of American society. But previously their efforts had been beaten back by a diverse coalition of interests whose leaders asserted that America should remain a land of opportunity to the foreign-born. Moreover, when restriction bills did pass in Congress they had been vetoed, first by President Theodore Roosevelt, then by Taft and later by Wilson.

The 1921 law, which overrode President Wilson's veto, established an annual quota which limited immigration from each country to three percent of its population in the U.S. as of the year 1910. Accordingly, no more than 30,977 Poles could henceforth enter the country, a significant fall-off from the 174,365 Poles who had been admitted in 1913, the last full year of pre war open immigration.

In 1924, an even more restrictive law passed, cutting annual immigration from Poland to 5,982, or two percent of the Polish population in the U.S. as of 1890, when relatively few Poles or other Eastern and Southern Europeans had as yet arrived. Together with restrictions upon emigration then being enacted in Poland, the U.S. legislation sharply curtailed Polish immigration for decades to come. As a result, Polonia was deprived of the opportunity to revitalize its ethnic life and the process of its assimilation into American society was accelerated.[5]

Yet no discussion of the climate enveloping Polonia between the wars would be complete unless it included some brief analysis of the changing nature of the community's own self-image. Clearly, for those who believed that Poland's independence was the sole justification for organized Polonia's existence, the decline in popular interest in Poland during the 1920s seemed to prove that the ethnic community was doomed to assimilation. One writer of the time put the matter rather dramatically when he argued, "If one was truly Polish he should already have begun to make plans to return 'home;' if he was American, what justified any further involvement in Polonia life?"[6] Others took the opposite route, emphasizing the "wychodztwo dla wychodztwa" argument.

The debate over the content of "Polishness" after the War was inevitable, since the nearly four million people of Polish birth or descent could no longer be accurately described as either "Poles in America" or "American Poles." Historically, the first designation had referred to immigrants who sought work in America but whose intention was to return to Poland with their savings; the second formulation emphasized that the immigrants possessed a cohesive Polish ethnic life distinct from their compatriots only because of their distance from the homeland. But by the 1920s, those who remained in America could hardly feel comfortable identifying themselves either as "Poles in America" or as "American Poles" since both terms implied a dual national loyalty, which few felt. Yet defining another kind of self-identity was difficult and it wasn't until the 1930s when this was achieved. As first formulated by the then Censor of the Polish National Alliance, Francis Swietlik, members of the Polish ethnic community in America were called upon to think of themselves as "Polish Americans," with primary loyalty to the United States but continuing ties of feeling, culture and tradition to the ancestral homeland.

Swietlik's first development of this idea, made in a speech he delivered in Warsaw as the chairman of a delegation of American Poles to an international meeting of Poles from around the world, caused him no little criticism from those in Polonia and Poland who interpreted his remarks as a rejection of future cooperation with Poland. This was, in fact, not at all what Swietlik had in mind and he later demonstrated the depth of his commitment to the homeland by his wartime leadership of the Polish American Council and its relief activities. What he did reject, however, was a trend toward extremism on the subject of ethnic identity. Obviously, withdrawal from ethnic activity was out of the question for Swietlik; equally important, however, was his belief that Polonia's members needed to integrate successfully into American society if they were to become an effective force working on Poland's behalf. To Swietlik, preoccupation with Poland's internal politics was simply frivolous since it drained talent and energy away from Polonia's primary objectives, which consisted of maintaining a high level of popular involvement in the activities of the ethnic community itself. And without a vital Polonia, he concluded, little good could be achieved for Poland.[7]

And what of the actual condition of the ethnic community during the interwar period? From even the most cursory overview of American Polonia in the "roaring twenties" one must conclude that even as they were gradually redefining the content of their ethnic heritage, Polish Americans of the time remained heavily involved in the internal affairs of their substantial and growing community. It was in the 1920s, after all, that economic conditions for large numbers of Polish Americans noticeably improved and increasing numbers of people were in a position to purchase insurance through the Polish fraternals. With the movement of masses of Polish Americans out of the old Polonia neighborhoods into outlying sections of their communities, new Polish parishes and schools were rapidly built to meet their needs.

Indeed by 1932, there were more than eight hundred Roman Catholic parishes in Polonia with six hundred of these operating their own schools. By this time, approximately 300,000 Polish children were in parish primary schools, about as many as were in the public schools. Forty-eight high schools and several colleges run by Polish religious teaching orders were in existence, along with the PNA school in Cambridge Springs, Pennsylvania which at the time included a junior college, a high school and a technical trades institute.

In 1930, the Polish language press also reached peaks that were only braked by the onset of the Great Depression. In that year, eighty-four Polish language periodicals were operating, including fifteen daily papers, the largest of which was the PNA *Dziennik Zwiazkowy* with 60,000 readers in the Chicago area. Overall circulation levels reached 1.3 million.

Further illustrating the dynamism of American Polonia was the growth of the fraternals. By the mid 1930s, the ten largest Polish ethnic fraternal associations could claim a combined membership of 680,000, fifteen percent of the total ethnic population of 4.5 million. This was nearly twice their size in 1915. Particularly successful in attracting members were the three major Chicago-based fraternals, the Polish National Alliance, the Polish Roman Catholic Union and the Polish Women's Alliance. The PWA experienced the largest proportional expansion and rose from 14,500 members in 1914 to 53,000 in 1935. The PRCUA reported a more gradual increase, but in total numbers far exceeded the PWA; in 1915 its membership was 85,000 while in 1931 it had grown to 169,000. Most impressive however was the breakneck expansion of the PNA. In 1913, the Alliance had become the first one hundred thousand member Polonia fraternal; by 1926 it also became the first to reach the two hundred thousand member mark. In 1930, it already included 287,000 members and appeared certain to grow even larger. Only the Depression would reverse so dramatic a trend; by 1935 membership had declined to about 265,000 and it was not until the late 1930s that the Alliance was able to resume its upward climb. Still, between 1920 and 1930, the PNA rose by 216 percent, from 133,000 to 287,000 insurance policy holders.

In the past, of course, the PNA had registered several other records of dramatic membership growth. But in one respect the expansion of the 1920s proceeded in a novel fashion. Historically, growth had come primarily through formation of new local lodge units in territories where the PNA had not previously been active or by decisions of independent Polish societies to affiliate with the national organization. Between 1890 and 1900, for example, membership increased nine times over, from 3,426 to 28,359, but the number of PNA lodges also rose significantly, from 113 to 451, or about four times over. From 1901 and 1910, when membership doubled, from 30,355 to 71,335, the number of lodges grew at approximately the same rate, from 469 to 1106. From 1911 to 1920, the expansion trend of the preceding twenty years continued although at a somewhat reduced pace; membership increased by sixty-three percent, from 77,825 to 126,521, and the number of lodges by thirty-nine percent, from 1,202 to 1,678.

Between 1921 and 1930, this historic pattern was nearly reversed, however, indicating that the territorial expansion of American Polonia had reached its peak. Although PNA membership rose meteorically, from 137,389 to 286,587, the number of lodges increased much more slowly, from 1,678 to 1,833. Put another way, the average PNA lodge included about sixty-three to seventy-five members in the years between 1900 and 1920. But by 1925, average lodge membership stood at one hundred and twenty-two; in 1930 this figure had risen to one hundred and fifty-six persons.[8]

This shift in its pattern of growth also caused the PNA to develop innovations in its recruitment of new members. Increasingly popular was the membership drive ("drajw") in which lodge organizers enrolling large numbers of insurance policy holders were offered various prizes for their efforts. Such contests were first established on an annual basis in 1919 and quickly assumed a major role in stimulating recruitment. Although the prizes varied practically every year, one feature about the membership campaigns did not change—the awards offered continued to grow larger and more attractive practically every year. Thus, one of the earliest contests held in 1919 provided individuals "signing up" the greatest numbers of new members with PNA posters and emblems. In 1922, anyone enrolling at least two hundred and fifty adults received a motorcycle valued at $200; those bringing in at least one hundred and seventy-five new people were promised "a record player with twelve records" worth $175. Signing up at least forty people brought the recruiter a camera. The 1924 campaign featured cash prizes and focused upon the recruitment of young people. An award of $150 went to agents bringing in three hundred policy owners under the age of sixteen, for example, and proportionately smaller prizes were provided for recruiters enrolling fewer youngsters. The response to this drive was astonishing—20,138 people joined the Alliance in only three months' time.

A 1925 contest building on the cash incentive offered awards of $450 to agents signing up at least one hundred and fifty members. This drive added 18,298 more policy holders to the ranks of the mushrooming movement. The 1926 campaign was even more ambitious. This time the drive extended through the entire year and aimed at doubling the overall membership of the fraternal! Not only did individuals earn cash prizes for each new recruit; their lodges were informed that they would receive a bonus of $2 for each new member. All they needed to do to be eligible for the windfall was to double in size during the campaign.

The 1928 contest witnessed a decline in enthusiasm, perhaps because the top award, a free trip to Poland, may have been less appealing than the previous prizes offered to enterprizing recruiters. Other tangible awards were in fact substituted later on for the ship tickets, including automobiles, radios and other appliances, and this decision revived the campaign. In 1929, vacations to Poland were combined with cash prizes and once again the drive did well. Among those who took the 1929 trip to the ancestral homeland, which included an audience with President Ignacy Moscicki in Krakow's historic Wawel castle, were the winners of several beauty contests sponsored by the PNA in Chicago. One young lady had been named Miss Alliance and other winners held the titles of Miss Polonia, Miss *Zgoda*, and Miss Council 75.

A 1930 contest, which coincided with the PNA's fiftieth anniversary, again provided a cash award to each person recruiting at least one new member. It also focused on a competition among PNA councils. This contest was won by Council 122 in Hamtramck, Michigan; its members brought in five hundred and twenty-three adults and one hundred twenty-two children. Councils 3 and 75 of Chicago placed second and third in the three month campaign.

Membership drives continued to play a major role in stimulating interest in recruitment during the 1930s and the years that followed and they were particularly important in helping preserve a measure of stability for the PNA during the darkest years of the Great Depression. Especially between 1930 and 1935, the enrollment campaigns served to brake what could have been a disastrous slide in membership caused by the country's economic collapse. As a matter of fact, thousands of unemployed PNA members who could not keep up their premium payments or were forced to cash in their policies did leave the Alliance. But most of them were replaced by new members who joined largely as a result of the aggressive recruitment campaigns directed out of the Chicago home office. In 1935, the PNA still included 264,839 members in its ranks, a net loss of only 21,687 from 1930. While it was not until 1945 that overall membership figures surpassed those of 1930, one can well imagine the destructive impact of the Depression on the future well-being of the PNA had mass recruitment efforts been ineffective.

For the Polish National Alliance, however, the 1920s proved to be years of dynamic growth in ways other than membership. After the War, the

PNA considerably expanded its entire life insurance program. Coverage was increased to a maximum of $2,000 in 1921 and in 1924, individuals under the age of sixty were permitted to purchase as much as $5,000 in life insurance. An insurance policy enabling its owner to fully pay all his or her premiums in twenty annual installments was introduced in 1921 to complement the fraternal's traditional plan in which a member paid monthly premiums as long as he lived. In 1918, juveniles were permitted to possess PNA insurance with the option of becoming full voting members in their lodge upon reaching age sixteen. This move in turn trained attention upon the organization of youth activities within the PNA, which rapidly developed during the next fifteen years.

PNA youth activities included the formation of baseball, basketball and football leagues in communities with large Polish populations. The popularity of such sports in one sense reflected the extent to which both the Alliance and Polonia had become "Americanized." Yet the success of the programs also demonstrated the fraternal's capacity to adapt to the changing interests of its members.

But successful as was the expansion of PNA membership and activities in a time of changing ethnic values and interests, even more dramatic was the great political fight that raged within the Alliance between the two world wars. This conflict pitted two nearly equal factions in a battle for control that was waged everywhere, at PNA national conventions, at lodge and council meetings, in the Polonia press and even in the courts.

Political factionalism itself was not new to the Alliance; indeed the two rival groups which vied for power in the 1920s and 1930s had antecedents which had joined in battle at a series of PNA conventions before World War I. What distinguished this power struggle from the others was its intensity and the character of the contestants. Each faction was well organized, possessed strong and visible leaders, well-defined ideological orientations, and enjoyed significant mass support. In some respects, the two sides more closely resembled the militant political parties that operated in Europe than the loose, more informal groupings of America.

In one corner was assembled the conservative faction, which was sometimes referred to as the "right wing" (or "prawica"), to use a European parliamentary term that many foreign-born Poles well understood. Most often, the conservatives were popularly known as "the old guard" in recognition of their leaders' past association with the pre war National Democratic movement headed by Dmowski and backed by Smulski's National Department. Headed by Casimir Zychlinski, President of the PNA since 1912, the old guard faction enjoyed solid ties with Polonia's conservative establishment which included the clergy and the Catholic fraternals. Its veteran leadership looked back proudly to PNA achievements on behalf of Poland's independence, which had finally come to fruition in 1918.[9]

Strongest in Chicago and the surrounding Midwestern states, the old guard had gained firm control of the administrative machinery of the Polish National Alliance by 1918. But its preeminence was undermined by the rising prestige of Jozef Pilsudski, Dmowski's nemesis, in Poland. During the 1920s Pilsudski became the central force in Poland's political life while Dmowski's position declined considerably; in America, these developments revived the fortunes of Pilsudski's supporters within the old Polish National Defense Committee and helped them play an unexpectedly large role in Polonia affairs. The old guard was further weakened by criticism from younger Polish Americans who considered its achievements as merely past history and believed it offered little to the new generation. One contemporary commentator described the old guard as hanging "suspended half way between the sky and the ground," since its members were regarded as Americans whenever they visited Poland but as foreigners in the United States.[10] A sign of the old guard's decline appeared in a 1923 editorial in the newsletter of the Chicago Society of the PNA, whose members included a number of business and professional men, members in Polonia's "new elite." Commenting upon Zychlinski's attendance at a function which had been attended by many non-Poles, the Society's president criticized his inability to speak effectively in the English language to his audience.[11]

Arrayed against the old guard was the "opposition" faction, which was frequently nicknamed the "left wing" (or "lewica"). Drawing much of its following from PNA lodges and councils located in the Eastern section of the United States, the opposition group also claimed roots which went deep into the past history of the Alliance. As early as the 1890s, there had been a small number of socialists who had joined the PNA and these men, together with individuals who were "free thinkers" or "independent Catholics" on religious matters frequently coalesced to make up a vocal minority at Alliance conventions. Prior to World War I, their leading spokesman was Alexander Debski, a political *emigre* and an organizer for the Polish socialist party in the U.S. Debski served a term as PNA vice censor and after the war returned to Poland where he was politically active in Pilsudski's government until his death in 1935.

The opposition faction's popularity had first risen within Polonia in the aftermath of the 1905 Russian Revolution. Debski and his colleagues stoutly supported Pilsudski, who organized armed resistance against the tsar in an effort to win autonomy for the Poles in the Empire. Dmowski, in contrast, promoted a passive line among his National Democrats in the forlorn hope that a show of loyalty to the Empire in its crisis would at least earn Polish aspirations some recognition in St. Petersburg. Though Pilsudski's uprising failed, his effort rekindled memories of the nineteenth century insurrectionist tradition and made him increasingly popular with the militant Falcons' Alliance and to a lesser degree the PNA. Too, after 1905 several thousand Poles entered the United States as political exiles. Many of these partisans of Pilsudski later became active in the PNA.

Though still a minority within the Alliance, the opposition faction gained several notable successes within Polonia before World War I. In December, 1912 Debski and his socialist colleague Bronislas Kulakowski were able to form the Polish National Defense Committee in cooperation with Falcons' President Teofil Starzynski, Zychlinski and the leaders of most of the other organizations in Polonia. And even after the conservative groups withdrew from *KON*, the left faction continued to be influential within the PNA. At the Alliance's convention in September, 1913, for example, six opposition leaders were elected to high national office, including its vice president. A majority of the delegates also approved a resolution to transfer the *Skarb Narodowy* fund to Pilsudski's forces in Poland, thereby bringing to a close the Alliance's financial support of the National Democratic movement. The roots of that relationship went back to 1886.

But the conservatives retained majority control over both the PNA board of directors and its supervisory council. In 1914 they took the Alliance out of *KON* and soon afterward forced most of the opposition faction's members in the fraternal leadership to resign from their posts. For the duration of the War, the PNA worked closely with the clergy and the Catholic fraternals on both humanitarian and political matters. *KON's* influence declined because of Pilsudski's war time collaboration with the Central Powers against America's eventual allies, Britain and France.

After the War, the opposition faction was considerably revitalized through its identification with Pilsudski, one of the "founding fathers" of modern Poland in 1918 and the hero of its 1920 war with Soviet Russia. Pilsudski's prestige also served to broaden the ranks of his followers in America and by the mid 1920s it was no longer accurate to brand the opposition group's members as "socialists." For example, Casimir Sypniewski, the opposition's most prominent figure after his election as PNA Censor in 1924, was a successful Pittsburgh attorney and a Republican. On Poland, however, he was a staunch Pilsudski man.

Perhaps the first sign of the opposition's resurgence in the PNA came at its 1921 convention, where the resolution to withdraw from the Polish

National Department was approved. But in spite of this embarrassment, the old guard easily retained its control over the central administration of the fraternal by winning fifteen of the eighteen national offices contested at the *sejm.* Only three opposition candidates, including Magdalena Milewska who was elected ladies' vice president, were able to win office.

In 1924, when the Alliance held its national convention in Philadelphia, the opposition slate made a far stronger showing; this time five of its candidates won national office while four others were elected as independents. Replacing the jocular old guard Censor, Michael Blenski, was Sypniewski, himself a PNA activist since 1909 and an unsuccessful candidate in 1920 for the presidency of the Falcons' Alliance. But the presidential election proved to be a better indicator of the already intense factional rivalry. In this contest, Zychlinski bested his opponent, Chicago druggist Stefan Sass, by a 220-217 margin. However, Sass, an unsuccessful presidential candidate for the fifth time since 1911, refused to accept his narrow loss. Charging that a miscount of the ballots had cheated him of victory, Sass took his claim to the Illinois Supreme Court. There he issued a *Quo Warranto* petition demanding that Zychlinski prove that he had won reelection fairly. Though Sass lost his suit in 1926, his action reflected acutely upon the growing factional bitterness enveloping the PNA. As ill-will and mutual distrust grew, each side became increasingly unable to abide by the decisions of internal PNA authorities when disputes had to be settled. With the erosion of faith in the legitimacy of actions made by the president, the board of directors, the censor and the supervisory council, unhappy members instead looked for recourse outside the fraternal and to the courts. The Sass *Quo Warranto* suit thus set a precedent of sorts and during the following decade, three similar legal actions were taken to settle differences within the PNA.[12]

A second dispute broke out soon after the Philadelphia convention within the new board of directors. When a majority agreed to send official delegates to a Spring, 1925 all-Polonia congress whose purpose was to establish a new inter-organizational federation to carry on the work of the nearly defunct National Department, five of the fifteen board members registered loud disapproval. They contended that PNA participation at the conference was expressly forbidden by the 1921 convention resolution which had taken the Alliance out of the National Department. That organization, which still existed on paper, was formally the sponsor of the 1925 conclave. Their view was rejected, however, by the old guard majority, whose members denied any conflict between their action and the earlier decision of the delegates. Still, to mollify its critics, the board majority did promise not to spend any PNA money in attending the conference, which was scheduled to take place in Detroit.

The minority faction rejected these assurances. Its members (Directors Frank Synowiec, Matt Majchrowicz, Casimira Obarska, Michael Tomaszkiewicz and Titus Jachimowski) immediately filed a court injunction against the majority bloc to restrain it from officially representing the PNA at the conference and commiting funds in support of its activities. This move infuriated President Zychlinski and his allies who then acted to suspend "the five" from any further participation in the meetings of the board of directors on the grounds that they had behaved in a disloyal fashion. What appears to have most incensed the old guard was its opponents' failure to have taken their complaint first to the supervisory council, the supreme judicial body of the PNA, before turning to the court with their grievance.

A conference of Polonia organization leaders was in fact held in April, 1925. It was attended by more than 1,600 delegates, perhaps a third of whom belonged to the PNA. There it was agreed to form a successor federation to Smulski's National Department. This new agency, the Polish Welfare Council in America *(Polska Rada Opieki Spolecznej w Ameryce, PROSA)*, was to direct its attention to Polonia's domestic concerns, including the preservation of the Polish language parishes, cultural exchanges with Poland, and resistance to immigration restriction. *PROSA* thus represented a major deviation from the aims that Smulski had sought to achieve. Sound in theory, its aims were not, however, actualized and the federation led only a shadowy existence over the next decade, never playing any major role in the community's affairs.

For their part, the five suspended PNA board members petitioned Censor Sypniewski to convene the supervisory council's judicial committee to review their status. Sypniewski did his best to have the board's action overruled but to no avail. Arguing that he was both the supreme judge and interpreter of the PNA constitution, he declared that the suspension of the dissidents could be sustained only by a three-fourths majority of the entire supervisory council. When only a simple majority voted in favor of suspension Sypniewski concluded that the five should resume their posts on the board. But PNA legal counsel Leon Mallek, a Zychlinski ally, then stepped in and ruled against Sypniewski; the *impasse* left the entire matter hanging until the issue could be settled by the delegates to the next national convention. This event was scheduled for Chicago in September, 1927.

Factional conflict was further intensified by the personalities of the major combatants, the proud and ageing Zychlinski and the cold, aloof and intellectual Sypniewski. But conflict was also a product of other factors that were associated with the dynamics of the PNA itself. For one thing, with the enormous surge in PNA membership, the fraternal's role as Polonia's leading movement had been considerably enhanced during the 1920s. To the Pilsudski government, which had come to power by means of a controversial military *coup* in May, 1926, an Alliance led by individuals sympathetic toward the new regime was crucial to its success in generating widespread approval of Polonia.

Moreover, the very organizational structure of the PNA invited open political competition and conflict. According to its own constitution, the Alliance was less a business corporation and more like a kind of mini-government of Polonia. For example, it conferred upon all adult members the right to participate in its activities. Further, a kind of "separation of powers" doctrine divided authority in the fraternal among three distinct national decision-making bodies.

Ultimate power was (and continues to be) shared by the PNA national convention or *sejm*, the national board of directors and the supervisory council. The national convention, which met every three years during the 1920s, served as the supreme legislature. The *sejm* possessed the power to rule on all past actions of the board, the executive branch of the PNA, to amend the fraternal's constitution, to set policy and budgets and to elect all national officers. Given its large size and the fact that its delegates were elected by the mass membership, the convention was a natural arena for open political conflict.

A second leading institution was the Alliance's "executive branch," composed of the board of directors and headed by the president. This fifteen member body was responsible for administering the fraternal in the period between conventions. Yet a third "branch" of PNA government was the supervisory council which was composed of a body of commissioners responsible for overseeing activities in the various territorial districts about the country into which the Alliance membership was divided. This quasi-judicial body met at the request of the censor, who served as its chairman. Among its major responsibilities, the council filled vacancies in the executive leadership whenever they occurred between conventions.

Like the president the censor was elected at the national convention and held a number of responsibilities. These ranged from interpreting the con-stitutionality of board decisions, overseeing the business activities of the fraternal, and calling conventions to order to serving as a kind of moral leader of the movement.

Throughout its history, the existence of two PNA powerful leaders had been a source of internal division whenever the censor and president represented divergent philosophies or were otherwise incompatible. The president was in charge of the practical administration of the organization; yet an aggressive censor could claim that his responsibilities carried greater weight and that the job of the president and his fellow board members was merely to manage fraternal insurance operations. Originally, the censor could even veto board decisions and only the convention itself could override him.[13]

Long before Sypniewski's election, of course, relations between the censor and the president had been stormy at times. True, the first Censor, Julius Andrzejkowicz, had been content to play a rather passive role in PNA affairs. This was due partly to his relatively advanced age and the fact that he lived in Philadelphia while the seat of the PNA executive board was in Chicago. Frank Gryglaszewski, Andrzejkowicz's successor, was a marked study in contrast. A Chicagoan and an early *Gmina Polska* society member, Gryglaszewski emerged as a dominant and forceful personality in the PNA leadership during his eight years in office (1883–1891.) He aggressively promoted its growth in his extensive travels about the country as a Federal inspector of public buildings and won for himself a large following. Gryglaszewski's immediate successor, Val Przybszewski of Bay City, Michigan, also tried to direct the PNA but instead only became embroiled in chronic conflicts with the Chicago–based board. After a single two year term, he declined to seek reelection in 1893.

The fourth Censor was another Chicagoan, Theodore Helinski, who for a time was able to rebuild harmonious relations with the central administration. Nevertheless, he too eventually became frustrated by his inability to shape PNA policy more effectively and refused to seek reelection in 1899, and instead ran successfully for the office of national secretary. (A major bone of contention of the time dealt with the admission of women to full membership status, a goal that was realized in 1900). Nonetheless, during the tenure of Helinski and those of his successors, Leon Sadowski of Pittsburgh, Anthony Schreiber of Buffalo, Anthony Karabasz of Pittsburgh and Michael Blenski of Milwaukee, tensions between the censor and the board diminished and for the most part, cooperation rather than confrontation characterized their relations.[14] As a result, the period between 1893 and 1924 (when Blenski lost to Sypniewski) was less traumatic and divisive for the PNA than it might otherwise have been and these years proved to be fruitful in many respects for the fraternal.

Several factors account for this development. For one thing, each censor from Helinski to Blenski was a professional person for whom involvement in PNA matters, no matter how interesting, was second to his career obligations. Helinski was a banker, Sadowski and Karabasz were physicians, Schreiber a brewery owner and Blenski a judge. Second, all these men shared a common ideological perspective with the majority on the board of directors, one committing the PNA to close cooperation with the National Democratic movement centered in Europe. Third, it was during their tenures that the men elected president of the Alliance became significant figures in their own right. The first highly visible president was Zbigniew Brodowski, a Chicago civic activist and former *Zgoda* editor who was widely known for his patriotic views on Polish independence. Though his immediate successors, Frank Jablonski and Stanislas Rokosz, were less dominant personages, after them came two strong and effective men who dedicated themselves completely to the Alliance, Marian Steczynski and Casimir Zychlinski.[15] It was during their lengthy tenures that the office of president began to overshadow that of the censor. During this time (which began with Steczynski's election in 1903 and continued until Zychlinski's death in 1927) only Schreiber attempted to reassert the preeminence of the censor's office. In 1913, he called upon the board of directors to restrict itself to the mundane responsibilities of managing the insurance and investment activities of the fraternal while he would serve as the movement's chief representative on patriotic and Polonia-wide issues. His proposal, coming shortly after the disclosure of fraudulent behavior by the PNA financial secretary, was seemingly well-timed. Nonetheless, it was soundly rejected by the delegates to the twentieth PNA convention, clearly demonstrating that they looked to the president and not the censor for leadership.

But Sypniewski's challenge was definitely of a different order; unlike Schreiber he headed a major PNA faction whose aim was to gain control over the entire organization. As censor Sypniewski did his best to check the old guard but during his first term in office (1924–1927), he enjoyed little success. This was due to the fact that practically all his powers were shared with the board and thus could not be exercised absolutely. A case in point was his failure to intercede effectively on behalf of the five suspended dissident board members to win their reinstatement. Another concerned the editorship of the PNA weekly, *Zgoda.*

Prior to the 1915 convention, the editorship had been an elective office but afterward the constitution was amended and the post made appointive. Consequently, the censor was granted the power to appoint a suitable person from candidates proposed for his consideration by the board of directors. This method had worked satisfactorily over the next decade, thanks to a consensus of opinion between President Zychlinski and Censor Blenski over *Zgoda* editorial policy.

When Sypniewski took office in 1924, he rejected the board's choice for editor, John Przyprawa, a competent journalist but a virulent critic of the opposition faction. Instead, he proposed one of his own supporters, Stanislas Zaklikiewicz, for the post. But the board refused to pay Zaklikiewicz his salary and Sypniewski was forced to accept Przyprawa's reappointment. Because of these difficulties it appeared evident that only by gaining control over the board of directors itself could the opposition faction be assured that the censor's rulings would be carried out.

In one area, Sypniewski did retain practically absolute power to make decisions affecting the Alliance. As censor he possessed full authority to plan and direct the national convention of the PNA, which was set for Chicago's Sherman Hotel in September, 1927. Seizing this opportunity, he went on to lead his forces to a stunning, if short-lived triumph over the old guard.

Formally, it was the censor's responsibility to issue the proclamation or "oredzie" which called the delegates to each conclave and to propose a tentative agenda for their consideration. More important, though, was his control over the appointment of a large proportion of the members of the various pre-convention planning committees responsible for arranging the event. One of these special bodies was the five member credentials committee. Its task was to review the eligibility of each delegate wishing to participate in the proceedings.

In more serene times, the work of the credentials committee was fairly uncomplicated and consisted of certifying that the elections in the PNA councils had been held legally and according to set constitutional procedures. But these were hardly serene times. In 17 out of 149 councils, the losing slates of convention candidates challenged the official results and demanded that the credentials committee seat them and not those who had earlier been declared the winners. Numerous allegations charging that certain local council election judges had purposely miscounted the ballots were heard. There were also shrill complaints of ballot box stuffing. Given the intense competition between the two nearly equal factions for control of the Alliance, it was obvious that the committee's decisions could determine which side would dominate the convention proceedings and elect the fraternal's future leadership.

When the first session of the convention was called to order on September 19, 1927, Sypniewski, as temporary chairman of the proceedings acted forcefully to ensure that the opposition faction would take full control. Even as many of the delegates were still looking for their seats, he asked the chairman of the credentials committee to submit its report listing the names of all approved delegates. In all, 461 delegates were certified as eligible to take part in the convention. Sypniewski promptly called upon them to stand and take their oath so that the business of the convention could proceed.

But a serious obstacle to the censor's expeditious handling of the credentials question still remained. About 540 men and women were on the convention floor expecting to hear their names read. Suddenly nearly eighty of them realized that the credentials committee had ruled against their claims and in favor of their council opponents. Shouts were heard throughout the hall appealing the committee's decisions, which turned out to be decidedly in favor of the opposition faction. But Sypniewski refused to entertain motions permitting anyone to address the assembly until after he had administered the oath of office. At this point, the proceedings fell into confusion with angry delegates and would-be delegates raising such a ruckus that the Censor was finally persuaded to call a recess without having administered the oath.

When the convention was called to order for a second time after dinner, the afternoon's events were replayed. This time, however, several old guard spokesmen were able to address the crowd but no solution to the crisis could be found. Given all the commotion, Sypniewski was again forced to adjourn the session with nothing accomplished.

The next day the Censor tried a new tactic and began to administer the oath without even attempting to call the roll of eligible delegates. His action infuriated the old guard who at this point stormed out of the hall *en masse* and marched over to the La Salle Hotel, located but a few blocks away from the Sherman. With each faction now in full control of its own meeting place, two conventions were called to order in relative calm.

At the opposition-controlled Sherman Hotel convention, approximately 260 delegates remained and they proceeded to elect their own slate of candidates to head the Alliance.[16] Over at the La Salle Hotel, there were approximately 275 delegates and they too initially elected several executive officers of their own, including a new president and censor.[17] But several respected old guard jurists questioned their action and advised instead that the delegates reelect only those officers who had been members of the board of directors at the start of the convention crisis.[18] As a result, Felix Garbarek, who had become President only a few weeks earlier upon the death of Casimir Zychlinski, remained as interim head of the fraternal.[19]

Sypniewski's bold attempt to rig the convention in favor of his partisans had not only failed; worse, the walk out by the so-called "La Sallowcy" threatened the very foundations of a united Alliance and sowed confusion in the ranks of the mass membership. What saved the PNA from even worse calamities was the fact that the old guard, which had controlled the central administration and treasury before the convention, remained intact after it bolted out of the Sherman Hotel. By retaining its own administration at the La Salle, it maintained a tight grip upon the organizational apparatus of the fraternal. Thus, to dislodge the old guard Sypniewski and his allies were obliged to once again turn to the court for a settlement of their factional fight. By means of a second *Quo Warranto* proceeding which was initiated late in 1927, the censor demanded that legal control over the PNA be turned over to the officers elected at the opposition-dominated Sherman Hotel meeting.

Judge Jacob Hopkins of the Superior Court of Illinois eventually ruled on Sypniewski's suit. After listening to extensive testimony from representatives of both sides and extracting from them a promise to abide by his final decision, Hopkins decreed that the Chicago convention reassemble as soon as possible and that the delegates be given the opportunity to decide among themselves who should direct their affairs. The judge rebuked Sypniewski for his handling of the credentials committee report and the manner in which he had run the meeting. Furthermore, he questioned the competence of the five member committee to determine which delegates should be seated, especially given the inordinate number of contested slates and the decisive impact its rulings were likely to have at the convention. The judge proposed, instead, that decisions on credentials at the reconvened conclave be made by the uncontested body of delegates and not the credentials committee.

In Judge Hopkins' opinion, Sypniewski had erred seriously in trying to ram through the oath of office without first having permitted dissident delegates the chance to present their cases to the entire assembly. The censor well understood that once the oath was administered, no one without delegate status could address the convention. Even if he could find someone to speak on his behalf, such an effort was bound to be futile since a majority of the delegates belonged to the opposition camp and were likely to reject any appeal. All in all, Hopkins concluded, the unfairness of the proceedings was largely responsible for the withdrawal of the old guard partisans from the convention.[20]

If Judge Hopkins' ruling was sensible enough in emphasizing the need for due process at the next convention, it brought little satisfaction to either side. Though the old guard was permitted to preserve its hold on the central administration, it was able to do so only on an *interim* basis. And, because of the death of its best known leader, President Zychlinski, in August, 1927, there was no one of comparable stature to present the old guard faction's position to the membership.

For the opposition, Judge Hopkins' decision proved to be an embarrassing, if temporary, set-back to its efforts to gain control over the Alliance. During the remaining months leading up to the reconvened *sejm*, Sypniewski's supporters worked hard to strengthen their hand and were backed by a steady outpouring of propaganda from the Polish government and its friends in Polonia.

The reconvened Chicago conclave was called to order on August 27, 1928. It proved to be a strangely anti-climactic event after all the drama and confusion of the preceding eleven months. At the first session, the names of 361 uncontested delegates were read and these individuals were duly sworn in by the censor. A point of order was then raised to consider the credentials of a group of contested delegates who had not yet been tendered the oath of office. This motion was voted down 180-163 and from then onward the opposition faction was able to hold a narrow but decisive working majority throughout the entire *sejm*.

John Romaszkiewicz, a Boston bank officer who had been elected President the year before at the Sherman Hotel convention was confirmed as head of the PNA by an overwhelming 268-184 margin over the old guard's nominee, Joseph Mallek. Mallek, like his son Leon, an attorney and a thorn in Sypniewski's side for several years, had also briefly served as a PNA President, having been elected overwhelmingly at the La Salle Hotel convention in 1927.[21]

In several other major elections, the margins of victory for the opposition's candidates were much narrower, however. Magdalena Milewska defeated the old guard leader, Mary Sakowska for ladies' vice president by only ten votes, 227-217, and Casimir Kowalski, a Milwaukee socialist, won over the incumbent national secretary, John Zawilinski, by a vote of 229-223. Max Hencel, the opposition's choice for treasurer, defeated the conservative incumbent Michael Turbak by only two votes, 226-224. Even Sypniewski's reelection over Detroit attorney and *PROSA* leader Leopold Koscinski was rather unspectacular. While he defeated Koscinski by a 235-214 margin, Sypniewski's victory was much narrower than it had been in 1924 when he had ousted Michael Blenski by ninety-three votes. Even in his glory, Casimir Sypniewski was hardly a truly "popular" figure.[22]

The 1928 convention saw the "rehabilitation" of the five dissident PNA board members who had been deprived of their offices over the dispute connected with the Alliance's participation in the founding of *PROSA* in 1925. One of "the five," Casimira Obarska was later elected a vice president of the Alliance and another, "Honest Mike" Tomaszkiewicz went on to serve as its national treasurer from 1939 until his retirement in 1955. But none of the dissident board members were recompensed for the salaries withheld during their suspensions.

An interesting sidelight to the proceedings focused attention upon some rather ill-chosen comments made by two old guard leaders about the character of the opposition faction. In the opinion of Adolf Rakoczy, who had completed Anthony Karabasz's term as censor in 1915, the opposition's delegates were best described as "rabble." Unfortunately for him, his observation was reported to the convention and several injured delegates called for his immediate expulsion from its proceedings. But Rakoczy publicly apologized for his indiscretion and was given back his mandate. A more serious blunder was committed by PNA Vice President Felix Garbarek, who had served as acting president following Zychlinski's death. Garbarek permitted himself to be interviewed by a reporter for the *Chicago Evening American* and was quoted as describing several opposition leaders as "Bolsheviks." When the story was printed, again there were calls for Garbarek's immediate suspension from office. Though he lamely denied having made the comments and was reelected vice president, a last minute decision by the opposition to field a competing candidate almost succeeded. Clearly, a bit of humor would have gone far at the 1928 Chicago convention.

If the opposition faction expected to establish firm control over the PNA following the *sejm,* it was sorely mistaken. Indeed the twenty-fifth convention proved to be but an early battle in a conflict that would extend to the PNA's next conclave in Scranton, Pennsylvania in 1931. There the old guard would reassert itself and hold power for the rest of the decade.

Greatly bolstering the old guard's chances was the appearance of a new standard bearer in the person of Francis Swietlik. Thirty-six years of age at the time of the 1928 convention, Swietlik was the first American-born Pole to rise to prominence within the PNA. An attorney who later became Dean of Marquette University's Law School and a Milwaukee County judge, Swietlik was an eloquent public speaker fluent in both English and Polish. Moreover, in Chicago he had earned wide recognition as a strategist for the old guard.

Swietlik's rise enabled the old guard to regroup so it might successfully challenge the opposition. But the new regime's cause was itself damaged by a series of unforeseen developments, themselves compounded by several errors in leadership by Censor Sypniewski.

A major blow was the advent of the great economic Depression only a year after it had come into office. In the wreckage of the Wall Street crash of October 29, 1929, twenty-five percent of the labor force was left jobless, thousands of companies, lending institutions and farms went bankrupt, and hundreds of thousands of families were evicted from their homes. The crash saw the *New York Times* stock index fall from 449 points in September, 1929 to 49 points in October, 1932 and led to an economic collapse and hard times that endured until America's entry into the Second World War.[23] For the PNA, it had a savage impact upon an organization that heretofore had been experiencing its greatest period of growth.

As thousands of PNA members lost their jobs, many were unable to continue making their insurance payments. Despite the energetic efforts of the leadership to promote its insurance programs through its annual drives (a goal of 50,000 new members was ambitiously set for 1930, the golden anniversary of the Alliance), the fraternal was soon treading water. To use another analogy, the PNA increasingly resembled a huge revolving door, with as many people dropping away as joining its ranks. At first, the Alliance seemed to be holding its own. In 1930, for example, 42,000 people purchased new insurance policies while 30,000 either cancelled their coverage or were terminated for non-payment of premiums. But as the Depression deepened the membership picture became darker. By 1935, overall membership had declined 7.7 percent from 286,526 members in 1930 to 264,839 policy holders.

Even more alarming was the Depression's impact upon the Alliance's financial condition. Historically the PNA had invested nearly all its assets in residential and apartment mortgage loans, a lucrative and socially beneficial strategy during the economic boom of the 1920s. But in the 1930s large numbers of mortgage holders were either themselves unemployed or unable to collect rents from their jobless tenants and as a result could not repay their debts. Not only was the PNA required to foreclose on many of these properties; it found itself managing hundreds of buildings which were yielding nothing on the fraternal's original investment. In 1935, the PNA held 1,349 buildings on which it had made loans; 177 of these were standing vacant while many more were in some stage of default. Further complicating its financial difficulties was the PNA's traditional practice of participating in so-called "split mortgages." Through such arrangements the Alliance agreed to provide a portion of the home loan in cooperation with another lending institution. When home owners defaulted on such mortgages, the PNA was unable to establish its clear title to the property and was forced to take legal action simply to protect its claims.

The Depression's threat to its financial stability brought rising demands from PNA members for changes in fraternal investment policies. It was only later, after 1935, that such changes began to be made under the leadership of Swietlik who had replaced Sypniewski as censor at the 1931 convention.

Gradually the PNA divested itself of most of its real estate portfolio and by 1943 owned only 142 properties. The search for profit combined with greater security led Swietlik and PNA President Charles Rozmarek (elected to succeed Romaszkiewicz in 1939) to switch from real estate and into investments in government and high quality corporate bonds. These prudent moves enabled the PNA to greatly improve its economic position by the mid 1940s.

A second shock to the Sypniewski faction came in the form of a fire that devastated Alliance College on the night of January 20, 1931. The result of an electrical short circuit, the blaze leveled the old Rider Hotel which served as the dormitory and main classroom building on the campus. It also housed the priceless library and museum which Henry Kalussowski had donated to the PNA in 1891. Fortunately, not a single student had been in the building at the time the fire broke out and there were no casualties. And, thanks to the energetic efforts of College President Stefan Mierzwa, winter clothing for the orphaned student body was quickly gathered through the cooperation of local Cambridge Springs churches and merchants. Suitable shelter was also found in town and classes were resumed almost immediately in some nearby buildings. But because of the prevailing economic conditions and the revelation that the hotel had been underinsured, reconstruction of the college proceeded slowly. Yet more than money and property were involved in the losses from the 1931 fire. More demoralizing was the seeming end of the historic dream of PNA ownership of its own educational institution. The loss of the Kalussowski library and museum further underscored the fire's significance to many PNA members.

But if ill-fortune stalked the new administration in its efforts to firm up its command over the Polish National Alliance, the opposition faction's cause was also damaged by Sypniewski himself. A major blunder was the censor's decision to establish cordial relations between the PNA and the Polish government. Only weeks after the close of the 1928 convention Sypniewski was in Warsaw trying to consolidate ties between the Alliance and the newly formed Organizational Council of Poles from Abroad *(Rada organizacyjna Polakow z zagranicy)*. This federation, headquartered in the Polish capital, had been created for the expressed purpose of building closer relations between Polonia communities around the world and the fatherland. Many Polish Americans worried that PNA involvement in the Organizational Council would infringe upon its freedom of action but the strongwilled Sypniewski pushed ahead nevertheless.[24] In fact, little came of his efforts. Regular tourist trips to Poland were sponsored by the PNA and a permanent Polish American pavilion at the Poznan international trade fair was built, underwritten mainly by the Alliance. Another forward step was PNA purchase of $30,000 in Polish government bonds on behalf of the Kosciuszko Foundation, which used the dividends to underwrite the expenses of scholars travelling to America. On the negative side, the heightened visibility of Polish consular and embassy officials at PNA events generated growing suspicion that the opposition faction was being used by Warsaw as an instrument of Polish foreign policy. This concern caused a good deal of controversy given the character of the regime Marshal Pilsudski headed after May, 1926.

Pilsudski had returned to power by means of a military *coup* and in the process he overthrew the parliamentary coalition headed by the peasant party leader Wincenty Witos. Pilsudski justified his action on the basis of the Polish democracy's failure to deal with the country's mounting economic and social problems; in its place he established a kind of "guided democracy" under his direction. The Marshal's decision to repress what remained of the democratic opposition to his rule in 1930 further eroded his popularity in Polonia and undermined the efforts of the Sypniewski group to rally around Pilsudski and enhance its own position in the Alliance. Particularly embarrassing were the appearances of Polish government representatives at the annual Third of May observances at which the PNA celebrated Poland's aspirations for democracy embodied in its 1791 constitution; this when in Poland an increasingly authoritarian regime held sway.

As the 1931 convention approached, resistence to Sypniewski's regime crystalized in favor of his opponent, Swietlik. The Milwaukee attorney aggressively challenged the censor and was aided in the effort by a warm and friendly style which stood in sharp contrast to the incumbent's aloof and icy manner. Sypniewski further alienated many PNA activists with the program he outlined for the future in the months just preceding the Scranton convention. In essence, the censor argued for two major changes in PNA policy, which he believed would enhance the fraternal's appeal throughout Polonia. His first proposal called for the transfer of the PNA financial reserves, then amounting to about $3 million, into a special "Alliance Auxiliary Fund" *(Zwiazkowa Fundacja Zapomogowa)*. This money would then be invested in high quality government securities under the direction of a special committee that he was to head. The interest and dividends from such investments would be made available to PNA families in search of home loans or funds to start their own businesses, to students in need of college tuition grants and to worthy community causes. As the Alliance grew, Sypniewski argued, so would the reserve fund providing with it the resources to benefit PNA members on an ever increasing scale.

Sypniewski's second major proposal, one that had long been promoted by one of his Chicago allies, former PNA Vice President K. B. Czarnecki, was to establish a system of PNA-owned lending and banking institutions throughout the country in communities where large Polish American communities existed. Such institutions would not only provide PNA members outside Chicago with their first opportunity to borrow money for home mortgages through the Alliance, they would serve to diversify the fraternal's activities and strengthen its economic position.

Swietlik, by 1931 the old guard's acknowledged spokesman, was a sharp critic of Sypniewski's ideas. Strong enough to force Stanislas Zaklikiewicz, the editor of *Zgoda,* to print his views in what had become the opposition faction's own organ, Swietlik argued that the censor's proposals were unrealistic given the existing nationwide economic crisis and if put into effect would jeopardize its financial position. More relevant to the problems before the PNA, he asserted, was the issue of Sypniewski's leadership style. Under the censor, the Alliance had been rent by chronic dissension and conflict. Sypniewski's relationship with the Pilsudski regime had also led to the PNA's isolation from the rest of Polonia, he charged. Swietlik's recipe for a brighter future called upon PNA members to put aside partisan conflict and to cease identifying with particular political factions in Poland. Instead, the Alliance would be better served by developing a non-partisan relationship toward Poland and giving greater attention to cooperation with other American Polonia organizations. Historically, Swietlik reminded his readers, the PNA's greatest achievements had occurred when it had followed these goals, as exemplified by the accomplishments of the World War years. When the PNA had sought to dominate Polonia however, its efforts, however well-intentioned, had yielded little.[25]

As the delegates convened in Scranton on September 20, 1931, it was soon evident that a slight majority adhered to the conservative faction. At the very outset, a motion to adopt Sypniewski's complicated and controversial proposals was tabled for consideration later in the convention. This prevented the censor's supporters from extolling the virtues of his farsighted thinking; during the interpellation sessions the old guard faction centered its attacks upon Sypniewski, Secretary Kowalski and Treasurer Hencel while extending only compliments to President Romaszkiewicz. In the elections, Swietlik trounced Sypniewski by forty-seven votes, although Kowalski and Hencel lost by extremely narrow margins, making their defeats a more accurate indicator of the relative strength of the two factions. Deeply wounded by his repudiation, Sypniewski retired from any further involvement in PNA and Polonia activities, though he lived until 1958.

The left faction, however, continued to elect candidates to high office even after 1931, although Sypniewski's ouster followed by Romaszkiewicz's

Table 1.   PNA Convention Results of Elections for National Office[26]

Faction	1924	1927–28	1931	1935	1939	1943
Old Guard	10	3	9	11	7	9
Opposition	7	15	8	7	8	7
Uncommitted or Unknown	1	0	1	0	3	2

loss of the presidency in 1939 were decisive blows from which it did not recover. Indeed, the opposition's peak year remained 1928, when it gained nearly all the top PNA offices, including those of president, censor, vice censor, secretary, treasurer and ladies' vice president. A check of the convention results for all elections between 1924 and 1943 provides a good barometer of the shifts in the factional fighting during the entire period.

The 1931 triumph of Swietlik and the old guard sharply reversed Sypniewski's pursuit of close cooperation between American Polonia and the Pilsudski regime inaugurated in 1927 with the formation of the Organizational Council of Poles from Abroad. In the Summer of 1934, an international congress of Polonia representatives was held in Warsaw to establish a more effective permanent world organization to coordinate the activities of Poles from abroad with the homeland. As ambitiously conceived by its creators, the aim of this World Union of Poles from Abroad (often known as *Swiatpol* for *Swiatowy Zwiazek Polakow z Zagranicy)* was not only to strengthen cultural ties between Poland and the foreign Polonia communities but "to subordinate the activities and the organizations of Polish immigrants living abroad to the interests of the Polish government." All Poles, wherever they lived in the world, were called upon to give "unconditional loyalty to Poland" even if they happened to be citizens of another country. Given its size and potential significance in American political life, the adherence of American Polonia to the semi-official government organization was crucial to its ultimate success.[27]

But it was Francis Swietlik, not Sypniewski, who headed the 45 member American delegation which travelled to Warsaw. Speaking on its behalf at the congress, he rejected the notion of American Polonia's formal involvement in *Swiatpol.* Though Swietlik agreed with the importance of cooperation with Poland in preserving the Polish ethnic heritage in the United States, he took strong exception to *Swiatpol's* arbitrary assumption that the

Polish Americans were Poles first and Americans second. Emphasizing that he and his colleagues had come to Warsaw not as Poles living abroad but as an inseparable element in American society, Swietlik argued that "Polonia in America (was) neither a Polish colony nor a national minority, but a component of the great American nation, proud of its Polish origin and careful to implant in the hearts of the younger generation a love for all that is Polish."[28]

Swietlik's redefinition of the content and meaning of the Polish ethnic identity in America was not well received at the congress and upon his return he was subjected to sharp criticism from both within and outside the Alliance. At its October, 1934 meeting, the PNA board of directors publicly embarrassed him by voting to join *Swiatpol* anyway, subject only to approval by the delegates to the 1935 national convention. As a result of this controversy, Swietlik redoubled his efforts to work on behalf of a complete conservative victory over the opposition members still holding high PNA office.

At the 1935 convention in Baltimore, the old guard dominated the proceedings and even the personally popular Romaszkiewicz barely won reelection over Swietlik's candidate, Charles Rozmarek. The opposition faction's frustration was best illustrated by the decision of several of its leaders to once more take their complaints to court after the convention. In what was to be the fourth civil suit and the third and final *Quo Warranto* action filed against the old guard in little more than a decade, the dissidents argued that the conservatives had rigged the Baltimore convention.[29] (Ironically, the same claim had been made by the old guard delegates who had stormed out of the convention hall in Chicago in 1927.) For their efforts, the *"Quo Warrancisci"* were stripped of their rights to vote and to hold office in the PNA. Eventually, their case was also thrown out of court. However, this particular conflict did lead to a much needed reform in the method the PNA had used to select national convention delegates, a method whose abuse had contributed so heavily to the 1927 crisis at the Chicago convention.

Prior to 1915, convention delegates had been elected directly from the local lodges, but this system had been changed when lodges were grouped together into district council units. Under the initial council set-up, convention delegates were still elected on the basis of popular votes cast in the lodges. This system afforded unscrupulous election judges an opportunity to tamper with lodge voting results by "stuffing the ballot boxes" before they were transferred to the council headquarters for tabulation. A veteran of the factional wars recalled that in one election, 420 votes were reported to have been cast from his lodge, although the lodge itself had only 400 members and considerably fewer individuals had actually taken part in the election! As a result of the 1935 *Quo Warranto* dispute, the method of convention delegate selection was altered. Power to elect delegates was placed solely in the hands of lodge representatives called together to a special meeting of their council where they alone decided who would attend the convention. This change enabled such council delegates to supervise directly the counting of ballots; thereafter, charges of vote fraud diminished considerably. Later at the 1943 convention, the delegates agreed to reinstate the partisans of the 1935 *Quo Warranto* dispute in return for their public apology for having gone to court with their complaint. Thereafter, several of the leading dissidents went on to play major roles in PNA affairs.

Swietlik also learned from the controversy over his statements in Warsaw, which showed that the subject of Polonia's relationship to Poland was too emotional to be minimized by the conservatives. In May, 1935 he met in Chicago with the leaders of the Polish Roman Catholic Union and the Polish Women's Alliance. Together they formed the Polish Interorganizational Council, whose purposes emphasized charitable activity on behalf of needy Poles wherever they lived, and which was reminiscent of the still-born Polish Welfare Council of 1925 *(PROSA)*. PRCUA President Joseph Kania and PWA President Honorata Wolowska accepted the posts of vice presidents of the Interorganizational Council, which soon evolved into the Polish American Council *(Rada Polonii Amerykanskiej)*. Upon the outbreak of World War II, the *Rada Polonii* became the chief humanitarian assistance organization working for Polish relief and the focus of Swietlik's activities as a Polish American leader.

Sypniewski had personified the intellectual side of the opposition faction's program for the PNA, with its emphasis upon building formal ties with the Polish government and expanding the fraternal's institutional activities throughout Polonia. But there was a second, emotional element in the ideology of the opposition faction, one represented by President John Romaszkiewicz, which remained significant within the PNA for yet another decade. Romaszkiewicz, who enjoyed enormous personal popularity, had won a rousing reelection victory in 1931. Even during the Scranton convention he was busy preaching his message and for the next eight years his energies were focused upon realizing a program which launched the PNA into one of the most exciting phases in its history.

Romaszkiewicz took up an issue of growing PNA concern, the preservation of ethnic feeling among the hundreds of thousands of American-born youngsters growing up in the United States. Other leaders had proposed their own answers to a question which concerned the very future of the ethnic community, especially following the end of mass immigration after 1920. But instead of promoting PNA sponsorship of such "American" youth activities as baseball, basketball and bowling, Romaszkiewicz reached far back into his own experience in the pre war Falcons' Alliance and came up with a singularly novel program. His idea was that of *Harcerstwo,* the traditional name of the Polish scouting movement, and Romaszkiewicz zealously called upon the Alliance to establish its own *Harcerstwo* groups in every lodge and council throughout the country.

The purpose of *Harcerstwo,* in Romaszkiewicz's view, was to deepen the ethnic consciousness of the youth in a direct way, by promoting its participation into a movement with an explicit Polish character. At the same time, *Harcerstwo* evoked memories about the rich ties that had existed before World War I between the Alliance and the Falcons' movement, which had combined physical fitness programs with cultural offerings designed to generate patriotic feeling among the youth of that era. While the Falcons had gone their own way after breaking with the PNA, the idea of creating a kind of new *Sokolstwo* among the youngsters already enrolled in the Alliance exerted considerable appeal. Indeed, as *Harcerstwo* took shape, Romaszkiewicz borrowed many of the slogans, watchwords and activities directly from the Falcons he remembered.

The *Harcerstwo's* essential characteristic was its Polish flavor. Romaszkiewicz expressly rejected the notion of forming a PNA-sponsored branch of the Boy Scouts of America (which itself belonged like the Polish *Harcerstwo* to the international scouting movement). Instead, he established his youth groups in conscious imitation of the Polish model and encouraged the wearing of uniforms of the Polish *Harcerstwo,* and the teaching of Polish songs, language and sports activities that were popular in the ancestral homeland. Through all these programs, Romaszkiewicz and his followers believed it possible to reinvigorate ethnic feeling among Polonia's youth by identifying with the post war Poland. And, at his height, the PNA *Harcerstwo* did achieve phenomenal success, with more than 50,000 young people in its ranks throughout the country. Youth activities also engaged several thousand older PNA members who took responsibility for organizing scouting units in their local lodges and councils and directing their various activities, which included camping, singing, dance, sports, craftswork and periodic jamborees.

Such was Romaszkiewicz's success that other Polonia fraternals soon established their own scouting organizations in imitation of the PNA example. John Romaszkiewicz thus succeeded where Sypniewski had failed. By breathing emotion and feeling into the opposition faction's program, he mobilized thousands of people in support of one of the PNA's central historic goals, the maintenance of Polish ethnic consciousness in America.

But Romaszkiewicz soon found himself fighting an uphill battle within his own organization to preserve the youth movement, since the Scranton convention witnessed the return of the conservative faction into preeminence. While the opposition faction rallied behind *Harcerstwo*, conservatives such as Swietlik were troubled when they analysed the principles of the youth movement. For one thing, the enthusiastic support given *Harcerstwo* by the Polish government underlined the PNA's continuing political ties with the Pilsudski regime, ties which Swietlik wished to terminate, or at least modify. The paramilitary flavor of the uniformed *Harcerstwo* activities was unsettling too. Most serious, however, was Swietlik's argument that the activities of *Harcerstwo* isolated Polish American youths from their non-Polish school-mates and neighborhood companions and slowed down their advance into full acceptance in American society. As a successful American-born professional of Polish-born parents, Swietlik's sensitivities in this regard were clearly different from the much older Romaszkiewicz, who had come to the United States as a teenager. As the 1935 convention drew near, Swietlik decided to do something about his objections and persuaded a Wilkes-Barre attorney named Charles Rozmarek to run against Romaszkiewicz for the presidency. Like Swietlik an American-born Pole, Rozmarek campaigned aggressively against the by-then ailing incumbent and lost to Romaszkiewicz by a margin of only eight votes. Having come so close on his first try for the presidency, Rozmarek never stopped campaigning for the job and in 1939 he defeated the "Grandfather of the *Harcerstwo*" by six votes, out of 531 that were cast.

But if *Harcerstwo* had its critics within the PNA, it was dealt an equally serious blow from outside. From the outset, officials of the Boy Scouts of America complained about *Harcerstwo*, arguing that as an American-based scouting organization the PNA group was required to operate under their jurisdiction. Furthermore, they demanded that *Harcerstwo*, as a division of the American movement, pay an annual membership fee to the parent body of $3 per head. The issue of affiliation with the American scouting organization was never settled during the tenure of Romaszkiewicz; afterward, Rozmarek reorganized the movement under the name of *Druzyny zwiazkowe*. He also dispensed with the uniforms and paraphernalia of the Polish movement so that the PNA would not be required to pay the head tax demanded by the Boy Scouts of America. With the entrance of the United States into World War II even these units went out of existence, never to be replaced either in size or scope of activities by any later ethnic youth movement in Polonia.

Conclusions

On September 1, 1939 the military forces of the Third Reich attacked Poland without provocation from the sea, air and land and within days had captured large portions of its western and northern territories. As these events unfolded in Europe, the delegates to the 28th Polish National Alliance convention were assembling in Detroit. Although the events of the convention were dramatic enough, the Polish crisis overshadowed the proceedings. In the months that followed, PNA activity centered on the Polish question and the means by which it, together with all of Polonia, could effectively assist the war-ravaged homeland for which so much had been offered a generation earlier. Given these realities, it is not at all surprising that the experience of the 1920s and 1930s was quickly relegated to the remote past, especially since so many events of the era had been bitterly divisive and emotionally draining. Polish Americans have always been at their very best in times of great crisis, when solidarity is called for and ideological and personal conflicts are put aside.

Nonetheless, a retrospective look at the political factionalism within the PNA tells much about the vitality of Polonia and the Alliance during the interwar period. The most impressive evidence demonstrating the importance of the PNA is in the enormous efforts of so many people to gain control over a movement they counted to be Polonia's most significant and influential organization. One measure of the turbulence of the period is in the number of candidates who competed for elective offices at the interwar PNA conventions. For example, in 1928, ninety-three men and women were nominated for the top eighteen national offices and three years later there were seventy-seven candidates for the same number of positions. In 1939, a grand total of one hundred and forty persons ran for national office. In contrast, even at the hectic 1967 convention thirty-nine people campaigned for the seventeen highest offices while in the less frenetic conditions of 1971 and 1975, the number of candidates was even lower with thirty-seven and twenty-seven individuals, respectively, seeking national office.[30] And, when one realizes that the struggle between the old guard and the left opposition was not simply over the material assets of a business operation but one centered on debates over complex ideological issues dealing with the meaning of Polish ethnicity, the future of Polonia and its proper relationship with

Poland, one can only be impressed that so many people "cared" during the years of interwar conflict to become actively engaged in the struggle.

Yet, it must also be recalled that the record of the 1920s and 1930s was not simply one of political and ideological conflict. Throughout all those years, thousands of people entered the Alliance to safeguard their families with life insurance policies and thousands of others were recipients of the various benefits which the PNA provided. And thanks to the conscientious efforts of its officers, even in the worst years of the Great Depression the financial solvency of the organization was preserved. Throughout the period, PNA-sponsored youth and sports activities mushroomed while hundreds of sons and daughters of PNA members received school loans and scholarships to advance their educations. Although these activities were less dramatic than the stories of convention fights and court suits, they gave substance and meaning to the work of the PNA as a center of Polish American life.

Chapter 6

THE ROZMAREK ERA: 1939–1967

September 10, 1939 found the delegates to the Polish National Alliance's 28th convention gathered in Detroit's Book Cadillac Hotel at a cataclysmic moment in the history of Poland. Just ten days earlier, Nazi Germany had invaded Polish territory without provocation and was driving into the heart of the embattled country. Only a day after the conclave's final adjournment, there was still worse news. Soviet forces from the East quickly occupied half the country in accordance with a secret agreement between Stalin and Hitler signed on August 22, 1939 in Moscow, which had called for the partition of Poland and the rest of Eastern Europe.

In Detroit, events in Poland dominated everyone's attention. One of the major actions taken by the delegates was to commit $100,000 in humanitarian relief for the victims of the invasion. Another $7,500 was raised by personal donations made by delegates in a collection taken at the convention hall. These substantial efforts backed up earlier donations from the PNA to Poland which Censor Francis Swietlik had organized during the Spring of 1939, when the gravity of the Nazi-inspired crisis had first become evident. At that time, PNA members had sent $250,000 to the ancestral homeland.

Furthermore, in mid-October, 1939 the PNA made yet another massive contribution in relief assistance when the PNA's leaders travelled to Washington, D.C. to present the American Red Cross with a check for $150,000 to spur its work for Poland. Thus, within the span of six months the PNA alone contributed more than one-half million dollars in humanitarian aid to Poland.[1] Moreover, Swietlik, who was resoundingly reelected to a third term as Censor in Detroit, took the lead in mobilizing the PNA, other Polonia fraternals and the Polish parishes around the country to raise funds through the *Rada Polonii Amerykanskiej,* or Polish American Council, which he chaired. Throughout the conflict, which soon expanded into the Second World War, the *Rada Polonii* acted in concert with the American Red

151

Cross and other relief agencies to gather food, clothing and medical supplies for refugees scattered about Europe and in Poland. By 1948, it had gathered approximately $20 million for the cause.[2]

The Polish National Alliance once again took the lead in relief work. Through its approval of a special monthly assessment of five cents per member, the PNA generated an enormous sum for the cause. In 1951, Treasurer Michael Tomaszkiewicz could announce that this assessment alone brought in $786,307.[3] And such aid did not include the donations in time, money and material contributed by individual members, lodges and councils throughout the country.

America's entry into the conflict in December, 1941 spurred the Alliance's purchase of war bonds, an activity also promoted at the local level. This enormous effort was duly recognized on December 9, 1944 when U.S. Treasury Department representatives appeared at the Chicago headquarters of the PNA to accept a check for a $5 million bond purchase. At that time it was announced that the Alliance had already bought $19.5 million in bonds. Earlier, PNA contributions to the war effort had been great enough to warrant a decision by the War Department in August, 1944 officially naming one of its bombers the "Polish National Alliance."[4]

As chairman of the *Rada Polonii,* Censor Swietlik's energies were stretched to the limit. Because he remained the Dean of the Marquette University School of Law throughout the war, Swietlik inevitably found less time for the PNA. He readily justified this, however, since he was confident that the Alliance was in good hands under its newly elected president, Charles Rozmarek. Rozmarek had been Swietlik's candidate for the presidency since 1935 and in 1939 he had defeated John Romaszkiewicz at Detroit. Swietlik fully expected Rozmarek's victory to signal the end of the internal political conflict coloring PNA affairs during the interwar years and assumed that he and his protege would work harmoniously in the future.

Swietlik's expectations were generally realized during Rozmarek's first term. Seven years younger than his mentor, Rozmarek focused his attention upon mastering the complex administration of the fraternal and establishing his authority over the organization. Also making for a smooth relationship was the fact of America's neutrality in the World War until December, 1941. This restricted Polonia's involvement to humanitarian work under the auspices of Swietlik's *Rada Polonii* confederation.

However, as time passed the relationship between protege and mentor changed substantially due to a combination of factors leading to Rozmarek's consolidation of power as PNA president and Polonia leader and to Swietlik's withdrawal from Alliance politics. These factors had much to do with the personalities and ambitions of the two leaders but also included the war's impact upon Poland and Polonia. After 1941, U.S. participation in the conflict as an ally of Poland transformed the Polish issue into a political cause for Polonia. The Polish American Congress which Rozmarek headed from its creation in 1944 thus overshadowed the *Rada Polonii* which ceased to be the sole organization working for the ancestral homeland.

To better appreciate the reasons for Charles Rozmarek's rise to leadership, one must recognize the skills and personal attributes he brought to the office of president. Only forty-two years old at the time of his election, Rozmarek was a man of impressive size and appearance. He was an eloquent and forceful public speaker in both the Polish and English languages. The son of an immigrant coal miner, Rozmarek had risen far from his humble Pennsylvania origins by attending the Harvard University law school; there he developed an urbane leadership style while earning his degree. Aside from his personal qualities Rozmarek possessed the will to achieve what no previous PNA leader had been able to do—to establish a seemingly invincible political organization whose central purpose was to perpetuate his rule. This "machine" was so effective that Rozmarek was able to preside over the PNA for an unprecedented twenty-eight years, making his the longest tenure in its history.

Rozmarek's political machine differed considerably from the factions that had vied for power in the years between the wars. Groupings like the "old guard" and the "opposition" had been organized largely along ideological lines. Their leaders held their posts largely because they were effective spokesmen of views shared by large numbers of PNA activists. In contrast, Rozmarek's organization existed in support of Rozmarek himself and those in the leadership who backed him. Later on, Rozmarek's election as president of the Polish American Congress in 1944 further enhanced his status within the PNA by enabling him to appear publicly throughout the country as Polonia's chief spokesman on the subject of U.S. relations with the post war communist regime set up in Poland. As president of the PAC, Rozmarek became more than a business or fraternal leader, he was confirmed as a kind of statesman linking Polonia to American officialdom and thus above attack.

In establishing his command over the PNA, Rozmarek, of course, benefitted greatly from the help he received from a number of talented allies and advisors. Within this group was his wife, Wanda, who was prominent in the PNA women's divisions and in the lodges and councils in the Chicago area; earlier, before Rozmarek became president, she had been active in the fraternal in Pennsylvania. Director of the summer Polish studies courses held at Alliance College where youth leaders were trained for many years, Wanda Rozmarek was in a position to identify talented individuals who could support her husband's administration in the future.

Several other individuals played important roles in Rozmarek's regime. One was Stanley Swierczynski, manager of the Alliance Printers and Publishers, a separate corporation controlled by the PNA Board of Directors. Informally, Swierczynski was also Rozmarek's campaign manager, and in this capacity he was continually busy lining up friendly delegates before each convention to assure the president's reelection.

Karol Piatkiewicz, editor-in-chief of the two Alliance newspapers, was another important *aide* to Rozmarek. Piatkiewicz was initially responsible to the censor, who according to the PNA constitution, oversaw the editorial policy of both newspapers. In 1944, Rozmarek successfully altered this arrangement when he demanded that *Zgoda* publish reports on the activities of the new Polish American Congress, of which he had just been elected president. Here, Rozmarek overrode Swietlik, who argued that such information was too partisan in tone and should not be included in the "nonpolitical" fraternal organ. Consequently, Piatkiewicz reported solely to the president and both newspapers reflected Rozmarek's views.

A third aide to Rozmarek was Frank Dziob, his personal secretary and along with Piatkiewicz the author of his speeches. Yet a fourth ally was Mrs. Frances Dymek, PNA ladies' vice president and head of its women's divisions between 1935–1939 and again between 1943–1967. Dymek's backing of Rozmarek through most of his administration won him the solid support of the large PNA women's constituency. In return, Dymek's pact with Rozmarek enhanced her own position. For example, it was Dymek's motion to make the ladies' vice president the first vice president of the PNA (and therefore the immediate successor of the chief executive in case of his death or incapacity between conventions) that was unanimously approved at the 1955 national convention in Minneapolis. By way of contrast, until 1921 the ladies' vice president had been but an honorary officer without any voting rights on the board of directors.

But Rozmarek's preeminence within the Polish National Alliance was not due solely to the skills he and his allies possessed, considerably as they were. As important was his political organization. An astute observer of Pennsylvania and Chicago politics, both of which were based heavily on patronage, Rozmarek soon realized that he possessed the means to create within the PNA a similar system so powerful that he would become practically invulnerable to criticism and invincible in any contest for power.

PNA council presidents around the country were assigned the duties of "precinct captains" and made responsible for bringing out a vote favorable to Rozmarek's delegate slate at each convention. In return for their loyalty, they often received bonuses (or "overrides") for all new insurance purchased in their districts. Such bonuses were doled out from the central office in Chicago. District commissioners were also expected to support Rozmarek's administration in their constituencies or face the loss of funds needed to finance fraternal, sports and cultural activities in their territories on a satisfactory level. At the national conventions, ample money was available to help undecided delegates make up their minds in favor of the administration and its candidates. Such funds were aggressively accumulated from Rozmarek's allies both in and outside the organization during the years between conventions. As for these affairs, one PNA leader who was also active in state and national partisan politics offered the opinion that more "politicking" went on at PNA conclaves during the Rozmarek era than at the party conventions she attended. A similar view was expressed by then Minnesota Senator Hubert Humphrey, who spoke at the 1955 PNA convention which was held in Minneapolis.

One Rozmarek fund raising tactic caused him no little embarrassment when it came to light in 1941. It involved a decision to assess each employee at the PNA home office five percent of his salary for the privilege of working for the Alliance. Individuals who refused to comply risked losing their jobs. Among the more than one hundred employees at the Chicago office, several particularly dissatisfied people organized a labor union to protect them from the assessment, a practice never previously followed in the PNA, though common in Chicago politics. In March, 1941 the dissidents, who had established a local of the Office Employees Union of the American Federation of Labor, failed to win Rozmarek's recognition of their right to bargain collectively with the PNA. In the months that followed, the PNA attempted to weaken the unionization effort by various pressure tactics culminating on October 6, 1941, when a worker named Anna Owsiak was dismissed for union activity. The following day saw 27 other employees initiate a strike against the PNA which continued until January, 1942 when the National Labor Relations Board ordered the employees' reinstatement and an end to PNA efforts to harass their unionization activities. Rozmarek's response to this decision was interesting and typical of his general approach; refusing to accept the decision of the Federal agency, he called on the PNA to appeal its ruling on the grounds that the NLRB had acted unconstitutionally. Rozmarek argued that the PNA was a fraternal benefit society operating on a not-for-profit basis and that it did not fall within the scope of the

Wagner Act, the Federal law prohibiting unfair labor practices by commercial institutions.

The unionists' position was made especially difficult because no fraternal leader openly backed their cause. A letter signed by forty-five employees to Censor Swietlik stated their grievances but failed to win his support, for example, although he was appalled to learn of the five percent fund. But Swietlik opposed the principle of legitimizing labor-management conflict since this seemed to be contrary to the idea of fraternalism. Hence he did nothing.

Rozmarek's argument was summarily rejected by the National Labor Relations Board when it ruled in favor of the PNA employees' union. The PNA then petitioned the U.S. Court of Appeals to review the decision. That court rejected the claim that the PNA was only a fraternal aid association and affirmed the NLRB's position that the Alliance was a commercial firm which had engaged in unfair labor practices. But Rozmarek was undeterred, and stubbornly initiated yet another petition before the United States Supreme Court.

The case of the Polish National Alliance versus the National Labor Relations Board did indeed reach the highest court of the land in January, 1944 when it agreed that the PNA's complaint dealt with a significant constitutional matter, whether or not fraternal insurance firms engaged in commerce and were thus obliged to obey legislation regulating commerce and labor relations. On June 5, 1944, the court ruled 8-0 against the PNA with Justice Felix Frankfurter writing the majority opinion. Frankfurter's opinion dealt with the constitutional issue alone; the Appeals Court had already condemned the anti-union practices which had brought about the problems in the first place. He sharply criticized the petitioners for their questionable reasoning in trying to avoid the obligations placed upon their organization by Federal law.

> When the conduct of an enterprise affects commerce among the states is a matter of practical judgment and not abstract notions . . . The exercise of this practical judgment the Constitution entrusts primarily and very largely to the Congress, subject to the latter's control by the electorate. Great power was thus given to the Congress, the power of legislation and thereby the power of passing judgment upon the needs of a complex society . . . To hold that Congress could not deem the activities here in question to affect what men of practical affairs would call commerce and to deem them related to such commerce merely by gossamer threads and not by solid ties, would be to disrespect the judgment that is open to men who have constitutional power and responsibility to legislate for the nation.

The unionists' victory proved to be Pyrrhic, however. Several of its early leaders were in military service when the courts made their rulings and those who remained at work in the Chicago office eventually disbanded the union local. A few employees may have even continued to pay for the right to work at the PNA during and after the dispute.[5]

But thanks to the combination of his personal gifts and the support he could count upon from his allies in the leadership, Rozmarek was able to overcome such errors in judgment and in a relatively short time built a formidable organization inside the PNA based on the principle of complete personal loyalty. Already at the 1943 convention held in Boston, Rozmarek's strength was evident. There he crushed Romaszkiewicz, himself a Bostonian, in the presidential balloting by a 444-87 margin. No other national candidate won so convincingly, not even Swietlik who was reelected by a 413-146 vote nor Treasurer "Honest Mike" Tomaszkiewicz, who won 423-74. Thus, even before Rozmarek was able to further enhance his prestige as president of the all-Polonia Polish American Congress in 1944, he was already the PNA's dominant leader. From 1943 onward, until he was defeated for an eighth four year term in 1967, Charles Rozmarek exerted a vice-like grip on PNA affairs and defeated nearly every opponent of his regime. Although remnants from the old "lewica" or "left" opposition faction continued to nominate candidates against Rozmarek and his slate, they won only a handful of national offices during his presidency.

If two pillars of Rozmarek's leadership included his own personal gifts and the political organization he built, a third was his command over the Polish American Congress from 1944 to 1968. As PNA President Rozmarek was already a considerable figure in American Polonia, but initially he operated in the shadow of his mentor, Swietlik, whose prestige as censor was considerably embellished by his leadership of the *Rada Polonii*. It was only as president of the Polish American Congress, therefore, that Rozmarek would supercede Swietlik as an all-Polonia leader. Through the Congress, a political action federation of organizations committed to Poland's independence, Rozmarek could justifiably claim that he was Polonia's chief spokesman; moreover, he could also assert that it was he who had realized a historic mission of the Alliance, the unification of Polonia, through the PAC. By presiding over both organizations, Rozmarek became Polonia's ambassador to a succession of Presidents from Franklin Roosevelt to Lyndon Johnson. His hold on the PAC further reinforced his position in the PNA, since any criticism of his administration of the Alliance could be labelled as but a veiled attack on his work for Polish independence.

Throughout Rozmarek's long tenure as president of the PNA, the issue of Poland once again became intimately connected with American Polonia, as it had been before 1918. During the war, the cause revolved around the recovery of national independence, victory over Nazi Germany and support for the Polish government in exile which operated after 1940 in London and was led by General Wladyslaw Sikorski. But the end of the conflict did not bring about the rebirth of a pro-Western democratic Poland as Polonia had hoped; instead a communist-run regime submissive to the Soviet Union was installed in Warsaw. The failure of the Western Allies "to win the peace" in regard to Poland thus became an issue of central importance to Polonia under Rozmarek for the next two decades. Given these developments, other traditional PNA concerns were overshadowed. One, youth activities, provides a case in point. Already in 1941 the Alliance's commitment to *Harcerstwo* had ended when it decided not to affiliate with the Boy Scouts of America. The reorganized PNA scouting circles which followed *Harcerstwo* also disappeared, but no alternative strategy was formulated to deal with ways to motivate young people into the Alliance. Due to the war, other PNA activities were also curtailed, particularly those in sports such as basketball and baseball. While Rozmarek did propose the creation of a four year liberal arts curriculum at the Alliance College, the actual development of the PNA school proceeded slowly during the 1940s and 1950s.

Thus, the one concern burning brightly throughout Rozmarek's administration focused upon Poland. Historically, many of the PNA's proudest moments had been devoted to working for national independence before and during World War I and, not surprisingly, the Nazi-Soviet partition of September 1939 rekindled mass commitment to this cause. There were nevertheless, several important differences between Polonia's response in the two wars. In the First World War era, many of the activists in patriotic organizations like the PNA and the Falcons considered themselves "American Poles" whose chief concern was for the homeland. Not surprisingly, one of the best expressions of Polonia commitment was its formation of a Polish army in the United States. By World War II, Polonia had changed considerably; most of its members and a large part of its leadership was composed of "Polish Americans" whose primary loyalties were to the U.S., although they maintained considerable affection and concern for the fate of the land of their ancestors. While Polonia's initial response to the invasion of Poland was to support humanitarian activities under the auspices of Swietlik's *Rada Polonii* (an organization comparable to the Polish Central Relief Committee of 1914), the effort to organize a new Polish army of American volunteers failed miserably.

On the diplomatic front the situation had changed considerably after 1939 too. Paderewski, the great pianist-patriot who had so energetically worked to mobilize American and Polonia public opinion on behalf of the Polish people in the First World War, was still on the scene. But his death in 1940 at the age of eighty dealt the Polish cause a heavy blow, since there was no one else who could approach him in stature. On the positive side, General Sikorski's government in exile did enjoy good relations with both London and Washington. Composed of all the major pre war political parties, his government also had the support of the underground forces inside occupied Poland, which included about 450,000 persons by the war's end. The Polish government in exile commanded a 100,000 member army, recruited mainly from *emigre* communities in France and Belgium, which in June 1944 took part in the Normandy invasion. After 1942, it directed a second army under the command of General Wladyslaw Anders, which was permitted to leave the Soviet Union and fought bravely in the North African and Italian campaigns.

Poland's plight in World War II was greatly imperiled by the ruthless tactics the two occupying powers employed to prevent its resurrection. Both sides systematically killed off the country's political, military, religious and cultural leadership. Though by far the greater damage was perpetrated by the German invaders, the USSR too was guilty of crimes against the Polish people. Occupying the Polish lands east of the Vistula River after September 17, 1939, the Soviets executed or exiled thousands of captured civilian and military officials. In 1940, the Soviet security police was responsible for the deaths of more than nine thousand Polish army officers taken prisoner the previous Fall, an action that came to be known as the Katyn massacre.[6]

In the U.S., Swietlik's *Rada Polonii* at first dominated things. However, because of its primarily charitable character, it could not operate openly as a political voice in support of Sikorski's government without jeopardizing its ties with organizations such as the Red Cross. Moreover, a few of the Polish exile government's actions after 1941 caused division and controversy within Polonia and some embarrassment to Swietlik. Sikorski's death in an airplane accident in 1943 was also a serious blow since it left the exile government in the hands of the able, but less prominent Polish peasant party politician, Stanislaw Mikolajczyk, whose moderate leadership was sharply criticized by militant elements in Polonia. As the war went on, it became increasingly evident that a growing need existed for a Polish American organization to articulate and mobilize Polonia opinion in behalf of the ancestral homeland, something clearly beyond the capacity of the *Rada Polonii.*

If Poland's plight was difficult between 1939 and 1941, the Nazi attack upon its erstwhile Soviet ally on June 22, 1941 complicated the situation even more. British Prime Minister Winston Churchill, whose government was allied with the Poles, immediately proposed an Anglo-Soviet alliance which ignored Moscow's earlier participation in the invasion and partitioning of Poland, and its absorption of nearly half its territory. On July 30, 1941, under British pressure, Sikorski's government agreed to a treaty with the USSR which reestablished diplomatic relations between the two sides and permitted the formation of a Polish-led army in the Soviet Union. However, while the treaty annulled the Nazi-Soviet pact of 1939, the Soviets refused to recognize the prewar border with Poland as the future boundary line between the two countries. Instead, the matter was left unsettled, in time becoming an emotionally divisive factor that adversely affected Polish-Soviet relations and significantly shaped the perspectives of Polonia.

In America, Polonia continued to respond generously to humanitarian assistance campaigns promoted by Swietlik's *Rada Polonii,* though neither the Nazis nor Soviets were particularly cooperative. The *Rada Polonii* did assist in resettling Poles who were permitted to leave the Soviet Union after 1941; through the International Red Cross its packages of clothing and supplies gradually began to reach their intended recipients. In addition, Swietlik met Sikorski in 1941 and 1942 during his visits to the United States; massive crowds welcomed the Polish leader on his tours to demonstrate their support for the London exile government.

But criticism of Swietlik and Sikorski surfaced from a small but articulate element within Polonia, whose members in 1942 organized the National Committee of Americans of Polish Descent *(Komitet Narodowy Amerykanow Polskiego Pochodzenia* or *KNAPP).* Led by Frank Januszewski, editor of the *Dziennik Polski* of Detroit and Max Wegrzynek, editor of the New York *Nowy Swiat,* this group questioned Sikorski's reconciliation policy toward the USSR and demanded that the Polish government-in-exile seek Soviet recognition of the prewar boundaries between the two countries as a condition for cooperation. Dominated by individuals influenced heavily by the thinking of Pilsudski, *KNAPP* was highly suspicious about the chances for friendly Soviet-Polish postwar relations and did its best to disseminate this view throughout Polonia. To better articulate its concerns to the government of the United States, *KNAPP* called for the formation of a new, distinctly political action organization to unite American Poles in defense of its view of Poland's true national interests. *KNAPP* also opposed cooperation with Swietlik's *Rada Polonii* because of its friendly ties with the Sikorski government as well as its essentially humanitarian character, which prevented it from playing too explicit a political role in influencing U.S. policy. As in World War I, when concern over Poland's future status caused the Polish Central Relief Committee to eventually give way to its political subcommittee, the National Department, so also in World War II was the *Rada Polonii* to be superceded by a specifically political body.

Two other developments helped spur the formation of the Polish American Congress. The first was Katyn. After resuming diplomatic relations with Moscow in 1941, the Sikorski government was repeatedly frustrated in its efforts to learn the whereabouts of thousands of military officers captured by the Soviets after September, 1939. These officers were essential for the creation of an effective Polish army in the USSR to fight Nazi Germany. In April, 1943, the Nazis uncovered a mass grave in the Katyn forest in Western Russia where the bodies of more than four thousand Polish officers were buried. Declaring this to be a Soviet atrocity, the Nazis called upon the International Red Cross to make its own investigation of the grisely remains. When the Polish government-in-exile supported such an investigation, the Soviets condemned the decision and summarily broke off diplomatic relations with Sikorski. From this point onward, Stalin committed the USSR to bringing the tiny and subservient Polish communist party to power, most of whose leaders were inside the Soviet Union. Stalin pressed Roosevelt and Churchill to accept "his Poles" as the heads of the future Polish state, even though they enjoyed practically no support in the occupied country.

A second stimulus for the Polish American Congress was in the activities of a relatively small number of pro-Soviet Polish Americans who claimed that their views reflected American Polonia opinion. Expressing full support of President Roosevelt and his military alliance with Stalin, the pro-Soviet Polish Americans initially seemed politically influential. One mass organization in which they took part was the American Slav Congress, formed in Pittsburgh in 1942, which claimed to represent the thinking of fifteen million Slavic Americans. A second was the American Polish Labor Council which called itself the voice of 600,000 Polish workers. Asserting that they alone reflected the will of Slavic and Polish Americans, both formations condemned *KNAPP* as divisive to the American-Soviet alliance.

At this critical point, it was clear that Polonia needed its own political voice if its leaders were to effectively support the aims of the Polish people in the occupied homeland and the policies of the democratic Polish government in exile. But *KNAPP* alone was too narrowly structured to play this role. It included only about 2,000 persons, most of whom were recent *emigres*. Essential to the success of any all-Polonia political action federation was the involvement of the large fraternals and the Polish clergy, which together enjoyed the trust of millions of people.

In the early months of 1944, Charles Rozmarek seized the opportunity to play what became his greatest role in the affairs of American Polonia. In early March, he addressed a gathering of fifty Polish American leaders in Chicago where he publicly called for a congress of Polonia to coordinate the defense of free Poland's interests in America. A week later he spoke to a larger group in New York and appealed for ethnic cooperation to assure the success of the proposed congress of Polonia which was scheduled for Buffalo at the end of May. One scholar has this to say about Rozmarek's contribution during these critical weeks:

> Rozmarek's role in bringing together the two centers of Polonia on the eve of the official convocation of the Polish American Congress was crucial in forging the united front that Polish Americans needed in order to speak with authority on behalf of Poland.[7]

On May 28, 1944 more than 2,500 people from twenty-six states gathered at a four day meeting to forge the Polish American Congress, or *Kongres Polonii Amerykanskiej.* Present were dignitaries and clergy from both the Roman Catholic and Polish National churches, a large number of politicians and government officials and hundreds of fraternal activists. Rozmarek was the dominant personality at the conclave. Elected PAC President, he enunciated as its two central aims cooperation with the United States government in its war effort and support of a just peace within the framework of the principles of the Atlantic Charter, which were understood to insure the restoration of an independent Polish state. In its resolutions the Polish American Congress criticized the Soviet Union on the border question and its backing of the tiny Polish communist party. Nevertheless, President Roosevelt was relieved to learn that the new organization supported his leadership and was nonpartisan in reiterating Polonia's full commitment to the war effort.

Roosevelt had good reason to be concerned about the Polish American Congress. In November, 1943 he had made a private agreement over the Polish border issue with Stalin when they and Churchill had held their first summit meeting in Teheran, Iran. Without attempting to negotiate a more equitable resolution of the dispute, Roosevelt volunteered his willingness to go along with Stalin's position. But since he was already planning a fourth campaign for the presidency, FDR worried that public awareness of his views would alienate the traditionally friendly Polish American voters and threaten his reelection hopes. Thus he asked the Soviet leader to keep their understanding confidential.

Charles Bohlen, a career diplomat who later served as ambassador to the Soviet Union, was the President's interpreter in his private talks with Stalin. In his memoirs, Bohlen sharply criticized FDR's serious blunder in giving Stalin what he wanted without extracting any concessions in return. In justifying their private agreement on the basis of cynical domestic political considerations Roosevelt only compounded his error, since he could have given Stalin a better argument for the American initiative, e.g., his desire to improve U.S.—Soviet understanding.[8]

During the first nine months of 1944, FDR remained evasive on the Polish border issue. He did meet with Prime Minister Mikolajczyk in June and urged the Polish leader to speak directly with Stalin in Moscow, as if the matter of boundaries was still negotiable. But Roosevelt avoided Polish American Congress leaders who made several attempts to present their views on the Polish situation, which reflected what had been approved in Buffalo. Only on October 11, 1944, did the President receive Rozmarek and his associates in the White House. The atmosphere surrounding the gathering was particularly somber. The Nazis were by then completing the crushing of a massive nationalist uprising in Warsaw by partisans of the London Polish government, one which had received practically no military assistance from the Allies. As a result, two hundred thousand people perished in the tragic affair and Warsaw itself was systematically razed. Still, Roosevelt was positive about United States support for Poland. While he avoided making any commitments to Poland's future political and territorial integrity, he implied the American government's support for Poland's eastern border by allowing a giant map of the prewar Polish state to hang behind his desk. Roosevelt's statement in support of a "strong and independent Poland" led one alert United Press reporter to observe in his story about the conference that FDR's choice of words was very similar to Stalin's earlier call for a "strong, independent and friendly Poland," led by people who favored the incorporation of the disputed territories into the USSR.[9]

Despite the October meeting Roosevelt remained concerned about the Polish vote and sought Rozmarek's endorsement of his reelection in the waning days of the campaign. But Rozmarek was unwilling to do this until he received a more definitive statement from the president on the Polish issues. On October 28, only a week before the election FDR spoke with Rozmarek in his special train during a stopover in Chicago. In exchange for Roosevelt's pledge to uphold the principles of the Atlantic Charter as they related to Poland, Rozmarek gave FDR his personal endorsement, which was widely publicized as representing the official positions of the PAC and PNA.[10]

Roosevelt's electoral vote victory of 432-99 over his Republican opponent, New York Governor Thomas Dewey, was impressive. But his popular vote margin of fifty-three percent was more indicative of the closeness of the contest. In the Polish ethnic communities, however, Roosevelt won ninety percent of the vote and he carried seven of the ten states with the largest Polish American population concentrations: New York, Illinois, Pennsylvania, Michigan, New Jersey, Massachusetts, and Connecticut. Dewey won Ohio, Wisconsin and Indiana.

According to historian Richard Lukas, whose study of the Polish question in World War II focused heavily on the 1944 election, FDR was overly concerned about the Polish American voting bloc's potential effect upon the outcome. Lukas also argues that Roosevelt exaggerated Rozmarek's influence over Polonia and states that for most Poles, loyalty to FDR's New Deal economic polices was too strong to be overcome by disappointment over his position on Poland.[11]

But this runs counter to several other considerations. For one thing, the ten "most heavily Polish" states possessed a total of 268 electoral votes. Had Dewey captured only these states, he would have won the presidency even if FDR had carried every other one of the remaining 38. Secondly, all ten heavily Polish states were fairly evenly balanced between the two major parties; thus a relatively small shift in voting support might easily have caused entirely different results. In Illinois, for example, FDR's victory margin was only 60,000 out of the nearly 4 million votes that were cast; in Michigan the president won by 23,000 out of a total vote of 2.2 million; in Pennsylvania, he won by 105,000 in a state where 3.8 million people cast ballots; in New Jersey, the president carried the state by 27,000 votes out of two million who went to the polls. In only one state with a substantial Polish ethnic population, New York, was FDR's victory substantial enough to have enabled him to win in spite of heavy Polish American voter defections.

It is unlikely that Rozmarek's endorsement of Dewey alone would have caused a large majority of Polish Americans to reject Roosevelt, especially given his Republican opponent's conservative posture on the domestic issues. But due to the closeness of the popular vote in so many states, had the PAC leader succeeded in leading even thirty-five percent of the Polish American voters out of the Democratic camp, his action might have been decisive. Moreover, criticism of the president for turning his back on Poland was not an issue of isolated concern only to Poles. Thus, had Rozmarek been certain of Roosevelt's true position and effectively broadcast his objections widely, he might well have changed the outcome of the election.

Charles Rozmarek's endorsement was made, presumably, without firm knowledge of Roosevelt's 1943 agreement with Stalin at Teheran. Also unclear is the extent of his awareness of the October 13, 1944 meeting in Moscow between Prime Minister Mikolajczyk, Soviet Foreign Minister Vyacheslav Molotov, Churchill, British Foreign Secretary Anthony Eden and U.S. representative Averill Harriman. There the Polish leader was shocked to hear Molotov state that Roosevelt had already agreed to Soviet border demands regarding Eastern Poland at Teheran and that it was Mikolajczyk's duty to go along.[12]

What accounts for Charles Rozmarek's decision to endorse FDR in spite of the president's dubious commitment to Poland? One should consider Rozmarek's relative inexperience in politics, the pressure applied by Chicago Mayor Ed Kelly to "play ball" and back the president, along with the awe FDR inspired in those he met. In addition, the Polish vote had been solidly Democratic; Rozmarek's endorsement of Dewey would have sharply divided Polonia and damaged his claim to leadership of a united community.

Given these factors, a more prudent man might have remained publicly neutral, but here Rozmarek's personal ambition coupled with his desire to win Polonia a greater say on the Polish question influenced his move. Also unfortunate was Rozmarek's decision to act without first consulting the top leadership of the Polish American Congress for its advice, a characteristic of his leadership style which generated a good deal of criticism.

To his credit, Rozmarek led the Polish American Congress in adopting a sharply critical stance on U.S. policy after the election, when Roosevelt and Churchill made public their actual views about Poland. At a time when few Americans openly questioned Soviet war aims as contrary to U.S. security interests, Rozmarek aggressively mobilized Polonia and its political friends in Washington to demand a new assessment of Soviet policies.

In London, Mikolajczyk failed to win his government's approval of the border changes Stalin had dictated and resigned. He was replaced as prime minister by the more intransigent underground leader and socialist politician, Tomasz Arciszewski. But events after November, 1944 made the border question second to a more serious issue—the complexion of the future Polish government. With the underground in ruins after the failure of the Warsaw uprising and Soviet troops overrunning the country, the USSR was in an excellent position to determine Poland's postwar political system. Of crucial importance was the tiny Polish Workers Party formed in 1942 out of the remnants of the prewar Communist Party that Stalin himself had dissolved in 1938. Claiming only 8,000 members in January, 1943 and but 30,000 members two years later, the Polish Workers Party enjoyed practically no indigenous support in a country of twenty-five million. But because of its slavish obedience to the policies the Soviets had devised for Poland, the PWP was the key element within the pro-Soviet Polish Committee of National Liberation that was formed in July, 1944 as the basis for an eventual communist government.

On New Year's eve 1944, the Committee of National Liberation declared itself the provisional government of Poland, a move that received immediate approval from Moscow. By extending its diplomatic recognition to the Committee of National Liberation, the USSR practically put an end to whatever dim hope non-communist Poles at home and abroad still harbored about governing the country after the War. When Roosevelt and Churchill met Stalin for the second and last time at the Yalta Black Sea resort in February 1945, they were unable to budge the Soviet leader from his view that the Communist-led group should serve as the nucleus for the future Polish provisional government. Though the Polish issue was brought up at seven of the eight sessions at the conference, the best that could be achieved by the two Western leaders was to augment Stalin's group with a few "democratic leaders from Poland and Poles abroad." Roosevelt did try to put forward Mikolajczyk's name and those of several other prominent Poles in the West or in the homeland, but Stalin flatly rejected the plan. In the end, the "Big Three" agreed to leave this matter up to their representatives who were to meet later in Moscow to hammer out all the specific details connected with the people and parties included into the Polish provisional government.

Churchill, Roosevelt and Stalin agreed at Yalta that as soon as this provisional government was formed, they would immediately recognize it as the legitimate government of Poland. Once constituted, its leaders were expected to hold "free and unfettered elections as soon as possible on the basis of universal suffrage and the secret ballot." All "democratic and anti-Nazi parties" were to be allowed to put forth candidates in the proposed elections. Nonetheless, FDR returned home dejected by what had transpired. Though he publicly expressed satisfaction with the results of the meeting, in private he agreed with a close associate's bleak assessment of the agreement on Poland that it was "so elastic that the Russians could stretch it all the way from Yalta to Washington without ever technically breaking it." Indeed, several terms of the Yalta agreement were practically meaningless and unenforceable. The signatories, for example, never defined what they meant by "democratic and anti-Nazi parties" and this lapse enabled the Polish provisional regime to exclude all conservative parties from post war politics. And, despite Soviet Foreign Minister Molotov's personal assurances that parliamentary elections to establish a permanent Polish government could be held within a month following the Yalta conference, the failure to set up an election timetable permitted the Communists to delay holding the vote for two years. When elections were finally held on January 19, 1947 they occurred in an atmosphere of violence and intimidation aimed at all who opposed the regime. The results themselves were falsified.[13]

Nevertheless, Roosevelt believed that despite the flaws in the Yalta agreement, he had done what he could for Poland. Churchill, too, concluded that the agreement was realistic, given Soviet military superiority in the region.[14]

Futhermore, he urged Mikolajczyk to return to Poland as a deputy prime minister in the Communist-run provisional government and to lead his followers in the democratic Peasant Party. This movement claimed 600,000 members in January, 1946 to 230,000 for the Communists and was the one mass organization with any hope of competing successfully for power. In the face of objections from many in and outside Polonia that the effort was hopeless and would simply add legitimacy to the Soviet-controlled Polish regime, Mikolajczyk joined the provisional government after he pledged his support for the new Soviet-Polish boundaries. He appears to have taken seriously the notion that his supporters would be permitted to participate in a fair election contest guaranteed by the Western Allies, one he was sure the Peasant Party would win. In fact, the situation was hopeless. Once Communist efforts to badger Mikolajczyk into joining its "popular front" coalition failed, the decision was made to break up the Peasant Party. Two of its top leaders were assassinated during the protracted election campaign, thousands of party activists were arrested including 149 of its 444 parliamentary candidates, and the organization's newspapers were censored and their distribution disrupted. The Communists campaigned relentlessly against the Mikolajczyk-led movement, labeling it a "trojan horse" filled with bankrupt reactionaries no longer able to operate openly.

In the January, 1947 elections, the regime claimed it had won eighty percent of the vote (Mikolajczyk stated that his forces had received ninety percent); it followed the victory by pressuring several remaining Peasant leaders to break with Mikolajczyk and to set up their own party, one willing to comply as a junior coalition partner in the new political order. In fear of imminent arrest, Mikolajczyk and a few close associates fled the country, eventually arriving in the United States in November, 1947.

If most Americans initially had regarded the Yalta agreements as "about the best that could be worked out" with the Soviet Union, Rozmarek and the Polish American Congress viewed the decisions as they related to the future of Poland as "a staggering blow to the cause of democracy." Practically alone at first the PAC leader urged Congress to condemn what had transpired at Yalta and travelled to San Francisco in the Spring of 1945 as an unofficial representative of Poland to argue his case at the founding sessions of the United Nations. When President Harry Truman (who had replaced Roosevelt following his death in April) did recognize the Communist-dominated Polish provisional government which was formed in July, 1945, Rozmarek condemned the move as "a tragic historic blunder." Describing recognition as nothing less than "a moral defeat for the democracies," he asserted that as loyal Americans, Polonians were obliged to express their outspoken opposition to the decision of their own government when it was in error. In Rozmarek's view the U.S. had repudiated the principles of the Atlantic Charter, the very rationale for its involvement in the War.[15]

By the Summer of 1946 the official position of the Polish American Congress toughened from calling for free elections in Poland (the policy of the Truman administration) to repudiation of Yalta on the grounds that adequate provisions had never been made in the "Big Three" agreement for genuinely free elections. Rozmarek asked Truman to withdraw American recognition from the Warsaw regime and to reestablish diplomatic ties with the London Poles until free elections were actually held, a proposal the United States government rejected.

A "bombshell" set off by Secretary of State James Byrnes further damaged the PAC's confidence in the administration. Speaking on September 6, 1946 in Stuttgart, Germany, Byrnes emphasized that the United States considered the new western border of Poland along the Odra and Nyssa Rivers to be provisional, a view which clearly implied that Germany was far more important to American interests than Poland. Since Byrnes had strongly supported the new Polish border at the Potsdam conference in July 1945, his remarks represented a major shift in policy. As a result, Rozmarek found himself joining both Mikolajczyk and the Polish Communist-led government in protesting the speech.

Yet despite his deepening frustration with Washington, Rozmarek took no partisan stance in endorsing candidates in the 1946 Congressional elections. This decision was probably a mistake, since the PAC lost an opportunity to influence the course of electoral politics at a crucial moment. In fact, the largely anti-Yalta Republican party captured both legislative houses for the first time in eighteen years. Rozmarek's "fear of jeopardizing internal support by backing losing candidates" seems to have been the best explanation for PAC inaction.[16]

The fraudulent 1947 Polish elections only confirmed the views of PAC leaders about Yalta and took the organization further along the road in opposition to the Truman administration, which limited itself to a formal protest to Warsaw. Following Arthur Bliss Lane's resignation as U.S. Ambassador to Poland, he and Rozmarek worked to set up a "Committee to Stop World Communism" which helped shape the increasingly anti-Soviet mood that gripped much of the American public.

Rozmarek's highly publicized activities also strengthened his position as PNA president. And, at the 1947 PNA convention in Cleveland, the path to even greater control was considerably eased when his one major rival, Swietlik, decided not to run for reelection as censor, an office he had held since 1931. Nonetheless, Swietlik subjected Rozmarek to considerable embarrassment in his convention report in which he summed up his work on behalf of the PNA and Polonia during the preceding four years. In his remarks, Swietlik brought up two concrete examples which he argued demonstrated Rozmarek's unwillingness to cooperate with his one-time mentor. The first concerned the editorial direction of *Zgoda,* which Rozmarek had assumed against Swietlik's wishes and the PNA by-laws. A second bone of contention had been the special audit of PNA finances which Swietlik had ordered, much to Rozmarek's displeasure. Swietlik summed up his criticisms with a succinct evaluation of the president's leadership style, declaring that "Rozmarek will not accept any control."

When his turn came to address the convention, Rozmarek pugnaciously took issue with Swietlik. He argued that the censor's refusal to permit information about Polish American Congress activities to appear in the pages of *Zgoda* had forced him to take a stronger hand in the paper's operation. Rozmarek defended his opposition to the special audit in a more roundabout fashion. He acknowledged the censor's historic responsibility in overseeing the management of Alliance finances. But in his opinion this function had become superfluous, since regular audits were now required by the state insurance commissions. Furthermore, Swietlik's audit had proven to be a waste of money since it uncovered no irregularities.

Rozmarek went on to characterize Swietlik's criticisms as having been motivated by his hostile response to the forming of the Polish American Congress, which meant the eclipse of the censor's *Rada Polonii* charitable federation. He recalled that Swietlik had opposed the concept of such a political action organization for Polonia and had played no role in its creation in 1944. Indeed, his appearance at the founding meeting of the PAC in Buffalo had prompted jeers from some of those in attendance.

Swietlik, while expressing himself publicly in criticism of Rozmarek, was unwilling to challenge him for the leadership of the Polish National Alliance.

Neither did he seek another term for himself as censor, although he would have very likely been reelected, according to several well informed participants at the convention. In his place, the Pittsburgh judge and Polonia activist Blair Gunther was overwhelmingly elected. While popular in his own right, Gunther was clearly "Rozmarek's man" for the censor's job. For most of his twelve years in office, Gunther operated largely in the shadow of the president, although he too broke with Rozmarek in the late 1950s.

The public spectacle of Polonia's two top leaders quarreling with one another caused quite a stir. At last, one delegate rose to urge the two to shake hands for the good of the Polish American people. In response, Rozmarek and Swietlik "buried the hatchet" to a round of applause mixed with relief. Four years later, however, Swietlik changed his mind and once again sought his old office. But at the Buffalo convention, his comeback effort failed badly and Gunther was reelected, 381-138.[17]

Rozmarek's tendency to act without first consulting the major constituent groups in the Polish American Congress continued to cause him some grief. In December, 1947 he and several other PAC leaders met Stanislaw Mikolajczyk in Chicago to determine how they might cooperate in presenting Poland's cause in America. Though Mikolajczyk enjoyed widespread recognition in the U.S. for his war-time leadership of the Polish government in London and his idealistic but doomed attempt to wrest control of the Polish government from the Communists after 1945, within much of Polonia he was virtually a *persona non grata*. Indeed, by traveling to Poland Mikolajczyk was viewed by many as having simply played into the hands of the Soviets by lending his name to the government they had imposed.

Still, Rozmarek went ahead and concluded an agreement with the Peasant Party leader, which was approved at the 1948 Polish American Congress convention. As a result the *KNAPP* group withdrew in protest from the PAC, followed by Polonia's second largest fraternal, the Polish Roman Catholic Union in America. (When the PRCUA at last returned to the fold in 1954 it was on the condition that the future president of the Polish American Congress be "an independent man, not connected with any organization in an official capacity."[18] Moreover, not only was the Rozmarek-Mikolajczyk alliance divisive, it also proved to be unproductive in another way since Mikolajczyk saw himself as no less than the leader of the Polish democratic government in exile. As such, he expected the PAC to serve him and carry out his policies, something Rozmarek was unwilling to do.

Rozmarek's second plunge into the game of endorsing presidential candidates proved to be as unsuccessful as his 1944 effort. Irreconcilably opposed to Truman by 1948, he along with Swietlik and Gunther publicly backed the Republican hopeful, Dewey. In making his move, Rozmarek underestimated Truman's growing hostility to Soviet foreign policy, which from 1947 onward had become increasingly evident, although the change did Poland itself little good. On March 12, 1947 the president spoke before a joint session of Congress asking for $400 million in military and economic assistance to Turkey and Greece, which were threatened by Soviet-sponsored communist movements. In announcing what became known as the Truman Doctrine, he established as policy the principle that the U.S. government would "support free peoples who are resisting attempted subjugation by armed minorities or by outside pressure." While the president did not call for the withdrawal of Soviet military power from Eastern Europe, his proposal coincided with Rozmarek's view that the USSR posed a genuine threat to American interests in the world. A few months later, Secretary of State George Marshall proposed an economic assistance program to enable Europe to recover from the devastation of World War II and to prevent the area from coming under communist control. His idea, known popularly as the Marshall Plan, was enacted the following year. By 1952 the United States had poured more than $12 billion in successfully reconstructing Western Europe, making the plan the single greatest achievement in the history of American foreign policy.

Following the Communist seizure of power in Czechoslovakia in February, 1948 and Stalin's blockade of West Berlin which began in June, American and European leaders moved quickly to establish a new military alliance, the North Atlantic Treaty Organization (NATO), to deter further Soviet expansion. By then too, the U.S. had at last devised a coherent and effective approach to foreign policymaking to meet the Soviet challenge. Called "containment," the approach called upon the United States to use its military and economic resources to block Soviet expansion and ultimately bring sufficient pressure upon the Russian communist dictatorship to cause its gradual internal liberalization.

Like Roosevelt before him, Truman worried about the Polish American vote in 1948 and did a good deal to impress Polonia with his concern for a variety of issues of importance to the ethnic community. Aside from his solid "Fair Deal" economic proposals which included a call for a federally sponsored health care program, Truman made sure that a resolution indicating the Democrats' commitment to a free Poland was inserted into the party's platform. Far more important was the passage of a Displaced Persons Act which enabled approximately 150,000 victims of the war who were unwilling to return to their original homelands in Communist Eastern Europe to enter the United States outside of the Immigration Bureau's quota system. While

Rozmarek had worked hard for this legislation, it was under Truman that it had become law.

The 1948 presidential election was extremely close and involved four major contestants: Truman, Dewey, Southern "states rights" leader Strom Thurmond and former Vice President Henry Wallace, who headed a faction of dissatisfied liberals backed by the American Communist movement calling itself the "Progressive party." Until the waning days of the campaign, Truman's cause appeared hopeless, but on election day he won a narrow popular vote victory over Dewey. Truman's election was helped considerably by Polish Americans who largely ignored Rozmarek's advice and voted Democratic by a 4-1 margin. At best, the PAC leader could seek some small consolation in having helped to pressure Truman into a more "hawkish" stance. But his failure to deliver a sizeable vote in Polonia for the Republican candidate was another blow to his political prestige.[19]

Yet it would be an error to conclude from Rozmarek's misadventures in influencing the outcome of presidential elections that the Polish American Congress' activities during and immediately after the War represented a failure for Polonia. At home, the PAC organized a "one million dollar" fund drive that netted more than $600,000; at the organization's second convention in 1948 Rozmarek was able to announce that its treasury held more than $305,000, an amount unequalled for many years to come.[20] These funds were eventually spent to assist more than one hundred thousand displaced persons in resettling in the United States. Rozmarek also made PNA resources generously available to the needs of Polish refugees. For example, Alliance College became a half-way house for approximately 350 orphans who had entered this country from Mexico.

Through the efforts of Rozmarek and other PNA members who turned their own homes into shelters for refugees without family sponsors, large numbers of the newcomers were able to become acquainted with American conditions and find employment in their new homeland. Many of these new arrivals later joined the PNA and added a spirit of vitality and ethnic consciousness to the fraternal.

In political matters there were also gains. Rozmarek at first linked the Polish American Congress with the most strident critics of U.S. foreign policy. He backed the liberation of the Eastern European peoples by "rolling back" the communist regimes imposed by the Soviet Union after the war. The PAC aligned itself with like-minded *emigre* organizations, most notably the Assembly of Captive European Nations, whose chief Polish spokesman was the wartime Peasant Party leader and underground activist, Stefan Korbonski. The Polish American Congress enthusiastically supported the creation of

Radio Free Europe, which beamed news from the West into the communist-ruled satellites, and Rozmarek frequently contributed interviews and speeches to RFE broadcasts into Poland.

In 1952, Rozmarek supported the candidacy of General Dwight Eisenhower, the nominee of the Republican party, in the expectation that if elected, he would carry out the GOP's pledge to bring about the liberation of Eastern Europe. But Eisenhower personally opposed "national liberation" and shortly after his election announced that he favored only the "peaceful liberation" of the region. Once in office the new administration generally adhered to Truman's containment policy, a tacit acknowledgement of Soviet preeminence in Eastern Europe.

In June 1956, the Poles vented their frustrations over poor economic conditions and political repression as thousands of workers took to the streets of Poznan to protest their demand for "bread and freedom." Though the demonstration was put down by the Polish army and police at the cost of hundreds of lives, the Stalinist regime in Warsaw was discredited and in October replaced by a more moderate Communist party faction headed by Wladyslaw Gomulka. A veteran party leader and its general secretary until 1948, when the PWP had merged with remnants of the Socialist Party to form the Polish United Workers Party, he had been purged from his post because of his stubborn opposition to a few of Stalin's orders. Nonetheless, in nearly every important respect Gomulka was an orthodox communist loyal to Moscow, whose major differences with the Stalinist faction concerned his appraisal of the Polish Catholic Church and the issue of private farming. Recognizing the significant role of the church in Polish national life, he opposed a frontal assault upon an institution which would only alienate millions of people. Further, though Gomulka agreed that in the long run Polish agriculture should be collectivized along Soviet lines, for the time being he believed it was better to leave the private farmers alone. Toleration of private farming would help Poland avoid a breakdown in food production that would cause widespread unrest throughout the cities. Fortunately, Gomulka was able to persuade the Soviet leadership that he could be trusted. Poland thus escaped the tragic fate of Hungary, where reform-minded communists led by Imre Nagy were thrown from power by a Soviet military invasion which caused thousands of casualties.

Committed only in rhetoric to the idea of "national liberation," the United States government remained an onlooker during the events of October and November, 1956. In this way were illusions dispelled in Eastern Europe about the readiness of the U.S. to intervene in support of a pro-Western revolt against the Soviets. For their part, after 1956 Eastern Europeans who sought economic and political reforms at home understood that they could expect little assistance from the West for their efforts. Rozmarek and the Polish American Congress also came to appreciate this reality, although "liberation's" emotional hold remained strong.[21] But even as he continued to condemn the Gomulka regime, so also did Rozmarek urge the Eisenhower administration to provide the Poles with economic assistance. In Washington, such help was justified in terms of "rewarding" Gomulka for his show of autonomy from Moscow. Already by 1957, the U.S. extended $95 million in credits to Poland (Rozmarek had asked for $125 million) in the hope that such assistance would encourage Gomulka to adopt a still more independent policy toward the USSR.

Between 1957 and 1964, the United States pumped $588 million in various forms of credits, loans and aid to Poland. But Gomulka disappointed those who believed the U.S. aid pipeline would turn him into a second Tito, or independent communist leader. To the contrary, the Polish party boss gradually established himself as Moscow's most reliable junior partner. One analyst of U.S. policies to Poland during these years concluded that the aid program had no noticeable impact upon Polish communist relations with either Washington or Moscow.[22]

Before 1956, it had been the Polish American Congress which had taken the lead in formulating proposals about the way in which the United States should view the communist regime in Warsaw. Rozmarek had aggressively backed the notion of national liberation, stridently condemning every aspect of communist rule in Poland while identifying Polonia with the democratic *emigre* groups operating in America. But things changed after the return of Gomulka. It was now Washington which took the initiative in developing an appropriate conceptual framework through which the United States might establish working relations with Warsaw. By the middle and late 1960s, U.S. officials were talking in terms of "building bridges" with Eastern Europe, "peaceful engagement" with the governments and peoples of the area, and "detente." In these changing conditions, Rozmarek's alliance with the ageing *emigre* leadership in the United States appeared increasingly irrelevant and his organization's antagonistic stance toward the Polish regime singularly unproductive.

In sum, however, Rozmarek's failure to influence U.S. policy toward Poland had less to do with the moral soundness of Polonia's evaluation of communist rule in Poland than with his unrealistic belief that it was in the national interest of the United Sttes to overthrow the regimes imposed in Eastern Europe by the Soviet Union after the War. The crowning touch of this failure came in 1956. When the Poles of Poznan rose up in frustration against their Stalinist masters, it was a competing communist faction which replaced them in power, not the democratic exiles in the West.

On the domestic front, the Polish American Congress' grudging realization that military liberation was out of the question permitted Rozmarek to establish closer ties with politicians who better represented "mainstream" thinking on the priorities of United States foreign policy. Not only did he repair his ties with the moderate wing of the Republican party, an achievement symbolized by the appearance of President Eisenhower at the 1960 Polish American Congress convention, he also built up relations with Democratic leaders in Congress.[23] After 1957, Rozmarek identified himself with Senator John Kennedy of Massachusetts, one of the most ambitious cold war Democrats. Kennedy became a strong proponent of economic assistance and "most favored nation" trade status for Poland and aggressively courted the Polish American vote in his successful bid to gain the 1960 presidential nomination. In the November elections, his enormous popularity in Polonia paid off handsomely. Though Kennedy defeated his Republican opponent Vice President Richard Nixon by only 120,000 votes out of 70 million that were cast, he carried the Polish vote by a 78-22 margin, winning 164 out of 214 electoral votes from the ten states with the heaviest concentrations of Polish Americans *en route* to a 303-219 victory. In comparison, in 1956 Eisenhower had won more than 50 percent of the Polish vote and carried all of the most heavily Polish states.

Throughout the 1950s, Rozmarek was a highly visible public figure on the Polish issue. His activities were reported not only in the PNA newspapers but throughout the still extensive Polonia press. Many of his speeches and appearances received coverage in such English language newspapers as the conservative *Chicago Tribune;* the *Chicago Sun-Times* where a supporter, Roman Pucinski worked; and the Wilkes-Barre, Pennsylvania *Times-Leader,* whose editor, John McSweeney, was a close friend. The Polish American Congress' monthly newsletter, published in both English and Polish, was also widely distributed. One 1954 article in this publication described Rozmarek's activities on behalf of the PAC in the following fashion:

> Over the past two years Rozmarek delivered addresses about the Polish American Congress and on topics concerning Poland on one hundred and twelve occasions in fifty-two cities of the United States. He spoke over radio stations thirteen times in various cities, four times on TV programs, and on Radio Free Europe to Poland seven times.

The article went on to praise him as "a man of boundless energy and intellectual capacity who was the finest kind of public relations man" for Polonia.[24]

A PNA publication filled with press clippings of Rozmarek's speeches between 1955 and 1958 further illustrates the character of his activities. During the period covered in that book, Rozmarek was reported to have made more than eighty speeches throughout the country. In addition, the publication included scores of his letters to newspaper editors along with dozens of photographs showing him in the company of President Eisenhower, Secretary of State John Foster Dulles, Senator John Kennedy and other national officials.[25] Also impressive was the size of the audiences which heard the PAC president, especially at the annual Third of May rallies in Chicago where crowds of more than one hundred thousand were usually on hand.

Rozmarek's activism as head of the Polish American Congress was made possible by the simple fact that he simultaneously served as president of the Polish National Alliance. It was the Alliance that underwrote the costs of his many trips on behalf of the PAC, which usually coincided with his visits to PNA councils and lodges. Rozmarek's fusion of his responsibilities as fraternal leader and ethnic political representative helped the Polish American Congress remain a force in American political affairs years after Poland's political fate had seemingly been decided. In contrast to John Smulski's National Department, which disintegrated within a few years after Poland's rebirth in 1918 largely because of growing PNA disinterest in its proposed program, Rozmarek forged solid and lasting ties between the PAC and PNA and thus guaranteed the persistence of the Congress as an ethnic lobby.

Just as Rozmarek's attentions as PAC leader were focused largely upon the Polish situation rather than upon American Polonia concerns, so also were PNA activities during his long administration geared heavily toward encouraging the new immigrants into the Alliance.[26] During the 1950s this strategy yielded some spectacular benefits and membership rose to the highest level in its history. In 1955, a record number of insured individuals belonged to the fraternal. The Alliance's net worth increased more than four times between 1939 to 1967, from $29 million to $133 million. The total amount of insurance coverage sold by the PNA during Rozmarek's tenure had also increased, though not as spectacularly. In 1939, total coverage provided by the PNA to its members amounted to $134 million. Twenty-eight years later, it had risen to $302 million.

Though such figures were impressive, some in the Alliance were convinced that Rozmarek had paid insufficient attention to the changing needs of the American-born descendants of the pre-World War I Polish immigration, whose fathers and mothers had built the PNA and who now constituted the great majority in Polonia. They noted that, under Rozmarek, there had been a gradual decline in the number of insurance policy holders under the age of sixteen. In 1935, the PNA had included 73,000 "juveniles" who made up twenty-seven percent of the total membership. By the 1960s, juveniles constituted only twenty-one percent of those in an organization which had itself begun to suffer noticeable losses in membership. Worrisome declines in overall membership, the number of insurance policies in force and the number of young members all pointed to problems for the future, and growing criticism of the president's stewardship.

In the field of educational activities, Rozmarek's tendency was to cut back upon the funding allotted for student loans and scholarships. And few initiatives were undertaken to develop the PNA's college. Between 1930-1939, the decade immediately prior to Rozmarek's election (and interestingly, the years of the Great Depression), the PNA's average annual expenditure for educational activities amounted to $124,000. Between 1940-1955, average yearly spending in this area dropped to $84,000.[27] Lack of interest and imagination are words that best typify the administration's policies in education during these years. Indeed, it was not until 1963 that the traditional $100 interest free student loan program for PNA members established in the 1920s was increased to $200 to at last reflect changes in the cost of living.

By the early 1950s there was evidence of growing opposition to Rozmarek's leadership within the PNA from various quarters. One critic was none other than Censor Blair Gunther, who had succeeded Swietlik in 1947 as Rozmarek's man. An issue between the two focused upon the power to appoint the editor-in-chief of the two PNA newspapers. Gunther claimed this right but Rozmarek argued that he, as president of the board of directors of Alliance Printers and Publishers (a separate corporation wholly controlled by the PNA) was empowered to make the appointment. The argument was eventually settled in court in Rozmarek's favor though Gunther was recognized as having the power to appoint the editor of *Zgoda* with the consent of the board of directors. This the Censor refused to do and Karol Piatkiewicz carried out the functions of running both papers throughout the remaining years of the Rozmarek presidency.

Another opponent was Adam Tomaszkiewicz, who was elected PNA treasurer in 1955 and served one four year term in office. The son of "Honest Mike" Tomaszkiewicz, who had held the same office from 1939 until his retirement in 1955, Adam was the one candidate elected against Rozmarek's slate; during his tenure as treasurer he was a lone but vocal opponent of the president and the rest of the board. Joining with Gunther, who found himself similarly isolated as the head of the minority faction in the supervisory council, Tomaszkiewicz sharply attacked the manner in which the organization was being administered.

For his part, Rozmarek worked aggressively to remove Gunther as Censor even before the next regularly scheduled convention of the Alliance in September, 1959. Throughout the first half of 1958, his backers publicly demanded that Gunther, as the presiding officer of the supervisory council, call this body into session. Their plan was to introduce a resolution charging that he had been derelict in his duties and requiring that he resign immediately from his office. But Gunther stubbornly refused to convene the council; instead he and Tomaszkiewicz called an extraordinary convention for December, 1958 to review the financial condition of the Alliance under the Rozmarek regime. Notwithstanding the president's objections, the by-laws of the PNA provided the censor with the power to call such extraordinary conclaves and twice before special conventions had been held. In 1884, Frank Gryglaszewski had convened the delegates from the preceding *sejm* to establish a workable insurance program under the auspices of the national leadership. In 1900, Leon Sadowski had called a special convention to revise the membership statutes of the Alliance. As a result, women were granted full equality with men to own insurance, vote and hold elective office.

But previous extraordinary conventions had not been held in opposition to the president and the board of directors. Indeed, Rozmarek and his allies aggressively opposed Gunther's action in every way available.

In September, 1958 Rozmarek convened a joint meeting of the board and the supervisory council, which Gunther and Tomaszkiewicz boycotted. Here, Rozmarek's opposition to the idea of the extraordinary convention was approved unanimously and the president's policies were given an enthusiastic vote of confidence. Charging not only that such a convention was "illegal" (since it had not been approved by the supervisory council), Rozmarek's allies also condemned Gunther and Tomaszkiewicz for wasting PNA money by calling a convention less than a year before the next regularly scheduled conclave.

In November, the president's faction on the council went a step further and called a special meeting without the censor's authorization, ostensibly to remove him from office *in absentia* and thus make academic the issue of the special convention. The meeting was scheduled to be held in Cambridge Springs, Pennsylvania. But Gunther immediately filed an injunction in the Crawford County Court House in nearby Meadville, Pennsylvania which prohibited the Council from formally meeting.

Stymied in his efforts to rid himself of Gunther by means of the supervisory council, Rozmarek next focused upon the task of preventing the special convention from taking place at all. All prospective delegates were sent a telegram from the president notifying them that they should not expect reimbursement for travel and lodging expenses if they did attend the meeting, which was set for December 6, 1958 at Chicago's Holy Trinity school hall. Gunther's appeal for the extraordinary convention was characterized over and over in the PNA newspapers as illegal, unnecessary, and financially wasteful. Several special issues of *Zgoda* were published in the weeks immediately before the convention to propagandize this view; one also printed Rozmarek's telegram to the delegates for all to read.[28]

The campaign to prevent the special convention succeeded when the dissidents were unable to muster the *quorum* of delegates from the 1955 conclave which was needed to conduct business. According to a controversial report of the proceedings which appeared in *Zgoda,* 212 delegates were in attendance, 56 fewer than was required. Listed as playing leading roles at the abortive meeting were Gunther, Tomaszkiewicz and his father, former National Secretary Albin Szczerbowski, Casimir Lotarski, John Ulatowski, Edward Plusdrak, Mitchell Odrobina, former Vice Censor Joseph Habuda, Medical Examiner Anthony Sadlek, Stanley Dybal, and Helen Dworczak.

Only nine months later, the regularly scheduled PNA convention was held in Hartford, Connecticut with Rozmarek's supporters in full control of the proceedings. His nominee for the office of censor was a New Jersey businessman and PAC leader, Edward Kozmor who handily bested Gunther in their contest. Tomaszkiewicz ran against Rozmarek for the presidency and he too was decisively defeated, 285-172. Gunther's proposal to henceforth limit all executive officers to two consecutive four year terms was soundly defeated at the convention. Moreover, Rozmarek pushed through a resolution declaring in *ex post facto* fashion that the 1958 effort to even call the extraordinary *sejm* had been "illegal." Furthermore, the PNA by-laws were revised to require a two-thirds vote of the supervisory council in support of a censor who called an extraordinary convention in the future. Nonetheless, those delegates who had heeded Gunther's call and travelled to the 1958 conclave received compensation to cover their expenses, in seeming contradiction to Rozmarek's claim that it had been "illegal."[29]

In 1963, Rozmarek faced another challenger, Aloysius Mazewski, a Chicago-born PNA activist who had been involved in its affairs since the early 1930s. An attorney who was also active in local Republican politics, Mazewski had served as a national director of the PNA between 1947 and 1955. Entering fairly late as a candidate for the presidency in 1963, he was as unsuccessful as Tomaszkiewicz in his first effort to unseat the incumbent. Nonetheless, Mazewski played a major role at the 1963 convention and succeeded in persuading a majority of the delegates to vote against several constitutional amendments which together would have given Rozmarek absolute control over the Alliance. (One proposal would have granted the president the right to appoint five of the ten members of the board instead of electing all ten at the convention; another designated the president the "supreme" leader of the PNA.) Furthermore, it was at the 1963 convention where Rozmarek's opponents won approval of a special independent investigative committee charged with looking into the various criticisms made about PNA investment practices under Rozmarek. Even some of the president's own supporters agreed with the plan, if only to clear the air. Chaired by Joseph Dancewicz and including fellow Directors Edward Moskal, Blanche Helkowski, Michael Holodnik, and Mitchell Odrobina, the committee was told to complete its task in time to report what it found at the 1967 convention.

Formally called into being at an extraordinary meeting of the PNA board of directors in March, 1965 as the "Real Estate Investigating Committee," Dancewicz's group focused its attention upon the procedures the Alliance used in making mortgage loans for apartment buildings. This was due to allegations of "irregularities and costly errors in the operations and management or mismanagement of the mortgage department." One irregularity among many discovered by the committee showed a mortgage for a building and land when in fact only a vacant lot existed. Originally, a building had stood on the lot but because of the owner's failure to correct numerous safety violations in the structure, the city had finally torn it down. Though the PNA had repeatedly been notified about the violations, it had taken no action in time to protect its investment.

Another committee finding revealed that the Alliance had made fifteen different mortgage loans to one individual with practically no financial assets. Four years after receiving his first PNA loan, the individual already owed the city $73,000 in unpaid property taxes. Several of the buildings purchased by this customer were later sold with no repayment of the loans originally made by the PNA.

Another individual was found to have received 83 mortgage loans amounting to $7.7 million from the PNA between 1962–1964, 18 of which were found to be delinquent. In nine cases, the properties were appraised to be worth a total of $983,000, of which $975,500 had been lent out by the PNA. This meant that the borrower had invested only $7,500 of his own funds in purchasing the buildings. Worse still, a subsequent appraisal of seven buildings purchased through loans available from the PNA showed them to be worth $492,500, though the same properties had been initially appraised for $1,059,500. These actions enabled the purchaser to apply for mortgages amounting to $667,500, a sum substantially higher than their fair market value. The Real Estate Investigating Committee also found that the owners of many properties with PNA mortgages were delinquent in paying their taxes and in meeting their obligations to maintain the properties.

The committee's investigation demonstrated an intensive effort by its members to deal with a serious problem facing the fraternal. A total of 286 PNA-mortgaged properties (a large fraction of the real estate portion of the Alliance's investment portfolio) were examined and as a result, the committee made seventeen recommendations to the 1967 convention to reform the PNA's loan and appraisal policies. These recommendations were later approved by the delegates. A separate statement written by Walter Andrzejewski, a real estate broker and PNA activist who assisted the committee and took over as the director of the PNA Mortgage Loan department in 1966, was more explicit in discussing the problem.

In summarizing the work of the committee Andrzejewski concluded that

> This investigation revealed that of the last $10 million of mortgages made by the Polish National Alliance since 1961, about 94 percent were made to Land Trusts, through Henry Banach, Jr., and of these, approximately 90 percent of the mortgage notes were not signed by applicants for loans, the alleged owners or purchasers of properties. Therefore, there is no personal responsibility to guarantee repayment of these loans. The excuse given by (the previous manager of the Real Estate Loan department) made to the Real Estate Investigating Committee during its hearings, that the PNA would lose most of its mortgage business if it were mandatory to sign a mortgage note by every person applying for a loan—does not make sense.

Contrasting the business practices of savings and loan associations with those of the PNA, Andrzejewski called the Alliance "system of making mortgage loans unbelievably slip-shod" and proposed that henceforth all loans be subjected to outside audits. Still, Andrzejewski assured the delegates that in every case where ordinary PNA members had received residential mortgage loans in which they had been required to sign repayment guarantees, none were in jeopardy of default. Presumably, such loans made up the great majority of mortgages held by the Alliance.[30]

Though the Committee's expose, presented at the convention by Director Edward Moskal, set off shock waves around the hall, the report might have been buried or perhaps never delivered at all had the Mazewski faction not already won a slight majority of the delegates in attendance. Indeed, the very first vote taken at the convention largely determined what was to follow when Mazewski's candidate for permanent chairman, Judge Edward Plusdrak of Chicago, narrowly defeated Rozmarek's choice, U.S. Congressman Roman Pucinski, 206-202. Plusdrak's election meant that the Mazewski faction would decide the convention's agenda and that its positions on controversial points of order would be upheld. Most significant was the chairman's decision to schedule the Real Estate Investigating Committee's report prior to the interpellation and election of officers. Mazewski's eventual victory over Rozmarek thus proved to be somewhat anti-climactic, with the challenger winning by a 221-189 margin.

Mazewski's victory was itself the product of years of campaigning and fund raising throughout the country. In his efforts to undermine Rozmarek's strength, he developed a variety of issues which included the incumbent's relatively advanced age (he was seventy at the time of the convention compared to Mazewski who was then fifty-one), the decline in insured membership during the previous decade, and the President's alleged insensitivity to the concerns of the new generation of PNA members. From 1965 onward, Mazewski's views were published in his own bulletin, *Wiadomosci* (The News), which was distributed to all past delegates and local PNA leaders around the country. *Wiadomosci* was essential since the opposition was not permitted to air its views in either of the Alliance papers. Edited under the direction of Joseph Gajda and Jan Krawiec, *Wiadomosci* also released many of the Real Estate Committee's findings several months before the 1967 convention.

Mazewski worked hard to build a large and diverse coalition of supporters from PNA units throughout the country. Among his backers were past Director Bonaventure Migala, John Radzyminski, Vice President Frank Prochot, Treasurer John Ulatowski, former Secretary Joseph Foszcz, Peter Kaczmarek, Director Mitchell Odrobina, and Commissioner Gladys Podkomorska, among many others. Mazewski's cause was further helped along when two veteran Rozmarek allies, Vice President Frances Dymek and Stanley Swierczynski (formerly the manager of Alliance Printers and Publishers and for many years the President's "campaign manager") broke with him and went over to the opposition.

In Rozmarek's "farewell address" to the convention the day after his defeat, he publicly acknowledged the end of a long and momentous era in PNA history. Rather bitterly he declared:

> If I were to tell you that I leave office without regrets this would not be true. But it is in the nature of people deeply dedicated to their work to seek to complete the tasks to which they have devoted their lives. I was and I remain sincerely and deeply committed to work on behalf of the Polish National Alliance

and its aims. In my heart there will always remain a bit of sadness for those trusted collaborators with whom I worked during the past 28 years in the service of the Polish National Alliance, Polonia and for the beloved land of our forefathers, Poland.

I never saw Poland, but I fought for the cause of a free Poland. Never did I and never will I waver in this struggle.

I leave office with a feeling that I have done my best to fulfill my duties. I gave everything I could for our organization and for our ten-million strong Polish American community. The struggle for a Poland truly free and independent will remain for me the most important order. Let us love Poland, the land of our fathers. Let us love America, the land of our children!

Rozmarek still remained president of the Polish American Congress until its quadrennial convention, which was set for the Summer of 1968. At this meeting, however, he stepped aside to enable Mazewski to assume the titular leadership of Polonia, as president of both the PNA and PAC. When the Congress celebrated its own twenty-fifth anniversary in Washington, D.C. a year later Rozmarek chose not to attend. In 1973, he passed away at the age of 76.

Any assessment of Charles Rozmarek's long and extraordinary public career must first take into account the many talents he brought to the leadership of the PNA and the PAC. A well-educated professional person, Rozmarek possessed great dynamism coupled with a pugnacious, combative approach to his responsibilities. All these features, along with his ability to speak effectively in both Polish and English gave him enormous self confidence. Only forty-two years old when he first won the presidency of the Polish National Alliance, Rozmarek had another advantage which enabled him to be an effective Polonia leader. One of the earliest Polonia activists to be born in the United States, he faced few rivals in the PNA who possessed similar personal attributes and as deep a commitment to fraternal politics. Indeed, only Francis Swietlik, his early mentor whom he eventually superceded as Polonia's top leader, seems to have been willing to devote himself heavily to ethnic affairs. Yet Swietlik never fully "made the plunge" into ethnic politics. Rather, he preferred to devote his primary professional attentions to his duties as a university law school dean and the quasi-judicial responsibilities of censor of the Polish National Alliance rather than to engage whole-heartedly in the rough and tumble infighting of PNA politics. Ultimately the difference between Swietlik and Rozmarek rested on this basic reality. Involvement in Polonia represented an important avocation for Swietlik, who was deeply interested in public service. To Rozmarek, Polonia political combat was at the core of his life.

As president of the Polish American Congress, Rozmarek has been subjected to some criticism because he failed to extract an explicit U.S. commitment to postwar Polish independence from President Roosevelt before the 1944 election. It is possible that a more experienced ethnic leader might have responded differently to FDR's vague assurances over the Polish issue, and a public rejection of Roosevelt just prior to the election could have decisively changed the outcome. Nonetheless, these considerations obscure the more serious problem Rozmarek faced in satisfactorily representing Polonia's concerns. Put bluntly, FDR was not the reincarnation of Woodrow Wilson in his orientation toward Poland. Though sympathetic to its plight, his primary wartime objective was to maintain a spirit of Soviet-American cooperation so that together they and Britain could crush the Axis alliance. Equally important was Roosevelt's aim of building a stable post war world order based on the principle of Soviet-American understanding. Events soon demonstrated that these objectives were unrealistic, given the tenor and purposes of Stalin's regime. In short order the two great powers found themselves engaged in a tension-filled cold war rivalry which has characterized relations between the United States and the Soviet Union for most of the period up to the present day. Thus, it is one thing to recognize that Rozmarek's view of the Soviet Union was more accurate than FDR's and quite another to expect him to have succeeded in changing the president's view about the principles of American foreign policy, something clearly beyond his capability.

A more telling criticism of Rozmarek's leadership must focus upon his continued commitment to the dream of liberation long after it ceased to find widespread acceptance as a practical instrument of U.S. foreign policy toward communist-controlled Eastern Europe. The rhetoric of liberation long remained popular among politicians, but no American administration chose to define the country's national interests in the region in terms of this idea. Indeed, liberation was a principle which would have represented the existence of a state of war between the United States and the Soviet Union, and thus risked a nuclear confrontation over a region beyond traditional American interests. Less dramatic but also significant, such a policy would have greatly impeded the ability of American Poles to provide continuing help to their relatives still living in the country.

By identifying the Polish American Congress with the liberation strategy, Rozmarek was unable to maneuver effectively in initiating new proposals for U.S. consideration and was less able to put pressure upon Washington to address itself to Polonia's concerns. Not surprisingly, by the mid 1960s PAC activity had reached a historic low point.

Furthermore, while the liberation idea won favor for Rozmarek with the relatively small but active post World War II political emigration in the United States, it failed to address the concerns of the American-born in Polonia. Making up the largest segment of the Polish American community, the American-born were deeply hostile to the Warsaw regime but equally concerned about the cultural survival of the ethnic community in a rapidly changing American society. But Rozmarek had little to say about this question other than to emphasize respect for the Polish heritage, exemplified in Polonia's observance of the "Millenium" in 1966. Thus, in one sense, Mazewski's triumph over Rozmarek represented a replay of the post World War I victory of the *wychodztwo dla wychodztwa* faction in the PNA, which sought to rededicate the Alliance to putting Polonia's domestic house in order after years of neglect.

However, Mazewski's tasks were all the greater than those of his predecessors. On the one hand, there was the erosion in ethnic life caused by the inevitable process of assimilation, which had gone on for a generation and which complicated the new administration's efforts to reinvigorate the PNA and the PAC. On the other, there was the impact of Rozmarek's leadership itself in stifling political competition inside the PNA. Indeed, perhaps Rozmarek's last legacy was the political machine he had fashioned, which perpetuated his near absolute command over the Alliance long after he had completed his contribution to American Polonia.

Chapter 7

THE MAZEWSKI YEARS—INTO A NEW ERA

Since September 1967, Aloysius A. Mazewski, a Chicagoan born in 1916, has served as the president of the Polish National Alliance. Trained as an attorney, he is one of the increasingly numerous "second generation" activists in the Alliance (his father was a lodge leader). During World War II, Mazewski compiled an impressive record as an Army administrator and left military service in 1946 with the rank of major. In the years that followed he coupled a successful law practice and an interest in local Republican party politics with a heavy involvement in PNA affairs. In 1947 he was elected a member of its board of directors, a post he held until 1955. Gravitating to the anti-Rozmarek faction in the Alliance, Mazewski was defeated for a third term on the board in 1955. In 1959, he supported Adam Tomaszkiewicz's unsuccessful bid for the presidency and in 1963 lost his own campaign for its highest office. Mazewski's victory over Rozmarek in 1967 thus represented the culmination of twenty years of nearly continuous involvement at the center of PNA politics.

Three factors helped to explain Mazewski's victory. For one thing, many PNA activists were ready for change after 28 years of Rozmarek rule and the 70 year old President was clearly vulnerable to his 51 year old challenger in this respect. Second, Mazewski focused concern about the future prospects of the Alliance in calling attention to the increasingly evident decline in its membership and by his criticisms of Rozmarek's controversial investment policies. Third, Mazewski and Rozmarek offered sharp contrasts in their styles of leadership that benefitted the challenger. Due perhaps to his many years of contact with national and international leaders as de facto head of American Polonia, Charles Rozmarek exuded a kind of imperial approach to his office and his public speaking style was replete with the already obsolete ideological rhetoric of cold war anti-communism. Though PNA members overwhelmingly accepted his views on Poland and communism, many in

187

the fraternal nonetheless had tired of his doctrinaire and aloof approach. Mazewski, in contrast, possessed a warm and friendly personality and his victory gave both the PNA and the Polish American Congress an opportunity to initiate a long needed process of renewal and review of their programs.[1]

Within the PNA, Mazewski's administration began the modernization of the fraternal's insurance program to enhance its operation in an increasingly competitive field. As a result, by the early 1980s the PNA was in an excellent position to present an array of insurance offerings to a new generation of Polish Americans, thus guaranteeing the fraternal a solid future. Equally significant was the work to restructure the PNA's investment portfolio. Changes in this area strengthened the financial foundations of the Alliance and made possible its considerable growth during the turbulent 1970s.

The formation of a new PNA leadership team was, however, only initiated at the Detroit convention since several top PNA leaders who had served under Rozmarek were reelected, including Vice President Frank Prochot, Secretary Adolph Pachucki and Censor Walter Dworakowski. Nonetheless, the first Mazewski administration (1967–1971), composed as it was of a mixture of veterans and new faces, achieved some early successes on the road to renewal. From the start, for example, Mazewski established a working majority on the all-important five member executive committee on the board of directors. This body, which includes the president, the two vice presidents, the national secretary and the treasurer, is responsible for the daily direction of the PNA and meets regularly several times each week in Chicago. (The remaining ten directors reside in various parts of the country and are called together at approximately three month intervals.)

Several other immediate changes were evident insofar as appointive positions were concerned. Karol Piatkiewicz retired after thirty-six years of service as editor-in-chief of *Zgoda* and *Dziennik Zwiazkowy* at the end of 1967. With his departure, the position of editor-in-chief was abolished and the papers placed under separate direction. Joseph Wiewiora, a veteran journalist who had worked for several Chicago Polonia dailies, was appointed editor of the bi-weekly *Zgoda* by Censor Dworakowski. He was charged with the task of transforming the Alliance's official organ into a truly bi-lingual and national publication reporting activities in the Polish American Congress, Polonia, as well as the PNA. Wiewiora was largely successful in making *Zgoda* a more important means of communicating news of ethnic and cultural significance to its readers, many of whom possessed no other source of information about Polonia due to the closings of a number of Polish language dailies in every major American city aside from Chicago and New York.

Taking over the editorship of Chicago's *Dziennik Zwiazkowy* was Jan Krawiec, a post World War II *emigre* who previously had edited *Wiadomosci,* the campaign publication of the Mazewski forces. Under Krawiec, the focus of the "Daily Zgoda" shifted to reporting local and world events entirely in the Polish language. This was in recognition of the fact that the paper could no longer compete with the metropolitan Chicago English dailies so long as its primary appeal was to English-speaking members of Polonia. After the *Dziennik Chicagoski,* operated by the Resurrectionist order, failed in 1970 the *Dziennik Zwiazkowy* became Chicago's one remaining Polish daily. Joseph Gajda, another Mazewski man, was named manager of Alliance Printers and Publishers. He was later elected vice president of the Polish National Alliance following the death of the popular Frank Prochot in 1974.

Appointed to the post of chief organizer, a title later changed to chief sales representative, was Joseph Foszcz, who had previously served a term as national secretary. Foszcz retired from this post in 1976 and was followed by the twenty-five year old Frank Spula. Toward the end of Mazewski's first term, a new position was created, that of director of fraternal activities, to support the work of the sales representative and to establish closer ties between the PNA central office and its lodges. Under Anthony Piwowarczyk, a long-time south side Chicago activist whose father had served on the national board of directors, efforts were made to build up lodge participation in local recreational and cultural activities and to stimulate their appeal to Polish Americans at the grass roots level. The tasks of the director of fraternal activities also involved a close association with the vice president, whose chief responsibilities deal with youth and sports activities.

Another office created in 1972 was that of director of public relations, a post filled by Edward Dziewulski. This position was established to develop new methods to communicate to Polish Americans about the work of the PNA, something the declining Polonia press could no longer accomplish alone. One major accomplishment of the director of public relations was to promote a better understanding of the PNA's mission and that of the PAC among representatives of the Chicago area print and electronics media. A symbol of this achievement since 1975 has become the annual December "Wigilja" luncheon hosted by the Alliance for media officials. Through this impressive event, attended by approximately two hundred executives, reporters and news commentators from the city's newspapers, television and radio stations, PNA leaders gained the opportunity to develop better relations with individuals whose understanding of Polonia was essential if they were to report accurately on the community and its organizations. One outcome of such contacts was the extensive coverage given President Mazewski's views and activities following the election of Pope John Paul II in 1978 and the rise of the Solidarity labor movement in 1980, along with Polonia's political and humanitarian efforts on behalf of Poland. Without such media attention to PNA activities large numbers of Polish Americans would have remained uninformed about organized Polonia's responses to such developments.[2]

On assuming the reins of leadership, Mazewski and his colleagues were confronted with several problems. One of the most serious was that of fraternal membership, which had been headed in a downward direction under Rozmarek. Historically, the membership picture in the Polish National Alliance had seen the organization experience four strikingly distinct phases of activity. From 1880 to 1900, the Alliance had grown very gradually as a men's only movement to the point where it possessed approximately 15,000 members at the turn of the century. From 1900 up to 1930, growth took off in an almost exponential fashion; with the approach of its golden anniversary the PNA included more than 286,000 men, women and children making it nearly nineteen times larger than it had been thirty years earlier. During this period, not only did the PNA grow in terms of total membership and active local lodges, it remained a "young" movement whose adult members averaged less than forty years of age, a figure not taking into account the juveniles who entered the movement in ever increasing numbers after World War I.

From the 1930s until the mid 1950s, membership in the Alliance entered a third distinctive phase, in which the PNA was able to maintain and even slightly increase its size despite the loss of thousands of members who were forced to withdraw because of the Depression. The Alliance even added a new crop of policyholders after World War II from among the thousands of displaced persons who chose to settle in the United States, instead of remaining in Western Europe or returning to live in Communist-dominated Poland.

But in the years that followed, the Alliance entered a fourth phase of its history in which it experienced a gradual decline in membership, a disturbing trend with which Rozmarek seemed unable to deal.[3] In retrospect, the causes of this decline seem fairly clear. They involved the assimilation and advancement of the Polish ethnic population in American society, processes which greatly increased the difficulty of enrolling new members into the Polish National Alliance and other ethnic fraternals as well.

Without going into any extended discussion of the meaning of assimilation in terms of the Polish ethnic experience during the past century, any observer of Polish Americans who happen to be the grandchildren and great grandchildren of immigrants ("the third and fourth generation" to live in America) cannot ignore its impact upon Polonia. Assimilation, whether described in the light of the growing incidence of intermarriage between Poles and non-Poles, in terms of name changing, loss of mastery of the Polish language, or resettlement out of traditionally Polish ethnic neighborhoods, deeply eroded the vitality of Polonia following the Second World War. One noted expert on the subject has distinguished between "behavioral assimilation" (the absorption of cultural behavioral patterns of the host society by members of the ethnic group) and "structural assimilation" (the entrance of the immigrants and their descendants into the social organizations, institutional activities and general civic life of the receiving society).[4] For most Polish Americans, particularly those of the "third" and "fourth generation," it should be noted that *both* structural *and* behavioral assimilation have taken place. As a result, by the 1960s increasingly large numbers of Polish Americans were becoming divorced from the organizations which continued to operate in Polonia and traditionally had served their needs. Sometimes, assimilation has been incorrectly understood as a form of "amnesia" which made Polish Americans forget their heritage. In reality, a far more accurate characterization would stress that for many, ethnic heritage has become irrelevant in their daily lives. This was so even as they retained a sentimental attachment to the customs practiced by their parents and grandparents, continued to enjoy Polish foods in their homes, spoke Polish with members of their families and took part occasionally in secular and religious ethnic activities.

For the PNA, the problem of assimilation appeared at a particularly inauspicious time. Historically, the fraternal's greatest growth had occurred during the 1920s and it was during the 1950s and 1960s that large numbers of individuals who had purchased insurance after World War I began leaving the scene, requiring the PNA to step up its recruitment efforts if only to maintain existing membership levels. Yet this effort was complicated by the massive post 1945 departure of thousands of Polish Americans from the central cities where they had traditionally resided into new outlying neighborhoods or the suburbs where they were hard to reach. In moving away, the new generation left behind the religious and secular institutions which had traditionally dominated Polonia; but in their new environs Polish Americans established few ethnic parishes or fraternal lodges to help in preserving their cultural heritage. Fraternals, which had been important community centers in the old Polonia neighborhoods, gradually declined in number and activity with the ageing of their memberships coupled with their inability to recruit younger people to fill their depleted ranks. Moreover, the post World War II immigration that did enter the fraternals tended to organize into its own lodges rather than to join already existing local units.

With so many of its lodges located in older and poorer urban areas and headed either by cohorts of ageing officers or members of the new emigration, the PNA's attractiveness among younger native-born Polonians could only diminish during the 1950s. While ethnic consciousness certainly did not die out during this period, involvement in ethnic activities definitely waned among the younger generation. This trend was to some extent hidden, however, because large numbers of older people living in the central cities continued to attend various Polonia manifestations.

For Polish Americans, assimilation was accelerated by other factors, including the attractiveness of various aspects of American society to the immigrants and their offspring, the support consequently given to Americanization by many Polonia organizations including the PNA, and the low level of awareness on the part of most Polish ethnics about their cultural heritage. Many contemporary American sociological critics of this country's attitudes toward East European immigrants before World War I have focused deserved attention upon the hostility, fear and condescension with which native Americans greeted them.[5] But such efforts to throw light upon a neglected and sorry chapter of American social history should not blind one to the equally relevant reality of ethnic enthusiasm for life in the new country, the "land of Washington." To hundreds of thousands of Polish immigrants, America was indeed a country of enormous opportunity, even if these opportunities were in the coal mines, steel mills and stockyards. While they endured difficult economic and housing conditions in America, those who remained here did so well aware that these conditions were "better" than what they had left behind in Poland.

Indeed, Polish Americans were enthusiastic about many aspects of American life including its democratic political system and the opportunity to participate openly in behalf of the Polish patriotic cause without fear of government repression. The "benign neglect" of American authorities toward the immigrant communities most certainly had harmful consequences upon those individuals who lost life and limb in work because government safety precautions were nonexistent or unenforced. Neither can the lack of government concern in assuring proper housing and sanitation for the newcomers be excused. At the same time, official indifference permitted Poles to readily establish uncensored newspapers which told their readers what they needed to know about events in America and their homeland. In America, no government authorities prevented the building of Polish churches and schools, nor the teaching of traditional values in their own language. "Laissez faire" economics also provided an opportunity for ambitious people to make their fortunes in their adopted homeland with little fear of official restriction.

To its credit, the PNA recognized the immigrants' attraction to American society from the start. Following Agaton Giller's injunction to create a Polonia organization aimed at "helping our people attain a good standard of life" so they might simultaneously become good Americans and better serve the patriotic cause, the Polish National Alliance committed itself to aiding immigrants in mastering the English language and attaining U.S. citizenship.

Yet a third factor speeding the assimilation process was the immigrants' relatively low level of national consciousness about Poland's history and culture. This was due to the lack of educational opportunities available to them in the homeland, coupled with the near absence of information about Poland in the American school system. Not only was the subject of Poland ignored, so also was the cultural life of the Polish ethnic community in America. Given this failure on the part of public and private schools alike, it is not surprising that large numbers of Polish Americans remained uninformed about their ethnic heritage, literature and history and increasingly unable to maintain their national language in the United States. Until the 1978 election of a Polish Pope and the economic and political crisis in Poland which brought the Solidarity labor movement into existence in 1980, very little about Poland or the Polish Americans was known in this country. Given this state of affairs, there was little the PNA alone could do to reverse the trend toward assimilation.

For the PNA after 1945, even the growth that did occur came to pose new problems as time passed. Under Rozmarek, the Alliance did enroll thousands of new immigrants, but a large number of the new recruits purchased "twenty year" insurance plans instead of signing up for programs in which they continued to pay premiums throughout their lives or at least until they reached the age of sixty-five. In one sense, their decision had adverse consequences. Once they had completed or "paid up" their twenty year policies, the holders of such certificates could no longer be counted as active PNA members unless they extended their insurance coverage or purchased a new policy. As inactive members, they were ineligible to receive the PNA newspaper, *Zgoda,* nor could they attend lodge meetings or hold any elective office. By the early 1980s approximately one-third of all PNA members had passed into this limbo state simply because of a decision they had made to buy a particular type of insurance plan. As a result, the Alliance lost a sizeable number of individuals as active fraternal members who otherwise might have considerably enlivened the movement.[6]

Despite the difficulties presented by assimilation, there were things that the Mazewski administration could and did accomplish to increase the PNA's attractiveness to potential members. One practical strategy was to develop a number of new and innovative PNA insurance programs to better meet the increasingly diverse interests of its audience. Originally, the Alliance had offered a single insurance plan to all of its members. A policy holder paid monthly premiums to the Alliance throughout his life; upon his death, his family received a lump sum amount ranging from 300 to 900 dollars which was usually more than enough to cover funeral expenses. Later, such "ordinary whole life" policies accumulated interest or dividends which enhanced their value as long term investments that the policy holder could borrow from when he was in need. By the post World War I era, policy purchasers could choose between two basic plans, the second of which was fully "paid up" when one was sixty-five years old. For children there was another plan, in which an individual was enrolled as a "juvenile" member prior to age sixteen. This policy could later be readily converted into a regular membership. The twenty year payment program was established in the 1930s.

Under Mazewski, the PNA introduced a number of new insurance plans to improve the competitive position of the PNA in its search for new members. A "term insurance" plan was also set up offering prospective members the chance to buy a larger amount of personal protection at relatively low cost, though this plan had no cumulative dollar value as a long term savings program. The PNA supplemented its programs with plans providing insurance to entire families, accident insurance, home owners insurance, annuities, endowments and disability benefits. Though it did not enter into the hospital insurance field, the PNA contracted with the Valley Forge National Liberty Insurance Company in 1973 to offer its members "group coverage" at low cost through this firm.

Several innovative plans aimed at children were put into effect as well. One program, the "Single Premium Payment Plan," enabled parents with children under fifteen to provide them with as much as $6,000 in term insurance at the cost of a single $160 premium payment. At age twenty-one the holder of this type of plan was automatically eligible to own a $12,000 whole life policy which would be paid up at sixty five. The annual cost of such a plan amounted to $160 and did not require the policy holder to pass a medical examination.

A second plan for youngsters was the "Juvenile Estate Builder" which enabled parents to purchase up to $10,000 of insurance coverage for their offspring. At age twenty-one the face value of such a policy could be increased to five times its original size with no increase in premiums and, once again, no need for the policy holder to demonstrate medical insurability.

Yet a third plan available to parents was the "Orphans Fraternal Benefit," which was established in 1972. According to this plan, the PNA agreed to provide a monthly benefit in addition to its insurance obligation to children whose parents had both died. Besides this, the PNA also promised up to $7,200 in college educational assistance to such orphans. Its sole condition was that all family members possessed whole life insurance with the PNA.

In addition, the Alliance established a special one payment insurance plan providing coverage for up to four years ("The PNA Centennial Special Program") and has worked energetically and successfully to retain "paid up" members as active participants by offering to extend their insurance coverage at low rates. During the first six months of 1982 alone, a campaign aimed at 80,000 insured members led more than 3,000 persons to extend their coverage.

These successes came largely from direct mail solicitations originating out of the PNA home office in Chicago, another innovation developed under Mazewski. Perhaps the most interesting solicitation so far devised by the central office was set to begin in late 1982. From a list of 125,000 people with Polish sounding surnames living in Michigan, Illinois, Indiana, Ohio and Wisconsin and compiled from census data, the PNA sought to reach out to an entirely new audience with which it was previously not in contact.

The expanding role of the central office in recruitment work was connected with the computerization of insurance operations that occurred during the 1970s. The modernization of its activities was nowhere better symbolized than by the transfer of the Chicago office in 1976 from its location on 1514-1520 North Ashland Avenue to a new and spacious home on 6100 North Cicero Avenue. This move away from the historic "Polish downtown" of Chicago's near northside was a prudent one given the area's gradual loss of ethnic character and its socio-economic decline. The new headquarters was singularly attractive and its location in the newer but still heavily Polish northwest section of Chicago demonstrated the PNA's continuing commitment to progress. In the new building are found not only the fraternal's business offices but also the headquarters of Alliance Printers and Publishers and the historically significant PNA library. In addition, hundreds of artistic artifacts, maps, sculptures, and portraits reflecting the history of Poland, Polonia and the PNA adorn the building along with scores of photographs which depict the organization's involvement in civic affairs on all levels of government.

The declining activity of many local lodges, which in the past had served as mainstays of fraternal life, remained a factor accounting for difficulties the PNA faced in attracting new members. Traditionally, the lodges had performed two important functions within the Alliance; one was that of providing erstwhile future leaders with a training ground in which to hold elective office and participate in fraternal affairs, the second was to serve as the primary agency for the recruitment of new members.

In the early decades of its existence, lodges had sprung up almost as rapidly as mushrooms after a rain storm and were as good an indicator of the vitality of the organization as were membership figures. In 1900, there were 451 lodges; ten years later a grand total of 1,106. In 1920, 1,678 local PNA units were in operation. Lodge expansion peaked in the mid 1930s at approximately 1,900 groups; in 1940 the PNA could count 1,827 member units. During the next four decades, however, the trend was contrary. Many lodges merged together or went out of existence because of significant declines in membership, an inability to recruit new blood, changes in the complexion of Polish neighborhoods, the ageing of their founding members or simply because too many competing PNA lodges had been formed in the same neighborhood. In 1950, 1,699 lodges were reported; by 1960 this figure had dropped to 1,516. In 1970, 1,357 local groups were in operation compared to 1,175 ten years later.[7]

Worse, among the lodges which remained, many were in reality inactive. While Rozmarek had given attention to the positive side of PNA lodge life by focusing upon those units which remained active, Mazewski candidly addressed himself to the larger problem. At successive national conventions he drew the delegates' attention to the fact that many lodges had failed to enroll even one new insured member during the four years since the previous convention.[8] Between 1975 and 1977 Mazewski also directed the PNA to make its first systematic effort to examine the actual problems facing many of its lodge units by organizing a detailed evaluation of the grass roots organizations. The analysis was named "Project Scan and Renovate."

This project was conducted primarily by means of on-site visits of PNA national officers to lodges located in their districts. More than 750 lodge units were eventually visited and a mass of useful information was accumulated about their condition, along with suggestions about ways of improving relations with the Chicago home office. On the positive side of the ledger, the project compiled data showing what many local units of the Alliance were doing and how they were contributing to meeting the needs of their members and communities. Eighty-one percent of the surveyed lodges reported that they held annual elections of local officers with sixty-one percent celebrating the installation of new officers by hosting some type of social event. Thirty-nine percent of the lodges conducted an activity of social or fraternal character for their members, the most popular of which were dances, parties and banquets. Common fraternal activities focused on sports, with dance classes and lodge participation in local civic projects trailing behind. Ninety lodges possessed a youth program of some type while an even one hundred units participated in sports activities, the most popular of which were bowling and golf. Nearly one-third of the groups reported that they were involved in community affairs in some way.

Interestingly, the PNA review found that the most commonly practiced lodge fraternal services still revolved around assisting families with ill or deceased members. Originally, the Alliance had been formed to perform just such duties, including visiting ill or hospitalized members, collecting money for the families of departed colleagues and serving as pall-bearers at funerals. A century after its creation, these activities were still being widely practiced even though American society itself had significantly changed over the years in nearly all other respects.

According to the survey, satisfaction with the Chicago home office (as measured by the favorable opinion of lodge leaders toward *Zgoda,* the official PNA publication and their general belief that communication between the lodges and the central administration was smooth and effective) was positive. Moreover, given the fact that the average age of lodge officers and secretaries was about fifty-seven years, the PNA appeared to possess a sizeable *cadre* of local salespeople and organizers capable of recruiting new members.

Project Scan and Renovate also documented a number of problems facing the lodges. Most significant was the seeming inability of lodge officers to encourage active participation by younger people in their units. Only eight percent of the survey respondents, for example, could identify any ways in which they might bring more young members into their activities and only nineteen percent considered younger members to be willing to hold office. One obstacle to participation by the younger American-born generation seemed to be associated with the use of the Polish language in lodge meetings. According to the survey, sixty-seven percent of the respondents reported that their units conducted meetings either in Polish or interchangeably in both languages, this in spite of the fact that eighty-five percent of the local secretaries corresponded with the Chicago office in English. The heavy use of Polish thus appeared to be a deterrent to participation for those lodge members who were unfamiliar with the ancestral tongue. Whether Polish will continue to be as heavily used in the future remains to be seen, however.[9]

Several questions about lodge life were, unfortunately, not covered in the survey and thus somewhat limited its value as a mirror reflecting the actual condition of the fraternal at its grass roots. For example, it was not determined how many members actually attended lodge meetings on a regular basis and what proportion of the total membership was composed of active participants. It would also have been interesting to learn whether or not active members were representative of the total lodge in terms of age, education, country of birth, or job status. More information about the regular activities taking place at lodge meetings would also have been of use; to what degree, for example, do lodges engage in community wide affairs and how often do they cooperate with other Polonia organizations, including the Polish American Congress? Are lodge members deeply interested in Poland or do civic and fraternal doings engage them? More information about these and other matters might have helped the PNA home office develop a variety of models for lodge members to consider adopting to spur their own activities. Unfortunately, the project appears to have been conducted solely for the benefit of the Chicago home office so that it might gain a more accurate perspective on the condition of its local units. It does not appear that plans existed to utilize the data collected in Project Scan and Renovate in a systematic fashion to upgrade lodge activities.

The interrelated problems connected with membership and the condition of lodge life remain the most serious problems facing the PNA as it entered its second century of operation. The roots of both problems are complex and go far back in time. To its credit, the current administration has begun to candidly address itself to both matters and to recognize their implications. It has sought to enhance the appeal of its insurance offerings and to better advertise its product. Beginning with the 1977 lodge survey, the PNA also initiated the process of identifying the needs of its grass roots organization for the first time. Yet much still needs to be done. More attention must be directed to studying those fraternals with which the PNA has contacts through the National Fraternal Congress whose local lodge units remain active and effective in serving both the fraternal and social needs of their members. Why are some lodge systems more successful than others and what might the PNA learn from the experiences of other organizations?

Second, local lodge leaders need to be provided with a more acute appreciation of their significant role in maintaining the general health of the national organization. Greater emphasis needs to be placed upon more effective publicizing of the insurance offerings of the Alliance, together with the fraternal benefits members can derive by joining the PNA. It is unlikely that many members have any clear awareness at all of the student loan and home mortgage loan benefits offered by the PNA or that possibilities do exist to set up youth and sports activities with funds originating out of the Chicago home office to help achieve their aims. The PNA might also be advised to establish a network of regional offices in Polonia centers outside of Chicago to better promote its activities.[10]

Under Mazewski, concern for lodge life and efforts to enhance PNA offerings have been supplemented by a program of professionalizing the promotion and sales of insurance. In 1979, he told delegates at the PNA convention in Washington of several activities in this area. For one thing, the central office had already published twenty-five different pamphlets and brochures advertising PNA insurance in an attractive and easily readable style. For another, the PNA had begun to hold regular training seminars for its sales force to better acquaint them with its various insurance offerings, new sales techniques and developments in insurance regulations affecting their work. These activities have continued to expand: in the first five months of 1982 alone, for example, the home office sponsored five seminars. During this period, an average of ten programs in different sections of the country were being held each month. In August, 1982 a special seminar held at the Alliance College was scheduled to which 250 sales persons were invited.

During Mazewski's tenure the number of local PNA insurance salespersons has generally been larger than was the case under his predecessor. In 1967, Rozmarek reported that the Alliance possessed 832 organizers, practically all of whom were lodge financial secretaries engaged in insurance sales on a part-time basis. In the years that followed, the number of organizers rose as high as 870 and in 1980 included 840 people, most of whom had been recruited during Mazewski's administration. Of these, twenty were "full-time" salespersons. Among the most successful of these individuals have been Richard Smoger of Detroit and Genia Gunther of Pittsburgh. Each has regularly sold more than a million dollars in PNA insurance for nearly every year during the past decade. In addition to Smoger and Gunther, several other PNA sales representatives have enjoyed notable success, among them John Ramza, Jan Chudy, Victoria Pietkiewicz, Thaddeus Radosz, Michael Pierzga, Bogdan Parafinczuk, Joseph Zdunczyk, John Radzyminski, Henry Puchalski, Thomas Wyszynski, Josephine May, August Gorski, and Frank Mazurek. Each sold at least one million dollars of insurance during one or more of the four-year periods between PNA conventions held between 1963 and 1983.

From the late 1960s, the number of active salespersons also rose. In 1967, for example, 106 organizers were made honorary members of the Alliance's "One Hundred Thousand Dollar Club," signifying that they had sold at least that much insurance during the previous four years. Under Mazewski, the "club's" membership has risen to as many as 146 sales representatives. Another sign of the central administration's increasing interest in promoting salesmanship is the PNA "President's Club," created in 1980. Membership in this select group extends to those sales representatives who enrolled at least twenty-five new policy holders during the preceding year. In its first year, the "club" recognized seventy-five sales representatives for their successful efforts in bringing new members into the PNA. In 1981 the group included sixty-five persons, and in 1982 it numbered sixty-six individuals. All told, forty-three outstanding sales representatives have been included in the "President's Club" in all three years.[11]

Yet another constructive move came in 1977 when the commissions earned by sales representatives were raised substantially. These and other initiatives taken during the past decade all helped the PNA continue to attract large numbers of newly insured members, as can be seen from the following table:

Table 1.   Number of Applications for PNA Insurance, Volume of Insurance Purchased and Average Amount of Insurance, 1972–1982

Year	Number of Applications	Insurance Purchased	Average Coverage
1972	8,836	$19,932,927	$2,256
1973	7,988	19,696,478	2,466
1974	8,051	21,152,345	2,627
1975	7,405	20,533,011	2,773
1976	7,810	21,346,173	2,733
1977	8,295	27,643,591	3,333
1978	6,760	23,317,581	3,449
1979	5,829	21,117,144	3,623
1980	7,208	23,231,758	3,223
1981	9,031	30,131,064	3,336
1982	8,754	31,933,880	3,648
Eleven Year *Totals*	85,967	$260,035,952	$3,025

Still before the Alliance remains the task of establishing field representatives to strengthen the sales activities of local organizers in each of the sixteen PNA supervisory districts around the country. The responsibilities of such individuals would involve promoting and advertising the PNA's product, a serious shortcoming at the present time, and stimulating salesmanship in the lodges and councils. In 1971, Mazewski had reported that three such representatives were active, but progress in the meantime has been slow. This seems due to indecision as to the relative merits of professionalizing sales efforts as opposed to placing continued reliance upon financial secretaries and district commissioners to carry out the work of recruitment. This dilemma is one the PNA shared with the other fraternals. On the one hand, a greater emphasis upon a network of professional sales persons might stimulate greater membership growth; on the other, it also discourages fraternal activities which have traditionally been directed by the lodges, councils and district commissioners.

Yet another area of activity dealt with Mazewski's handling of PNA investments. Up until the Depression years, nearly all Alliance assets had been invested in real estate mortgages in the Chicago area. With the economic crisis of the 1930s such investments had become an enormous burden to the PNA and by 1939 its total losses amounted to $6.8 million, no less than twenty-three percent of its net worth.

Led by Censor Swietlik and President Rozmarek, the PNA Board of Directors shifted investments away from real estate after 1939 and into stocks and bonds. This move combined a greater degree of liquidity with a smaller if more certain rate of return and helped the PNA resume its financial expansion. By 1959, the fraternal's net worth had reached $98.1 million, nearly three and one-half times what it had been twenty years before.

These gains seemed impressive, however, only so long as the value of the dollar was not seriously eroded by high inflation, since many PNA investments yielded very low dividends over extremely long time periods, sometimes as long as fifty to sixty years. Yet it was in the mid-1960s that the United States entered into just such a prolonged period of inflation, turning dividend yields of three and four percent on securities purchased in the 1950s into as much a burden as an asset. Moreover, Rozmarek's tendency to invest heavily in "interest free" municipal bonds did the fraternal no good since the Alliance, a "non-profit" association, paid no taxes itself.

Under Mazewski, low yielding bonds were systematically sold off with the proceeds placed immediately in Federal treasury bills bringing far higher rates of return. By 1971, more than $3.4 million in the low yield investments had been exchanged for securities returning thirty-four percent more in dividends. Between 1975 and 1979, $8.2 million in low return bonds were also sold off at a loss, and replaced with new investments yielding an average of 11.1 percent annually in dividends. Such actions enabled the PNA to quickly make up its losses and to exchange unattractive holdings for more productive investments. As a result of such decisions, the average rate of

Table 2.   Areas of PNA Investment, 1935–1982

	1935	1939	1943	1947	1951	1955	1959	1963	1967	1971	1975	1979	1982
Total Investments in Millions of Dollars	24.5	29.3	33.5	43.1	60.7	78.4	98.1	117.4	133.4	145.7	158.4	161.0	176.3
Percent Invested in Home Loans	84.1%	63.5%	6.7%	12.3%	26.7%	31.0%	23.7%	16.3%	12.8%	14.8%	14.2%	18.4%	24.0%
Percent Invested in Bonds, Stocks Government Securities	4.5	16.4	59.7	78.0	64.3	62.8	70.9	77.1	80.7	77.5	78.4	74.7	69.3
Other investments*	11.4	20.1	33.6	9.7	9.0	6.2	5.4	6.6	6.5	7.7	7.4	6.9	6.7

*"Other investments" have included real property of the Alliance such as the College and the Central Office, and funds invested in bank accounts. On December 31, 1982 the PNA reported that it held funds in surplus to meet any unforseen emergency that amounted to $17.1 million, or 9.7 percent of its assets. This compared very favorably to previous years and reinforced the fraternal's ranking as an efficiently managed organization. In comparison, the PNA reported a surplus of less than $8.4 million in 1965, or 6.7 percent of its assets of $125,400,000 at the time. Standard Analytical Service, Inc. *Certificateholders' Report on the Polish National Alliance of the United States of North America* (Chicago, 1983).

return on all PNA investments steadily rose during the 1970s, despite the fact that it was still saddled with more than $35 million in stocks and bonds yielding less than 3.5 percent annually. Taking all investments into account, however, the picture looked bright by 1980. Between 1967 and 1979, the Alliance could report that its average rate of earnings had increased by forty-six percent, from 3.97 percent in 1967 to 5.80 percent in 1979. During this period, the PNA's net worth rose by twenty-one percent even though the organization raised the dividends it paid all life insurance policy holders from 3.5 to six percent. In 1982, dividends were increased even further. In 1981, Mazewski could also report that the sum total of all PNA gains for the year amounted to $8.16 million, the highest in its history. At the same time, individuals continued to be able to borrow from their insurance deposits at the extremely favorable rate of five percent. (And at its 1983 convention it was reported that PNA investments were yielding an annual return of 7.24 percent, an increase of 25 percent compared to 1979. By this time the Alliance had also reduced its low-yield bond holdings to $14.8 million.)

Changes were also instituted to better protect the Alliance in its real estate investments. Though home mortgages no longer constituted the primary target of PNA investments, rigorous changes were instituted in the policies of the mortgage loan department following the 1967 convention to insure the security of the fraternal's investment in housing stock. For example, a $50,000 ceiling on all mortgage loans was put into effect with only PNA members eligible to apply.[12] For the first time, members living outside of the Chicago metropolitan area were permitted to enter into such loan agreements.

The real estate reforms thus provided more PNA members with greater opportunities to borrow at favorable interest rates and terms from the Alliance in order to become residential home owners. This valuable service was in the spirit of the organization's historic commitment to assisting its members in their upward socio-economic advancement in America. It also brought to an end the dangerous practice of awarding loans for speculative purposes on investment properties located in declining areas of Chicago, a practice that had subjected the PNA to unnecessary risk.

A notable development in recent years has been the trend on the part of new members to purchase increasingly larger insurance policies. Not only was this sensible in view of inflation's impact upon the real value of insurance plans offered by the PNA; the purchase of larger policies positively affected the position of the fraternal as well. It also demonstrated the success of Mazewski's efforts to upgrade and modernize the Alliance's insurance program. A glance at the average value of certificates held with the PNA during the period between 1939 and 1983 dramatizes this development.

Even these figures somewhat obscure the dramatic increases in the average size of new PNA policies purchased in recent years. Between 1963 and 1967, for example, new policies written over that four year period averaged

Table 3.   Average Amount of PNA Insurance Per Certificate

	1939–1983		
Year	Average Size of Policy	Rate of Increase over the Previous Period	Rate of Overall Increase
1939	$477.48	1.00	1.00
1947	$636.21	1.33	1.33
1955	$744.11	1.17	1.56
1963	$806.63	1.08	1.69
1971	$983.23	1.22	2.06
1979	$1292.47	1.32	2.70
1983	$1482.80	1.15	3.10

about $1,529. During those years a total of $59,476,571 worth of insurance was written. Between 1979 and 1982, $106,413,846 in insurance was written and the average amount of every new policy in the PNA equalled $3,453, an increase of 126 percent over the earlier four year period. Indeed, in 1982, a record $31,933,880 in insurance was sold to 8,754 applicants, for an average of $3,647 per policy.[13]

These figures demonstrated the PNA's dynamism in the insurance field. Over the past two decades the PNA continued to be the most successful insurance association appealing primarily to Polish Americans; for most of this period it consistently sold more insurance than all other Polish fraternals combined. Ranked as the eighth largest fraternal in the United States in terms of its net worth, and the eleventh largest in terms of the insurance "in force" on behalf of its members, the PNA was also the largest ethnically based fraternal in America.[14] Still lacking, however, was sufficient popular awareness both within and outside the PNA of these realities, plus the fact that the Alliance provided an insurance product which could compete favorably in terms of quality, diversity and security with those offered by the heavily advertised commercial carriers.

Confidence, a certain dynamism and a commitment to adapt to changing conditions facing Polonia have been easily recognized characteristics of the

Polish National Alliance during the Mazewski administration. Mazewski himself, an energetic individual who enjoys travelling about the country meeting PNA lodge, council and district representatives to establish direct personal contacts with the membership, has become the very personification of the Polish National Alliance. At the same time, he has become Polonia's chief spokesman in Washington by virtue of his presidency of the Polish American Congress since 1968. Mazewski has worked effectively to present Polonia's concerns to every American president from Lyndon Johnson to Ronald Reagan and has frequently appeared in Congress to press home the interests of the ethnic community on a variety of issues.

The "Mazewski era" has meant innovation and adaptation to changing conditions facing Polonia in other respects as well. In 1974, the annual Third of May parade and observances held since 1904 in Chicago's near north side Polonia were moved to a new location in view of the old neighborhood's decline as a center of Polish ethnic life. Since then this great manifestation of patriotic sentiment has been held in Chicago's downtown "loop" area, the center of the city's cultural, commercial and political activity. There it has been revived as an event for all, Poles and non-Poles alike, and not simply an observance primarily for the old north side Polonia (which in fact was but one of the windy city's three historic Polish American enclaves).[15] In addition, the Kosciuszko monument was itself moved in 1978 from Humboldt Park to Grant Park on Chicago's magnificent lakefront. Today, the monument, replete with a new and informative inscription provided by the PNA, is to be found near the Adler Planetarium, one of the city's most popular attractions.

The move of the PNA home office away from the declining district where the fraternal had been based since the 1880s was yet another response to the need for change, as was the revitalization of *Zgoda* and *Dziennik Zwiazkowy.* Youth and sports activities also began to receive more attention from Mazewski and his colleagues, many of whom had taken part in the *Harcerstwo* movement prior to World War II. In 1970 they organized the first quadrennial youth jamboree on the Alliance College campus. The first three-day event brought together more than 1,100 young people from around the country for an ethnic festival celebrating their heritage; it was followed by similar events in 1974, 1978 and 1982.

In sum then, as the PNA looked forward to its thirty-ninth national convention in Orlando, Florida in September, 1983, its members could be confident that the fraternal was moving effectively along the road to renewal in the face of changing conditions. Under Mazewski and his fellow officers the Alliance had already strengthened its financial foundations while moving resolutely toward preserving its traditional commitment to both fraternalism and its historic Polish character. A favorite Mazewski phrase, that the PNA's past but the prologue to an even brighter future, appeared especially accurate as the Alliance moved into its second century of activity on behalf of Poland and Polonia.[16]

Partitioned Poland at the founding of the Polish National Alliance in 1880.

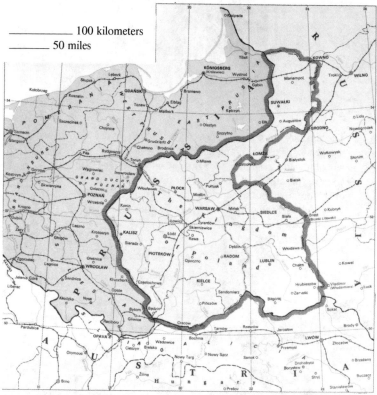

Source: A. Gieysztor, *et. al., A History of Poland,* second edition (Warsaw, 1979).

The historic PNA emblem represents the aspirations of a restored and independent Poland (symbolized by a crowned eagle) united again with Lithuania (signified by a knight on horse) and Ruthenia or Ukraine (the archangel Michael). The three peoples had all been part of the pre-partition kingdom in the eighteenth century. The shield was used practically from the birth of the Alliance.

The new PNA home office located at 6100 North Cicero Avenue in Chicago. The building was dedicated on June 4, 1977.

The founders of the Polish National Alliance, as depicted in this painting by Michael Rekucki, from left to right are: John Blachowski (standing), Julian Lipinski, John Popielinski, Julius Andrzejkowicz and Julius Szajnert. Agaton Giller's image is in the Polish sky above.

Teofila Samolinska   Henry Kalussowski   Erasmus Jerzmanowski

The offices of the PNA and *Zgoda* in Chicago, 1889. Fifth from the left is President Stanislas Kociemski, and to his left stand Secretary Ignace Morgenstern, Censor Frank Gryglaszewski and *Zgoda* Editor (and later PNA President) Zbigniew Brodowski. The others are employees of the printery.

Early Leaders of the Polish National Alliance

Val Przybyszewski

Rev. Casimir Sztuczko

Max Kucera

Theodore Helinski

Anthony Schreiber

The "Central Government" of the Polish National Alliance (1894). Seated at the lower left is John Smulski, then a director. Behind him is *Zgoda* Editor Frank Jablonski, who was later a president of the PNA. President S. F. Adalia Satalecki is in the center.

The monument to Tadeusz Kosciuszko in Lafayette Park across from the White House, a gift of the Polish National Alliance on behalf of Polonia to the American people (1910).

Members of the PNA's Michael Wolodyjowski society of Chicago in military regalia, about 1910. This lodge, like many others of the time, was much influenced by Henryk Sienkiewicz's romantic and patriotic epic novels about seventeenth–century Poland's wars with Sweden, Russia, and the Turks and named itself after one of his fictional heroes.

John Smulski

RECEPTION

GIVEN BY

PRESIDENT THEODORE ROOSEVELT

AT

THE WHITE HOUSE

THURSDAY AFTERNOON, SEPTEMBER 26, 1907

AT 2:30 O'CLOCK

TO

THE DELEGATES TO THE BIENNIAL CONVENTION

OF

THE POLISH NATIONAL ALLIANCE

OF THE UNITED STATES OF AMERICA

HELD AT BALTIMORE, MARYLAND

ADMIT THE BEARER

Pass admitting PNA convention delegate to a White House meeting with President Theodore Roosevelt.

President William Howard Taft speaking at the dedication of the Alliance school in Cambridge Springs, Pennsylvania, October 26, 1912.

The PNA board of directors following the historic 1913 convention. In the front row are Director Mary Sakowska, Vice President Stanislas Mermel, President Casimir Zychlinski, Secretary John Zawilinski, Treasurer Joseph Magdziarz and Director Casimira Obarska. Among those in the second row are Directors Leon Mallek (left) and Nikodem Zlotnicki (fourth from left).

PNA cooperation with the Polish Falcons' Alliance in organizing a Polish Army in America in World War I; an officer's training course at the Alliance school (1914).

Polish Army recruiters (1918). Second from right is Josephine Rzewska.

Ignacy Jan Paderewski at the first commencement ceremonies of the Alliance school, June 1916. To his right is Marian Steczynski, business manager of the school and president of the PNA from 1903 to 1912. To his left is Madame Paderewska and Romuald Piatkowski, the school's first rector. Roman Abczynski, chairman of the school board, carries the American flag. The short, balding man at right is John Przyprawa, later editor-in-chief of the Alliance publications. Others in the photo include the faculty of the school.

Paderewski awards medals to PNA leaders in recognition of their service on behalf of Polish independence at a 1921 ceremony. Pictured at the left is President Zychlinski. Receiving his medal from Paderewski is Julian Szajnert, one of the founders of the Alliance, established forty-one years earlier.

The central PNA library and reading room in Chicago, 1940.

Thomas Siemiradzki

Valerie Lipczynska

Stefan Mierzwa

PNA *Harcerstwo* leaders with officers of the Alliance (1933). Fifth from the left in the front row sits President John Romaszkiewicz, "the father of the *Harcerstwo*." To his left: Director Michael Tomaszkiewicz, Henry Lokanski and *Harcerstwo* Director Stanislas Kolodziejczyk.

August 1936 *Harcerstwo* leadership course at Alliance College. More than 170 Polish Americans took part in this program along with 21 visitors from the movement in Poland.

Censor Francis Swietlik, President Romaszkiewicz, *Harcerstwo* Director Kolodziejczyk and local Polonia activist Roman Kwasniewski at a Milwaukee Scouting jamboree, 1935.

Harcerki (girl scouts) in camp, Wisconsin, 1938.

The PNA board of directors about 1937. Presiding in the high-backed chair is President John Romaszkiewicz. Clockwise about the table are Assistant Secretary Michael Kostecki, Karol Piatkiewicz, editor-in-chief of Alliance publications, Directors Berniece Zawilinska, Angela Wojcik, Matt Majchrowicz, Frank Glowa, Frank Synowiec, Al Sobota, Treasurer Joseph Spiker, Vice Presidents Frances Dymek and Chester Hibner, and Counsel Leopold Koscinski. In the center is Secretary Albin Szczerbowski. Only the Chicago directors are present at this meeting, which was held each month. Directors from other parts of the country were called together every three months. This practice was ended in 1968; since then, meetings of the board of directors have been held on a quarterly basis.

The first permanent PNA home office located at 1404 West Division Street, Chicago, was dedicated on November 26, 1896.

The second PNA home office at 1520 West Division Street, dedicated on May 8, 1938.

Judge Edmund Jarecki speaks at Chicago's Humboldt Park in a Polish Constitution Day observance in the late 1920s.

Marchers representing PNA lodge "Gmina Polska 2" make their way to Humboldt Park for the "Third of May" ceremonies in a photograph taken in the early 1940s.

General Joseph Haller visits PNA home office, 1940.

Polish Prime Minister Wladyslaw Sikorski and Censor Francis Swietlik meet in Chicago (1941).

Casimir Sypniewski

October 11, 1944: President Franklin D. Roosevelt meets with leaders of the Polish American Congress. The map shows the prewar Polish boundaries, which Roosevelt and Stalin had secretly altered at their meeting in Teheran in November 1943. Among those shown are U.S. Congressman John Dingell of Michigan and Thaddeus Adesko (from the left), Frank Dziob (sixth from left), PRCUA President John Olejniczak, and from the right PNA/PAC President Charles Rozmarek, Polish Women's Alliance President Honorata Wolowska and Polish Falcons' Alliance President Teofil Starzynski.

World War II relief efforts in high gear. Charles Rozmarek and Albin Szczerbowski stand atop and inspect a shipment.

The first Polish refugees arrive in Chicago and are welcomed by PNA leaders (1948). To the left stands Bonaventure Migala, later a national director. Next to him is President Rozmarek, Vice President Frances Dymek and Mrs. Wanda Rozmarek.

Part II

THE PUBLICATIONS OF THE POLISH NATIONAL ALLIANCE

On October 3, 1981 nearly one thousand friends of the Polish National Alliance gathered for a banquet to celebrate the one hundredth anniversary of the founding of its official publication, *Zgoda*. In a true sense this event brought to a close the observances throughout the country connected with the centennial anniversary of the PNA's founding. These had been initiated at the Alliance's 38th national Convention in Washington, D.C. in August, 1979, peaking in Chicago with a grand banquet held on September 20, 1980 at Przybylo's White Eagle Restaurant. There, the President of the United States, Jimmy Carter, had honored the fraternal by delivering an eloquent speech to a massive audience of nearly three thousand Alliance and Polonia leaders.

The hundredth anniversary of the founding of *Zgoda,* the oldest Polish and Polish American newspaper published continuously anywhere also commemorated a remarkable and historic event. From its inception at the second PNA Convention in New York City on September 24, 1881, the Alliance's "organ" or official publication was intimately connected with the fraternal's efforts to mobilize and lead the Poles in America. Throughout its existence, *Zgoda* has also reflected the life of Polonia's largest organization and, indirectly, the development of Polonia. And, with a bi-weekly circulation of 94,000 copies in 1983, it has become the largest Polonian publication in America, informing perhaps as many as four hundred thousand persons about events taking place within the Polish American community, the Polish American Congress, Poland and the Alliance in both the English as well as the Polish languages.

Zgoda's early importance in promoting patriotic feeling and popular awareness of the PNA mission can also be appreciated by reviewing the names of the paper's editors, individuals who were Polonia leaders in their own right. For example, *Zgoda's* very first editor, Edward Odrowaz, also

209

served as the PNA's first national secretary in 1880. The paper's third editor, Zbigniew Brodowski and its fifth head, Frank Jablonski, were each later elected presidents of the Alliance. Many of the individuals connected with *Zgoda* ranked among the leading intellectuals and political activists of Polonia. Both Ignace Wendzinski, the paper's second editor, and Thomas Siemiradzki, its seventh chief were formidable publicists in behalf of the PNA cause. Stefan Barszczewski, who succeeded Jablonski, wrote several plays and was also the author of the first official history of the Polish National Alliance in 1894. Stanislas Osada, an assistant editor of *Zgoda* published the second PNA history on the occasion of its silver anniversary in 1905 and became one of Polonia's most prolific writers.

During the World War I era, the editorship position was made appointive and thereafter the men in charge of *Zgoda* were for the most part professional journalists whose views generally conformed with those of the censor, to whom they were responsible, and the majority faction within the board of directors. Between 1913 and 1931, three men held the responsibilities of *Zgoda* editor, Stanislas Orpiszewski, a blacksmith by training and self-educated writer; John Przyprawa, perhaps the most polemical of the paper's editors and a strong defender of the "old guard" faction during the turbulent 1920s, and Stanislas Zaklikiewicz, Censor Casimir Sypniewski's choice to run the paper after the victory of the "opposition" faction following the stormy Chicago convention sessions of 1927–1928.

Editor-in-chief of both *Zgoda* and the *Dziennik Zwiazkowy* (the Chicago Polish daily the PNA established in 1908) between 1931 and 1967 was Karol Piatkiewicz, who was both a talented writer and an able historian. Upon his retirement, Piatkiewicz was succeeded as editor of *Zgoda* by Joseph Wiewiora, a veteran Chicago newsman who had previously worked for several dailies, including the PRCUA's *Dziennik Zjednoczenia.*

The idea of setting up its own newspaper originated with the creation of the Polish National Alliance in 1880. At their first convention the delegates approved a set of goals which included "the political direction of the Polish immigration as American citizens through the aid of the Alliance's own organ . . ." At the Alliance's second *sejm* held in New York a year later, delegate Stanislas Artwinski proposed that the PNA put this goal into effect. In Artwinski's words, such a publication was needed "to explain the purposes, objectives and pursuances of the organization and to defend its own interests against attacks by elements opposed to the Alliance."[1] Immediately after approving his resolution in principle, the delegates agreed to raise $2,000 to start up the paper. There and then, they pledged $694 to demonstrate their faith in the proposed project, a significant act since the Alliance's total assets at the time amounted to only $622.71. Because PNA membership then included only 346 men, it was also agreed to sell the new publication to non-members and to include in its pages news of general interest along with internal fraternal activities.[2] This decision established *Zgoda* from the start as an all-Polonia publication.

The convention's one disagreement over the paper revolved around its title. Censor Andrzejkowicz proposed *"Niepodleglosc"* (Independence) but Frank Gryglaszewski argued in favor of a different name, *"Zgoda"* (Harmony or Unity.) By a single vote, Gryglaszewski's proposal prevailed. Under its first editor, Odrowaz, who like Artwinski had worked for the *Ogniwo* weekly paper, the office of the newspaper was established in New York City at 16 Rivington Street. Odrowaz was himself a veteran of the 1863 Revolution who had knocked about in Europe before arriving in America in 1875. He was a prolific writer who had been a strong advocate of the PNA from the outset. Odrowaz was also a confirmed New Yorker who refused to continue to edit the paper after the delegates at the third PNA convention voted in 1882 to transfer its office to Chicago. "A man of mystery" in the words of Polonia historian Arthur Waldo, Odrowaz died in poverty in 1889. Since the copies of the first year of *Zgoda* have been lost, it is difficult to judge the quality of his work; however, Henry Nagiel, an early Polonia journalist wrote that Odrowaz "created a publication well edited in the patriotic spirit. From its first issue *Zgoda* played an important role among New York Poles, appealing to them to organize themselves and to advance everywhere . . . the awareness of national identity." Nagiel characterized Odrowaz's writing style as "clear, concise, objective and didactic."[3] An epigram Odrowaz used regularly on the first page of his paper conveys both his sense of style and patriotic zeal for the PNA cause: "There is more life in the grave of Poland than the emperors imagine."

Odrowaz's successor as editor was Ignace Wendzinski, another exile who had become involved in not one but two insurrections for independence. Active as a student in the conspiracy to overthrow German rule in the Grand Duchy of Poznan in 1848, Wendzinski also took part in the revolution against Russian rule in 1863 and had to flee the country after its defeat. By 1870 he was in America working as a parish school teacher. But Wendzinski also worked for several Polish newspapers, including *Orzel Bialy* (the White Eagle, published in Krakow, Missouri), *Gazeta Polska* (the Polish Gazette, Chicago), and *Przyjaciel Ludu* (the People's Friend, Chicago).

In fact, Wendzinski did not bring *Zgoda* to Chicago but rather to Milwaukee where he was then living. Under his editorship, *Zgoda* continuing its polemics with the clerical faction led by Barzynski. Though such conflicts stimulated the newspaper's circulation, a majority on the board of directors disliked the paper's editorial posture and sought to gain greater control over *Zgoda* by pushing the move to Chicago. In 1885, Zbigniew Brodowski was elected to replace Wendzinski. Curiously, because of uncertainty over the future location of the PNA central headquarters (in 1886 it was moved from Chicago to Bay City, Michigan for one year), no action was taken to establish *Zgoda* in the windy city until the matter was finally put to a vote of the delegates at the St. Paul convention in 1887. Of one hundred and twenty-two delegates, fifty-six supported a Chicago headquarters to thirty-one who backed Milwaukee, with the rest favoring other options or not voting. Thus it was that in January, 1888 *Zgoda* finally appeared as a Chicago-based publication.[4]

Brodowski, who was born in Poznanian Poland in 1852, arrived in America in 1876. Like Odrowaz and Wendzinski before him, he was not only well educated but had gained some journalistic experience working in New York. Brodowski later travelled to California where he worked in the construction of San Francisco's street car system. It was there that he met several of the most notable Poles of the day, including the actress Helena Modrzejewska (Modjeska), the novelist Henryk Sienkiewicz, and Civil War general Wlodzimierz Krzyzanowski. Moving to Chicago, he gained some notoriety in 1885 when he authored a widely publicized memorandum calling for Polish independence, a statement subsequently sent to Berlin and Vienna. That Fall, he was elected *Zgoda* editor, a post he held until 1889 when he refused to seek reelection after a dispute with Censor Gryglaszewski. Such was Brodowski's influence, however, that his choice for editor, Stanislas Nicki, defeated Gryglaszewski's nominee, Henry Nagiel, even though Nagiel was a professional journalist and Nicki had no previous experience qualifying him for the job.[5]

After serving four frustrating years trying to master the duties of editing the paper, Nicki stepped down from the job and was replaced by Frank Jablonski. (A life-long PNA activist, he later served for many years in the Alliance's Chicago business office, performing work for which he was better suited.) Under Jablonski, another professional journalist, the editorial quality of *Zgoda* was restored even as the paper maintained its steady assault upon its conservative critics headed by Barzynski. Thirty years old at the time of his election, Jablonski was something of a "boy wonder" in Polonia. Born in Prussian Poland, he later studied at the Louvain University in Belgium before coming to America in 1886. Working in Chicago as both a teacher and a newspaperman, Jablonski became deeply involved in the dispute over Holy Trinity parish, which had been closed since the later 1870s due to the opposition of Barzynski. Arguing for the "Trojcowanie," who were loyal to Rome but wished their parish to be independent of the Resurrectionist order, Jablonski quickly became a spokesman for the dissidents, many of whom were active in the PNA. In 1890 he headed a delegation that journeyed all the way to the Eternal City to appeal for the church's reopening. This effort proved ultimately successful; in June, 1893 the Vatican's Apostolic Delegate in Washington visited Chicago and formally made the Holy Cross religious order headquartered in South Bend, Indiana responsible for the church. Later the same year, the Reverend Casimir Sztuczko was named Holy Trinity's pastor, a post he would hold for fifty-six years. Always cognizant of the circumstances leading to his appointment, Sztuczko established cordial and lasting ties with the Polish National Alliance and became its unofficial chaplain.

Jablonski's achievement led in 1893 to his unanimous election as *Zgoda* editor, a post he held until 1897, when he was elected president of the PNA. After resigning from that office in 1901 and returning to full-time newspaper work in Milwaukee, Jablonski was elected in 1907 to once again edit *Zgoda.* This time, however, new responsibilities were added to those of putting out the PNA's weekly organ. At its 1907 convention in Baltimore, the delegates also approved a motion by Paul Kurdziel of Cleveland to create a PNA daily newspaper to operate in Chicago using the reserve funds of the weekly *Zgoda.* This newspaper, *Dziennik Zwiazkowy,* the "Alliance Daily," was also placed under Jablonski's direction. This decision was itself controversial and followed years of debate.

For over a decade there had been proposals for a daily PNA newspaper to provide Chicago's Polonia with information and opinion reflecting the editorial stance of the fraternal.[6] This had become an increasingly serious concern, since the other Polonia dailies in the city were not favorably disposed to the PNA. *Dziennik Chicagoski,* for example, was owned by the Resurrectionist order and *Dziennik Ludowy* was socialist in its leanings. In 1899, PNA members had actually committed funds to another daily, *Dziennik Narodowy,* in the expectation that it would promote Alliance editorial policies in Chicago. But growing differences between the owners of the paper and the fraternal ended this tie and led to renewed interest in the idea of a PNA-owned daily.[7] One particularly controversial problem arose out of the PNA's involvement in settling the accident claims on behalf of the victims of a catastrophic railroad disaster near Valparaiso, Indiana in October, 1906. In the accident, sixty Polish immigrants were killed and the Alliance took the responsibility of pressing the company to pay damages to their families. Although the railroad eventually paid over $2,000 in each case, critics of the settlement charged that PNA officers had received far more money and had pocketed the difference. These allegations were widely publicized by hostile newspapers, including its erstwhile ally, *Dziennik Narodowy.* The charges, like many others directed against the PNA during the era of Polonia "yellow journalism" proved to be baseless.[8]

In May, 1906, the board of directors approved Vice President Michael Rzeszotarski's motion to establish a PNA-owned daily, but final action was made contingent upon a favorable referendum vote by the membership. But in the referendum, the proposal was narrowly defeated. This led the newspaper's proponents to make a last ditch try to achieve their aim at the next Alliance *sejm,* which was scheduled to be held in September, 1907 in Baltimore.

At the convention, the supporters of the PNA daily included the presiding officers of the gathering who agreed to bring up the proposal for a vote before it was scheduled on the official agenda. With most of the opposition delegates unaware of this maneuver and still at lunch, the paper's supporters quickly approved the idea. Thus the *Dziennik Zwiazkowy* was born.[9] With Jablonski in charge, the paper's first issue appeared on January 15, 1908. But on February 23, 1908 Jablonski suddenly passed away at the age of 45, bringing to a premature end the still burgeoning career of one of Polonia's most highly regarded early leaders.[10]

Zgoda's sixth editor was Stefan Barszczewski, who ran the paper from 1897 to 1901. Like his predecessors, Barszczewski was young (twenty-seven years old), Polish born, well-educated and trained in journalism when he took over as editor. Only eighteen when first employed by the Catholic *Dziennik Chicagoski,* he had also run the Falcons' newspaper *Sokol* before he also assumed the responsibility of guiding *Zgoda.* Throughout his journalistic career in America, Barszczewski was one of the major publicists for the National Democratic cause within the two progressive Polonia movements.

In 1894 Barszczewski was commissioned to write the Alliance's first commemorative history on the occasion of the one hundredth anniversary of Kosciuszko's uprising. His work, spare in style but filled with zeal for the patriotic cause, suffered an unusual fate. Following its initial distribution, what few copies remained in the PNA home office were unaccountably lost for many years. Indeed, Osada refers only once in his 1905 PNA history to what he termed "a little brochure" but does not identify the book anywhere as a source he used himself. Piatkiewicz and Olszewski do not even mention the 1894 study in their histories. Only in the 1970s was a single badly damaged copy rediscovered and through the efforts of the PNA Educational Department and Dr. Edward Rozanski reprinted in 1980 as part of the centennial observances.

In 1901, Barszczewski declined a third two year term as editor and returned to Poland where he worked as a newsman for the rest of his life. Succeeding him was Thomas Siemiradzki, who served practically without interruption as editor of *Zgoda* until 1913. Born in Russian Poland and educated at the University of Saint Petersburg, Siemiradzki had entered the United States in 1896 and almost immediately became a major voice for the independence cause. At first engaged by the PNA to lecture throughout the country on Poland's history, Siemiradzki turned to writing and composed a series of popular studies that effectively presented the homeland's story to the immigrant community. Siemiradzki soon gained the nickname "professor," mainly in recognition of his erudite writing style although he was also in fact employed as a school teacher. Elected to edit *Zgoda* at the Toledo PNA convention in 1901, he was reelected in 1903 and 1905, but lost out to Jablonski at the 1907 convention at which the Alliance established its own daily.[11]

Siemiradzki's defeat was partly attributable to his decision to switch political allegiances from the nationalist pro-Dmowski wing of the PNA to Pilsudski's socialists. He made this shift because he strongly favored Pilsudski's commitment to taking direct action against tsarist Russia during the 1905 Revolution. Dmowski's National Democrats, in contrast, had opposed revolt and took a passive position during the crisis.

But despite his loss, Siemiradzki was soon back as editor of both Alliance newspapers following Jablonski's untimely death and he was reelected to this post in 1909 and 1911, although his influence in the PNA was waning. In November 1911, the board of directors voted to separate the responsibilities of editor of *Dziennik Zwiazkowy* from those of *Zgoda,* reserving to itself the power to select future heads of the Alliance daily. In 1913, Siemardzki decided not to seek reelection and ran instead for the office of censor. Following his defeat he was never again connected with either PNA newspaper, although he was appointed to the board of trustees of Alliance College in the late 1920s.

Although a devoted Pilsudski supporter, Siemiradzki hued to a deeply nationalistic commitment to Polish independence. As such, he became the leading exponent of the theory of Polonia as "the fourth partition of Poland." He argued that the three to four million immigrants and their children in America comprised a segment of the divided nation comparable to the rest of the Polish lands and distinguished only by their distance from the homeland. As members of this fourth partition, American Poles were responsible for mobilizing their economic, political, intellectual, and even military resources behind the independence cause. While many in Poland and Western Europe regarded Polonia primarily as a source of financial assistance, Siemiradzki argued that the ethnic community possessed resources sufficient even to establish an army to fight for freedom when the opportunity arose. Similarly, he championed the convocation of a world congress of Poles to publicly demand independence, an event that was held in Washington, D.C. in 1910. Siemiradzki also supported the establishment of a Polish college under PNA sponsorship and consistently argued that such a school should aspire to become nothing less than a new Jagiellonian university training Polonia's leadership.[12]

To succeed Siemiradzki, the delegates to the 1913 PNA Convention in Detroit unanimously elected Stanislas Dangel, a man who shared his political views. Dangel had fully expected that the board of directors would interpret his election as a mandate to choose him to edit the Alliance daily too, but here he was disappointed. Once he learned that the board had named Stanislas Orpiszewski, a loyal member of the nationalist faction, to the second post Dangel challenged its action before the supervisory council, the supreme judicial body of the PNA. When the council ruled against him, Dangel resigned from *Zgoda*. His departure, which was highly acrimonious, left the board free to appoint Orpiszewski to run both papers. Furthermore, in 1915 the delegates to the PNA Convention in Schenectedy, New York were persuaded to amend the by-laws and make the editorship of *Zgoda* appointive, rather than elective in character. The board justified the change by emphasizing the need to maintain a single editorial line for all PNA publications, one in harmony with the leadership.[13]

Though this reason for placing the editorships of the two papers under the authority of the board of directors made sense, the rise in factionalism within the PNA after World War I made the two papers the object of intense conflict. Until 1928, the papers continued to be edited by supporters of the nationalist or "old guard" faction, Orpiszewski (until 1921) and John Przyprawa (1921–1928). But in 1928, the "opposition" faction headed by Censor Sypniewski gained a dominant position on the board for the first time. As a result, Przyprawa was dismissed and replaced by a Sypniewski partisan, Stanislas Zaklikiewicz. But Francis Swietlik's victory over Sypniewski in 1931 led to a restoration of "old guard" control; consequently Zaklikiewicz was replaced by Karol Piatkiewicz who guided both PNA papers for the next 36 years, or until his retirement in December, 1967. Piatkiewicz's regime ushered in a long, second stage of history for the PNA press, one which witnessed the rise of the Alliance daily and the overshadowing of *Zgoda*.

From the time of its inception in 1908 onward, the Alliance daily seemed to have superceded the weekly *Zgoda* as a medium of mass communication within the vast Chicago Polonia. As a paper providing the burgeoning community with coverage of local and worldwide events, the "Polish Daily

Zgoda" (as it soon became known) found itself in hot competition with a number of other ethnic dailies as well as the many English language papers then in operation. During World War I, it met with great success and by 1918 it had become the most widely read Polish paper in the city. Indeed, in 1923 when the *Dziennik Zwiazkowy* took over its old rival, the *Dziennik Narodowy*, its circulation jumped to more than 54,000. Furthermore, under Piatkiewicz, who had served as city editor of the *Zwiazkowy* before becoming head of both PNA papers, the "Daily *Zgoda*" adopted a variety of innovative techniques to cover Chicago Polonia in ways that recognized the interests of both its Polish-born and the American-born readers.

Under Piatkiewicz, the newspaper focused heavy attention on the activities of the many Polish parishes and Polonia districts around the city; he even hired district correspondents whose responsibility was to provide regular reports of news from these communities. In this set-up, the district correspondents became more important that the two or three persons Piatkiewicz employed to sift through the city's English language dailies for stories to be translated into Polish. The attention Piatkiewicz paid to local Polonia happenings helped build up the paper's circulation by promoting community events not regularly covered by the English language papers and thus established for it a secure place in the sun where it could thrive as an alternative newspaper.

Another factor accounting for the "Daily *Zgoda's* growth under Piatkiewicz involved the decision to establish sports and society pages in the English language under the direction of journalists such as Matt Majchrowicz, Joseph Kowal and Helen Moll. These sections reflected Piatkiewicz's recognition of the fact that the new generation of American-born Poles possessed reasons different from their parents for reading the Polish language press which could not be ignored without risking losses in circulation and advertising.[14] At the same time, however, Piatkiewicz's heavy involvement with the Alliance daily led him to give less attention to the PNA weekly. *Zgoda's* pages gradually filled with reprints of stories earlier appearing in the daily paper along with notices of an official business nature and news items about specific lodge, council and district activities which were of only limited interest to most readers. *Zgoda's* decline was made evident when it became a fortnightly instead of a weekly in 1947 and few readers bothered to complain about the loss. President Rozmarek's dominance over the paper also limited its role.

A third chapter in the story of *Zgoda* began after 1968 when the PNA supervisory council, acting upon recommendations earlier made by the new President, Aloysius Mazewski, established a special press committee to evaluate the newspaper and propose ways to improve its format. The council also entrusted the committee's chairman, Censor Walter Dworakowski and *Zgoda's* new editor, Joseph Wiewiora, with the task of determining how these improvements were to be implemented.

Two significant innovations were soon effected. One dealt with the use of English in the newspaper, the other with its editorial content. Prior to 1968, most of the paper was published in the Polish language with English language inserts made up mainly of articles reprinted from the *Dziennik Zwiazkowy*. The new format established English as the primary language used in the paper and relegated the use of Polish language material to its second section. (In 1983, a typical issue of *Zgoda* included 12-16 pages with the last 4-6 pages in Polish.) This move was favorably received; indeed, in the first two months after the change in language emphasis, the editor received three hundred letters from his readers but only one complained about the deemphasis of the Polish language.

A more significant policy change dealt with the paper's content. While recognizing the need to provide information and publicity about individual members, lodges, councils and district organizations in *Zgoda,* the supervisory council agreed that greater emphasis needed to be given to general news of interest to PNA members in their roles as participants in the Polish American community:

> Since the Polish National Alliance is an integral part of the ten million member American Polonia, therefore *Zgoda* should consider those news items and problems which are relevant to Polonia, its standing, purposes and attainments.[15]

In retrospect the two moves were significant to the future operation of *Zgoda* and were made in recognition of the great changes within Polonia that were becoming evident in the 1960s. With the gradual passing of the generation of immigrants who had come to America before the First World War, there was an acute need to refashion *Zgoda* and enhance its attractiveness to a new generation of PNA members, for whom the Polish language was at best a second language or one not known at all. Moreover, with the 1960s came the rapid decline of the Polish language press in America: where as many as nine Polish dailies had once operated, including two in Chicago, two in Milwaukee, and one each in Cleveland, Buffalo, Detroit, Boston and New York, only five remained in 1970 and two in 1982, the Chicago "Polish Daily *Zgoda*" and the New York *Nowy Dziennik*. Combined readership of these papers was no more than 75,000 compared to probably more than 500,000 in the years immediately following the Second World War.

Given these changes, Polish Americans wee increasingly starved for information about the issues confronting Polonia and Poland, and the activities and achievements of fellow Polonians in politics, the Church, business, the arts and the professions. By adapting its format and subject matter to these needs *Zgoda* regained relevance as a mass communications medium. Particularly important too, was the fact that *Zgoda* was not directly affected by declining circulation and increasing costs, since the paper was issued free of charge to all PNA policy holders above the age of sixteen.

Zgoda's evolution into a nationwide all-Polonia publication also made possible a redefinition of the aims of the Alliance daily. Where *Dziennik Zwiazkowy* had once focused attention upon the activities of parishes and community organizations in Chicago's Polonia, the paper increasingly began to serve a different set of needs. These were connected with providing the immigrants who had settled in the city after World War II with their own publication, one heavily emphasizing Polish language coverage of news at the local, national and international levels. Under its editor, Jan Krawiec, *Dziennik Zwiazkowy* thus continued to operate as an alternative medium of mass communications, as it had under Piatkiewicz. But while the paper once focused its attention upon the activities of the organized local Polonia community, its function has become one of preserving its readers' contact with the world through a newspaper published in their traditional language. Thus, after 1967 the Polish National Alliance succeeded in defining a specific role for each of its newspapers. With *Zgoda* directed increasingly to the interests of the American-born membership of the PNA throughout the country, *Dziennik Zwiazkowy* could establish itself as a publication for recent immigrants. More than any other Polonia organization, perhaps, the PNA kept faith with all its members, providing both the foreign-born and the American-born with a means of mass communication they could call their own.

The PNA leadership's commitment to *Zgoda* can also be appreciated by briefly reviewing its efforts to place its operation on a sound financial footing. As far back as 1882, the delegates to the third PNA convention authorized the creation of a private joint stock publishing company with a capital investment of $2,500. At their sixth convention in 1886, the delegates agreed to buy out the shareholders of the independent *Zgoda* company and in its place formed a "Corporation of the Polish National Alliance for Publication" sponsored by the PNA.

In 1934 this corporation was reorganized and renamed Alliance Printers and Publishers. Formed as a separate agency within the PNA and operating under Illinois regulations, this subsidiary was governed by the board of directors of the fraternal. Its chief administrator, or general manager, was appointed by and responsible to the board. Alliance Printers and Publishers was created for two purposes; to establish better supervision by the parent organization over its various publications and to limit the PNA's financial liability were the newspapers to experience significant operating deficits. The first manager of the business operations was Casimir Kowalski, who had previously been PNA national secretary. In 1939, Charles Rozmarek appointed one of his strongest backers, Stanley Swierczynski, to the post. Swierczynski served in this capacity until 1964 and combined his business responsibilities with the management of Rozmarek's presidential campaigns.

From 1964, three men held the responsibility of managing Alliance Printers and Publishers, Emil Kolasa, Joseph Gajda and Edward Rozanski. Kolasa who previously had worked as an advertising agent for the PNA papers left the post in 1971 to become a national director. Gajda, a veteran worker in the Chicago home office of the PNA and a one-time activist in the *Harcerstwo* youth movement succeeded him but he also resigned in 1974 when he was elected vice president upon the death of Frank Prochot. In his place came Edward Rozanski, a one-time photographer for the "Daily *Zgoda*" who had later served a term as a director.[16]

Throughout its history, the Polish National Alliance has engaged in printing a wide variety of materials in addition to *Zgoda* and *Dziennik Zwiazkowy*. From 1914 onward, the PNA published its own annual "Poor Richard's Almanac," *Kalendarz Zwiazkowy*. This magazine has provided its readers with a potpouri of useful and interesting information ranging from helpful advice on procedures to be followed in gaining U.S. citizenship to features on Polish and American history, cooking, and culture, supplemented by large doses of the poetry and literature of the day.

Another publication is *Promien* (The Sunbeam), the organ of the Youth and Sports Department, which is issued on a somewhat irregular basis to the directors of sports and dance groups under PNA sponsorship. Since it first appeared in 1948, *Promien's* quality has improved noticeably. At first it was filled with reprints of articles published previously in *Dziennik Zwiazkowy*. Frequently, such pieces had little to do with the supposed interests and activities of *Promien's* intended readers. Beginning in the early 1970s, however, the magazine's contents underwent a significant change; features focusing upon the educational training programs for youth leaders held each Summer at Alliance College began to appear regularly, for example. Highlights of the quadrennial PNA youth jamborees received lavish attention, along with such sports events as the annual bowling, golf and softball tournaments run by the PNA. Another positive development has been the effort to print stories in *Promien* about aspects of PNA history thought to be relevant to young activists in the fraternal. For example, a 1979 issue of the magazine presented a beautifully photographed retrospective study of *Harcerstwo,* the PNA scouting movement of the 1930s, which drew attention to one of the Alliance's most significant efforts to inculcate ethnic feeling, pride and fellowship among the youth of that period.

Over the years the PNA has also sponsored the publication of scores of books and pamphlets to stimulate greater awareness of Poland's history, heritage and literature, as well as the Alliance's place in Polonia. One of its earliest publications was a work with a contemporary ring titled "By What Right does Moscow claim responsibility for the Slavic Peoples?" Other early works published by the Alliance included Libelt's "On Polish Patriotism," Sawicka's "Outline and Significance of the May Third Constitution," and Siemiradzki's work, "The Political History of Poland in Outline." In 1894, the PNA published its own first history written by Barszczewski. Since then it has published histories of the Alliance in 1905, 1940 and 1957 as well. In addition to a variety of political tracts and histories of Poland, the PNA underwrote the publication of scores of original novels, plays and short stories by writers of the time and also reissued several major literary works to meet the growing demand for such materials within Polonia. Particularly in the era before Poland regained its independence in 1918, this effort was extremely significant since it was only in the Austrian section of the partitioned homeland where serious reading materials in the Polish language were available. Without activities such as those sponsored by the PNA the vast majority of Polish immigrants would have been left with little access to Polish language reading materials in America. Furthermore, the effort to stimulate ethnic consciousness through its publications of newspapers, pamphlets and books was reinforced by the Alliance's systematic establishment of libraries and reading rooms throughout the U.S. Though the Alliance has been less engaged in such enterprises in recent years, it has continued to print useful pamphlets on aspects of PNA and Polonia history. In 1958, for example, it published a brief study commemorating the 350th anniversary of the landing and settlement of the first Poles in America at the Jamestown, Virginia colony. In 1973, *Zgoda* editor Wiewiora brought out a brief outline history of the PNA entitled "In the Mainstream of American Life," a useful thumbnail sketch which was revised and reissued in 1980. In 1980, the PNA reprinted its very first history in commemoration of its centennial.

In short, then, the creation of Alliance Printers and Publishers as a subsidiary of the PNA greatly advanced the fraternal's continuing work to disseminate information pertaining to Poland and Polonia in accord with its original aims. Only one problem developed out of its creation and this had to do with a matter that was not foreseen at the time of incorporation in 1934. At that time the board of directors headed by the president of the PNA was made responsible for guiding its operations, and not the censor, who had originally been named in the Alliance constitution to direct *Zgoda* editorial policy. In the 1940s and 1950s a serious disagreement arose between Rozmarek and Swietlik (and later his successor Gunther) as to who exactly was responsible for overseeing the PNA newspapers. In fact, Censor Gunther took the matter to court out of his conviction that the PNA by-laws explicitly placed him in command. Rozmarek disagreed, basing his position on the articles of incorporation of Alliance Printers and Publishers, and was vindicated, although it was clear that the intent of the PNA constitution had been contradicted. It was not until the 1963 PNA convention that the confusion was cleared up when the delegates voted to explicitly return to the censor his traditional powers over *Zgoda.*

No brief review of the editorial orientation and history of the Alliance press during the past century can do justice to the subject of the quality of the writing that has appeared in *Zgoda* or *Dziennik Zwiazkowy* over the years. Both papers, particularly before 1920, employed an exhortatory and didactic approach in reaching their readers. Their purpose was as much to educate and uplift as to inform and thereby to instill among its readers a sense of patriotic feeling as members of the Polish nation, something few had brought with them to America.

The papers' editorial orientation has usually been progressive and moderate in tone; their readers consistently urged to work together to improve their status in America, to become better educated and to play an active role in public affairs. As such both *Zgoda* and *Dziennik Zwiazkowy* have generally occupied a middle of the road position distinguishing them from the radical and conservative wings of the Polonia press. Prior to the First World War, the Alliance's "swoj swojego" or ethnic solidarity orientation made its papers the object of sharp attacks from the Polish socialist press, which emphasized that working class Poles could never expect help from economically "better off" members of Polonia. At the same time, PNA patriotic activities caused conservative and clerical voices in the ethnic community to question its papers' lack of reverence for the leading role of the Catholic Church on the issues of the day.

The interwar years saw the two PNA publications reflecting the internal partisan conflict that wracked the Alliance. When the "old guard" controlled editorial policy, "opposition" elements had to find channels of mass communication outside the PNA to express their positions on the issues and personalities of the day. When the opposition came into power on its own in 1928, it simply turned the tables on its adversaries. The situation began to change gradually after Swietlik's election as censor in 1931. In his victory speech, he promised that the PNA publications would henceforth be open to all points of view and that no faction should use the papers to promote a single position on controversial matters.

But the Second World War and its consequences for Poland made it difficult to maintain so liberal a perspective. The times called for solidarity on behalf of the restoration of a sovereign and democratic Polish state and the staunchly anti-communist editorial position of both papers reflected support of Charles Rozmarek's initiatives as leader of the Polish American Congress.

Since 1968, both newspapers have broadened their editorial direction considerably in a fashion which has made the two publications more responsive to the changes occurring within American Polonia. While maintaining the Alliance's traditional commitment to Poland's independence, both papers have increased their awareness of the concerns of the generations of American-born Poles.

Still, both papers might do much more to better serve the intellectual and informational needs of their readerships. Given the precipitous decline in the number of Polonia publications in recent years, *Zgoda* and *Dziennik Zwiazkowy* occupy an extraordinarily important place in providing Polish Americans with information, ideas and opinion about matters pertaining to their cultural concerns and ethnic life. Each publication in its own fashion has an opportunity to provide needed and valued printed material on issues facing Polish Americans and commentary on books, films and personalities relevant to Polonia life.

A particularly important responsibility falls to *Zgoda* a national publication with an enormous circulation, in comparison with the Chicago-oriented *Zwiazkowy,* whose readership is also smaller. As a bi-weekly *Zgoda* is in the favorable position of not having to report the latest events under restrictive deadlines. Hence, its editor can deal with topics of broader significance in a thought-provoking fashion. Furthermore, there is the fortunate circumstance of the paper's freedom from direct dependence upon subscriptions or advertising revenues.

Given these considerations *Zgoda's* possesses the potential to become a truly nationwide Polonia publication. Dealing not only with such time-honored subjects as PNA fraternal and insurance matters, the Alliance College, the Polish American Congress and the work of the top Alliance leadership, the paper could also serve as a forum of Polonia opinion about issues facing the ethnic community as well as a place where views about books, films and people might be aired. *Zgoda* might also make better use of many of the articles that presently appear in the Chicago *Zwiazkowy,* whose quality deserves a wider audience. One serious observer of the scene well articulated the needs of Polonia in the following fashion:

> Let us be truthful. Even if we (in Polonia) were somehow to arrive today at one great thought, who would know about it besides those present (at our meeting) and possibly, a few others who might accidently hear about it? How are the thoughts expressed here to be disseminated into the community?

> We can ask: 'Where is the forum where our leaders and thinkers can express their opinions? Where can we, where can our youth, or where can our interested adults look for mental stimulus? Where will the ideas presented here be published?'

> The fraternal press is still the only vehicle we have today which is providing this kind of opportunity to communicate within our community. It is the only press that is to some degree adequately funded. It has been reported that the fraternal press reaches only seven percent of the Polish American population. It is nevertheless reaching a greater percentage of our population than anything else we are doing . . . The fraternal press, therefore, is what we have to work with.[17]

Clearly a more vital *Zgoda,* strengthened by an enhanced staff and budget, would not only better serve the interests of the PNA, it would be more capable of meeting the many cultural and intellectual needs of Polonia. By operating in this fashion, the newspaper would be fulfilling once again the ambitions of its greatest and most effective editors, men such as Odrowaz Jablonski, Siemiradzki and Brodowski.

The approach of its centennial as the world's oldest Polish language newspaper in continuous publication led many contributors to the publication to speculate on the meaning of the very word "zgoda," a term with a variety of definitions and nuances having no specific English language equivalent. Traditionally, PNA members translated "zgoda" as meaning "agreement," "harmony," or "unity."[18] However one translates the word, one can readily understand what Frank Gryglaszewski had in mind when he proposed the name for the PNA's publication in 1881. For one thing, in opposing Andrzejkowicz's suggestion of "Niepodleglosc," he was hardly rejecting the idea of continuing to do what was possible on behalf of the cause of Poland's eventual independence. Rather, in making his suggestion Gryglaszewski realized that understanding and cooperation within the still small Polish immigrant community was absolutely essential if its members were ever to contribute to Polish independence and the successful resettlement of the immigrant population. Such unity could not be automatically established, from the top down, but had to develop in a democratic, consensual manner. Given this insight, what better way for the PNA, whose leaders aspired to bring together the people of Polish origin living in the United States, than to offer its most basic message as the name of its official publication?

One might point out, of course, that little in the way of genuine "zgoda" has characterized the history of Polonia or for that matter that of the PNA over much of the past one hundred years. Indeed, conflict, whether ideological or personal, has often better reflected the realities than harmony and understanding. Nonetheless, Polish Americans in times of great crisis have tended to put aside their differences when the future of Poland depended upon their effective cooperation, as during the First and Second World Wars and in the homeland's time of troubles which surfaced in the late 1970s. Ironically too, much of the conflict within the Polish American community has been in pursuit of "zgoda" and an effective way to deal with the problems facing the ethnic community. Yet, conflict among competing forces sharing similar ultimate goals has generally proved to be as much a sign of the continuing vitality and attractiveness of Polish ethnic values as it has been a source of disappointment following from the failure to realize genuine agreement.

As it looks forward to a second century of operation, the Polish National Alliance is in an excellent position to promote genuine unity and cooperation within the ethnic community. With many of the internal religious and class differences that once divided Polonia largely settled, PNA members can more effectively direct their energies to lead the millions of Americans of Polish origin and heritage in their efforts to play influential roles in this country's national life. Increasingly composed of better educated and more affluent members of American society, Polonia itself needs sound leadership. What better watchword could be developed to symbolize the future basis of Polish American activity than "zgoda"?[19]

Chapter 9

PNA YOUTH AND SPORTS ACTIVITIES

Formally, the Polish National Alliance's sponsorship of youth-directed programs dates back to its 1918 convention in Pittsburgh where the fraternal approved a resolution permitting "juveniles" (children under the age of sixteen) to be insured for the first time. Two years later, the PNA established a Youth Department to coordinate activities for its juvenile members. In 1931, the delegates to the Scranton convention went further and approved the funding of a Youth and Sports Department. They also established a scouting movement modelled after the Polish *Harcerstwo*. In the years that followed PNA youth activities reached their peak, both in terms of the diversity of programs and the extraordinary number of participants. By 1940, nearly one hundred thousand people were engaged in some type of PNA youth-oriented sports, cultural or scouting activity. Though the onset of World War II made it impossible to maintain these levels of participation, the youth and sports work of the Alliance originating in the 1920s and 1930s mobilized a new generation into greater involvement in the PNA and strengthened the fraternal for years to come.

But the PNA was committed to youth work long before the 1918 decision. Indeed, during its first four decades of existence, the Alliance was not simply dedicated to youth, it was itself a youthful organization. Statistics published regularly by the fraternal through the 1920s show the average age of its members to be thirty-five to forty years, with a large proportion of these individuals in their late teens and twenties. And from the PNA's earliest years, its leaders were actively engaged in programs aimed at preserving the ethnic consciousness of young people in the burgeoning Polonia settlements.

In 1887, a number of Chicago PNA activists organized the first "nest" or group of an organization of young people that grew into the Polish Falcons' Alliance. The Falcons' movement had originated in Bohemia in 1862 and its first Polish unit formed in Lwow in 1867. The Falcons' basic purpose, put well by its motto "A healthy spirit in a healthy body," combined gymnastics activities for young people with educational programs involving singing and dance to inspire patriotic pride. Active in forming this first group were PNA members Frank Sowadzki, Stanislas Slominski, Felix Piotrowicz, John Samolinski and Frank Stefanski.

A second Falcons' nest in Chicago formed in 1888 on the city's near south side. Centered at St. Adalbert's parish, it was led by Casimir Zychlinski. In 1894 Zychlinski became the first president of the Polish Falcons' Alliance when a number of local units coalesced. (A lifetime activist in the Falcons' movement, Zychlinski in 1912 was elected president of the Polish National Alliance.) In 1896 the Falcons' federation established its own newspaper, *Sokol* (The Falcon) under the editorship of Stefan Barszczewski. A year later Barszczewski was elected editor of the PNA organ, *Zgoda*.

In the years that followed the Falcons not only grew into a nationwide movement but remained closely identified with the PNA. For its part, the Alliance considered its duty to be one of assisting the Falcons' development into a mass membership youth organization. PNA leaders such as Zychlinski, Marian Steczynski (president of the fraternal from 1903 until 1912), Julius Smietana and John Chrzanowski all doubled as Falcons' activists and worked on its behalf.[1]

Moreover, by the turn of the century, the idea of making the Falcons a special department of the PNA became popular. Accordingly, entire Falcons' nests were invited to enter the PNA as autonomous units. So long as their members took out life insurance with the Alliance, they were made eligible for substantial monetary assistance to expand their activities and reach more young people. But while the PNA emphasized that the Falcons would retain their separate identity through the arrangement (which went into effect by mutual agreement in 1905), several factions in the youth movement broke away in opposition to the plan. Although the schism was healed in 1912 at a special unity convention, the reconstituted Polish Falcons' Alliance became fully independent of the PNA.[2]

Yet despite its formal separation from the Alliance, the Falcons' movement under its President, Teofil Starzynski, actually maintained a close working relationship with the great fraternal. Within both organizations there were powerful feelings in favor of actively supporting Polish independence on a number of levels. Not only did they cooperate in founding the Polish National Defense Committee *(KON)*, they also established an officers' training camp at the Alliance school in Pennsylvania in the Spring of 1914. Its purpose was to create a *corps* of military leaders to head an army of Poles raised in America, which PNA and Falcons' activists planned to establish and send to Europe to fight for independence when the opportunity arose. When the United States entered the World War in 1917, the two movements once again spearheaded the mobilization of a force of more than 22,000 men which eventually sailed to Europe and became part of the Polish army headed by General Jozef Haller. Nevertheless, these activities notwithstanding, the Falcons and the PNA did not reestablish their old close formal ties.

In 1917 the PNA gained a new and quite different opportunity to advance its aims in promoting ethnic consciousness within Polonia's new generation. A change in Governmental regulations dealing with fraternals was announced, one which permitted the Alliance to actively recruit children as insured members for the first time. In 1918, Zychlinski won convention approval to admit individuals under the age of sixteen and to establish a special youth department to look after their specific interests. This department went into operation in November, 1919. According to Zychlinski's proposal it was also understood that such "juvenile members" would automatically be accepted as full-fledged members of their lodges upon their attainment of the age of sixteen.

From the start, the PNA Youth Department was viewed as an important factor in the fraternal's future growth, though its early activities were hampered by a lack of funds. At first the Department relied upon donations from the lodges and councils and in 1923 the situation required Censor Michael Blenski to obtain a loan of $5,000 from the PNA National Fund so the Department could continue to function. Despite these difficulties, activists in the Youth Department remained optimistic about its potential. An early Department publication put its purposes as those of "strengthening our organization with the energies of our young people, preserving their sense of Polish identity and protecting them from Americanization."[3] Another called upon PNA members to remember that "the noble blood of Poles flows through the veins of the generation born here in America, among those who enthusiastically participate in Alliance sports activities."[4]

Ironically, the sports programs of the Youth Department reflected more about the Americanization of Polonia's new generation than many of its supporters cared to admit. This was hardly surprising inasmuch as the 1920s represented the beginnings of mass enthusiasm for professional and amateur athletics in the U.S. Unprecedented attention was focused upon the exploits of Babe Ruth, Red Grange, Jack Dempsey, Bill Tilden and Bobby Jones and the sports in which they excelled. This development also greatly affected the interests and athletic activities of Polish American youth.[5] In contrast, popular interest waned in traditionally "Polish" sports such as soccer and gymnastics.

Already between 1923 and 1925, the Youth Department was supporting ninety-two sports groups affiliated with its lodges and councils in thirteen states. Baseball, basketball, tennis and bowling were must popular and the first PNA bowling league was already in operation in Chicago in 1925. By 1930 twenty-five different leagues with more than one hundred and fifty teams were in action. The first PNA-sponsored baseball league was formed in 1923 and in the same year the organization held its first tennis tournament. Basketball was yet another American sport that soon captured a large following. The first PNA basketball league was established in 1926 and in 1929 the Alliance inaugurated an intercity tourney in Chicago. National tournaments bringing together the best PNA aggregations from around the country in basketball, tennis, bowling and baseball soon became annual affairs. Another popular event of the era was the annual match between the top PNA and PRCUA baseball clubs for the "Polish championship" of Chicago. Increasingly, young women also participated in PNA sports programs and by 1930, women's leagues in tennis, basketball, softball and bowling were in action.

In addition to the department's support of athletic activities at the lodge and council levels, there were other signs of PNA support for sports activities. By the mid 1920s, for example, both of the Alliance's newspapers were giving extensive coverage to sports events. Matt Majchrowicz, sports editor of *Dziennik Zwiazkowy* gave particular attention to such activities and in 1924 the weekly *Zgoda* began to regularly publish the results of sports contests involving PNA teams. Increasingly, sports news was handled in the English language in deference to the younger generation.

In all, the PNA sports movement could claim approximately 40,000 regular participants by 1940. Although they did not provide many participants in American professional sports, the PNA leagues nonetheless helped revitalize the lodges and councils and served to introduce large numbers of young people into fraternal life. Still the "American" character of the sports promoted so successfully by the Department led to debate about the future of ethnic consciousness in the Alliance and spurred opponents of Americanization to organize their own youth activities.

This concern became more serious after 1926; in that year the Falcons' Alliance established its own insurance program and thereby extinguished the last hope for some future reunification with the PNA. Yet for some old partisans of *Sokol* type youth activities, the idea of forming a similar organization under PNA auspices continued to exert an appeal. Some recalled that as far back as 1912, a youth group modelled after the Polish scouting organization, *Harcerstwo,* had been formed at the Alliance school in Cam-

Table 1.   Number of Teams Participating in Activities Sponsored by the PNA
Sports Department, 1932–1939

	1932	1933	1934	1935	1936	1937	1938	1939
Total Number of Teams	324	341	299	517	573	661	799	896
Men's Sports								
Baseball	206	182	119	232	156	138	147	112
Basketball	102	91	92	114	125	161	208	241
Softball	10	21	18	36	73	116	168	259
Bowling	N.I.	N.I.	N.I.	N.I.	42	56	78	96
Tennis	11	11	11	32	37	21	34	29
Men's Light Athletics	0	0	3	12	15	12	17	14
Women's Sports								
Basketball	12	13	18	29	38	44	32	35
Softball	0	4	9	14	22	29	34	30
Tennis	12	18	18	29	28	25	31	23
Bowling	N.I.	N.I.	N.I.	N.I.	21	26	23	35
Women's Light Athletics	0	0	3	6	8	10	13	9

N.I.: "no information" available on these activities. Data are from the reports of the PNA Sports Department made to the delegates at the 1935 and 1939 conventions.

bridge Springs. Involved in that activity had been several individuals who later became leaders in the PNA, such as Jerome Pawlowski, a physician who was elected a vice censor. In 1922, the Polish Army Veterans' Association (composed of the members of the Polish army in America) had called on the Alliance to create such a scouting movement but on the condition that it be autonomous from the PNA. The suggestion was turned down; it reminded too many people of the disappointing experience with the Falcons.

In 1929, the PNA Youth Department itself recommended the forming of *Harcerstwo,* a proposal that was enthusiastically backed by the new president of the Alliance, John Romaszkiewicz. An old Falcon himself,

Romaszkiewicz pushed the plan through the 1931 convention and within a few months had organized a *Harcerstwo* executive committee to establish scouting groups in every PNA district. Serving on the committee were Romaszkiewicz, Vice President Chester Hibner, Directors George Piwowarczyk, Berniece Zawilinska, and Michael Tomaszkiewicz, along with Henry Lokanski and Walter Strojny. Named as the movement's executive director was Stanislas Kolodziejczyk, a veteran gymnast who had just completed an instructional course in scouting held in Warsaw.

Romaszkiewicz was a "true believer" in *Harcerstwo's* potential as a force preserving ethnic consciousness and pride among the new generation of American-born youth. To emphasize its Polish character he required that *Harcerstwo* members follow the aims, principles and activities of the movement in the ancestral homeland and not those of the Boy Scouts of America. Romaszkiewicz asserted that the PNA *Harcerstwo*

> must be a Polish organization, to which only youth of Polish heritage may belong, in contrast to the American scouting movement which enrolls members of all ethnic groups . . . The PNA *Harcerstwo* must be faithful to the United States but at the same time it will be respectful of the land of its members' ancestors, Poland. The American boy scouts, in contrast, recognize no other loyalty than to the United States . . .[6]

Romaszkiewicz's organization embraced two goals. One was to train Polish American youngsters to "be good citizens, healthy and strong in mind and body." But equally significant was the task of instilling a love for the ethnic heritage through the *Harcerstwo* program. As Romaszkiewicz put it, "If our *Harcerstwo* is just like the English or American scouts it will be an artificial movement, since it is our aim to preserve our Polish heritage and language here in America through our activities."[7]

So deeply convinced of the importance of *Harcerstwo's* Polish ethnic character was Romaszkiewicz that he even called for the suspension of any member who used the word "scout" in its activities. What is more, the PNA president was not alone in his dedication to *Harcerstwo* as the instrument by which Polish ethnic consciousness was to be preserved. In an article he published titled "In What Way is *Harcerstwo* Different From American Scouting? In Every Way!" Henry Lokanski emphasized that only *Harcerstwo* provided youngsters with a firm appreciation of their national culture, language and religion. Ethnic identity, he went on, was further reinforced by the wearing of Polish *Harcerstwo* uniforms at meetings and by using Polish language commands and watchwords. Lokanski concluded by noting,

> These differences between the two scouting movements are so profound that

there can be no compromise between them. *Harcerstwo* will provide our youth
with a sense of their heritage and will brighten the future of the PNA. American
scouting is indifferent to the fate of our people. . .[8]

Although many PNA members remained skeptical about the movement
and its aims, *Harcerstwo* grew rapidly during the first four years of its
experience, fueled by the enthusiasm of Romaszkiewicz and his allies.
Enrollment activities got underway in early 1932 and by June of that year,
thirty-two units had formed with 1,400 members. By March, 1933 the
movement included 13,486 members; by December, 1934 its ranks had
swelled to 23,486 youngsters organized in 486 units. A year later, *Harcerstwo*
reached its zenith; by then 934 units were in operation with approximately
52,000 members. Despite the Depression, which caused many PNA members
to give up their insurance policies, the youth movement seemed to stimulate
new interest in the Alliance. Between 1931 and 1935, for example,
approximately 18,000 juvenile PNA members continued in the fraternal
upon reaching the age of sixteen largely because of their previous involvement
in its scouting activities. For many who took part in *Harcerstwo,* the activities
of the youth movement generated a continued interest in the PNA, which
had committed itself to the work of preserving ethnic identification at a
formative period in their lives. One author who covered the movement
in some detail has termed the era of *Harcerstwo* activity "the golden age"
of PNA involvement with Polonia's youth.[9]

Kolodziejczyk's own work, *The Handbook of the PNA Harcerstwo in
North America* became the basic guide for its organizational activities and
was printed in both Polish and English. The book directed *Harcerze* (boys)
and *Harcerki* (girls) in ten different skills they needed to master to attain
higher rank in the movement. Five of these concentrated upon traditionally
Polish sports such as gymnastics, marksmanship, cycling, swimming and
archery. American sports like baseball, football and basketball were also
played, however.

Despite its impressive record, *Harcerstwo* never enjoyed unqualified support
within the Alliance. Its first great youth jamboree, held at Chicago's Riverview
amusement park on July 22, 1934 was a case in point and reflected conflicting
attitudes about the wisdom of having *Harcerstwo* in the first place as well
as its aims. While more than three thousand uniformed *Harcerze* and *Harcerki*
took part in the day of programs, picnics, sports and amusements sponsored
by what was then District 15 of the Alliance (presently districts 12 and
13 which together cover Chicago), only eleven of its twenty-three member
councils were represented at the event. Indeed, the other twelve councils

did not then possess a single *Harcerstwo* unit, even though two years had gone by since recruitment efforts had commenced.

Harcerstwo, in fact, was the object of considerable concern for several reasons. To many PNA members, the basic purpose of *Harcerstwo* was both wrong-headed and futile. For one thing, the idea of instilling ethnic consciousness among young Polish Americans by organizing them into units which accentuated their Polish identity simply isolated them from the dominant cultural currents in American society. Another criticism dealt with the close identification of *Harcerstwo* and its leaders with the Polish government. The cordial relationship between the Pilsudski regime and the PNA leadership between 1928 and 1935 seemed far from altruistic to its opponents. The tie was underscored by the frequent appearances of Poland's ambassadors and consular officers at *Harcerstwo* events. (Among those who attended such functions were General Marian Gorecki, a member of the Polish government, who made a special point of praising the youth movement's aims. Another was General Jozef Haller, one of the most widely known World War I era heroes of Polish independence.)

But a more serious problem complicated Romaszkiewicz's task, the stance of the American scouting movement toward *Harcerstwo*. From the start, Boy Scouts of America officials argued that any organization based in the U.S. and founded upon the precepts of scouting had to be under their jurisdiction. Protests from Alliance leaders that theirs was an ethnic youth movement based upon Poland's example notwithstanding, the U.S. organization relentlessly demanded that the PNA either affiliate with it and pay annual dues amounting to $3 per scout or dissolve its *Harcerstwo* units. Because Poland's *Harcerstwo,*like the Boy Scouts of America, belonged to the same international federation, it had to abide by the U.S. body's ultimatum, one it was ready to press in court.

Faced with a dilemma of no small consequences, Romaszkiewicz was nevertheless unable to win PNA approval for an annual expenditure amounting to $150,000 to continue *Harcerstwo* activities. On the other hand, perhaps because of the depressed state of the economy, he was unwilling to call upon parents with children in the organization to absorb the added costs. Sponsorship of *Harcerstwo* in turn became an important campaign issue in the hotly contested 1939 fight for the PNA presidency, when Romaszkiewicz's challenger, Charles Rozmarek expressed his opposition to the whole idea. At the convention in Detroit, the end finally came. A majority of the delegates voted to drop the very name of the movement along with its uniforms, which together symbolized *Harcerstwo's* ties with the Polish organization. Renamed the PNA Youth Groups *(druzyny mlodziezowe),* these units were merged into the Alliance's Youth and Sports Department. Within a few years and largely due to America's involvement in World War II, most of these groups also went out of existence. At the 1939 convention, Romaszkiewicz was himself defeated for reelection.

Romaszkiewicz, "the father of the *Harcerstwo*," had done his best to make the youth movement a success. One year, for example, he had even donated ten percent of his own salary to help fund its activities. He had taken part in innumerable events around the country promoting the cause. And, in 1935 he backed the purchase of 224 acres of farm land near the town of Yorkville, some forty miles from Chicago, so that local *Harcerstwo* units might have their own permanent camping site. But in the end, the PNA turned away from the *Harcerstwo* idea, despite all his efforts.

In retrospect, one cannot help but wonder whether the decision of 1939 was correct. It is a fact that no Polonia organization subsequently mobilized as many young people into ethnic activities as attractive as *Harcerstwo*. But was enthusiasm for the Polish scouting idea simply a fad of the 1930s, one which would have lost popularity as increasing numbers of American-born Polish youngsters became integrated into non-ethnic organized activities in their schools, parishes and neighborhoods? Surely, the onset of World War II significantly altered the conditions before Polonia making relief efforts, rather than youth activities, the community's highest priority. Moreover, with America's entry into the conflict in 1941, thousands of young men and women departed for military service, leaving Polonia bereft of the very individuals who in peacetime would have served as ethnic youth leaders. The political realities of post war Poland would have further complicated the activities of a PNA *Harcerstwo* had it remained, since the youth movement had always emphasized its ties with the ancestral homeland.

Nevertheless, even during its brief decade of existence *Harcerstwo* represented a largely successful effort to mobilize thousands of people around the cause of preserving the ethnic heritage in America. For many of these people it was through *Harcerstwo* and its programs that they gained a knowledge and pride of their culture, which might otherwise have never been developed. Through group activities focusing upon camping, the singing of patriotic songs, the learning about Polish legends and history, thousands of young people not only made lasting friendships, they also came into contact for the first time with the aims of the Polish National Alliance. For many of them a continued involvement in the PNA would follow, largely thanks to their years in *Harcerstwo*.

Perhaps nothing better illustrates the impact of the PNA effort than the responses of others to *Harcerstwo*. For one thing, the success of the PNA Youth movement led other Polonia fraternals to establish their own scouting groups. One may also wonder whether the Boy Scouts of America would have been so unalterably opposed had *Harcerstwo* recruitment efforts attracted only a small number of youngsters into its ranks.

The other youth activities sponsored by the PNA also were adversely affected by the War. Thus, the Alliance's annual national basketball tournament was suspended permanently following the 1942 event at Pittsburgh's Duquesne University. Already by 1947, the chairman of the Youth and Sports Department felt obliged to report that the Alliance faced real problems in the future unless it reinvigorated its work with the younger generation. On the surface, the Alliance's programs remained fairly impressive both in size and scope but in fact the number of lodges retaining their own youth activities was diminishing. Even in 1947, only 368 out of 1,600 lodge units continued to sponsor some type of youth or sports-oriented program.

Since the Second World War, the record of PNA activity in sponsoring sports and youth programs can be succinctly summarized. It has been one of steady decline in participation both in terms of the number of lodges and individuals. The explanation for this trend is also fairly evident and is primarily due to three interrelated developments that have occurred during the past forty years. One concerns the growing involvement of Polish Americans in sports and youth activities sponsored by non-Polonia institutions in the community, such as little league and scouting. Another involves the movement of large numbers of younger Polish Americans out of the old ethnic neighborhoods where lodges sponsoring sports and youth activities were concentrated. Yet another factor to be considered concerns the ageing of the PNA membership itself and changes in recreational and leisure habits on the part of those individuals who have remained active in the Alliance. For example, participation in baseball and basketball, sports for younger persons which also require quite a bit of organization and fairly large numbers of participants, has fallen off precipitously. On the other hand, there has been a continuing involvement in bowling and golf. These appeal to men and women of various age groups, call for fewer participants and a lower level of organization, and stress social comaraderie as much as athletic prowess. Thus, the annual national PNA bowling tournaments have continued to attract between one thousand and twelve hundred participants since the mid 1960s. Held in various cities throughout the country, the largest turnout for the tournament was in 1978 when 1,264 bowlers gathered in Allen Park, Michigan, a suburb of Detroit, for the two day affair.[10]

Table 2. Youth and Sports Activities Sponsored by the Polish National Alliance, 1951-1979

Type of Youth Activity	Time Period						
	1951-55	1955-59	1959-63	1963-67	1967-71	1971-75	1975-79
Youth Circles	79	57	48	55	54	44	--
Singing Groups	46	36	39	42	37	26	19
Drum and Buglers	18	8	9	9	5	3	3
Dance Groups	18	36	33	39	26	32	54
Drama Circles	--	7	7	6	4	4	--
Totals	161	154	136	151	126	109	76

Type of Sports Activity	1951-55	1955-59	1959-63	1963-67	1967-71	1971-75	1975-79
Baseball Teams	55	57	52	15	10	15	--
Softball Teams	110	117	105	29	17	19	--
Soccer Teams	5	9	9	9	8	4	--
Volleyball Teams	9	15	12	--	--	--	--
Bowling Teams	708	905	980	--	--	--	--
Bowling Leagues	--	--	--	61	60	69	33
Basketball Teams	95	98	90	17	6	1	--
Golf	--	31	38	N.I.	13	14	13
Duckpins	--	26	26	N.I.	--	--	--
Others	--	--	--	14	16	14	33
Totals	982	1258	1312	145	130	136	79

N.I.: No information.

These national tournaments, of course, represent but the tip of the iceberg insofar as PNA involvement in bowling is concerned. Many lodges and councils sponsor teams and leagues of their own and for numerous teams, bowling goes on practically all year around.

Golf tournaments have also been popular events; as with bowling many lodges and councils promote their own local golf outings in addition to participating in the national tourney directed by the PNA Youth and Sports Department each year since 1963. Though these events have involved fewer participants than the bowling competitions, golf tournaments held in such locations as Dunkirk, New York (in 1975 and 1980), Beaver Falls, Pennsylvania (1978), Cranston, Rhode Island (1976), Jackson, Michigan (1979), Johnstown, Pennsylvania (1974), Monaca, Pennsylvania (1968), and Akron, Ohio (1982) each attracted more than 150 participants. The record for the greatest number of golfers at a PNA tournament was set in 1980 when 190 men and women took part in the competition held at the Shorewood Country Club in Dunkirk, New York. A PNA sponsored national softball tournament was also set up in 1980. Nine teams representing lodges and councils from around the country took part in the first competition, which has since become an event held annually at the Alliance College campus during the summer.

Yet another aspect of the work of the Youth and Sports Department has involved its support of dancing and singing groups for children and teenagers which are organized by lodges and councils throughout the country. Instructors for these programs are trained in special summer courses which operate for three weeks each year at the Alliance College and regularly enjoy enrollments of forty to fifty young people. The instructional programs carry on the tradition of training in Polish history, culture, language and music which began in the 1930s under the direction of PNA Ladies' Vice President Florence Dymek and Wanda Rozmarek.

Efforts were also made to improve the editorial content and overall attractiveness of the Youth and Sports Department's magazine *Promien* after 1970. This magazine, which is distributed to PNA youth group leaders and instructors throughout the country, was established during the 1940s. For many years, however, it contained reprints of articles published earlier in *Zgoda* and *Dziennik Zwiazkowy* and possessed no clearly defined focus relating to the interests of its intended readership. This changed during the first Mazewski administration when the new President and Vice President Frank Prochot reorganized the magazine to provide its readers with a better appreciation of the mission of the Youth and Sports Department. Since then, the publication has given special attention to youth events and has provided the instructors of PNA dance and singing groups with a wealth of useful information about ethnic music, folk art and dance to help them better perform their responsibilities. *Promien* has also included a number of lavishly illustrated color features on topics deemed to be of special interest to young people. One article dealt with the 1972 launching of the American space satellite named in honor of Copernicus and another focused upon the history of the PNA *Harcerstwo* movement, for example. Special biographical articles on the lives of Ignacy Paderewski, Prochot, and Charles Rozmarek as well as an essay on the history of the Alliance at the time of its ninetieth anniversary in 1970 have given readers of *Promien* a better insight into the fraternal's role.

In 1970, the Polish National Alliance made a new effort to enliven ethnic feeling and pride among the present generation of young people by sponsoring a novel mass-oriented event, the Youth Jamboree. The first Jamboree was held over a three day period in July, 1970 on the Alliance College campus. Under the general supervision of Melanie Winiecki, then a member of the PNA board of directors, the event brought together more than 1,100 young people active in local dance and singing groups along with more than 200 adults involved in such programs. Its sole purpose was to enable them to meet and to perform their specific programs for one another. The 1974 Jamboree was also directed by Winiecki and attracted nearly 1,100 people. The 1978 and 1982 Jamborees were directed by Genevieve Gajda and brought together approximately one thousand and eight hundred people, respectively.

On one level, the jamborees might be characterized as ethnic dance and music festivals and as such they have proved to be at one and the same time colorful spectacles and educational events. Clearly it is useful for instructors, PNA leaders and children alike to have the opportunity to experience what people in other groups throughout the country are doing to preserve Polish music and dance in their communities. But perhaps even more important, the Jamborees have stimulated a deeper sense of pride and awareness among participants in their common heritage. Occurring in the pleasant atmosphere of the richly Polish and historic Alliance College and emphasizing contacts with fellow PNA members from other parts of the country, the jamborees have provided their participants the chance to gain new insights into their heritage. At the events, young people proudly wear their costumes around the campus and exchange friendly words with other PNA members from communities far from their homes. The jamborees have traditionally closed with Mass replete with Polish hymns sung enthusiastically by all and followed by a campfire sing-along featuring ethnic songs. The three day affairs have thus allowed those in attendance to become immersed in the best aspects of their ancestral cultural heritage embodied in Polish music, dance, healthy recreational activities and fellowship.

Looking into the future, it is just such activities as the youth jamboree that the PNA must build upon to make its youth programs attractive once more to Polonia. The programs themselves may vary from those which have been traditionally popular, but whatever their specific content they can succeed if they remain based upon a knowledge and enthusiasm for the Polish heritage. The current leaders of the Polish National Alliance, who themselves are products of the banner years of the *Harcerstwo* and other youth programs the fraternal directed during the 1930s, recognize this. But it will be up to the next crop of PNA national officers to fan the coals of ethnic feeling which the people in charge during the 1970s sought to rekindle.

While the PNA sponsored sports programs have generally succeeded in involving a large number of members and becoming integral elements in the activities of many of the lodges, the Alliance's youth activities have suffered a precipitous decline in recent years. Clearly, the PNA must upgrade both the quality of its singing and dance programs and attract greater participation in their activities if it is to continue to fulfill one of its traditional functions as an ethnic movement. Successful youth activities can also help in revitalizing local lodge life and bring more young people into contact with the fraternal. A well organized youth ensemble can be an educational and enjoyable experience for its participants and a great source of pride for their parents and friends as well.

To succeed, these programs need to be more effectively promoted and publicized so that parents and grandparents belonging to the PNA will enroll their youngsters into existing ensembles and establish new units where none presently are to be found. Great concern must be placed upon properly training instructors and youngsters alike in the authentic cultural traditions and history of Poland, too, if these programs are to realize their mission in stimulating interest and pride in the PNA. If these concerns can be met, the activities of the Alliance's youth groups will once again begin to be an important factor in enriching the contributions of the fraternal to its members.

Chapter 10

WOMEN IN THE POLISH NATIONAL ALLIANCE
AND HUMANITARIAN WORK

Women in the Polish National Alliance

Throughout its history women have played an important, if little recognized, role in the growth of the Polish National Alliance into a significant mass movement, just as they have influenced the development of practically every other Polish American organization. Women activists worked for the Alliance from the start and during the past century members of the fair sex have steadily become more significant actors at every level of PNA life, from the lodge hall to the board of directors.

In 1982, for example, two of the five executive officers of the PNA were women. Helen Szymanowicz held the post of first vice president and Lottie Kubiak was its national secretary, the first woman incidentally to hold that office in the fraternal's history. Four of the ten members of the PNA board of directors were women as were sixteen of its district commissioners, who with the fraternal's censor and vice censor constitute its supervisory council. Hence, 102 years after its founding, 22 of the 49 national elected officers of the Polish National Alliance were women.

Women comprise a significant part of the membership of the PNA as well. In the early 1980s, more than one hundred of its nearly 1200 lodges were "women's only" groups (more than 800 lodges are open to both men and women members while the others are composed of men). Moreover, approximately 130,000 adult women and 14,000 girls under 16 belonged to the Alliance, more than in any other fraternal. Even the Polish Women's Alliance, Polonia's third largest fraternal included fewer female members, 77,000, than the PNA. Were the women in the PNA to form their own separate fraternal this organization would immediately become the second largest in American Polonia.[1]

Thus, more than a century after its founding, the PNA was truly a movement in which all its active members, whether men or women, have come to play major roles in shaping its development and policies. Indeed, as of 1983, women had achieved every elective office in the Alliance but those of president and censor, and many excellent female leaders had been chosen to direct its operations as appointed officers as well. But the drive for full equality of the sexes was not easily nor speedily achieved, despite the considerable efforts of many women and men to realize this aim.

One of the spiritual founders of the Polish National Alliance was a woman, Teofila Samolinska. Born in the Russian zone of partitioned Poland in 1848, Samolinska took part in the 1863 uprising and afterward left Poland with her family into foreign exile. Arriving in America at the end of the Civil War, she and her parents settled in Chicago where she became an early supporter of the *Gmina Polska* patriotic society which formed in 1866. A talented writer and poet, Samolinska contributed regularly to the embryonic *Polonia* press and later even corresponded with several of Poland's leading authors of the day, including Ignacy Kraszewski. In 1878, Samolinska, like Henry Kalussowski, wrote to the *emigre* leader, Agaton Giller, in Switzerland in pursuit of his advice and encouragement regarding the organizing of a patriotic organization to unify the growing immigrant population around the country. Though Kalussowski rather than Samolinska was to receive the credit for spurring Giller's call to Polonia to form such a movement, one Polonia historian, at least, has remembered Samolinska's effort. In his view, she deserves the title of "the mother of the Polish National Alliance."[2]

A colleague of a number of early PNA activists in Chicago, Teofila Samolinska increasingly urged that they include women with men into their patriotic society on an equal basis. But her efforts were in vain. Though the founders of the Alliance included a number of progressive ideas into their constitution they were cool to accepting full female equality. One reason may have simply been practical; having already extended PNA membership to non-Catholics and even to peoples such as Jews, Lithuanians and Ukrainians who had once been part of the old pre-partition Polish kingdom, they feared alienating the more conservative elements of the immigrant community by endorsing yet another rather radical idea, that of female participation in the new movement.

Of course, there was a more fundamental reason behind their decision and this had to do with the patriarchal character of Polish immigrant life at the time, a condition that was reinforced by cultural values which then dominated both Polish and American societies. The sociologist Helena Lopata well summarizes this problem when she writes:

Polish culture contained at the time of migration . . . many assumptions as to
the nature and proper roles of women in each major stage of their life course.
Peasant families (not greatly unlike upper class members) expected girls to continue
the work of their mothers—learning to keep the home, sew, cook and take care
of younger children. Formal education was not considered important for them
because the knowledge and skills they required could be learned only at home.
The girls, as their brothers, learned to work early in life, contributing what they
could to the economic welfare of the family and carrying out tasks around the
home and farm . . . . This attitude toward women's education was carried over
by the peasant to this continent . . . .[3]

Lopata adds that once in America, the parents' concern for their daughter's
morality created an early dilemma. On the one hand they needed their
children's earnings to supplement family income, on the other they were
anxious to protect them in every way, even from gossip. Thus, when girls
did work, they were initially employed as domestics, a job that also gave
them good training for their roles as wives and mothers. Given these
considerations, a powerful climate of opinion prevailed in the outside Polonia
against the participation of women in social organizations.

Although Samolinska failed to win full female equality within the early
PNA, the Alliance nevertheless did agree that women could be insured by
the fraternal through their husbands. At the third PNA *sejm,* held in 1883,
a resolution was approved providing the survivors of a male insured member
with a $500 death benefit along with a $200 benefit to a husband should
his wife die. This idea, however, was not put into effect until 1886 when
the PNA approved a similar plan which raised the wife's death benefit to
$250. To cover the cost of this insurance, special one time assessments of
50 and 25 cents were imposed whenever one of the insured members died.[4]

Although the PNA failed to grant full membership rights to its female
members, cooperation between the Alliance and a variety of women's groups
that did exist in the last years of the nineteenth century continued. In 1883,
Samolinska herself helped found a group, the Central Association of Polish
Women, to foster cultural and patriotic activities in Chicago. This organization,
which remained active through the 1930s, frequently staged plays and musical
events in league with various PNA lodges. In 1885, another group of women
appeared at the fifth PNA convention in St. Paul and there appealed for
unity within Polonia. In 1894, women activists organized their own drive
in support of the PNA *Skarb Narodowy.* And in 1897, a large group of
PNA wives presented a banner to the delegates at the national *sejm* in
Philadelphia; the banner's inscription once again emphasized the need for
Polonia unity in support of Poland's freedom.

By the turn of the century, pressure was building within the PNA to extend full membership rights to women. Two developments largely account for the changed atmosphere which in 1900 did produce this objective within the Alliance. For one thing, female activists such as Samolinska, Valerie Lipczynska, Emilie Napieralska and Stefanie Chmielinska were stepping up their own agitation for equal rights (or *rownouprawnienie*) throughout Polonia. For another, their activities coincided with a change in community attitudes about the place of women in the immigrant society. Already, more women were entering the labor force and beginning to develop different attitudes about their roles and responsibilities within the family and ethnic community. While a dramatic transformation in the status of women would not be evident until the World War I era, when large numbers of female workers entered the labor market in place of men called to military service, change was already in the air by 1900.

For many immigrant women, life in America was itself a kind of liberation. With their parents far away in Poland, they were freed from many of the traditional obligations which had occupied their time in the old country. As wives in America, some increased the family income by turning their homes into boarding houses or by opening taverns or grocery stores. Others worked as seamstresses or cleaning ladies in the hotels of urban America. All these activities raised their status both within the family and the ethnic community. Moreover, women played an active role in parish doings, which after all, presented them with their one significant social, cultural and recreational outlet away from the drudgery of domestic work.

Given the heavily structured character of Polish immigrant community life and its emphasis upon mutual self-help as defined by both the church and the fraternals, it should not be surprising that by the turn of the century a number of women activists were becoming increasingly insistent in seeking a greater role for themselves within such associations as the PNA and the Polish Roman Catholic Union. If few Polish women of the day were as well educated or emancipated as Teofila Samolinska, women already possessed a number of educated and middle class spokespersons who were able to assert their concerns. Some were themselves the wives or daughters of fraternal leaders, while others were engaged in teaching and nursing work.

In 1897, the Polish Roman Catholic Union agreed to admit women into its ranks as voting members. But the fraternal's conservative posture did not satisfy those activists who possessed a more progressive and nationalist outlook and who preferred to participate in the Polish National Alliance. Their drive was supported by many in the PNA leadership but at first met with failure when the Alliance rejected a resolution to admit women as equal members at its 1899 *sejm* in Grand Rapids, Michigan. In response they organized their own group, the Polish Women's Alliance or *Zwiazek Polek*. At its first meeting on November 12, 1899 in Chicago, a number of PNA leaders including former Censor Theodore Helinski were present. There Helinski urged all women to join the new movement, not only the wives of PNA members but also their sisters, mothers and daughters. He completed his remarks by stressing that he had spoken "not as a PNA officer but as a fellow Pole."[5]

The forming of the PWA spurred the PNA to act swiftly in reconsidering its policy toward women. In 1900, Censor Leon Sadowski, another advocate of *rownouprawnienie*, called an extraordinary convention of the Alliance for the specific purpose of revising its constitution on membership. It was at this *sejm*, which was held in Chicago in March, only four months after the founding of the Polish Women's Alliance, that the PNA granted full equality to women by a delegates' vote of 187-10. The resolution itself recognized "women (as) a formidable force who are able to work even more effectively here in America for Poland's good and to deal with the loss of Polishness among our young people . . ."[6]

The 1900 decision proved to be one of the best the PNA ever made and greatly benefitted both the Alliance and American Polonia. For one thing *rownouprawnienie* was the major reason for the unprecendented surge in PNA membership that began in 1900 and reached its peak in 1913. At the 1899 convention where "emancipation" had been turned down, the Alliance included 15,288 members. In December, 1900, only nine months after the extraordinary convention, membership had increased to 28,366 insured men and women, a leap of 86 percent. By 1907, women accounted for more than 20,000 members in a PNA whose ranks had swelled to 54,000 persons. In 1913, the year the fraternal reached the 100,000 membership mark, more than 35,000 *"Zwiazkowczyni"* could be counted in its members. When the Alliance reached the level of a 200,000 members movement in 1924, this figure included approximately 75,000 women. Ever since, not only have more women continued to enter the PNA, so also has the proportion of women belonging to the Alliance consistently risen. In the early 1980s, approximately 48 percent of all insured PNA members were women.

But there were even greater effects upon the Polish National Alliance resulting from the 1900 vote which had to do with the expansion of PNA activities on behalf of Polonia. Given their special interest in the care of the youth, women PNA members were active from the start in organizing "Saturday schools" to educate the children in their language and heritage.

In time thousands of children attended the schools, which were sponsored by PNA women's lodges. Women also took the lead in establishing libraries and reading rooms in lodges and councils throughout the country supported by the *Wydzial Oswiaty,* or PNA Educational Department. Yet another early concern was the conditions of work facing women in the factories, a problem that led many PNA women activists into wholehearted support of the organized labor movement, even before the First World War.[7]

Throughout the War, PNA women and the female contingents of other Polish fraternals were busy organizing clothing committees with the tasks of producing shirts, stockings, scarves and gloves for the people of war-ravaged Poland. Later organized into the League of the White Cross in response to the appeals of Madame Paderewska, they sent trained nurses led by Agnes Wisla, a PNA member, to join the Polish army raised in America when it traveled to France. Women PNA activists participated in countless fund raising efforts throughout the War and helped collect approximately $10 million for Polish relief.[8] They were also persuasive recruiters for the Polish army, a force that eventually numbered more than 20,000.

During the interwar years, Polish National Alliance women continued to focus much of their work in humanitarian areas. In Chicago on December 4, 1928 they formed the PNA Benevolent Society for the purpose of producing, purchasing and distributing clothing and food to needy Polish families during each Christmas season. The significance of the Society can be measured by the fact that traditionally all the highest ranking female officers of the Alliance took an active part in its work. In turn, the formation of a central benevolent society in Chicago also spurred the creation of similar charitable activities by PNA lodges and councils around the country, all of which were especially significant during the economic depression of the 1930s.

In 1936, these groups joined together in support of the *Rada Polonii Amerykanskiej* charitable federation organized by PNA Censor Swietlik to coordinate humanitarian activities throughout Polonia. The *Rada Polonii* would eventually play its greatest role during World War II and provide PNA women with an important means by which to coordinate their efforts during the conflict. During the 1930s too, women in the Alliance continued their educational work not only in the traditional Saturday schools but also by playing a major role in organizing the PNA scouting movement, *Harcerstwo,* after 1931. Hundreds of women directed scouting activities at all levels of its operation.

In the Second World War, PNA women expanded upon their humanitarian efforts on behalf of occupied Poland by sending thousands of packages of new and used clothing, rolls of bandages, medical supplies and foodstuffs to prisoners of war, refugees and foreign exiles. Cooperating with both *Rada Polonii* and the American Red Cross, the women's divisions of the PNA throughout the country eventually shipped more than 70,000 packages to those in need. They also helped to staff USO centers in the United States, organized blood drives on behalf of the Red Cross and promoted the sale of War bonds. For their extraordinary services the PNA's women were honored with a special citation of merit from the American government.

Another activity involved assisting in the resettlement of Polish orphans during and after the War. For example, when approximately 350 orphans were brought to the United States from Siberia, the women's lodges assisted in their adjustment to their new surroundings. Initially the children were quartered at Alliance College under the supervision of Vice President Frances Dymek and Wanda Rozmarek, wife of the president of the fraternal. After the War, hundreds of PNA women signed assurance agreements with the Government in which they pledged to help displaced persons entering this country to find housing and work. In addition, the PNA Benevolent Society spearheaded a campaign which raised more than $250 thousand for orphans and blind children in and outside Poland. After the Polish situation became critical in 1980, they once again stepped up their humanitarian work on the homeland's behalf.[9] Looking back at these many and varied efforts, one veteran PNA women's activist put it bluntly when she declared, "Men may have been in the top positions, the leaders of the PNA, but the women were the doers. They were always ready and willing to roll up their sleeves and work for the cause." While this opinion might somewhat exaggerate things, it is no understatement to assert that the women participating in the Polish National Alliance added considerably to its record of contribution to Poland, America and Polonia.

On the organizational level, the trend since 1900 has been decidedly in the direction of an ever expanding role for women in leadership positions within the Alliance. At first, the early women's activists led by Valerie Lipczynska of Grand Rapids, Michigan worked toward the goal of organizing their own "Women's Department," an autonomous agency enabling female representatives in PNA lodges to get together and share information on their interests and concerns. In April, 1906 the PNA board of directors formally approved such a Department and chose Lipczynska, who had been elected vice censor in 1905, to direct its activities under the general supervision of the board. Until 1935, when it was dissolved and replaced by a system of women's divisions in each supervisory district of the PNA, the Women's

Department spearheaded most of the activities of female members of the fraternal.

In 1909, PNA women made another major advance. In that year the delegates to the organization's national convention approved a change in the constitution requiring that at least one of the ten national directors of the PNA be a woman. This action enabled Mary Sakowska to become the first woman to join the board as a voting member. In 1911, the rule was revised to provide for at least two female directors and Sakowska and Wladyslawa Chodzinska were then elected. In 1915, the minimum was once again raised to require at least three female directors. The same year witnessed the election of a woman vice president, Casimira Obarska. But Obarska's office was honorary in nature and she had no vote in board proceedings. The first ladies' vice president with the right to vote was Magdalena Milewska, who was elected in 1921. From then on women were insured at least four places on the fifteen member national board of directors.

The entry of women into the PNA supervisory council was less immediate. Although that body was established in 1907, no women except for Lipczynska were able to win entry into its midst until 1935. Even Lipcznyska held her post on the council for most of the period between 1907 and her death in 1929 thanks to her honorary designation as "commissioner for all states." The failure of women to win election as commissioners was simply due to the fact that they were unable to defeat male opponents in contests held at the national conventions which involved only the delegates from the territorial district from whence they came. Recognizing this problem the delegates at the 1921 convention approved the creation of the offices of special women commissioners in each supervisory district. Women holding such posts were restricted to working with the women's lodges in their areas, however.

In 1935, the women delegates to the Baltimore convention were finally successful in pushing through a proposal to place two ladies on the supervisory council as "at large" representatives. They also established on a formal basis the office of lady commissioner in every supervisory district. From 1935 onward, there were in fact two commissioners in each district, one (usually a man) elected by the convention delegates and another representing the women's lodges in the district. These lady commissioners headed the "women's divisions" in their districts and were responsible for organizing youth, cultural and humanitarian activities that heretofore had been under the control of the central Women's Department headquartered in Chicago. That office was disbanded.

Though these moves represented progress (further advanced by the 1939 decision to create three supervisory seats reserved for women), it was not until 1951 that women achieved genuine parity with men in this body. In that year the delegates at the PNA *sejm* in Buffalo created two equal commissioners for each of the sixteen supervisory districts, one to be filled by a man, the other by a woman. Most responsible for the realization of parity was Frances Dymek, who was first elected Ladies' Vice President in 1935. Defeated for reelection in 1939, she won again in 1943 and held the post until her retirement in 1967. An expert political leader and a strong ally of President Charles Rozmarek, Dymek shrewdly capitalized upon her political ties with Rozmarek and the support she provided for his reelection campaigns to win a series of tangible gains for women. It was in return for her backing in 1951, for example, that Dymek won Rozmarek's endorsement of parity between male and female commissioners. In 1955, Rozmarek also backed her proposal that the office of ladies' vice president become second only to his in authority. Through this change in the constitution, the ladies' vice president became acting president upon the death or incapacitation of the chief executive. Such was Dymek's stature that her decision to oppose Rozmarek's reelection effort in 1967 was a major factor contributing to his defeat.

From even this brief discussion it is evident that women have contributed significantly to making the Polish National Alliance the force within American society that it has become during the past eighty years. Without the involvement of Teofila Samolinska, Valerie Lipczynska, Mary Sakowska, Casmira Obarska, Magdalena Milewska, Frances Dymek and many others, the legacy of the PNA would have been far less than what it is today. Unfortunately, if it is accurate to state that the achievement of male PNA activists have received all too little recognition from later historians of Polonia, the fate of women leaders in the Alliance has been even more severe. If there is any single "untold story" of Polonia that needs telling because of its particular relevance to issues of the 1980s, it is in the description and analysis of the lives of women in the PNA and Polonia. Overcoming tremendous barriers against female involvement in public affairs imposed upon them by the societies in which they lived, the women activists of the PNA went on to vastly enrich the work of Polonia's greatest fraternal by their dedicated service.

Humanitarian Activities Through the Years

An all too seldom recognized PNA activity has consisted of its humanitarian efforts on behalf of the Polish immigrants and their offspring, whether or not they belonged to the Alliance. Such neglect is in some ways understandable given the attention that PNA leaders themselves have trained upon Poland and the organization's many other activities. As a result, however, relatively few people have become aware of the PNA's continuing role in assisting people in need. Indeed, not a single published work has properly credited the Alliance (or for that matter any other Polonia fraternals) in this area. Yet despite the fact that its humanitarian labors have gone generally unheralded, the PNA has continued to provide millions of dollars over the years to assist people in dire straits and in this fashion has made one of its greatest contributions to American society.

One turn of the century observer of the conditions of the Eastern European immigration rather vividly described its plight when he remarked, "My people do not live in America; they live underneath America. A laborer cannot afford to live in America."[10] Indeed, the Polish immigrants to the United States who brought with them neither work skills nor a fluency in the English language found themselves holding jobs that were at the bottom of the economic ladder. One scholar of the time who used census data for 1910 provided detailed statistical information to underscore this reality. He found that while Polish immigrants made up 15 percent of the foreign born populations in such states as Pennsylvania, Massachusetts, Illinois, Michigan, New York and Wisconsin, they constituted 48 percent of the foreign born workers in the coal mines, 75 percent of the employees in the clothing mills, 46 percent of the packing house workers, and 51 percent of those laboring near the blast furnaces. In contrast they made up only 3.5 percent of the foreign born sales personnel, 2.4 percent of the professional workers and 5.7 percent of the foremen.[11]

Though systematic data on the salaries earned by Polish workers in the pre World War era are difficult to find, the information that exists shows that they were very poorly paid despite the arduous and often hazardous nature of their jobs. Some estimates show Polish workers earning approximately $10 per week by 1914, but a report from the U.S. Immigration Commission published the very same year and based upon a survey of more than 13,200 laborers found that 34 percent earned less than $400 in one year. Seventy percent earned less than $600. This at a time when $500 was defined by the agency as the minimum amount required by a family to maintain an adequate diet.[12]

During the industrialization of the United States (1870–1930), an era that coincided with the massive migration of Poles into this country, wages tended to fluctuate greatly. For example, coal miners in Pennsylvania who earned about $3 a day in 1870 were getting about $2.25 a day in 1900 for the same kind of work. In the early 1890s freight car builders employed by the Pullman Company outside Chicago were receiving $2.61 per day. Their 1893 strike was precipitated by a salary cut that reduced their wages to $1.54 a day. During economic "panics" (the term used to describe the depressions that regularly occurred before 1929), great numbers of laborers were thrown out of work altogether without the benefit of unemployment compensation or any other systematic forms of relief or welfare. All these considerations led the PNA and other fraternals of the day to establish some type of minimal relief assistance to worker-members and their families when they were in need. By the early 1900s this program was an important part of PNA activity both at the national and the local lodge levels. Another early action was the work of the Alliance among new immigrants. The Alliance established its first immigrant home in New York in 1886 and continued to operate its own facility until after World War II. The aim of the center was to provide newcomers just off the boat and without friends or nearby relatives with temporary lodging and meals until they might find their bearings.

Still, the primary humanitarian concern of the Alliance was best expressed by its providing low cost life insurance to its members and their families. The PNA established its first working insurance program in 1886, one which enabled a male member to be insured for $500 and his wife for $250. By 1897 husbands could purchase up to $900 insurance with their spouses holding certificates paying a $300 death benefit. After 1900, when women won full membership status, insurance benefits were equalized. In 1907, maximum coverage through the PNA was raised to $1,000 and a variable payment system based upon the age of the insured member was set up to replace the old fixed method of assessment insurance. Thanks to this reform the old restriction requiring individuals to be less than fifty years of age in order to quality for admission was lifted. Thereafter, anyone in acceptable medical condition between the ages of 16 and 65 could qualify for insurance protection.

To the Polish immigrant, insurance was very important for a variety of reasons. Obviously, given the hazardous nature of work in the foundries, mines and slaughterhouses and the disastrous impact a breadwinner's death would have upon his family's survival, the immigrants understood the economic value of insurance. Another factor was the concern the immigrant placed upon his funeral. Although even modest funerals were expensive (one scholar who studied funeral bills in 1920 found that even the least expensive ones cost about $120 not including church expenses and headstone), often placing the family in debt, a proper funeral was important to the typical Polish immigrant. One writer observed that the Pole "wants to die decently, ceremonially, socially (because) the funeral is the most conspicuous event in his life . . . It leads to speculation on how well off or poor he was . . ."[13] Thus for both economic and cultural reasons, it was important that burial insurance be available and at a modest cost to the immigrant and his family.

And while the great majority of PNA members prior to World War I were fairly young (in 1909 it was reported that the average insurance holder was 34 years old with children not yet eligible for membership), the Poles' concern about insurance was hardly misplaced. The problem after all centered on the hazardous working conditions so many immigrants experienced, a situation that was illustrated vividly by the PNA itself. At its 1909 convention, the fraternal provided an analysis on the causes of death of insured members during the previous two year period. Of 487 fatalities, 179 were directly the result of on-the-job accidents and constituted by far the greatest single cause of death. Most work-related deaths took place in the mines but foundry and railway accidents were also responsible for a considerable number of fatalities.[14]

Thus, it is not at all surprising that thousands of Polish immigrants turned to the fraternals for insurance protection, particularly since such insurance was not then readily available through commercial firms nor their employers. In one study conducted in 1920 by the Illinois Health Insurance Commission among approximately 3,000 randomly selected Chicago families, more than 82 percent owned some type of life insurance. Of the eleven ethnic and racial groups into which the respondents were categorized, Poles ranked third in the proportion of family units with 88.5 percent owning insurance. Among European ethnic groups, only Czechs were more likely to own insurance, with 88.9 percent doing so.[15]

But the Polish National Alliance provided more than life insurance to its members, valuable as such assistance was at the time. In 1890, the PNA also established a special committee on assistance *(komitet wsparc i pomocy)* to aid those in dire need. Over the years, this committee, using funds raised through a special one or two cent monthly assessment on every member, continued to broaden its rationale for providing assistance. Originally, help was furnished only to members who were forced to relocate their families to another city in search of work. Later, individuals who suffered injury at work or were incapacitated by serious illness or disease could also apply for assistance through their lodge by appealing to the committee. By the 1920s, destitute elderly PNA members were included into the committee's humanitarian work. Indeed, for the next thirty years a major subject of discussion at nearly every national convention focused on whether or not the PNA should establish its own home for aged members. Only in 1951 was the proposal to do so finally tabled after a survey of the lodges showed a majority opposed the idea.

Still, in the era before the U.S. government created its own social security and old age assistance programs, efforts such as the PNA committee on assistance remained a significant part of the fraternal's work. In 1910, for example, it was reported that 1,150 members in need had received some financial assistance from the Alliance during the previous two year period, 2.1 percent of the fraternal's total membership. Moreover, these figures reflect only the work of the national committee and not the efforts of local lodge committees created for the same purposes and operating with their own funds.

From 1963 onward, the committee's responsibilities were substantially redefined at each succeeding PNA convention. This was in recognition of the expansion of state and Federal welfare programs and the consequent lessened importance of fraternal-sponsored charitable assistance. Thereafter, the Alliance redirected its emphasis into another area, that of relieving aged insurance holders of their continuing obligations to pay regular insurance premiums. By 1980, members over the age of 65 who owned any one of four different life insurance policies had become eligible to request that they be relieved of paying regular premiums in the future. In all, nearly 20,000 persons were affected by these decisions.

Yet another type of humanitarianism unique to fraternals characterized PNA actions on behalf of its members who participated as soldiers or sailors in America's wars. The PNA patriotically supported the United States in both World Wars, not only out of hope that victory would bring Poland's freedom but also out of its members' deep loyalty to their adopted homeland. Nevertheless, these conflicts also meant that many insured members were called into military service and combat. In World War I, more than 6,000 PNA members eventually served, either in the American armed forces or in the Polish army formed in the U.S. In World War II, nearly 36,000 men and women of the Alliance took part in some way in the conflict. Later in Korea and in Vietnam, several thousand PNA members once again answered their country's call to duty. In each of these conflicts, there were many Alliance members who were casualties. In the First World War more than three hundred perished and in World War II, 1,017 individuals lost their lives while 4,730 others were wounded. Several hundred PNA members were casualties in America's two later wars on the Asian mainland.[16]

In each of these struggles, the Polish National Alliance decided that it was its duty to provide full death benefits to the families of those members who lost their lives in action, even though the organization had the option to limit insurance payments to deaths occurring in peacetime conditions. In World War I, the PNA, faced with the possibility of paying extraordinary insurance liabilities voted a special 2 cent per month assessment on all members to cover the costs of the conflict. In World War II, no special assessment was set up, even though the Alliance eventually paid out nearly one million dollars in battlefield death benefits. Such actions in themselves could not begin to nullify the tragedy visited upon families which lost members in war. Nevertheless, they were more significant expressions of commitment than patriotic speechmaking on behalf of the American war efforts and showed the PNA's dedication to the well-being of its members and their loved ones. This commitment was backed up by deeds.

In yet another noteworthy way was the PNA's humanitarianism evident and this concerned its support of better wages and working conditions for the immigrant worker and the defense of workers' rights. From the outset, the PNA was seen by both Polish socialist and labor union activists as a genuine defender of the immigrant working man. Indeed, a delegation of Polish workers belonging to the Alliance put forth a resolution at the 1893 PNA *sejm* in Chicago calling upon the fraternal to rename itself the Polish National Alliance of Working People and to focus its priorities on their needs. Though this effort failed, leftist and socialist PNA members continued for years to press their case at national conventions of the Alliance. Moreover, by World War I, a sizeable proportion of the PNA membership possessed a distinctly working class character and many PNA lodges were composed exclusively of bricklayers, miners, foundry workers, packing house workers, and carpenters. At the 1913 *sejm* in Detroit, the proletarian character of the Alliance was underscored when numerous resolutions having a definitely socialist tone were passed and the *Skarb Narodowy* fund was transferred into the hands of Pilsudski's socialist forces in Poland.

But there were other and perhaps more significant expressions of concrete PNA identification with workers' concerns. After the massacre of 19 Polish and Slovak coal miners by a sheriff's posse near Lattimer, Pennsylvania in August, 1897, the PNA delegates then holding their national convention in Philadelphia voted to send a delegation headed by former Censor Frank Gryglaszewski to western Pennsylvania to assist the state authorities in prosecuting the officials responsible for the violence. These men served as translators for the workers who had witnessed the shootings in which thirty-nine men had been wounded. The PNA also voted $1,000 to aid in this effort to see that justice was served.[17]

Consistently, the PNA played an important part in supporting the aspirations of working people struggling to organize labor unions in the difficult years before 1933, when the U.S. government opposed that movement. The existence of lodges entirely made up of union members of course added weight to this stance. In 1909, PNA activists in Massachusetts were helpful in mediating the textile worker strike in Ludlow on behalf of the workers. One of the participants in this effort was John Romaszkiewicz, who later rose to become the president of the Alliance.[18] After World War I, PNA members were conspicuous participants in the waves of strikes that occurred in the steel and meat packing industries in Chicago. Two PNA leaders, Stanislas Rokosz, a past PNA president, and John Kikulski were killed in the violence accompanying their efforts to organize the packing house workers. The PNA newspapers lent their editorial encouragement to unionization efforts and for years afterward, many union locals in cities like Detroit and Chicago held their headquarters in PNA lodge halls. Given the close cooperation that existed in many Polonia communities between labor and fraternal leaders, it is unfortunate and innaccurate to assert that the PNA's philosophy made it unfriendly to organized labor. Though the Alliance did espouse the slogan "swoj swojego" (cooperation among all Poles in business and commerce) rather than the idea of class solidarity, the PNA was generally sympathetic to the working people, who after all, comprised the overwhelming majority of its own membership.[19]

Such concerns also led the Alliance to provide funds to workers to assist them when they became embroiled in prolonged strikes or were laid off from their jobs. On numerous occasions the PNA board of directors voted substantial sums of money for these causes, notably in 1910, 1914, 1922 and 1927 on behalf of miners in Pennsylvania. As frequent were PNA decisions to free unemployed or striking workers from their obligations to meet their insurance premiums until they were back at work. The Alliance also provided aid to its members when they were the victims of natural disasters. For example, it sent help to those who were affected by the 1906 San Francisco earthquake; in 1973 residents of Johnstown, Pennsylvania whose homes were devastated by floodwaters also received assistance.[20]

Through these varied humanitarian activities, the PNA showed that its aims were not limited to working on behalf of Poland or providing for its members' social and recreational needs, important as those activities were.

Operating in the spirit of its founders, the PNA continued to be more than a fraternal insurance association and patriotic movement by working conscientiously in the humanitarian realm. Though these works have seldom received the attention they have deserved, together they constitute some of the greatest achievements in the fraternal's first century of service.

Chapter 11

EDUCATION AND THE ALLLIANCE

Important to the founders of the Polish National Alliance was the subject of education. They correctly realized that formal education was a necessary acquisition if the thousands of Polish immigrants streaming into the country were to advance socially and economically in American society, and eventually win an audience for their views on Poland's independence. From the outset, therefore, the PNA included among its aims "the moral and material betterment of the Polish immigration and its interests," an idea that became the basis of its commitment to learning.

Initially, PNA educational work was focused in *Zgoda,* where Poland's history was frequently discussed and the immigrants exhorted to commemorate patriotic observances honoring the fallen heroes of past insurrections. But in time, the question of education became recognized as one requiring different strategies, since PNA members knew that their children were receiving little if any instruction about Polish history in the schools, even those operated by the Polish clergy.

If the situation was not promising for patriotic education in the parochial schools it was far worse in the public schools. There, not even the Polish language was taught, let alone Polish history. By the early 1890s it was clear that if Poles in America were to retain their ethnic heritage, the PNA would have to take a different approach to the task of educational work. An early stratagem was to urge public schools located in heavily Polish communities to include courses in Polish history, language and literature. In this way, the youth would successfully preserve its heritage while adapting to American society and the English language. As early as 1891, the PNA national convention had passed a resolution encouraging "all Poles to become naturalized citizens since the U.S. Constitution in no way interferes with efforts on behalf of Poland or love for the Fatherland." The Alliance published its own naturalization handbook *(Podrecznik Naturalizacyjny)* including the fifty most frequently asked questions of applicants for American citizenship. These questions have since been reprinted in nearly every volume of the PNA almanac for later generations of newcomers. In essence, therefore, the ideology of the Polish National Alliance stressed the harmony, not conflict, between Polish ethnic identity and loyalty to the U.S. Given this orientation, the primary issue was one of preserving Polish feeling in America.

In Cleveland in 1895, the delegates to the eleventh *sejm* created a special committee or department concerned with educational matters. This committee was named the *Wydzial Oswiaty* and immediately set out to organize lectures and courses in Polish history and literature presented by visiting scholars from Poland. In 1896, Professors Kurcjusz and Siemiradzki, who had recently arrived in America, were commissioned to tour the country and lecture about Poland to its lodges. A second aim of the committee was to provide qualified children of PNA members with no-interest loans to assist them in their high school (and in later years college) educations. By the turn of the century the loan program was in full swing. Eligibility rules for the programs were explicitly defined in 1909; loans were to be made to children of PNA members belonging to the Alliance for at least five years or to applicants who themselves had held policies for at least three years. That year, $3,000 was set aside for the loans; over the years, the amounts increased steadily. The program itself was intended to be "self-funding" with earlier recipients who had found jobs after completing their educations repaying what they had been awarded to assist later applicants. With new money continuing to be earmarked for the program, the loan repayments significantly increased the size of the fund by the 1930s.

A glance at reports of the *Wydzial Oswiaty* over the years shows an active and influential committee. In 1913, for example, its chairman reported that 47 individuals had received $4,456 (or approximately $95 per student) during the previous two years. In 1925 the committee made loans to 60 recipients, of whom 22 were attending the PNA school in Cambridge Springs, Pennsylvania. Between 1924-1926, $15,000 in interest-free loans were granted. In 1929, 122 loans amounting to $18,000 were made. Of the 140 young people who had applied that year for assistance, 38 were identified as planning to attend the Alliance school, with the rest enrolled at other institutions. Of all applicants (128 of whom were men), 22 planned careers in Law, 20 in Medicine, 13 in Dentistry, 10 in Teaching, 10 in Engineering, 10 in Pharmacy.[1]

In 1930, $19,825 in loans went to 162 students, 41 of whom were in one of the programs offered in Cambridge Springs. In 1932, $22,785 in loan money was made available, but the program was sharply reduced in the following year to $14,500 because of the Depression. Jacob Twardzik, chairman of the *Wydzial Oswiaty* reported that the number of applicants had risen to 524, but only 192 students could be helped. Indeed, a budget of $117,900 would have been necessary for the *Wydzial* to have satisfied all the requests for educational assistance, he concluded. As it was, however, between 1932–1934, 673 students did receive loans totaling $72,982.

In 1935, the delegates to the PNA convention in Baltimore even further deemphasized their support of the student loan program. Four years later, Frank Synowiec, chairman of the *Wydzial Oswiaty* reported that a total of $50,748 had been made available to 875 recipients during the years between 1935 and 1939 for an average of less than $60 per student. Synowiec also noted a severe decline in the rate of loan repayment. In a wide-ranging review of the committee's practices, he pointed out that of all loans granted between 1901–1929, $50,611 had not yet been paid back. Indeed, loans totalling $151,656 were still outstanding if one included disbursements which had been made between 1929 and 1939 (although the committee did not consider such recent loans to be delinquent until ten years had elapsed). This revelation, though not particularly surprising in view of the large amounts of money loaned out to students over a period extending over more than forty years, the limitations facing the PNA in bringing about repayment, plus the Depression's effects, led some to question the value of the program. Still, there were defenders of the student loan effort. In 1940, Mary Czyz, ladies' vice president and chairman of the committee proudly reported that more than 1,500 students had received approximately $257,000 in loan assistance over the years. Czyz went on to defend the program by offering the observation that "there is not a single American university where Polish American students in need of financial assistance to complete their studies had not benefitted from aid provided by the *Wydzial Oswiaty*."[2]

The coming of the Second World War significantly changed the character of the PNA student loan program, however. At the 1947 PNA convention in Cleveland, committee chairman Angela Wojcik noted that only $950 in loans had been made during the entire four year interval since the preceding conclave; in contrast, $38,630 in earlier loans had been repaid since 1943. The student loan program had in fact practically ceased to operate, she declared, because so many young men and women had entered the Armed Forces instead of going to school. Wojcik also drew attention to the impact of the post war GI education act, through which thousands of returning veterans were able to go to college with Federal government aid, a development likely to make PNA student loans less attractive. Wojcik also described how the *Wydzial Oswiaty* had become increasingly involved in other programs. For example, it had become responsible for underwriting the costs of the annual May 3rd Constitution Day observance at the Kosciuszko monument in Chicago. As far back as 1935, the committee had been authorized to direct annual summer Polish studies courses in Cambridge Springs. The committee also had raised around $57,000 from within the PNA membership to assist in the resettlement of Polish orphans who had come to the United States from Russia *via* Mexico and was active in other charitable projects as well.

Between 1947 and 1967, Vice President Frances Dymek headed the committee. During her tenure, the loan program declined still more in status. Between 1947 and 1963, for example, only $12,550 in student loans was granted and the amounts available to qualified students were not allowed to exceed $100. During this same 16 year period, more than $40,000 in earlier loans were repaid, but these monies were diverted into other activities, including the publication of Polish language books for the growing post war immigration in America and the sponsorship of the always impressive Third of May observances. Reprinting Sienkiewicz's great historical and patriotic novels, *Pan Wolodyjowski* and *Ogniem i Mieczem* cost the committee $10,000; another expensive publication effort was that of Waclaw Lednicki's *Russia, Poland and the West.* A rather serious blow to the loan program occurred in 1951, when the convention delegates in Buffalo voted to discontinue the penny per month assessments of PNA members for educational activities. During the next twelve years the committee's funds depended totally upon its own money raising projects, which included the annual appeals for contributions at the Third of May observances. Loan repayments continued to trickle in too, but at a slower rate. Between 1959 and 1963, only about $4,400 was received, compared to $17,000 between 1947 and 1951.[3]

Several changes in the loan program approved in 1963 greatly revitalized *Wydzial Oswiaty* activities. Most significant, $150,000 was set aside for scholarships to students at the Alliance College in an effort to encourage more young people to attend the PNA school. In 1967, Dymek reported that more than $121,000 of this amount had actually been spent. In addition the maximum amount on student loans was doubled to $200 in belated recognition of rising educational costs. As a result nearly $9,000 was loaned out between 1963 and 1967 in contrast to only $2,800 during the previous four year period.

Following Dymek's retirement as Ladies' Vice President, Irene Wallace (1967–71) and Helen Szymanowicz (since 1971) continued the scholarship and loan policies initiated in 1963. For Alliance College students the only eligibility requirement was membership in the PNA for at least two years. An additional scholarship of $100 was also established for students earning a grade of "B" or better in the Polish language courses offered at the College.[4] Due to the substantial increase in college enrollment during the years of Wallace's tenure, nearly $160,000 was expended in scholarships while she presided over the *Wydzial Oswiaty*. But when a precipitious decline in the student body occurred in the years after 1971, scholarship activities of the committee were also affected: between 1971 and 1979 less than $125,000 was actually spent. The loan program, however, grew in significance and between 1967 and 1983 more than $70,000 was expended for this purpose, while a nearly equal amount was paid back by earlier recipients. Thus while only about $1,100 in loans had been distributed per year in the 1947–1967 period, from 1967 to 1983 the average annual amount awarded rose to $4,500. Still, a general lack of awareness about the loan program among many PNA members with children and grandchildren in college hindered its greater utilization, despite its increasing value in an era of dwindling Federal aid to higher education.

Two initiatives extending beyond the concepts of student loans and scholarships to those at Alliance College were approved at the 1979 PNA national convention in Washington, D.C. There, PNA convention chairman Adam Tomaszkiewicz's proposal to award fifty merit scholarships of $500 each to young PNA members attending college was approved and in 1980, implemented by the board of directors. These "special recognition" scholarships were to commemorate the PNA centennial. These awards were made to outstanding students who were themselves involved in PNA and Polonia activities or whose parents had made significant contributions to the Polish ethnic community. This merit program deserves continuation, expansion and greater publicity, and can benefit both its recipients and the PNA by linking their academic efforts with the traditional educational goals of the fraternal. A second program inaugurated at the same time set aside a total of $150,000 for the next four years for scholarships to college students belonging to the PNA but not attending Alliance College. This program was continued by the delegates to the 1983 convention under the chairmanship of Vice President Szymanowicz.

Another side of *Wydzial Oswiaty* work over the years was in its organizing of the so-called Saturday Polish school movement. In existence from the beginning of this century, the Polish schools mushroomed in the 1920s, thanks largely to the efforts of dedicated women members of the Alliance, and emphasized instruction in Polish language, literature and history. By 1930, 146 schools were in operation providing instruction for 10,404 children.

In 1935 there were 238 schools with 17,000 children and in 1940, 195 schools with approximately 14,000 students. Besides underwriting the instructional costs of these programs, the PNA also published educational materials and song books for the courses, such as the widely used *Wypisy Polskie.* The Polish Saturday school program was less adversely affected by World War II than was the loan program and many PNA members, whether they were born in America or happened to be recent immigrants, took a renewed interest in organizing language, singing and dance programs coordinated by the schools. A decline in the program did begin in the late 1950s and accelerated in the 1960s as younger Polish Americans and their families moved out of the old Polonia neighborhoods into the suburbs, where few organized Polish American communities were to be found. In 1963 the Alliance financed 80 schools. By 1967 this number had dropped to 71 and four years later it had fallen to 43 schools. In 1979, thirty schools remained in existence with a combined enrollment of fewer than one thousand children. In 1983, Vice President Szymanowicz reported to the delegates attending the thirty-ninth convention that the Educational Department had supported the activities of between 32 and 36 Saturday schools during the previous four year period.

The *Wydzial Oswiaty* also sponsored educational conferences in Chicago, New York, Buffalo and Cleveland to further the training of the schools' instructors. After 1935 the Summer Polish studies course at Cambridge Springs, Pennsylvania was established to improve and regularize the instructional program and through the years several thousand persons received formal training that many put into practice in their lodges and councils.

Another PNA educational activity was its support of libraries and reading rooms which provided its members with access to popular Polish literature, history and political tracts, as well as useful information about the citizenship tests they were required to pass to become naturalized Americans. A PNA Library and Museum committee had been formed in 1891 when the Alliance accepted the personal library of the venerable patriotic leader, Henry Kalussowski, as a gift to Polonia.[5] Kalussowski made his donation on the condition that the Alliance open the library to the general public and that it continue to build up the collection. In 1892, the library officially opened with a collection of approximately 6,000 titles. Its formal dedication took place on October 22, in conjunction with Polonia's celebration of the 400th anniversary of Columbus' discovery of America. Working with the then sizeable budget of $1,000, the committee was initially chaired by Stanislas Kociemski, a former PNA President and Treasurer. When the *Wydzial Oswiaty* was formed in 1895, its members cooperated closely with the library committee to purchase, print, and disseminate reading materials for the growing Chicago Polonia along with the rest of the country. By 1908, more than 120 local PNA libraries and reading rooms had been set up and possessed approximately 20,000 books in all. In 1929, the *Wydzial Oswiaty* chairman reported that more than one hundred lodges and councils continued to maintain their own reading rooms and libraries; in 1930, the 114 libraries and 36 reading rooms in operation contained about 45,000 titles valued at $60,000.[6]

The central PNA library and museum gradually accumulated a remarkable collection of materials that was heavily used in Chicago. Even though a large portion of the original Kalussowski collection was later transferred to the Alliance School library in Pennsylvania in 1912 (where it had grown to more than 12,000 titles in 1931), the PNA library in Chicago continued to expand. In 1924, it included 7,757 titles and by 1937 the collection had nearly doubled, including 13,492 titles. In 1956 there were 25,428 titles in the collection, most of these in the Polish language.

Particularly in the heyday of Chicago Polonia activity, the PNA central library was a center of cultural life. One estimate of library usage made in 1916 determined that 11,000 persons had borrowed 26,000 titles during the course of the year while another 8,400 persons had spent time in the reading room without, however, borrowing any materials. In 1937, a similar count showed that about 8,000 persons had borrowed 27,000 titles while 13,400 used the reading room over a year's time. Between 1959 and 1963, 17,012 people used the library and borrowed 31,975 titles. Between 1967 and 1971, however, 10,622 persons used the library over the entire four year span and this number has declined further in recent years. Nonetheless under the care of Mrs. Josephine Rzewska, a long time PNA veteran, the library remains an attractive place filled with photos and Polish artifacts which underscore its museum-like atmosphere. It is unfortunate that more persons, particularly school teachers, do not take the opportunity to walk their children through the library to provide them with a greater appreciation of this aspect of Polonia history and activity.

Through the years the *Wydzial Oswiaty* has underwritten the publication and dissemination of dozens of books, magazines and brochures, including Oskar Halecki's *History of Poland*, the work *Polish Pioneers of Jamestown* which commemorated the 350th anniversary of the first appearance of Poles in America in 1608, and Wanda Rozmarek's 1963 handbook, *Polish for Americans,* intended for Polish language courses taught at night and in high schools. In 1980, the Educational Department authorized the reprinting of the first PNA history, originally published in 1894.

All these activities exemplify the Alliance's ongoing commitment to educational enlightenment. Within the movement, nonetheless, many continued to hold the view that education in the Polish heritage ought not to be left solely to the Alliance's newspaper, its Saturday schools, libraries or to non-Polish academic institutions which Polonia's youth attended with the aid of student loans. They argued vigorously that the PNA should organize its very own school. Such an institution they hoped, would explicitly promote the patriotic and social values of the Alliance on an intellectual level in its curriculum and thus help to form the next generation of PNA and Polonia leaders. A stimulus behind this concept already existed in the form of the schools which parishes and religious orders operated. Already by 1900, a number of parochial high schools had been established in Chicago, Milwaukee, Buffalo and other Polonia centers.

At the PNA's 14th national convention in Grand Rapids, Michigan (1899), the importance of education as a means of preserving Polish consciousness among the youth was evident from a series of resolutions the delegates approved in which they called for the teaching of Polish in the public schools ("like the Germans receive") and the expansion of PNA publications about Poland. In 1901, PNA and PRCUA representatives met at Holy Trinity Church in Chicago where they issued a call for the preservation of the Polish language, culture and traditions in the parishes, greater autonomy of these parishes from the non-Polish hierarchy and opposition to Americanization.

In 1903, however, the delegates at the Wilkes-Barre, Pennsylvania PNA convention went a step further and approved the formation of a special education and school commission charged with the task of raising funds to create a school owned and operated by the Alliance. Moreover, they put teeth into the resolution by voting a monthly one cent assessment upon all members to help realize this aim. In 1905, this assessment was doubled.

The fund raising campaign was temporarily eclipsed by a second action taken at the 1905 convention to underwrite the costs of constructing a monument in Washington, D.C. to honor Tadeusz Kosciuszko. PNA Secretary Theodore Helinski spearheaded the all-Polonia drive to achieve this goal; only after the Kosciuszko monument was completed and dedicated in May, 1910, simultaneously with a Government-funded statue honoring Pulaski, could attention again be directed to the Alliance school project. Fortunately, once the costs of the Kosciuszko monument had been covered, more than $75,000 remained in the school fund to pursue this activity.

At the 1911 Alliance convention in St. Louis, a motion was approved urging the leadership to establish a school where students might obtain on modest terms an education "that would be conducted in a genuinely civic and patriotic spirit . . . identifying the best of American and Polish culture . . ."[7] The board of directors and the censor were authorized to move swiftly to identify appropriate sites for such a school. Soon after the convention the Reverend Seweryn Niedbalski of Erie, Pennsylvania, working with two Pittsburgh PNA leaders, Anthony Karabasz and former Vice Censor Roman Abczynski (whose responsibilities had involved the school project) informed Censor Anthony Schreiber that the Rider Hotel located in the town of Cambridge Springs, about 20 miles south of Erie, was available as a potential site. Named after W. D. Rider, who had opened the hotel in 1897, the building had later become known as the Vanadium and was a popular health resort. Besides the hotel, which included several hundred rooms and sat atop a hill overlooking the small town, 160 acres of adjacent woodlands and fields were also available for the sum of $175,000. Schreiber inspected the property and immediately invited the board of directors and the supervisory council to consider it as the site for the proposed Alliance school. On December 4, 1911, they travelled to Cambridge Springs and there approved Schreiber's recommendation to make the purchase. All agreed that the Rider Hotel could be readily transformed into the main building of the school and that the surrounding land could serve as a campus where other school buildings might eventually be constructed. A major reason for the vote, aside from the modest price, was Cambridge Springs' healthful resort atmosphere and its central location, roughly equidistant from the great Polonia centers of Chicago and Milwaukee in the west and New York, Buffalo and Philadelphia in the east. Moreover, the proximity of the school to large Polish populations in Western Pennsylvania, Ohio and Southern Michigan was also given consideration. The site seemed to be ideal.[8]

In the spring of 1912, PNA President Marian Steczynski resigned to assume personal responsibility for the speedy conversion of the hotel into a school ready to open that fall. Steczynski's efforts proved successful; what is more, he continued in the capacity of business manager of the Alliance school for the rest of his life. A skilled horticulturalist, he devoted considerable time to develop the natural beauty of the grounds. In one of his projects, Steczynski directed the planting of hundreds of fir trees which presently line the college. These he transplanted from seedlings which were brought to the school from Poland after the War and symbolized the ties between the PNA school and the homeland. Steczynski's very presence on the campus gradually made him a living symbol of the founders' commitment to the school.

The first faculty of the institution (which was originally conceived as a four year secondary school together with a finishing program for young boys in the primary grades) included seven men. Romuald Piatkowski supervised the academic program. Piatkowski was a Polish born educator who had earlier taught at the Orchard Lake Seminary near Detroit. A PNA activist for a number of years, he was appointed to be the first head of the Alliance Press Agency in 1908 and in 1910 he played a leading role organizing the Polish National Congress held in Washington, D.C. Described as "a gentleman and a scholar" by a later Alliance College President, Stefan Mierzwa, Piatkowski originally headed an institution whose academic program emphasized mathematics, English, Polish, French and Latin and which admitted boys up to the age of twenty at a total cost (including tuition, room and board) of $200 per year.

The school's formal dedication took place in a memorable ceremony held on October 26, 1912. The main speaker for the occasion was none other than the President of the United States, William Howard Taft. Taft's visit to Cambridge Springs was remarkable for several reasons. For one thing, it involved a rather arduous trip taking the President out of Washington for days. For another, Taft chose to make the visit only a few days before a Presidential election in which he was locked in a bitter four-way contest with Woodrow Wilson, Theodore Roosevelt and the socialist candidate Eugene Debs. Given these circumstances, his visit reflected not only his regard for the Polish National Alliance's achievement in education; it also signified the importance he attached to the PNA in the coming election.[9]

Taft's address included the usual praise for the industry of the Poles in America and a review of Poland's history which included some criticisms of the flaws in its political life that had led to its partition. More interesting, however, was the president's prescient remarks about what nowadays is called "ethnic pluralism". Expressing confidence that the Polish "immigrants could become solid citizens of their new homeland while preserving the valuable traits of their ancestors," Taft stated:

> I have an abiding faith in the influence of our institutions upon all who come here, no matter how lacking in education they may be, if they have the sturdy enterprise to leave home and to come out to this new country to seek their fortunes. It is not the uneducated who scoff at education—they value it. They sacrifice everything to enable their children to obtain that which they are denied. The second generation of a sturdy but uneducated peasantry, brought to this country and raised in an atmosphere of thrift and hard work, and forced by their parents into school to obtain an instrument of self-evaluation, has always contributed to the strength of our people, and will continue to do so. The difficulty that they do not speak our language makes the process of amalgamation slower perhaps, but it does not prevent it.

The President concluded his remarks with a strong justification of a liberal immigration policy:

> I am proud of our country that we have had its doors swinging easily open for the industrious peoples of other countries that have sought ours . . . He would be blind indeed who would deny that a substantial part of our progress is due to this policy of generosity toward those who are seeking the atmosphere of freedom and the land of equal opportunity.[10]

In its first year of operation, the Alliance school attracted an impressive enrollment of 326, but questions about its failure to receive accreditation from the Commonwealth of Pennsylvania caused doubts about the future. Piatkowski's strict disciplinary system also encouraged the withdrawal of a number of students. In September 1913, the institution's second year, enrollment had fallen to only 135 boys. Responding to its problems the school authorities focused their attentions upon winning accreditation, which was at last awarded in 1914. In 1915 a technical training program, originally called the *Instytut Rzemieslniczy,* was added so that young men could obtain instruction in such fields as mechanics, tool design, and electrical work. Later renamed the *Instytut Techniczny,* this program proved to be very successful and continued to operate as an integral element of the school until it was phased out in 1965. Liberal arts students were then entering the school in large numbers and a technical training program was judged unnecessary to the college's future operation. In 1975, however, the Institute was reopened with graduates of its two year program earning an associate degree in applied science.

During the World War years of 1914–1918, the Alliance school doubled as a training ground for future army officers. In 1914, the PNA established its first officers training program in anticipation of America's involvement in a conflict its leaders hoped would bring Poland's independence. They believed that America's entrance into the war would enable them to organize an army of Poles in the U.S. and lead many Polish Americans to be recruited into the U.S. military forces as well. These expectations made it crucial to design a training program to enable Poles to assume command responsibility once war broke out. When the United States actually declared war in 1917, approximately five hundred Polish Americans planning to serve in the Polish army in France travelled to Cambridge Springs to take part in the program, along with 220 non-Poles. Under the direction of Frank Dziob, the officers training program continued on a smaller scale the next year.

The officers program not only served the patriotic cause; it also provided the Alliance school with a new function in a time of declining student enrollment. In 1915, 197 students were in the high school and another 102 were in the trade school. By 1917, 169 remained in the high school and 68 were in the technical training program. Indeed, it was not until after the war's end that this trend was reversed.

At the newly accredited school's first commencement in June, 1916, it was Ignacy Paderewski who delivered a stirring speech to the graduates. An emotional orator whose flashing eyes and bushy red hair gave him a charismatic appearance, the virtuoso pianist and patriot praised the PNA for having never rested on words when deeds were needed on behalf of Poland. "That is why they have created this school for the immigrants," he declared. Paderewski urged the graduates to remember that though they had been raised in America, their parents had brought with them to the United States "the elements of your life. They have formed your character as young men of Polish heritage and through their efforts they have insured Poland a rich future harvest on the abundant fields of America. Polish youth! You today are setting off on a long road. You are off to work, to toil, even to battle. Go in Poland's name, in God's name and you will succeed. The eternal land of your fathers blesses you that God will grant you happiness."[11]

In 1916, Rector Piatkowski resigned to protest the school board's decision to make English instead of Polish the language of instruction at the *Kolegium.* A Polish-born writer, Waclaw Gasiorowski, eventually succeeded him. A veteran of the Polish army, Gasiorowski struggled to increase enrollment but was unable to bring it beyond the 250 mark. In 1924 Gasiorowski did introduce the two year college program; in its first year of operation, 18 students enrolled. New facilities were also planned, which included a men's dormitory and classroom building named for Kosciuszko.

In 1928 Gasiorowski resigned and later returned to Poland. He was replaced as president of the school by Professor Stefan Mierzwa, creator of the Kosciuszko Foundation in 1925 and a close associate of Censor Casimir Sypniewski. "An excellent organizer and a man of practical dreams," Mierzwa firmly believed in the institution's possibilities, provided that the PNA commit itself to transforming the little rural school into a first rate academic center. This view was shared by Sypniewski and the school board. Mierzwa worked successfully to regain accreditation, which the school had lost under Gasiorowski. He improved the instructional level of the college program to enable its graduates to be readily admitted into four year American colleges. Mierzwa ended the finishing school program in 1930, another sign of his commitment to push the institution ahead. Under Mierzwa, the Kosciuszko building was completed and an imaginative development plan entitled "Yesterday, Today and Tomorrow" won the approval of the school board for submission to the delegates attending the 1931 PNA convention. This building plan presented four sets of proposals by different architects to create new buildings on the campus, including a library-auditorium complex, another dormitory, a classroom building, and a combined administrative office-cafeteria center. The estimated cost of the expansion project was pegged at $600-650,000.

But these proposals were not approved due to a combination of developments, which included Mierzwa's own resignation. Most directly responsible was Sypniewski's defeat in his quest for a third term at the hands of Attorney Francis Swietlik of Milwaukee. As the PNA officer chiefly responsible for the operation of the college, Swietlik had the right to select his own man to head the school and Sypniewski's close association with Mierzwa disqualified him from continuing in his post. Second, by 1931 the Great Depression's affects were being felt upon college finances and downward trends in student enrollment undermined arguments for expansion. In the 1928-1929 school year, for example, 313 students had enrolled— 145 in the high school, 143 in the technical institute and 23 in the junior college. But by September 1930 the size of the student body had dwindled by 17 percent, to 260 students. As the Depression wore on enrollment steadily declined; in the 1936-1937 school year only 192 students were in attendance.

But the most dramatic blow came on January 20, 1931 when a fire caused by an electrical short circuit totally consumed the Rider Hotel. The building had served as the school's main classroom area, its administrative center, dormitory and library housing the invaluable Henry Kalussowski collection. Fortunately, not a single student was caught in the building at the time of the fire and Mierzwa was able, with the cooperation of the local citizenry, to find clothing and adequate shelter for the boys. Mierzwa declared that a building had burned down, not the college, but the destruction of the old hotel caused enormous problems in the school's operation for the remainder of the academic year and left many PNA members pessimistic about its prospects.

In the years following the Rider Hotel fire, the PNA did commit resources to the rebuilding of the college, although its pace was tortuously slow. In 1934, a combined classroom-administrative center-science structure, Alliance Hall, was completed and in the following year the athletic field was set up. The school's next major project was a combined auditorium-cafeteria-library and reading room named Washington Hall which was dedicated in 1942. These two newer structures together with Kosciuszko Hall had a similar traditional architectural style and were all built of red brick with Spanish tile roofs. All remain particularly impressive and beautiful edifices accented with Polish and PNA symbols. Except for a couple of other minor buildings these structures constituted the entire campus until the early 1960s, although the PNA purchased the Bartlett Hotel located in the town of Cambridge Springs and transformed it into a women's dormitory when the college became co-educational in 1948.

A chronic problem facing the college during the 1930s and 1940s was that of low enrollment. In 1940, President John Kolasa reported that the entire student body included 177 young men, with 43 graduates completing their studies. If these figures were a source of concern, the onset of the World War II caused even deeper problems. In September, 1942 total enrollment was 116 and by March, 1943 it had declined to only 70. When the PNA held its national convention in Boston in September, 1943 it was reported that enrollment had further declined to only 32, with seven faculty members on the staff. To preserve the school in the face of the crisis, President Rozmarek proposed an emergency assessment of 60 cents a year on all insured members. Also approved was a resolution to house at the school several hundred Polish war orphans who had been brought to America from Siberia. Moreover, Rozmarek, who in June, 1942 had asserted the need for positive thinking about the college and its future development into a four year co-educational liberal arts institution, repeated his appeal at the 1943 convention. His recommendation was put into effect after the war, when the school's prospects brightened for the first time in years.

In September 1946, nearly three hundred students were on the campus, most of them veterans. In September, 1948 the college became a four year co-educational institution and its new president, Arthur Prudden Coleman, made strengthening the curriculum a top priority. Coleman, a linguist who had previously taught at Columbia University, headed the school for fourteen years and during his tenure Alliance College generally maintained an enrollment of approximately 300 students.[12] By 1963, a year in which Edward Kruszka served as acting president of the College following Coleman's departure, the faculty of the school included 26 members and the student body 316, of whom 77 were in the graduating class. In 1951, its technical programs were reorganized with admissions requirements raised to the college level. Thereafter, students enrolled in the technical institute could earn an associate degree in applied science with specializations in tool design, drafting, applied electricity and tool and die making.[13]

By the early 1960s, new concerns surfaced at the Alliance's national conventions about the future of the college. One worry focused upon the school's failure to expand its enrollment. Equally serious was growing recognition that the college required an enormous infusion of new money to build modern campus facilities, both to attract students and to satisfy the expectations of state accrediting agencies. This challenge to the PNA's continued involvement with the College was, however, met thanks largely to a notable change in the leadership of the Alliance.

In 1959, Edward Kozmor, a New Jersey businessman and longtime Polonia leader was elected censor. In Kozmor, the college gained a great friend who was the first censor since Sypniewski to make the school's revitalization a high priority. Kozmor worked hard to promote popular awareness and greater financial support from PNA members for its development, mincing no words in speaking directly about the college's needs. Declaring at the 1963 PNA convention that "despite everything we do, the school is standing still," Kozmor nonetheless helped to generate a new attitude supportive of the school's development. Between 1955–1959, for example, the Alliance's financial contribution to the college had slipped to less than $76 thousand a year. But between 1959 and 1963 it rose to $130 thousand, with the PNA also approving a $125 thousand loan to the college. Between 1963 and 1967, direct assistance increased to $151 thousand per year and the PNA granted three new mortgage loans amounting to $1.185 million. In addition, $150 thousand was set aside for scholarships for students attending the college. Indeed, between 1967 and 1979, direct subsidies from the PNA to its college increased to an average annual amount of $230 thousand, with $37,500 provided each year for scholarships. So great was the commitment Kozmor had inspired that President Mazewski was able to report that between 1975 and 1983 alone, the Alliance had provided more than $4 million in assistance to the college.[14]

Kozmor's efforts came at a critical time in the history of the college, which was once again facing a ten year accreditation review. In response to his appeal, the delegates at the 1963 convention not only increased the PNA's annual subisdy to the college to expand enrollment but also agreed to an aggressive building program to provide it with the means to at last attain major status.

In 1964, with accreditation once again retained, construction began on a new science building named in honor of Maria Sklodowska-Curie, the two-time Nobel laureate in physics and chemistry and the discoverer of radium. Completed in 1966, the Sklodowska-Curie building was but the first of a series of major additions to the campus in the 1960s, largely under the direction of Censor Walter Dworakowski, who succeeded Kozmor upon his death in 1965, and Dr. Henry Parcinski, President of the College between 1963 and 1970.[15] In 1967, the PNA secured a Federal government loan for $2.13 million from the Department of Housing and Urban Development and was given 50 years to satisfy the debt at an interest rate of 3 percent. Through this loan and additional PNA assistance, a new men's dormitory on the campus was completed in 1969. This edifice was named in memory of Stanley Luter, who for many years was the school disciplinarian. At the same time a new women's dormitory was also completed, along with a new student union-cafeteria complex and a third building dedicated to Censor Kozmor which presently provides accomodations for special guests at the college. The most recent addition to the school is the residence of the president of the college, which is located just off the campus grounds.

As a result of these and earlier decisions taken by the Polish National Alliance, the college complex in 1983 included eight major structures and several minor buildings in a heavily wooded 220 acre campus. Situated in the foothills of the Alleghenies and reminiscent of the Tatra mountains of Southern Poland, the entire area possesses a natural beauty which is complemented by the Polish character of its buildings. In addition, the college also features several monuments which symbolize its roots. One is dedicated to President Woodrow Wilson, who supported the reestablishment of an independent Poland in 1917; a second honors the young men who served in the Polish army in America, whose officers were trained at the school. Yet a third, a grotto, is dedicated to the Virgin Mary. The library of the college contains numerous artifacts underscoring the school's Polish past, including the Stanley Piatkiewicz reading room which is filled with more than 12,000 books in Polish history and culture, along with a great bust of Paderewski. It is difficult for anyone visiting the campus not to be moved by the experience of simply walking about the tree lined grounds and reflecting upon the patriotic emotions that inspired the founders of the school.

During the 1960s, the reconstruction of the college was coupled with a dramatic growth in its enrollment, due largely to a number of coincidental developments including the "arrival" of the post World War II baby boom generation to college age and the decision of many to go on with their studies during the United States' participation in the Vietnamese War. In 1960 enrollment was down to 230 but in 1964 it had risen to 300; in 1966 it had increased to more than 500 and in 1968 peaked at 629 students. Indeed, overly optimistic projections about the future guessed that by 1970, 800 students would be on campus served by a faculty of fifty (twice the number of instructors in 1963). In the fall of 1971, Alliance college admitted a record 223 students into its freshman class and at its spring commencement ceremonies graduated 224 individuals, the largest class in its history.

But just as rapidly as enrollment climbed in the 1960s so also did it decline in the 1970s. In the Fall of 1973, enrollment plunged below 500 when only 414 students started the school year. In 1975, 237 students were admitted, while in 1977, 182 students began the year. Although the college has made a modest recovery since then (in 1982, 230 students began the school year) it must also be noted that a large portion of the present student body is presently involved in the restored two year technical program rather than in its four year liberal arts curriculum.

During its history, Alliance College has produced a number of outstanding young men and women who have gone on to contribute significantly in the various professions to which they devoted themselves upon their graduation. To mention just a very few representative *alumni* of the school who have remained committed to its continued betterment long after their graduation, one could include Professors Walter Smietana (class of 1943), Thaddeus Haluch (1950), Louis Rotter (1918), and Blair Kolasa (1944), all of whom later taught at the College; William Miesczak (1925), Norbert Soltys (1952), Matthew Pliezga (1940), Walter Drake (1940), John Wronowski (1926), Walter Golaski and Frank Jarecki, all businessmen and industrialists; Helen Kotecki (1966), Henry Majdecki (1954), and Ronald Wilga (1970), educators; and John Szwarc (1964), a professional chemist. Particularly involved in service to the College as members of its Board of Trustees over the years have been Hilary Czaplicki (1949, presently PNA Censor), Stanley Krzywicki (1941), John Czajka (1952), Patricia Sikora (1964), Edward Sitnik (1952, elected PNA Vice Censor in 1983), and Regina Jaworski (1970).

Among the many faculty members who have devoted themselves to the goal of making academic excellence the watchword at Alliance College, one might include a wide-ranging list of outstanding teachers whose students will remember with nostalgia. Edward Kruszka served fifty-two years at the school beginning in 1915 with the formation of the Technical Institute and was the acting president of the College for a year. Louis Rotter, who had graduated from the school in 1918 also served in the Technical Institute until his retirement in 1965. John Jadus, a professor in the social sciences department taught at the college from 1934 until 1964 and also served a term as its acting president. Leo Krasowski, a professor of Business and Economics retired in 1979 after twenty-seven years of service at the college. William Page taught mathematics for twenty-four years and Owen Friend gave thirty years to the teaching of Biology. Among *alumni* presently at the college are Professor Smietana, a specialist in Psychology and another former acting president; Blair Matejczyk, a professor in Physics and Mathematics as well as the photographer of college events through the years; and

Thaddeus Haluch, professor of Physical Education, coach of school inter-collegiate sports and presently Director of Athletics. Professor Robert Ilisevich has taught History and Political Science at the college for twenty-five years. Among other well-remembered college staff personnel is Stanley Luter, the school's dean of men and its stern disciplinarian who learned his responsibilities through service in the Polish army raised in America during the First World War.

One of the best known student activities bringing recognition to Alliance College in recent years has been the *Kujawiaki* dance ensemble, which was born on the campus in 1964. Rooted in growing student interest in the music and dance heritage of Poland, along with an increased awareness of the popularity of other student dance groups, such as the Duquesne University Tamburitzins, the *Kujawiaki's* first leader was Gardenia Woju-tuszewska. In 1965, Jan Sejda, an original member of the world famous *Mazowsze* ensemble, took over as director of the *Kujawiaki.* During his tenure, the Alliance College group became recognized around the country for its commitment to authentic Polish dances, music and costumes from various regions of the country, and was even invited to perform at the White House. In 1973, Ronald Galasinski took over the reins of leadership and added a new dimension to the *Kujawiaki* choreography, an American set of old hoe-down music and square dancing.

In 1974, Christine Marchewka, one of the first *Kujawiaki,* became the ensemble's director after having pursued doctoral studies in Slavic literature at Indiana University and a year of Theater study at Southern Illinois University. She incorporated dramatic elements into the ensemble's program based upon literary and historical research. The current director of the *Kujawiaki* group is Lawrence Kozlowski, whose background in Polish ethnography has enabled him to further enrich the folkloric character of the many dances and songs performed by the ensemble, helping it to better reflect the variety of Polish peasant music through the past. Undoubtedly, each phase of *Kujawiaki* activity has strengthened its role as an ambassador of Polish folk culture to Americans, PNA members and non-members alike. The group's existence has also generated interest and enthusiasm among Polish Americans in their own heritage and helped contemporary Polonia find its own place in the burgeoning world of folk song and dance activities throughout the United States.

Responsible for the College in its most recent decade of difficulty has been the present censor of the PNA, Hilary Czaplicki. An *alumnus* of the College, Czaplicki has actively worked to raise funds by strengthening the relations between the school and its three thousand past graduates, many

of whom have enjoyed professional success in business. As chairman of
the PNA school commission, which is composed of all members of the
Alliance's board of directors and its supervisory council, and as a member
of the school's board of trustees, Czaplicki has done much to place the
operations of the college on a sound footing and to frankly present its actual
situation to the PNA membership.

In his work, Czaplicki received significant support from PNA President
Mazewski. During his administration, Mazewski generated approximately
$200,000 for the college through a variety of fund raising activities. These
have included the annual sale of PNA Christmas cards to the membership,
banquets on behalf of the school, and personal solicitations. Mazewski's
own commitment to the College, however, was no better symbolized than
by his son Aloysius Jr.'s attendance and graduation from the institution
in 1972. Among previous PNA presidents only Marian Steczynski had had
a child enrolled at the school.[16]

In November, 1982 Alliance College observed the 70th anniversary of
its founding at a fund raising banquet held in Philadelphia attended by
more than 500 hundred *alumni*, PNA leaders, Polonia activists and other
friends of the school. In retrospect, it was evident that the commitment
of the Polish National Alliance to the principle of educating the youth of
Polonia in their heritage has been awesome. Through the years, nearly 4,000
men and women have been educated at the school at a cost of approximately
$20 million. In the beginning, the Alliance school emphasized the objective
of training its students in the Polish spirit, whether at the high school, technical
school or junior college level. After World War II, when the institution
became a four year coeducational liberal arts college, this commitment
remained even though the student body increasingly became one composed
of individuals of non-Polish ethnic origins who resided in the area. No other
Polish American organization, it ought to be added, has made a commitment
to education in any way comparable to that of the PNA.

Yet even as PNA members could look back proudly upon their achievement, problems about the college continue to require attention. One concerns
the school's capacity to attract an enrollment sufficient to make it viable.
Historically, the school has been unsuccessful in gaining students from the
great Polish American communities located in Chicago, Milwaukee, New
York and New Jersey. Even nearby Polonia centers in Cleveland, Buffalo
and Pittsburgh have declined as targets for recruitment with the growth
of publicly supported colleges and universities in those cities since the 1950s.
Given the school's enrollment problems, the financial burden placed upon

the PNA has increased every year during the past decade. Indeed, in addition to its regular support which included mortgage subsidies, scholarships and direct aid to the college amounting to appoximately $2 million during the period between 1979 and 1983, the PNA board of directors found it necessary to provide an additional $300,000 to the school at its meeting of April 30, 1982.

Regardless of Alliance College's fate, which after all will be decided only after serious deliberations among the membership and leaders of the PNA, it remains paramount that the Polish National Alliance's record of commitment to education not be forgotten or minimized in discussions about the school. This record is a proud one and is fully in keeping with the Alliance's traditional commitment to the education and advancement of its youth in America, along with the development of greater appreciation of the rich Polish cultural heritage and all that this means among Polish Americans and non-Poles alike.[17]

Heads of the Alliance School*

Romuald Piatkowski, first Rector (1912–1916)
Edmund Dolewczynski, Stanislas Popiel and George Harrington, acting directors of the three sections of the school: High School preparatory program, Junior and Senior High School (1916–1918)
Felix Mikolajczyk, Director of the School (1919)
George Harrington, Acting Director (1920)
Waclaw Gasiorowski, Chief Administrator and Director of the School and the Technical Institute (1920–1928)
Stefan Mierzwa, President of the School including its Junior College (1929–1932)
Edward Kuberski, Director and Manager of Alliance College (1932–1936)
William Powers, Acting Dean of the College (1937)
John Kolasa, President of the College (1937–1947), Acting President (1948–50)
John Jadus, Acting President (1947–1948)
Arthur Coleman, President of the College (1950–1962)
Edward Kruszka, Acting President (1962–63)
Henry Parcinski, President of the College (1963–1970)
Walter Smietana, Acting President (1970–1972)
Herman Szymanski, President of the College (1972–1977)
Arthur Auten, President of the College (1977–1981)
Lawrence Carlson, Acting President (1981–1982)
Casimir Kowalski, President of the College (Since April, 1982)

Edward Kruszka served as Dean of the Technical Institute of the Alliance School for nearly the entire period between 1917 and 1965, when the Institute went out of existence.

In 1977, the Technical Institute was reorganized and Peter Mathews was appointed Director of Technical Programs at the College.

---

*Terms of service were generally for the school year which begins in September.

Alliance College Honorary Degree Recipients (1955–1983)

Polish National Alliance Leaders
Joseph Habuda, Vice Censor (1956)
Francis X. Swietlik, Censor (1956)
Charles Rozmarek, President (1972)
Casimir Lotarski, Censor (1977)
Joseph Wiewiora, Editor, *Zgoda* (1978)
Walter Dworakowski, Censor (1976)

Polonia Leaders
Joseph Osajda, President, Polish Roman Catholic Union (1973)
Adele Lagodzinska, President Polish Women's Alliance (1972)
John Cardinal Krol (1967)
Very Reverend Michael Zembrzuski, Vicar General Pauline Fathers (1968)
Bishop Alfred Abramowicz (1979)
Rev. Stanley Milewski (1978)
Prime Bishop Francis Rowinski (1981)

Businessmen and Industrialists
Henry Kawecki (1964)
Richard Switlik (1966)
Leo Schmidt (1966)
Tadeusz Sendzimir (1967)
John David Wright (1967)
Frank Bobrytzke (1968)
Walter Golaski (1968)*
George Karch (1969)
Walter Poranski (1969)
Ignatius Nurkiewicz (1969)
Frank Piasecki (1970)
Edward Piszek (1971)

Dennis Voss (1973)
Chester Sawko (1975)
Stanley O'Brakta (1977)
Victor Owoc (1979)
Frank Jarecki (1980)*
Richard Lelko (1980)
William Miesczak (1982)*
George Korey-Kreczkowski (1983)
Henryk de Kwiatkowski (1983)

Politicians
Thaddeus Adesko (1963)
John Gronouski (1964)
John Dent (1965)
Edmund Muskie (1970)
John Volpe (1972)
Michael Balzano (1973)
John Tabor (1974)
Clement Zablocki (1975)
Joseph Kuszynski (1975)
Mary Anne Krupsak (1977)
Roman Pucinski (1979)
Daniel Rostenkowski (1980)
Lt. Gen. Edward Rowny (ret.) (1981)
Walter Baran (1982)

Labor Leaders
David McDonald (1955)
I. W. Abel (1970)
Lech Walesa, In absentia (1981)

Academic Persons
Henry Parcinski (1956)
Alfred Sokolnicki (1961)
Arthur Coleman (1962)
Edward Kruszka (1963)
Zbigniew Brzezinski (1966)
Leon Twarog (1969)
George Janczewski (1970)
Viola Andrews (1976)
Blair Matejczyk (1979)
Stanley Luter (1973)

Philanthropists
Blanka Rosenstiel (1978)

Alumni
Myron Steczynski (1972)*
Valery Fronczak (1976)*

Graduates of Alliance College

Chapter 12

LEADING POLONIA: THE POLISH NATIONAL ALLIANCE
AND THE POLISH AMERICAN CONGRESS

From its origins the Polish National Alliance was envisioned to be a political movement representing the concerns of the burgeoning immigrant community on behalf of Poland. While the PNA soon established an insurance program for its members, this aspect of its activities did not detract from its political aims; indeed its insurance feature helped provide the necessary financial means and the mass membership base for the Alliance to become a viable and influential force in Polonia.

Between 1880 and the onset of the First World War, the PNA dedicated itself to the task of working for Poland's independence by seeking to unify Polonia under its auspices. These efforts, however, were largely unsuccessful, except for the Polish National Department which operated during the conflict under the leadership of the banker, politician and PNA activist, John Smulski. But Smulski's movement disappeared only a few years after the War and once again Polonia was without a political action organization to articulate its interests and concerns.

With the outbreak of World War II, the sole federation of Polonia groups in existence was the Polish American Council *(Rada Polonii)*, a charitable and humanitarian association linking the fraternals and parishes and chaired by Francis Swietlik, then the censor of the PNA. During the War, the *Rada Polonii* did much for Polish refugees by gathering food parcels, clothing and medical supplies but it was unable to double as a political movement without jeopardizing its charitable status. By 1944, Swietlik and the *Rada Polonii* had given way to the newly formed Polish American Congress *(Kongres Polonii Amerykanskiej)* headed by PNA President Charles Rozmarek and geared to speak for Polonia on the political issues facing occupied Poland. Including practically every significant ethnic organization, secular and religious, the Polish America Congress (PAC) quickly became the authoritative representative of Polonia. Moreover, it continued to operate as an interest group in American politics long after the War, unlike Smulski's National Department.

Throughout its history, the PAC has been intimately associated with the Polish National Alliance in various ways. For one, the president of the Congress has always been the president of the PNA. For another, not only has the national PNA leadership participated actively in PAC work, hundreds of local lodges and councils of the Alliance have also belonged to the Congress as members of its various state divisions throughout the country. This linkage from top to bottom has given thousands of PNA members the opportunity to take part regularly in the affairs of the PAC in their communities. Indeed, it might even be argued that without the Alliance the PAC could never have long existed. But PNA members valued the Congress and have willingly worked for its objectives for good reason—in bringing together the organizations of Polonia the PAC represented nothing less than the realization of the historical PNA aim of uniting the entire Polish American community on behalf of Poland's independence and its own betterment.

Charles Rozmarek's stormy twenty-four year career as president of the Polish America Congress has been described earlier. In retrospect, Rozmarek made two lasting contributions as PAC leader. His first great achievement was in rallying Polonia behind the cause of Poland's independence in its darkest days during and immediately following the War. By 1944 the devastated country was under Soviet military occupation and Moscow had installed a provisional communist-led regime in power, even though it enjoyed practically no popular support among the Polish people. At Yalta President Roosevelt and Prime Minister Churchill conceded Poland to Stalin. Faced with this seemingly hopeless situation Rozmarek might have also come to terms with the reality of a Soviet-ruled Poland; instead he became an outspoken critic of the Western Allies in their failure to win the peace and was one of the first Americans to publicly question the wisdom of the U.S. alliance with the Soviet Union.

Second, Rozmarek's unwavering opposition to Soviet and Polish communism gradually reshaped Polonia's ideological perspective to reflect his thinking. The cold war PAC stance in turn reinforced the attitudes of other ethnic Americans of Eastern European origins toward the USSR and even affected the outlook of larger bodies of people within the Roman Catholic Church, the organized labor movement and the Democratic party, each of which included large numbers of Polish Americans. Together these forces helped define the character and conduct of American foreign policy for more than a decade after the Second World War had ended.

Poland's wartime ambassador to the United States, Jan Ciechanowski, later wrote a book whose title, "Defeat in Victory," appropriately characterized his nation's fate in the conflict. Though an important member of the Alliance that defeated the Axis powers and a major contributor to victory on several fronts, Poland fell under Soviet control in 1944 and has remained at best a semi-sovereign state ever since. In such conditions it was critical that Polonia be prepared to express Poland's cause with the United States and do what it could to assist in the resettlement of thousands of *emigres* and refugees who were admitted into this country after 1945. The PAC's existence also made possible a greater role for Polonia in American politics and from 1944 its leaders on several occasions attempted to affect the outcome of elections on both the national and statewide levels. Since the 1960s in particular, the Congress has increasingly also reflected Polonia's growing concern about its own future. Accordingly, during the past decade and a half, the organization has sought to formulate a domestic agenda for Polonia, one involving the preservation of ethnic culture and its religious and secular institutions, the defense of the Polish self image from derogatory attacks, and support for the appointment of talented Polish Americans to government service. Aloysius Mazewski, who succeeded Rozmarek as president of the Polish American Congress in 1968 put the problem bluntly when he first took office, asserting that it was time to "upgrade the image of ten million Americans of Polish heritage."

After 1968, PAC activity was considerably revitalized. To deal with its many concerns the Congress established eighteen standing commissions charged with formulating and executing coherent strategies in such areas as the teaching of the Polish language in the schools, the publishing of books disseminating information about Poland and Polonia, relations between Polonia and the Catholic Church, and the appointment of Polish Americans to government office. Three particularly effective commissions focused on defamation, Polish-Jewish relations, and Polish affairs.

Headed by Chicago attorney Ted Kowalski and Connecticut judge Thaddeus Maliszewski, the PAC Civil Alertness Commission has been active in combatting defamation of Poland and Polonia appearing in the American mass media. This phenomenon itself became increasingly noticeable and troubling to Polish Americans during the 1960s. Attacks often took the form of demeaning ethnic humor, but there were also occasional allegations about anti-semitism and racism which were linked to Polish ethnicity. Due to the prompt and energetic protests from the Commission and President Mazewski directed toward television networks, book publishers, film producers and distributors responsible for making derogatory materials available to the public, defamation against Polish Americans declined substantially during the 1970s.

A second activity initiated by the new PAC leadership after 1968 was in establishing regular contacts between the Congress and America's influential Jewish community. Historically, Poland had been the ancestral homeland for perhaps one-half of all American Jews and prior to World War I at least one-third of all those who had emigrated from Poland to the United States had been Jews. Before World War II, Poland's population of 34 million had included more than 3.5 million Jews and the country was a recognized center of Judaic culture. But in the United States, Jews and Poles had had little contact with one another before the 1960s. Not only employed in different sectors of the nation's economy but also concentrated in diverse parts of the country far from one another, the two peoples had been preoccupied with their own adjustment to American society.

However, World War II's tragic impact upon Jews and Poles in the ancestral homeland, together with each community's own educational and economic advances in America after 1945 served to bring members of the two groups into increasingly regular contact. Given these changed circumstances, it was important that the organizations representing each community also develop more formal relations, both at the national as well as the local levels. With the Polish American Congress representing Polonia, meetings with American Jewish leaders have occurred periodically since 1968. Their aims have been (1) to create better understanding among Poles and Jews alike of the actual history of their pre War relationship in Poland, one that endured for nearly eight centuries; (2) to foster greater sensitivity within each community about the existence of both anti-semitism and anti-Polish feeling in the United States and its corrosive effects upon intergroup relations; and (3) to cooperate where possible on matters in which Poles and Jews were in substantial agreement. Such issues included the question of "reverse descrimination" in hiring, promotions and admission into educational programs in the U.S.[1] Among the positive results flowing from the dialog have been the lectures organized in various cities under PAC co-sponsorship and dealing with the history of Jewish-Polish relations. These lectures have been named in memory of Janusz Korczak (1878–1942), a Polish citizen of Jewish cultural origins, and a noted physician, author, educator and patriot who perished in the Treblinka concentration camp. Korczak's life along with the lectures honoring his memory have come to symbolize the principles of mutual understanding and tolerance between Jews and Poles. Other fruits of the dialog were the highly favorable reactions on the part of American Jews to the election of Pope John Paul II in 1978 and the rise of the

Solidarity labor movement in 1980. In that same year, Mazewski was one of the two Polish Americans whom President Carter appointed to serve on the sixty-one member United States Holocaust Commission. This body was charged with the task of planning a fitting memorial to the Holocaust in Washington, D.C.

In its approach to Poland, the PAC after 1968 remained consistent in opposing the Soviet-sponsored communist regime in Warsaw. For example, the Congress' leaders declined to participate in ceremonial meetings with Polish United Workers' Party First Secretary Edward Gierek during his 1974 visit to the U.S. Further, the PAC persuaded officials of the State Department not to invite Gierek to cities with substantial Polish populations. In sharp contrast was the organization's cordial relationship with representatives of the Polish Roman Catholic Church who periodically have made their way to the United States. One churchman to meet PAC leaders was Karol Wojtyla, who visited America in 1969 and 1976 as Archbishop of Krakow and again in 1979 as Pope John Paul II. The Pontiff also spoke with Polish American leaders in subsequent audiences in Rome. During Poland's economic crisis after 1980, these relations paid important dividends when the PAC was able to organize shipments of food and medical supplies worth millions of dollars to Poland under the auspices of the Church.

The PAC remained equally firm in pressing for U.S. recognition of Poland's western frontiers which had been defined by the Great Powers in 1945 on a provisional basis. Accordingly, Poland had absorbed a significant amount of historically Polish territory which had fallen under German control in compensation for its eastern provinces seized by Stalin in 1939. This effort bore some fruit in 1975 when the United States government and thirty-four other nations signed the Helsinki Final Act. Among the provisions of this international agreement was the signatories' recognition of the permanence of European borders established after World War II.

Yet in other ways, the PAC orientation toward Poland underwent a subtle but significant shift under Mazewski. It became less preoccupied with its past emphasis upon the doctrine of "liberation," which had already lost whatever credibility it once possessed in Washington by the late 1950s. At the same time, the Congress stepped up its support of the "human rights" cause in Poland, a concept which won increasing public support throughout the country during the mid 1970s because of disenchantment with the unfulfilled promise of Soviet-American *detente*.

President Richard Nixon's administration (1969–1974) had been committed to *detente* and its greatest achievement came in 1972 with the signing of the first Strategic Arms Limitations agreements in Moscow. But Nixon's downfall caused by his involvement in the Watergate scandal together with growing disillusionment about Soviet military expansion into Africa and Asia (actions which seemed to contradict the spirit of superpower cooperation embodied in *detente*) undermined support for the policy. In December, 1974 the United States Congress took an action which showed in dramatic fashion the depth of public disappointment with *detente*. In approving a trade agreement which the USSR had long sought that granted it "most favored nation" status in its dealings with the United States, Congress also attached a provision requiring that an unspecified number of Soviet citizens be permitted to emigrate without reprisals. Moscow immediately repudiated the entire treaty, asserting that the amendment represented interference into its internal affairs. Nonetheless, with the trade agreement, the notion that *detente* should include a "human rights" dimension was bolstered. Solidly behind this idea were the Polish American Congress, the leading American Jewish organizations, many other ethnic associations and the U.S. labor movement.

In 1975, President Gerald Ford signed the Helsinki Final Act on behalf of the United States. In addition to recognizing the post war European frontiers, the international agreement also included a section calling upon all signatory states to respect the fundamental human rights of their own citizens. Included in these rights was individual freedom of thought, conscience and religion; moreover, the Helsinki document called for periodic meetings of the signatories to monitor each state's actual compliance with the provisions of the agreement.

For its part, the Polish American Congress supported the Helsinki agreement because of its human rights provisions and its guarantee of Poland's western border with East Germany. President Mazewski led a delegation of Eastern European ethnic leaders to Washington which met with President Ford just prior to his departure for Europe. There, the PAC head persuaded his colleagues to support the Government on the agreement, despite their expressed reservations about the wisdom of granting international recognition of Soviet control over Eastern Europe.

In retrospect, the Helsinki conference marked the high water mark for pro-*detente* thinking in America. Already, doubts were being raised as to the genuine benefits of increased economic relations with the Soviet Union and these concerns were accompanied by growing dissatisfaction with the USSR's behavior in the international arena. Contrary to Nixon and Secretary of State Henry Kissinger's view that *detente* in strategic arms development and trade would "spill over" into greater cooperation in other areas of superpower interest, critics of American policy toward Moscow argued that the Soviets had actually used *detente* to "catch up" with this country in terms of its overall military power. Soviet assertiveness in the third world only further clouded the atmosphere which once had been so propitious for *detente*. In fact, it was "human rights" and not *detente* which became the watchword of several major party presidential candidates in the 1976 election, including Jimmy Carter of Georgia, who defeated Ford for the nation's highest office.

Polish American Congress concerns about human rights grew during the 1970s, a decade of failed expectations and chronic unrest inside Poland. In December, 1970 the regime of party leader Wladyslaw Gomulka was brought down following massive workers demonstrations against a precipitious consumer price increase. Gomulka, who had himself come to power in 1956 as a reformer, was replaced by Edward Gierek. Gierek rescinded the price increases and promised to make more consumer goods available to the population. He also adopted a conciliatory policy toward political critics to restore a semblance of public acceptance following his predecessor's forcible repression of the demonstrations.

Gierek's regime then embarked upon an ambitious and risky economic modernization policy based on enormous loans from the West and designed to make Polish products more competitive abroad. These exports would then earn the hard currency revenues needed to pay for the better life he had promised the Polish consumer. But the plan was shortcircuited as early as 1973 when the Organization of Petroleum Exporting Countries drastically raised oil prices and thereby brought about a recession throughout Western Europe and a sharp decline in their importation of Polish products. Gross errors in planning further aggravated the country's economic woes as did the disadvantageous trade agreements Poland had negotiated with the Soviet Union. The USSR's decision to raise the price of the oil it sold to its Polish ally compounded the country's problems. Ultimately, Poland found it nearly impossible to repay even the interest on the huge foreign debt it had incurred to finance Gierek's modernization scheme; by 1980 this debt exceeded $20 billion.

Already by 1976, increasing consumer demand fueled by salary increases Gierek had ordered coupled with lagging exports to the West forced the regime to resort to the very same tactic that had caused Gomulka's demise. In July, 1976 food prices were sharply increased in an effort to limit consumption on one of the few products the Poles were still successfully exporting. But widespread workers' demonstrations once more caused the regime to retreat. Earlier in the same year, the government had also backed down from its effort to change the language of the constitution, an action which many politically conscious Poles opposed as a transparent attempt to restrict further the few freedoms they still enjoyed. Both defeats not only

embarrassed Gierek's regime; they also led to the formation of an organized
opposition within the country in the form of the Workers' Defense Committee
(Komitet Obrony Robotnikow, KOR). Headed by intellectuals but supported
by politically conscious people in all economic and social *strata*, KOR initially
sought the reinstatement of all laborers who had been fired from their jobs,
a punishment for having taken part in the 1976 demonstrations. But gradually,
the movement broadened its demands to include the democratization of
Polish political life, greater freedom of speech and the teaching of the actual
events of Polish history in the country's universities. In 1980, KOR was
active in the formation of the Solidarity trade union movement. Particularly
important was the support it received from the nation's chief religious leader,
Stefan Cardinal Wyszynski, Archbishop of Warsaw and Gniezno and Primate
of the Polish Roman Catholic Church.

In July, 1980 the Gierek regime openly admitted the failure of its entire
economic gamble and for the second time tried to impose steep increases
in food prices upon the people. This time, however, the workers responded
differently from 1970 and 1976. Then their street protests had led the
government to resort to force and to claim it was simply restoring order.
In 1980, they organized strikes in their workplaces, demanding wage increases
sufficient to offset the consumer price hikes. In the face of these actions,
which spread to factories, mines and shipyards throughout the country, the
authorities quickly gave in.

But at the Lenin shipyards in Gdansk, a massive sit down strike in August
went beyond economic grievances. There, the organizers focused their
attention upon the need for political reform. Their demands included the
right to organize independent trade unions with the power to strike, their
own newspaper, an end to censorship, Church access to the mass media,
and the release of political prisoners, along with a list of proposals calling
for improvements in their working conditions. When the government
ultimately yielded to the strikers' demands on August 31 and accepted all
twenty-one points presented by the Gdansk workers, the stage was set for
one of the most incredible developments in modern history. Within a few
weeks of the settlement, a democratically organized independent trade union
federation calling itself *Solidarnosc* (Solidarity) had emerged. Under the
leadership of Lech Walesa, a hitherto obscure electrician and union activist
from the days of the 1970 seacoast demonstrations who became the chief
spokesman for the Gdansk shipyard workers, Solidarity grew to include
approximately ten million people in its ranks and won the support of Cardinal
Wyszynski. Identifying Solidarity with the principles of democratic socialism
popular in Western Europe (rather than the Soviet brand found wanting

in Poland), Walesa and his colleagues stressed their ties with the Church and the role that Pope John Paul II had played in inspiring their movement by his 1979 visit to the country.

Solidarity also made deep inroads into the ruling Communist party, whose membership had been badly shaken by the years events. Thousands of party members became enthusiastic supporters of Solidarity out of the conviction that the labor movement possessed the capacity to help bring about a badly needed economic and political "renewal" of the entire system. They pushed for an extraordinary congress of the Polish United Workers' Party to reshape its future policies, internal organizational structure and top leadership. This congress was held in July, 1981 and its democratically elected delegates chose a largely new leadership to direct the party; perhaps as many as forty of the two hundred people elected to the party's Central Committee were identified as members of Solidarity.[2]

For Polish Americans, already heartened by the election of a Polish Pope, the formation of Solidarity was greeted with a mixture of excitement, hope and anxiety. To many, what had transpired vindicated the PAC's historic policy toward Poland which distinguished between giving support to the aspirations of the Polish people (or nation) while rejecting any close ties or recognition of the Polish regime. The latter was seen as illegitimate. Over the years, some in Polonia had criticized the PAC for an "unrealistic" stance toward the Warsaw regime, particularly in those brief interludes in post war Polish politics when the ruling elite had decreed some kind of "liberalization" to gain favor in the West along with the appearance of greater acceptance at home. In focusing its support upon the Polish Church, whose leaders it considered to be the sole authentic representatives of the nation, the PAC had interpreted the upheavals of 1956, 1968, 1970, and 1980 as manifestations of widespread and chronic discontent which reflected the nation's rejection of an alien political system imposed from the Soviet Union and historically unable to develop any roots of indigenous support on its own.

Already in August, 1980, in the midst of the Gdansk strike, the Polish American Congress issued its first memorandum on the situation. The PAC called upon the American government to remain dedicated to its own human rights position and the principles of the Helsinki accords of 1975 and to use its influence in restraining the Soviet Union from military intervention in Poland's internal affairs. At the same time, the organization urged Washington to provide economic assistance to enable Poland to begin the task of dealing with its deepening economic crisis. This crisis, the PAC document asserted had been "brought about mainly by the inefficient, wasteful

and corrupt Communist system of centralized planning and management
. . ." Because of this situation, the statement went on, U.S. aid should be
conditional upon the Polish government's introduction of remedial structural
reforms—the prerequisites for its future economic progress.

Calling upon Radio Free Europe and its sister station Radio Liberty to
keep up the flow of information into Poland and the communist world
about events inside the country, the PAC spoke for Polonia in expressing
"its full support and solidarity for the efforts of Polish workers as they
seek a greater measure of human rights and freedom. Demands formulated
by the strike committee are just," the memorandum emphasized. Though
the strike would not be settled for another week, the Polish American Congress
had taken a stand behind the workers from the very beginning. In the ensuing
months, it never wavered from this stance.[3]

In the weeks that followed the historic agreement of August 31, 1980
between the Polish government and Walesa's committee, the United States,
under firm and continuing PAC prodding, took an increasingly bold, two-
pronged stance toward Warsaw. On the one hand, the Carter administration
grew more insistent in asserting that the crisis be settled by the Poles themselves
and without Moscow's interference. On the other, its announcement in
September, 1980 of its decision to provide Poland with $670 million in
agricultural and technical aid in the form of credits to support its economic
recovery showed a willingness on the part of the United States to deal
practically and constructively with the crisis. PAC efforts to win greater
U.S. support for Poland continued into the Reagan administration, which
came into office in January, 1981. Indeed, before its decision to withhold
economic assistance in response to the Polish regime's imposition of martial
law and its crackdown upon the Solidarity movement in December, 1981,
the Reagan administration had approved the granting of $1.2 billion in
various types of economic credits and debt deferrals. Indeed, before martial
law, the Senate Foreign Relations Committee's chairman, Charles Percy
of Illinois was reported to have been ready to approve another billion dollars
in economic credits and loan guarantees to Poland. All of the efforts were
strongly endorsed by the PAC.

On the humanitarian level, PAC work began in earnest at the end of
1980 when it responded to Walesa's appeal to coordinate an international
Polonia fund drive to purchase $5.5 million in medical supplies for Poland.
Because of Poland's worsening economic crisis, foreign currency to purchase
medical supplies and drugs from Western manufacturers had become scarce
and as many as 58 different types of medications and surgical goods were
either exhausted or in dangerously short supply. Through the tax exempt

Polish American Congress Charitable Foundation, a "bank lekkow" was quickly set up to generate funds from around the United States and seventeen other countries with organized Polish emigrant communities. By December 1981, more than $2 million in money and materials had already been collected in the drive, which was tightly monitored by a joint PAC-Solidarity commission to ensure the prompt and proper distribution of supplies within Poland.[4]

In the spring of 1981, the Polish American Congress initiated a Food for Poland campaign in recognition of the fact that the country was experiencing significant shortages of many staples. With long lines of consumers building up at the entrances of nearly every food store in Poland, shortages of meats, vegetables and even dairy products were causing special hardships upon mothers with small children, the elderly and invalids. The regime's move to impose rationing did little to alleviate the growing crisis.

PAC leaders concluded that the heads of the Polish Church were in the best position to determine whose needs were greatest. By January, 1982, more than 3.7 million pounds of food had been shipped to Poland under PAC auspices, each package bearing the inscription, "Dar Polonii Amery-kanskiej" or "Gift of the PAC Charitable Foundation." Further, after a June, 1981 agreement between officials of Poland and CARE to ship 600,000 packages of food to Poland's needy over the next two years, the Polish American Congress made its own commitment to purchase $500,000 in food packages to be distributed to the elderly, to pregnant and nursing women and to mothers with infants below normal birthweight. In addition, the PAC shipped $1.1 million in medical supplies for a total contribution of $3.6 million in relief for Poland. Another major PAC effort in 1982 was its sponsorship of the "solidarity express" train which gathered nearly 900 thousand pounds of food and medical supplies valued at $7 million for shipment to the beleaguered Poles.[5] By the end of April, 1983, total PAC-sponsored aid was estimated to have exceeded $33 million in net worth.

Throughout its existence as an independent democratically organized trade union movement, Solidarity enjoyed full cooperation from the Polish American Congress. Not only did the PAC back Solidarity politically in the United States and support its humanitarian concerns by raising funds and materials for Poland, it enthusiastically received several of Solidarity's leading representatives who came to the U.S. to inform Polish Americans about actual conditions inside the country. One such spokesman, attorney Zbigniew Gryszkiewicz, made an extensive speaking trip throughout Polonia when he visited the United States in March, 1981. When he appeared on the McNeil-Lehrer national news program, Mazewski served as his translator.

A second Solidarity representative, Stanislaw Sila Nowicki, took part in the annual Third of May observances sponsored by the Polish National Alliance in Chicago two months later. Mazewski met with Lech Walesa when he travelled to Warsaw and Gdansk on May 31, 1981, as part of the U.S. delegation attending the funeral of Cardinal Wyszynski.

The PAC's original estimation of the character and aims of Solidarity did not change throughout its existence as an open mass movement. Mazewski summed up the views of the organization and indeed Polonia on this score in his May 3, 1981 speech to thousands gathered in Chicago's downtown civic center:

> *Solidarnosc* is not a political movement. *Solidarnosc* does not reach out for government powers in Poland. *Solidarnosc,* fundamentally, is a social movement born of a desperate need for decent living conditions and a measure of internal freedom guaranteed by the universal principle of Human Rights. In simple words, *Solidarnosc* is a movement toward humanization of living conditions within the communist bloc. Obviously, this concept . . . cannot be understood by . . . the Kremlin tyrants . . . As American Polonia, we fully and resolutely support the *Solidarnosc* movement in Poland . . . We are aware of the deprivations and economic chaos created by faulty communist planning. We are doing all that is within our means of power to alleviate the poverty of the Polish people . . .[6]

Thanks partly to loud and clear expressions by PAC representatives about the danger of Soviet intervention to Western security, the U.S. under both Carter and Reagan took tough postures increasingly critical of such an action, even though there was little that the United States and its NATO allies could do to retaliate if the Soviets moved into the country.[7] The stance of the PAC was consistent throughout the period. It involved supporting the moderate elements within the Solidarity movement who appeared to be interested in building a viable trade union movement in the country. It also was committed to looking to the Polish Church for leadership. The Church, whose support for the workers' movement had legitimized Solidarity in the first place, was seen to be of crucial significance to the future success of "renewal" in Poland. Not unexpectedly, the PAC and Polonia looked to its leaders for direction in fashioning an orientation toward Solidarity, a large but loosely organized movement whose own representatives lacked experience in dealing with the official authorities in Warsaw.

On December 12, 1981, General Wojciech Jaruzelski (who had also become the head of both the communist party and the government) imposed martial law upon the country, ordering the arrest of thousands of Solidarity activists and the dissolution of the union. The regime justified its action by claiming to have evidence that Solidarity was planning a *coup d' etat* aimed at installing itself in power to overthrow communism in Poland.[8] The PAC response was prompt and clear in its complete support of Solidarity and renewal and its denunciation of the regime's action.

On December 21, 1981, President Mazewski; Helen Zielinski, President of the Polish Women's Alliance and Vice President of the Polish American Congress; Joseph Drobot, President of the Polish Roman Catholic Union and Treasurer of the PAC; and John Cardinal Krol of Philadelphia travelled to Washington where they met with President Reagan and Vice President George Bush to discuss the Polish situation. There, Mazewski presented a memorandum from the PAC which called for the immediate end of martial law, the release of all political prisoners confined by the military regime, the release of Solidarity leader Walesa and the restoration of the gains of Solidarity previously acceded to by the government. Not only were these points incorporated into Reagan's Christmas message a few days later, the entire discussion served as a basis for the developing U.S. response to the Polish crisis, which emphasized its condemnation of the role of the Soviet Union in orchestrating the acts of the Polish regime. In June, 1982, when the U.S. acted temporarily to block completion of the development by a major Soviet-European consortium to pipe natural gas into the West, the reason it offered was Soviet involvement in the Polish crisis.

Nearly forty years after its creation in Buffalo, the Polish American Congress was indeed playing the very role its founders had hoped for the organization, that of representing the concerns of American Polonia about the situation of Poland's people to the highest officials in the government of the United States. By establishing firm and enduring relations with American government leaders and by developing an accurate vision of the situation within Poland itself, the PAC was indeed as relevant in the 1980s as it had been in defending Poland's rights in its earlier crises. Indeed, throughout his presidency Mazewski helped make the PAC an increasingly visible and significant organization whenever Polonia's needs required action.

As Polish American Congress President, Mazewski proved to be an articulate and aggressive spokesman for Polonia, both in national as well as international arenas. He met frequently with Presidents Nixon, Ford, Carter and Reagan in the White House and hosted both Carter and Reagan when they visited the Chicago headquarters of the Polish National Alliance. Mazewski regularly communicated with leading foreign policy makers on Polish issues, including Henry Kissinger, Zbigniew Brzezinski and Alexander Haig. America's ambassadors to Poland have also come to know well the position of the Polish American Congress through regular conversations with its leaders both in Washington and in Chicago.

Mazewski was appointed to several prestigious commissions during his tenure as head of the Polish National Alliance and the PAC, a sign of Washington's growing recognition of both organizations. In 1970, he became the first Polish American to serve as delegate to the United Nations and thanks to the support he received from the PNA (which permitted him to spend an average of three days each week away from Chicago performing his duties in New York), Mazewski was able to take an active role for three months in the work of the U.S. delegation. During Nixon's presidency, Mazewski was also appointed a member of the Volunteer Action Committee which was charged with promoting greater involvement in civic life by people belonging to voluntary associations. This appointment was eloquent testimony to official recognition of the historic work of the Polish National Alliance and indeed all American fraternals, whose members have traditionally dedicated time, energy and money to civic and charitable causes. Later, Mazewski served on the Federal Ethnic Studies Commission which supported the successful passage of legislation creating the Ethnic Heritage Studies Act of 1972. This law represented a milestone in that for the first time in its history the U.S. government committed itself to supporting scholarly research to preserve knowledge and appreciation of ethnic and immigrant contributions to the country. In 1980, a year in which Mazewski was named to the U.S. Holocaust Commission, he and Helen Zielinski became the first Polish Americans to participate in the international conference held in Madrid to monitor compliance with the human rights articles of the Helsinki treaty. (Mazewski was succeeded in this capacity by another leading Polish American, Illinois Congressman Edward Derwinski).

As PAC leader, Mazewski expressed Polonia's positions on numerous domestic and foreign issues to the U.S. Government. Along with helping the Ethnic Heritage Studies Act become law in 1972, he was responsible, with Illinois Congressman Frank Annunzio, for winning passage of legislation providing medical benefits to Polish veterans living in this country who had fought on the side of the Western Allies during the World Wars. President Gerald Ford signed the Polish Veterans' Act in 1976.

Mazewski also worked for the appointment of qualified Polish Americans to responsible Federal, state and local offices. One was Mitchell Kobelinski of Chicago, who was named Director of the United States Import-Export Bank and later Director of the U.S. Small Business Administration.

Leonard Walentynowicz of Buffalo became Assistant Secretary of State for Consular Affairs. Mitchell Kafarski of Detroit was included on the Pennsylvania Avenue Development Commission. (On this body, which oversaw the reconstruction of one of the Capital's main thoroughfares,

Kafarski was instrumental in making sure that the Casimir Pulaski monument would be placed in a location where it could be readily seen each day by thousands of people. The statue had been dedicated in 1910 along with the Kosciuszko statue under PNA auspices.) Other appointments have gone to Dr. Blair Kolasa, Floyd Placzek, and most recently to General Edward Rowny, who was confirmed as Chief U.S. Negotiator, Strategic Arms Reduction Talks under President Reagan.

Throughout his tenure, Mazewski consistently expressed the PAC's position on behalf of a free Poland while stressing the country's importance in U.S. foreign policy. In 1970, he sharply criticized a NATO proposal to defend Western Europe from Soviet attack which would have called for barraging Eastern Europe with nuclear weapons, even though no such weapons had been based in the area. As a result of his comments, NATO strategy was reconsidered and Mazewski himself was invited to attend meetings of both the military alliance and the European common market as a U.S. observer. In 1976, he publicly condemned the so-called "Sonnenfeldt doctrine" in hearings held by the Congressional Committee on Foreign Affairs. Allegedly, Helmut Sonnenfeldt, an aide to Secretary of State Kissinger, had argued in favor of a *detente*-based policy toward Eastern Europe which would accept Soviet preeminence in the region through its recognition of the area's "organic" relationship to the USSR. After Mazewski made his strongly worded condemnation of Sonnenfeldt's views, they were categorically repudiated by President Ford; indeed, Kissinger personally informed Mazewski that no such proposals had in fact been made.[9]

As PAC head, Mazewski frequently represented American Polonia abroad. In 1969, he visited Rome where he personally presented Pope Paul VI with a memorandum expressing Polonia's concern for the future of ethnic parish life and the absence of Polish Americans in the Roman Catholic hierarchy. (Though a similar memorandum had been drawn up during Charles Rozmarek's presidency, it had simply been mailed to the Vatican and never received a reply.) Mazewski first met Cardinal Karol Wojtyla, the future John Paul II in 1969 and again in 1976 when Wojtyla headed a large delegation of Polish bishops to the International Eucharistic Congress in Philadelphia. In 1978 Mazewski attended Wojtyla's installation in Rome and he again met him on the Pontiff's 1979 visit to America; in 1981 when a special hostel for Eastern European pilgrims funded by donations from the world's Polonia was dedicated in the Eternal City, Mazewski was at the head of the U.S. delegation attending the ceremonies. Not surprisingly, the Polish National Alliance played a major role in the fund raising project, contributing more than $125,000 toward the completion of the hostel.

Mazewski has played an important role in strengthening closer and more cordial ties among the Polonia communities throughout the world and helping formulate a more coherent orientation among the many disparate groups toward Poland. He has attended a number of joint meetings bringing together the Polish American Congress and its northern neighbor, the Polish Canadian Congress. In 1978, he was a major speaker at a world congress of Polonia held in Toronto. Mazewski also attended numerous other international gatherings of Poles abroad held in Denmark, Britain and Greece and in 1981 he was named chairman of the worldwide Polonia effort to raise funds for medical supplies for the homeland. In the same year, Mazewski travelled to Warsaw where he attended the funeral of Cardinal Wyszynski as an official representative of the United States and American Polonia.[10]

Throughout his years as President, Mazewski has had considerable success in developing a working relationship with U.S. policymakers who deal with Poland. During the Carter administration he helped to arrange a series of meetings bringing together Polonia representatives and foreign service officers at the U.S. State Department where they could effectively exchange information and views about Poland for the first time. On several occasions, Carter's National Security Advisor, Zbigniew Brzezinski, met with Mazewski and other PAC leaders to discuss international affairs. Such contacts provided Polonia with its first substantial opportunities to have some input in U.S. foreign policy by articulating its views to the Government.

Following the economic crisis which ushered the birth of Solidarity, Mazewski's meetings with U.S. officials increased markedly. On frequent occasions he spoke with Presidents Carter and Reagan and with other PAC and Polonia leaders presented Polish America's perspective on the situation. Always the purpose of the PAC remained consistent—that of supporting Solidarity's right to exist as a constructive force in reforming Polish economic and political life and opposing Soviet military intervention into Poland's internal affairs. As such, the Polish American Congress has remained true to the historic goals with which it identified itself in 1944. Whatever, the future holds for Poland, the PAC is certain to remain dedicated to supporting its reemergence as an independent nation with strong cultural, economic, moral and human ties with the West, where so many millions of Poles have settled during the past 150 years.

Table 1.   National Organizations Affiliated with the Polish American
Congress and Having Representatives on its National Board of Directors, 1983

Name of Organization and Date Founded	Headquarters	Character	Estimated Membership	Number of representatives on the PAC National Board
Polish Roman Catholic Union (1873)	Chicago	Fraternal Insurance	120,000	5
Polish National Alliance (1880)	Chicago	Fraternal Insurance	300,000	8
Polish Singers' Alliance (1889)	New York	Cultural	2,000	1
Alliance of Poles of America (1895)	Cleveland	Fraternal Insurance	16,000	1
Union of Poles in America (1898)	Cleveland	Fraternal Insurance	10,000	1
Polish Women's Alliance of America (1898)	Chicago	Fraternal Insurance	78,000	5
Polish National Alliance of Brooklyn (1903)	Brooklyn	Fraternal Insurance	13,000	1
Polish National Union (1908)	Scranton	Fraternal Insurance	31,000	1
Polish Alma Mater (1910)	Chicago	Fraternal Insurance	5,000	1
United Polish Women of America (1912)	Chicago	Fraternal Insurance	4,000	1
Association of Polish Women of U.S. (1913)	Cleveland	Fraternal Insurance	2,000	1
Polish Union of America (1917)	Buffalo	Fraternal Insurance	12,000	2
Union of Polish Women (1920)	Philadelphia	Fraternal Insurance	9,000	1
Polish Army Veterans Association (1921)	New York	Veterans	7,000	1
Polish Legion of American Veterans (1921)	Detroit	Veterans	8,000	1
Polish Falcons (1928)	Pittsburgh	Fraternal Insurance	26,000	3
Polish Veterans of World War II Association (1952)	New York	Veterans	5,000	1

Table 1.   (Continued)

Name of Organization and Date Founded	Headquarters	Character	Estimated Membership	Number of representatives on the PAC National Board
Sea League of America	Chicago	Social-Cultural	*	1
American Council of Polish Cultural Clubs	Baltimore	Cultural	*	1
Western Association of Polish Schools	New York	Educational	*	1
Polish Western Association of America	Chicago	Political	*	1
Alliance of Polish Clubs	Chicago	Cultural	*	1
Polish Teachers Association in America	Chicago	Educational	*	1
National Advocates Society	Chicago	Professional	*	1
Polish National Relief Fund Committee	Chicago	Cultural	*	1
North American Study Center for Polish Affairs	Ann Arbor, Michigan	Educational	*	1
Polish Highlanders Society	Chicago	Cultural	*	1
Dmowski Institute	Chicago	Cultural-Political	*	1

*Fewer than 5,000 members.

*Also having representatives on the National Board of Directors are the 31 state divisions of the Polish American Congress, whose allotment of representatives is based upon the number of Polonia organizations affiliated with these units. The largest state divisions are those representing Illinois and Michigan (with 6 delegates each), New Jersey (5), Downstate New York (4), Connecticut, Indiana, Western New York, Eastern Pennsylvania, Western Pennsylvania and Wisconsin (3 apiece). In all, in 1983 a total of 46 delegates represented Polonia organizations affiliated with the PAC and 63 persons from the state divisions.

The highest decision-making body of the PAC between 1944 and 1976 was the national convention, which met every four years during this period, with an additional convention held in 1970. Since 1976, the highest body in the organization has been its National Board of Directors which meets annually to review the organization's activities and set its agenda. Directing its work in the *interim* is a five-member National Executive Committee based in Chicago and headed by the President.

Table 1.   (Continued)

Polonia organizations not belonging to the Polish American Congress on the national level (although many of these organizations are active in various state divisions of the PAC) include five fraternal insurance associations, Federation Life Insurance of America, the Association of the Sons of Poland, the Polish Union of the U.S.A., Northern Fraternal Insurance of America, and the Polish Beneficial Association.

Cultural associations not affiliated with the national PAC include the Kosciuszko Foundation, the General Pulaski Heritage Foundation, the Pilsudski Institute, the Copernicus Foundation, the Polish American Historical Association and the Polish Institute of Arts and Sciences in America. Other associations include the National Medical and Dental Association and the Polish American Guardian Society. Active at the state level have been the many Roman Catholic and Polish National Catholic parishes affiliated with the PAC.

National headquarters of the Polish American Congress are in Chicago and the organization maintains an office in Washington, D.C. It has published its own *Newsletter* on a somewhat irregular basis since 1950. The PAC also directs its own charitable foundation through which tax deductible donations can be made for humanitarian, relief and cultural activities it sponsors. For further information see Pienkos, "The Polish American Congress."

Chapter 13

SOME CONCLUSIONS AND A GLANCE AHEAD
INTO THE SECOND CENTURY

This study has covered not only the Polish National Alliance's first century but the years between 1980 and 1983 as well. It was during this period that I was engaged in the research and writing of this book. In looking over the preceding chapters it seems that a few generalizations about the record of the PNA are appropriate at this point.

For one thing, the PNA has succeeded in its insurance commitment to its members. It has kept faith, in good times and bad, with every individual who ever invested his hard earned dollars into the fraternal by providing the insurance benefits it promised when they were needed. This was achieved in spite of the fact that America endured several economic panics and depressions in the years after 1880; such conditions were responsible for the failure of many other insurance and savings institutions. It was in such hard times, when insurance benefits were especially important to those in need, that the PNA continued to come through.

Second, the Alliance compiled an enviable record of service on a variety of levels—humanitarian, cultural and political—in behalf of Polonia and Poland over the years. From the outset it looked after the needs of its less fortunate members. It worked for the educational advancement of the immigration by establishing libraries and reading rooms where people could learn about their new homeland and the "old country" as well. It set up its own newspaper to spur learning and community action and created a publishing company to further the availability of reading materials to a still wider audience. It created a student loan program to aid in the educational aspirations of Polonia's youth. Most of the monuments in honor of Kosciuszko and Pulaski were the products of PNA-led campaigns whose purpose was largely to enlighten Poles and non-Poles alike about the exploits of these heroes. The culmination of all these efforts came in 1912 when the Alliance established its own school. Politically, the PNA was forever in the leadership of Polonia's efforts on behalf of Poland's independence. And since 1944 it has continued to champion this cause through its involvement in the Polish American Congress.

Third, the PNA was a considerable factor in the successful Americanization of the immigrants and thus helped to ease their adaptation to life in this country. From its inception, the leadership of the Alliance followed the injunctions of its "godfather," Agaton Giller, and urged the immigrants to become familiar with the English language and to apply for American citizenship, even as it called upon them to cherish their Polish heritage. It organized night school courses in language, citizenship and U.S. history while at the same time it sponsored lecture series in the main centers of Polonia life where people could learn about conditions facing partitioned Poland. In retrospect, the PNA was probably overly optimistic about the maintenance of strong attachments to Poland among people who with their families had chosen to make their fortunes in America. In time, large numbers of Polish Americans were lost to Polonia through assimilation. Still, the PNA remained committed to the idea that both cultures had much to offer and its leaders have stressed this throughout the movement's entire history.

Fourth, the PNA consistently identified with a number of progressive political and social ideas that were important elements in both American and Polish thinking at the close of the nineteenth century. These included a respect for education, participatory democracy, equality of rights regardless of religious and ethnic differences, and the value of the printed word. The PNA's espousal of full equality for its female members as early as 1900 was another sign of its progressive character. The Alliance's leaders never considered the notion of operating as anything other than as an open and public mass membership association; just as important, they rejected the idea of a class-oriented movement in favor of ethnic solidarity. To the extent that the PNA has remained dedicated to these perennially attractive ideas, it has succeeded in remaining a significant force in the Polish American community.

This record of past achievement is impressive and merits more widespread recognition. But recalling with pride its past accomplishments cannot serve as the sole reason for studying the history of the PNA. In the light of this record, one can also appropriately ask how well the fraternal's present leadership has done in continuing to work for its goals and what, in turn, are the organization's future prospects?

Any observer of the Polish National Alliance at the present time would be less than objective if he failed to recognize that the fraternal faces several

serious problems that require attention if it is to retain its status as a significant
ethnic movement and viable insurance association capable of realizing its
historic aims. The most important problem concerns the condition of the
PNA's network of local lodges. Historically, the lodges were crucial because
of their role in recruiting new members, engaging them in a variety of social
and fraternal activities in their communities and training them for leadership
responsibilities in Polonia and PNA affairs. During the past two decades,
however, not only has the number of PNA lodges suffered a significant
decline (from 1,516 in 1960 to 1,123 in 1983); a large proportion of the remaining groups are in reality inactive, having failed for years to enroll a single
new member.[1]

But while its leaders have been aware of this situation for a number
of years they have failed to act effectively to deal with the challenge this
decline poses to the PNA's future viability. Concerted strategies have not
been devised to strengthen and support the activities of those lodge units
which remain vital. Nor have alternative methods to recruit new members
been developed.

Especially unfortunate, the PNA has failed to use the means presently
at its disposal to reinvigorate and better direct its lodge activities. For one
thing, it does not appear that the information derived from the one publicized
lodge survey the PNA home office did conduct in 1977 was used to assist
in the strengthening of the local units. Too, it seems apparent that many
PNA members remain uninformed about the various fraternal benefits to
which they are entitled, such as the student loans and scholarships that
are available through the Alliance's Educational Department, and the home
loan mortgages the PNA provides at favorable terms. Nor does the home
office in Chicago effectively publicize its financial support of lodge-sponsored
youth and sports programs, even though such activities could help greatly
enliven the local groups' appeal to young and older members alike. The
PNA organ, *Zgoda,* is nowhere as effective as it should be in stimulating
interest in the Alliance's role in preserving ethnic pride and consciousness,
even though it possesses the potential to do so and in fact still reaches
several hundred thousand people every other week. And, despite its active
membership in the federation of American fraternal insurance associations
known as the National Fraternal Congress, the PNA has derived little if
any benefit from information its leaders receive about the experiences of
other fraternals in successfully reinvigorating their lodges.[2]

Within the PNA the sale of insurance remains for the most part the
responsibility of lodge financial secretaries, who for the most part are engaged
in this work on a part-time and semi-professional basis. Continuing reliance

upon such individuals has some benefits but in recent years this practice has significantly limited the fraternal's capacity to more aggressively and effectively promote its product, not only to the families and friends of current policy holders but also to individuals with no previous contact with the Alliance. Rarely, in fact, is PNA insurance advertised and promoted at its own lodge meetings. Nor has the organization developed the necessary advertising techniques to establish visibility for its product in a manner that would bring the PNA to the attention of potential members. Both these problems are due to the character of its present sales force, many of whose members do not possess a highly developed commitment to "sell" others on the value of PNA insurance.

The PNA's incapacity to face its lodge and recruitment problems squarely has had a significant impact upon the fraternal's membership.[3] On the one hand it has not attracted a substantial portion of the post World War II Polish emigration into its ranks, even though success in this area would have benefitted the new arrivals and reinforced the Alliance's ethnic identity. On the other hand, the lodges have been equally unsuccessful in encouraging more Americans of Polish ancestry to participate in its activities, especially those in Polonia who have, since the early 1960s, been establishing careers in business and the professions, in ever larger numbers.[4] While there ought to be room for both of these significant elements of contemporary Polonia within the Polish National Alliance, the organization's leadership has failed thus far to determine how such an objective might be attained. Clearly, however, if the PNA is to better meet this challenge, it must once again be open to all, just as it was in the past. Then, working people rubbed shoulders with members of Polonia's business and professional classes, yet at the same time found ways in which to cooperate to realize the PNA's objectives.[5]

At the root of its present difficulties is its national leadership, which has been unable to develop strategies to deal with the problems of membership and lodge life. Moreover, given the highly competitive and political character of the fraternal's organizational structure, the leaders of the Alliance have traditionally been unwilling even to express their concerns to the membership out of a conviction that such actions would provoke only criticism of their policies and efforts to oust them from office at the next opportunity. This observation appears to be accurate enough in the case of the administrations of the two most recent presidents of the PNA, Charles Rozmarek and Aloysius Mazewski, who have in turn led the fraternal since 1939.

On a rather superficial level, one can readily identify several differences between the two men's leadership styles. Rozmarek, who headed the fraternal from 1939 to 1967, was a combative personality and frequently controversial, given his tendency to make decisions affecting the PNA and the Polish American Congress without first having consulted other responsible officers. In contrast, Mazewski's approach has been more friendly and casual; he is less domineering in his relations with others and seldom invites open conflict.

Yet on a more substantive level, Mazewski's approach to leadership has borne striking resemblance to that of his predecessor. Both men sought to monopolize decision-making functions within the PNA and the Polish American Congress and to dominate the latter organization as Polonia's most visible spokesman. Indicative of both leaders' attitude toward the PAC has been their reluctance in permitting its development of a significant presence in Washington, D.C. with a staff lobbying for Polonia demands in the nation's capital. Instead, the real headquarters of the Polish American Congress has remained the Chicago home office of the PNA. Each man acutely appreciated the symbolic value of the presidency of the Polish American Congress in bringing him recognition as Polonia's leader; each in his own fashion made "recognition" (usually measured in terms of well publicized meetings between PAC officers and U.S. government leaders) a top priority item on his agenda.

Within the PNA, both men gradually established themselves in full command, although they used different strategies to achieve this aim. Rozmarek set up a clearly defined political organization within the fraternal whose members identified with his leadership; Mazewski has avoided creating so visible a faction connected with his regime. Instead, he has carefully cultivated his own personal popularity, which he rarely shared, although others have frequently sought his backing to win office for themselves. As a result, since 1967 PNA politics has lost its historic factional and ideological character and become highly personalized in tone. This development has brought both greater stability to the organization and considerable benefits to the incumbent. Because no ruling faction is to be found with definite links to Mazewski, so also is it true that no clearly defined anti-administration faction has formed either. The decline of the once influential Polonia press and the impact of assimilation have also helped strengthen Mazewski's position. No longer do opponents possess the communications means to reach large numbers of PNA members, as was the case even as recently as the 1960s. Then, Mazewski's own challenge of Rozmarek was boosted by the publicity he received in the still influential Chicago daily *Dziennik Chicagoski,* for example. But like Rozmarek, Mazewski has tended to avoid dealing with potentially controversial problems of a substantive character (e.g., the condition of the lodges, recruitment, the fate of Alliance College, the role of *Zgoda* as a more influential Polonia publication of news and ideas) by focusing his attention upon less divisive matters and upon the drive for greater public recognition for his leadership in Polonia. And, several of these efforts have met with considerable success. Mazewski's investment policies helped place the fraternal upon solid footing in the early 1970s and under his leadership there have been several noteworthy moves toward modernizing the insurance operations.

Mazewski helped resuscitate the Polish American Congress back in the late 1960s and early 1970s and restated the PNA's identification with its aims. Especially during the past decade he was increasingly successful in winning greater recognition for Polonia as well. On September 20, 1980, for example, President Carter journeyed to Chicago for the sole purpose of speaking to the PNA on the occasion of its centennial. And on June 23, 1983 President Reagan flew by helicopter to the PNA home office to salute the fraternal and to assert his solidarity with Mazewski on United States policy toward Poland. These events and others of a similar character were by no means trivial and demonstrated growing official American awareness of the PNA and the PAC on the national political scene.

Aside from its specific successes and failings, there is a larger significance to the Mazewski presidency, however, one which holds special importance for the fraternal's future. For it has been under Aloysius Mazewski that the Polish National Alliance remained deeply identified with the historic aims of the founders of the fraternal and the generations that followed. Coming into office in the late 1960s when doubts were being raised about the relevance of ethnicity in a Polish American community heavily affected by assimilationist ideas and trends, Mazewski might well have directed the fraternal away from its historic traditions and instead emphasized its American business character. That he refused to do so suggests a solid faith in the principles of the Alliance and their validity for the future. Though the task for the next leadership of the organization will be difficult in many practical respects, it is very unlikely that it will seriously consider abandoning the ethnic and patriotic interests which Mazewski reasserted during his years in office.

A panoramic view of Alliance College today. Beyond is the city of Cambridge Springs, Pennsylvania, with the Allegheny Mountains in the background.

The Rider Hotel (or "Vanadium") in the early 1920s. Originally built as a health resort, the hotel and the surrounding grounds were purchased by the PNA as the site for its school in 1912. The building was destroyed in a 1931 fire.

Alliance Hall in the late 1970s.

The early days of the Alliance school, about 1916.

Alliance College commencement ceremonies in 1978.

A collage of lead articles appearing in *Zgoda* over the years, along with several of its mastheads. The paper's first editor, Edward Odrowaz, is shown to the left.

POGODA

Dziennik Związkowy

POLISH DAILY ZGODA
Published Since 1908
AN AMERICAN DAILY IN THE POLISH LANGUAGE — MEMBER OF UNITED PRESS INTERNATIONAL

KALENDARZYK

No. 111   Rok (Vol.) LXXI   CHICAGO, ILL., Czwartek, 7 Czerwca (June 7), 1979   Telefon wszystkich Biur 286-0141.   25c

JAN PAWEŁ II NA JASNEJ GÓRZE

Europa i Azja Uziemia DC-10

Aresztowania i Rewizje w Czechosłowacji

FAA Odbiera Licencję Producentowi
Mc Donald Douglas Musi Wykazać Prawidłowość Konstrukcji

Uśmiech Papieża

Kazanie o Prawach Ludzi i Narodów
Podniosłe, Jasnogórski Apel z Udziałem Prymasa Węgier

Przykre Incydenty w Częstochowie

Reżym PRL Zadowolony z Wizyty

WARSZAWA — Papież Jan Paweł II ukląkł i ucałował ziemię po przybyciu do Polski.

Strajk Zagraża Odcięciem Dostaw

Ładunek Marihuany Zniszczony w Wypadku

Wybory Do Parlamentu Egipskiego

Jan Paweł II w Wadowicach i Auschwitz

Kanclerz NRF w Białym Domu

Zaledwie Początek

Wznowienie Rokowań

ZPRK i Zw. Polek Także "Sponsorami" Reportażu z Polski

"Sojuz 34"

Oskarżenie Panamy

Nikła Zniżka

Page one of the June 7, 1979 issue of the *Dziennik Zwiazkowy*.

A sample of the work of long–time *Dziennik Zwiazkowy* editorial cartoonist K. J. Majewski. This piece appeared on the fifth anniversary of the signing of the Yalta agreement and graphically illustrates the artist's view of Soviet aims and Roosevelt's willingness to "agree to everything."

Censor Blair Gunther inaugurating the 1951 PNA convention in Buffalo. To the left, Director Aloysius Mazewski, then 35 years of age; to the right is President Charles Rozmarek. Behind Gunther is Treasurer Michael Tomaszkiewicz.

President Dwight Eisenhower at the 1960 Polish American Congress convention in Chicago. From left to right: U.S. Senate candidate Samuel Witwer, PRCUA President Joseph Osajda, Eisenhower, U.S. Congressman Roman Pucinski (Illinois), PNA/PAC President Charles Rozmarek and Rev. Valerian Karcz, PAC National Secretary.

Democratic party presidential nominee John Kennedy's appearance at the same convention. Seated from left to right: Chicago Mayor Richard Daley, President Rozmarek, Senator Kennedy. Standing to the right is PNA Censor Edward Kozmor. At the podium, Illinois Appellate Court Judge Thaddeus Adesko.

U.S. Senator Edmund Muskie of Maine, guest speaker at the annual Polish Constitution Day ceremonies in Chicago in 1971. Left to right—Vice President Frank Prochot, Secretary Adolph Pachucki, President Aloysius Mazewski, Mayor of Chicago Richard Daley, Senator and Mrs. Muskie, Governor of Illinois Richard Olgivie, Vice President Irene Wallace, and Censor Walter Dworakowski.

President Aloysius Mazewski, delegate to the United Nations twenty–fifth General Assembly (Fall, 1970) seated next to Ambassador Charles Yost.

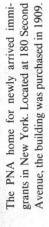

The PNA home for newly arrived immigrants in New York. Located at 180 Second Avenue, the building was purchased in 1909.

PNA President Mazewski with President Richard Nixon and New York Governor Nelson Rockefeller in 1971 at the dedication of the Ellis Island Immigration Museum.

President Gerald Ford signs into law the Polish Veterans' Assistance Act (October, 1976). To the left is Congressman Frank Annunzio of Illinois, sponsor of the bill. Second from the right is President Mazewski.

All PNA officers and directors and several Polish American Congress representatives were at this August, 1979 meeting with President Jimmy Carter in the White House. U.S. Congressman Clement Zablocki of Wisconsin sits at Carter's right, President Mazewski is to his left. Across the table is National Security Advisor Zbigniew Brzezinski.

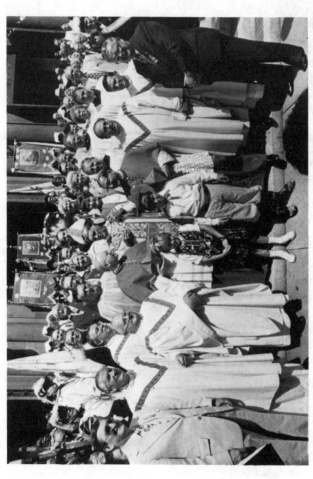

Following the High Mass inaugurating the 1979 PNA convention. At left is Censor Hilary Czaplicki and to the right President Mazewski. In the center (carrying the crozier) is Chicago auxiliary bishop Alfred Abramowicz. To his right is Gregory Cardinal Baum of Washington and to his left Wladyslaw Cardinal Rubin of Rome, whose responsibilities include the care of the religious needs of Polonia throughout the world.

Mazewski, Cardinal Rubin, U.S. National Security Advisor Brzezinski and Lt. General Edward Rowny (ret.) during the thirty-eighth PNA convention in Washington, D.C., August, 1979.

The PNA board of directors in the Alliance's centennial year, 1980. From left to right are Directors Florence Wiatrowska, Thaddeus Radosz, Mitchell Jeglijewski, Emil Kolasa, Henry Burke, Vice President Helen Szymanowicz, Censor Hilary Czaplicki, President Aloysius Mazewski, Vice President Joseph Gajda, Directors Jean Kozmor, Adele Nahormek, Mitchell Odrobina, John Radzyminski and Helen Orawiec. In the corner at left is Treasurer Edward Moskal; to the right is Secretary Lottie Kubiak.

Leaders of the PNA Benevolent Society in the Alliance's library in Chicago, about 1975. Standing at left is former Director Melanie Winiecki and next to her is Secretary Lottie Kubiak. At the far right is Vice President Helen Szymanowicz; next to her is Director Florence Wiatrowska. Seated in the foreground at right is PNA librarian Josephine Rzewska.

PNA Lodge 1001, Anthony, Rhode Island, Softball Champions, 1978-1979.

National golf tournaments, like bowling meets, have been popular annual PNA-sponsored events in the past quarter-centry.

Participants in the PNA Sports—Youth Instructors' course at Alliance College in 1980 with Vice Presidents Helen Szymanowicz and Joseph Gajda (third and fourth from right in the front row).

Eagles' Society Soccer Team, PNA Lodge 315, Bridgeport Connecticut.

A few of the groups participating at the 1982 PNA Youth Jamboree.

Concluding Mass at the PNA Youth Jamboree, Alliance College.

President Carter is greeted in the age-old Polish tradition when he accepts bread and salt from his hosts, Vice President Helen Szymanowicz, Censor Hilary Czaplicki and President Aloysius Mazewski, at the centennial banquet of the PNA on September 20, 1980 in Chicago.

President Ronald Reagan speaks to PNA and Polonia leaders after flying to the PNA home office by helicopter (June, 1983). With him are Rev. Edward Pajak, President Mazewski and U.S. Senator Charles Percy of Illinois.

On December 20, 1981 PAC leaders Mazewski, Helen Zielinski, Joseph Drobot and John Cardinal Krol met with President Ronald Reagan and Vice President George Bush in the White House to discuss the American government's response to the imposition of martial law in Poland. The story was front page news in the *New York Times.*

Mazewski and Polish Solidarity Union Chairman Lech Walesa in Warsaw at the time of the funeral of Stefan Cardinal Wyszynski (July, 1981).

Giller's tomb in Warsaw's Powazki Cemetery. The remains of the Alliance's "spiritual father" were reinterred through the efforts of the PNA in 1982 from their place of burial in the Soviet Union.

PNA/PAC President Aloysius Mazewski and Pope John Paul II in Rome during ceremonies opening the Polish Pilgrims' hostel in November, 1981. This edifice was purchased in honor of the Holy Father after a fund drive supported by Polonia communities throughout the world.

Employees at work in the Insurance Department in the new PNA home office.

Presidium for the 1979 convention in Washington, D.C. with President Mazewski, left. To his right stand former Censor and First Vice Chairman Casimir Lotarski, Chairman Adam Tomaszkiewicz, Ladies' Vice Chairman Alice Posluszny, Second Vice Chairman Wilhelm Wolf, and Secretary Alexander Wachel.

PNA leaders at the thirty-ninth convention in 1983 at Orlando, Florida herald the fraternal's entrance into its second century by singing the great patriotic anthem of 1910, *"Rota."* In the foreground, left to right, are Judge Frank Sulewski, Raymond Dembski, Mrs. Wanda Rozmarek and Adam Tomaszkiewicz. Composed by Nowowiejski with words by Maria Konopnicka, the hymn testifies to the Poles' commitment to their heritage. It begins, *Nie rzucim ziemi skad nasz rod! Nie damy pogrzesc mowy."* (We'll hold our land, our father's land, we'll keep alive our language.)

The newly elected board of directors in October, 1983 leading the PNA into its second century. (From left to right) Directors Mitchell Jeglijewski, Helen Piotrowski, Adele Nahormek, John Ramza, Felix Hujarski, Treasurer Edward Moskal, Vice President Helen Szymanowicz, Censor Hilary Czaplicki, President Aloysius Mazewski, Vice President Anthony Piwowarczyk, Secretary Emil Kolasa, Vice Censor Edward Sitnik, Directors Paul Odrobina, Casimir Musielak, Stanley Stawiarski, Stanley Lesniewski, Genevieve Wesolowska.

Part III

APPENDIX A

A Chronology of Major Events in American, Polish, Polonia
and PNA History

Date	AMERICA	POLAND	POLONIA	PNA
966		Baptism of Mieszko and his countrymen; birth of a recognized Polish state		
1226		Teutonic knights invited into Poland		
1241		Tartar invasion		
1364		University in Krakow founded		
1386		Union of Poland and Lithuania through marriage between Jadwiga and Jagiello		
1410		Victory over the Teutonic knights at Grunwald		
1425-33		Law of *"neminem captivabimus" (Habeus corpus)* promulgated		
1492	Columbus discovers America			
1543		Appearance of Copernicus' treatise, *On the Movements of Heavenly Bodies*, a high point in the "Golden Age" of Polish culture along with the literary work of Mikolaj Rej, Jan Kochanowski and others		

Year		
1569		Union of Lublin cementing ties between Poland and Lithuania
1607	Jamestown Colony	
1608	Polish Settlers at Jamestown	
1612		Polish troops occupy the Kremlin in Moscow; zenith of the country's power and territorial expansion
1620	Mayflower Compact	
1636	Harvard College founded	
1648		Chmielnitsky rebellion against Polish rule in the Ukraine
1648-60		"The Deluge" or occupation of the country by Swedes, Germans and Russians. (This period is the subject of Nobel Prize recipient Henryk Sienkiewicz's epic "Trilogy")
1683		King Jan Sobieski's victory over the Turks at Vienna
1755-63	French and Indian Wars	

Date	AMERICA	POLAND	POLONIA	PNA
1764		Stanislaw August, the last king, elected		
1768		Pulaski involved in the confederation of Bar revolt against Russian influence		
1772		First partition of Poland by Russia, Austria and Prussia		
1775-83	War of Independence			
1776	Kosciuszko's arrival			
1779	Death of Pulaski at the battle of Savannah			
1787	Constitution			
1788-92		The "great *Sejm*"—Old Poland's effort at national renewal		
1789	George Washington inaugurated President			
1791		Promulgation of "Third of May" Constitution		
1793		Second partition by Russia and Prussia		
1794		Kosciuszko insurrection		
1795		Third partition by Russia,		

Year		
1797		Austria and Prussia; Poland erased from the map
		Dabrowski's legion in Italy (inspiration for the Polish national anthem)
1797-98	Kosciuszko's second stay	
1803	Louisiana Purchase	
1807-15		Duchy of Warsaw created loyal to Napoleon; serfs freed there
1812	War with Great Britain	Napoleon invades Russia
1815		"Kingdom of Poland" formed under Russian Tsar Alexander I
1823	Monroe Doctrine	
1830-31		"November Insurrection"; its failure forces thousands into exile including Fryderyk Chopin and Poland's greatest Romantic epic poet, Adam Mickiewicz, author of *Forefather's Eve* and *Pan Tadeusz*

Date	AMERICA	POLAND	POLONIA	PNA
1842			Henry Kalussowski organizes Society of Poles in America, a patriotic organization of exiles from the November insurrection	
1846–48	Mexican War	Polish revolt in Krakow; Galician peasants' attack on Polish nobility (1846) "Spring of Nations" insurrections in Galicia and Poznania; serfdom abolished (1848)		
1854–58			First Polish settlements in Texas, Michigan and Wisconsin	
1861–65	Civil War	"January Insurrection;" serfs emancipated in Russian Poland (1863–64)	Brigadier General Krzyzanowski in the Union forces among numerous Polish officers on both sides Echo z Polski (1863): first Polish newspaper in America	
1865–70	Passage of the 13, 14, 15th amendments to the Constitution abolishing slavery, racial discrimination and granting Negroes the right to vote		The first mutual and fraternal associations are formed, Gmina Polska and Saint Stanislas societies of Chicago (1866)	

1870 — First group of Resurrectionist priests in America (1866)

"Union of Poles in America" formed in New York; this first national fraternal society is stillborn

1873–74 — Polish Roman Catholic Union in America founded; first national fraternal society

1876 — First visit of actress Helena Modrzejewska to America; Sienkiewicz in America

1877 — Peter Kiolbassa, PRCUA leader, elected first Pole in the Illinois legislature

1879 — Letter from Agaton Giller on the "Organization of Poles in America," inspiration of the Polish National Alliance

1880 — Birth of the Polish National Alliance in Philadelphia (February 15); first *Sejm* in Chicago (September) elects J. Andrzejkowicz Censor and M. Kucera President

1881 — *Zgoda* established in NY

1882 — Marcin Kopankiewicz—first insured member to die

Date	AMERICA	POLAND	POLONIA	PNA
1886	Founding of American Federation of Labor, first lasting workers' organization		Polish seminary founded in Orchard Lake, Michigan	PNA adopts new by-laws naming its leadership the "central government" for the Poles in America and establishes a firm insurance program
1887	The Statue of Liberty Enlightening the World dedicated	*Liga Polska* patriotic movement formed in Switzerland		
			Falcons' group formed in Chicago (a national Falcons' Alliance formed in 1894)	PNA establishes *Skarb Narodowy* (Polish National Fund) to raise money in cooperation with the *Liga Polska*
1889			Polish Singers' Alliance founded in Chicago	Withdrawal of "Alliance Priests" from PNA at eighth *Sejm* over issue of membership by non-Catholics
1890			First Polish socialist group formed, in New York	
1891			First Paderewski concert in U.S.	Kalussowski's library donated to PNA as the basis of the Alliance's own library and museum
1892	Ellis Island replaces Castle Garden as the main port of entry for European immigrants			
1893	Economic depression	Emergence of first mass oriented patriotic political movements (Socialists, National Democrats, and Peasants' parties)		Followers of National Democrats dominate the tenth PNA *Sejm*

Year			
1893–99	Populist William Jennings Bryan's "Cross of Gold" speech helps win him the Democratic party nomination but he loses election to William McKinley (1896)	Polonia solidarity shown in protests against Russian-American treaty and at Columbian Exposition (1893), in opposition to Lodge immigration restriction bill (1898), and at the Hague Peace Conference (1899)	First PNA home office on Chicago's Division St. dedicated (July, 1896) PNA formerly chartered as a fraternal insurance association under Illinois law (1896)
	War with Spain (1898)	PNA activist, inventor and philanthropist Erasmus Jerzmanowski helps form the Polish League to unite Polonia; it fails out of PNA indifference (1894) Beginnings of Polish National Catholic Church (1897) Founding of Polish Women's Alliance (1898)	PNA gives money and legal aid to Polish miners to bring to justice those responsible for the "Lattimer (Pennsylvania) Massacre" (1897) Extraordinary PNA *Sejm* votes equal rights to women members
1900			
1901	Assassination of President McKinley by Polish-born anarchist, Leon Czolgosz	First volume of Rev. Wenceslaus Kruszka's history of the Poles in America; in 1903 he travels to Rome to appeal to the Pope for the appointment of Polish bishops in America	

Date	AMERICA	POLAND	POLONIA	PNA
1904-1905	Pilsudski and Dmowski both travel to Chicago to mobilize Polonia behind their policies (1904)	Russo-Japanese War; Disturbances in Russian zone of partitioned Poland	PNA President Steczynski heads "National Committee" to rally Polonia; Growing support for Pilsudski's activist stance	PNA effort to incorporate Falcons', Singers' and Youth Alliances as special departments
1906				PNA Women's Department created
1907				PNA *Sejm* delegates visit the White House and are greeted by President Theodore Roosevelt
1908			Consecration of Paul Rhode, first Polish Roman Catholic bishop in America	First appearance of *Dziennik Zwiazkowy* (Polish Daily *Zgoda*)
1910		Following the Washington congress, PNA leaders including President Steczynski, Vice Censor Abczynski and Casimir Zychlinski attend ceremonies in Krakow commemorating the 500th anniversary of the victory at Grunwald and visit Rappersville Polish Museum, onetime center of *emigre* patriotic movement. These activities reemphasize PNA ties to Polish independence movement	Dedication of monuments to Kosciuszko and Pulaski in Washington, D.C. followed by a Polish National Congress (May); both events are spear-headed by the PNA	

Year				
1912	Wilson defeats Roosevelt and Taft for the Presidency		Reunification of Falcons' Alliance as an independent movement; Formation of a Committee for National Defense (*KON*) on behalf of Polish independence (December)	Dedication of the PNA school at Cambridge Springs, Pennsylvania; President Taft in attendance
1913	High point of immigration reached as 174,000 Poles enter the country		Division in *KON*; formation of Polish National Council by conservatives in Polonia (June)	*Skarb Narodowy* funds transferred to Pilsudski's forces in Poland; membership reaches 100,000
1914		World War I begins; Pilsudski's Legions	Polish Central Relief Committee (*PCKR*) formed with PNA support (October)	PNA Independence Department formed after its withdrawal from *KON* to work for Poland's cause (June)
1915	Paderewski's arrival in U.S.	Sienkiewicz's *Appeal to Civilized Nations* on Poland's behalf		
1916		Two Emperors' Manifesto, first pronouncement in favor of an autonomous postwar Poland	*PCKR* forms the National Department focusing on political action and led by PNA leader and banker John Smulski (August)	
1917	Wilson's "Peace without Victory" speech; U.S. enters the War (April)	Competing declarations on Poland; Bolshevik revolution (November)	Polish Army in America formed	
1918	Fourteen Points (January); Armistice (November)	German-Soviet treaty of Brest-Litovsk (March); Polish republic formed with Pilsudski's return to Warsaw (November)	Polish White Cross created through the initiative of Helena Paderewska; first *Sejm* of the Polish Emigration meets in Detroit	PNA *Sejm* in Pittsburgh establishes Juvenile Department enabling youth to be insured

Date	AMERICA	POLAND	POLONIA	PNA
			(August). $10 million fund drive eventually collects $5 million for Poland; first Polish U.S. Congressman elected, John Kleczka of Milwaukee First volume of Thomas and Znaniecki's *Polish Peasant in Europe and America* (the work appears in a Polish translation in 1976)	
1919		Versailles Treaty	Second *Sejm* of the Emigration in Buffalo (November)	
1919–20	Prohibition approved by the 18th amendment to the Constitution (1919); Women's suffrage granted by the 19th amendment (1920)	Polish-Soviet War; battle of Warsaw (August 1920)	Stanley Kunz elected to Congress from Chicago (1920)	
1921	First immigration legislation creating quotas passes; first visit of Nobel Laureate Maria Sklodowska-Curie to U.S.		Polish Army Veterans' Association, Polish Legion of American Veterans both organized	
1924	More restrictive immigration legislation approved	Wladyslaw Reymont received Nobel Prize in literature for his novel, *The Peasants*; death of the great author Joseph Conrad (Korzeniowski)		PNA surpasses 200,000 members; Election of Casimir Sypniewski as PNA Censor at 24th *Sejm*, a victory for the "left" or "Pilsudski faction"

Year		
1925	Kosciuszko Foundation created	Fifth Congress of Emigration (Detroit); liquidation of National Department and creation of Polish Welfare Council in America (*PROSA*)
1926	Pilsudski's *Coup* (May)	
1927		Death of President Zychlinski, longtime PNA and Falcons leader 25th PNA *Sejm* in Chicago; dissatisfied delegates organize counter-convention and the factional fight is settled only in court
1928		"Left" faction wins in reconvened 25th *Sejm* (September)
1929	Wall Street Crash (October); beginning of Great Depression	
1931		Alliance College fire (January); Conservatives retake control over PNA at Scranton *Sejm*; Francis Swietlik elected Censor
1932	Roosevelt elected over Hoover; a massive majority in Polonia backs his "New Deal"	PNA *Harcerstwo* scouting movement underway led by President John Romaszkiewicz

Date	AMERICA	POLAND	POLONIA	PNA
1934			Swietlik leads American delegation to world congress of Poles from abroad in Warsaw; there he declines to join the organization and emphasizes Polonia's first loyalty is to America	
1935		Death of Marshal Pilsudski		
1936–38			Formation of Polish Interorganizational Council in Chicago headed by Swietlik; in 1938 it becomes Polish American Council dedicated to relief work for Poland and Polonia	New PNA central office on Division Street in Chicago (1938)
1939		Nazi attack on Poland, World War II begins (September 1); Soviet attack from the East (September 17); Warsaw falls (September 23)		Charles Rozmarek elected President of PNA in Detroit, $100 thousand voted by Sejm delegates for Polish relief (September)
1940		Death of Paderewski		
1941–42	General Sikorski, head of Polish Exile Government makes first visit to U.S.; America in the War (December, 1941)	Nazi invasion of USSR (June, 1941); Polish-Soviet cooperation against Nazi Germany	Polish Institute of Arts and Sciences in America formed in NY (1942)	
1943	Moscow Conference (October); Teheran Conference (November-December); issue of	Katyn discovered; USSR breaks relations with Sikorski government;		

	Poland's postwar boundaries settled by Great Powers	Warsaw Ghetto destroyed (April); Sikorski killed (July); Mikolajczyk succeeds him as Premier	Polish American Congress founded in Buffalo (May); Rozmarek publicly supports reelection of FDR unaware of his actual stance on Poland; Polish American Historical Association formed in Chicago	PNA surpasses 300,000 members
1944	Mikolajczyk meets FDR (June); D-Day in Europe Roosevelt wins fourth term (November)	Monte Casino; Polish Committee of National liberation led by Communists formed at Lublin (July); Warsaw Uprising (August-October); Mikolajczyk resigns (November)		
1945	Yalta Conference (February); FDR dies (April); War in Europe ends (May); Potsdam Conference (July)	USSR recognizes Communist-led provisional government (January); Polish Government of National Unity recognized by U.S. (July)	Rozmarek attends opening session of UN in San Francisco championing cause of a free Poland	
1946	Secretary of State Byrnes' Stuttgart speech	Referendum (May); Communist effort to intimidate democratic opposition		
1947	Truman Doctrine; Marshall Plan	Falsified Elections (January); Mikolajczyk flees country (October)		Alliance College becomes a four year coeducational institution
1948			Special legislation backed by PAC allows 150,000 Polish refugees and exiles into U.S.	
1949	National Committee for a Free Europe formed; NATO (April)	Council of Mutual Economic Assistance (COMECON) formed linking USSR and East European States	PAC "Million Dollar" fund drive ends with over $600,000 raised	Death of Rev. Casimir Sztuczko, pastor of Holy Trinity Parish in Chicago from 1893 and ally of PNA

Date	AMERICA	POLAND	POLONIA	PNA
1950–53	Korean War Republican Party endorses "Liberation" of Eastern Europe in its Platform (1952)		Polish Veterans of World War II Association formed (1952)	Women achieve full equality as district commissioners with men (1951)
1953	Dwight Eisenhower inaugurated but repudiates "Liberation" by force	Death of Stalin; Khrushchev eventually succeeds him		
1955		Warsaw Pact Military Alliance linking USSR and Eastern European states		Frances Dymek elected First Vice President of PNA at Minneapolis *Sejm*
1956		Khrushchev "Secret Speech" denouncing Stalin's crimes (February); Poznan workers riots (June); Gomulka elected new first party secretary (October) as Stalinist leaders are removed		
1957	U.S. economic aid to Poland begins			
1958			Edmund Muskie (Maine) elected first Polish American in U.S. Senate	Censor B. F. Gunther and Treasurer Adam Tomaszkiewicz fail in effort to call extraordinary *Sejm* to investigate investment policies; PNA assets reach $100 million

Year			
1959	Vice President Nixon in Warsaw		
1960	John Kennedy elected president over Nixon with overwhelming support of Polonia	President Eisenhower attends Polish American Congress convention	
1961		John Gronouski becomes a member of the Cabinet as U.S. Postmaster General; appointed Ambassador to Poland (1965)	PNA *Sejm* authorizes a special development committee to find ways to stimulate membership growth
1962	Cuban Missile Crisis		
1963	Assassination of Kennedy; Lyndon Johnson replaces him		
1965–73	Vietnam War President Johnson signs bill greatly liberalizing immigration and removing the old quota system (1965); in 1970 President Nixon approves further liberalization of the new law		
1966	"Millenium" of Poland's Christianity and nationhood	100,000 attend mass in Chicago celebrating Poland's Millenium	
1967		Archbishop Krol of Philadelphia, first Polish American named a Cardinal	Aloysius Mazewski elected President over Rozmarek at Detroit *Sejm*

Date	AMERICA	POLAND	POLONIA	PNA
1968	Richard Nixon defeats Hubert Humphrey for presidency; Muskie was Humphrey's vice presidential running mate	"March" crisis in Warsaw; liberal critics of regime repressed and "Zionists" expelled from their government posts	Mazewski succeeds Rozmarek as PAC President	*Zgoda* transformed into a bi-lingual publication dealing with all-Polonia matters
1970		Treaty with West Germany; workers' revolt in the Baltic coast cities ends Gomulka regime; Gierek replaces him	*Dziennik Chicagoski* newspaper fails leaving *Dziennik Zwiazkowy* the one remaining Polish daily in the city	First quadrennial PNA Youth Jamboree at Alliance College
1972	Congress passes Ethnic Heritage Studies Act	Nixon visit to Poland and the USSR		
1973			Observance of 500th anniversary of birth of Copernicus	
1974	Nixon resigns; Gerald Ford replaces him	Gierek visit to U.S.		
1975	Helsinki Agreement	Ford visits Poland		Special scholarship funds first set aside for promising students at PNA *Sejm* in Milwaukee; plan put into effect in 1980
1977		President Carter visits Poland	Brzezinski named National Security Advisor by President Carter	Third PNA Central Office in Chicago dedicated
1978		Cardinal Wojtyla elected Pope John Paul II	World meeting of Polonia leaders in Toronto attended by PAC/PNA President Mazewski	

Year				
1979	Pope John Paul II visits the U.S., celebrates mass for Poles in Chicago	Pope John Paul II's first visit to his homeland following his election	First "Polish Day" at the State Department; Polonia leaders actually present views for first time; Jagiellonian University hosts significant American-Polish scholarly symposium on Polonia, co-sponsored by U.S. government	President Carter travels to Chicago to attend PNA Centennial celebration
1980		Massive worker demonstrations bring down Gierek; Rise of Solidarity democratic labor movement and Lech Walesa (July-September); Czeslaw Milosz awarded Nobel prize for literature	Muskie named Secretary of State; major scholarly conference on American Polonia held in Toronto	Centennial celebration of Zgoda, oldest continuing Polish newspaper in the world and most widely read Polonia publication in U.S.; PNA assets surpass $175 million
1981	Inauguration of President Ronald Reagan; he carried every state with large Polish population concentrations in 1980 election; Director Andrzej Wajda honored in Washington for such films as "Man of Marble" and "Man of Iron" (October); Reagan voices sharp U.S. disapproval of Soviet-sponsored Polish martial law and leads international protest calling	General Jaruzelski becomes head of Polish government (March); Communist Party Congress held on more democratic lines (July); First national Solidarity union congress (September); Unprecedented Jaruzelski-Walesa-Archbishop Glemp meeting to stabilize Polish political situation (November); Jaruzelski imposes martial law	Death of Cardinal Wyszynski, Primate of Poland; PAC/PNA President Mazewski travels to Warsaw for the funeral and meets with Walesa; PAC fund raising campaign for Polish relief begun; by 1983 $34 million has been raised; PAC leaders meet Reagan; their views are accepted as in agreement with U.S. policy (December)	

Date	AMERICA	POLAND	POLONIA	PNA
	for negotiations to solve Poland's problems (December)	and imprisons leaders of the now outlawed Solidarity movement (December)		
1982		Unsuccessful assassination attempt on the life of Pope John Paul II; 600th anniversary of the installation of icon to the Virgin in Czestochowa; Solidarity union officially dissolved by decree (October)	Massive shipments of medicine, food and clothing to Poland sponsored by PAC	Seventieth anniversary dinner of founding of the Alliance school celebrated in Philadelphia as the kick-off for a fund raising campaign
1983	President Reagan speaks to PAC leaders by phone in Washington, visits PNA headquarters in Chicago (June)	Second visit of Pope John Paul II to Poland (June) Government announces its lifting of martial law (July) Walesa awarded Nobel Peace Prize (October)	Conference on PNA organized at Polish American Historical Association convention in San Francisco	Seventy-fifth anniversary observance of founding of *Dziennik Zwiazkowy* Thirty-ninth PNA *Sejm* held in the South for the first time, Orlando Florida (September)

APPENDIX B

Tabular Data on PNA Membership; National Officers of the PNA,
1880–1983; The Conventions of the PNA

TERRITORIAL ORGANIZATION OF THE POLISH NATIONAL ALLIANCE

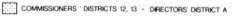

COMMISSIONERS' DISTRICTS 12, 13 - DIRECTORS' DISTRICT A

COMMISSIONERS' DISTRICTS 1, 2   - DIRECTOR'S DISTRICT B

COMMISSIONERS' DISTRICTS 3, 4   - DIRECTOR'S DISTRICT C

COMMISSIONERS' DISTRICT 5, 6, 7 - DIRECTOR'S DISTRICT D

COMMISSIONERS' DISTRICTS 8,9   - DIRECTOR'S DISTRICT E

COMMISSIONERS' DISTRICT 11

COMMISSIONERS' DISTRICT 14   DIRECTOR'S DISTRICT F

COMMISSIONERS' DISTRICT 16

COMMISSIONERS' DISTRICT 10

                                 DIRECTOR'S DISTRICT G
COMMISSIONERS' DISTRICT 15

Table 1.   The Polish National Alliance: Membership and Financial
Position, 1880–1980

By Decade	Total Membership	Number of Lodges	Net Worth
1880[a]	189	9	$ 162.50
1890	3,426	113	5,144.73
1900	28,358	451	98,339.05
1910	71,335	1,106	1,154,918.38
1920	126,521	1,678	5,656,562.71
1930	286,526	1,833	20,286,870.52
1940	274,839	1,827	30,365,843.00
1950	323,794	1,699	56,298,000.00
1960	336,159	1,516	102,417,460.00
1970	329,241	1,357	137,998,552.00
1980	294,761	1,175	$167,355,216.00

[a]As of August 10, 1880. Data for other years are as of December 31.

Of 115 insurance associations belonging to the national federation of fraternals, the National Fraternal Congress, the Polish National Alliance ranked eighth in terms of net worth in 1980. The PNA ranked eleventh in the total amount of insurance in force at the time protecting its members.

The leading fraternal insurance societies operating in the United States in 1980 were the Aid Association for Lutherans, the Lutheran Brotherhood, the Knights of Columbus, the Woodmen of the World Life Insurance Society, the Independent Order of Foresters, the Modern Woodmen of America, the Royal Neighbors of America, the Polish National Alliance of the United States of North America, the Catholic Order of Foresters, and the Catholic Knights.

In 1980, the Polish Alliance remained by far the largest ethnically-based fraternal insurance society in the U.S. and thus the largest Polish-American fraternal as well. *Source: The Fraternal Monitor,* July, 1981.

Table 2.   Polish National Alliance, 1931–1983: Certificates in Force, Insurance in Force, Net Worth as of the Summer Prior to Every PNA National Convention[a]

Year	Certificates in Force	Insurance in Force	Net Worth
1931	296,120	$126,134,500	$23,216,984
1935	280,785	124,563,109	28,376,427
1939	279,539	133,474,057	29,308,803
1943	279,159	166,150,016	33,536,954
1947	302,449	192,420,717	43,132,041
1951	327,441	226,045,694	60,688,343
1955	339,222	252,417,224	78,426,382
1959	336,502	268,698,159	98,099,918
1963	351,166	283,260,209	117,370,088
1967	344,963	302,040,786	133,416,423
1971	328,600	323,088,103	145,736,045
1975	312,923	351,918,984	154,941,085
1979	301,590	389,796,708	160,871,595
1983	292,439	433,770,867	176,417,404

[a]All data are from the pre-convention audit reports which were dated between April 30 and June 30, just before the fall conventions. All policies, whether fully paid up or not, are included under the heading of "Certificates of force." In 1983, more than 100,000 policies were fully paid for. An individual may own more than one insurance policy in the PNA and such "multiple certificate holders" accounted for approximately 10,000 policies. On the other hand, children of parents holding "family plan" type insurance policies were not counted in the membership since they held no individual certificates.

Table 3.   Amounts of Insurance Written by Polish American Fraternals, 1980[a]

Fraternal	Number of Policies Written	Insurance in force	Average Insurance Coverage for New Policies
Polish National Alliance	7,661	$19,552,345	$2,552
Polish Roman Catholic Union	2,141	5,072,000	2,369
Polish Falcons	1,193	1,035,068	868
Polish Women's Alliance	1,178	1,605,000	1,363
Polish Union of USA	509	695,224	1,366
Polish National Union	487	1,056,969	2,170
Alliance of Poles	372	508,500	1,367
Northern Fraternal (Polish Association)	265	1,311,535	4,949
Union of Polish Women	230	234,400	1,019
Federation Life	170	828,489	4,874
Polish Union of America	158	465,000	2,943
PNA of Brooklyn	143	376,526	2,633
Totals	14,507	$32,741,056	$2,257

[a]*Source: The Fraternal Monitor,* July 1981. According to the February 1, 1982 issue of *Zgoda,* the PNA increased its total insurance sales to 9,030 new policies in 1981 and sold $30,131,064 in total coverage. The average policy written in 1981 was for $3,336.

Table 4.   Changes in Membership in Selected Polish Fraternals Listed According to Their Year of Founding

Fraternal	Year Organized	Headquarters	World War I Era	Mid 1930s	1955	1978
Polish Roman Catholic Union	1873	Chicago	85,208	154,622	175,502	114,941
Polish National Alliance	1880	Chicago	110,331	284,289	337,829	302,137
Polish Union	1890	Buffalo	18,900	21,000	17,598	11,280
Falcons Alliance	1894	Pittsburgh	7,000	26,000	20,423	26,447
Alliance of Poles	1895	Cleveland	7,000	9,000	15,080	16,000
Polish Association	1895	Milwaukee	10,700	8,700	6,000	4,800
Polish Alma Mater	1897	Chicago	8.000	8,000	N.I.	5,300
Polish Women's Alliance	1899	Chicago	14,500	53,000	85,407	78,030
Polish Beneficial Association	1899	Philadelphia	25,500	35,000	N.I.	24,600
Sons of Poland	1903	Jersey City	N.I.	16,000	17,159	12,100
Polish National Alliance of Brooklyn	1903	Brooklyn	5,442	16,112	20,652	13,800
Polish National Union	1908	Scranton	3,870	17,000	30,570	31,351
Polish Union	1908	Wilkes-Barre	18,987	17,936	21,232	13,500
Federation Life	1913	Milwaukee	1,000	3,000	6,000	5,600
Share of Fraternal Membership belonging to PNA			33.6%	42.4%	42.8%	46.0%

N.I.: No information

Sources: *Statistics of Fraternal Benefit Societies, 1980;*
    Joseph Wytrwal, *America's Polish Heritage,* p. 327; Andrzej Brozek,
    Polonia Amerykanska 1854–1939, pp.202-217;
    Donald Pienkos, "The Polish American Congress: An Appraisal,"
    Polish American Studies (1979).

Table 5. Rank Order of the Five Largest Polish American Fraternals, 1970–1980 in Terms of Membership, Assets, Total Insurance in Force[a]

Fraternal	Membership			Assets (in 000's)			Insurance (in 000's)		
	1970	1980	Growth Index	1970	1980	Growth Index	1970	1980	Growth Index
Polish Falcons	25,055	26,597	1.06	$7,901	$11,352	1.44	$16,089	$18,638	1.16
Polish National Union	32,871	30,356	.92	12,641	16,581	1.31	28,605	34,846	1.22
Polish National Alliance	326,611	294,761	.90	137,999	167,355	1.21	322,622	404,779	1.26
Polish Women's Alliance	87,084	75,347	.87	28,724	33,559	1.17	58,285	57,680	.99
Polish Roman Catholic Union	139,071	104,254	.75	53,381	59,097	1.11	110,632	111,346	1.01

[a]The growth index divides 1980 data by data for 1970. Indices greater than 1.0 measure increases, less than 1.0, decreases.

Table 5A. PNA Share of Membership, Net Assets and Insurance in Force in Comparison with the Four Next Largest Polish American Fraternals Combined
(Polish Roman Catholic Union, Polish Women's Alliance, Polish National Union and Polish Falcons of America)

	1967	1982
PNA Share of Membership	53.2%	55.4%
PNA Share of Net Assets	57.0	58.7
PNA Share of Insurance in Force	59.5	65.1

Source: Statistics of Fraternal Benefit Societies for 1967 and 1982.

Table 6. The Territorial Structure of the Polish National Alliance, 1980

	Total Number of PNA Councils	Total Number of Lodges	Territory Represented and Supervisory Districts
Directors' District "A" (represented by four directors) *Total Membership:* 68,135	26	210	District 12 (South section of Chicago and Southwest section of Illinois, 14 councils and 111 lodges)
			District 13 (North section of Chicago and North section of Illinois, 12 councils and 99 lodges)
Directors' District "B" (one director) *Total Membership:* 31,440	16	123	District 1 (Massachusetts, Rhode Island, New Hampshire, Maine, 9 councils and 78 lodges)
			District 2 (Connecticut, 7 councils, 45 lodges)
Directors' District "C" (one director) *Total Membership:* 39,001	29	170	District 3 (Eastern New York state, 14 councils and 94 lodges)
			District 4 (Western New York, 15 councils and 76 lodges)
Directors' District "D" (one director) *Total Membership:* 52,891	39	224	District 5 (New Jersey excluding Camden, 10 councils and 62 lodges)
			District 6 (Maryland, Washington, D.C., Delaware, Southern Pennsylvania, Camden, New Jersey, 12 councils and 64 lodges)
			District 7 (Northeastern section of Pennsylvania, 17 councils and 98 lodges)

Directors' District "E" (one director) *Total Membership*: 44,390	38	District 8 (Western Pennsylvania, 25 councils and 122 lodges)
	204	District 9 (Ohio, West Virginia and Virginia, 13 councils and 82 lodges)
Directors' District "F" (one director) *Total Membership*: 21,356	38	District 11 (Southern section of Indiana, Southern Illinois, Missouri, Nebraska, Kansas, Arkansas, Texas, Colorado, Florida, 15 councils, 55 lodges)
	152	District 14 (Wisconsin, Iowa, Minnesota, Upper Peninsula of Michigan, North Dakota, Manitoba, 17 councils and 70 lodges)
		District 16 (California, Oregon, Washington, Arizona, 6 councils, 27 lodges)
Directors' District "G" (one director) *Total Membership*: 40,365	20	District 10 (Michigan, excluding its upper Peninsula, 13 councils and 96 lodges)
	122	District 15 (Northern section of Indiana, 7 councils and 26 lodges)
10 Members of the National Board of Directors	206	32 Commissioners belonging to the national Supervisory Council, 2 from each of the 16 districts
	1205	

Aside from the national convention of the Polish National Alliance, the organization's chief legislative body which meets every four years, there are two other main institutions, the PNA Board of Directors and the Supervisory Council. The Board of Directors, the main executive and administrative body, includes fifteen members, all of whom are elected by the delegates at the quadrennial convention. Included on the 15 member Board are the president, two vice presidents, the secretary and treasurer of the PNA along with 10 national directors who represent 7 specific territorial regions or districts (obwody) of the United States. These directors' districts are identified alphabetically, as "Obwod A," "B" and so forth.

The PNA Supervisory Council, the Alliance's supreme judicial body, includes 34 individuals, namely the censor (its chairman), the vice censor, and 32 district commissioners. These 32 persons are elected by delegates representing the 16 supervisory districts (*okregi*) of the PNA, or two from each district. Each okreg must have one male and one female commissioner. The manner in which the commissioners' supervisory districts interlock territorially with the directors' districts (*obwody*) is detailed here.

336 APPENDIX B

Table 7.   Leading PNA Insurance Sales Persons, 1981 and Town of Residence

---

Individuals with sales totalling more than $1,000,000

Genia Gunther   Langhorne, Pennsylvania

Individuals with sales totalling more than $500,000

Richard Smoger   Detroit, Michigan

Individuals with sales totalling more than $200,000

Josephine May	Chicago, Illinois
Thaddeus Radosz[b]	Chicago, Illinois
John Ramza	Streeter, Illinois
August Gorski[c]	Philadelphia, Pennsylvania
Bogdan Parafinczuk	Chicago, Illinois
William Kozerski	Hamtramck, Michigan
Joseph Grajewski	Steubenville, Ohio
John Sulima	Bethany, Connecticut
John Radzyminski[b]	Pittsburgh, Pennsylvania
Sophie Litwa[c]	Ogden, Pennsylvania
Gladys Podkomorska	Milwaukee, Wisconsin

Individuals with sales totalling more than $150,000

John Zubriski	Elmira, New York
Michael Pierzga	Nazareth, Pennsylvania
Walter Noga, Jr.	Battle Creek, Michigan
Vincentia Majka[c]	Belleville, Illinois
Hedy Rabiega	Milwaukee, Wisconsin
Stella Lemanek	Inkster, Michigan
Joseph Czepiel	Pittsburgh, Pennsylvania
Marian Przybylski	Detroit, Michigan
Stanley Gruszka[c]	Waterbury, Connecticut
Timoteusz Sujka	Akron, Ohio
Thomas Wyszynski	Cuyahoga Falls, Ohio

Table 7. (Continued)

Individuals with sales totalling more than $100,000

Kazimiera Bidas	Garfield, New Jersey
Joseph Szczech	Chicago, Illinois
Stanley Stawiarski	Joliet, Illinois
Julian Matkowski	Philadelphia, Pennsylvania
Mitchell Jeglijewski[b]	St. Louis, Missouri
Marie Jaje	Philadelphia, Pennsylvania
Magdalena Dziedzic-Versusky	Clark Township, New Jersey
Josephine Polomski	Philadelphia, Pennsylvania
Felix Urbaniak	Wethersfield, Connecticut
Richard Szlenkier	Detroit, Michigan
Stanley Jaskowski	Cleveland, Ohio
Darlene Zaren	Milwaukee, Wisconsin
Theodore Chojnacki	Cleveland, Ohio
Joseph Wojtowicz	Ypsilanti, Michigan
Frank Mazurek	Norwalk, California
Frank Dudek	Philadelphia, Pennsylvania
Joseph Gajda[a]	Chicago, Illinois
Walter Kornacki	Philadelphia, Pennsylvania
Jerome Serak	Chicago, Illinois
Stanley Pilch	Chicago, Illinois
Joseph Bieszczad	Olyphant, Pennsylvania
Felix Hujarski[c]	Cleveland, Ohio
John Dlugosz	South Bend, Indiana
Joseph Sikora[c]	Chicago, Illinois

[a]Vice President of the PNA
[b]National Director of the PNA
[c]District Commissioner of the PNA

Table 8.   **Location of PNA Lodges by State at Selected Periods**

State	1894	1905	1921	1947	1979	1983
Illinois	46	124	423	398	227	205
Pennsylvania	28	113	387	379	263	252
New York	31	69	218	233	165	151
Michigan	16	41	109	174	101	94
Wisconsin	11	25	63	71	49	46
Ohio	10	27	105	112	72	67
New Jersey	9	33	67	84	68	63
Minnesota	8	14	29	25	14	14
Indiana	5	10	33	36	26	24
Missouri	5	7	16	13	10	8
Massachusetts	3	17	56	94	66	62
Washington	3	6	14	8	7	7
Texas	3	2	5	7	12	12
Arkansas	2	2	3	2	1	1
Maryland	2	7	21	22	16	13
Colorado	2	3	4	4	2	2
California	2	3	6	6	17	16
Oregon	1	2	3	2	2	2
Connecticut	1	11	46	58	45	39
Rhode Island	1	4	9	9	6	6
Nebraska	1	1	5	5	4	4
Kansas	--	1	2	7	3	2
New Hampshire	--	1	3	0	5	5
West Virginia	--	1	15	14	9	8
Delaware	--	1	3	3	3	3
Canada	--	1	0	1	0	0
Virginia	--	--	2	0	2	2
Washington, D.C.	--	--	1	0	1	1
Florida	--	--	1	2	10	9
Oklahoma	--	--	3	0	0	0
Iowa	--	--	--	--	1	1
Arizona	--	--	2	3	2	2
Montana	--	--	1	0	0	0
Wyoming	--	--	1	0	0	0
Maine	--	--	1	0	1	1
North Dakota	--	--	--	--	1	1
Total Lodges	190	526	1,657	1,772	1,205	1,123

Major Election Results

Year	Convention site, dates	Office	Winner	Loser	Vote
1880	Chicago (1st Convention) Palmer House, September 15-18	Censor President V.P. Secretary Treasurer	J. Andrzejkowicz M. Kucera J. Rewerski E. Odrowaz St. Kociemski	All elected by Acclamation	

13 delegates at the convention, 18 groups in the Alliance representing about 900 persons. Assets were $162.30.

Year	Convention site, dates	Office	Winner	Loser	Vote
1881	New York (2); Convention Hall near 17 Rivington Street September 21-24	Censor President V.P. Secretary Treasurer Editor, Zgoda	J. Andrzejkowicz* M. Kucera* J. Rewerski* M. Osuch St. Kociemski* E. Odrowaz	All elected by Acclamation	

11 delegates; 9 groups representing 345 members; net assets of $622.71.

Year	Convention site, dates	Office	Winner	Loser	Vote
1882	Chicago (3); Vorwaerts Turn Halle on 251 West 12 St. September 21-23	Censor President V.P. Secretary Treasurer Editor	J. Andrzejkowicz* St. Kociemski J. Rozenski Ig. Morgenstern Ig. Mikitynski Ig. Wendzinski	All elected by Acclamation	

15 delegates; 11 groups representing 455 members; assets of $1,145.06.

Year	Convention site, dates	Office	Winner	Loser	Vote
1883	Milwaukee (4); Parish Hall of St. Stanislas Bishop and Martyr Church September 21-24	Censor President V.P. Secretary Treasurer Editor	Fr. Gryglaszewski St. Kociemski* Edw. Dankowski Ig. Morgenstern* J. Kowalski Ig. Wendzinski*	All elected by Acclamation	

16 Voting and 3 non-voting delegates, 12 groups or lodges representing 448 members; $175.55 in assets.

Table 9. (Continued)

1885	LaCrosse, Wisconsin (5); Hall of St. Vitus Church, a Czech parish February 14-17	Censor	Fr. Gryglaszewski*	All elected by
		President	St. Kociemski*	Acclamation
		V.P.	A. Blaszczynski	
		Secretary	Ig. Morgenstern*	
		Treasurer	M. Kucera	
		Editor	Z. Brodowski	

12 delegates; 10 lodges with 295 members; $639.52 assets.

1886	Bay City, Michigan (6) Polish Church Hall July 5-7	Censor	Fr. Gryglaszewski*	E. Jerzmanowski	36-18
		President	W. Przybyszewski		
		V.P.	A. Meczarski	Elected by	
		Secretary	Fr. Wisniewski	Acclamation[a]	
		Treasurer	J. Breski		
		Editor	Z. Brodowski*	M. Sadowski	40-9

56 delegates; 48 lodges with 1893 members; Assets of $3,660.63.
Prior to the vote for officers, a motion to make Bay City instead of Chicago the headquarters of the PNA passed 31-25.

1887	St. Paul (7) St. Adalbert Church Hall September 12-15	Censor	Fr. Gryglaszewski*	W. Czechowicz	57-3
		President	M. Osuch	K. Dorszynski	55-7
		V.P.	T. Wozny	Ig. Mikitynski	44-15
		Secretary	Ig. Morgenstern	A. Mallek	53-13
		Treasurer	A. Kowalski	Ig. Mikitynski	58-10
		Editor	Z. Brodowski*	By acclamation	

81 delegates; 87 lodges with 3210 members; $8530.05 assets.
Chicago was restored permanently as the headquarters of the PNA at this convention.

1889	Buffalo (8) St. Adalbert Church Hall September 10-15	Censor	Fr. Gryglaszewski*	A. Kopankiewicz	34-18
		President	St. Kociemski	S.F.A. Satalecki	29-25
		V.P.	S.F.A. Satalecki	By acclamation	
		Secretary	A. Mallek	Ig. Morgenstern*	39-29
		Treasurer	M. Majewski	J. Kostrzewski	53-8
		Editor	St. Nicki	H. Nagiel	43-21

1891	Detroit (9) St. Josaphat Parish Hall September 21-29			
		Censor	W. Przybyszewski	Fr. Gryglaszewski*	53-32
		President	S.F.A. Satalecki	St. Kociemski*	57-32
		V.P.	St. Slominski	St. Kociemski	unknown
		Secretary	A. Mallek*	By acclamation	
		Treasurer	M. Majewski*	By acclamation	
		Editor	St. Nicki*	H. Nagiel	58-32

92 delegates; 111 lodges with 3865 members; assets $5,216.83.

1893	Chicago (10) Pulaski Hall near Holy Trinity Parish September 4-9			
		Censor	T. Helinski	By acclamation	
		President	S.F.A. Satalecki*	W. Bardonski	81-57
		V.P. (I)	St. Slominski*	By acclamation	
		V.P. (II)	W. Bardonski	By acclamation	
		Secretary	A. Mallek*	C. Zychlinski	83-53
		Treasurer	M. Majewski*	By acclamation	
		Editor	Fr. Jablonski	St. Nicki*	90-20

148 delegates; 167 lodges with 5654 members; $19,331.38 assets.

1895	Cleveland (11) St. Stanislas Bishop and Martyr Parish Hall September 9-14			
		Censor	T. Helinski*	By acclamation	
		President	Z. Brodowski	A. Blaszczynski	74-33
		V.P. (I)	A. Blaszczynski	By acclamation	
		V.P. (II)	T. Kodis	By acclamation	
		Secretary	M. Sadowski	C. Zychlinski	66-46
		Treasurer	Val Wleklinski	M. Majewski*	73-14
		Editor	Fr. Jablonski	By acclamation	

120 delegates; 210 lodges; 7515 members; assets of $28,182.71.

1897	Philadelphia (12) Convention Hall September 6-11			
		Censor	T. Helinski*	By acclamation	
		President	Fr. Jablonski	W. Poszwinski	104-23
		V.P.	J. Polczynski	By acclamation	
		Secretary	M. Sadowski	By acclamation	
		Treasurer	Val Wleklinski*	J. Szostakowski	107-33
		Editor	St. Barszczewski	St. Osada	87-55

165 delegates; 12,231 members; 338 lodges; assets of $39,419.

Table 9. (Continued)

Year	Location / Hall / Dates	Office		Vote
1899	Grand Rapids, Mich. (13) Church Hall October 16-21	Censor	L. Sadowski	S. Sleszynski	147-16
		President	Fr. Jablonski*	A. Kolakowski	126-33
		V.P.	St. Rokosz	W. Syzmanski	118-45
		Secretary	T. Helinski	J. Szajnert	122-33
		Treasurer	M. Majewski	J. Szostakowski	152-11
		Editor	St. Barszczewski*	T. Siemiradzki	113-50

170 delegates; 412 lodges; 15,288 members; assets of $96,530.

Year	Location / Hall / Dates	Office		Vote
1901	Toledo (14) Parish Hall October 14-20	Censor	L. Sadowski*	By acclamation	165
		President	St. Rokosz	M. Steczynski	100-70
		V.P.	J. Szostakowski	A. Centella	70-64
		Secretary	T. Helinski	J. Szajnert	164-21
		Treasurer	M. Majewski*	B. Maciejewski	169-9
		Editor	T. Siemiradzki	J. Chrzanowski	166-28

196 delegates; 464 lodges; 29,762 members; assets of $132,886.

Year	Location / Hall / Dates	Office		Vote
1903	Wilkes-Barre (15) Church Hall October 19-24	Censor	L. Sadowski*	J. Sliwinski	241-103
		President	M. Steczynski	By acclamation	310
		V.P.	M. Rzeszotarski	J. Herman	189-159
		Secretary	T. Helinski*	By acclamation	292
		Treasurer	M. Majewski*	By acclamation	293
		Editor	T. Siemiradzki*	St. Osada	268-102

382 delegates; 551 lodges; 36,312 members; assets of $239,981.

Year	Location / Hall / Dates	Office		Vote
1905	Buffalo (16) The Polish Home October 23-28	Censor	A. Schrieber	L. Sadowski*	223-119
		President	M. Steczynski*	St. Rokosz	245-90
		V.P.	M. Rzeszotarski*	A. Majewski	231-108
		Secretary	T. Helinski*	Fr. Rosenthal	224-104
		Treasurer	M. Majewski*	B. Maciejewski	274-52
		Editor	T. Siemiradzki*	St. Orpiszewski	177-165

375 delegates; 622 lodges with 44,022 members; assets of $321,931.

Year / Location	Office			Votes
Baltimore (17) Broadway Institute Hall September 23-28	Censor	A. Schreiber*	By acclamation	314
	President	M. Steczynski*	S. J. Napieralski	214-121
	V.P.	F. Ksycki	K. B. Czarnecki	188-138
	Secretary	S. Czechowicz	R. Piatkowski	243-82
	Treasurer	M. Majewski*	W. Bardonski	252-70
	Editor	Fr. Jablonski	T. Siemiradzki*	167-159

352 delegates; 773 lodges with 52,448 members; assets of $469,233.

Year / Location	Office			Votes
1909 Milwaukee (18) Kosciuszko Armory Hall October 11-16	Censor	A. Schreiber*	L. Sadowski	249-155
	President	M. Steczynski*	By acclamation	
	V.P.	F. Ksycki*	K. B. Czarnecki	236-162
	Secretary	S. Czechowicz*	Fr. Karcz	307-86
	Treasurer	M. Majewski*	W. Perlowski	262-136
	Editor	T. Siemiradzki	By acclamation	

446 delegates; 956 lodges with 55,033 members; assets of $763,668.

Year / Location	Office			Votes
1911 St. Louis (19) Convention Hall October 9-14	Censor	A. Schreiber*	A. Skarzynski	192-95
	President	M. Steczynski*	S. Sass	157-131
	V.P.	F. Ksycki*	K. B. Czarnecki	164-118
	Secretary	S. Czechowicz*	By acclamation	
	Treasurer	M. Majewski*	St. Rokosz	179-110
	Editor	T. Siemiradzki*	Cz. Kozlowski	194-92

290 delegates; 1202 lodges; 75,665 members; assets of $1,483,563.

Year / Location	Office			Votes
1913 Detroit (20) Dom Polski September 15-22	Censor	A. Karabasz	T. Siemiradzki	327-259
	President	C. Zychlinski	S. Sass	352-231
	V.P.	St. Mermel	A. Czechowicz	374-228
	Secretary	J. Zawilinski	J. Karasiewicz	312-268
	Treasurer	J. Magdziarz	By acclamation	
	Editor	St. Dangiel	By acclamation	
	Lady Commissioner for all states	V. Lipczynska	J. Bonczak	302-272

704 delegates; 100,198 members; 1433 lodges; $2,152,020 in assets.

Table 9. (Continued)

1915	Schenectady (21) St. Adalbert Hall September 27 - October 3	Censor	M. Blenski	R. Abczynski	227-195
		President	C. Zychlinski*	S. Sass	224-195
		V.P.	K. B. Czarnecki	J. Szymanski	218-191
		Hon. Lady V.P.	C. Obarska	Wl. Chodzinska	204-200
		Secretary	J. Zawilinski*	By acclamation	285
		Treasurer	J. Magdziarz*	By acclamation	281
		Editor	St. Orpiszewski	By acclamation	278

437 delegates; 110,331 members; 1576 lodges; assets of $2,936,607.

1918	Pittsburgh (22) Moose Temple September 16-21	Censor	M. Blenski*	By acclamation	373
		President	C. Zychlinski*	Fr. Wiernicki	317-147
		V.P.	K. B. Czarnecki*	R. Kowal	278-147
		Secretary	J. Zawilinski*	Leon Nowak	314-145
		Treasurer	J. Magdziarz*	S. Gorecki	339-112

470 delegates; 125,860 members; 1697 lodges; assets of $4,934,834.

1921	Toledo (23) Memorial Hall September 26 - October 1	Censor	M. Blenski*	T. Butkiewicz	346-143
		President	C. Zychlinski*	S. Sass	282-206
		V.P. (I)	F. Garbarek	A. Piwowarski	395-87
		V.P. (II)	M. Milewska*	By acclamation	
		Secretary	J. Zawilinski*	Theodore Sakowski	348-135
		Treasurer	J. Magdziarz*	S. Gorecki	354-128

496 delegates; 1679 lodges with 123,468 members; assets of $6,333,543.

1924	Philadelphia (24) Lulu Temple August 25-30	Censor	C. Sypniewski	M. Blenski*	266-173
		President	C. Zychlinski*	S. Sass	220-217
		V.P. (I)	F. Garbarek*	E. Placzek	273-162
		V.P. (II)	M. Sakowska	M. Milewska*	285-143
		Secretary	J. Zawilinski*	Unopposed	408
		Treasurer	M. Turbak	J. Magdziarz*	221-216

432 delegates; 1695 lodges with 108,211 members; assets of $9,152,660

1927 — Chicago (25)
Sherman Hotel
September 19-20, 1927;
August 27 - September 1, 1928

Office			
Censor	C. Sypniewski*	L. Koscinski	235-214
President	J. Romaszkiewicz	J. Mallek	268-184
V.P. (I)	F. Garbarek*	Fr. Synowiec	233-210
V.P. (II)	M. Milewska	M. Sakowska*	227-217
Secretary	C. Kowalski	J. Zawilinski*	229-223
Treasurer	M. Hencel	M. Turbak*	226-224

468 delegates; 1789 lodges with 266,265 members; assets of $16,657,532 (1928).[a]
Election results are for 1928.

1931 — Scranton (26)
Town Hall Building
September 20-26

Office			
Censor	F. X. Swietlik	C. Sypniewski*	282-235
President	J. Romaszkiewicz*	L. Koscinski	318-194
V.P. (I)	Cz. Hibner	F. Spychalski	277-244
V.P. (II)	C. Obarska	M. Milewska*	293-214
Secretary	A. Szczerbowski	C. Kowalski*	260-257
Treasurer	J. Spiker	M. Hencel*	259-253

533 delegates; 1844 lodges; 288,619 members; assets of $23,216,984.

1935 — Baltimore (27)
Lord Baltimore Hotel
September 15-21

Office			
Censor	F. X. Swietlik*	L. Lipowicz	285-225
President	J. Romaszkiewicz*	K. Rozmarek	260-252
V.P. (I)	Cz. Hibner*	J. Michalak	264-246
V.P. (II)	Fr. Dymek	M. Milewska*	295-210
Secretary	A. Szczerbowski*	C. Kowalski	285-227
Treasurer	J. Spiker*	M. Hencel	263-245

520 delegates; 1907 lodges; 280,785 members; assets of $28,376,427.

1939 — Detroit (28)
Book Cadillac Hotel
September 10-16

Office			
Censor	F. X. Swietlik*	W. E. Stankiewicz	300-228
President	K. Rozmarek	J. Romaszkiewicz*	269-262
V.P. (I)	P. Kozlowski	W. Krawczewski	300-206
V.P. (II)	M. Czyz	Fr. Dymek*	312-212
Secretary	A. Szczerbowski*	C. Kowalski	301-228
Treasurer	M. Tomaszkiewicz	J. Spiker*	286-245

533 delegates; 1836 lodges; 279,533 members; assets of $29,308,803.

Table 9. (Continued)

Year	Location	Position	Candidate	Candidate	Vote
1943	Boston (29) Statler Hotel September 19-24	Censor	F. X. Swietlik*	S. A. Gutowski	413-146
		President	K. Rozmarek*	J. Romaszkiewicz	444-87
		V.P. (I)	P. Kozlowski*	L. Witecki	372-90
		V.P. (II)	F. Dymek	M. Czyz*	335-221
		Secretary	A. Szczerbowski*	C. Kowalski	365-91
		Treasurer	M. Tomaszkiewicz*	J. Malinowski	423-74

577 delegates; 1821 lodges, 279,690 members; assets of $33,547,121.

Year	Location	Position	Candidate	Candidate	Vote
1947	Cleveland (30) Hotel Cleveland August 24-29	Censor	B. F. Gunther	A. Maciejewski	342-150
		President	K. Rozmarek	J. H. Mikulski	391-102
		V.P. (I)	P. Kozlowski	no opposition	415
		V.P. (II)	Fr. Dymek	Karolina Spisak	343-150
		Secretary	A. Szczerbowski	W. Andrejewski	352-134
		Treasurer	M. Tomaszkiewicz	J. Pyrzynski	426-36

493 delegates; 1776 lodges, 304,830 members; assets of $43,132,041.

Year	Location	Position	Candidate	Candidate	Vote
1951	Buffalo (31) Statler Hotel September 23-28	Censor	B. F. Gunther*	F. X. Swietlik	381-138
		President	K. Rozmarek*	J. Roszkowski	372-94
		V.P. (I)	P. Kozlowski*	E. Plusdrak	287-237
		V.P. (II)	Fr. Dymek*	K. Spisak	378-152
		Secretary	A. Szczerbowski*	B. Migala	279-245
		Treasurer	M. Tomaszkiewicz*	F. Wrobel	293-223

523 delegates; 1677 lodges with 330,563 members; with assets of $60,688,343.

Year	Location	Position	Candidate	Candidate	Vote
1955	Minneapolis (32) Hotel Nicolet September 18-23	Censor	B. F. Gunther*	J. Godlewski	301-206
		President	K. Rozmarek*	St. Piotrowicz	420-78
		V.P. (I)	Fr. Dymek*	S. Gondek	301-202
		V.P. (II)	S. Lisowski*	M. Mokrzycki	345-149
		Secretary	J. Foszcz	J. Dancewicz	272-235
		Treasurer	A. Tomaszkiewicz	J. Rychlicki	297-188

501 delegates; 1617 lodges with 339,801 members; with assets of $78,426,382.

1959 — Hartford (33), Hotel Statler-Hilton, September 20-25

Office			
Censor	E. Kozmor	B. F. Gunther*	260-200
President	K. Rozmarek*	A. Tomaszkiewicz	285-172
V.P. (I)	Fr. Dymek*	S. Gondek	275-183
V.P. (II)	Fr. Prochot	A. Piwowarczyk	275-177
Secretary	J. Foszcz*	W. Andrzejewski	304-154
Treasurer	J. Ulatowski	L. Trawinski	364-78

462 delegates; 1529 lodges with 335,135 members; with assets of $98,099,918.

1963 — Philadelphia (34), Benjamin Franklin Hotel, September 15-20

Office			
Censor	E. Kozmor*	no opposition	394
President	K. Rozmarek*	A. Mazewski	292-146
V.P. (I)	F. Dymek*	S. Gondek	285-150
V.P. (II)	Fr. Prochot*	Cz. Mikolajczyk	318-118
Secretary	A. Pachucki	J. Foszcz*	239-200
Treasurer	J. Ulatowski*	H. Spindor	265-141

440 delegates, 1475 lodges with 351,166 members; with assets of $117,370,088.

1967 — Detroit (35), Hotel Sheraton Cadillac, September 17-22

Office			
Censor	W. Dworakowski	E. Maziarz	263-144
President	A. Mazewski	K. Rozmarek*	221-189
V.P. (I)	I. Wallace	W. L. Podkomorska	209-196
V.P. (II)	Fr. Prochot*	K. Lotarski	221-187
Secretary	A. Pachucki*	J. Foszcz	212-199
Treasurer	E. Moskal	J. Swiderski	257-132

406 delegates; 1423 lodges with 344,963 members; with assets of $133,416,423.

1971 — Pittsburgh (36), Hotel Pittsburgh Hilton, September 19-24

Office			
Censor	K. Lotarski	W. Dworakowski*	230-139
President	A. Mazewski*	Z. Tuczynski	349-10
V.P. (I)	H. Szymanowicz	I. Wallace*	216-153
V.P. (II)	Fr. Prochot*	C. Grabowski	297-55
Secretary	A. Pachucki*	no opposition	322
Treasurer	E. Moskal*	no opposition	312

371 delegates; 1352 lodges; 325,724 members; $145,736,045 in assets.

Table 9. (Continued)

	Office			Votes
1975 Milwaukee (37) Hotel Marc Plaza September 21-26	Censor	H. Czaplicki	A. Czelen	183-156
	President	A. Mazewski*	no opposition	315
	V.P. (I)	H. Szymanowicz*	no opposition	307
	V.P. (II)	J. Gajda	no opposition	288
	Secretary	L. Kubiak	no opposition	320
	Treasurer	E. Moskal*	no opposition	311

342 delegates; 1289 lodges with 312,923 members, with assets of $154,941,085.

	Office			Votes
1979 Washington, D.C. (38) Capital Hilton Hotel August 24-31	Censor	H. Czaplicki*	A. Czelen	165-96
	President	A. Mazewski*	E. Sitnik	273-46
	V.P. (I)	H. Szymanowicz*	A. Rychlinska	201-119
	V.P. (II)	J. Gajda*	no opposition	279
	Secretary	L. Kubiak*	S. Pilch	245-72
	Treasurer	E. Moskal*	no opposition	283

325 delegates; 1,195 lodges with 301,590 members; with assets of $160,871,595.

	Office			Votes
1983 Orlando, Florida (39) Sheraton Twin Towers Hotel September 18-23	Censor	H. Czaplicki*	no opposition	285
	President	A. Mazewski*	A. Czelen	263-49
	V.P. (I)	H. Szymanowicz*	H. Orawiec	165-132
	V.P. (II)	A. Piwowarczyk	L. Ciaston	235-83
	Secretary	E. Kolasa	S. Pilch	195-124
	Treasurer	E. Moskal*	no opposition	255

324 delegates; 1,123 lodges with 292,439 members; with assets of $176,417,404.

*Denotes incumbent

[a]1927 statistics just prior to the twentieth convention were: 249,402 members and $10,857,456 in assets. Extraordinary conventions were held in Chicago on February 21-23, 1884 and March 19-24, 1900. A third extraordinary convention was scheduled to begin on December 6, 1958 in Chicago but failed for lack of a quorum.

Table 10.   Elected National Officers, Polish National Alliance, 1880–1983[a]

Julius Andrzejkowicz[+], Censor (1880–1883)

Maximilian Kucera[++], President (1880–1882); Treasurer (1885–1886); Vice Censor (1889–1901)

Joseph Rewerski, Vice President (1880–1882)

Edward Odrowaz, Secretary (1880–1881), Editor, *Zgoda* (1881–1882)

Henry Zielinski, Vice Secretary (1880–1881)

Stanislas Kociemski[++], Treasurer (1880–1881); President (1882–1886, 1889–1891)

Francis Borchardt, Legal Advisor (1880–1881)

Michael Osuch, Secretary (1881–1882), President (1887–1889)

W. Sowadzki[++], Vice Secretary (1881–1882, 1883–1885)

Frank Gryglaszewski, Vice Censor (1882–1883); Censor (1883–1891); Commissioner (1909–1913)

John Rozenski, Vice President (1882–1883)

Ignace Morgenstern, Secretary (1882–1886, 1887–1889)

Roman Stobiecki, Vice President (1882–1883)

Ignace Mikitynski, Treasurer (1882–1883)

Ignace Wendzinski[++], Editor *Zgoda* (1882–1886)

Peter Wodzicki, Vice Censor (1883–1885)

Edward Dankowski, Vice President (1883–1885)

Joseph Kowalski, Treasurer (1883–1885)

Val Przybyszewski, Vice Censor (1885–1886); President (1886–1887); Censor (1891–1893)

Adam Blaszczynski, Vice President (1885–1886); First Vice President (1895–1897); Director (1907–1909)

John Wleklinski, Vice Secretary (1885–1886)

A. Grodzki, Vice Censor (1886–1887)

Al. Meczarski, Vice President (1886–1887)

Frank Wiszniewski, Secretary (1886–1887)

Al. Leszczynski, Vice Secretary (1886–1887)

John Breski, Treasurer (1886–1887)

J. Muszynski, Director (1886–1887)

Frank Glaza, Director (1886–1887)

J. Welter, Director (1886–1887)

Zbigniew Brodowski, Editor *Zgoda* (1886–1889); President (1895–1897)

Val Czechowicz, Vice Censor (1887–1889)

T. Wozny, Vice President (1887–1889)

Peter Arkuszewski, Vice Secretary (1887–1889)

August Kowalski, Treasurer (1887–1889)

K. Nowak, Vice Censor (1889)

F.S.A. Satalecki, Vice President (1889–1891); President (1891–1895)

Anthony Mallek, Secretary (1889–1895)

Table 10.   **(Continued)**

Albert Kowalski, Vice Secretary (1889-1891)

Michael Majewski[++], Treasurer (1889-1895, 1899-1913)

Theodore Helinski, Vice Censor (1891-1893); Censor (1893-1899); Secretary (1899-1906)

Stanislas Slominski, Vice President (1891-1893); First Vice President (1893-1895)

Stanislas Nicki, Editor, *Zgoda* (1889-1893); Comptroller (1895-1905)

Stanislas Lewandowski, Vice Censor (1893-1895)

Victor Bardonski, Second Vice President (1893-1895)

Frank Jablonski, Editor, *Zgoda* (1893-1897, 1908); President (1897-1901)

Frank Smietanka, Director (1893-1895)

John Smulski, Director (1893-1895)

Anthony Groenwald, Director (1893-1895)

Val Welzant, Vice Censor (1895-1897)

Theodore Kodis, Second Vice President (1895-1897)

M. J. Sadowski, Secretary (1895-1899)

Val Wleklinski, Treasurer (1895-1899)

J. Czernik, Vice Censor (1897-1899)

Joseph Polczynski, Vice President (1897-1899)

Stephen Barszczewski, Editor, *Zgoda* (1897-1901)

Leon Sadowski, Censor (1899-1905)

A. Nowak, Vice Censor (1899-1901)

J. N. Cukierski, Vice Censor (1899-1901)

A. Olszewski, Vice Censor (1899-1901)

Stanislas Rokosz, Vice President (1899-1901); President (1901-1903)

Marian Steczynski, Director (1899-1901); President (1903-1912)

Casimir Zurawski, Director (1899-1901); Medical Examiner (1909-1911)

M. Wleklinski, Director (1899-1901)

S. Lanferski, Director (1899-1903)

M. Zolkowski, Director (1899-1901)

Peter Beczkiewicz[+], Vice Censor (1901-1903)

John Kucki, Vice Censor (1901-1903); Commissioner (1907-1911)

John Welzant, Vice Censor (1901-1903)

Peter Szelazkiewicz, Vice Censor (1901-1903)

John Szostakowski, Vice President (1901-1903)

W. A. Kuflewski, Medical Examiner (1901-1909, 1911-1913); Director (1903-1909; 1911-1913)

Thomas Siemiradzki, Editor, *Zgoda* (1901-1913)

L. Czeslawski; Director (1901-1905)

W. Pijanowski, Director (1901-1905, 1907-1909, 1915-1921)

A. Dziadul, Director (1901-1903)

A. Majewski, Director (1901-1903); Commissioner (1913-1918)

Table 10.   (Continued)

Alexander Debski, Vice Censor (1903–1905)
Michael Blenski, Vice Censor (1903–1905); Censor (1915–1924)
Joseph Tuchocki, Vice Censor (1903–1905)
Walter Sawa, Vice Censor (1903–1907)
Michael Rzeszotarski, Vice President (1903–1907)
Walter Jelen, Director (1903–1907)
Leon Wild, Director (1903–1904)
John Kikulski, Director (1904–1905)
A. Ambrozewski, Director (1903–1909)
Frank Zawadzki, Director (1903–1905)
Anthony Schreiber, Censor (1905–1913)
S. Pruss, Vice Censor (1905–1907); Commissioner (1907–1909)
W. Siwinski, Vice Censor (1905–1907)
John Romaszkiewicz, Vice Censor (1905–1907); Commissioner (1907–1909); President
    (1928–1939)
J. Kaczmarski, Vice Censor (1905–1907); Commissioner (1907–1911)
W. Waligorski, Vice Censor (1905–1907)
S. Napieralski, Vice Censor (1905–1906); Secretary (1906–1907)
F. Uriwal, Vice Censor (1905–1907)
Joseph Kruszka, Vice Censor (1905–1907); Commissioner (1907–1909)
Joseph Nowakowski, Vice Censor (1905–1907)
Valerie Lipczynska, Vice Censor (1905–1907); Commissioner (1907–1921, 1924–1929)
K. B. Czarnecki, Director (1905–1907); Vice President (1915–1921)
Stanislas Osada, Director (1905–1909)
J. Chmielinski, Director (1905–1907)
Chester Hibner, Director (1905–1907); Vice President (1931–1939)
John Sliwinski, Vice Censor (1907–1909)
Filip Ksycki, Vice President (1907–1912, 1912–1913); President (1912)
S. Czechowicz, Secretary (1907–1913)
Bialecki, Commissioner (1907–1909)
W. Urbanski, Commissioner (1907–1909, 1911–1913)
M. F. Poniecki, Commissioner (1907–1909, 1913–1915)
Frank Danisch, Commissioner (1907–1909)
Thomas Blazejewski, Commissioner (1907–1909, 1915–1918)
M. L. Mucha, Commissioner (1907–1911)
M. Glowczewski, Commissioner (1907–1913)
A. Tubielewicz, Commissioner (1907–1909)
Roman Abczynski, Vice Censor (1909–1911), Commissioner (1913–1915)
John Wlekinski, Director (1909–1911)
M. Kmieciak, Director (1909–1915)

Table 10.   **(Continued)**

M. Wojtecki, Director (1909–1911)

Mary Sakowska, Director (1909–1918); Vice President (1924–1928)

Nikodem Zlotnicki, Director (1909–1921)

J. Hatmanowicz, Director (1909–1911)

Anthony Wojczynski, Commissioner (1909–1911)

W. Gorski, Commissioner (1909–1911)

Val Przybylinski, Commissioner (1909–1911)

Albert Nowak, Commissioner (1909–1911)

Paul Kurdziel, Commissioner (1909–1911); Director (1939–1940)

J. Jaworski, Commissioner (1909–1928)

A. Tomkiewicz, Commissioner (1909–1913)

W. Orzechowski, Commissioner (1909–1911)

A. Gregorowicz, Commissioner (1909–1911, 1913–1915)

K. Schmiedehausen, Commissioner (1909–1911)

Stephen Dydek, Commissioner (1909–1911)

Henry Niedzwiecki, Vice Censor (1911–1913)

Leon Mallek, Director (1911–1915)

Casimir Zychlinski, Director (1911–1912); President (1912–1927)

Wladyslawa Chodzinska, Director (1911–1913, 1918–1921, 1924–1928)

J. P. Szymanski, Director (1911–1913)

Stanislas Mermel, Director (1911–1913); Vice President (1913–1914)

Julius Szajnert[+], Commissioner (1911–1929)

J. Zabielski, Commissioner (1911–1913)

M. Burzynski, Commissioner (1911–1913, 1915–1921, 1924–1931)

Anthony Karabasz, Commissioner (1911–1913); Censor (1913–1915)

J. Rosinski, Commissioner (1911–1913)

E. Szydlowski, Commissioner (1911–1913)

A. Rusin, Commissioner (1911–1913)

A. Zwolinski, Commissioner (1911–1913)

J. Groszewski, Commissioner (1911–1913)

P. Lipinski, Commissioner (1911–1913)

A. Mikiewicz, Commissioner (1911–1913)

M. Powicki, Commissioner (1911–1931); Vice Censor 1935–1947)

S. T. Yezerski, Commissioner (1911–1913)

A. Jankiewicz, Commissioner (1911–1913, 1915–1918, 1921–1924)

Adolf Rakoczy, Vice Censor (1913–1915); Censor (1915)

John Zawilinski, Secretary (1913–1928)

Joseph Magdziarz, Treasurer (1913–1924)

W. Sutkiewicz, Director (1913–1915)

John Jankowski, Director (1913–1915)

Table 10.   (Continued)

Henry Anielewski, Director (1913–1915)
Casimira Obarska, Director (1913–1915, 1921–1931); Honorary Vice President (1915–1918);
    Vice President (1931–1932)
Frank Wleklinski, Director (1913–1915, 1918–1921)
Anthony Mazur, Director (1913–1918)
Casimir Olszowy, Director (1913–1915)
Anthony Balcerzak, Medical Examiner (1913–1928)
A. Wawrowski, Commissioner (1913–1915)
John Maternowicz, Commissioner (1913–1921)
Paul Borowicz, Commissioner (1913–1921)
E. Brachowski, Commissioner (1913–1915)
J. S. Karpanty, Commissioner (1913–1924)
F. Zawacki, Commissioner (1913–1915, 1918–1921)
L. Terski, Commissioner (1913–1918)
Alexander Heller, Commissioner (1913–1921)
A. Grabarkiewicz, Commissioner (1913–1921)
F. Grodzki, Commissioner (1913–1915)
John Grodzki, Commissioner (1913–1915)
Joseph Werwinski, Vice Censor (1915–1921)
W. Szymanski, Director (1915–1918)
Magdalena Milewska, Director (1915–1921); Vice President (1921–1924, 1928–1931,
    1932–1935)
S. J. Dudek, Director (1915–1918, 1921–1924)
Frank Nowak, Director (1915–1928)
J. F. Singer, Director (1915–1924)
W. Wrzesinski, Director (1915–1918)
S. Wleklinski, Director (1915–1918)
H. Kwasniewski, Commissioner (1915–1918)
A. B. Brzozowski, Commissioner (1915–1918)
J. Asbert, Commissioner (1915–1918)
Stanislas Skura, Commissioner (1915–1918)
W. Stachowski, Commissioner (1915–1918)
John Froncek, Commissioner (1915–1918)
J. Krupa, Commissioner (1915–1918, 1924–1928)
Casimir Janowski, Commissioner (1915–1921)
Leon Chlebinski, Commissioner (1915–1918, 1924–1928)
M. Lukaszewicz, Commissioner (1915–1921, 1924–1928)
F. Kuczynski, Commissioner (1915–1918)
F. Gizynski, Commissioner (1915–1918)
J. Czarnecki, Commissioner (1915–1918)

Table 10.   **(Continued)**

W. Laskowski, Commissioner (1915–1918, 1921–1924)

M. Kuflewska, Director (1918–1921)

K. Wisniewski, Commissioner (1918–1921)

S. Majewski, Commissioner (1918–1921)

Frank Yagocki, Commissioner (1918–1924)

Roman Kopytecki, Commissioner (1918–1921)

F. Michalski, Commissioner (1918–1921)

J. Fraczek, Commissioner (1918–1921)

J. B. Wleklinski, Commissioner (1918–1921)

A. Brzezinski, Commissioner (1918–1924)

W. Ogrodowski, Commissioner (1918–1921)

Ignace Cylkowski, Commissioner (1918–1921)

J. J. Trzesniewski, Commissioner (1918–1924)

Frank Sedziak, Commissioner (1918–1921)

Felix Furtek, Commissioner (1918–1924, 1935–1947)

Leopold Koscinski, Vice Censor (1921–1924)

Felix Garbarek, Vice President (1921–1927, 1928–1931); President (1927–1928)

Angela Skierczynska, Director (1921–1924, 1928–1931)

Frank Glowa, Director (1921–1939)

Frank Synowiec, Director (1921–1928, 1935–1939)

M. Kitkowski, Director (1921–1924)

Val Kozuch, Director (1921–1929); Commissioner (1955–1963)

Stanislas Strzelecki, Director (1921–1924)

Frank Oklejewicz, Commissioner (1921–1928)

M. Dziob, Commissioner (1921–1924)

S. K. Kowalski, Commissioner (1921–1928)

Thomas Jarzebowski, Commissioner (1921–1924)

Rosalia Skura, Commissioner (1921–1924)

Stanislas Chudzinski, Commissioner (1921–1924)

J. Saja, Commissioner (1921–1924)

M. W. Rozycki, Commissioner (1921–1924)

A. Rogalski, Commissioner (1921–1924)

J. Kosinski, Commissioner (1921–1924)

Michael Tomaszkiewicz, Commissioner (1921–1924); Director (1924–1939); Treasurer (1939–1955)

John Gronczewski, Commissioner (1921–1928); Director (1940–1947)

Rev. John Kromulicki, Commissioner (1921–1924)

P. Wojciechowski, Commissioner (1921–1928)

Casimir Sypniewski, Censor (1924–1931)

Walter Cytacki, Vice Censor (1924–1931)

Table 10.   (Continued)

Michael Turbak, Treasurer (1924-1928); Commissioner (1943-1947)
Frances Siniarska, Director (1924-1928)
Matt Majchrowicz, Director (1924-1928, 1935-1943, 1951-1959)
Titus Jachimowski, Director (1924-1926)
Stanislas Ogrodnik, Commissioner (1924-1928)
A. Piotrowski, Commissioner (1924-1928)
J. A. Faltyn, Commissioner (1924-1928)
Stanislas Lubinski, Commissioner (1924-1928)
J. Lenczewski, Commissioner (1924-1928)
P. Swaszkiewicz, Commissioner (1924-1928)
J. Tudek, Commissioner (1924-1939)
M. Grzybala, Commissioner (1924-1928)
Stanislas Stawski, Commissioner (1924-1931)
J. Raczka, Commissioner (1924-1928), Director (1928-1931)
J. Sobieski, Commissioner (1924-1931)
Stanislas Traczyk, Commissioner (1924-1935)
W. J. Miller, Commissioner (1924-1935)
R. J. Wrona, Commissioner (1924-1928)
M. Jasudowicz, Commissioner (1924-1928)
Casimir Kowalski, Secretary (1928-1931)
Maximilian Hencel, Treasurer (1928-1931)
S. F. Wietrzynski, Medical Examiner (1928-1935)
Joseph Spiker, Director (1928-1931); Treasurer (1931-1939)
Gregory Piwowarczyk, Director (1928-1935, 1939-1943)
Helen Prokesz, Director (1928-1931)
Walter Krawczewski, Director (1928-1931)
Frank Spychalski, Director (1928-1931)
J. M. Zarembski, Commissioner (1928-1935)
Peter Kozlowski, Commissioner (1928-1939); Vice President (1939-1954)
T. Zaborski, Commissioner (1928-1935)
M. Turman, Commissioner (1928-1935)
D. Gajewski, Commissioner (1928-1931)
J. Mankowski, Commissioner (1928-1931)
Constance Aleksalza, Commissioner (1928-1931)
Walter Grodziecki, Commissioner (1928-1931)
Peter Iwaszkiewicz, Commissioner (1928-1939)
A. Zaluga, Commissioner (1928-1935)
J. Rosowicz, Commissioner (1928-1931)
A. Hinkelman, Commissioner (1928-1931)
J. Biesiada, Commissioner (1928-1931)

Table 10.   (Continued)

Frank Reichert, Commissioner (1928–1931)
Frank Kustra, Commissioner (1928–1931)
Frank Zielinski, Commissioner (1928–1935)
Stanislas Kowalewski, Commissioner (1928–1935)
A. Broda, Commissioner (1928–1935)
Francis Swietlik, Censor (1931–1947)
Jerome Pawlowski, Vice Censor (1931–1935)
Albin Szczerbowski, Secretary (1931–1955)
Bronislawa Zawilinska, Director (1931–1939)
Jacob Twardzik, Director (1931–1935)
Stefanie Dworak, Director (1931–1935)
B. Menczynska, Director (1931–1935)
I. K. Werwinski, Director (1931–1939)
A. Sobota, Director (1931–1939)
Stanislas Zawilinski, Director (1931–1935)
A. A. Maciejewski, Commissioner (1931–1939)
W. Dawidowski, Commissioner (1931–1935)
Frank Gregorek, Commissioner (1931–1935)
J. Lenkiewicz, Commissioner (1931–1935)
J. J. Twardzik, Commissioner (1931–1935)
Stephen Nowakowski, Commissioner (1931–1939)
J. Bochmowski, Commissioner (1931–1935)
J. P. Michalak, Commissioner (1931–1935)
T. J. Kuberacki, Commissioner (1931–1935)
Stanislas Tomczak, Commissioner (1931–1935)
W. Kasperski, Commissioner (1931–1935)
Stanislas Ciborowski, Commissioner (1931–1935)
Frances Dymek, Vice President (1935–1939, 1943–1967)
Frank Dulak, Medical Examiner (1935–1939)
Angela Wojcik, Director (1935–1951)
Eugene Jaworek, Director (1935–1939)
D. T. Sakowski, Director (1935–1939)
John Rudek, Commissioner (1935–1947), Director (1947–1955)
A. Karwan, Commissioner (1935–1943)
Frank Lankowski, Commissioner (1935–1943)
Stephen Sudek, Commissioner (1935–1951)
Joseph Ostrowski, Commissioner (1935–1939)
John Juszczyk, Commissioner (1935–1939)
John K. Wieczorek, Commissioner (1935–1943)
Thomas Gratzek, Commissioner (1935–1943)

Table 10.   (Continued)

F. M. Sianiuk, Commissioner (1935-1939)

Anna Pytek, Commissioner (1935-1939)

Genevieve Szymczak, Commissioner (1935-1939)

Charles Rozmarek, President (1939-1967)

Mary Czyz, Vice President (1939-1943)

A. Z. Sampolinski, Medical Examiner (1939-1943, 1959-1963)

Joseph Wattras, Director (1939-1951)

Jacob Rekucki, Director (1939-1947)

Ignace Zwarycz, Director (1939-1943)

Josephine Migala, Director (1939-1951)

Stanley Basinski, Director (1939-1951)

Ignace Postanowicz, Director (1939-1943)

Stanley Niedzwiecki, Commissioner (1939-1959)

G. Tuchewicz, Commissioner (1939-1943)

Henry Dudek, Commissioner (1939-1951); Director (1951-1959)

Michael Holodnik, Commissioner (1939-1959); Director (1959-1967)

Joseph Habuda, Commissioner (1939-1947); Vice Censor (1947-1955)

John Slodkiewicz, Commissioner (1939-1951)

Louis Witecki, Commissioner (1939-1943)

Wenceslaus Fabiszewicz, Commissioner (1939-1943)

John Jezierski, Commissioner (1939-1943)

Anna Tuman, Commissioner (1939-1947; 1955-1967)

Mary Majka, Commissioner (1939-1943)

Lawrence A. Sadlek, Medical Examiner (1943-1959)

Caroline Spisak, Director (1943-1947; 1955-1963)

Joseph Jozwiak, Director (1943-1947)

John Ulatowski, Director (1943-1959); Treasurer (1959-1967)

Frank Wrobel, Director (1943-1951)

John Nowak, Commissioner (1943-1971)

Edward Kozmor, Commissioner (1943-1955); Vice Censor (1955-1959), Censor (1959-1965)

Joseph Wojcik, Commissioner (1943-1951)

Joseph Tobola, Commissioner (1943-1959)

Walter Daniszewski, Commissioner (1943-1947)

Pelagia Lukaszewska, Commissioner (1943-1947)

Anna Petyk, Commissioner (1943-1947)

Blaire F. Gunther, Censor (1947-1959)

George Wrost, Director (1947-1955)

Stefanie Gondek, Director (1947-1955)

Aloysius Mazewski, Director (1947-1955); President (from 1967)

Edward Karolkiewicz, Commissioner (1947-1951)

Table 10.   **(Continued)**

Leopold Babirecki, Commissioner (1947–1983)
Louis Sliwinski, Commissioner (1947–1951, 1955–1975)
Anthony Szczypinski, Commissioner (1947–1953)
John Wojciechowski, Commissioner (1947–1951)
Thaddeus Wachel, Commissioner (1947–1951, 1959–1983)
Peter Kus, Commissioner (1947–1951)
Wanda Slupska, Commissioner (1947–1955)
Anna Kazmierczak, Commissioner (1947–1955)
Leokadia Misiora, Commissioner (1947–1951, 1959–1971)
Mary Godlewska, Commissioner (1947–1951)
Anna Zdunek, Commissioner (1947–1951); Director (1951–1955)
Stefan Lisowski, Vice President (1954–1959)
Catherine Ziemba-Dienes, Director (1951–1971)
Walter Pasciak, Director (1951–1955)
Joseph Dancewicz, Commissioner (1951–1963); Director (1963–1979)
Josephine Karolkiewicz, Commissioner (1951–1955)
Theodora Drozd-Zegota, Commissioner (1951–1959)
Mary Tuchewicz, Commissioner (1951–1967)
Walter Szczygiel, Commissioner (1951–1959)
Helen Rozajewska-Dworczak, Commissioner (1951–1959)
Emilie Janowska, Commissioner (1951–1963)
Andrew Golec, Commissioner (1951–1955)
Veronica Kopec, Commissioner (1951–1955)
Frank Odrobina, Commissioner (1951–1955); Director (1955–1959)
Josephine Wolas, Commissioner (1951–1963)
Henry Kubicki, Commissioner (1951–1955)
Mary Godlewska, Commissioner (1951–1963)
Michael Mokrzycki, Commissioner (1951–1955)
Mary Gierut, Commissioner (1951–1959)
Edward Krysinski, Commissioner (1951–1955)
Rosalie Wojcik, Commissioner (1951–1959)
Gladys Podkomorska, Commissioner (1951–1967, 1971–1975)
John Ziemba, Commissioner (1951–1959); Director (1959–1971)
Valerie Mackowiak, Commissioner (1951–1955)
Andrew Spulniak, Commissioner (1951–1955)
Bronislawa Czarnecka, Commissioner (1951–1959)
Joseph Foszcz, Secretary (1955–1963)
Adam Tomaszkiewicz, Treasurer (1955–1959)
Bonaventure Migala, Director (1955–1963)
Henry Spindor, Director (1955–1963)

Table 10.   (Continued)

Bronislawa Helkowska, Director (1955–1967)
Adolf Pachucki, Director (1955–1963); Secretary (1963–1975)
Bronislawa Niemyska, Commissioner (1955–1967)
Thaddeus Giergielewicz, Commissioner (1955–1963)
Felice Zochowska, Commissioner (1955–1963)
Walter Dworakowski, Commissioner (1955–1959); Vice Censor (1959–1965); Censor (1965–1971)
Irene Wallace, Commissioner (1955–1959); Director (1959–1967); Vice President (1967–1971)
Jacob Lewandowski, Commissioner (1955–1959)
Frank Kawa, Commissioner (1955–1959)
Frank Jendryaszek, Commissioner (1955–1967)
Constance Czarnecka, Commissioner (1955–1959)
Constantine Dombrowski, Commissioner (1955–1959)
Edward Gembara, Director (1959–1963)
Frank Prochot, Vice President (1959–1974)
Henry Borowy, Commissioner (1959–1963)
Evelyn Gawalis, Commissioner (1959–1975)
John Jaje, Commissioner (1959–1967)
Apolonia Danielewicz, Commissioner (1959–1963)
Sophie Wojcik, Commissioner (1959–1983)
Anthony Czelen, Commissioner (1959–1967); Vice Censor (1967–1971)
Alexander Kopczynski, Commissioner (1959–1979)
Genevieve Gratzko, Commissioner (1959–1963)
Mitchell Odrobina, Commissioner (1959–1963); Director (1963–1983)
Stanley Sulkowski, Commissioner (1959–1983)
Mary Szelag, Commissioner (1959–1963)
Adele Cwik, Commissioner (1959–1963)
Jacob Fatla, Commissioner (1959–1967)
Victoria Basinska, Commissioner (1959–1963)
William Wojcik, Commissioner (1959–1963)
Louise Kobylak, Commissioner (1959–1963)
Melanie Winiecka, Director (1963–1975)
Edward Moskal, Director (1963–1967); Treasurer (from 1967)
Stanley Jozefiak, Director (1963–1971)
John Siderski, Commissioner (1963–1975)
Joseph Zdunczyk, Commissioner (1963–1979)
Theodore Pajak, Commissioner (1963–1967)
Stefanie Jedwabnik, Commissioner (1963–1967)
Wladyslawa Opatkiewicz, Commissioner (1963–1967, 1971–1979)
Marianna Golembiewska, Commissioner (1963–1971)

Table 10.   (Continued)

Joseph Rychlicki, Commissioner (1963–1967)
Bernice Barc, Commissioner (1963–1975)
Pauline Gorska, Commissioner (1963–1975)
Helen Orawiec, Commissioner (1963–1971); Director (1975–1983)
Zygmunt Sokolnicki, Commissioner (1963–1967)
Sofie Buczkowska, Commissioner (1963–1975)
Wladyslawa Wawrzyniak, Commissioner (1963–1967)
Sam Brown, Commissioner (1963–1967)
Stanislawa Nieder, Commissioner (1963–1971); Director (1971–1979)
Anthony Sliwa, Commissioner (1967–1971)
Jadwiga Sochaczek, Commissioner (1967–1971)
Edward Rozanski, Director (1967–1971)
Hilary Czaplicki, Director (1967–1975); Censor (From 1975)
Helen Szymanowicz, Director (1967–1971); Vice President (from 1971)
Thaddeus Radosz, Director (1967–1983)
Florence Wiatrowska, Director (1967–1983)
Eugene Zegar, Commissioner (1967–1975)
August Gorski, Commissioner (1967–1983)
Frank Lysakowski, Commissioner (1967–1975)
John Kozaren, Commissioner (1967–1971)
Adele Nahormek, Commissioner (1967–1971, 1975–1979), Director (From 1979)
Helena Piotrowka, Commissioner (1967–1983), Director (From 1983)
Joanna Kowalska, Commissioner (1967–1983)
Jean Kozmor, Commissioner (1967–1975); Director (1975–1983)
Anna Jasionowska, Commissioner (1967–1971)
Casimir Lotarski, Censor (1971–1975)
Chester Mikolajczyk, Commissioner (1967–1971); Director (1971–1975)
John Radzyminski, Director (1971–1982)
Alfred Ulman, Vice Censor (1971–1975)
Henry Burke, Director (1971–1983), Commissioner (From 1983)
Anthony Akus, Commissioner (1971–1979)
Joseph Krawulski, Commissioner (1971–1983)
Thomas Paczynski, Commissioner (1967–1975)
Peter Kaczmarek, Commissioner (1971–1975)
Frank Zielony, Commissioner (1971–1975, From 1979)
Julia Beben, Commissioner (1971–1975)
Angela Turochy, Commissioner (1971–1979)
Mary Grabowska, Commissioner (1971–1983)
Mary Drewno, Commissioner (1971–1975)
Wladyslawa Wilk, Commissioner (1971–1975)

Table 10.   (Continued)

Leopold Ciaston, Vice Censor (1975–1983)
Joseph Gajda, Vice President (1974–1983)
Lottie Kubiak, Commissioner (1967–1971); Secretary (1975–1983)
Emil Kolasa, Director (1975–1983); Secretary (From 1983)
Stanley Jendrzejec, Commissioner (1975–1983)
Victoria Mocarsky, Commissioner (1975–1983)
Stanley Lesniewski, Commissioner (1975–1983); Director (From 1983)
Clara Puchalska, Commissioner (1975–1979)
Thaddeus Swigonski, Commissioner (1975–1983)
Walter Miszczak, Commissioner (1975–1983)
Stella Lemanek, Commissioner (1975–1979)
Roman Kolpacki, Commissioner (1975–1983)
Genevieve Wesolowska, Commissioner (1979–1983), Director (From 1983)
Casimir Musielak, Commissioner (1975–1979); Director (From 1983)
Victoria Kolman, Commissioner (1975–1979)
Karol Matras, Commissioner (1967–1979)
Virginia Posanski, Commissioner (1975–1979)
Phyllis Ausenbaugh, Commissioner (1975–1983)
Stefanie Gafkowska, Commissioner (1975–1983)
Mitchell Jeglijewski, Director (From 1979)
Dolores Fedorka, Commissioner (1979–1983)
Mary Kozerska, Commissioner (1979–1983)
Vincentia Majka, Commissioner (From 1979)
Stanley Fidler, Commissioner (1979–1983)
Lottie Zisk, Commissioner (1979–1983)
Antonia Morawska, Commissioner (From 1979)
Felix Hujarski, Commissioner (1979–1982); Director (From 1982)
Edward Gornikiewicz, Commissioner (From 1979)
Joseph Sikora, Commissioner (1979–1983)
Stanley Gruszka, Commissioner (From 1979)
Casimira Pytel, Commissioner (From 1979)
Sofie Litwa, Commissioner (From 1979)
Robert Borowicz, Commissioner (From 1979)
June Grudichak, Commissioner (1979–1981)
Anthony Piwowarczyk, Vice President (From 1983)
Edward Sitnik, Vice Censor (From 1983)
Paul Odrobina, Director (From 1983)
John Ramza, Director (From 1983)
Stanley Stawiarski, Director (From 1983)
Pauline Rykowski, Commissioner (From 1981)

Table 10.   (Continued)

Regina Kobzi, Commissioner (From 1983)
Frances Syrk, Commissioner (From 1983)
Jean Binkowski, Commissioner (From 1983)
Casimir Jasinski, Commissioner (From 1983)
Alfred Pomianowski, Commissioner (From 1983)
Helen Kujawska, Commissioner (From 1983)
William Wolf, Commissioner (From 1983)
Jean Jasinski, Commissioner (From 1983)
Sophie Michaels, Commissioner (From 1983)
Leo Jankowiak, Commissioner (From 1983)
Helen Okrasinska, Commissioner (From 1983)
Michael Pierzga, Commissioner (From 1983)
Ernest Zarnowski, Commissioner (From 1983)
Helen Krause, Commissioner (From 1983)
Cecylia Posluszny, Commissioner (From 1983)
Joanna Chlus, Commissioner (From 1983)
Stella Rutkowska, Commissioner (From 1983)
Stanley Soja, Commissioner (From 1983)
Thomas Wyszynski, Commissioner (From 1983)
Alex Wachel, Commissioner (From 1983)
James Griffith, Commissioner (From 1983)
Stanley Sciblo, Commissioner (From 1983)

---

[a]The Editor of *Zgoda* was elected at the conventions held between 1881 to 1913. From 1915 onward, the office was appointive. *Zgoda* editors since then have been Stanislas Orpiszewski (1913–1921), John Przyprawa (1921–1928), Stanislas Zaklikiewicz (1928–1931), Karol Piatkiewicz (1931–1967) and Joseph Wiewiora (since 1967). From Orpiszewski's appointment to Piatkiewicz's retirement, the Editor of *Zgoda* was Editor-in-Chief of both Alliance newspapers. The position was abolished in 1967 and Jan Krawiec appointed Editor of *Dziennik Zwiazkowy*.

The first members of the PNA board of directors were elected in 1886 and until 1895 their official title was that of "Guardian of the Purse." Directors were elected regularly after 1899.

Two vice presidents were first elected in 1893 and 1895. Thereafter the PNA reverted back to its earlier practice of electing a single vice president until 1915. In that year a woman was chosen for the first time to serve as an honorary vice president but without voting rights. In 1921, the office of second vice president was established once more and reserved for a female PNA leader, this time possessing full voting rights. In 1955, the Ladies' Vice President was made its first vice president due to a constitutional change approved by the delegates to the thirty-second convention in Minneapolis.

A vice censor was first elected in 1882. In 1899, the PNA approved the creation of four vice censors for the first time, with each of these officers representing a distinct section of the country

Table 10.   (Continued)

---

and made responsible for specific supervisory tasks, namely immigration, colonization, education and employment. In 1907 the Alliance reverted to electing a single vice censor and established a new set of officers charged with coordinating fraternal activities in various regions around the country. These officers were named district commissioners and in 1909 they were organized into a quasi-judicial body chaired by the censor named the supervisory council.

Valerie Lipczynska was named to be the PNA's first female vice censor in 1905 when she was elected one of eleven vice censors at its sixteenth convention in Buffalo. Lipczynska remains the only woman to have ever been a vice censor in the history of the Alliance.

Beginning in 1935 two female commissioners were elected to the supervisory council as "at-large" representatives guaranteeing women a place in that body. From 1939 onward, each of the sixteen supervisory districts were required to elect two commissioners, one male and one female. Until 1951, however, women commissioners were elected only by delegates from the women's lodges and received only a small salary in comparison with their male counterparts. Full parity was gained only at the 1951 convention.

The office of Medical Examiner was elective between 1901 until 1963. Since then the position has been appointive and held by Dr. Lawrence Sadlek.

Other major appointive positions have been those of PNA General Counsel, Chief organizer, Chief Underwriter, and Controller.

The first counsel was Frank Borchardt of Milwaukee, who took part in the founding convention as a delegate from the Kosciuszko guard. Thereafter, a number of attorneys served on an occasional basis in this capacity, including Julius Smietana of Chicago. The 1918 convention, however, decreed that henceforth a full-time counsel be appointed by the board of directors on a fixed salary. Leon Mallek became the first PNA general counsel, followed by Louis Pinderski, Leopold Koscinski, Casimir Midowicz, Valery Fronczak and Czeslaw Rawski.

At the eleventh PNA *sejm* in 1895, former Censor Frank Gryglaszewski was unanimously elected to a newly created appointive post, that of Chief Organizer. Among Gryglaszewski's successors have been Stanislas Litko, Joseph Mierzynski, Jacob Fafara, Thomas Paczynski, Joseph Majerczyk, Joseph Foszcz, and Frank Spula. Spula's title is presently that of Director of Insurance Sales.

To safeguard the PNA insurance programs, an underwriters' department was established in 1937. The first head of this department was Walter Andrzejewski; he was succeeded upon his retirement by Thaddeus Jasiorkowski.

The office of Controller was elective from 1895 to 1905. In 1935 the controller was made responsible to the censor and remained so until 1975 when the thirty-seventh convention of the PNA made this officer responsible to the board of directors. Joseph Bronars was controller from 1935 until 1970. His successor was Walter Prosniewski, who was followed upon his retirement by Alexander Przypkowski.

Note: In the list of elected PNA officers (+) denotes that an individual was a founder of the PNA; (++) denotes that an individual was one of the members of the *Gmina Polska* patriotic club in Chicago.

Table 11. Chairmen of National Conventions of the PNA 1880–1983

Convention	Chairman	Other National Offices
1880, 1881, 1882	Mr. Julius Andrzejkowicz, Philadelphia	Founder, PNA, Censor (1880–1883)
1883; Extraordinary Convention of 1884; 1885, 1886, 1887, 1889	Mr. Frank Gryglaszewski, Chicago	Vice Censor (1882–1883), Censor (1883–1891), Commissioner (1909–1913)
1891	Mr. Val Przybyszewski, Bay City, Michigan	Vice Censor (1885–1886), Censor (1891–1893), President (1886–1887)
1893	Mr. Stanislas Lewandowski, Cleveland	Vice Censor (1893–1895)
1897	Mr. Julius Lipinski, Buffalo	Founder, PNA
1899	Mr. Julian Szajnert, Minneapolis	Founder, PNA, Commissioner (1911–1929)
Extraordinary Convention of 1900; 1901	Mr. Stanislas Sleszynski, New York	--
1903, 1909	Mr. Albert Nowak, Buffalo	Commissioner (1909–1911)
1905, 1907	Mr. John Sliwinski, Pittsburgh	Vice Censor (1907–1909)
1911	Atty. Karol Wagner, Milwaukee	--
1913	Atty. Casimir Sypniewski, Pittsburgh	Censor (1924–1931)

1915, 1918	Mr. Frank Piekarski, Chicago	--
1921, 1924	Atty. Roman Abczynski, Pittsburgh	Vice Censor (1909–1911), Commissioner (1913–1915)
1928, 1935	Mr. Casimir Kowalski, Milwaukee	Secretary (1928–1931)
1931	Mr. Eugene Jaworek, New Bedford, Massachusetts	Director (1935–1939)
1939	Atty. Arthur Koscinski, Detroit	--
1943	Judge Blair Gunther, Pittsburgh	Censor (1947–1959)
1947, 1951, 1959, 1963	Judge Thaddeus Adesko, Chicago	--
1955	Mr. Edmund Lewandowski, Cleveland	--
1967, 1971	Judge Edward Plusdrak, Chicago	--
1975, 1979	Mr. Adam Tomaszkiewicz, Chicago	Treasurer (1955–1959)
1983	Judge Frank Sulewski, Chicago	--

From 1880 through 1886 the Censor served as permanent chairman of the PNA convention. From 1887 onward, the Censor was responsible for opening the convention and served as temporary chairman until the delegates elected a permanent chairman to preside over their activities.

From 1880 until 1905, the chairman of the convention was officially known as the President or *Prezes sejmu*. Thereafter the title was changed to *Przewodniczący*. The office of Chairman has always been viewed as conveying great honor and responsibility, since the individual elected is expected to insure that convention proceedings are handled according to proper parliamentary procedures.

Other officers elected to serve at the conventions have been those persons serving as deputy chairmen, secretaries of the convention and sargeant-at-arms.

APPENDIX C

Leaders of the Polish National Alliance:
A Selective Biographical Listing

Julius Andrzejkowicz (1821–1898)

Founder and first Censor of the Polish National Alliance. Born in Lithuania, Andrzejkowicz participated in a patriotic group of young people who planned an insurrection against Russian rule in 1848. When the group was discovered, Andrzejkowicz fled the country and emigrated to France. In 1854 he was in America and probably spent some time in California after the Gold Rush. Brought to Philadelphia by distant relatives, he worked as a chemist in a paint-making company in which he later purchased a partnership. This firm, "Andrejkovicz and Dunk," expanded considerably and established offices in various cities throughout the country. Andrzejkowicz himself wrote a book on Chemical dye processes which went into several editions and he introduced the use of analine colors in the U.S.

In 1880, Andrzejkowicz (who though well informed about Polish developments was not active in Philadelphia Polonia life) was approached by Julian Lipinski for a contribution on behalf of famine stricken Silesia. Andrzejkowicz not only agreed to help but proposed to call a meeting to bring together others in the settlement to learn about the appeal. At that meeting, held in Andrzejkowicz's office on February 15, 1880, he proposed the formation of a permanent nationwide patriotic federation of Polish societies along the lines Agaton Giller had suggested in his 1879 published letter. This organization, named the Polish National Alliance by Andrzejkowicz, was approved and he was elected its temporary President. Later in September, 1880 he was elected Censor at the founding national convention of the PNA in Chicago with responsibility of providing moral leadership and general supervision over the work of the administrative officers of the Alliance.

Because of ill health, Andrzejkowicz declined to serve as Censor in 1883 and at that time was voted an honorary member for life in the movement he had founded. He was again honored in special fashion at the PNA convention of 1897, which was held in Philadelphia.

Stefan Barszczewski (1870–1937)

Editor of Zgoda. Born in Poland, Barszczewski came to America in 1887 where he gained employment in newspaper work. Already an editor of *Dziennik Chicagoski* at the age of nineteen, he became Editor-in-Chief of *Sokol,* the organ of the Falcons' Alliance in 1890. In 1897 he was elected

Editor of *Zgoda* and held both positions until 1901, when he returned to Poland. There, he worked on several newspapers, including the *Kuryer Warszawski*. Barszczewski wrote several plays and a number of short stories and authored the first history of the Polish National Alliance in 1894.

Peter Beczkiewicz (1857–1934)

Founder of the Polish National Alliance. Born in Poland, Beczkiewicz took part in the first meeting to establish the Alliance in Philadelphia on February 15, 1880. In 1901 he was elected a vice censor of the PNA at its national convention in Toledo. Beczkiewicz died in South Bend, Indiana.

Constantine Bialynski (1848–1918)

Founder of the Polish National Alliance. Born in Poland, Bialynski was the second member to join the Alliance and took part in its initial meeting in 1880. A modest and reserved individual who never sought national office, he was involved for many years in Group 1 of the PNA in Philadelphia.

John Blachowski, Anthony Wojczynski and Teofil Kucielski

Founders of the Polish National Alliance. Next to nothing is known of these men aside from their initial support for the PNA at its first meeting and their later participation in Group 1 in Philadelphia.

Michael Blenski (1862–1932)

Censor of the Polish National Alliance. Born in the Pomorze district of German-ruled Poland, Blenski was a Kaszub who "became Polish" only in America and never ceased practicing his command of the language in his long career as a public official. Coming to Milwaukee in 1880 from Poland, Blenski worked first as a pattern maker and later gained employment as a bookkeeper. Active in local politics, he was elected to the Wisconsin legislature in 1892 and in 1893 appointed by President Grover Cleveland to be the first executive secretary of the U.S. Weather Bureau in Washington, D.C. Earning a law degree at Georgetown University, he returned to

Milwaukee where he won election as a civil court judge in 1909. He held this post until his death. In 1916 Blenski was a member of the "Kosciuszko Guard," a Polish-American unit of the Wisconsin National Guard and he took part in General John Pershing's campaign to capture "Pancho" Villa in Mexico. Blenski joined the Polish National Alliance in 1902 and won election as a vice censor of the PNA in 1903. From 1915 to 1924 he served three terms in the office of censor.

Zbigniew Brodowski (1852–1901)

President of the Polish National Alliance and *Zgoda* Editor. The son of a judge in Poznan, Brodowski studied at the Universities of Breslau (Wroclaw) and Lipsk and came to America in 1876 after completing his education. Originally employed as an editor of the New York *Kuryer,* he won some notoriety by writing an article condemning a shabby history of Poland which had earlier appeared in *Gazeta Polska.* Travelling to California where he worked in the construction of the San Francisco cable car line, Brodowski knew a number of Polish personalities of the day including the actress Helena Modrzejewska (Modjeska), General Krzyzanowski (a civil war veteran, Polish patriot and himself a member of the Polish National Alliance), and the novelist Henryk Sienkiewicz. His writing won much praise and Brodowski's stories appeared in Polish and American newspapers.

In 1884, he travelled to Chicago where he first edited the *Gazeta Chicagoska.* From 1885 to 1889 he was editor of *Zgoda.* At this time he wrote a memorandum calling for Poland's independence which was sent to Berlin and Vienna. As a commissioner of the Chicago Parks in 1890, Brodowski found employment for hundreds of Polish immigrants. In 1895 he was elected president of the Alliance but served less than two years. In August, 1897 he resigned to accept the post of U.S. Consul in Breslau. However, because of his previous work on behalf of Polish reunification and independence, the German government refused to accept his appointment. Eventually, Brodowski was reassigned to American consulates in southern and western Germany. He died during an outbreak of influenza.

Hilary Czaplicki (Born 1928)

Censor of the Polish National Alliance. A native of Philadelphia, Czaplicki is a graduate of Alliance College and has since been active in the PNA and the Polish American Congress for a number of years. He was a national director of the PNA from 1967 to 1975 and has held the office of censor since then. Holder of a masters degree in Journalism from Columbia University, Czaplicki's professional career included work for the U.S. Army and Navy in public relations.

Mary Czyz (Born 1901)

Vice President of the Polish National Alliance. Born in the Sanok district of Poland, Czyz was brought to America as a child by her parents who settled in Chicago. She took courses in real estate at the La Salle Extension University and joined the PNA in 1927. Czyz was active in lodge and council affairs and twice was a delegate to the PNA Benevolent Society of the Women's Department. She was elected to a single term as Ladies' Vice President over Frances Dymek in 1939 but lost to Dymek in her try for reelection in 1943. Czyz devoted an extraordinary amount of energy to promoting the purchase of U.S. bonds among PNA members during the Second World War.

Alexander Debski (1857–1935)

Leader of the Polish socialists in America and Vice Censor of the Polish National Alliance. Born in the Russian zone of partitioned Poland, Debski, an engineer by training, took part in 1892 in the founding of the Polish Socialist Party (PPS), a democratic patriotic movement committed to the betterment of the conditions of the Polish working class and to national independence. Travelling to America in 1899, Debski tried unsuccessfully to unite the Poles in America belonging to the PPS and those who had joined the American socialist party (which made the problems facing the U.S. worker its top priority).

Debski recognized the importance of the Polish National Alliance as the most important Polonia patriotic movement and sought to turn it away from the National Democratic party of Roman Dmowski and in favor of Pilsudski's PPS. He was partially successful here. In 1903, he was elected a vice censor of the Alliance and a large number of PNA members came to identify with his views, particularly after the 1905 Polish uprising against the Tsar when the independence struggle was led by Pilsudski and his followers. Several PNA leaders identified with Pilsudski in the years that followed, including Thomas Siemiradzki, editor of *Zgoda;* however, the PNA National Democratic faction headed by Presidents Steczynski and Zychlinski eventually prevailed.

In 1912 Debski and his colleagues won a last victory when they were able to organize an all-Polonia Polish National Defense Committee *(Komitet Obrony Narodowej)* which included the socialists, the clergy and the conservative fraternals, along with the Alliance. This unity did not last long, however and by 1914 *KON* included only the socialists and the Polish National Catholic Church. Debski left for Poland in 1919 and actively backed Pilsudski's leadership. In 1930 he was elected to the Polish Senate.

Vincent Domanski (1849–1935)

Founder of the Polish National Alliance. Born in Poland, Domanski settled in America where in 1875 he established what is believed to be the first Polish-owned bank in the United States. One of those who in February 1880 organized the PNA, Domanski was a delegate to the first convention of the Alliance which was held at the Palmer House in Chicago in September, 1880.

Walter Dworakowski (Born 1917)

Born in Akron, Ohio, Dworakowski returned to Poland with his parents in 1920. Educated in the universities of Warsaw and Wilno, he earned a law degree before the outbreak of World War II. A participant in the Warsaw uprising of 1944, Dworakowski was captured and imprisoned by a Soviet military unit but was able to leave Poland because of his American citizenship. Gaining an American law degree, Dworakowski served as Assistant Attorney General of Ohio between 1959 and 1963.

Active in the PNA and the Polish American Congress, he was elected a PNA commissioner in 1955, vice censor in 1959 and became censor in 1965 upon the death of Edward Kozmor. Dworakowski was elected to that office in his own right in 1967. The greatest expansion of Alliance College took place during Dworakowski's tenure.

Frances Dymek (1895–1979)

Vice President of the Polish National Alliance. Born in Chicago, Dymek held the office of Ladies' Vice President of the PNA for twenty-eight years (1935–1939, 1943–1967). An energetic organizer and shrewd politician, she was greatly responsible for enlarging the representation of women on both its executive board and supervisory council. In 1955, Dymek was elected First Vice President of the Alliance with the right to succeed the president on a provisional basis in case of his death or incapacitation. Thanks to this change in the fraternal's by-laws, women PNA leaders gained the second highest executive office in the organization. Dymek was also active in leading the charitable work of the women's divisions and was involved in humanitarian efforts organized by the USO and the Red Cross during the Second World War.

Wladyslaw Dyniewicz (1843–1928)

Newspaper publisher and early Polonia nationalist leader. Born in Poland, Dyniewicz came to Chicago after the defeat of the 1863 insurrection and was one of the organizers of the *Gmina Polska* patriotic club. He later established the first successful Polish paper in America, *Gazeta Polska* of Chicago, and in its pages promoted the idea of a national alliance of patriotic groups to work for independence. In 1875 he issued a call for such a federation, but this brought no tangible results. In 1880 he became one of the greatest backers of the embryonic PNA and participated in the founding convention of the Alliance. The Dyniewicz publishing company along with the Smulski printing operation were the two most active disseminators in Chicago of materials on Poland's literature, language and history during the early decades of Polonia life.

Frank Dziob (1890–1983)

PNA activist and Polonia leader. Born in Poland, Dziob was brought to America as a child. Active in the Falcons' Alliance, he volunteered for service in the Polish army organized in the U.S. during World War I and rose to the rank of captain. During the war Dziob was an aide to both Ignacy Paderewski and General Jozef Haller. He also directed the early training of commissioned and non-commissioned officers at the Polish National Alliance school in Cambridge Springs in 1917. After the war Dziob was active in Polish veterans' groups and became national commander of the Polish Army Veterans' Association. Dziob was the personal secretary of President Charles Rozmarek from 1939 to 1967, wrote many of his speeches and served as his advisor.

Joseph Gajda (Born 1916)

Vice President of the Polish National Alliance. A Chicago native whose father was active in the PNA, Gajda was enrolled as a child in the Alliance and became a participant in his lodge's activities almost immediately after he was sworn into adult membership in 1931. Following his graduation from high school in 1934 he was employed in the PNA home office until 1941, when he entered the Navy. He was active in the effort to unionize the workers in the home office, a matter of great controversy within the Alliance which led to a legal battle that was taken all the way to the United States Supreme Court. After the War, Gajda worked for an electrical contracting firm until 1969. In that year he was appointed manager of Alliance Printers and Publishers. In 1974 he was elected PNA Vice President to complete the term of the late Frank Prochot. He was twice reelected to this office. Gajda declined to seek a third term in 1983 for health reasons although he was unopposed for the office.

As Vice President, Gajda carried on the work of Prochot in strengthening youth and sports activities and in enhancing the attractiveness and editorial quality of *Promien,* the PNA youth leaders' magazine. Both Gajda and his wife, Genevieve (who coordinated the PNA Summer instructors' courses and the quadrennial youth jamborees held at Alliance College) were themselves onetime leaders in the PNA scouting movement, *Harcerstwo,* during the 1930s.

Felix Garbarek (1881–1953)

President of the Polish National Alliance. Born in German-occupied Poland, Garbarek came to Chicago as a child and received an excellent education. By profession he was a successful attorney and an accountant. Founder and first president of Council 120 and later a president of the Chicago Society of the PNA, he was elected vice president of the Alliance in 1921 and filled the office of president upon the death of Casimir Zychlinski in August 1927, on the eve of the PNA convention. When the convention collapsed after the "old guard" faction walked out to hold its own assembly, the "opposition" faction went to court to gain control over the administration of the Alliance.

Garbarek served as acting president of the PNA during the twelve month period in which the rightful leadership of the Alliance was uncertain. He did not seek the presidency in 1928 when the meeting was reconvened but was reelected vice president. During the 1928 convention Garbarek was quoted in a Chicago newspaper for some incendiary comments made about the opposing faction. Though he denied making the statements attributed to him, the article provoked a storm of controversy. Garbarek was barely reelected to the vice presidency and did not again seek national office in the Alliance.

Agaton Giller (1831–1887)

The "Godfather" of the Polish National Alliance. Giller, from his youth a political activist, spent seven years in Siberian exile for his efforts. A participant in the 1863 insurrection, he became a leader in the Polish "National Government" (or revolutionary council) and was eventually forced into exile in the West following its defeat. In 1879 he responded to letters from Henry Kalussowski and Teofila Samolinska and authored a long essay on the subject of the way in which the immigrant population should unite on behalf of Polish independence. This piece, titled "On Organizing the Poles in America," was first published in Poland and later reprinted in various Polonia newspapers.

Giller's views, the considered judgment of one of the most widely respected veterans of the patriotic forces in exile, were the inspiration for the formation of the Polish National Alliance less than a year later. On February 15, 1880 in Philadelphia, a small group of men agreed to establish a nationwide federation of patriotic societies in line with his ideas. When they wrote to Giller of their action, he responded enthusiastically and congratulated them on their achievement. His letter, read later at the second national convention of the Alliance in 1881, has been lost.

Frank Gryglaszewski (1852–1918)

Censor of the Polish National Alliance. Born in Lwow, Gryglaszewski came to America as a youth and settled originally in Chicago where he joined the *Gmina Polska* patriotic society. One of the earliest PNA members and a delegate to its second convention in 1881, Gryglaszewski stoutly supported the creation of the Alliance's very own newspaper and contributed a considerable sum of money to make it a reality. It was also Gryglaszewski's suggestion to name the newspaper *Zgoda* to symbolize the PNA commitment to unity and harmony within Polonia. In 1882 Gryglaszewski was elected to the newly created office of Vice Censor and the following year he became Censor, a position he held until 1891. For several years Gryglaszewski held a Federal government office, that of Inspector of Public Buildings. In this capacity he was able to travel throughout the country and to promote the PNA to Polish settlers wherever he found them. Thus, as a kind of "Johnny Appleseed," Gryglaszewski enrolled hundreds of new members into the fraternal and helped organize dozens of lodges, particularly in the Midwest.

As chairman of the PNA Colonization commission after 1894, he helped several hundred immigrants set up their own farms on lands available through the Federal Homestead Act. In 1895 he was named by the Alliance to be its first Chief Organizer. A dedicated PNA member throughout his life, Gryglaszewski was elected Commissioner for the state of Minnesota in 1909 and 1911. A brilliant organizer and agitator, he worked effectively to make possible the early growth of the PNA at a time when its ranks were thin, assets practically nil and the fraternal subjected to incessant assault from its opponents. Gryglaszewski also founded the Grygla-Selden cast iron works in Minneapolis. He died in Santa Fe, New Mexico.

Blair F. Gunther (1903–1966)

Censor of the Polish National Alliance. A native of western Pennsylvania, Gunther was a graduate of Saint John Kanty College in 1922 and Duquesne University, where he earned a law degree in 1928. Active for many years in local and state politics, he became a county judge in 1942 and later served on the Pennsylvania Superior Court. A president of PNA Council 38 in Pittsburgh, Gunther was elected censor in 1947 and served three terms in the office. An excellent public speaker, Gunther's great contribution to American Polonia was his work in helping in the resettlement of Polish war victims in the United States. He was connected with the publication of the Polish newspaper, *Pittsburgczanin.*

Gunther and PNA Treasurer Adam Tomaszkiewicz were unsuccessful in 1959 in wresting the leadership of the Alliance from President Charles Rozmarek and Gunther subsequently limited his activities to his judicial responsibilities. In 1957, there was considerable speculation that Gunther would be nominated to the United States Supreme Court and thus become the first Polish American to belong to that august body. However, President Eisenhower chose William J. Brennan instead.

Theodore Helinski (1856–1921)

Censor and Secretary of the Polish National Alliance. Born near Poznan, Helinski came to America as a boy and was educated mainly in this country. A resident of Poniatowski, Wisconsin at the time the PNA was formed in 1880, he organized a lodge in town and himself became the 245th member of the Alliance. Helinski later served as head postmaster in Duluth, Minnesota and in 1906 became treasurer of the Northwestern Trust and Savings Bank of Chicago, founded by John Smulski. He held this post until his death.

Elected by unanimous vote to the office of censor in 1893, Helinski was a strong advocate of progressive policies and championed the admission of women as full voting members in the Alliance, an aim that was realized in 1900. He also argued for a PNA open to all Poles regardless of their politics or religious inclinations. In 1894, Helinski took the lead in opposing immediate PNA participation in the newly-created Polish League, a nation-wide federation of Polonia societies dominated by the Reverend Vincent Barzynski which he believed would lead to the demise of the Alliance as a patriotic movement.

Helinski later headed the fund drive to build the monument in honor of Tadeusz Kosciuszko in Washington, D.C., an effort that was realized in 1910. During World War I he served first as President of the Polish Central Relief Committee and later was First Vice President of the Polish National Department. Helinski also chaired the Military Commission of the National Department which was responsible for organizing the Polish Army in America. He is buried in St. Adalbert Cemetery in Chicago.

Frank Jablonski (1863–1908)

President of the Polish National Alliance and Editor of the PNA newspapers. Born in Inowroclaw, near Poznan in German-ruled Poland, Jablonski received an extensive education including theological studies at the University of Louvain in Belgium. Coming to Chicago around 1885 he worked as a teacher and took a leading part in the struggle to win

Church approval for the opening of Holy Trinity parish. (During the previous decade members of Holy Trinity had fought a losing battle against the Resurrectionist fathers of St. Stanislas Kostka parish and the Archbishop of Chicago for control over their church.) Jablonski was sent to Rome to urge the opening of the church in the heavily Polish near-northside community of Chicago and in 1893 the Vatican concurred. The Reverend Casimir Sztuczko of the Holy Cross order took over as pastor and served in that capacity as a strong ally of the PNA until his death in 1949. Thanks to this success, Jablonski became famous and at the 1893 PNA convention he was unanimously elected editor of *Zgoda,* a post he held until 1897 when he was chosen President of the Alliance.

As editor, Jablonski's work centered on defending the PNA from attacks from the conservative Polish clerical faction. In early 1901, Jablonski resigned the presidency of the Alliance to accept the editorship of the Milwaukee *Kuryer Polski.* In 1907 the delegates at the Baltimore convention voted to create a Polish daily *Zgoda* and elected Jablonski to edit the new paper, along with its weekly organ. He died only one month after assuming his new post. Buried in Chicago's St. Adalbert Cemetery, the inscription on Jablonski's tombstone reads, "Here rest the remains of the dearly departed Jablonski, able defender of Holy Trinity Parish and Guardian of the Polish National Alliance."

Erasmus Jerzmanowski (1844–1909)

Polonia activist, patriot, philanthropist and supporter of the Polish National Alliance. Born of an aristocratic family near Kalisz in the Russian zone of Poland, Jerzmanowski took part in the 1863 insurrection and later fled into exile in France. Taking up studies at the University of Paris, he graduated from its Polytechnical Institute in the field of chemistry and became engaged in work connected with natural gas, a new fuel with great potential once it could be safely burned. Jerzmanowski later was awarded the Legion of Honor for his service in the Franco-Prussian war.

In America in 1875, Jerzmanowski invented the modern gas lamp and patented scores of his creations while organizing the Equitable Gas Company of New York. This firm won the rights to produce and sell gas street lamps for the city and almost overnight made Jerzmanowski Polonia's first millionaire. He then turned his attention to philanthropic and patriotic matters. Joining the PNA, he organized the Central Welfare Committee of the Alliance in New York in 1886 to help immigrants upon their arrival in the new land. Jerzmanowski also established an immigration bureau, a reading room and a library which all remained in operation under PNA sponsorship for many years.

Jerzmanowski helped organize a number of PNA lodges in the East, and vied with Frank Gryglaszewski for leadership of the fraternal. But his campaign failed and he never held elective office in the Alliance. In 1894 he was chosen to be the American commissioner responsible for raising funds for the Polish National Treasury headquartered in Rappersville, Switzerland after having been involved in an unsuccessful effort to form a new Polonia-wide movement—the Polish League. The league failed because of PNA opposition and Jerzmanowski retired in 1896 to live his remaining years in Poland. After his death near Krakow, his entire estate was given to the Jagiellonian University, helping to make possible the creation of what today is known as the Polish Academy of Sciences.

Henry Kalussowski (1806–1894)

Early Polonia activist, patriot and spiritual father of the Polish National Alliance. Born in Poland, Kalussowski participated in the 1830 revolution and left the country after its defeat. In 1842 he was a founder of one of the first Polish patriotic groups in the U.S., the Society of Poles in America. Active in the 1848 Polish revolt, he returned to the United States where he organized another *emigre* organization, the Democratic Society of Polish Refugees in America. During the 1863 revolution, Kalussowski was the insurrectionists' representative in America. From 1850, he worked in the Treasury Department in Washington, D.C. and was engaged in representing the Polish independence cause in the capital.

In 1878 Kalussowski wrote to Polish exile leader Agaton Giller for advice in support of the efforts of American Poles interested in organizing a patriotic movement among the immigrants. Giller's response led to the formation of the Polish National Alliance in 1880.

In 1891 Kalussowski donated his extensive personal library and collection of papers and memorabilia to the PNA in return for its pledge to sponsor a library and reading room open to Polonia. This offer proved to be the basis for a variety of PNA educational and cultural programs central to the movement ever since. Kalussowski was later named an honorary member of the Alliance in recognition of his life of service to Poland and Polonia.

During his years in Washington, Kalussowski frequently lectured at nearby colleges on the Polish question and in 1867 he translated the Russian documents for the U.S. purchase of Alaska. Kalussowski was a personal friend of the Hungarian freedom fighter, Louis Kossuth.

Anthony Karabasz (1867-1934)

Censor of the Polish National Alliance. Born in the German-dominated section of partitioned Poland, Karabasz came to America as a teenager and became a teacher and church organist in Pittsburgh. In 1889 he opened a pharmacy. Karabasz belonged to the same PNA lodge as Censor Leon Sadowski and in 1911 was himself elected a commissioner for the Pittsburgh region. As commissioner he was influential in the selection of the site of the Alliance school in Cambridge Springs, Pennsylvania. In 1913 Karabasz was elected censor.

In the Spring of 1914 he and Vice Censor Adolph Rakoczy (1869-1941) travelled to Poland to make their own first hand review of the activities of the political parties with which the PNA had become aligned in 1912 when it joined the Polish National Defense Committee *(KON)*. Their report was unfavorable to continuing the ties with the Polish coalition, which included the socialist forces headed by Jozef Pilsudski. As a result, the PNA formally withdrew from *KON* and organized its own political action committee, the Independence Department. Soon after his return from Poland, Karabasz was embarrassed by allegations that he had originally left the country as a youth because he was wanted by the police for theft. Though he strenuously denied the charges, Karabasz resigned from his office in March, 1915. Rakoczy, who filled out the remaining months of his term, did not seek election as censor in September, 1915.

Stanislas Kociemski (1827-1904)

President of the Polish National Alliance. Born in the Poznan district of German-ruled Poland, Kociemski came to America in 1854 and settled in Chicago where he became the proprietor of a picture frame making factory. The great Chicago fire of 1871 destroyed his business; until then he had been "one of the wealthiest Poles in the city." Kociemski was a founder of the *Gmina Polska* patriotic club in 1866 and one of the earliest supporters of the Polish National Alliance, winning election as treasurer between 1880-1882. Kociemski served four terms as president "during the darkest era in PNA history," and later chaired the PNA library and museum at the time of its establishment in 1894.

380

Stanislas Kolodziejczyk (1897–1960)

National Director of the Polish National Alliance Scouting Movement *(Harcerstwo)*. Born in Poland, Kolodziejczyk entered this country as a youngster and was active in the Falcons' Alliance. In his prime he was known as an excellent gymnast. Within the U.S. Army Kolodziejczyk served as an instructor in sports activities for the officers' corps and he later took part in Olympic trials for the American team. In 1929, Kolodziejczyk completed the scouting training course at the Central Institute of Physical Education in Warsaw and he applied the lessons learned from this program when he was appointed by President Romaszkiewicz to organize the PNA *Harcerstwo* in 1932.

As director he led a movement which at its height included more than fifty thousand youngsters and constituted the greatest success in building ethnic consciousness ever recorded in Polonia among the American-born Poles. In 1938 Kolodziejczyk was succeeded as *Harcerstwo* director by George Hawrylowicz. After 1940, he was chief youth activities organizer for several other Polonia fraternals, including the Polish Alma Mater and the Polish Roman Catholic Union in America.

Casimir Kowalski (1883–1944)

National Secretary of the Polish National Alliance. Born in Poland, Kowalski emigrated to Pennsylvania where he worked in the coalfields before coming to Milwaukee around 1910. Both he and his wife were active trade unionists and became leaders in organizing socialist party units in the Milwaukee Polish community. In 1918 he was elected to a seat on the Milwaukee city council as an alderman-at-large and he later served as a secretary to Mayor Daniel Hoan.

Active in the PNA from the time of the First World War, Kowalski rose to prominence within the "opposition" or "lewica" faction of the Alliance during the 1920s. He chaired the controversy-filled 25th PNA convention in September, 1927 following the walkout by the "old guard" and was then elected national secretary by the delegates who remained. When the convention was reassembled by court order in August, 1928 Kowalski was confirmed as secretary and went on to serve one three-year term. Defeated for reelection in 1931, he was then appointed manager of Alliance Printers and Publishers and held this post for four years. Kowalski was one of the leaders of the opposition faction in the Alliance along with Censor Casimir

Sypniewski and Treasurer Max Hencel. A fiery speaker committed to socialism and Pilsudski, he seemed always to be in the eye of the hurricane.

Peter Kozlowski (1888-1954)

Vice President of the Polish National Alliance. Commissioner from 1928-1939 representing Connecticut, Kozlowski was elected vice president in 1939 and held this post until his death in 1954. He was the first vice president to have general responsibilities over the youth and sports activities of the Alliance. During his first term, *Harcerstwo* was phased out of existence and replaced by the PNA youth circles. Born in Poland, Kozlowski joined the PNA in 1910 and was a factory foreman prior to his election to the vice presidency and his subsequent relocation to Chicago.

Edward Kozmor (1905-1965)

Censor of the Polish National Alliance. Born in Jersey City, Kozmor was a businessman by profession who was active for many years in the Alliance. He served as commissioner of its fifth district between 1943 and 1955. During this period he dedicated his efforts to the resettlement of displaced persons in America. Elected censor in 1959, Kozmor focused his activities on revitalizing Alliance College. He succeeded in raising funds toward the construction of necessary new buildings on the campus in Cambridge Springs, Pennsylvania. His death in 1965 prevented his witnessing the completion of the Curie Sklodowska science building and the women's dormitory. The latter building has been named in his memory. Kozmor's widow, Jean, served as a director of the Polish National Alliance between 1975 and 1983.

Jan Krawiec (Born 1919)

Editor of *Dziennik Zwiazkowy,* the "Polish Daily *Zgoda.*" Born near Przemysl in Southeastern Poland, Krawiec graduated from the army officer training unit just prior to the Nazi invasion in September, 1939 and participated in the heroic defense of the country. During the occupation, he belonged to the Polish underground and there began his newspaper career writing for the conspiratorial press. In 1943 Krawiec was arrested and spent the next two years in prison, first at Auschwitz and later at Buchenwald, from which he was liberated in 1945.

After working for Polish newspapers in Germany until 1949, Krawiec emigrated to America where he worked as a laborer in Chicago. In 1954 his college studies began in the night school classes of Loyola University, where he earned his degree in 1963 in Political Science. During this period he was also employed with the *Dziennik Chicagoski*. Between 1963 and 1967 he was a social worker with the County and also edited the newspaper published by the supporters of Aloysius Mazewski's successful presidential campaign, *Wiadomosci* (The News).

In 1967 Krawiec was appointed editor-in-chief of *Dziennik Zwiazkowy*. In 1972 he was the first representative from an ethnic paper to travel officially as a correspondent to the Soviet Union when President Nixon held a summit meeting with Communist Party leader Leonid Brezhnev.

Lottie Kubiak (Born 1919)

Secretary of the Polish National Alliance. Born in Gary, Indiana, Kubiak became the first woman to hold this national office when she was elected to the post in March 1975 to fill the vacancy resulting from the death of Adolph Pachucki. She was then twice elected to this post in her own right. Between 1963 and 1971 she was a PNA commissioner and was also active in the Indiana division of the Polish American Congress. She also held responsible positions in the United States Steel Company.

In addition to her work in the PNA, Lottie Kubiak for more than thirty years has broadcast a weekly radio program in Polish dealing with news and cultural matters which is heard in Gary and Southeast Chicago. In 1983 she declined to seek reelection to a third full term and at the thirty-ninth PNA convention was succeeded by Emil Kolasa.

Maximilian Kucera (1840–1904)

President of the Polish National Alliance. Kucera came to America after the 1863 insurrection. Employed initially as a laborer, he opened up his own business, a grocery store, after arriving in Chicago where he was one of the founders of the *Gmina Polska* patriotic society. A delegate of the *Gmina Polska* group at the first PNA convention in September 1880, Kucera was elected the first president of the tiny organization (Andrzejkowicz was chosen temporary president of the Alliance at its February 15, 1880 meeting in Philadelphia but accepted the post of censor at the September convention in Chicago).

After serving two one year terms as president, Kucera was treasurer of the PNA from 1885–1886. In 1899, Kucera (by then a resident of Milwaukee) was elected a vice censor of the Alliance and in 1903 he became an honorary member of the organization he had helped found. He was active in Milwaukeee raising money for the construction of a monument to Tadeusz Kosciuszko which was dedicated in 1905.

Valerie Lipczynska (1847–1930)

Polish National Alliance Leader. Born in Poland, Lipczynska was a nurse during the 1863 insurrection and came to America in 1869. A resident of Grand Rapids, Michigan she supported the PNA from 1883 onward and was active in the effort to win equal rights for women in the movement. After 1900 (when women were admitted as full members), Lipczynska immediately became a leader within the Alliance.

Lipczynska participated in every PNA convention from 1901 onward (she was the first woman convention delegate in PNA history) and played a major role in organizing the Women's Division of the Alliance. Elected first and only lady vice censor in the history of the Alliance at the 1905 convention, she became a commissioner in 1907 and was elected honorary commissioner for all states from 1915 through the remainder of her life. An educated person who was both intellectually gifted and a good organizer, Valerie Lipczynska earned recognition for her work in recruiting young men for the Polish Army in 1917. For her efforts on behalf of Polish independence, Lipczynska was awarded the Golden Cross of Merit in 1927 by the government of Poland. She was the first women's leader of the Polish National Alliance.

Julian Lipinski (1834–1898)

Founder of the Polish National Alliance. Born in the Russian-ruled section of partitioned Poland, Lipinski was a weaver by trade and self-educated. He fought in the 1863 insurrection and afterward spent a number of years in Paris exile. Active in the *Gmina Polska* patriotic club in Europe, he remained involved in exile politics after coming to Philadelphia and was elected treasurer at the founding meeting of the PNA in February 1880, becoming the fourth member to join the new organization. At its 1897 convention he was elected an honorary lifetime member of the PNA. Lipinski died in Buffalo, New York.

Casimir Lotarski (Born 1918)

Censor of the Polish National Alliance. Born in Buffalo, New York, Lotarski accompanied his parents when they returned to the newly reborn Poland after the First World War. After a few years, the Lotarski family returned to America and lived for many years in Youngstown, Ohio. As a young man, Lotarski became active in the PNA and was a close associate of Joseph Habuda, vice censor of the Alliance and the proprietor of a flourishing lumber and building supplies firm in Youngstown. Both in Youngstown and in Buffalo, where he later resided, Lotarski was an active and successful salesman for the PNA. He, together with a number of other men (including Joseph Foszcz, Aloysius Mazewski, Adam Tomaszkiewicz, George Wrost and John Ziemba) was one of a new generation of American-born activists who became a leader in the PNA in the years immediately following World War II.

In 1958, Lotarski was the secretary at the extraordinary convention called to meet in Chicago which failed for want of a quorum. In 1971, Lotarski, who had become active in banking in Buffalo, was elected censor of the PNA and served one four-year term in office. It was during his tenure that enrollment at Alliance College reached its peak.

Anthony Mallek (1851-1917)

Polish National Alliance Activist and Cultural Leader. Born in the Prussian zone of occupied Poland, Mallek came to America in 1871 where he taught in the parish schools of Chicago and Wisconsin and was also a church organist. From 1880 to 1916 Mallek performed these tasks at Holy Trinity parish. One of the organizers of the Polish Singers' Alliance in 1888, Mallek gained renown by organizing a number of choirs which performed at Polonia-wide patriotic observances. He published choir music in seventeen song books and between 1886 and 1903 edited the journal of the Singers' Alliance, *Ziarno*. Mallek was committed to establishing close ties between the Singers and the Polish National Alliance, which shared common patriotic aims. In 1889 he was elected national secretary of the PNA.

Aloysius Mazewski (Born 1916)

President of the Polish National Alliance. Born in North Chicago, Illinois
of parents who were themselves participants in local PNA life, Mazewski
became active in Alliance activities as a teenager, rising to a leadership
role in Council 41 during the 1930s. He energetically organized Polish
American youth activities as a high school and college student and was
President of the Polish Students' club at Lane Technical High School, the
Chicago Polish Students' Association and the Polish American Junior League
(which included seventeen Chicago high school units). Earning a law degree
from De Paul University on the eve of World War II Mazewski volunteered
for military duty and served as an intelligence officer and later as an army
hospital chief administrator. He left the army in 1946 with the rank of
major.

In 1947 he was elected to the national board of directors of the PNA
and won reelection to the board in 1951. In 1967 he was elected President
of the PNA in a spirited contest against Charles Rozmarek and he has
been reelected at each successive national convention. In 1968 Mazewski
was elected President of the Polish American Congress.

Under Mazewski's direction, the PNA thoroughly modernized its insurance
program to meet the increasingly diverse needs of its membership. In addition,
he directed the restructuring of the investment portfolio of the Alliance.
Thanks to these reforms, the Polish National Alliance has been provided
with the means to remain a large and dynamic institution into the next
century. Similarly, Mazewski's leadership of the Polish American Congress
enabled it to become the universally recognized voice of a unified American
Polonia that it is in the 1980s. It is no exaggeration to state that PAC
views on foreign and domestic matters concerning Polish Americans are
recognized as authoritative in Washington.

During Aloysius Mazewski's administration, the Polish National Alliance
has successfully transformed itself from a Polish-American organization into
a truly indigenous institution both proud of its rich ethnic heritage and
able to compete successfully in the insurance field with the largest commercial
firms.

Magdalena Milewska (1877–1957)

Vice President of the Polish National Alliance. A talented speaker and
organizer, Milewska was an outspoken advocate of women's equality in

the PNA and the American labor movement. She was elected a national director of the Alliance in 1915 and served as vice president between 1921–1924, 1928–1931 and 1932–1935. Milewska was deeply involved in World War I era humanitarian and patriotic activities and in educational work among young people. Born in Poland, she died in Chicago. Milewska was the foremost female leader in the "opposition" or "lewica" faction during the interwar years.

Edward Moskal (Born 1924)

Treasurer of the Polish National Alliance. A Chicago native whose father was active in Council 75 of the Alliance, Moskal was elected to the PNA national board of directors in 1963 and since 1967 has served as its national treasurer. A member of the special committee studying the practices of the PNA in real estate investment in 1965, Moskal contributed to the recommendations that were adopted at the 1967 convention. These brought needed reforms to this major area of Alliance finance activity.

As treasurer Moskal introduced computerization into the billing system of mortgages held by the PNA, a practice that has practically eliminated the problem of delinquencies in payments. Moskal is an active member in St. John Kanty parish, one of Chicago's oldest Polish churches.

Casimira Obarska (1875–1932)

Vice President of the Polish National Alliance. Born in 1875 near Poznan, Obarska came to America as a child. After her marriage she and her husband settled in South Chicago. An early activist for women's equality in the Alliance, Obarska was elected to its Board of Directors in 1913 and named honorary vice president of the organization in 1915, the first woman to hold so high an office. President of the Women's Division of the Alliance, Obarska won considerable praise for her work on behalf of U.S. Liberty Bond sales drives, the Polish Red Cross and in recruitment for the Polish Army during the First World War. A talented speaker and organizer, she played a major role in the Polish National Department and later organizations attempting to unify Polonia after the War. Obarska was instrumental in organizing youth activities within the Alliance. Elected Vice President of the Alliance in 1931, she died suddenly of a heart attack the following year.

Edward Odrowaz (1840–1889)

Founding editor of *Zgoda*. A product of a renowned aristocratic family, Odrowaz took part in the 1863 insurrection and lost his entire estate. For a time he lived in exile in Paris. Coming to New York in 1875, he participated in the founding convention of the Polish National Alliance in 1880 and was elected the organization's first secretary. In 1881, he was nominated by his friend Stanislas Artwinski to edit the newly-created PNA weekly, *Zgoda*. Odrowaz ran the paper in New York. When the delegates to the 1882 PNA convention voted to move the paper's headquarters to Chicago, Odrowaz refused to continue on. A contemporary journalist, Henry Nagiel, wrote of Odrowaz's work as *Zgoda* editor: "The publication was well edited in a patriotic spirit. From its first issue, *Zgoda* played an important role among New York Poles . . . *Zgoda's* language was clear, concise and its style well-turned, its editorials objective and its general tone truly didactic."

Michael Osuch (1853–1906)

President of the Polish National Alliance. Born in Poland and an early immigrant to Chicago, Osuch was one of the first supporters of the PNA. He was the eighty-third man to join the Alliance. A member of Group 4, Harmonia Society, he was elected national secretary at the second convention and in 1887 he won office as President. Osuch's wife Mary was also active in the PNA after women were admitted to full membership in 1900 but was even more involved in the PRCUA, becoming its vice president in 1908.

Karol Piatkiewicz (1895–1971)

Editor-in-Chief of *Zgoda* and *Dziennik Zwiazkowy*. Born in Poland, Piatkiewicz began his career as a newspaperman with *Nowy Wiek*, published in Lwow. Coming to the United States in 1914 he worked for the Milwaukee *Kuryer Polski* and the New York *Kuryer Narodowy* before coming to Chicago to work at the *Dziennik Zwiazkowy*. There Piatkiewicz later became city editor and worked effectively to make it the most widely read Polish daily in the city. The "Polish Daily *Zgoda*" under Piatkiewicz made certain that Chicago Polonia news was covered by a large staff of correspondents who reported on the activities of practically every Polish parish and community organization in the metropolitan area. He was also influential in reporting sports and society news in the English language which attracted the American born generation as well as their parents. In 1923 the *Dziennik Zwiazkowy* took over the failing *Dziennik Narodowy* to give the PNA paper a combined circulation of 54,000.

In 1931 Piatkiewicz was appointed editor in chief of both newspapers by Censor Francis X. Swietlik and he held this post until his retirement in 1968. He was a speechwriter for Swietlik and later composed many of the talks given by President Charles Rozmarek. Piatkiewicz was active in the Polish Newspapermen's Guild of America.

As editor in chief, Piatkiewicz gave primary attention to the "Daily *Zgoda*" and treated the weekly PNA paper (after 1947 a bi-weekly) with benign neglect. As such, *Zgoda* was published primarily in Polish and its content made up of reprints of feature stories appearing first in the Daily, along with information about lodge and council doings.

A good writer, Piatkiewicz authored the condensed history of the Polish National Alliance to coincide with the movement's sixtieth anniversary in 1940.

Romuald Piatkowski (1857–1939)

First rector of the Alliance School. An immigrant in 1892 from Russian-ruled Poland, Piatkowski taught first at the Polish Seminary in Orchard Lake, Michigan between 1892 and 1909. During this time he also became active in the Polish National Alliance. In 1907 Piatkowski was an unsuccessful candidate for the post of national secretary but in 1908 he was appointed to head the Polish Press Information Bureau of the Alliance. Piatkowski played an important role in helping to organize the PNA-sponsored Polish National Congress (in fact a world congress of Polish activists) in Washington, D.C. This event was held in May, 1910 and coincided with the unveiling and dedication of monuments honoring Kosciuszko and Pulaski.

Piatkowski's 1911 *Pamietnik wzniesienia odsloniecia pomnikow Tadeusza Kosciuszki i Kazimierza Pulaskiego tudziez polaczonego z ta uroczystoscia pierwszego Kongresu Narodowego Polskiego w Washingtonie, D.C.,* (On the Dedication of the Monuments to Kosciuszko and Pulaski and the Proceedings of the First Polish National Congress held together in Washington, D.C.) is a masterful and luxurious report on these great events in the history of American Polonia. Appointed to be the first rector of the PNA school in Cambridge Springs, Pennsylvania in 1912, Piatkowski resigned the post in 1916 over a dispute concerning the use of English instead of Polish in classroom instruction. A believer in the use of Polish, Piatkowski returned to teach at the Orchard Lake seminary.

John Popielinski

Founder of the Polish National Alliance. Born in Poland, Popielinski had been a past president of the Kosciuszko patriotic club in Philadelphia when he attended the first meeting of what became the Polish National Alliance. His letter, written late in his life to Stanislas Osada, author of the 1905 PNA history, gives one a glimpse of those earliest moments in the century old movement. "We called Poles together at 347 Third Street in Philadelphia on February 14, 1880 . . . Besides Szajnert, Andrzejkowicz, I, Lipinski around fifteen others came to the meeting . . . Andrzejkowicz called the meeting to order, stated its aims, and a majority backed the idea and elected Andrzejkowicz president, Szajnert secretary, Lipinski treasurer. At the first meeting eleven people signed the declaration and decided to send Giller a letter and to send out an announcement to other groups as well. Some groups praised us, others criticized, but they didn't stop us."

Frank Prochot (1911–1974)

Vice President of the Polish National Alliance. Born in Chicago, Prochot was an active member of the PNA throughout his life. A popular figure in the PNA and an organizer, Prochot enrolled more than 3,500 new members and was an Alliance officer at both the lodge and council levels.

Prochot was deeply involved in developing the youth and sports department of the PNA, which came under his responsibilities as vice president. An active sportsman himself, he was successful in developing the annual national bowling and golf tournaments sponsored by the PNA into highly successful mass participation events. Prochot was editor of the PNA youth leaders' magazine, *Promien.*

Val Przybyszewski (Died 1924)

Censor and President of the Polish National Alliance. The only person to ever hold the two highest offices in the history of the Alliance, Przybyszewski came to America in 1873 and settled in the heavily Polish town of Bay City, Michigan. A fiery leader who was active in both local politics and Polish patriotic affairs, Przybyszewski organized the St. Casimir Society, Group 12 of the PNA, in 1880 and himself was the 312th member of the Alliance. Elected vice censor at the La Crosse convention in 1885, the next year he was elected president at the PNA convention held in Bay City. In fact, the entire board elected at this convention was from Bay City and Przybyszewski succeeded in moving the national headquarters of the organization out of Chicago for the one and only time in history.

At the 1887 convention, however, the Chicago faction headed by members of the *Gmina Polska* group won back control and brought the administration "home" to the Windy City. In 1891, Przybyszewski defeated Frank Gryglaszewski for the office of censor but was unable to accomplish much because of persistent conflicts with the central administration and the editor of *Zgoda*. In 1893, he declined to seek reelection and Theodore Helinski was elected by unanimous vote to succeed him, thereby ending the contest between Chicago and Bay City. Przybyszewski remained active in the Alliance for many years and in 1912 Lodge 192 in Philadelphia honored Przybyszewski by naming itself after the early PNA leader.

Stanislas Rokosz (1857–1921)

President of the Polish National Alliance. Born in Poland, Rokosz came to America from England in search of work in 1885. Active in the labor movement in Chicago, he helped organize a meatcutters' union and was president of one of its locals. Later he operated a restaurant.

Rokosz joined the PNA in 1889 and was an officer in Lodge 128 throughout his life. One of the organizers of the *Dziennik Narodowy* newspaper in Chicago (which served for several years as the daily of the Alliance before the PNA began its very own paper, *Dziennik Zwiazkowy*), Rokosz was elected vice president in 1899 and became president when Frank Jablonski resigned. He was elected in his own right in 1901. During the wave of strikes that swept Chicago after the First World War, Rokosz was murdered, probably in connection with his labor activities.

John Romaszkiewicz (1873–1949)

President of the Polish National Alliance from 1928 to 1939. Born in eastern Poland, Romaszkiewicz came to America as a high school age youth and completed his education in business in Boston. He later was in banking. Active in the Polish National Alliance from the time he first joined in 1893, he was elected a vice censor at the national convention of 1907 and a commissioner of the PNA two years later. Involved in work on behalf of the Polish National Fund *(Skarb Narodowy)*, Romaszkiewicz later took part in East Coast activities of the Polish National Department during the First World War.

Romaszkiewicz was a strong supporter of the idea of preserving patriotic feeling among Polish young people and he backed the Falcons' Alliance in its cooperation with the PNA. An enthusiast of Marshal Jozef Pilsudski, he was active in the "opposition" faction of the PNA in the 1920s and was elected President of the Alliance at its controversial twenty-fifth convention in Chicago's Sherman Hotel in 1927. A year later his election was confirmed when the delegates of a reunified PNA convened a second time on court order. As president, Romaszkiewicz's great contribution was in his forming of the PNA scouting movement or *Harcerstwo*. During the 1930s *Harcerstwo* possessed a peak membership of 52,000 youngsters and the movement rejuvenated interest among American-born Poles in their ethnic heritage.

Romaszkiewicz's leadership of both the PNA and *Harcerstwo* was, however, severely restricted after 1931 and especially after 1935. Within the PNA board of directors, the "old guard" faction became dominant and was headed by Vice President Chester Hibner, a Polish born Chicagoan and tavern keeper. Romaszkiewicz is buried in Boston.

Edward Rozanski (Born 1915)

Manager of Alliance Printers and Publishers, Inc. Born in Chicago, Rozanski has been active in the PNA since 1932. Except for the war years when he was in military service, he worked for *Dziennik Zwiazkowy* as a photo reporter between 1939–1950. In 1948, Rozanski earned a doctoral degree in optometry.

A national director of the Alliance in 1971–1975, Rozanski became manager of the PNA newspapers in 1975. Bibliophile and Polonia historian, Rozanski preserved many valuable materials about Polonia and has authored numerous articles on PNA history and personalities. He is the editor of the Alliance almanac, *Kalendarz Zwiazkowy*. Dr. Rozanski belongs to the Illinois Division of the Polish American Congress. Due to the illness which incapacitated *Zgoda* Editor Joseph Wiewiora in the Spring of 1982, Rozanski and Edward Dziewulski assumed the responsibilities of acting co-editors of the PNA organ in addition to their regular duties.

Charles Rozmarek (1897-1973)

President of the Polish National Alliance. Born in Wilkes Barre, Pennsylvania, Rozmarek earned a law degree from Harvard University and served in various public offices in the field of justice in his home town. A PNA member from 1917, he became the president of the Polish students' circle in Boston in 1925. In 1931, he was appointed to the school board of Alliance College and in 1935 was an unsuccessful candidate for the presidency of the Alliance, narrowly losing to John Romaszkiewicz.

Elected president in 1939, he held office for twenty-eight years, the longest tenure in the history of the Alliance. Under Rozmarek's leadership membership surpassed 300,000 for the first time and the organization's net worth rose from approximately $30 million to $133 million. Possessing a leadership style both autocratic and charismatic in nature, Rozmarek was an eloquent speaker and a great politician both in and outside the Alliance.

Rozmarek's great accomplishment was in organizing and leading the Polish American Congress, the all-Polonia political action federation, in 1944. The PAC symbolized the realization of the hopes of generations of PNA members to unite Polonia's energies in support of a free Poland. Moreover, this movement, unlike earlier efforts such as the Polish National Department created in World War I, remained in existence as a permanent fixture in American Polonia and has maintained its commitment to the original purposes for which it was established. As head of the PAC Rozmarek's greatest success was in winning congressional approval after World War II for special legislation enabling approximately 150,000 Poles to enter the U.S. and to build new lives for themselves in this country. Rozmarek's wife, Wanda, was deeply involved in the PNA and for many years directed the annual summer courses in Polish studies for teachers at the Alliance College.

Leon Sadowski (1868-1927)

Censor of the Polish National Alliance. Born in German-ruled Poland, he was brought to America as a youth. His family settled in Detroit; there Sadowski studied at the Polish seminary. Later he completed his medical training at the University of Pittsburgh and became a practicing physician.

Sadowski joined the PNA in 1890 and was elected censor in 1899, serving in that office for six years. This was a period of enormous growth as membership tripled from 15,000 to 45,000 and the assets of the Alliance rose from $88,000 to $300,000. A strong supporter of women's equality, he called a special convention in 1900 to revise the membership rules of the PNA constitution to achieve this goal.

As U.S. Commissioner for the Polish National Fund in Switzerland, Sadowski was sent to Europe by the delegates of the 1903 convention to determine how money from America was being used by the exile movement. On his return in 1904 he stoutly defended the Alliance's continued support of the Fund in a report he published in *Zgoda*. Sadowski further urged that the Alliance maintain its traditionally close ties with the National Democratic movement in Europe in the face of growing criticism from the socialists in the PNA who called for a transfer of allegience to Pilsudski. His stance earned him strong opposition and he was defeated for reelection at the 1905 convention.

Mary Sakowska (1879–1965)

Vice President of the Polish National Alliance. Born in Nanticoke, Pennsylvania, Sakowska was one of the earliest women's leaders in the Alliance and the first woman to be elected a member of the Board of Directors in 1909. She served in that capacity until 1918. In 1924 she was elected Vice President. Sakowska was deeply involved in the organization of the PNA Saturday schools and in the organizing of Alliance libraries throughout the country. During the war she was active in recruitment for the Polish Army in America. Sakowska was a leading member of the old guard faction during the internal struggle for control of the PNA during the interwar years.

Teofila Samolinska (1848–1913)

Polonia leader, patriot and author. One of the earliest pioneers of cultural and educational work in the Polish immigrant community, Samolinska is considered by many as one of the spiritual founders of the Polish National Alliance. Samolinska's activities were centered in writing; she authored plays, poems, essays and fictional stories and was a passionate public speaker whose ideas focused upon the building of patriotic awareness among the immigrant population in Chicago. Samolinska wrote in a variety of Polish newspapers, such as *Orzel Polski* and *Przyjaciel Ludu* and was an active member of the *Gmina Polska* patriotic club in Chicago. Believing that a nationwide federation of Polish patriotic clubs was needed to advance the Polish independence cause in America. Samolinska corresponded with Agaton Giller, Ignacy Kraszewski and Court Plater, major leaders of the patriotic movement in Europe, urging them to promote this idea.

Samolinska was a strong proponent of the PNA, but was unable to convince its founders that women should be able to join with equal rights in the patriotic movement. In 1887 she founded the Central Association of Polish Women in Chicago, a movement of educated feminine activists that remained an important element in Chicago Polonia cultural life into the middle of the 20th century. Into this association came women who later organized the Polish Women's Alliance in 1898 and who led the women's divisions in the PNA and the Falcons when they agreed to admit women into their ranks.

S. F. Adalia Satalecki (1848-1910?)

President of the Polish National Alliance. Born in Lwow, he settled in Chicago and practiced law. Satalecki was a fine public speaker and was fluent in several languages. He was also a prolific essayist and ran unsuccessfully for local public office on a number of occasions.

Elected Vice President of the PNA in 1889, Satalecki served as President for two terms (1891-1895), a period that proved particularly eventful for the fraternal. During his tenure, the competing elements in Polonia cooperated to raise money to put up an exhibition hall in Lwow to commemorate the centennial of the Kosciuszko uprising. They also worked together in sponsoring the "Polish Day" celebration during the Columbian Exposition of 1893 in Chicago and collaborated in opposing a proposed American-Russian treaty considered to be adverse to the cause of an independent Poland. It was also during Satalecki's presidency that the Polish League, inspired by the Reverend Vincent Barzynski was formed, only to collapse due to PNA opposition led by Censor Theodore Helinski. (Several PNA leaders initially supported the ideas of the Polish League including Vice President Victor Bardonski and Erasmus Jerzmanowski. Satalecki's position is unclear.)

Satalecki's friendship with Henry Kalussowski is believed to have led Kalussowski to donate his personal library to the PNA. This collection of more than six thousand volumes served as the basis of the Alliance's later efforts to provide the immigrants with reading materials on Poland's history and literature and led to the creation of a PNA library and reading room in Chicago. Satalecki's connections with Polish *emigres* in Western Europe also strengthened their ties with the PNA. In 1894, a North American branch of the Polish National Treasury was set up under PNA direction to facilitate the collection and forwarding of money to assist the work of the Polish national democratic movement centered in Switzerland.

Satalecki did not seek reelection in 1895 and disappeared from the scene, except for the years between 1899 and 1901 when he was once more in Chicago and again active in PNA matters. "A mysterious and romantic figure," in the words of the PNA historian Adam Olszewski, he apparently spent a good deal of time in the American West and even in Alaska engaged in various business interests. He is believed to have died in Poland while employed by the Austrian government in the resettlement of Poles returning from America.

Anthony Schreiber (1864–1939)

Censor of the Polish National Alliance. Born in the German zone of divided Poland, Schreiber earned a doctoral degree in chemistry at the University of Berlin, later immigrating to the United States as a young man. He joined the Alliance in 1886, the 1,797th member of the still small movement. At the turn of the century Schreiber established his own brewery in Buffalo; one of his products was a beer named after Paderewski's opera "Manru." In 1905 he was elected censor of the PNA and held this post for eight years before retiring from office at the tumultuous convention of 1913.

During Schreiber's tenure, the PNA was extraordinarily active. Within the rapidly growing organization, district commissioners were elected for the first time with the responsibility of connecting the activities of the local lodges with the policies of the central administration in Chicago. Councils were created to coordinate the activities of the local lodges. A system of variable insurance based upon age was first introduced which considerably increased the attraction of the PNA throughout Polonia. And the Polish daily *Zgoda* was established.

On the national level, Schreiber took part in the fund drive to build the Kosciuszko monument in Lafayette Square across from the White House, a project that was realized in 1910. He supported the work to organize the Polish National Congress which in May 1910 brought together representatives from Polonia and Poland for the first time. And it was Schreiber who initiated the establishment of an Alliance School (later Alliance College) in Cambridge Springs, Pennsylvania in 1911. At the 26th PNA convention in Scranton (1931), Schreiber was awarded the Legion of Honor for his past services by the Polish National Alliance.

Thomas Siemiradzki (1850–1939)

Editor of *Zgoda* and intellectual. Born in the Russian zone of partitioned Poland, Siemiradzki was a graduate of the University of Saint Petersburg and was educated to be a teacher. He came to America in 1896 and was employed initially as a speaker on Poland's history for a PNA-sponsored lecture tour that took him around Polonia. In this way Siemiradzki rapidly became a respected and popular publicist on Polish affairs in America. He later taught at the Polish seminary near Detroit.

At first a partisan of the Polish National Democratic movement led by Dmowski that dominated the PNA, Siemiradzki threw in his lot with the patriotic socialists headed by Pilsudski in 1905. His central view, however, remained unchanged throughout his lengthy career as a journalist. For "Professor" Siemiradzki (a nickname earned more because of the scholarly character of his writings and speeches rather than his holding of any academic degrees or college teaching positions), what was crucial was to stimulate Polonia's awareness that it had a major role in Poland's independence struggle. He advocated the idea of Polonia as the "fourth partition of Poland," meaning that the four million Poles in the U.S. comprised a crucial resource. Polonia, he felt, was not merely a source of funds but of human talent and leadership. Siemiradzki was enthusiastic about the youth movements in Polonia, particularly the Falcons' Alliance, and he backed close ties between them and the PNA. It was the Falcons' Alliance which would provide the manpower, Siemiradzki correctly thought, to fight for independence in the future.

Elected editor of *Zgoda* in 1901, Siemiradzki became editor-in-chief of *Dziennik Zwiazkowy* only weeks after its creation due to the death of its first editor, Frank Jablonski. In 1913 he was unsuccessful in his campaign to become Censor and his support of the left leaning Polish National Defense Committee (KON) instead of the Polish National Department curtailed his influence in the PNA. In 1928, when Casimir Sypniewski was elected Censor, Siemiradzki, then an editor with the Cleveland *Wiadomosci Codzienny,* joined the board of directors of Alliance College. His book, *The Political Outline History of Partitioned Poland* was published in various additions and printed in *Zgoda*.

John Smulski (1867-1928)

Polonia leader and patriot. Born and educated in the German-dominated section of partitioned Poland, Smulski's parents brought him to America as a young man. Thanks partly to his father's success as a publisher in Chicago, John Smulski earned a law degree at Northwestern University in 1890.

Even as a young man, Smulski was recognized as a leader in the growing Chicago Polonia community. In 1893 he was elected a director of the Polish National Alliance, the one elective office he ever held in the PNA. Smulski experienced extraordinary success in local and state politics, gaining the offices of the state treasurer and Chicago city comptroller. His only failure in politics came when he was defeated in his campaign to become mayor of Chicago in 1911. In 1906 Smulski organized the Northwestern Trust and Savings Bank of Chicago, popularly known as the "Smulski Bank." This institution became the largest Polish-owned commercial lending operation in the United States.

During World War I, Smulski worked together with Ignacy Paderewski and the leaders of Polonia to organize and lead the Polish National Department (or *Wydzial Narodowy*). The National Department lobbied for American support of Poland's independence, raised millions of dollars for Polish war victims and organized the twenty-five thousand man Polish Army in America which in 1918 took part in the War in Europe. For his enormous contributions to the success of the Allied war effort and the recovery of Polish independence, Smulski received the French Legion of Honor and the Polish government's highest tribute, the order of *Polonia Restituta*.

Frank Spula (Born 1951)

Director of Sales of the Polish National Alliance. A Chicago native who earned a degree in Business Administration from De Paul University (1973) and a fellowship in Life Insurance Office Management (1979), Spula has served as PNA director of Sales since 1976. Among his predecessors in

APPENDIX C

this position, previously known as Chief Organizer were Joseph Majerczyk, Thomas Paczynski, Joseph Foszcz, Jacob Fafara and Frank Gryglaszewski.

Marian Steczynski (1866–1939)

President of the Polish National Alliance. Born in the Krakow region in Austrian-ruled Poland, Steczynski was a horticulturist by training whose early activities in Polonia were with the Falcons' Alliance. Associated with Polish *emigre* politics centered in Switzerland, Steczynski joined the Polish National Alliance in 1896 and rapidly rose to leadership in the movement. Elected President in 1903 Steczynski led the PNA until 1912, when he resigned to become the business administrator of the newly established Alliance School, a post he held until his death. Steczynski personally planted the trees that line the college today from seedlings brought from Poland.

Steczynski's presidency was a time of enormous intellectual and organizational ferment; efforts were made to unify the PNA with the Falcons', Singers' and Youth Alliances; the Polish Daily *Zgoda* was established; the fund drive to build a monument to Kosciuszko in Washington, D.C. was realized; and an Alliance School was created in Pennsylvania. Steczynski's significance was such that during his tenure, leaders of the PNA were able to meet with two American Presidents, Theodore Roosevelt and William Taft. And, he played a major role in organizing the Polish National Congress held in 1910. It was Steczynski who proposed the resolution that symbolized the PNA's patriotic commitment to Poland at the 1910 convention: "We Poles have the right to existence as an independent nation and we believe it is our sacred duty to strive for the political independence of our fatherland, Poland."

J. Stanley Swierczynski (1889–1979)

Business manager of Alliance Printers and Publishers. Born in Jersey City, Swierczynski was involved in New York area PNA activities as a manager of its Immigrants Home and as a lodge organizer. Later he became a district manager of the Poland American Steamship lines in Pittsburgh. In 1939 Swierczynski was appointed manager of Alliance Printers and Publishers and held this post until he resigned in 1964. Swierczynski served in the unofficial capacity of "campaign manager" for Charles Rozmarek's presidential campaigns between 1939 and 1963. In 1967 he worked on behalf of Aloysius Mazewski. He died in Miami, Florida.

Francis X. Swietlik (1890–1983)

Censor of the Polish National Alliance. Swietlik received a law degree from Marquette University in 1914 and soon afterward became involved in PNA affairs. During the First World War the Alliance delegated him to evaluate the conditions of Polish refugees living in Canada and later on he served in the American armed forces in Europe, rising to the rank of captain. From 1930, a member of the Law faculty of Marquette University, Swietlik became the Dean of its Law School in 1934 and held this post until he was appointed to the State Circuit Court in 1953.

During the 1920s Swietlik became a recognized leader of the PNA faction opposed to Censor Casimir Sypniewski and in 1931 he defeated Sypniewski for that office. Swietlik served in this capacity until 1947. His tenure was marked by three major efforts. First, it was Swietlik who in 1934 declared American Polonia's "independence" from Poland at the Second World Congress of Poles from Abroad in Warsaw. There he emphasized that the ethnic community's first loyalty was to the United States, though cultural ties with Poland remained important. Second, Swietlik redirected the investment policies of the PNA away from heavy reliance upon home mortgages, a risky business in the Depression, and into stocks and bonds. This move led to the enormous economic growth of the Alliance over the next forty years. Third, he ended the PNA's confrontation with the other major Polish fraternals in favor of greater cooperation in charitable and benevolent work.

A result of this policy was the creation of the Polish American Council in 1936, an organization that raised more than $20 million on behalf of Poland during and after the Second World War. A professional man born in America, Swietlik was perhaps the first PNA leader to fully comprehend that the future of the Alliance depended upon its transformation from a Polish into a Polish American mass movement and in its greater involvement in U.S. society.

Casimir Sypniewski (1877–1958)

Censor of the Polish National Alliance. Born in Poznan, Sypniewski came to America with his family and settled in Pittsburgh where he eventually became an attorney. He was active in PNA national conventions as early as 1909. During the First World War, he served as the chairman of the Polish National Department under the leadership of John Smulski and represented this patriotic Polonia federation in Paris.

An admirer of Jozef Pilsudski's leadership in Poland, Sypniewski became active within the "opposition" or "left" faction in the PNA, which was particularly influential in the East. Nearly chosen president of the Falcons' Alliance after World War I, in 1924 he was elected Censor and reelected to this post in 1928. As censor, Sypniewski appointed Dr. Stefan Mierzwa, organizer of the Kosciuszko Foundation, to head Alliance College. During Sypniewski's tenure, the Alliance was torn by chronic internal conflict between two nearly equal factions, the "old guard" and "the opposition." The fight was punctuated by legal suits and battles at nearly every level of Alliance political life.

Sypniewski's aim, ultimately, was to strengthen PNA ties with the Polish government in Warsaw, and to expand the activities of the Alliance in the areas of cultural affairs, the college, and financial investment. But his plans were rejected as too impractical in an era of economic depression. His defeat for reelection at the 1931 PNA convention marked the beginning of the end for the left faction's dominance in the Alliance; throughout the remainder of his life Sypniewski took no part in the activities of the organization.

Julian Szajnert (Died 1929)

Founder of the Polish National Alliance. Born in Poland, his early years in America were spent in Philadelphia where he was one of the organizers of the Tadeusz Kosciuszko society in 1871. At the founding meeting of the PNA on February 15, 1880 Szajnert was elected the group's secretary and together with Andrzejkowicz authored the first announcement calling upon Poles throughout America to join the Alliance. As the years rolled by Szajnert assumed the role of an "elder statesman" who in critical times offered his counsel to the movement. Between 1911–1918 and 1924–1929 he held the office of honorary Commissioner for all states and during the latter period took an active leadership role within the "old guard" faction in its struggle against the "opposition" headed by Censor Casimir Sypniewski. Szajnert died in Minneapolis.

Albin Szczerbowski (1884–1961)

National Secretary of the Polish National Alliance. Born in Krakow, Szczerbowski was brought to America as a child by his parents. Szczerbowski was active in the PNA at a young age, working in the Chicago home office and later serving in the 1920s as the manager of the Alliance papers. He served for many years as a lodge officer in Group 149 and in Councils 3 and 149. In 1931 Szczerbowski was elected Secretary General over Casimir Kowalski and served 24 years in office before being defeated in 1955. For many years Szczerbowski owned and operated a furniture store on Chicago's northwest side.

Helen Szymanowicz

Vice President of the Polish National Alliance. A native of Erie, Pennsylvania, Helen Szymanowicz was a district PNA organizer, president of Lodge 2205 and Council 72 and member of the national board of directors (1967–1971) before her election as vice president in 1971. Her responsibilities include maintaining contacts with the women's divisions of the Alliance which are organized in each of its sixteen regional districts throughout the country. She is head of the PNA Benevolent Society which since 1928 has been active in the Chicago area collecting food and clothing for needy Poles, both in the community and in Poland itself.

A special concern of Szymanowicz has been to assist members of the post-1970 Polish immigration in adapting to conditions they find in Chicago. Another responsibility is that of chairing the Educational Department of the PNA, which includes the awarding of scholarships and student loans, maintaining the Alliance library and archives, and organizing the annual May Third parade and commemorative activities directed by the PNA. Szymanowicz is credited with the idea of moving this event to the "downtown" section of Chicago in 1974, thereby enhancing its significance and attractiveness to the entire Polish American population of the city.

Adam Tomaszkiewicz (Born 1916)

Treasurer of the Polish National Alliance. Tomaszkiewicz succeeded his father, Michael, as PNA treasurer in 1955 and served a single term before failing in his effort to defeat Charles Rozmarek for the presidency of the Alliance in 1959. In 1958 he and Censor Blair F. Gunther tried unsuccessfully to call an extraordinary convention to examine the financial policies of the fraternal; the effort failed for lack of a *quorum*. Earlier, Tomaszkiewicz was active in the Polish American Congress and chaired its $1 million fund raising campaign after the War.

In recent years Tomaszkiewicz, a tax accountant and insurance salesman by profession, has once more become active within the PNA and has served the Alliance in a number of responsible capacities. In 1975 and 1979 he chaired its quadrennial conventions and in 1975, 1979 and 1983 he chaired the convention's budget and finance committee. In 1982 he headed a special advisory committee to determine PNA policy toward Alliance College. Tomaszkiewicz has served as a PNA leader at both the lodge and council levels and is presently President of the Cicero society of the Alliance.

Michael Tomaszkiewicz (1885–1967)

Treasurer of the Polish National Alliance. Born in Poland, Tomaszkiewicz migrated to Chicago where he gained employment at the R. T. Crane Valve Company. Active in the Polish National Alliance from the time he joined in 1912, he was elected a commissioner in 1921 and three years later won office as a member of its national board of directors. Tomaszkiewicz held this post until 1939 when he was elected PNA Treasurer. He held this position until 1955 when he retired after having served a record thirty-four consecutive years in national elective office.

Known as "Honest Mike," Tomaszkiewicz was an independent-minded member of the national PNA leadership. In 1925 he was one of the "group of five" in the PNA central administration which challenged President Zychlinski's decision to keep the PNA in the Polish National Department after the delegates to the 1924 convention had voted against participation. Taking their complaint to court, the group's members were suspended from the Board and threatened with loss of participatory rights in the Alliance. Vindicated in 1928 at the twentieth PNA convention in Chicago, Tomasz-kiewicz went on to become one of the most popular and respected members of the movement.

During the 1930s he stoutly supported the formation of *Harcerstwo* and as Treasurer raised hundreds of thousands of dollars from Alliance members in behalf of the Polish nation during World War II.

Irene Wallace (Born 1924)

Vice President of the Polish National Alliance. A native of Campbell, Ohio, Wallace was active in the *Harcerstwo* movement, the Polish American

Congress and in PNA lodge and council affairs before her election as a district commissioner in 1955. Elected to the PNA board of directors in 1959 and 1963, Wallace succeeded Frances Dymek as Ladies' Vice President in 1967 upon her retirement. She was unsuccessful in her 1971 reelection campaign and withdrew from PNA politics. Initially employed as a secretary, Wallace studied Business Administration at Miami University of Ohio and later became a specialist in data processing and programming.

Ignace Wendzinski (1828–1901)

Editor of *Zgoda*. Born in Bydgoszcz in German ruled Poland and educated as a teacher, Wendzinski took part in patriotic efforts during the "Spring of the Nations" and was imprisoned for two years for his activities. In 1863 he participated in the Polish insurrection against Russia and after a few years in exile in Western Europe he came to America in 1870. Employed as a teacher and a newspaper editor Wendzinski worked for such papers as *Orzel Bialy, Gazeta Polska* and *Przyjaciel Ludu* before becoming editor of *Zgoda* at the 1882 PNA convention. Because the paper's founding editor, Edward Odrowaz, refused to move to Chicago from New York, when the newspaper's headquarters were transferred at the convention, Wendzinski was chosen in his place and served in this capacity until 1886. (During this time, *Zgoda* was actually published in Milwaukee.)

Under Wendzinski, a sharp critic of those in the Polish clerical camp who accused the PNA of being an anti-religious organization, *Zgoda* grew rapidly in circulation. But, by the mid-1880s a majority in the Alliance favored a less combatative policy towards its clerical opponents and Zbigniew Brodowski replaced Wendzinski. Later, he worked as an editor for several Milwaukee Polish papers and as a teacher.

Joseph Wiewiora (Born 1912)

Editor of *Zgoda*. Wiewiora came to America in 1926 with his parents from the region around Zywiec in Southwest Poland. Residing in East Chicago, Indiana Wiewiora first worked at the daily newspaper *Dziennik*

Zjednoczenia published by the Polish Roman Catholic Union and in 1930 worked in Stevens Point for the *Gwiazda Polarna* Polish weekly. Returning to Chicago, Wiewiora was again employed by the *Dziennik Zjednoczenia* until World War II, when he worked in the military supply division of the Pullman Standard company before joining the army. After the war, Wiewiora was active in Hammond, Indiana politics before working as a writer for the Polish American Congress and as an assistant editor of *Dziennik Zwiazkowy.*

From January, 1968 he served as Editor of *Zgoda.* In this capacity, Wiewiora made the newspaper a true dual language publication with the paper's first section in English followed by information in the Polish language. Equally important, he transformed the function of *Zgoda* from one largely limited to PNA lodge and council doings into something much broader. Through his efforts, backed by the leadership of the PNA, *Zgoda* is once again the newspaper it was when it was founded in 1881. Providing news about Poland, American Polonia and the Polish American Congress along with PNA stories, *Zgoda* has become the most important Polish American newspaper in the nation.

Casimir Zychlinski (1859–1927)

President of the Polish National Alliance from 1912 to 1927. Born and educated in Poland, Zychlinski came to America in 1876 where he lived for a time in New York. He joined the PNA in 1881. In 1883 he moved to Chicago where he was active in the south side Polonia community centered about St. Adalbert parish. In 1887 he was a founder of the Falcons' Alliance and for the next ten years served as the first president of the fledgling youth movement.

Active for many years in the PNA he was elected to its Board of Directors and chosen to be the Vice President of the Alliance when President Marian Steczynski resigned in 1912 to direct the newly created Alliance School. When Vice President Filip Ksycki (1867–1954), who succeeded Steczynski, himself resigned the Presidency only weeks after his appointment because of business conflicts, Zychlinski became the new President and was subsequently elected for five terms in his own right. A dynamic speaker and excellent organizer, Casimir Zychlinski led the PNA during the momentous years of the First World War and the recovery of Poland's independence after 123 years of foreign partition. Under his leadership, the Polish National Alliance grew from 80,000 to 250,000 members.

Sources: Stanislas Osada, *Historia Zwiazku Narodowego Polskiego* (1905).

Adam Olszewski, *Historia Zwiazku Narodowego Polskiego* (1957–1963).

Zgoda, organ of the PNA.

Rev. Francis Bolek, ed., *Who's Who in Polish America,* 3rd edition (New York: Harbinger House, 1943).

APPENDIX D

Speeches of Presidents of the United States to the PNA

Over the years, a number of presidents have addressed representatives of the Polish National Alliance in their role as Polonia leaders on matters of national importance.

During the First World War, President Woodrow Wilson met with Polonia leaders as did President Franklin D. Roosevelt during the Second World War. In 1937, Roosevelt also participated in the ceremonies connected with the reinterrment of the remains of General Wlodzimierz Krzyzanowski at the Arlington national cemetery. After World War II, every president met with the leaders of the PNA in their capacities as officers in the Polish American Congress and several took advantage to deliver public addresses to national conventions of the PAC. Thus it was on September 30, 1960 that President Dwight Eisenhower spoke to the PAC at its fifth quadrennial convention in Chicago. Sixteen years later, both President Gerald Ford and presidential candidate Jimmy Carter addressed the Polish American Congress at its convention in Philadelphia. In 1966, Lyndon B. Johnson hosted PNA and Polonia leaders at the White House for ceremonies celebrating Poland's one thousandth anniversary as a Christian nation. At that event, a special commemorative stamp was issued recognizing Poland's millenium.

On five occasions, a president has addressed the PNA apart from the rest of Polonia and in this section three of these speeches have been reprinted in their entirety. While different from one another in tone and style, they provide an insight into what America's leaders have understood to be the main values in the Polish culture through history and the dominant themes of United States foreign policy toward Poland.

The very first meeting of PNA leaders with the President took place at the White House on September 26, 1907. On that day, President Theodore Roosevelt greeted approximately four hundred delegates from the PNA convention taking place in nearby Baltimore. There is no record, however, of his exact remarks on this occasion. Before their trip to the White House, the delegates toured the Capitol building and laid wreaths at the foot of the Washington monument. They also placed flowers at busts of Kosciuszko and Pulaski which were to be found at the places where monuments to the two patriots were later to be erected through the efforts of the Polish National Alliance.

At the White House, Roosevelt received the thanks of the PNA for his support of the monuments project. Speaking for the Alliance, Theodore Helinski emphasized the feelings of loyalty toward their adopted homeland which characterized the orientation of Polonia and expressed the hope that

407

Roosevelt would use his influence to bring the speedy release of political prisoners exiled in Siberia for their involvement in the Polish uprising against tsarist Russia in 1905. Roosevelt thanked those in attendance for their loyalty and sent his well wishes to all Poles in America. He completed his comments by extending his regards for a productive convention to the PNA delegates.

On August 24, 1979 President Carter also greeted PNA leaders in the White House during a break away from the thirty-eighth convention of the Alliance being held in the nation's capital. A photograph of the event is to be found in this work.

Address of President William Howard Taft at the dedication of the Polish National Alliance school in Cambridge Springs, Pennsylvania

October 26, 1912

Mr. Chairman, Members of the Polish National Alliance of America, Ladies and Gentlemen:

We are met to-day to dedicate a college founded by, and to be conducted under the auspices of, the Polish National Alliance. This expression, on the part of the Poles of the United States, of a desire to perpetuate in this the land of their adoption the highest institution of learning, for the purpose of furnishing to their educated youth an opportunity for the study of the language, the literature, and the history of Poland, presents an interesting phase of the settlement of this country by immigrants from European countries. If such an institution as we are now welcoming into life were to have the effect of separating into an isolated community the Poles who came to this country, or preventing them from learning the English language, of reducing their interest in the political life of the United States, and of minimizing their sense of loyalty to the government and country of their adoption, then it might be questioned how far those of us who are not Poles, and whose first interest is that of the country at large, should encourage this effort. But fortunately no such narrow limiting motive actuates the movement, the consummation of which we dedicate to-day.

Experience has shown that the free air of America creates a natural tendency, on the part of those who come to live with us, and enjoy our institutions, to learn the language, to amalgamate with other peoples, and to take an active interest in the politics of the country, and that this is so strong as to arouse no fears that in the end it will not be the natural and prevailing force in all our foreign population. If a family of foreigners comes here it finds that its children quickly pick up the English language, and if it would preserve its own language it must be insisted on by family discipline. In other words, our long experience has confirmed the view that there is nothing at all inconsistent in the respect and in the cultivation of respect, by those who come to us from other countries, for their national traditions, their national language, their national literature, and the assimilation of their aims, political, social and economic, to those of the people of their adopted country. Indeed, the fervor with which they celebrate their national anniversaries, the enthusiasm with which they sing their national songs, and review the great deeds of their national heroes, instead of detracting from their loyalty to their new home and its government, seem, as the years go on, to strengthen that loyalty, and to make them better Americans, because, as in the present instance, they are better Poles. Therefore, I have not hesitated to come, upon the kindly invitation of the Polish National Alliance of America, to join you in celebrating this foundation of a Polish university, in which the more fortunate of the Polish youth, who wish to perfect themselves in the language and its literature, and at the same time acquire a liberal education, may spend a few years at the formative state of their lives in acquiring what will contribute to their happiness all through their lives, and will enable them to enjoy the literature, history and spirit of two languages and two countries instead of one.

The history of Poland records the story of a wonderful people whose peculiar form of government, and whose geographical position in Europe first gave them great influence and great power for good in the protection of western European Christian civilization against the invasion of the Tartars and the pagan tribes of the East, and then led to misgovernment and offered their territory, lying as it did, without natural boundaries, in the center of Europe, to be divided between the three countries having more stable governments, but altogether forgetful of the gratitude due to Poland for what she had done in saving Europe.

Time does not permit more than a passing reference to the noble record that the Polish people made while a nation. Their territory in its greatest length exceeded 700 miles, and in its greatest width was a little less than that. It covered a space of 282,000 square miles, and a country which now has a population of 24,000,000. It reached from the Baltic, at one corner, to the Black Sea, at the other. The Carpathian Mountains separated it from Austria and the Danube provinces, and it lay in mid Europe, a rich agricultural country, with no natural protection on any side sufficiently extended to be important. It had a landed nobility and a peasant class, and there seems to have been no burgher or middle class engaged in business who lived in the cities. The people of Poland in early days were adapted to farming and fighting. The government control was in a Diet of the landed aristocracy. It conformed to a constitution that contained seeds of its destruction, for in that Diet every noble was given a "liberum veto", so-called,—the right to stop proceedings, and to prevent action, and this exaltation of the individual as a member of the Diet promoted a factionalism that greatly weakened the strength of the union of the constituents of the government.

Continuing the idea of equality in power among the landed nobility, the selection of a King was by election of the Diet. The jealousy and dissension among the nobles tempted other governments to propose candidates for the sovereignty of Poland, and there were a number of such candidates elected. Early in the history of the Kingdom there were strong men selected from Polish families who maintained the power of the Kingdom, and exercised a wide influence, and at times they would recur to the practice of electing a Pole instead of a foreigner. The rivalry that the elections engendered, and the presence that it seemed to invite of large escorts for each candidate, contributed to the turbulent scenes that attended every election. These unfortunate peculiarities, together with the geographical position I have already referred to, are the circumstances that made possible the partition of the ancient Kingdom of Poland, and their strength as the cause of the misfortunes in the history of Poland can not be escaped. It can not be denied, indeed it is manifest, and has been always, that no people of Europe have had stronger in their hearts the feeling of nationality than the Poles. In the first place, they were the natural guardians, because of their geographical position, of the Christian civilization of West Europe. For a large part of the time they were so situated, their nationality was embodied in and represented by the Roman Catholic Church. They were on the boundary where the rivalry of the Greek and Byzantine Catholicism manifested itself against the religion of Rome, and never for an instant did they yield. The result was that their nationality and their religion were completely identified, and even in the days of Luther, and the subsequent thirty years' war, the number of Poles who became independent, or left the church to join in the new movement, was insignificant. When then we consider the history of Poland, and see that, in the face of this strongest spirit of nationalism, identified with the spirit of religion the various partitions of Poland took place, we must recognize the powerful agency that their form of government, their political structure and their geographical situation had in working out their mournful fate as a nation; and in accepting such people as our fellow-citizens, as constituents in our body politic, and as amalgamating with all our other peoples here, we must recognize and rejoice in the value and weight of that spirit of nationalism and undying loyalty to an idea, that are certain to make Poles strong in the support of American sovereignty and loyal to the core, in a free country in which they can develop all their best traits, and enjoy the political, social, economic and religious freedom that they so prize.

It is indeed a sad commentary on the gratitude of peoples and nations to read the history of John Sobieski, the greatest of the Kings of Poland and of the Polish Kings, and note how the fate of Europe hung upon the contest that he, with his comparatively small force, carried on successfully against the hordes of warriors that Islam and the Grand Turk were enabled to throw across the Austrian and Polish boundaries and attack Vienna and the other cities. The wonderful cavalry that Sobieski was able to gather in Poland, led by the Polish nobility, and the fighting qualities of the peasant Poles, constituted an army which was able to meet a force ten to twelve times its strength, and overcome it through its dash and solidarity, on the one hand, and through the strategic genius of its great leader, upon the other. The tender letters which Sobieski wrote to his wife, describing the victory at Vienna, gleam like sunlight in the history of Europe. While they give the valuable details observed by a contemporaneous and interested witness, they suffuse the scene with the color of the chivalrous and gallant love that we like to see manifested by one engaged in such heroic service to mankind as that which Sobieski performed. And when in later years, in an effort to rescue his country and restore its rended parts to a whole, Thaddeus Kosciuszko won another battle, which, however, was fruitless in its results, we are rejoiced in studying his character to find the same knightly chivalry, the same effectiveness as a warrior, and the same high purposes as a statesman that we recognize in Sobieski centuries before; and it furnishes exquisite pleasure to an American to know that Kosciuszko, and another valiant Pole, Pulaski, were attracted to this country to aid it in its struggle for liberty and independence in the War of the Revolution; that Pulaski, after having led many a valiant charge, gave up his life for his adopted country, and that his ashes now rest in the soil of the nation that sacrificed his all, to create. It was not the fate of Kosciuszko to lose his life in the Revolution, or to remain with us after its successful event. He returned to his beloved Poland. We are glad to recognize the debt we owe to these heroes, and the bronze statues to their memory that now adorn beautiful squares in Washington are a true expression of a grateful nation for most valuable services in a time of need.

The Poles are a people having qualities that we can well afford to incorporate into the composite American citizen that our policy of national hospitality is creating. Having, in the first place, the highest spirit of hospitality themselves, they are able to appreciate it and treat it with proper consideration when they are themselves the object of it. Brave and generous to a fault, warm-hearted, they have both the winning ways of the Irishman and the urbanity and delightful manners of the French. With an innate love of the picturesque and the poetic, they cherish all the traditions and legends and customs that add so much pleasure to their home life. They are a farming people. They love the soil, and they know how to treat it. By force of circumstances they have been brought into industrial employment in this country, more so perhaps than they would themselves like, and more so than they will themselves be compelled to accept in the development of our country. We are suffering from a congestion of labor in the large cities and a dearth of labor in the country. We need farmers. We need farm laborers. The increase in the value of the products of the soil and the better emoluments now derived from farming, are in the end certain to attract laborers and farmers to the country, and in this movement there are no people in the world who are better adapted to be successful than the Poles. Farming has now become a scientific profession. The problems we have here are the problems of the old world, intensified, and we are bound to make one acre in the future grow as much as two acres grow now. In this struggle with nature, in this effort to wrest the secret of her productions from her in such a way as to increase our yearly product, the Poles may be counted on as some of our best future agents.

The great body of our people are of English descent, and they have inherited that tendency to take their pleasures sadly which was characteristic of the Puritans, and indeed of all Englishmen. The Poles are Celts, or rather they are Slavs, and like the Celts they have the philosophy of getting pleasure out of life that the Puritan-descended American may profitably acquire. They are artists in every sense. Chopin, and the list of composers I am sure I may be excused from attempting to pronounce, have furnished to the world an evidence of the Polish love of harmony that needs no further proof. The Polish artists who paint, the Polish poets who write, all confirm the love of beauty that prompts the nation to every form of artistic development. Then, too, they properly claim, as one of their nation, the great philosopher and astronomer, who set our ideas right with reference to the universe, Copernicus. The views he advanced at the time he advanced them were so radical as to prevent his then securing the gratitude that he deserved, but he stands out now in the history of our men of science as one of the pioneers with Galileo, Sir Isaac Newton, Keppler and Humboldt.

Finally, of recent years only, one of the most brilliant novelists of modern times, who paints history into his stories, is Sienkiewicz, who has opened to the world a vision of Poland as she was, and the Poles as they were and are, with a strength and vividness of description that secure to them a permanent place among the novels of the world. With a language thus rich in poetry, in legend, in history and in fiction, there is no wonder that the sons of Poland who have gathered in this country feel moved to establish an institution of learning in which their children may continue to enjoy and imbibe the spirit of their ancestors, and maintain a love among them for the best of their national heritage.

Nearly five hundred years ago Casimir, the great King of Poland, in the luxurious generosity of a Polish King, founded a library in Cracow, the then capital of Poland, and gave a charter for a university with three schools, of law, of philosophy, and of theology, but war intervened and his plan for the university was suspended, until under another King, Jagiello, in 1400, the University of Cracow was founded. And now for five hundred years that institution of learning has continued to thrive, and to furnish a place for the preparation of most of the Poles in higher education. This University and that of Lemburg are the two that have maintained the highest standards of Polish literature.

Of course I understand that this university we are founding is not the first institution of liberal learning that the Poles of this country have inaugurated, and that there are many seminaries and colleges and schools all over the United States that owe their institution to the Polish-Americans but I understand this to-day to be the most ambitious of these enterprises, and to represent the yearning of Polish-Americans for a broad and liberal institution of learning for the preservation of the Polish artistic spirit, its love of high literature, and its encouragement of all the arts and sciences. May it grow to strength and influence! May it retain in the Polish-American the valuable traits of its Polish ancestors, and may it enable the Polish-Americans to carry into the make-up of the composite American those high, chivalrous and artistic qualities, together with the spirit of undying loyalty and nationalism, so as to help round out the American race and continue it to be worthy of the great inheritance that the Lord has seemed to desire it to receive.

I can not close without some reference to the question of immigration, and the attitude that ought to be taken by the lovers of our country. I am one of those who believe that America is greatly better in her present condition, and will have a still greater advantage in the future, because of the infusion into our body, politic and social, of the sturdy peasantry and the better educated classes who have come to us from the nations of Europe. In the actual development of the country, it would have been impossible for us to have done what has been done in the construction of railroads, in the development of our farms, and in the establishment of our industries, had we not had the strong arms and the steady heads of those who have come to us from continental Europe. Assuming that the foundation of our country and the original people here were from the islands of Great Britain and Ireland, and treating the foreign question as one now of immigration from continental Europe, I repeat that I do not share in the fear that our citizenship is ultimately likely to suffer by the coming from other continental countries for the purpose of permanent settlement of any of the peoples who are now coming. We have a right to have, and ought to have, immigration laws that shall prevent our having thrown upon us undesirable members of other communities, like the criminals, the imbeciles, the insane and the permanently-disabled, but we have a vast territory here not yet filled, in the development of which we need manual labor of a constant and persistent kind, and I think we have shown in the past, as we shall show in the future, that our system of education is sufficiently thorough and sufficiently attractive to those who come here that they of all others avail themselves of it with promptness and success. I have an abiding faith in the influence of our institutions upon all who come here, no matter how lacking in education they may be, if they have the sturdy enterprise to leave home and to come out to this new country to seek their fortunes. It is not the uneducated who scoff at education—they value it. They sacrifice everything to enable their children to obtain that which they were denied. The second generation of a sturdy but uneducated peasantry, brought to this country and raised in an atmosphere of thrift and hard work, and forced by their parents into school to obtain an instrument for self-elevation, has always contributed to the strength of our people, and they will continue to do so. The difficulty that they do not speak our language makes the process of amalgamation slower perhaps, but it does not prevent it.

I am proud of our country that we have had its doors swinging easily open for the industrious peoples of other countries that have sought ours for greater happiness and quicker development, and he would be blind indeed who would deny that a substantial part of our progress is due to this policy of generosity toward those who are seeking the atmosphere of freedom and the land of equal opportunity.

Text of President Jimmy Carter's Remarks at the one hundredth anniversary dinner of the Polish National Alliance in Chicago, Illinois

September 20, 1980

I want to thank Al Mazewski for that fine introduction. In his capacity as president of both the Polish National Alliance and the Polish-American Congress, Al is a frequent visitor at the White House. He knows how to get things done.

He also knows how to get re-elected. So far, he's in his fourth term. Myself, I'll settle for two.

It is good to see him again, and also so many of his colleagues in the leadership of the Polish-American community. I cannot name you all, but I do want especially to recognize the national president of the Polish Roman Catholic Union, Joseph Drobot; the president of the Falcons, Bernard Rogalski; the chairman of the board of Alliance College, Hilary Czaplicki; the vice president in charge of the women's division of the Polish National Alliance, Mrs. Helen Szymanowicz; and the president of the Polish Women's Alliance, Mrs. Helen Zielinski. The motto of her organization is, "The ideals of our women are the strength of a nation"—and I agree. Someone else who would agree with that is the mayor of this great city of Chicago, the second largest Polish city in the world, Mayor Jane Byrne.

Chicago is also known as the "city of the big shoulders." During the early years, the tough years of building, those were Polish shoulders—here and in many other cities. Nor should we forget the contributions of artists and thinkers such as Nobel Laureates Henryk Sienkiewicz and Madame Curie, Joseph Conrad, Arthur Rubenstein, Ignacy Paderewski, Hyman Rickover, and, I might add, Dr. Zbigniew Brzezinski.

With Zbig in the White House and Ed Muskie at the helm of the State Department, I am getting used to hearing about our "bipolar" foreign policy. But with Clem Zablocki serving as Chairman of the House Foreign Affairs Committee, what we actually have is a tri-polar foreign policy.

The Polish-American contribution to our country has enriched all our lives. It has been estimated that about 30 percent of all Americans can trace at least one of their ancestral lines to Poland. And for generations, the Polish National Alliance has been the mortar that has held the Polish-American community together. I am honored to join you in celebrating your 100th birthday. I am sure your second century will be as successful as your first.

As Al mentioned, I am only the second President in history to appear before you. The first—William Howard Taft— was a Republican. I'm proud to be the Democrat who has evened the score.

I'm not going to talk politics tonight, but I can't help noticing an interesting coincidence. When President Taft spoke to you, it was also an election year—1912. There was one Democratic candidate and two Republicans—just like this year. Here's the part I like: the Democrat won.

I like this part, too: The winner of that election—President Woodrow Wilson—played a decisive role in the history of Poland. He made Poland's freedom one of his famous Fourteen Points—and because of that, after more than a century of foreign oppression, Poland's existence as a state was restored.

I have a special feeling for the sons and daughters of Poland. Poland was the first foreign country to which I made a state visit as President of the United States. And the Polish people have been among the earliest and most consistent fighters for human rights—not just for a year, not just for a hundred years, but for a thousand years.

All of us were reminded again of that heritage last year—when Pope John Paul II visited our country.

What an impact this good and holy man had on our people. His spirit, his kindness, his radiance conquered our hearts.

That was a proud and special moment for all Americans. It was doubly so for Polish-Americans. Pope John Paul II, a faithful son of his nation and his Church, became a living symbol of Polish contributions to our common values.

The Pope is only the latest of the millions of Poles who have come to America—as visitors and as immigrants—bringing with them a love of human rights.

Everyone knows that Thaddeus Kosciuszko helped America win her independence. What most people do not know is what Kosciuszko did just before he returned to Poland to fight for Polish freedom. He had a large sum of money coming to him from the Continental Congress. He left that money in the care of Thomas Jefferson—with instructions to him to purchase the freedom of as many black slaves as possible. The great Polish general very simply believed that slavery was as repugnant here in America as in his own country.

Let me remind you of one more incident in the long history of Polish-Americans and human rights. It goes back a long time—more than 350 years—yet it is as fresh as today's newspaper.

In 1608, in what is now Virginia, Captain John Smith brought a small group of Polish glassmakers to Jamestown to set up the first factory in America. But the Polonians, as they were then called, were denied the rights of free citizens.

These proud people endured these indignities for eleven years. Then, in 1619, they staged the first sitdown strike in American history—not for money, but for human rights. Because of that, the House of Burgesses—the first legislature in America—passed a bill giving the Polonians the right to vote and the other rights of free people.

Think of that, three and a half centuries ago—and then think of the Gdansk workers of 1980. The spirit of the Jamestown Polonians is very much alive—here in this room and across the ocean. The events of recent weeks in Poland have inspired the world.

During this period of exciting change in Poland, the U.S. government has pursued a careful policy—a policy based on the need for a calm atmosphere, free from outside interference. We will not interfere in Poland's affairs—and we expect that others will similarly respect the right of the Polish nation to resolve its problems on its own.

It now appears that the crisis may be on its way to a peaceful and constructive resolution. But Poland's economic problems remain very severe. Besides the dislocations, there have been terrible floods. Poland needs food.

That is why I ordered quick approval of Poland's full request for $670 million in new credit guarantees for four million tons of American grain and other farm products—the largest such guarantee we have ever made. We have also substantially increased Pacific Coast allocations of fish to Poland.

These steps, urged by many of you here tonight, are intended to meet an urgent and basic need for food.

They are also intended to show our admiration for the dignified manner in which the entire Polish nation is conducting itself in this time of wrenching and positive change.

And they are intended to demonstrate to the new leadership of Poland our desire for better relations. We want to strengthen even further the human ties between our two countries.

The shipyard workers in Gdansk—the coal miners in Silesia—the store clerks and workers in Warsaw have sent a powerful message around the world.

Poland has reminded us that the desire for human rights and human dignity is universal.

Freedom of thought and expression—freedom from arbitrary violence—freedom from violations of personal integrity—due process—participation in government—civil and political and economic rights. These are the very stuff of human rights.

And, tonight, I pledge to you this: As long as I am President, this nation will stand for its beliefs, will stand for its ideals, will stand for its values, will stand up for human rights.

To those who criticize our human rights policy, who say it is not in our national interest, who say it hampers American foreign policy, I say: How can we—as free people—be indifferent to the fate of freedom elsewhere? How can we, as people with the most abundant economy on the globe, be indifferent to the suffering of those elsewhere who lack food, and health care and shelter?

We cannot be indifferent—and we will not retreat one step from our human rights policy.

Human rights is the very soul of our foreign policy—because it is the soul of our identity as a nation. We support human rights because our conscience demands it. But the fact is that our human rights policy— in general—also pragmatically serves our national interest.

Both our nation and the world are more secure when basic human rights are respected.

Our words and our actions have left their mark:

Governments have released political prisoners, lessened political repression and economic misery.

Hundreds of thousands of people have emigrated to freedom from the Soviet Union, Cuba and elsewhere.

Increased trade with African and Third World nations has resulted in part from the growing trust generated by America's human rights policy.

The Soviet Union may not like our human rights policy. The generals, colonials, and dictators may not like it. Those who tyrannize others will always fear the ideas of freedom and human dignity. But the people in the villages, the factory workers, those who farm the land and populate the cities—they care and they applaud and they pray that Americans will never abandon them.

I say to them: We are one, we are together. We will not abandon you.

Here at home, our nation's commitment to fundamental values is strengthened by advancing human rights—the rights of all Americans, regardless of color or national origin or accent or sex. That commitment makes us proud to be Americans. And it makes us realize that America's foreign policy in the 1980s must always emanate from those values.

We cannot return to the days when we too often gave unquestioning support to repressive regimes.

We cannot return to the days when secrecy in foreign policy was used to hide policies and acts the American people would never support.

We must continue to strengthen our defenses—as I have done every year since I became President, as I will continue to do in the future. But we cannot sap our strength by returning to the days when some would advocate a military solution for every international disturbance.

We have learned too much from the past twenty years. Too many American families have made too many sacrifices for their leaders to have their vision blurred by nostalgia for a world that no longer exists.

I say to you that America's military might should be used to seek peace and avoid war.

And I say to you that America's human rights policy should be used to pierce the curtain of oppression—to throw the searchlight of world conscience on those who smother the winds of freedom.

The cause of human rights is a slow process. Results are not always immediately evident. Progress is often painfully slow. Sometimes there are reverses.

But when the cause triumphs and the winds of freedom blow, no power on earth can withstand their force.

We will stand up for human rights in Madrid at the European security conference—and Al Mazewski will be there as a member of the American delegation.

Will this nation abandon its human rights policy? I answer—never.

I pledge to you that as long as America stands true to itself and as long as I am President, our voice of liberty will not be stilled.

America is human rights. That is what America has meant to the rural people of Poland—the potato farmers of Ireland—the Jews of Eastern Europe—all the oppressed who built and peopled our country.

Those inalienable human rights—of life, liberty and the pursuit of happiness, so eloquently penned by Thomas Jefferson, so profoundly demonstrated by the Polish workers—will endure and will prosper and will thrive.

Thank you.

**Remarks of President Ronald Reagan to the Polish National Alliance
and representatives of the Polish American Community at the
home office of the PNA in Chicago, Illinois**

June 23, 1983

Thank you, Mr. Mazewski. Our country is composed of many cultures, races and ethnic groups. But there's one thing we all have in common, something that ties us together as one people and is at the very heart of our national character and that is a fervent love of liberty.

It's this heartfelt conviction that today binds us, not just Polish Americans, but all Americans—(Applause.) And it binds us with those who struggle for freedom and independence in Poland.

Let no one mistake our fortitude. Time may pass, but the American people will never, never forget the brave people of Poland and their courageous struggle. (Applause.) It seems like only yesterday when all of us were so filled with hope. Solidarity, a truly independent labor union, had emerged. And with it came new recognition of freedoms of speech, press and the right to free association to strike and to reap the fruit of one's labor.

Perhaps nothing more clearly demonstrates the repressive and insecure nature of communism than the tremor felt throughout the communist world as a result of Polish workers and citizens exercising inalienable human rights, the rights that are so fundamental to free Western societies and that we too often taken for granted.

Solidarity was born not only of the failure of the Polish government to meet the needs of its people, but also from a noble tradition of freedom preserved and nourished by the proud Polish people through two centuries of foreign and domestic tyranny.

Symbolizing the battle of real workers to sustain fundamental human and economic rights in a so-called worker's state, Solidarity sought to address and to resolve Poland's deep-rooted economic ills. It acted in good faith and it pursued a path of constructive dialogue with the Polish government. Despite these peaceful efforts on the part of Solidarity, a brutal wave of repression descended on Poland on December 13th, 1981.

The imposition of martial law stripped away all vestiges of the newborn freedom. Polish authorities resorted to arbitrary arrests, imprisonment, and the use of force. The free flow of people, ideas, and information was suppressed. A darkened cloud descended on Poland. But not all has been darkness.

Despite the unyielding repression of the last 18 months, the will of the Polish people has not yet been broken and we've seen that on television over these last several days. And the Papal visit to Poland which ends today is truly a ray of hope for the Polish people and an event of historic importance. (Applause.)

During these eight short days, the Pope's message of hope and faith has helped to inspire millions of Poles to continue their struggle to regain the human rights taken from them by the Polish authorities on December 13th. (Applause.)

I was deeply moved, as I know you were, by the Pope's outspoken defense of the Polish people's human rights. His frequent statements of support for the interned, the imprisoned, and those dismissed from work for their political activities were poignant reminders to the Jaruzelski regime and the Soviets that they cannot hope to permanently erase the historic August accords.

Freedom loving people everywhere support His Holiness' call for social renewal, social justice, and reaffirmation of national sovereignty. I've long felt that many, if not all, of the problems faced by the Polish people could be resolved if Poland's neighbors would permit that beleaguered nation to work them out undisturbed. (Applause.) And you're aware of the neighbor particularly that we're talking about. (Applause.)

I've developed a new hobby. It is one of finding and then verifying from some of the dissidents who are here in our country, who have escaped, the jokes that the Russian people are telling among themselves which shows their cynicism about their own government. And one of the recent ones is that they were saying that if the Soviet Union let another political party come into existence, they would still be a one-party state because everybody would join the other party. (Laughter. Applause.)

I have to tell you the latest one that I have found is so typical. And this, too, is of the Soviet Union and its failures. The story is that a commissar visited a collective farm, and grabbed one of the workers to talk to him and said, "How are things here?" "Oh," he said, "everything is just wonderful." He said, "there are no complaints, haven't heard a single complaint." "Well," he said, "how are the crops?" "Oh," he said, "the crops—never better, everything just fine." "What about potatoes?" He said, "potatoes," he said, "if we piled them up in one pile, they'd reach the foot of God." (Laughter.) And the commissar said, "this is the Soviet Union. There is no God." (Laughter.) He said, "that's all right; there are no potatoes." (Laughter.) (Applause.)

But seriously, the need for dialogue and reconciliation in Poland has never been more evident than it was during the Pope's visit. The gulf separating the Polish people from their government remains vast. And nothing showed this more clearly than the faces, the words, and the signs carried by the millions of Poles who traveled great distances to see and hear the Pope. His call on the need to find a humane way for a peaceful and rational solution to the conflict offers the only prospect of bridging this gap between the people and their government.

I suspect that the Polish people are even more ready in the aftermath of his visit to begin a dialogue. But the real question is not the willingness of the Polish people, but that of the Warsaw government. I urge the Polish authorities to translate the restraint they showed during the Papal visit into willingness to move toward reconciliation rather than confrontation with the Polish people. (Applause.)

I was, also, impressed by the Pope's words on the importance of free trade unions, and his quote of Cardinal Wyszynski—the comment that there is an innate right to form free associations and that the State's only role is to protect it, to protect that right. (Applause.)

The actions of the millions of Poles who attended the Masses around the country, inspiring the spirit which gave rise to Solidarity still flourishes in Polish hearts. There is only one way for the Polish government to gain the confidence and trust of its own people. And that is to end martial law, to release political prisoners—(Applause)—to restore freely formed trade unions, and to embark on a path of genuine, national reconciliation. (Applause.)

We are currently consulting with our allies on the Polish question. Once these consultations are complete, we'll decide on how to proceed in our relations with Warsaw. In the meantime, I would only repeat what I said in my December 10th speech. "If the Polish government takes meaningful, liberalizing measures, we are prepared to take equally significant and concrete steps of our own." (Applause.)

Moreover, the United States will continue to provide humanitarian assistance to the Polish people. I know the great sacrifices which so many of you and the Polish-American community have been making to send assistance in the form of food and medical supplies.

We, too, have participated in this humanitarian effort with more than $40 million worth of aid distributed through CRS and CARE. As I've said before, if the Polish government will honor the commitments it has made to basic human rights, we in America will gladly do our share to help the shattered Polish economy just as we helped the countries of Europe after both World Wars. (Applause.)

I've talked of freedom. We've talked of freedom many times. Many of you have seen first-hand there, in visits to relatives, or in being there before you came here, what is going on. But to many of us, freedom becomes a word, and particularly to our young people. They hear it so often. And they don't have an opportunity to know what is so important about that word.

And just a few days ago I received a letter from a woman who has just returned from a visit to relatives in Poland. And yet it was her first visit there. And she said, "I felt that I owed you this letter. Until three weeks ago I supported a nuclear freeze and arms reduction," and she went on with some of the other things. But, she says, "Not any more. Not after what I've seen."

I'll only read a few paragraphs. She said: "Poland is a concentration camp encircled by the same double strands of barbed wire that is displayed at Auschwitz and Buchenwald—camps so atrocious they have been preserved so that we shall never forget and never permit this sort of thing to happen again. But it is happening today in the great nation state of Poland. The fear in the faces of men, women and children is also a reminder of things past. People speak in whispers, look over their shoulders constantly. And a few brave young people will tell you that people still disappear daily from their jobs and their homes. As an American observer, I see little difference between the gestapo and the KGB." (Applause.)

She goes on eloquently about other things there that she's seen—the differences. She says, "I, too, support human rights. I was in Warsaw and Krakow. And I was asked by the people there if people in America understood what was happening in Poland under Russian domination. I said, No. No, because we don't know fear, oppression, religious censorship. We have never known the hopelessness that comes from living under a dictatorship. If there could only be one protest march in Poland today, Mr. President, it would not be for arms reduction or jobs or food or even clothing. But rather for the most prized and valued fundamental right of all—of every living soul in this universe: freedom." (Applause.)

And then she asked that we keep that light of freedom burning here, because the whole world is watching and living by its glow. The visit by John Paul II to his homeland was an inspiration to all who cherish freedom. It vividly showed that no one can crush the spirit of the Polish people. (Applause.) In the moving words of the Polish National Anthem: "Poland has not died while we yet live," are more true today than ever. The spirit of solidarity that unites the Polish people with free people everywhere has never been stronger.

I thank you for letting me be with you this brief time here today. God bless you all. And we shall stay together and we'll let Poland be Poland. (Applause.) Thank you.

NOTES

Introduction

1. In its centennial year, for example, the PNA included 295,000 members and possessed assets of more than $167 million. These figures compared very favorably to the second largest Polish and ethnic fraternal, the Polish Roman Catholic Union in America, which counted 104,000 members and $59 million in assets in 1980. *Statistics of Fraternal Benefit Societies* (Chicago, 1982).

2. The previous histories were published in 1894, 1905 and 1940.

3. The record of scholarly neglect of Polish fraternalism is sad and long. Among the large number of monographs on Polonia written since 1960, not one has dealt directly and substantially with any of the major fraternals. Consideration of fraternals has generally been limited to tangential discussions of their activities in works dealing with the relationship between the immigrants and American Catholic Church authorities or the role of Polish Americans in political matters. Thus, there is some limited discussions of the fraternals in works such as Edward Kantowicz's *Polish American Politics in Chicago (1975)*, Angela Pienkos' edited work, *Ethnic Politics in Urban America: The Polish Experience in Four Cities* (1978), Richard Lukas' *The Strange Allies: The United States and Poland, 1941-1945* (1978), Joseph Parot, *Polish Catholics in Chicago, 1850-1920* (1980), Anthony Kuzniewski, *The Polish Church War in Wisconsin, 1896-1918*(1980), and Piotr Wandycz, *The United States and Poland* (1980). But only three recent studies have given much more than passing notice to the fraternals, Victor Greene's *For God and Country: The Rise of Polish and Lithuanian Ethnic Consciousness in America* (1975), Joseph Wytrwal's *Behold! The Polish Americans* (1977), and a Polish language work, Andrzej Brozek's *Polonia Amerykanska, 1854-1939* (1977). Scholarly disinterest in the fraternal movement is also evident from even a cursory glance at the major journals devoted to Polish and Polish-American matters in the United States, the *Polish Review* and *Polish American Studies.* And according to a recent survey of doctoral dissertations completed

at American universities on Polonian topics between 1940 and 1980 only three of sixty-nine Ph.D. theses dealt with fraternals in any substantial fashion. See Angela Pienkos, "The Polish American Historical Association and its Role in Research on Polish America: An Assessment," *Polish American Studies,* 38, Number 1 (Spring, 1981), 63-73.

Fraternal leaders too have received little recognition for their services to Polonia. A look at the supposedly definitive study of the Polish ethnic group which appeared in the widely heralded *Harvard Encyclopedia of American Ethnic Groups* in 1980 did not include the name of a single twentieth century Polish fraternal leader. See in this connection my review of Wandycz's book in *Polish American Studies,* 38, Number 2 (Autumn, 1981), 91-94.

4. For a succinct summary of the PNA contribution to American Polonia see Donald Pienkos, "The Polish National Alliance: One Hundred and Two years of Service," *Zgoda* (February 15, March 1, and March 15, 1982) reprinted in the New York Polonia publication, *New Horizon* (September, 1982) and in the 1983 edition of the Alliance *Almanac.* The article originally appeared in the magazine of the United States Information Agency, *Ameryka,* and was distributed in Poland under the title "Zwiazek Narodowy Polski: Sto Lat w Sluzbie Polonii Amerykanskiej," (Spring, 1982).

Sources

1. Translated, The Polish National Alliance of the United States of North America, its Development, Activity and Present Status.

2. Translated, A History of the Polish National Alliance and the Rise of the Polish National Patriotic Movement in America.

3. *Pamietnik Jubileuszowy ZNP, 1880-1940,* translated, A PNA 60th Anniversary History. Piatkiewicz wrote a shorter review in 1955 on the occasion of the 75th anniversary of the Alliance.

4. Or History of the Polish National Alliance. Olszewski's work was published as volumes 2 through 6 with Osada's study posthumously identified as Volume 1.

5. During this time I also made frequent trips to Chicago where I visited Saint Adalbert Cemetery, the final resting place of scores of major PNA officers and activists since 1900, Holy Trinity Church and Saint Stanislas Kostka Church, the historic religious centers of Chicago's most important and influential Polonia community located in the near North Side of the city, the present and former home offices of the PNA, and the Polish Museum of America. In addition, I much appreciate the opportunity I had to serve as an officer of one of the PNA's more active lodges, the Milwaukee Society, Group 2159, as a delegate to Milwaukee PNA Council 8, as a member of the board of directors of the Wisconsin Division of the Polish American Congress and as a director representing Wisconsin on the national board of the Polish American Congress. All these experiences were invaluable first hand

opportunities to become exposed to the realities of fraternal and ethnic life and to meet people dedicated to preserving their heritage through these organizations. They enhanced my understanding of what I read and had heard from others. As a parent whose three eldest sons participated in a PNA dance group sponsored by the Women's Division of District 14, I gained an additional insight into the meaning of fraternalism through attending their regular practice sessions and performances and talking with the dance group's sponsors, instructors and other parents. Last, I benefitted immeasurably from numerous conversations I had with family members who have been involved in the PNA through the years, including my wife, her mother Angeline Dubiel Mischke, Joseph Dubiel, and Stanley Sciblo.

6. Angela T. Pienkos, "The Polish American Historical Association and Its Role in Research on Polish America: An Assessment."

Chapter 1

1. This observance recalled the Polish monarchy's successful effort at reforming the country's political system in a progressive and republican fashion by putting into effect Europe's first modern written instrument of government. Promulgated on May 3, 1791, the event became widely recognized in Polish American communities around the time of its centennial.

2. Few peoples anywhere on earth have experienced greater tragedy coupled with dramatic recovery as have the Poles. Devastated by a surprise attack from Nazi Germany and Soviet Russia in 1939, Poland lost more than 6 million people during its occupation, or 22 percent of its entire prewar population. Among the casualties was an extraordinarily high proportion of its most talented intellects, cultural figures, military, political and spiritual leaders. Many of Poland's major cities, including Warsaw the capital, were levelled as was a great proportion of the country's industry, transportation system, seaports and mining areas. In spite of the occupation, approximately one million Poles fought for the Allied cause and served in every European theater of the conflict. Falling, against its people's will, under Soviet domination after the War, Poland nonetheless achieved an amazing recovery in the years which followed. This rebirth, which few would have dared to predict in 1945, has made Poland a significantly more urban, industrialized, and highly educated nation than it was in the past. The country has experienced an enormous population explosion which has transformed Poland into the youngest nation in Europe. Intellectually and spiritually, Poland has come to symbolize vitality around the world; politically, the Poles have retained their national identity and their commitment to human rights, values which link them closely to Western Europe, Canada and the United States, where millions of emigrants settled.

3. Helena Lopata, *Polish Americans* (Englewood Cliffs, New Jersey, 1976), pp. 33-42. This analysis attempts to exclude persons who originated from Poland

but who did not identify themselves as Polish but rather as Jews, Lithuanians, Germans, Ukrainians or other ethnic groups. Data for 1973–1980 are from *The Annual Report of The Immigration and Naturalization Service* (U.S. Department of Justice: Washington, D.C.).

4. W. S. Kuniczak, *My Name is Million: An Illustrated History of the Poles in America* (Garden City, New York, 1978), p. 107.

5. There are many examples of these attitudes among immigrants from scholarly works which appeared in pre World War II Poland, including the study of Babica, a village in Galicia, written by Krystyna Duda-Dziewierz (*Wies Malopolska a Emigracja Amerykanska* [Warsaw, 1938]). Numerous peasant letters included in Thomas and Znaniecki's book also bring home these feelings as do memoirs of peasants published by the sociologist Ludwik Krzywicki, under the title, *Pamietniki Chlopow* (Warsaw, 1936).

6. Stanislaw Pigon, *Z. Komborni w Swiat* (From Kombornia into the World, Krakow, 1957), p. 54.

7. Cited in Angela T. Pienkos, *A Brief History of Federation Life Insurance of America* (Milwaukee, 1976), p. 3. This study recounts the activities of a Milwaukee-based Polish fraternal.

8. Andrew Greeley, "The Ethnic Miracle," *The Public Interest* 45 (1976), 20-36; Eugene Obidinski, "Polish American Social Standing: Status and Stereotypes," *The Polish Review* 21 (Fall 1976), 97-100; Lopata, pp. 88-95. According to economist Thomas Sowell, who has studied I.Q. test scores for children of a variety of ethnic and racial groups over the years, Polish Christians had the second highest overall results, with Polish Jews scoring highest. Thomas Sowell, "Ethnicity, Intelligence and Upward Mobility," *Commentary* magazine (September, 1979), 8-10.

9. A useful review of the origins and development of the Polish National Catholic Church is by Laurence Orzell, "A Minority within a Minority: The Polish National Catholic Church, 1896-1907." *Polish American Studies,* 36, number 1 (Spring, 1979), 5-32.

10. Andrzej Brozek, *Polonia Amerykanska 1854-1939* (Warsaw, 1977), p. 45. This author estimated that at least up until the 1930s the Polish Roman Catholic and Polish National parishes included upwards of 75 percent of Polonia's population.

11. Sienkiewicz noted that the heavily peasant migration to America was composed of people who were "by nature religious, who had come to America ignorant of its language and customs. They thus looked upon the church as the center of their lives, about which they gathered, the thread linking them to Poland, something of their own which at the same time protected them. The parish was an entity that not only had spiritual but also social meaning to them." Brozek, p. 46.

12. Joseph Wytrwal, *America's Polish Heritage* (Detroit, 1961), pp. 159-167. A good recent discussion of Barzynski's leadership is in Joseph Parot, *Polish Catholics in Chicago, 1850-1920* (DeKalb, Illinois, 1981), pp. 84-91. St. Stanislas Kostka parish at its height included as many as 50,000 members, making it probably the largest parish in the world at the time. Barzynski, as head of the Resurrectionist order, was responsible for perhaps 90,000 Polish parishioners in Chicago and almost

their *de facto* bishop. A major blow to his leadership came with the disclosure that the parish bank he established in 1875 had accumulated a deficit of more than 400 thousand dollars. (It eventually reached 505 thousand dollars in 1901 and was not cleared until the early 1920s.)

13. By 1939, the major orders of Polish sisters directed 299 primary and 34 secondary schools. Brozek, pp. 148-149.

14. Jan Wespiec, *Polish American Serial Publications, 1842-1966* (Published by the author in Chicago, 1966; cited in Lopata, *Polish Americans,* p. 65). Frank Renkiewicz, compiler. *The Poles in America, 1608-1972* (Dobbs Ferry, New York, 1973).

15. Brozek, pp. 153-159.

16. As recently as 1982, for example, more than four thousand local Polish fraternal lodge units were in existence at the neighborhood level. The largest network of lodge organizations belonged to the PNA, with 1,135 groups.

17. The origins of American fraternalism go back earlier and the first such association, the Order of the Sons of Herman, was created in 1840, in Texas. But it was not until the years after the Civil War that interest went into high gear. Economic crises in 1873 and 1893 caused the collapse of a number of commercial insurance firms and the growing insurance needs of both immigrant and native-born workers required the creation of an alternative and inexpensive system of protection.

According to data for those U.S. fraternals operating in 1980, it is worth noting that most were formed between 1870 and 1910. Specifically, two currently operating fraternals were established between 1841 and 1860, five came into existence between 1861 and 1870, twelve between 1871 and 1880, twenty-one between 1881 and 1890, thirty-nine between 1891 and 1900, sixteen between 1901 and 1910, ten between 1911 and 1920, six between 1921 and 1930, and four in the years since 1931.

Fraternals by definition are "not for profit" associations. As such they have no stockholders or owners, although their officers are elected by the policy holders. All gains above operating costs go back to the members, either in the form of dividends on insurance or as scholarships, old age relief, social benefits or loans. In 1980 alone, the fraternals together contributed more than $50 million in charitable activities to needy members and non-members alike as part of their activities.

At present, approximately 1.5 percent of all life insurance sold in the United States is through fraternals, the largest of which happens to be the Aid Association for Lutherans. This organization in 1980 possessed a net worth of $850 million and $13 billion of insurance in force.

Initially, all fraternals required their members to pay a flat monthly insurance fee or assessment in order to collect sufficient funds to provide burial insurance and underwrite their various charitable activities. This assessment was the same regardless of the member's age or health. One of the earliest to introduce a different system of payments was the Polish National Alliance, which in 1907 approved a plan providing for variable insurance rates based upon the applicant's age. This reform significantly contributed to the PNA's expansion during the next two decades and helped keep it competitive with commercial and mutual insurance companies, the fraternal's rivals.

See S. S. Huebner and Kenneth Black, Jr. *Life Insurance* (Englewood Cliffs, New Jersey, 10th Edition, 1982), pp. 551-558.

18. See Murray Hausknecht, *The Joiners: A Sociological Description of Voluntary Association Membership in the United States* (New York, 1962), pp. 9-11, 118-122; Peter Berger, *To Empower People: The Role of Mediating Structures in Public Policy* (Washington, D.C., 1977).

19. Perhaps the most vivid depiction of the immigrant's unhappy fate is to be found in Upton Sinclair's celebrated novel, *The Jungle* (1906) which relates in almost hair raising style the experience of a Polish-Lithuanian family in Chicago's stockyards district at the turn of the century. For a contemporary description and analysis of ethnic immigrant conditions see Joseph Parot, "The 'Serdeczna Matko' of Sweatshops: Marital and Family Crises of Immigrant Working Class Women in Late Nineteenth Century Chicago," in Frank Renkiewicz, ed., *The Polish Presence in Canada and America* (Toronto, 1982), pp. 155-182.

20. For discussions of these early efforts, see Stanislas Osada, *Historia Zwiazku Narodowego Polskiego,* Vol. I (Chicago, 1905, 1957), pp. 3-94; Miecislas Haiman, *Zjednoczenie Polskie Rzymsko-Katolickie w Ameryce, 1873-1948* (Chicago, 1948), pp. 23-60.

21. Traditionally, winning election to serve as a convention delegate has been one of the most highly prized and hotly contested activities in the Alliance. For one thing, the expenses delegates incur in participating at a convention are covered by the Alliance. But more important is the set of powers that convention delegates possess in determining future PNA policies. Not only do they elect all national officers of the fraternal, delegates also have final approval over the organization's future budget, the power to alter its constitution, and the right to interrogate each national officer on all matters connected with his or her past performance, an important democratic prerogative known as interpellation.

22. Between 1886 and 1897, the PNA executive leadership was renamed the central government *(rzad centralny)* of the Alliance and, presumably, all Polonia, an unhappy move that met with much adverse reaction and was rescinded when it had become clear that other strategies to unite the ethnic community showed greater potential.

23. On several occasions there have been concerted, if unsuccessful efforts on the part of large numbers of delegates to actually abolish the very post of censor. One such action was taken in 1895 and won the backing of most delegates but failed because a change in the constitution required a two-thirds vote. Similarly, a vote taken at the 1918 convention also failed for lack of the required two-thirds majority, as did a motion proposed as recently as 1979.

24. An important sign of this trend within the PNA was in the formation of a number of lodges composed largely of men in business, politics, and the professions of medicine, law, dentistry and education. These individuals were representative of

a growing contingent of upwardly mobile and increasingly successful individuals of Polish birth or descent who generally saw themselves as Americans but who were interested in enhancing their status in their communities by associating with likeminded persons on the basis of their shared ancestral heritage. The first such PNA lodge was the Chicago Society, which was formed in 1912. After the First World War, it was followed by the Milwaukee Society, the Cleveland Society, the Buffalo Society and by similar groups organized in Toledo, Grand Rapids, Michigan, Detroit, South Bend, Indiana, and Manhattan. These lodges have not only continued to be active in the PNA through the years; they have also served as centers of Polonia leadership in the their local communities and have often exerted considerable influence outside of Polonia too.

Chapter 2

1. Thus the invitation extended in 1226 by Polish leaders to the German Knights Hospitaller, a crusading order of warriors better known as the Teutonic Knights to pacify the pagan tribes north of Poland along the Baltic seacoast, proved to be a grievous error. After exterminating the pagans, the Knights established their military hold over what was later called East Prussia and for the next two hundred and fifty years were a source of continuing conflict and instability. Fortunately, however, the Mongol invasion of 1241 had a more ephemeral effect; after defeating a Polish-German army and destroying Krakow, the country's capital, the Horde retired to the Volga River, where it ruled over Russia for nearly two hundred years.

2. Useful discussions of the 1791 Constitution and the events leading to its promulgation appear in W. J. Wagner, ed., *Polish Law Throughout the Ages* (Stanford, California, 1970), pp. 249-250; Piotr Wandycz, *The United States and Poland* (Cambridge, Massachusetts, 1980), pp. 42-47; and Stefan Kieniewicz, *The Emancipation of the Polish Peasantry,* (Chicago and London: 1969), pp. 18-29, 247-248.

3. Discussions of the currents of political romanticism and realism in nineteenth century Polish politics are found in Wandycz, pp. 94-103; M. K. Dziewanowski, *Poland in the Twentieth Century* (New York, 1977), pp. 31-62; Adam Bromke, *Poland's Politics: Idealism versus Realism* (Cambridge, Massachusetts, 1967); and Stanislaus Blejwas, "The Origins and Practice of 'Organic Work' in Poland: 1795-1863," *Polish Review,* 15, number 4 (Autumn, 1970), 23-54.

4. About 600,000 left to settle permanently in Germany and Western Europe, while 400,000 found themselves in Russia. Brazil was the destination for approximately 100,000 emigrants, Canada, about 45,000 and Argentina another 32,000. In addition, between 1870 and 1914 as many as one half million Poles emigrated to Germany and other Western European countries each year to find seasonal employment. Tadeusz Manteuffel, *et al., Historia Polski,* Volume III, Part One (Warsaw, 1967), pp. 100-107; Jerzy Zubrzycki, "Emigration from Poland in the 19th and 20th Centuries," *Population Studies: A Journal of Demography,* 6 (1952-1953), 248-272.

5. In all, between 1870 and 1910, the combined populations of towns having more than 10,000 inhabitants more than doubled, from about seven to sixteen percent. Donald Pienkos, "Communist Policy and the Polish Peasant: The Impact of Traditional Society Upon Revolutionary Goals," Ph.D. Diss., University of Wisconsin, 1970.

6. Kieniewicz, pp. 190-235.

7. Frank Renkiewicz, "The Profits of Non-Profit Capitalism," unpublished manuscript, pp. 3-4.

8. Membership in these organizations is also impressive, though it is difficult to determine with certainty how many peasants belonged to them. For example, in 1912, membership in all Polish rural credit and savings cooperatives had reached 1,904,500, or 7.3 percent of the entire population. This figure was twice the proportion for tsarist Russia. In all, 300 million rubles had been invested into these concerns compared to 470 million rubles for all the cooperatives in Russia excluding its Polish provinces. Donald Pienkos "Communist Policy . . ."

9. This was the opinion of Sienkiewicz, for example, and that of the important sociologist Ludwik Krzywicki, editor of the two volume interwar study, *Pamietniki Chlopow.*

10. More to the point, perhaps, was the enormous economic assistance provided by the emigration to families back in Poland. One estimate of the amount of money sent back by American Poles to their families in Galicia concluded that the figure exceeded $52 million by 1914 or approximately $4 million annually. This from relatively poor people whose numbers never exceeded five hundred thousand in any given year.

11. Barszczewski, *Zwiazek Narodowy Polski w stanach zjednoczonych Ameryki Polnocnej: jego rozwoj, dzialalnosc, i stan obecny na pamiatke stuletniej rocznicy powstania Kosciuszkowskiego* (Chicago, 1894, second edition 1980), p. 4. A recent presentation of the same view is by Victor Greene, *For God and Country: The Rise of Polish and Ethnic Consciousness in America, 1860-1914* (Madison, Wisconsin, 1975), pp. 6-7. Favorable evaluations of the emigration's experiences in America and its impact upon the homeland are numerous. One here might include the memoirs of the great peasant politician, Wincenty Witos, *Moje Wspomnienia* (Paris, 1964), Volume I, pp. 188-189; those of another peasant leader, Jan Stapinski, *Pamietnik,* edited by K. Dunin-Wasowicz (Warsaw, 1959), pp. 250-306; Pigon; K. Duda-Dziewierz, *Wies Malopolska a Emigracja Amerykanska* (Warsaw-Poznan, 1938); and K. Zawistowicz-Adamska, *Spolecznosc Wiejska* (Warsaw, 1958), second edition, pp. 213-215.

12. Zubrzycki; Victor Greene, "Pre World War I Polish Emigration to the United States, Motives and Statistics," *Polish Review,* 6 (1961), 45-68.

13. For a rather vigorous effort to contrast the "political" reasons behind the emigration out of the German provinces with those from the other regions, see Zubrzycki. A large seasonal migration out of the German provinces continued unabated up to the War and helps account for the drop in emigration to the U.S. See also Kieniewicz, pp. 197-202; Wandycz, pp. 87-89.

14. The Galicians also brought with them to America a deeply felt sense of identification with their home village, which led many to later even establish societies to organize shipments of goods and money to assist those who remained back home. Their sense of village consciousness also gave them a slightly different reason from the German Poles for establishing a solid parish community life in America. For the latter, the Church provided a defense against loss of national identity; for the Galicians it was a way to maintain a sense of the village they remembered in the old country.

15. Background about Kalussowski is in Joseph Wieczerzak, "Pre- and Proto-Ethnic: Poles in the United States before Immigration 'After Bread,' " *Polish Review*, 26 (Fall, 1976), 19-38.

16. Arthur Waldo, *Teofila Samolinska: Matka Zwiazku Narodowego Polskiego w Ameryce* (Chicago, 1980).

17. Kalussowski's last major contribution to American Polonia came in 1891 when he donated his entire personal library to the Polish National Alliance in return for its promise to maintain the collection and add to it so that it would become a significant library and reading center. After the establishment of the PNA school in 1912, the Kalussowski collection was transferred to Cambridge Springs, Pennsylvania, where it was housed for nearly twenty years. The collection was destroyed during the fire that levelled the school in January, 1931.

In 1893, a year before his death, the 87 year old Kalussowski was granted honorary lifetime membership in the Polish National Alliance in recognition of his contributions to Poland and the immigrants.

18. Greene, pp. 85-90; Joseph Parot, *Polish Catholics*, pp. 31-46.

19. Osada, pp. 56-65.

20. Greene, p. 62. Vincent Barzynski's thinking and activities are described by *Osada*, pp. 310-327; Haiman, pp. 38-179; and Wenceslaus Kruszka, author of the first history of the Polish people in America, *Historya Polska w Ameryce*, part 10 (Milwaukee, 1905-1908).

21. Barzynski, born in Poland in 1848, had come to America in 1870 and for the next two years taught school in Panna Maria, Texas. In 1872 he began publishing his newspaper, which he moved to Detroit and then Chicago. Later, Barzynski was involved in several immigrant colonization schemes in Nebraska and Minnesota. He died in 1889.

22. Giller's letter is reprinted in its entirety in Osada, pp. 97-108. Selections in English translation appear in Frank Renkiewicz, compiler, *The Poles in America 1608-1972,* (Dobbs Ferry, New York, 1973), pp. 64-65.

23. Wieczerzak, "Pre- and Proto-Ethnics," pp. 37-38.

The PNA for its part did not forget Giller's signal contribution to its formation and commemorated the great patriot regularly at its anniversaries as well as on occasions recalling the Polish struggle for independence. In 1980, as part of its centennial activities, the PNA arranged to have Giller's remains moved from their obscure grave in territory located in Soviet Russia and reinterred in Poland. In 1982, this was accomplished; Giller's grave is presently to be found in Warsaw's

Powazki cemetery together with a portrait and description of his great service to American Polonia and the cause of Poland's freedom. The inscription, from Polonia, recognizes Giller as a member of the National Revolutionary Government in 1863, a Siberian exile, writer, historian, journalist and spiritual father of the Polish National Alliance.

24. Though Andrzejkowicz was known to subscribe to a half-dozen foreign newspapers, he had not been active in the Polish community before his meeting with Lipinski, aside from having attended a meeting of the Kosciuszko society. Both Szajnert and Popielinski later recalled having first made Andrzejkowicz's acquaintance there.

25. Osada, p. 120.

26. *Posiedzenie I, 15 Lutego, 1880, Philadelphia* (Minutes of the first meeting of the Polish National Alliance).

27. Barszczewski, p. 11; Osada, pp. 120-123.

28. Osada, pp. 125-128.

29. From its earliest days, a number of goals that remained significant within the Alliance were already clearly defined. For example, at its March 14, 1880 meeting, the members approved PNA participation in the upcoming Third of May commemoration in Philadelphia and organized a library committee.

30. Reprinted in *Zgoda,* August 1, 1980, p. 1.

31. They were Ignace Wendzinski, Roman Stobiecki, Frank Gryglaszewski, and Frank Sowadzki, all listed formally as representing the Chicago *Gmina Polska* society; Joseph Krzemieniecki (Kosciuszko Society of Chicago); Edward Wilkoszewski (Polish Club of Chicago); Dyniewicz (Polish National Society of LaCrosse, Wisconsin); Max Kucera (Foundry Workers Society of Chicago); Konstanty Mallek (Pulaski Guard of Northeim, Wisconsin); Joseph Rewerski (Chicago Harmonia Singing Society). Domanski was accredited as representing the *Opieka* Society of New York, although he came from Philadelphia.

32. Osada, p. 151; Barszczewski, pp. 14–15. It was only in 1896, with Chicago confirmed as the PNA's headquarters, that it sought and received a charter from the state of Illinois to operate as a fraternal insurance association.

33. Barszczewski, p. 11.

34. See the photograph included in Karol Piatkiewicz, *Pamietnik Jubileuszowy ZNP, 1880–1940* (Chicago, 1940), p. 89.

35. Osada, p. 140, letter of July 30, 1880. If one goes along with including Odrowaz as a PNA "founder" one might as well add the names of a number of other early enthusiasts who supported the Polish National Alliance from the outset but who resided in other parts of the country. These include Dyniewicz, editor of the Chicago *Gazeta Polska,* Kalussowski, and Samolinska, and all fourteen delegates to the first PNA convention in September, 1880. Piatkiewicz in his 1940 PNA history also includes as "founders" Val Przybyszewski, Theodore Helinski, Michael Osuch, and Michael Majewski.

36. A list containing the names of all PNA national officers is in the Appendix of this work.

37. Constance Grodzka, "Historical Outline of the Polish National Alliance," unpublished paper, 1954, p. 119. Haiman, 58.
38. Osada, pp. 127-128, Barszczewski, pp. 12-14.
39. *Ibid.,* p. 14; Osada, p. 164.
40. Osada, p. 160.
41. Krzyzanowski (1824–1887) had been a participant in the abortive Krakow uprising of 1846 and had later emigrated to the United States. During the Civil War he served with distinction in the Union army and rose to the rank of Brigadier General. During the postwar Reconstruction era he held several government posts in the South. He was an early supporter of the PNA in Brooklyn and a backer of Erasmus Jerzmanowski in his efforts to build the Alliance in the East. On October 11, 1937 Krzyzanowski's remains were removed from their obscure burial place in Brooklyn to the Arlington National Cemetery thanks to the efforts of organized Polonia. In his speech honoring Krzyzanowski, President Franklin D. Roosevelt called him "the embodiment of the Polish ideal of liberty" and identified him with Pulaski and Kosciuszko. James Pula, *For Liberty and Justice: The Life and Times of Wladimir Krzyzanowski* (Chicago, 1978).
42. Barszczewski, p. 19. The idea continued to be brought up for years at national conventions, however, and one of the vice censors elected in 1901 was even specifically charged with directing PNA colonization activities.

Chapter 3

1. Of interest was an appeal to the delegates made by a group of Polish women in support of the Alliance. There is no record that any proposal was offered to admit women into the Alliance at this time, however. Osada, pp. 216-217.
2. Haiman, p. 71.
3. Osada, pp. 219 ff.
4. Osada, pp. 387-394; Barszczewski, pp. 43-56; Haiman, pp. 139-146.
5. For an excellent biography, see "A Tribute to Erasmus J. Jerzmanowski," published by the American Polish Engineering Association of Detroit in 1981. Osada blames Jerzmanowski's inability to win high office on popular resentment to his dictatorial actions at an East Coast meeting of PNA delegates in New York just before the national convention, but another factor was the widely held feeling against voting for a nobleman in the PNA, regardless of his qualifications. Interestingly, the banker and politician John Smulski was also unable to win high elective office in the Alliance after one term as a director. Osada, pp. 425-426.
6. Gryglaszewski was the chairman or presiding officer of the convention.
7. Barszczewski, pp. 28-29.
8. The delegates also approved a number of other resolutions emphasizing their fidelity to the Church and their commitment to preserving Polish feeling among their members. One resolution praised Archbishops Ireland and Foley for their support of the PNA; another committed the Alliance to continuing its patriotic activities to preserve Polish consciousness among the youth. But a third called upon *Zgoda* to restrain itself from taking up theological issues in its future editorializing, an activity

NOTES

many delegates believed had been a sore point with the clergy. Osada, pp. 334-335.

9. Haiman, pp. 88-90.

10. Osada, pp. 519-522.

11. Osada, pp. 289-291; *Kalendarz Zwiazkowy* (1923), "Zwiazek Narodowy Polski w Polnocnej Ameryce." Barszczewski, p. 31; *Zgoda,* October 2, 9, 30; November 20, 27, 1889.

12. Because of the circumstances of Majer's withdrawal and the hostility that greeted his effort to organize the *Unia Polska* fraternal, his constructive efforts on behalf of the PNA have tended to be underestimated. In fact, Majer's great achievement was to reinforce the PNA's position in Polonia as a patriotic movement deeply identified with the Church and to win approbation from the Catholic hierarchy for the fledgling organization when such an endorsement was crucial to its very survival. Moreover, Majer's success in building up priestly support for the PNA was most impressive, especially given the strength of its adversary, Barzynski. For example, in 1887 when the PNA held its national convention in St. Paul, Majer's home diocese, six of the eighty-one delegates were priests and eleven other priests were present as guests. In 1889, while only Majer and Domagalski were voting delegates in a convention with sixty-nine participants in all, their influence was even more pervasive, since thirty-eight clergymen were guests at the *sejm!*

Yet, the PNA's very character as a secular movement respectful of the Church but unwilling to be ruled by churchmen could not be altered by the Reverend Majer. Structured democratically, the Alliance and its members were unwilling to bow to the authority of clergymen even as they acknowledged the priests' right to direct parish affairs and to participate as equals in fraternal work.

13. Osada, pp. 542-544; Zlotnicki, pp. 105-106.

14. Adam Olszewski, *Historia Zwiazku Narodowego Polskiego,* Vol. III (Chicago, 1957), pp. 21 ff; *Zgoda,* May 1, May 22, 1913.

15. The problem of financial scandal was hardly unique to the PNA. In 1910, for example, several high PRCUA officers including its president were implicated in an affair involving the misuse of more than $92,000 in fraternal funds. Haiman, pp. 250 ff.

16. Osada, p. 431.

17. In 1906, the staunchly Catholic and patriotic Alliance of Poles included 1,500 members; in 1935 it claimed 9,000 in its ranks. In the mid 1970s, it had grown to approximately 16,000 insured members.

18. Olszewski, II, pp. 62-63. The official reaction of the PNA Board to Rhode's elevation was actually rather diplomatic, particularly when compared to responses published in the Polish Catholic paper, *Dziennik Chicagoski.* The *Dziennik Zwiazkowy* article reporting the news noted simply that "Many Poles who feel honored by the occasion . . . will participate (in the installation ceremonies)" *Dziennik Zwiazkowy,* June 27, 1908. In 1912, PNU membership was about 2,000; in 1935 it had grown to 17,000 and in 1975 stood at about 33,000.

19. Reverend Wenceslaus Kruszka, *Historya Polska w Ameryce* (Milwaukee, 1906), part 4, p. 32.

20. My own random sample of 277 of the 2,520 lodges formed after 1905 (after PNA-PRCUA tensions had eased) showed that, contrary to Kruszka's assertion, the use of secular symbols for the names of lodges actually became more frequent than had been the case earlier. In all, sixty-seven percent of the sampled lodges chose secular names to only thirteen percent selecting religious symbols. During the first twenty-five years the figures had been 65-20.

After 1905, lodges continued to choose Kosciuszko more than any other heroic figure while Sobieski's stock declined sharply. Not unexpectedly, lodge identification with more contemporary personages has led to groups naming themselves after Pilsudski, Paderewski, Wilson, Sklodowska, Gabriel Narutowicz (independent Poland's first president), Wladyslaw Sikorski (leader of the Polish government in London during World War II), and even Pope John Paul II.

21. Osada, pp. 314-317.

22. The goals of the Polish League approved at its founding convention included the general aim of working for the good of Polonia, developing learning by supporting the parish schools and promoting reading and the organization of libraries, helping the poor, improving the material conditions of the immigrants, and collecting money for the National Fund. Haiman, pp. 139-146; *Dziennik Chicagoski,* April 23, 1894.

23. As Helinski feared, Barzynski's supporters dominated the meeting. For example, PRCUA leader Peter Kiolbassa was elected to chair the proceedings over PNA Vice President Bardonski, 123-99.

24. *Dziennik Chicagoski,* May 12, 1894; Brozek, *Polonia Amerykanska,* pp. 71ff.; Barszczewski, pp. 43-56.

25. *Dziennik Chicagoski,* September 6, 1895, Osada pp. 244ff; Olszewski, volume III, p. 77.

26. Leon Blaszczyk, "The Polish Singers' Movement in America," *Polish American Studies,* 38 (1981), 50-62; *CFLPS,* "Polish Singers' Alliance, 1899–1934," Reel 52.

27. Indeed, between 1906 and 1912 the number of Falcons' nests increased from 60 to 248.

28. The motion to establish a reunited movement carried by a vote of 217 to 17 with 113 abstentions. Teofil Starzynski, head of the Independent Falcons, was elected President of the reunified Alliance.

29. This was made explicit in the document formally presenting the Kosciuszko monument to the United States on May 11, 1910 and signed by the members of the committee. "We, the undersigned, officers of the Polish National Alliance of the United States of North America and members of the executive committee of the Kosciuszko monument, acting in behalf of the said Polish National Alliance and of all Americans of Polish extraction do hereby tender to the people of the United States the monument to General Thaddeus Kosciuszko situated on the North East corner of Lafayette Square in the city of Washington, District of Columbia, erected by and at the expense of the Polish National Alliance, as an expression

438

NOTES

of our loyalty and devotion to our adopted country, for the liberty of which Thaddeus Kosciuszko nobly and gallantly fought and for the welfare and safety of which we, the Poles in America are at any time ready to shed our blood, as those two illustrious Poles and our predecessors, Kosciuszko and Pulaski did."

30. Olszewski, Volume II, p. 154.

31. Romuald Piatkowski, *Pamietnik wsniesienie i odsloniecia pomnikow Tadeusza Kosciuszki i Kazimierza Pulaskiego i kongresu narodowego Polskiego 1910 roku* (The Dedication of the Kosciuszko and Pulaski monuments and the Polish National Congress in Washington, D.C., 1910: A Memorial, Chicago, 1911). This remarkable work includes a discussion of the early history of the PNA.

32. In 1893 Kalussowski was granted an honorary membership in the Polish National Alliance in recognition of his many contributions over the years. His selection was one of the first to be made by the PNA and stimulated an interesting practice of honoring Poles and Polish Americans alike who had made some type of substantial commitment to the cause of preserving national consciousness in the arts, politics or in humanitarian work.

Until the practice was discontinued in 1911, more than a hundred persons were granted honorary membership in the Alliance. Among these were writers such as Jozef Ignacy Kraszewski, Henryk Sienkiewicz, Maria Konopnicka, Wladyslaw Reymont, Adam Asnyk, Stefan Zeromski, Eliza Orzeszkowa and Aleksander Glowacki (Boleslaw Prus). Others in this early PNA "hall of fame" included Ignacy Paderewski, Bishop Wladyslaw Bandurski, Helena Modrzejewska (Modjeska), the artists Wojciech Kossak and Jan Matejko, the sculptor Antoni Popiel, historian-philosophers Aleksander Swietochowski and Stefan Buszczynski, and the early American authority on Russian affairs, George Kennan the elder. A host of political activists from the nationalist movement were included over the years including Giller, Count Wladyslaw Plater, Roman Dmowski, Zygmunt Milkowski, Karol Lewakowski, Zygmunt Balicki, Jakub Bojko, and Boleslaw Limanowski. Among the many PNA leaders who were granted honorary membership were Andrzejkowicz, Kucera, Blachowski, Beczkiewicz, Helinski, Lipinski, Gryglaszewski, Kociemski, and Valerie Lipczynska. The peak year for awards came in 1911 when twelve individuals were named.

It should be mentioned that the practice of granting honorary memberships was revived in 1928, when Jozef Pilsudski and Poland's President Ignacy Moscicki were so recognized. And in 1983, yet another hero of a new era was similarly honored when Solidarity leader Lech Walesa was named a member of the PNA at its thirty-ninth convention. Only two weeks afterward, Walesa was awarded a Nobel Prize and joined Sienkiewicz, Reymont, Maria Sklodowska-Curie and Czeslaw Milosz in this most select of groups.

33. The PNA actively supported the work of the "universytet ludowy" (or people's university), which offered night school educational opportunities to immigrants in Chicago and other Polonia centers before the First World War.

34. Olszewski, Vol. II, pp. 39ff.

35. See for example, the remarks of PNA President Steczynski to PWA leaders in *Dziennik Zwiazkowy,* November 18, 1911; also *Chicago Chronicle* article of 1905, summarized in *CF LPS.*

Chapter 4

1. Indeed in Article IV of its very first constitution, the founders of the Alliance had asserted that "the Polish National Alliance arose from the will of the Polish people in America; therefore in its name, the central administration, as its legal representative will act to help bring about Poland's independence by whatever peaceful means possible." Indeed, they went so far as to state that "the authority and obligations of the central administration will cease with the regaining of Poland's independence." Edward Rozanski, "PNA Took Leading Part in Call to Arms," *Zgoda,* January 15, 1968.

2. Besides the work of the Departments, the PNA in 1903 established a formal set of standing commissions under the direction of the four vice censors elected at the national convention. Thus, Walter Sawa became chairman of the School Commission, Joseph Tuchocki, Trade (and also responsible for helping PNA members find employment); Michael Blenski, Colonization, and Alexander Debski, Immigration. Most successful was Debski. Olszewski, Volume II, p. 14.

3. Olszewski, Volume III, pp. 5-10, 20-30, 97-113; Rev. Louis Zake, "The Development of the National Department *(Wydzial Narodowy)* as Representative of the Polish American Community in the United States, 1916-1923," Diss. University of Chicago, 1979, pp. 22 ff. William Galush, "Building Polonia," Diss. University of Minnesota, 1975.

4. Zake, p. 23; Galush, pp. 196-197.

5. Olszewski, vol. III, p. 80. The "left" faction in the PNA was not, of course, exclusively composed of socialists although a number of its best known representatives were active in the PPS, including Alexander Debski, Bronislas Kulakowski and J. S. Sienkiewicz. Others who supported the "left" were partisans of armed insurrection such as Siemiradzki, or critics of Dmowski's pro-Russian orientation.

6. Olszewski, III, pp. 51-85.

7. *Dziennik Zwiazkowy,* February 18, 1915; Zlotnicki.

8. Olszewski, III, pp. 90-94.

9. Wandycz, pp. 171 ff.; Wytrwal, p. 199.

10. Edward Kantowicz, *Polish-American Politics in Chicago, 1888-1940* (Chicago and London, 1975), pp. 29, 60-64, 111-112; *Dziennik Zwiazkowy,* September 20, 1980.

11. It was in Schenectedy that the PNA position on Poland was once again expressed by its leaders. President Zychlinski asserted, "We do not want a Poland without Galicia, a Poland without its kingdom, a Poland without Pomerania." Censor Rakoczy declared, "We do not believe the promises of the bloody Russian or the Prussian descendants of the Knights of the Cross, or of hypocritical Austria . . . It

would be a hundredfold better for us to fight longer for independence than to receive it from the hands of our sworn enemies."

12. *Dziennik Zwiazkowy,* November 14, 1914.

13. Zake, *passim,* Galush, pp. 195-216; Olszewski, III, pp. 130-260.

14. Kuniczak, p. 134.

15. Wandycz, *Poland and the United States,* pp. 104-130, provides a good presentation of the relationship between Paderewski and Wilson along with the United States' role in helping to bring about Poland's restoration.

16. Kantowicz, pp. 100-109; Donald Pienkos, "Politics, Religion and Change in Polish Milwaukee, 1900-1930," *Wisconsin Magazine of History,* 61 (Spring, 1978), 185-186.

17. Wandycz, pp. 110-113. For a controversial analysis of the election, one disputed by Wandycz, see Louis Gerson, *Woodrow Wilson and the Rebirth of Poland, 1914-1920* (New Haven, Connecticut, 1953).

18. The estimate on volunteers is found in *Dziennik Chicagoski,* December 12, 1921. See also Brozek, p. 144. Company K was formed in 1874 and was popularly known as the "Kosciuszko Guard." It was an early group belonging to the PNA. Its members took part in the Spanish-American War of 1898 and the Pershing expedition to Mexico to capture "Pancho" Villa in 1916. See also Wytrwal, *Behold!,* pp. 223-232.

19. Olszewski, III, p. 240. In Chicago alone, PNA members had purchased about $3 million in bonds as of June, 1918.

20. *Polish Heritage* magazine (Detroit), 34, number 1 (Spring, 1983), 5.

21. J. Orlowski, *Helena Paderewska w Pracy Narodowej i Spolecznej* (Helena Paderewska's involvement in patriotic and social work, Chicago, 1929).

22. Joseph Hapak, "The Polish Military Commission, 1917-1919," *Polish American Studies,* 38, number 2 (Autumn, 1981), 36.

23. Aside from the contingents from the United States, Canada and Western Europe the Polish Army also included prisoners of war who had been compelled to fight in German units.

24. Rozanski.

25. Brozek, p. 144. For detailed information about the Polish army in America see Arthur Waldo, *Sokolstwo,* Volume III; and Hapak, "The Polish Military Commission," 26-38.

26. Zake, pp. 136-216; William Galush, "American Poles and the New Poland: An Example of Change in Ethnic Orientation," *Ethnicity,* 1, number 3 (1974), 209-221.

27. Olszewski, III, pp. 242-243, 370. So great was the enthusiasm among PNA members for their organization's commitment to Poland that returning emigrants made a short-lived effort in 1919 to establish Alliance lodges in the ancestral homeland. Though their attempt failed because of bureaucratic complications, it illustrated the zeal of Alliance members who wanted to spread the gospel of the fraternal abroad. In fact, this was not the first attempt to make the alliance an "international movement;" at the turn of the century unsuccessful tries in Canada and Brazil had also been made to promote its patriotic and self-help ideology.

28. From Roman Dmowski's letter to John Smulski, October 20, 1920, in *Czyn Zbrojny Wychodztwa Polskiego w Ameryce* (New York, 1957), p. 793.

29. Olszewski, III, pp. 246-247.

Chapter 5

1. M. Szawleski, *Wychodztwo Polskie w Stanach Zjednoczonych Ameryki* (Lwow-Warsaw-Krakow, 1924). The 1920 U.S. Census identified 2,443,329 people who were either born in Poland or were the children of foreign born Poles living in America. This figure did not include the grandchildren of immigrants, the members of the "third generation" in this country.

2. Stefan Mierzwa, *The Story of the Kosciuszko Foundation* (New York, 1972), p. 82. Mierzwa organized the Foundation in 1925 and was President of the PNA college between 1929 and 1932.

Wandycz estimates that between 1919 and 1923 alone, private deliveries of money from American Poles to families in the homeland amounted to more than $250 million. Another commentator, Alexander Rytel, assesses the total Polish American contribution to Poland during the entire First World War era as coming to one half of one billion dollars. Cited in Waclaw Soroka, *Polish Immigration in the United States* (Stevens Point, Wisconsin, 1976), p. 157.

3. Galush, pp. 247-248.

4. Smith suffered a crushing defeat to Herbert Hoover and carried only two states outside the traditionally Democratic "solid south." This despite his winning a majority of the vote in each of the country's twelve largest cities and his success among Catholic ethnics such as the Poles. See William N. Chambers and Walter D. Burnham, editors, *The American Party Systems: Stages of Political Development* (New York, 1967), p. 160.

5. For a penetrating analysis of the forces behind restriction, see James Pula, "American Immigration Policy and the Dillingham Commission," *Polish American Studies*, 37, number 1 (Spring, 1980), 5-31.

Restriction remained in force until the passage of new immigration legislation in 1965 when a new system creating equality among all European nations was set up. In this arrangement, 20,000 persons from Eastern Europe were eligible each year to enter the U.S. After World War II, however, 151,978 persons born in Poland were admitted as refugees through the passage of a series of Displaced Persons Acts. These individuals entered the United States outside the quota system. Some of the credit for this legislation belongs to the Polish American Congress, which lobbied heavily for its approval.

6. Andrzej Brozek, "The National Consciousness of the Polish Ethnic Group in the United States, 1854–1939," *Acta Poloniae Historica*, 37 (1978), 107-110. A leading advocate within the PNA of this position after the War was Roman Abczynski, who had been a vice censor and later led the Polish Falcons' Alliance.

7. Miecislas Haiman, the foremost historian of pre World War II American Polonia, has described Swietlik's speech in Warsaw as nothing less than Polonia's

"declaration of independence from Poland" and its historic status as a kind of colony or reserve force in relationship to the homeland. Haiman, pp. 422-434.

8. It was not until 1935 that the PNA reached its historic peak in terms of lodges when 1,907 were recorded. By then, however, average lodge membership was down to one hundred and forty-nine.

9. K. Groniowski, "Polonia Amerykanska a Narodowa Demokracja, 1893-1914." *Kwartalnik Historyczny,* 45, 1 (1972). Among the best known old guard leaders were Julian Szajnert, one of the founders of the PNA, Judge Joseph Sawicki of Cleveland, a major figure in the post war Emigration Congresses, Censor Michael Blenski, PNA Treasurer Michael Turbak and Mary Sakowska, a long time member of the board of directors. For a particularly interesting statement of the old guard's perspective, see Szajnert's article in the PNA Almanac, *Kalendarz Zwiazkowy,* for 1927, pp. 163-165.

10. Brozek, "National Consciousness . . ."

11. *Ibid.*

12. In traditional English practice, the writ of *Quo Warranto* (Latin for "by what authority or warrant") was available to citizens who questioned the legality of a public official's use of his powers in office. In such situations, it was necessary for the defendant to show "by what authority" he governed. In modern British and American law, this writ gave way to an "information in the nature of a *Quo Warranto.*" This civil remedy was used to determine the title to a corporate or public office. In the PNA *Quo Warranto* suits of 1925, 1928, and 1936 the plaintiffs in each case questioned the legitimacy of actions taken by PNA officers which kept them in power or strengthened their hold on the organization. See Henry Campbell Black, *Black's Law Dictionary,* third edition (St. Paul, 1933), p. 1485.

13. In 1963, the veto power was limited by the convention; henceforth any such action by the censor could be overridden by a two-thirds majority of the board of directors. The censor's power to call extraordinary conventions was similarly restricted by an amendment requiring two-thirds approval by the supervisory council.

14. Yet even then motions were made to abolish the office of censor at both the 1895 and 1918 conventions. The latter move actually won a majority vote of the delegates but failed for lack of a two-thirds vote necessary to amend the constitution. In 1979 a similar effort to abolish the office also failed.

15. Jablonski saw himself primarily as a newspaper man and Rokosz was a union organizer and tavern owner.

16. In the voting, John Romaszkiewicz became president, Frank Synowiec and Magdalena Milewska vice presidents, Casimir Kowalski secretary, Max Hencel treasurer, F. S. Wietrzynski medical examiner, and Gregory Piwowarczyk, John Raczka, Frank Spychalski, Walter Krawczewski, Matt Majchrowicz, Michael Tomaszkiewicz, Joseph Spiker, Stefanie Dworak, Casimira Obarska, and Helen Prokesz directors. Censor Sypniewski and Vice Censor Walter Cytacki were reelected unanimously. Of the five dissident board members who had been suspended from office in 1925, four won major office at the convention with the fifth, Jachimowski, narrowly missing renomination in the primary election held for directors.

17. Initially elected President was Joseph P. Mallek, father of Leon Mallek and also an attorney. Leopold Koscinski, a former Vice Censor was elected Censor.

18. Chief among these counselors were former Censor Blenski and Judge Sawicki. They also spoke with Sypniewski after the walkout in an unsuccessful effort to mediate the dispute. Olszewski, volume IV, pp. 157-184.

19. The old guard leadership that emerged out of the La Salle Hotel convention thus included Garbarek, Vice President Mary Sakowska, Secretary John Zawilinski, Treasurer Michael Turbak and Directors Wladyslawa Chodzinska, Frances Siniarska, Frank Nowak, Val Kozuch, and Frank Glowa. The other offices remained vacant.

20. Olszewski, *ibid.; State of Illinois, County of Cook in Superior Court: re.: The People of the State of Illinois relation of Max Hencel v. F. P. Garbarek, et. al.,* number 465223 (1928).

21. A long-time activist, in 1915 he had organized the Alliance building and loan association at Chicago's Holy Trinity church.

22. Still, opposition dominance over the convention was such that fifteen of the candidates elected to national office at the 1927 Sherman Hotel convention were confirmed in their posts a year later.

23. Richard Strout, "The Great 1929 Crash," *Christian Science Monitor,* October 1-5, 1979.

24. For an interesting discussion of this issue as it affected American Polonia, see Stanislas Osada, *Jak sie ksztaltowala Polska dusza wychodztwo w Ameryce* [How the Polish Spirit shaped the Immigration in America] (Pittsburgh, 1930).

25. Sypniewski's ideas also included a proposal to create a variety of new insurance programs aimed at young people. He further argued that PNA members be permitted to borrow from their insurance policies to avoid having to "cash in" their certificates when in need of money. Another Sypniewski idea was to establish a system of PNA youth clubs throughout the country to attract more of the American-born into the Alliance. See also *Zloty Jubileusz ZNP* [The PNA's Golden Anniversary] (Pittsburgh, 1930).

Swietlik's position statement in *Zgoda* was coupled with a rejoinder by editor Zaklikiewicz, who unfavorably compared the Milwaukee leader's vague proposals with the detailed and ambitious program for the future presented by Sypniewski. Zaklikiewicz also added a touch of unintentional humor when he made light of Swietlik's call for a return to harmony inside the PNA. He declared that this young man needed to learn a few things about the history of the Alliance, which had been filled with perpetual conflict! *Zgoda,* July 2, 1931.

26. President, Vice President, Ladies' Vice President, Treasurer, Secretary, Censor, Vice Censor, ten Members of the Board of Directors, Medical Examiner. The last office was made appointive in 1963.

27. Stanislas Blejwas, "Old and New Polonias: Tensions within an Ethnic Community," *Polish American Studies,* 38, 2 (Autumn, 1981), 55-58.

28. *Ibid.,* 57.

29. The plaintiffs included former Treasurer Max Hencel, Commissioner Joseph Michalak, Director Jacob Twardzik, Atty. Joseph Waynne (Waynowski), Walter Kalisz, and Bonaventure Migala. Olszewski, Volume IV, pp. 464ff.

30. Indeed in that tranquil year, 1975, all five executive offices went uncontested, president, ladies' vice president, men's vice president, secretary and treasurer.

Chapter 6

1. Olszewski, IV, pp. 687 ff.; Helen Moll, "Wspomnienia z Historycznego Sejmu ZNP w roku 1939" (Reflections on the Historic PNA Convention of 1939), *Dziennik Zwiazkowy,* June 10-11, 1983.

2. Andrzej Brozek, "Polonia w Stanach Zjednoczonych wobec inicjatyw Pade-rewskiego oraz Sikorskiego w czasie I i II Wojnej Swiatowej" (American Polonia's Responses to Paderewski and Sikorski's efforts during the First and Second World Wars), *Przeglad Polonijny,* 7, 2 (1981), 41-67; Francis Swietlik, *Sprawozdanie z dzialalnosci Rady Polonii Amerykanskiej od Pazdziernika 1939 do Pazdziernika 1948 na Zjazd Rady Polonii Amerykanskiej odbyty dnia 4-go i 5-go Grudnia 1948 r.* (Report on the Activities of the Polish American Council from October, 1939 to October, 1948. Made at its national convention in Buffalo in December, 1948), (Chicago, 1948).

3. *Zgoda,* April 15, 1951.

4. Olszewski, Volume V, pp. 292-317.

5. However, Rozmarek was considerably embarrassed by the episode; he was still defending his actions on the matter in the 1960s. See *United States Reports,* volume 322, *Cases adjudged by the Supreme Court at the October, 1943 term from April 10, 1944 to June 12, 1944* (Washington, D.C. 1945), pp. 643-653. Polish National Alliance of the United States of North America versus National Labor Relations Board, number 226. Also *Federal Reporter* Second Series, *Cases Argued and Determined in the U.S. Court of Appeals for the District of Columbia, U.S. Circuit Courts of Appeals* (St. Paul, 1943). Seventh Circuit, pp. 175-182; volume 136, F 2d; Interviews with Walter Andrzejewski and Joseph Gajda, March 16, 18, 1983. Mr. Andrzejewski graciously sent the author a copy of the letter to Swietlik along with an affidavit from another PNA employee, Joseph Lopatowski, confirming the allegations made by the pro-union activists.

6. The story of the Katyn massacre is summarized below and presented in detail in J. K. Zawodny's book, *Death in the Forest* (Notre Dame, Indiana, 1962). The Soviet government has heatedly and consistently denied its involvement in the massacre and the Polish Communist regime has either followed the same line or remained silent on the question.

7. Richard Lukas, *The Strange Allies: The United States and Poland, 1941-1945* (Knoxville, Tenn., 1978), p. 116.

8. Charles Bohlen, *Witness to History, 1929-1969* (New York, 1973), pp. 144-152.

9. Olszewski, Volume V, pp. 305-307.

10. The Charter, announced by Roosevelt and Churchill in July 1941 and reaffirmed on January 1, 1942 set eight objectives in the Allied war effort against

the Axis powers. Among these were pledges to make no territorial changes without the consent of the peoples concerned; to respect the rights of all peoples to choose their own form of government without foreign interference; and to establish peace and security for all nations.

11. Lukas, pp. 126-127.

12. Averill Harriman and Elie Abel, *Special Envoy to Churchill and Stalin, 1941-1946* (New York, 1975), pp. 359-360; Peter Irons, "America's Cold War Crusade: Domestic Politics and Foreign Policy, 1942-1948," Diss. Boston University, 1972, pp. 293 ff.

13. For full discussions of this period see John Snell, ed., *The Meaning of Yalta* (Baton Rouge, Louisiana, 1956); Floyd Rodine, *Yalta-Responsibility and Response, January-March, 1945* (Lawrence Kansas, 1974); Stefan Korbonski, *Warsaw in Exile* (New York, 1966), volume three of the memoirs of a leading actor in wartime Polish affairs; Stanislaw Mikolajczyk, *The Rape of Poland* (New York, 1948).

14. However, the British leader objected strongly but unsuccessfully to compensating Poland for its territorial losses in the East with lands in the West taken from Germany. As he put it, too much German food would stuff the Polish goose. Had Churchill's view prevailed, the postwar Polish state would have been whittled down to less than half its pre 1939 size and reduced to the status of a Soviet province.

15. Charles Rozmarek, *Stany Zjednoczone, Polska i Polonia Amerykanska* [The United States, Poland and Polonia], Remarks at the meeting of the Executive Council of the Polish American Congress, October 11, 12, 1945). (Chicago, 1945). The PAC has ceaselessly attacked Yalta for nearly forty years. As for Katyn, it strenuously backed the forming of a select investigative committee of the U.S. House of Representatives, which in 1952 found the USSR guilty of the atrocity.

16. Irons; Richard Lukas, "The Polish American Congress and the Polish Question, 1944-1947," *Polish American Studies*, 38, number 2 (Autumn, 1981).

17. From the *Minutes of the 1947 PNA Convention*, pp. 44ff. Rozmarek dominated the conclave but three young activists won seats on the board of directors in opposition to his slate—Stefanie Gondek, George Wrost and Aloysius Mazewski. All played notable roles in the years which followed. In 1955, 1959 and 1963 Gondek campaigned unsuccessfully against Dymek for ladies' vice president. Wrost and Mazewski both lost reelection bids in 1955, but Mazewski went on to overturn Rozmarek himself in 1967.

18. Donald Pienkos, "The Polish American Congress—An Appraisal," *Polish American Studies*, 36.

19. George Janczewski, "The Significance of the Polish Vote in the American National Election Campaign of 1948, *The Polish Review*, Volume 13, Number 4, (Autumn, 1968) 101-109.

20. One 1954 PAC report noted that in its first decade, the Congress had spent $1.2 million, largely on relief activities.

21. Even after the United States government had rejected the idea of liberation, its leaders continued to assure Rozmarek of their commitment to the eventual overthrow of the "temporary nightmare" of communism in Eastern Europe. For example, in 1960, President Eisenhower told the delegates of the PAC convention

446

that liberation, though not fulfilled, remained a hope. Bennett Kovrig, *The Myth of Liberation: East Central Europe in U.S. Diplomacy and Politics since 1941* (Baltimore, 1973), p. 273. See also Stephen Garrett, "The Ties that Bind: Immigrant Influence on U.S. Policy toward Eastern Europe," in A. A. Said, ed., *Ethnicity and U.S. Foreign Policy* (New York, 1977), pp. 59-82.

22. Stephen Kaplan, "U.S. Aid to Poland, 1957-1964; Concerns, Objectives and Obstacles," *Western Political Quarterly*, Volume 28, Number 1 (March, 1975), 147-166. The best analysis of the actual character of Gomulka's political outlook is that of Z. K. Brzezinski, *The Soviet Bloc: Unity and Conflict* (New York, 1960), pp. 58-64, 262-265.

23. For the text of Eisenhower's remarks, see *Public Papers of the Presidents, 1960-1961* (Washington, D.C., 1961), pp. 737-741.

24. Pienkos, "The Polish American Congress," 12.

25. *The Polish National Alliance in the Press of America: A Partial Collection of Clippings from Leading U.S. Newspapers, Covering the Period from 1955 to 1958* (Chicago, 1959). For a review of PAC activities during the Rozmarek era offered by a major supporter, see Rev. Valerian Karcz, "The Polish American Congress, 1944-1959," *Polish American Studies*, 16, numbers 3-4 (1959), 89-94.

26. Aside from Rozmarek's support for the creation of the New York-based Polish Institute of Arts and Sciences in America and the Polish American Historical Association, centered in the Midwest, his chief activities in preserving Polish ethnic cultural awareness was in lending PAC and PNA support for observances of a commemorative nature. For example, in 1958 the PAC sponsored a major observance memorializing the landing of the first Poles in America at the Jamestown, Virginia colony in 1608. This event was itself recalled in a special book entitled *Jamestown: Pioneers from Poland* (Chicago, 1958, 1976).

27. Hon. Thaddeus Machrowicz, "Remarks in the U.S. House of Representatives," *Congressional Record,* July 27, 1955.

28. The dissidents, though unable to publicize their views in the PNA newspapers, were nonetheless able to propagandize their appeals in other Polonia dailies, most notably the *Dziennik Chicagoski,* which covered the conflict in exhaustive fashion.

29. *Zgoda,* June 15, 1958; December 1, 1958; June 15, 1959; October 1, 1959; December 15, 1960; and the special issues of the paper dated November 8, 1958 and December 8, 1958.

30. *Urzedowy Protokol Sejmu XXXV-go ZNP* (Chicago, 1967), pp. 93-115.

Chapter 7

1. Mazewski also succeeded Rozmarek as president of the Polish American Congress in 1968.

2. Yet another contribution was the extensive televising of Pope John Paul II's 1979 visit to Poland in Chicago under PNA, PRCUA and Polish Women's Alliance sponsorship.

3. There were several leaders in responsible positions who were deeply concerned about the problem. For example, Censor Blair Gunther called attention to the matter

when he issued his formal message to the PNA membership convoking its 1959 convention. *Zgoda,* June 15, 1959.

4. Milton M. Gordon, *Human Nature, Class and Ethnicity* (New York, 1978), pp. 202-208.

5. For example, Michael Novak, *The Rise of the Unmeltable Ethnics* (New York, 1971).

6. The membership question, though complex, ought not to be a cause of misunderstanding. For one thing, the overall number of people belonging to the Polish National Alliance in the early 1980s was roughly the same as it had been in 1930, when it was fifty years old. In contrast, most other American fraternals (and practically every ethnically-based fraternal) has experienced far more severe declines in membership during the same period than the PNA.

Furthermore, the PNA experienced impressive growth during the years in terms of its net financial worth, the sum of all its assets which were invested to generate dividends for policy owners. In 1983, for example, the net worth of the PNA amounted to $176 million, nearly eight times what had been the case in 1931. A total of $434 million in insurance was in force for PNA members in 1983, compared with $126 million in 1931. For detailed information on this subject, see the Appendix of this work.

7. One way to look at the picture of lodge growth is that of marking the year in which certain "benchmark" lodges came into existence. This term simply refers to those lodges whose number is connected with the month and year in which it formally came into being. One means of selecting such benchmark lodges would be to identify the year in which every 250th PNA lodge was created.

Year of Admission of Benchmark Lodges into the PNA

Number of Lodge	Name of Lodge	Location	Year of Admission
Lodge 250	Kosciuszko Society	Palisades Park, New Jersey	1894
Lodge 500	Progress Society	Pullman, Illinois	1900
Lodge 750	Polish Falcons' Gymnastics Society	Glassport, Pennsylvania	1906
Lodge 1001	Fraternal Aid Society of our Lady of Czestochowa	Anthony, Rhode Island	1908
Lodge 1250	Tatra Society under the Protection of Saint Florian	Chicago, Illinois	1910
Lodge 1501	Sobieski Society	Barton, Ohio	1912
Lodge 1750	Freedom Society	Hamilton, Ohio	1914
Lodge 2002	United Poland Society	Chicago, Illinois	1917
Lodge 2250	Star of Youth Society	Jersey City, New Jersey	1923
Lodge 250	Women of the Rainbow Ladies' Society	Chicago, Illinois	1928
Lodge 2750	Polish Sharpshooters Society	Chicago, Illinois	1934
Lodge 3000	Pilsudski Society	Iron River, Missouri	1942
Lodge 3230	Space Coast Society	Titusville, Florida	1977

8. More than four hundred lodges fit into this category. Worse still, as Mazewski correctly pointed out, the failure of these units to satisfactorily handle routine insurance business such as the collection of premiums and the processing of claims for the members they retained damaged the reputation of the entire fraternal. See also President Mazewski's statement prior to the thirty-ninth PNA convention, *Zgoda*, August 1, 1983. One way of dealing with the problems posed by the inactive lodges lately has been to merge them with vital local units. Between 1979 and 1983, for example, eighty-two lodges met this fate along with ten councils. PNA lodge activities are summed up in the annual publication, *Statistics of Fraternal Benefit Societies* which appears under the auspices of the National Fraternal Congress of America.

9. Interestingly, the proceedings of the national conventions continue to be conducted in Polish.

10. Ann Mikoll, "Leadership: Fraternal and Cultural," in Alfred Bochenek, editor, *American Polonia: The Cultural Issues* (Detroit, 1981), p. 45.

11. These men and women were Julia Beben, Henry Kotarba, Stanley Gruszka, Joseph Zdunczyk, Kazimiera Lopatniuk, John Zubriski, Magdalena Dziedzic-Versusky, Frank Dudek, August Gorski, Genia Gunther, Sophie Litwa, Julian Matkowski, Stanley Nicgorski, Michael Pierzga, Joseph Czepiel, John Radzyminski, Theodore Chojnacki, Joseph Grajewski, Stanley Jaskowski, Raymond Okorowski, Tymoteusz Sujka, Thomas Wyszynski, Stella Lemanek, William Kozerski, Walter Noga, Jr., Richard Szlenkier, Richard Smoger, Elizabeth Gancarz, Aurelia Frenzel, Joseph Gajda, Edward Kempa, Josephine May, Thaddeus Radosz, John Ramza, Florence Wiatrowska, Stanley Stawiarski, Bogdan Parafinczuk, John Dlugosz, Ben Macalka, Joseph Mytyk, Alexander Wachel, Frances Syrk, and Frank Mazurek. From A. A. Mazewski, *Highlights of the President's Report to the 39th Convention* (Orlando, Florida, 1983).

A list of the top sales representatives for 1981 in terms of the amount of insurance sold is to be found in Appendix B, Table 7.

12. The maximum limit on home loans was later raised to $100,000.

13. *Zgoda*, February 1, 1983.

14. Indeed, between 1975–1980, the Alliance sold nearly twice as much insurance as all other Polish American fraternals together. *Fraternal Monitor*, 1981. For additional membership data see A. A. Mazewski, *Highlights of the President's Report*.

15. First held in 1891 to commemorate the centennial anniversary of the promulgation of the historic constitution, the parade became an annual manifestation of patriotism in 1904 and often attracted more than 150,000 participants. A colorful spectacle in which thousands of people dressed in traditional folk costumes or military uniforms marched or sat aboard carriages or floats proclaiming some patriotic or ethnic value, the parade culminated at the foot of the Kosciuszko monument. There the leading political figures of the day extolled Poland's historic greatness and its people's aspirations for independence, after which all present took part in a day long picnic. Among those who spoke at the Third of May observance were Ignacy Paderewski, General Jozef Haller, General Tadeusz Bor-Komorowski (leader of the tragic Warsaw Uprising of August, 1944), Stanislaw Mikolajczyk, General Wladyslaw

Anders, and Bogdan Kozuchowski (a pilot who flew his plane to freedom from Stalinist Poland). Through the years, numerous Polish American political leaders also addressed the gatherings, including U.S. Postmaster General John Gronouski (1964), Senator Edmund Muskie (1971), Congressman Roman Pucinski (1972), Congressman Daniel Rostenkowski (1979), Assistant Secretary of Commerce Jerry Jasinowski (1980), and Alaska Senator Robert Murkowski (1981). Vice President Albin Barkley spoke at the occasion in 1949 as was also true for Vice President Richard Nixon in 1960 and Vice President Lyndon Johnson in 1963. Hubert Humphrey addressed Third of May crowds on three separate occasions, once in 1959 as a United States Senator from Minnesota and twice (in 1965 and 1968) as Vice President.

In 1961 United States Attorney General Robert Kennedy enjoyed the honor and in 1978 Mrs. Rosalyn Carter represented her husband the President and became the first woman to deliver the main address at the historic ceremony. Other dignitaries who have spoken at the Third of May gathering have been United Nations Ambassador Arthur Goldberg, Senators Birch Bayhe of Indiana, Adlai Stevenson III and Charles Percy of Illinois, Directors of the United States Information Agency Edward R. Murrow and Charles Wick, and Astronaut Eugene Cernan. Needless to add, perhaps, a host of Illinois and Chicago area politicians and office seekers have traditionally been present at the event over the years, including the Governor of the state of Illinois and the Mayor of the city of Chicago.

16. The 1983 convention in fact witnessed the election of an unusually large number of new people in all areas of national PNA leadership. Mazewski himself was reelected to a fifth term as President as was Treasurer Edward Moskal; Vice President Helen Szymanowicz was also elected to a fourth term. But due to the decisions of Secretary Kubiak and Vice President Gajda not to seek reelection, the convention chose two new people to take their places in the key five member PNA executive committee. Elected Vice President was Anthony Piwowarczyk, who previously had served as Director of Fraternal Activities in the Chicago Home Office. Emil Kolasa, the newly elected National Secretary, had just completed two terms of service on the board of directors.

Due to an amendment to the PNA constitution approved in 1975, all directors and commissioners were limited to serving two consecutive terms in office. This change significantly affected elections to both bodies and eight of the ten members of the board of directors along with twenty-four of thirty-two commissioners were newly elected to these posts. And, while Censor Czaplicki was reelected without opposition, Vice Censor Leopold Ciaston did not seek another term and was replaced by Edward Sitnik.

In sum, while thirty-two of forty-nine national PNA officers elected at the fraternal's 1979 convention had held the exact same posts after the 1975 conclave, twenty-nine persons elected in 1983 had held no national posts in 1979. And six others made major changes in going from one office to another. The 1983 convention thus represented the largest turnover in national leadership since 1967.

Chapter 8

1. Earlier in 1881, Artwinski had tried unsuccessfully to make the New York paper, *Ogniwo,* the PNA's newspaper. Edward Rozanski, "Two Solutions—A Century Ago and Now," *Zgoda* Centennial Album (Chicago, 1981), p. 10.

2. A single copy at first cost six cents and a yearly subscription two dollars.

3. *Zgoda,* January 1, 1981; Henry Archacki, "So *Zgoda* Went West," *Zgoda* centennial album, pp. 15-16. Unfortunately readership remained low and even worse, only 512 of the paper's 1,140 subscribers were reported to have actually paid for the publication in April, 1882. One factor accounting for the paper's problems was Rev. Barzynski's sharp attacks on the PNA but another was connected with the failure of New York area Poles to rally around the new enterprise. Still, opposition to the transfer to Chicago was strong and the motion to move the paper's editorial office west prevailed by a single vote.

4. The results of the vote by lodges are interesting and show the strength of the Chicago-based PNA leadership and its allies in Minnesota. In comparison, support for Milwaukee was scattered throughout the midwestern lodges of the Alliance and disinterest in the entire matter was greatest among the eastern lodges which had already lost out.

Location of PNA Lodges	For Chicago	For Milwaukee	Other Choice, Not Voting
Illinois	16	4	3
Minnesota	6	1	0
Missouri	1	0	0
California	1	0	0
Michigan	4	2	2
Wisconsin	1	5	3
Indiana	0	1	0
Ohio	1	1	2
New York	0	2	9
New Jersey	0	1	0
Pennsylvania	1	3	3
Maryland	0	0	1
Not Known	5	4	10
Totals	36	24	33

Source: *Zgoda,* October 5, 1887.

5. Brodowski was elected president of the Alliance in 1895 but resigned twenty months later to accept an appointment from the U.S. State Department as Consul General in the city of Breslau, Germany (now Wroclaw, Poland). Due to his activities on behalf of Polish independence, the German authorities refused to approve his appointment to a city so near its Polish provincial territories in Silesia. Eventually, Brodowski was reassigned to the less politically sensitive Rhineland region.

6. PNA National Secretary M. J. Sadowski was the first to raise the matter publicly in a proposal he presented at the 1895 PNA convention.

7. Osada, pp. 471-472, 492.

8. Olszewski, II, pp. 35, 68-73.

9. The leader of the opposition forces was Michael Kruszka (1860–1918), a PNA member and editor-publisher of the Milwaukee *Kuryer Polski* and later, the *Dziennik Narodowy*. Throughout his newspaper career, Kruszka was a provocative and nettlesome force both in Milwaukee and in national Polonia affairs. In the early 1890s he fought the PNA leadership on the issue of the *Skarb Narodowy*, demanding that the fund be kept in a Milwaukee bank and that only the interest earned on contributions be sent to the Polish patriotic movement centered in Switzerland. In Milwaukee in the mid 1890s he led the fight to have the Polish language taught in the public schools, a successful battle which nevertheless earned him the enmity of local pastors who were convinced that his goal was really one of encouraging parents to take their children out of the parochial schools. One of the earliest successful politicians in Polonia (he was a Wisconsin State Senator from 1892 to 1896), Kruszka's fierce nationalism brought him into conflict with Church authorities in Milwaukee after 1900 when he joined with his half-brother, the Reverend Wenceslaus Kruszka (1868–1937), in demanding the appointment of a Polish bishop to serve the needs of the growing Catholic Polonia. Because of the incendiary nature of his paper's editorializing on the issue, the Milwaukee archbishop issued an edict in 1912 forbidding anyone to read a Kruszka paper under pain of excommunication. Kruszka sued the bishop in the state supreme court, but failed to show that the churchman's action was an unconstitutional abridgment of freedom of speech and press. Needless to add, all of Michael Kruszka's efforts, including his fight against the PNA daily, had a stimulative effect upon his papers' circulation and advertising revenues. See Donald Pienkos, "Politics, Religion and Change in Polish Milwaukee, 1900–1930," *Wisconsin Magazine of History,* 61 (1978), 178-209.

Despite his anger over what he derided as a parliamentary "trick," Kruszka otherwise took his convention defeat in stride. This was mainly due to the prudence of the partisans of a PNA daily, who decided that the paper would have to base its operations solely upon the surplus in the budget of *Zgoda.* With more generous PNA support out of the question, Kruszka concluded that the new paper's life-span would be short and pose no threat to his business interests. *Kuryer Polski* (Milwaukee), October 1, 1907.

10. Joseph Wiewiora, "*Dziennik Zwiazkowy* Born Amid Stress and Strife," *Zgoda,* January 15, February 1, 1983. For an interesting account of the origins of the *Dziennik Zwiazkowy* see Arthur Waldo, "Pierwsze Walne Zwyciestwo 'Dziennika,' (The Daily *Zgoda's* First Great Triumph), *Dziennik Zwiazkowy,* June 10-11, 1983.

A touching tribute to Jablonski occurred at the 75th anniversary banquet commemorating the founding of *Dziennik Zwiazkowy* on June 10, 1983. At the ceremonies, Jablonski's daughter, Ludmilla Jablonska Cummings, appeared and was awarded a special medal in honor of her father's many contributions to the PNA and Polonia.

11. Another decision made in Baltimore was in the form of a resolution creating the post of editor of the women's edition of *Zgoda*, a paper which had been established in 1900 at the time of admission of women as equals in the PNA. The first editor of the women's *Zgoda* was Casimira Walukiewicz. The women's *Zgoda*, whose creation along with that of the *Zwiazkowy* made the PNA suddenly the publisher of three separate newspapers, continued in operation until 1935 when a women's section was added to both the weekly *Zgoda* and the daily *Zwiazkowy*, and the women's weekly discontinued.

In 1976, *Zgoda's* women's page was dropped in favor of a column on Polish-style cooking. Through most of its existence, the women's edition of *Zgoda* was distinctive in many respects from the general edition of the PNA organ, although major news stories affecting the entire membership and editorials with universal importance were carried in both papers. The women's *Zgoda* featured stories on successful women in America and Poland and gave emphasis to contemporary romantic novels which it serialized for its readers. At the same time, the paper widely publicized the activities of the women's suffrage movement and applauded this early expression of feminism in its pages. One especially prominent British suffragette, Emmeline Pankhurst was the subject of enormous attention prior to 1920 as was the fight for improved working conditions for women.

Editors of the women's *Zgoda* after Walukiewicz included Mary Iwanowska, Iza Pobog, Jadwiga Michalska, Wladyslawa Tyrakowska, Helen Setmajer, Mary Weldowa, Anna Wyczolkowska, Janina Dunin, Jadwiga Krassowska-Stopowa, Agnes Wojcik, Anna Skibinska, and Helen Moll.

Women were not the only "special interest group" addressed by the PNA. For years, *Zgoda* carried regular columns directed at members involved in the Falcons' movement, the Singers' Alliance and various para-military formations, all of which shared many of the same aims as the PNA.

12. Siemiradzki's intellectualism was also evident when he persuaded the 1909 PNA convention in Milwaukee to transform *Zgoda* from a weekly paper providing news and features focusing upon fraternal activities as well as Polonia matters into a monthly forty-eight page magazine of literary and political ideas. The restyled *Zgoda* first appeared on August 15, 1910 in two editions, one for men, the other for women, but the experiment to make the publication into a kind of early *Commonweal* or *Commentary* was short-lived. After eight issues *Zgoda* reverted to its standard weekly format, its demise attributed to its high cost and a lack of receptivity from its readership. Nevertheless, even a brief look at the yellowed pages of Siemiradzki's experiment provides ample evidence about his ambitions for the redesigned publication, which is filled with articles focusing upon Polish history and then-current patriotic issues, plus pieces written by or about a number of prominent literary figures of the era.

13. The Dangel dispute is covered by Olszewski, Volume III, pp. 89-90. One

consequence of the 1915 convention action was that the editorship of *Zgoda* ceased to be a political springboard within the PNA. For background information on Dangel's career, see issues of the Milwaukee *Kuryer Polski* for September 18-24, 1907 and Laurence Orzell, "Franciszek Hodur and His Followers," in Renkiewicz, ed., *The Polish Presence in Canada and America,* pp. 118-128.

14. In an advertisement that appeared during the twenty-fifth anniversary year of the founding of the *Dziennik Zwiazkowy,* Piatkiewicz stressed that "only in a Polish newspaper may be found vital news of Polish life . . . news about their own life—social and commercial." Significantly, the ad was in English; a story about the Daily *Zgoda's* rival, the *Dziennik Chicagoski* (which already lagged behind in circulation) appeared in the Polish language. Anthony Tomczak, compiler, *Poles in Chicago: Their Contribution to a Century of Progress* (Chicago, 1933), pp. 163, 259.

15. *Zgoda,* July 15, 1981.

16. Prior to 1935, a large number of individuals served as business manager of the Alliance publications, beginning with Joseph Olbinski who held the post from the early 1880s until 1908. Succeeding him were Michael Rzeszotarski (1908), Stanislas Dangel (1908–1910), Constantine Wiechecki (1910–1917), Stanley Grzybowski (1917–1918), Stanislas Orpiszewski (1918 and simultaneously editor of both PNA papers), Anthony Chonarzewski (1918–1923), Basil Paszkowski (1923–1929), J. S. Sienkiewicz (1929–1931), Bronislas Czuwara (1931–1933), Czeslawa Mlotkowska (1933–1934, the one woman to hold the job), and Max Hencel (1934–1935, a past PNA Treasurer). In 1971, Karol Synowiec was temporarily business manager following Kolasa's resignation. See Paul Migacz, "Zarzadcy Wydawnictw Zwiazkowych" (Business Managers of the PNA Press), *Dziennik Zwiazkowy,* June 10-11, 1983. See also *Zgoda,* November 1, 1981.

In 1983 Kolasa succeeded Lottie Kubiak as National Secretary after Kubiak declined to seek reelection. Rozanski and Dziewulski served as acting co-editors of *Zgoda* in addition to their other responsibilities after April, 1982, due to Joseph Wiewiora's lengthy illness.

17. Marian Baruch, "Leadership: Fraternal and Cultural," in Alfred Bochenek, editor, *American Polonia: The Cultural Issues* (Detroit, 1981), pp. 48-49. Baruch's talk was one of eleven presentations delivered in two public conferences held in Buffalo and Chicago under the sponsorship of the American Council of Polish Cultural Clubs. The purpose of these gatherings, which took place in May and June, 1980, was to discuss the problems facing Polonia and the ethnic community's future in American society.

18. *Zgoda,* December 1, 1980; Hilary Czaplicki, "*Zgoda's* Founding Signalled Solidarity of Poles in U.S.," *Zgoda,* October 1, 1981.

19. For this study, both *Zgoda* and *Dziennik Zwiazkowy* were read extensively to provide a greater understanding of the PNA experience over the years. *Zgoda* was systematically consulted for every convention and nearly every pre-convention proclamation by the PNA's censor was also reviewed. *Zgoda* was also covered for the following specific periods, 1886–1887, 1889, 1910–1913, 1925–1931, 1958–1960, 1965–1968, and from 1974 to the present.

The women's edition of *Zgoda* was reviewed from 1906 to 1910, a time when, unfortunately general editions of the paper could not be located. The literary-political monthly *Zgoda,* published between 1910 and 1911, was read thoroughly.

The *Dziennik Zwiazkowy* was given close examination at a number of controversial conventions after 1908 and for the following periods, November-December, 1927, September-October, 1928, October-December, 1932, and for the years 1931, 1934, 1944, 1958 and 1967. Numerous selected editions of the paper were read for the years 1979–1983, when many articles appeared in connection with the PNA centennial.

English language translations of selected articles appearing in *Zgoda* and *Dziennik Zwiazkowy* were part of the Chicago Public Library Omnibus Project, sponsored in 1942 by the Federal Works Projects Administration. Selections from *Zgoda* were for the years 1887–1894, 1897–1903, and 1931. Pieces from *Zwiazkowy* were from the years 1908–1918.

Chapter 9

1. In 1903, for example, eleven of the top seventeen elected national PNA officers were also members of the Falcons including its President, Steczynski, Secretary Helinski, Censor Sadowski, Vice Censor Debski and *Zgoda* Editor Siemiradzki. Waldo, *Sokolstwo,* II, p. 399.

2. Falcons' historian Arthur Waldo has concluded that several issues were responsible for the separation of the two movements. One involved the fear of some Falcons' leaders that they would lose their identity through a close association with the larger PNA. Indeed, in 1909 the Falcons included 4,700 members to about 58,000 who belonged to the PNA.

Another difference was ideological; the Falcons were simply more militant than the PNA in their approach to Polish independence. Indeed, some saw their gymnastics exercises as a kind of paramilitary training for a future Polish army whose goal was nothing less than to liberate Poland.

In 1910 at the Polish National Congress in Washington, D.C. this question had come to a head during debate over a resolution which asserted that "We Poles have the right to our own independent national existence and we consider it our duty to support the achievement of political independence for our homeland." Some PNA delegates, including John Wleklinski, President of the pro-PNA Falcons faction, objected to the resolution on the grounds that it was unnecessarily provocative and would lead to repression of the patriotic forces in the homeland. The resolution passed and when Wleklinski returned to Chicago, he was immediately removed from office and expelled from the Falcons' organization! Waldo, *Sokolstwo,* Vol. III, pp. 259-264.

3. Roman Korban, *Sport wsrod Polonii Amerykanskiej* [Sports in American Polonia] (Warsaw, 1980), p. 97.

4. *Ibid.*

5. Several Polish athletes also achieved a measure of fame in the olympic sports. Stella Walsh (Walasiewicz) was a member of the U.S. track squad in 1932 games

held in Los Angeles. Stanislaw Pietkiewicz was another athlete who exemplified Poland's rise in sports when he won a two mile race in Boston before a crowd of 12,000 in 1930.
   6. Korban.
   7. *Ibid.*
   8. In *Dzien Zwiazkowy; Pierwszy Zlot Harcerstwa* [Alliance Day—First *Harcerstwo* Jamboree], July 22, 1934, Chicago.
   9. Korban, p. 105.
   10. The exact number of participants in the national bowling tournaments since 1957 is as follows: 280 (in 1957); 407 (1958), 598 (1959), 513 (1960), 628 (1961), 674 (1962), 966 (1963), 846 (1964), 1,014 (1965), 1,052 (1966), 1,208 (1967), 1,300 (1968), 1,400 (1969), 1,000 (1970), 1,100 (1971), 1,105 (1972), 900 (1973), 1,070 (1974), 1,243 (1975), 1,172 (1976), 1,120 (1977), 1,264 (1978), 864 (1979), 1,053 (1980), 1,164 (1981), 1,230 (1982). The following cities have hosted the tourneys: Buffalo; Cleveland; Detroit; Addison, Illinois (near Chicago); Milwaukee; South Bend, Indiana; Jackson, Michigan; Sharon, Pennsylvania; Erie, Pennsylvania; Muskegon, Michigan; Youngstown, Ohio; Allen Park, Michigan; Schenectedy, New York; and Toledo, Ohio.

Chapter 10

   1. *1979 Statistics of Fraternal Benefit Societies* (Chicago, 1980), pp. 146, 151.
   2. Arthur Waldo, *Teofila Samolinska, Matka Zwiazku Narodowego Polskiego w Ameryce* (Chicago, 1980).
   3. Helena Znaniecka Lopata, "Polish American Families," paper presented at a symposium on American Polonia held at the Jagiellonian University, Krakow, July, 1979.
   4. Osada, p. 206; Barszczewski, p. 22.
   5. J. Karlowiczowa, *Historia Zwiazku Polek w Ameryce* [History of the Polish Women's Alliance in America] (Chicago, 1938), p. 29. See also Thaddeus Radzialowski, "Immigrant Nationalism and Feminism: *Glos Polek* and the Polish Women's Alliance in America, 1898–1917," *Review Journal of Philosophy and Social Science,* II, 2(1978), 183–197. A Polish women's society had already been born in meetings held in Chicago between April and August, 1898. However, the impetus behind *Zwiazek Polek* was clearly the PNA's initial decision not to admit women into its ranks at its 1899 *sejm.*
   6. Olszewski, IV, pp. 95 ff. *Dziennik Zwiazkowy,* July 28, 1911.
   7. Radzialowski, *ibid.,* particularly the remarks of PNA leader Magdalena Milewska. In 1900, another important step forward was made by women when the idea of a women's edition of *Zgoda* was approved. This weekly publication was directed by female PNA activists for many years. Their names are to be found in chapter 8, footnote 11.
   8. *Dziennik Zwiazkowy,* January 15, 1915; February 12, 15, 1917.
   9. Helen Moll, "Fifty Years of Humanitarian Efforts by the PNA Benevolent

Society," an unpublished manuscript provided to the author by Vice President Helen Szymanowicz and written in 1978. See also Helen Moll, "Eighty Years of Women's Equality in the PNA," *Dziennik Zwiazkowy,* September 20, 1980, page 1, part two. Moll was the editor of the Women's page of the PNA publications for many years and an active member of the Polish National Alliance.

10. William Leiserson, *Adjusting Immigrant and Industry* (New York, 1924), p. 128.

11. *Ibid.*

12. S. P. Breckinridge, *New Homes For Old* (New York), 1921, pp. 92-96.

13. Breckinridge, *ibid.,* p. 96; William I. Thomas, *Old World Traits Transplanted* (Chicago, 1921), p. 125.

14. *Sejm XVIII ZNP* (1909), pp. 64-65.

15. Breckinridge, p. 95.

16. Olszewski, III; Grodska, p. 201; *Dziennik Zwiazkowy,* March 2, 1918; also Miecislas Haiman, "The Polish American Contribution to World War II," *Polish American Studies,* 3, Numbers 1-2 (1946), 35-37.

17. Osada, p. 462; See also A. Brozek and D. Piatkowska, "Prasa Slaska o masakrze robotnikow w Lattimer Pennsylvania, 1897" [The Silesian Press on the Lattimer Massacre of 1897], *Zaranie Slaska,* volume 5, number 2 (1978). See also *Zgoda,* February 1, 14, 1898; *Narod Polski,* February 9, 1898. Unfortunately, Michael Novak's otherwise excellent semi-fictional account of the massacre omits mention of the PNA role. Novak, *The Guns of Lattimer* (New York, 1978).

18. *Dziennik Zwiazkowy,* January 3, 1909.

19. *Zgoda,* December 26, 1894; *Dziennik Zwiazkowy,* November 3, 4, 1910; July 10, 1912.

20. In all, the PNA provided 506 of its members living in the Johnstown area with relief from making premium payments on their insurance for a full year after the flood. This benefit amounted to $16,215.

Chapter 11

1. Olszewski, Volume IV, pp. 136 ff.

2. Piatkiewicz, p. 187.

3. Under Dymek, *Wydzial* activities diminished in an across the board fashion. For example, between 1947–1955, $11,284 was spent annually, compared to $15,164 between 1943–1947.

From its earliest years the PNA had determined its expenditures in administering its business operations along with its various cultural and membership assistance activities in a rather novel fashion. It required that every member be assessed a total of twenty-one cents per month (in addition to the cost of his regular insurance premium) to cover the fraternal's financial obligations in running its Chicago office, operating its newspaper, and directing the work of its Educational, Youth and Sports, and Membership relief departments.

At each convention, the delegates voted how they would slice up the twenty-one cent pie and their judgment served to define the limits of spending for each PNA agency during the period up to the next convention.

This method of budgeting had several shortcomings, one of which might be mentioned here. Since Departments possessed no definite idea of what they could spend (their resources being determined by the recruitment and collection activities of the local lodges), they had little incentive to engage in ambitious projects to expand their activities. Such activities might lead to overspending and sharp criticisms at the next convention.

In 1951, the PNA departed from what had proven to be an antiquated method for alloting its funds and adopted a four year budget for all its major departments.

4. During the 1970s students at Alliance College taking courses in Polish language, history and culture saw the amount of this incentive scholarship doubled to $200. And, thanks to a bequest left in the estate of Stanley Janas, Alliance College students demonstrating financial need could apply for another set of grants of $500 per year. This program has been supplemented by the PNA since its inception in 1970. In all, students proving financial need and enriching their educational program at the College receive a reduction in their annual tuition amounting to $1,200 thanks to the PNA.

5. The first mention of a PNA sponsored library committee is to be found in the minutes of the March, 1880 meeting of its founding lodge in Philadelphia.

6. Olszewski, Volume IV, pp. 268-269; *Dziennik Zwiazkowy,* December 3, 1908. The Library and Museum committee remained a distinct entity until after World War II when its functions were merged with those of the *Wydzial Oswiaty.*

7. From the original mission statement of the Alliance School, cited in the *Alliance* (college) *Report,* December 1981, p. 2.

8. The announcement of the school's creation was nothing less than ecstatic. A front page editorial of the *Dziennik Zwiazkowy* began, "Rejoice, for the dream of the founders and pioneers of the Alliance has become a reality." The editorial went on to emphasize that the school would be open to all young men and that it would promote Polish national feeling while providing sound religious training as well. In closing, the editorial sounded an optimistic note in emphasizing that an organization 80,000 strong as the PNA would have little difficulty maintaining the school. *Dziennik Zwiazkowy,* "A Great Step Forward," December 11, 1911.

9. His biographer argues, however, that Taft had given up any serious hopes of re-election as early as July, 1912 when Roosevelt had decided to run as a third party "Progressive Republican" candidate. If this is so, it is even better testimony to the president's regard for the work of the Polish National Alliance. See Herbert Taft, *William Howard Taft* (New York, 1930), pp. 298-300. See also Olszewski, vol. II, pp. 246-370.

Taft's visit to the Alliance school dedication marked the first appearance of a President at a PNA event. On September 20, 1980 President Jimmy Carter became the second American chief of state to honor the Alliance in such fashion when he travelled to Chicago to speak to more than 3,000 PNA activists at the centennial banquet of the fraternal. And on June 23, 1983, President Ronald Reagan visited the PNA Home Office and spoke briefly to a large gathering. All three speeches can be found in their entirety in the appendix of this work.

PNA leaders have frequently met other American presidents as representatives of patriotic federations such as the Polish American Congress. On two notable occasions they have been welcomed as fraternal leaders to the White House in connection with PNA conventions held in Baltimore and Washington. In 1907, President Theodore Roosevelt greeted them; seventy-two years it was Carter who welcomed his guests to the White House.

10. Taft's comments about immigration and pluralism were of course, not without political weight and were aimed directly against his Democratic opponent, New Jersey Governor Woodrow Wilson. A professor at Princeton University before entering politics, Wilson had written a book entitled *A History of the American People* which had become the object of ethnic criticism during the campaign.

Wilson had written in disparaging fashion about the Poles while seeming to call for sharp restrictions in free immigration. In his book, Wilson had this to say: "Now there comes multitudes of men of the lowest class from the south of Italy and men of the meaner sort out of Hungary and Poland, men out of the ranks where there was neither skill nor energy or any initiative or quick intelligence . . . The Chinese were to be more desired, as workmen if not as citizens, than most of the coarse crew that came crowding in every year at the Eastern ports."

Wilson spent some energy explaining these words to unhappy immigrant politicians during the campaign but still lost a large portion of the Polish vote in cities such as Chicago and Milwaukee. It was only because the Republicans divided between Taft and Roosevelt that he won office. As president, Wilson did espouse a strongly liberal policy regarding immigration and was a firm proponent of a restored and independent Poland during World War I. Ray Stannard Baker, editor, *Woodrow Wilson: Life and Letters* (New York, 1931), volumes covering the years 1910–1918.

11. *Pamietnik Jubileuszowy Kolegium ZNP, 1912-1937* (Alliance Alumni Association, 1937), pp. 60-62. The editor of this 25th anniversary album was the then president of the school's *alumni* association, Atty. Valery Fronczak. One of the school's initial graduating class in 1916, he contributed greatly to the *alumni* association and to the school itself for many years and served as the PNA's legal advisor as well. In 1976, sixty years after hearing Paderewski's stirring words he was a recipient of an honorary degree from the college. The Alliance School *alumni* association, founded in 1916 by Professor Anthony Piwowarczyk, remains in existence supporting the institution.

12. With the appearance of the first female PNA student on the campus, Coleman's wife Marianne Moore Coleman initiated the tradition of Sunday teas at the home of the president. One of the purposes of these occasions was to introduce new students to proper manners befitting their collegiate status.

13. When the technical institute was reestablished in 1975, a major component in its program focused upon computer science training.

14. For a succinct description of the college's needs at the time, see "What can Alliance College Become?" ("Czem Moze byc Kolegium Zwiazkowe?") *Kalendarz Zwiazkowy*, 1958, pp. 95-100.

15. Parcinski, who was popular with *alumni* and possessed the "common touch," was an engineer by training. With Piatkowski, Mierzwa, and Coleman he ranks as one of the best leaders in the school's history.

16. Myron Steczynski was a member of the first high school graduating class of 1916. In 1972, he was awarded an honorary degree from Alliance College in recognition of his life-long support of the institution. The sons of two Censors also attended the College, Frank and Blair Gunther, Jr., and James and Edward Kozmor, Jr.

17. At its thirty-ninth convention in Orlando, Florida in September 1983, the Alliance increased its total financial assistance to the College to $2.1 million dollars over the next four years. Serious questions remained as to the school's status, however. See, for example, the *Dziennik Zwiazkowy* editorial of September 27, 1983 and an article in the same paper on September 28, "Kolegium zwiazkowe wobec krzyzsu: Brak funduszy, zbyt malo studentow, zniszczone budynki, rosna dlugi." Also, A. A. Mazewski, *Highlights of the President's Report to the 39th Convention of the PNA* (Orlando, 1983), pp. 14-16.

Chapter 12

1. In the late 1970s the PAC and several Jewish organizations cooperated in issuing briefs on behalf of Allan Bakke and Brian Weber in their reverse descrimination suits, which were ultimately heard by the United States Supreme Court.

2. By the end of 1981, approximately one third of the party membership also belonged to Solidarity and perhaps one half were identified as practicing Catholics, a dramatic sign of its internal transformation during the crisis. With the introduction of free elections at every level of party organizational life, the great majority of PUWP officials was replaced as well. See David Mason, paper presented at the annual national convention of the American Political Science Association, September, 1983.

3. *Polish American Congress Newsletter,* September, 1980.

4. Particularly active in coordinating the delivery of medical supplies were Dr. Walter Cebulski, Chairman of the PAC Medical Commission, and commission members Bonaventure Migala, Dr. Mitchell Kaminski, Dr. Antoni Mianowski, Dr. Arthur Wolski, Hans Midunsky, Professor Stanislaw Smolenski and Jerzy Przyluski.

5. Fund raising was carried out in various ways, and various state divisions in the Polish American Congress were especially active in soliciting funds and materials, particularly those in Michigan, Illinois, New Jersey, New York and Washington, D.C. For the first time in its history the Polish American Congress attempted to raise large sums through the vehicle of the telethon. The first such event, held in the Buffalo area and in nearby Canadian towns raised $205,000 in pledges within 2 hours in June, 1981. In August, Bobby Vinton was master of ceremonies for

a four hour telethon staged in Chicago over television station WGN. This effort brought in more than $1.2 million in pledges and a second such event was planned for 1982 in the Windy City. Another Buffalo telethon in 1982 raised an additional $192,000. Other local telethons in Detroit, Milwaukee and Cleveland were being planned in late 1981 as well. Coordinating the Chicago telethon was Alderman and former Congressman Roman Pucinski. The Buffalo telethon was organized under the leadership of Richard Solecki and Bryan Rusk. Polish American Congress Charitable Foundation *Newsletter*, April, 1982 (Chicago); PAC Charitable Foundation *Report,*June 1982 (Chicago).

6. *Zgoda,* May 15, 1981.

7. There were options, however, as noted in Zbigniew Brzezinski, *Power and Principle: Memoirs of the National Security Advisor, 1977-1981* (New York, 1983), pp. 465-469.

8. At their national congress in September, 1981 the Solidarity delegates approved an unfortunate resolution calling upon workers in other socialist bloc countries to form similar movements, an appeal that could only be taken as provocative by the Soviets and their Polish allies. At its last meeting, on December 12, 1981 the union leadership proposed a national referendum asking the people to choose the kind of government for Poland they preferred. This decision, which was taken against the advice of Walesa, a political moderate who generally opposed a confrontationist stance himself, was based upon growing disillusionment with the government's failure to honor its original agreements with Solidarity to work for renewal. It was used as a pretext for the imposition of martial law the next day and the imprisonment of nearly the entire union leadership. And, while the government initially promised to cooperate with a "reconstituted" Solidarity in the future, on October 11, 1982 it approved legislation which dissolved the movement.

9. Gerald Ford, Speech to the Polish American Congress at its tenth national convention, Philadelphia, September 24, 1976, in *Public Papers of the Presidents of the United States, 1976-1977,* Volume III (Washington, D.C., 1977), pp. 2313-2316. For specifics about Sonnenfeldt's actual comments, which had been made at an Ambassadors' meeting in London, see Wandycz, pp. 405-406.

10. Following upon Rozmarek's example, Mazewski adopted a leadership style in guiding the Polish American Congress that has been distinctively personal in nature. This approach has brought him both praise and criticism. By attempting to represent the PAC in all its major contacts with America's political leaders over the years, Mazewski has won wide recognition as Polonia's top spokesman on a variety of substantive and symbolic issues. But his activities have also brought forth complaints.

One has focused upon the failure of the Polish American Congress to maintain its commitments developed in the early 1970s to Polonia's many and varied domestic concerns. Increasingly, the issue of Poland, a special interest of PAC activists belonging to the relatively small post World War II Polish political emigration, has occupied the attentions of the President.

Secondly, Mazewski has been criticized for his seeming inability to delegate greater responsibility to competent Polish Americans in and outside of the PAC in developing and promoting commonly shared objectives for Polonia. Worth noting in this connection is the fact that the Polish American Congress has never established a strong and visible Washington, D.C. branch office to more effectively lobby on Polonia's behalf. Instead, the true locus of PAC operations has remained in the Chicago headquarters of the Polish National Alliance.

See Donald Pienkos, "The Polish American Congress—An Appraisal," *Polish American Studies,* 36, 2(Autumn, 1979), 5-43; and Thaddeus Gromada, "How Can a National Consensus be Developed?", Leonard Walentynowicz, "Polish American Professionals," and Eugene Kusielewicz, "What are the Priorities?" in Bochenek, ed., *American Polonia,* pp. 18-26, 39-42.

Chapter 13

1. In 1979, the President of the PNA reported that approximately four hundred and fifty lodges were inactive, more than one third of all its local units at the time.

2. In conversations with representatives of several non-Polish fraternals I learned that they too have experienced difficulties in revitalizing their grass roots organizations. Those which have retained the lodge system have increasingly depended upon a professionally trained sales force to expand their recruitment efforts. At the same time they have placed much greater emphasis upon assisting local units to better serve their memberships by providing a wider array of activities for members of varying age levels. They have more aggressively maintained contacts with lodge officers so as to better inform them about ways to improve their activities and the need to follow through upon such suggestions.

The PNA has taken an active role in National Fraternal Congress in another area, it should be noted. Its leaders have aggressively and successfully defended the fraternals from efforts by state legislatures and government agencies to alter their tax exempt status and to impose restrictive regulations upon their insurance sales operations.

3. The leadership's tendency in recent years has been to "emphasize the positive," especially the steadily increasing net worth of the fraternal and the rise in total insurance provided for its members. Though impressive in dollar terms, these figures do not hold up well when inflation's effects are considered. For example, if one notes that the purchase of some item presently requires three times as many dollars as it did in 1967, it follows that the PNA's assets and insurance in force have actually declined by more than one-half during this period. Though the PNA's record here as well as in terms of membership has generally been "better" than for nearly every other Polonia fraternal, it is questionable whether the standard of comparative achievement should be set so low.

4. Note Chapter 1 of this study on the educational and professional advancement of Polish Americans.

5. Illustrative of the PNA's present condition, perhaps, is the relative dearth of professionally trained individuals within its leadership. One might note here that

only five of the thirty-five men and women who competed for the seventeen highest national offices in the fraternal at its most recent convention were known to have college educational experience. *Zgoda,* August 15, 1983.

BIBLIOGRAPHY

Background studies in Poland's history, political development and dominant ideological trends from the Eighteenth Century onward

Blejwas, Stanislaus: "The Origins and Practice of 'Organic Work' in Poland: 1795–1863," *The Polish Review,* 15: No. 4 (1970).

Bromke, Adam: *Poland's Politics: Idealism vs. Realism* (Cambridge, Massachusetts: Harvard University Press, 1967).

Dziewanowski, M. K.: *Poland in the Twentieth Century* (New York: Columbia University Press, 1977).

Fountain, Alvin M., II: *Roman Dmowski: Party, Tactics, Ideology, 1895–1907* (Boulder, Colorado: East European Monographs distributed by Columbia University Press, 1980).

Kieniewicz, Stefan: *The Emancipation of the Polish Peasantry* (Chicago: University of Chicago Press, 1969).

Kos-Rabcewicz-Zubkowski, Ludwik: "Polish Constitutional Law" in W. J. Wagner, editor, *Polish Law Throughout the Ages,* (Stanford, California: Hoover Institution, 1970).

Pienkos, Donald: "Education and Emigration as Factors in Rural Societal Development: The Russian and Polish Peasantries' Responses to Collectivization," *East European Quarterly,* 9 number 1 (Spring 1975), 75-95.

Pigon, Stanislaw: *Z Komborni w Swiat,* (Krakow, 1957).

Wandycz, Piotr: *The United States and Poland* (Cambridge, Massachusetts: Harvard University Press, 1980).

Other Selected Fraternal Histories

Haiman, Mieczyslaw: *Zjednoczenie Polskie Rzymsko-Katolickie w Ameryce, 1873-1948* (Chicago: ZPRK w A, 1948).

Karlowiczowa, Jadwiga: *Historia Zwiazku Polek w Ameryce,* (Chicago: The Polish Women's Alliance, 1938).

Pienkos, Angela T.: *Federation Life Insurance of America, 1913–1976* (Milwaukee: Haertlein Publishers, 1976).

Waldo, Arthur: *Sokolstwo przednia straz Narodu,* 4 vols. (Pittsburgh: Polish Falcons of America, 1953–1974).

American Polonia, Its cultural and ideological Development to 1939; Polonia's Response during the First World War to Poland's Needs

"A Tribute to Erasm J. Jerzmanowski," (Detroit: American Polish Engineering Association, 1981).

Baker, Ray Stannard, ed.: *Woodrow Wilson: Life and Letters* (New York: Scribners, 1931).

Blaszczyk, Leon: "The Polish Singers Movement in America: An Attempt at an Historical Synthesis," *Polish American Studies,* 38, Number 1 (1981), 50-62.

Bolek, Frances, ed.: *Who's Who in Polish America,* 3rd edition (N.Y.: Harbinger House, 1943).

Breckinridge, S. P.: *New Homes For Old* (New York: Harper and Brothers, 1924).

Brozek, Andrzej: *Polonia Amerykanska, 1854–1939* (Warsaw: Interpress, 1977).

———. "The Polish Ethnic Group in the American Labor Movement," *Studia Historiae Oeconomicae* (Poznan), 13 (1978), 173-182.

———. "The National Consciousness of the Polish Ethnic Group in the United States, 1854–1939: A Proposed Model," *Acta Poloniae Historica,* 37 (1978), 95-127.

———. "Proby Zjednoczenia Polonii Amerykanskiej i ich ideologie," unpublished paper (1978).

———. "Polonia w Stanach Zjednoczonych wobec Inicjatyw Paderewskiego oraz Sikorskiego w czasie I i II wojnej swiatowej," *Przeglad Polonijny,* 7, Number 2(1981), 41-67.

Brozek, Andrzej and D. Piatkowska: "Prasa Slaska o masakrze robotnikow w Lattimer, Pennsylvania, 1897," *Zaranie slaska,* 1978, Number 2.

Emmons, Charles F.: "Economic and Political Leadership in Chicago's Polonia: Some Sources of Ethnic Persistence and Mobility," Diss. University of Illinois at Chicago Circle, 1971.

Florkowska-Francic, Halina: "Agaton Giller i Powstanie ZNP w Stanach Zjednoczonych (1880)," *Przeglad Polonijny,* 6, Number 1(1979), 79-89.

Galush, William: "American Poles and the New Poland: An Example of Change in Ethnic Orientation," *Ethnicity,* 1, Number 3(1974), 209-221.

———. "Forming Polonia: A Study of Four Polish-American Communities, 1890–1940," Diss. University of Minnesota, 1975.

———. "American Polonia, A History," unpublished manuscript.

Gerson, Louis: *Woodrow Wilson and the Rebirth of Poland, 1914–1920* (New Haven, Connecticut: Yale University Press, 1953).

Greene, Victor: *The Slavic Community on Strike, Immigrant Labor in Pennsylvania Anthracite* (Notre Dame, Indiana: University Press, 1968).

_____ . *For God and Country: The Rise of Polish and Lithuanian Ethnic Consciousness in America, 1860–1910* (Madison: State Historical Society of Wisconsin, 1975).

Groniowski, Krzysztof: "Socjalistyczna Emigracja Polska w Stanach Zjednoczonych (1883–1914)," *Z Pola Walki* (Warsaw), 13 (1977), 3-35.

Hapak, Joseph: "The Polish Military Commission, 1917–1919," *Polish American Studies,* 38, Number 2 (Autumn, 1981), 26-38.

Kantowicz, Edward R.: *Polish American Politics in Chicago: 1888–1940* (Chicago: University of Chicago Press, 1975).

Korban, Roman: *Sport wsrod Polonii Amerykanskiej* (Warsaw: Wydownictwo Interpress, 1980).

Pliska, Stanley: "The Polish American Army, 1917–1921," *The Polish Review,* 10, Number 3 (Summer 1965), 46-59.

_____ . "The Polish American Community and the Rebirth of Poland," *Polish American Studies,* 26 (1969), 41-60.

Pula, James: *For Liberty and Justice: The Life and Times of Wladimir Krzyzanowski* (Chicago: Polish American Congress Charitable Foundation, 1978).

_____ . "American Immigration Policy and the Dillingham Commission," *Polish American Studies,* 37, Number 1(1980), 5-31.

Radzialowski, Thaddeus: "Immigrant Nationalism and Feminism: *Glos Polek* and the Polish Women's Alliance in America, 1898–1917," *Review Journal of Philosophy and Social Science,* 2, Number 2 (1978), 183-197.

Renkiewicz, Frank, ed.: *The Poles in America, 1608–1972* (Dobbs Ferry, New York: Oceana Press, 1973).

Renkiewicz, Frank: "The Organization of the Polish American Worker, 1880–1980," unpublished manuscript.

_____ . "An Economy of Self-Help: Fraternal Capitalism and the Evolution of Polish America," in Philip Shashko, Donald Pienkos and Charles Ward, editors, *Studies in Ethnicity: The East European Experience in America* (Boulder, Colorado: University of Colorado Press, 1980).

_____ . "The Profits of Non-Profit Capitalism: Polish Fraternalism and Beneficial Insurance in America," unpublished manuscript.

Soroka, Waclaw: *Polish Immigration in the United States* (Stevens Point, Wisconsin: University of Wisconsin-Stevens Point, 1976).

Szawleski, M.: *Wychodztwo Polskie w Stanach Zjednoczonych Ameryki* (Lwow-Warszawa-Krakow, 1924).

Taft, Herbert: *William Howard Taft* (New York: Minton, Balch and Company, 1930).

Thomas, William I.: *Old World Traits Transplanted* (Chicago: University of Chicago Press, 1921).

Thomas, William I, and Florian Znaniecki, *The Polish Peasant in Europe and America,* 2 vols. (1927; reprinted New York: Dover Publications, 1958).

Wachtl, Karol: *Polonia w Ameryce* (Philadelphia: Naklad autora, 1944).

Wiewiora, Joseph, ed.: *Jamestown: Pioneers from Poland,* Second Revised edition (Chicago: Polish American Congress Charitable Foundation, 1976).
Wytrwal, Joseph: *Behold! The Polish-Americans* (Detroit: Endurance Press, 1977).
————. *America's Polish Heritage* (Detroit: Endurance Press, 1961).
Zake, Rev. Louis J.: "The Development of the National Department *(Wydzial Narodowy)* as Representative of the Polish American Community in the United States, 1916–1923," Diss. University of Chicago, 1979.

Historical Material on the Polish National Alliance

Barszczewski, Stefan: *Zwiazek Narodowy, Polski w stanach Zjednoczonych Ameryki Polnocnej: Jego Rozwoj Dzialalnosc i Stan Obecny* (Chicago: Polish National Alliance, 1894, second printing 1980).
"O dzialalnosci zwiazkowcow w Pittsburghu, Pennsylvania" in *Zloty Jubileusz ZNP* (Pittsburgh, 1930).
Olszewski, Adam: *Historia Zwiazku Narodowego Polskiego* (Chicago: Alliance Printers and Publishers, 1957–1963), five volumes.
Osada, Stanislas: *Historia Zwiazku Narodowego Polskiego, 1880–1905* (Chicago: Alliance Printers and Publishers, 1957), originally published in 1905.
————. *Jak sie ksztaltowala Polska Dusza Wychodztwa w Ameryce* (Pittsburgh: Falcons Publishers, 1930).
Piatkiewicz, Karol: *Pamietnik Jubileuszowy ZNP, 1880–1940* (Chicago: Alliance Publishers, 1940).
Czyn Zbrojny Wychodztwa Polskiego w Ameryce (New York: Polish Army Veterans' Association, 1957).
Mazewski, Aloysius: "Polonia i ZNP." *Kalendarz Zwiazkowy* (1977), 40–45.
Midowicz, Casimir: "The Polish National Alliance of the United States of North America," *Milwaukee Society Fifth Anniversary Bulletin* (Milwaukee, 1927).
Piatkowski, Romuald: *Pamietnik Wzniesienia Odsloniecia Pomnikow Tadeusza Kosciuszki i Kazimierza Pulaskiego tudziez Polaczonego z ta Uroczystoscia Pierwszego Kongresu Narodowego Polskiego w Washingtonie, D.C.* (Chicago: Polish National Alliance, 1911).
Pienkos, Donald E.: "The Polish National Alliance—One Hundred and Two Years of Service," *Zgoda,* 101 (February 15 through March 15, 1982).
Rozanski, Edward: "PNA Took Leading Part in 'Call to Arms,' " *Zgoda,* January 15, 1968.
Walka o Narodowy Charakter Zwiazku Narodowego Polskiego w Swietle Pism Zmarlego Prezesa Kazimierza Zychlinskiego (Chicago: Alliance Publishers, 1927).
Wiewiora, Joseph: *In the Mainstreams of American Life: A Centennial Outline of the Polish National Alliance History,* Third edition (Chicago, Alliance Printers and Publishers, 1980).
Zgoda: A Century of Service, 1881–1981, Centennial Commemorative Booklet (Chicago: Alliance Printers and Publishers, 1981).

Zlotnicki, Nikodem: "Zwiazek Narodowy Polski w Polnocnej Ameryce," *Kalendarz Zwiazkowy* (1923).

The World War II Era, The Creation of The Polish American Congress and the Consolidation of Communist Rule over Poland

Bethell, Nicholas: *Gomulka: His Poland, His Communism* (New York: Holt, Rinehart and Winston, 1969).

Bohlen, Charles E.: *Witness to History, 1929–1969* (New York: Norton, 1973).

Burks, Richard V.: "Eastern Europe," in Cyril Black and Thomas Thornton, editors, *Communism and Revolution: The Strategic Uses of Political Violence* (Princeton, New Jersey: Princeton University Press, 1964).

Churchill, Winston: *Triumph and Tragedy* (Boston: Houghton Mifflin Company, 1953).

Ciechanowski, Jan: *Defeat in Victory* (Garden City, New York: Doubleday, 1947).

Ciechanowski, Jan M.: *The Warsaw Uprising of 1944* (Cambridge: University Press, 1974).

Dallek, Robert: *Franklin D. Roosevelt and American Foreign Policy, 1932–1945* (New York: Oxford University Press, 1979).

Foreign Relations of the United States, 1947, Volume 4 (Washington: United States Government Printing Office).

Hammond, T. T.: "The History of Communist Takeovers," in T. T. Hammond, editor, *The Anatomy of Communist Takeovers*, (New Haven: Yale University Press, 1975).

Harriman, Averill and Elie Abel: *Special Envoy to Churchill and Stalin, 1941–1946* (New York: Random House, 1975).

Irons, Peter: "America's Cold War Crusade: Domestic Politics and Foreign Policy, 1942–1948," Diss. Boston University, 1972.

———. " 'The Test is Poland': Polish Americans and the Origins of the Cold War," *Polish American Studies*, 30, Number 2(1973), 5-65.

Janczewski, George: "The Significance of the Polish Vote in the American National Election Campaign of 1948," *The Polish Review*, 13, Number 4 (Autumn, 1968), 101-109.

Jedrzejewicz, Waclaw: *Polonia Amerykanska w Polityce Polskiej: Historia Komitetu Narodowego Amerykanow Polskiego Pochodzenia* (New York: National Committee of Americans of Polish Descent, 1954).

Korbonski, Andrzej: *Politics of Socialist Agriculture in Poland, 1945–1960* (New York: Columbia University Press, 1965).

Korbonski, Stefan: *Warsaw in Exile* (New York: Praeger, 1966).

Lotarski, Susan S.: "The Communist Takeover in Poland," in T. T. Hammond, editor, *The Anatomy of Communist Takeovers* (New Haven: Yale University Press, 1975).

Lukas, Richard C.: *The Strange Allies: The United States and Poland, 1941–1945* (Knoxville: University of Tennessee Press, 1978).

———. "The Polish American Congress and The Polish Question, 1944-1947," *Polish American Studies,* 38, Number 2(1981), 39-53.

Mikolajczyk, Stanislaw: *The Rape of Poland: Pattern of Soviet Aggression* (New York: McGraw-Hill, 1948).

Rodine, Floyd H.: *Yalta-Responsibility and Response, January-March, 1945* (Lawrence, Kansas: Coronado Press, 1974).

Rozmarek, Karol: *Stany Zjednoczone, Polska i Polonia Amerykanska; Uwagi na Zjazd Rady Naczelnej w Detroit, 11-12 go Pazdziernika, 1945* (Chicago: Alliance Printers and Publishers, 1945).

Sadler, Charles: "Pro-Soviet Polish-Americans: Oskar Lange and Russia's Friends in the Polonia, 1941-1945," *The Polish Review,* 22, No. 4 (Autumn, 1977), 25-39.

———. "'Political Dynamite': The Chicago Polonia and President Roosevelt in 1944," *Journal of the Illinois State Historical Society,* 71 (May, 1978), 119-132.

Sherwood, Robert E.: *Roosevelt and Hopkins, An Intimate History* (New York: Harper, 1948).

Sikorski Institute: *Documents on Polish-Soviet Relations, 1939-1945.* 2 volumes (London: Heinemann, 1961, 1967).

Snell, John, ed.: *The Meaning of Yalta* (Baton Rouge: Louisiana State University Press, 1956).

The Polish National Alliance, The Polish American Congress, Polonia and Poland after the Second World War.

Berger, Peter: *To Empower People: The Role of Mediating Structures in Public Policy* (Washington, D.C.: American Enterprise Institute, 1977).

Blejwas, Stanislaus A.: "Old and New Polonias: Tensions within an Ethnic Community," *Polish American Studies,* 38, Number 2(1981), 55-83.

Bochenek, Alfred, ed.: *American Polonia: The Cultural Issues* (Detroit: American Council of Polish Cultural Clubs, 1981).

Garrett, Stephen: "The Ties that Bind: Immigrant Influence on U.S. Policy toward Eastern Europe," in A. A. Said, editor, *Ethnicity and U.S. Foreign Policy,* Second edition (New York: Praeger, 1981).

Gerson, Louis: *The Hyphenate in Recent American Politics and Diplomacy* (Lawrence: University of Kansas Press, 1964).

Gordon, Milton: *Human Nature, Class and Ethnicity* (New York: Oxford University Press, 1978).

Greeley, Andrew: "The Ethnic Miracle," *The Public Interest,* 45 (1976), 20-36.

Iranek-Osmecki, Kazimierz: *He Who Saves One Life* (New York: Crown, 1971).

Kaplan, Stephen S.: "United States Aid to Poland, 1957-1964, Concerns, Objectives and Obstacles," *The Western Political Quarterly,* 28, Number 1 (March, 1975), 147-166.

Kovrig, Bennett: *The Myth of Liberation: East-Central Europe in U.S. Diplomacy and Politics since 1941* (Baltimore: The Johns Hopkins University Press, 1973).

Lafeber, Walter: *America, Russia and the Cold War* (New York: Wiley, 1966).

Laqueur, Walter: *The Terrible Secret: Suppression of the Truth about Hitler's Final Solution* (Boston: Little, Brown, 1980).

Lopata, Helena Znaniecka: *Polish Americans: Status Competition in an Ethnic Community* (Englewood Cliffs, New Jersey: Prentice-Hall, 1976).

"Mazewski lists Achievements of Polish American Congress, States Case for Its Continued Viability," *Zgoda,* 98 (December 1, 1979).

Novak, Michael: *The Rise of the Unmeltable Ethnics* (New York: MacMillan, 1971).

Modras, Rev. Ronald: "Jews and Poles: A Relationship Reconsidered," *America* (January 9, 1982), 5-8.

Obidinski, Eugene: "Polish American Social Standing: Status and Stereotypes," *The Polish Review,* 21, Number 3 (Summer, 1976), 79–102.

Pienkos, Donald E.: "The Polish American Congress—An Appraisal," *Polish American Studies,* 36, Number 2(1979), 5-43.

———. "Polish American Ethnicity in the Political Life of the United States," in Joseph Roucek and Bernard Eisenberg, editors, *America's Ethnic Politics* (Westport, Connecticut: Greenwood Press, 1982).

Piwowarczyk, Anthony: "Project Scan and Renovate," Internal PNA publication, 1977.

Polish American Congress Charitable Foundation Newsletter, 1981 (Chicago).

Polish American Congress Newsletter, Irregular 1950–1979 (Chicago); replaced by *PAC Bulletin.*

The Polish National Alliance in the Press of America: Partial Collection of Clippings from Leading U.S. Newspapers from 1955 to 1958, (Chicago: 1959).

Sowell, Thomas: "Ethnicity, Intelligence and Upward Mobility," *Commentary,* (September, 1979), 8-10.

Sprawozdania (Officers' reports) and *Protokoly* (minutes of the proceedings) of the national conventions of the Polish American Congress from 1944 through 1976.

Wytwycky, Bohdan: *The Other Holocaust: Many Circles of Hell* (Washington, D.C.: Novak Report Research Project, 1980).

Women and the PNA

Dunin, Janina: "Rola kobiety w Zwiazku Narodowym Polskim," *Kalendarz Zwiazkowy* (1934), 65-71.

Dziewulski, Edward: "Zgoda Salutes the Women of the Polish National Alliance," *Zgoda,* September 1, 1975.

Lopata, Helena Znaniecka: "Polish American Families," unpublished paper presented at the Symposium on American Polonia, Jagiellonian University, Krakow, 1979.

Moll, Helen: "50-cie Lecie Pracy Kobiet w ZNP," *Kalendarz Zwiazkowy* (1950), 89-96.

———. "50-cie Lecie Pracy Humanitarnej Stowarzyszenia Dobroczynnosci przy ZNP," ms. probably published in *Dziennik Zwiazkowy,* December, 1978.

———. "80 Lecie Rownouprawnienia Kobiet w ZNP," *Dziennik Zwiazkowy,* September 20, 1980.

The Polish National Alliance School

Alliance College Report, December 1981 (includes President William Howard Taft speech inaugurating the school in 1912), and preceding annual issues from 1971 onward.

Alliance College, List of Honorary Degrees since 1955.

Alliance College Presents the Kujawiaki Polish Folk Song and Dance Troupe, L. G. Kozlowski, Director (1981).

Coleman, Arthur: "Alliance College, American Cradle of Polish Heritage," *Zgoda,* June 1, 15, July 1, 15, August 1, 15, 1957.

"Czem Moze byc Kolegium Zwiazkowe?" *Kalendarz Zwiazkowy* (1958), 95-100.

Fronczak, Walery, ed., contributor and compiler: *Pamietnik Jubileuszowy Kolegium ZNP, 1912-1937* (Cambridge Springs, Pennsylvania: Alumni Association, 1937).

Machrowicz, Thaddeus: "Remarks in the U.S. House of Representatives," *Congressional Record,* July 27, 1955.

Mierzwa, Stefan: *Kolegjum Zwiazkowe: Wczoraj, Dzis, Jutro* (Cambridge Springs, 1931).

Smietana, Walter: "Alliance College, A Masterpiece of America's Polish Immigration," *Association for the Advancement of Polish Studies Newsletter,* 5, Number 1 (May, 1980), 1-11.

Tomaszkiewicz, Adam: "Report on the Status of Alliance College to the Board of Directors of the PNA," April 28, 1982.

Other Sources

Chicago Public Library Omnibus Project, *Chicago Foreign Language Press Survey,* (Chicago, 1942), of Chicago-based Polish language newspapers and periodicals between 1887 and 1931. *Zgoda* articles printed from 1887-1894 and 1897-1903 are translated, along with *Dziennik Zwiazkowy* articles from 1908-1918. In all, eight Polish language newspapers were included for translation work. Eleven microfilm reels, 16,368 sheets.

Sprawᵥ̤ lania Na Sejm: Reports of the executive officers, members of the Board of Directors, Censor vice-censor district commissioners and administrative personnel for every PNA national convention after 1901.

Urzedowy Protokol Sejmu ZNP: Minutes of the proceedings of each PNA national convention after 1901.

Minutes of the meetings of the PNA Board of Directors, 1920 to the present.

Statistics of Fraternal Benefit Societies (Indianapolis: The Fraternal Monitor), annual publication appearing between 1895 and 1957 and since 1966. Between 1958 and 1965, fraternal membership and financial data were published under the title *Consolidated Chart of Fraternal Societies.*

Wiadomosci (The News), bi-monthly, later monthly publication of the Greater Alliance Society faction which supported the presidential candidacy of Aloysius Mazewski (1966-1967).

Wyrok Sadu Apelacyjnego Stanu Illinois Podtrzymujacy Wyrok Sedziego M. Gridley z Sadu Wyzszego w Sprawie, "Quo Warranto" (Chicago: Alliance Printers, 1936). People of the State of Illinois ex. rel. Jacob Twardzik, *et. al.,* vs. F. X. Swietlik, *et. al.* in Appellate Court of Illinois, First District, October, 1936. Number 39173.

Polish American Patriot (Monessen, Pennsylvania), dissident periodical published since 1975 by Anthony Czelen.

Sass, Stefan K. vs. Robert E. Crowe, *Abstract of Record* and *Brief and Argument for Plaintiff in Error* in the Appellate Court of Illinois, 1926.

State of Illinois, County of Cook in the Superior Court re: People of State of Illinois relation of Max Hencel vs. F. P. Garbarek, *et. al.,* no. 465223. *Quo Warranto* suit filed in 1928.

Zgoda, June 15, 1958; November 8, 1958; December 1, 1958; December 8, 1958; June 19, 1959; October 1, 1959; December 15, 1960.

Other publications consulted: *Dziennik Zwiazkowy, Dziennik Chicagoski, Zgoda, Polish American Journal* (Scranton), *Polish American* (Chicago), *Am-Pol Eagle* (Buffalo), *Polish American World* (New York), *Narod Polski* (Chicago), *Gwiazda Polarna* (Stevens Point, Wisconsin), and *Post-Eagle* (Clifton, New Jersey).

Jubilees and Commemorative Albums and Brochures published by PNA Lodges and Councils.

A valuable resource for the study of the activities and accomplishments of local PNA lodge and council organizations over the years is the information often included in commemorative albums or brochures published by these units to celebrate the anniversary of their formation. Most local PNA organizations holding banquets to recall their 25th, 50th and 75th anniversaries engaged someone active in the unit to write a brief history for the occasion. Many of these booklets are to be found in the library of the Polish National Alliance in Chicago. They provide the contemporary reader with an excellent picture of the activities of the Alliance's "grass roots" organizations and the individuals who played an active role in PNA and Polonia life in their local communities. Among the most informative of these albums are the following:

Lodges

Radiant Society of Pittsburgh, Group 205, 60th anniversary (1953); Polish National Crown Society of Chicago, Group 771, 50th anniversary (1953); White Eagle Society of Kenosha, Group 704, 50th anniversary (1955); Gmina Polska Society Number 1 of Chicago, Group 20, 50th anniversary (1946); Prince Jozef Poniatowski Society of Chicago, Group 662 (1954); Kosciuszko Society of Hegwisch district of Chicago, Group 198, 40th anniversary (1929); Adam Mickiewicz Society of New Haven, Connecticut, Group 432, 40th anniversary (1938); Polish Eagle Society of Chicago, Group 523, 55th anniversary (1955); Kosciuszko Guard Society of Carnegie,

Pennsylvania, Group 416, 40th anniversary (1938); Kosciuszko-Pilsudski Society, of Erie, Pennsylvania, Group 224, 40th anniversary (1935); Kosciuszko Guard Society of Southington, Connecticut, Group 684, 50th anniversary (1954); Polish Artillery-George Washington Society of Chicago, Group 760, 50th anniversary (1955); General Dwornicki Society of Detroit, Group 1277, 50th anniversary (1961); Saints Michael and Andrew Society of Detroit, Group 679, 50th anniversary (1954); Polish Eagle Society of Pittsburgh, Group 506, 55th anniversary (1954); Polish Cadets Society of McKees Rock, Pennsylvania, Group 615, 50th anniversary (1953); Lech Society of Minneapolis, Group 1042, 35th anniversary (1944); Polish Falcons Society, of Steubenville, Ohio, Group 652, 55th anniversary (1954); Sons of Freedom Society of Chicago, Group 694, 50th anniversary (1955); Polish Women's Society of Chester, Pennsylvania, Group 2369, 25th anniversary (1950); Zamoyski Society of Hamtramck, Michigan, Group 1264, 50th anniversary (1960); Polish Youth Society of Chicago, Group 1030, 65th anniversary (1954); Veterans of a Free Poland Society of Detroit, Group 1613, 50th anniversary (1963); Love for the Fatherland Society, Group 1792 of Chicago, 20th anniversary (1935)1; Florian Society of Minnesota, 25th anniversary (1971); Polish National Alliance Society, Group 1 of Philadelphia, 65th anniversary (1945); and 70th anniversary (1950); Polonia Society of Milwaukee, Group 3100, 30th anniversary (1980); Thousand Brave Fighters Society of Chicago, Group 877, 25th anniversary, (1932); Free Poland Society of Johnstown, Pennsylvania, Group 832, 50th anniversary (1957); Falcons Gymnastic Society Number 1, Group 1060 of Chicago, 50th anniversary (1938); Kosciuszko Guard Society of Indian Orchard, Massachusetts, Group 1484, 50th anniversary (1954); Industrial Society of Polish Mechanics of Chicago, Group 3, 75th anniversary (1955); and Giewont Society of Chicago, Group 2514, 50th anniversary (1981).

PNA Councils

Council 23 of South Chicago, Indiana, 25th anniversary (1939); Council 41 of Chicago, 25th anniversary (1938); Council 2 of Chicago, 25th anniversary (1938); Council 150 of Yonkers, New York, 10th anniversary (1937); Council 120 of Chicago, 25th anniversary (1945); Council 92 of Buffalo, 25th anniversary (1938); Council 8 of Milwaukee, 1931 and 1940 albums; and Councils 38 and 145 of Pittsburgh, 1930 album celebrating PNA's fiftieth anniversary.

A last useful source is the PNA convention commemorative album (pamietnik), which appears just prior to every national *sejm.*

SUBJECT INDEX

NAME INDEX

Names preceeded by asterisk (*) have separate biographies in Appendix C.

476

Matejczyk, Blair, 274, 278
Matejko, Alexander, 431n
Matejko, Jan, 80
Mathews, Peter, 277
Matkowski, Julian, 337, 448n
May, Josephine, 199, 336, 448n
Mazewski, Aloysius, xi, xviii, xix, 27, 31-3, 61, 179, 181-3, 185, 187-90, 194-6, 199-201, 203-5, 217, 238, 271, 275, 281, 283-4, 289-94, 302-4, 323-5, 382, 385, 399, 445n, 446n, 449n, 459n, 460n
Mazewski, Aloysius Jr., 275
Mazurek, Frank, 199, 337, 448n
Mazzini, Giuseppi, 54
McDonald, David, 278
McKinley, William, 315
McSweeney, John, 175
Mermel, Stanislas, 102-3
Metelski, M., 57
Mianowski, Antoni, 459n
Michalak, Joseph, 443n
Michalska, Jadwiga, 452n
Mickiewicz, Adam, 37, 39, 89, 311
Midowicz, Casimir, xvii, 363
Midunsky, Hans, 459n
Mierzwa, Stefan, 141, 266, 268-9, 276, 441n, 458n
Mierzynski, Joseph, 363
Miesczak, William, 273, 278
Mieszko I, King of Poland, 35, 308
Migala, Bonaventure, xviii, 182, 443n, 459n
Mikolajczyk, Felix, 276
Mikolajczyk, Stanislaw, 159, 163, 165-8, 170, 321, 445n, 448n
Mikoll, Ann, 448n
Milewska, Magdalena, 108, 130, 138, 248-9, 385, 442n, 455n
Milewski, Rev. Stanley, 277
Milkowski, Zygmunt (T.T. Jez), 82, 84, 438n
Milosz, Czeslaw, 325, 438n
Mischke, Angeline, 427n
Mlotkowska, Czeslawa, 453n
Moczygeba, Rev. Leopold, 10, 48
Modrzejewska, Helena (Modjeska), 4, 212, 313, 369, 438n
Moll, Helen, xviii, 217, 444n, 452n, 455n
Molotov, V.M., 165-6
Monroe, James, 311

Morgenstern, Ignace, 75-6
Morton, Levi, 83
Moscicki, Ignacy, 126, 438n
Moskal, Edward, xviii, 180-1, 386, 449n
Murkowski, Robert, 449n
Murrow, Edward R., 449n
Muskie, Edmund, 278, 322, 324-5, 449n
Mytyk, Joseph, 448n

Nagiel, Henry, 211-2, 387
Nagy, Imre, 173
Napieralska, Emilie, 244
Napoleon I, 36, 311
Neumann, Anna, 107
Nicgorski, Stanley, 448n
Nicholas I, Tsar of Russia, 38
Nicki, Stanislas, 212
Niedbalski, Rev. Seweryn, 265
Nixon, Richard, 175, 283-4, 291-2, 323-4, 382, 449n
Noga, Walter, 336, 448n
Novak, Michael, 447n, 456n
Nowak, Albert, 364
Nowak, Frank, 443n
Nowicki, Stanislaw, Sila, 290
Nurkiewicz, I., 277

Obarska, Casimira, 131, 138, 248-9, 386, 442n
Obidinski, Eugene, 6, 428n
O'Brakta, Stanley, 278
Odrobina, M., xviii, 179-80, 182
Odrowaz, Edward, 56, 58, 63, 209, 211-2, 224, 387, 403
Okorowski, Raymond, 448n
Olbinski, Joseph, 453n
Olszewski, Adam, xvi, 115-6, 214, 395, 405n, 426n, 436n, 437n, 438n, 439n, 440n, 441n, 443n, 444n, 451n, 452n, 456n, 457n
Orlowski, J., 440n
Orpiszewski, Stanislas, 210, 216, 362, 453n
Orzell, Laurence, 428n, 452n
Orzeszkowa, Eliza, 12, 438n
Osada, Stanislas, xvi, 52, 57, 62-3, 65, 69, 74, 210, 214, 389, 405n, 426n, 430n, 433n, 434n, 435n, 436n, 437n, 443n, 450n, 455n, 456n
Osajda, Joseph, 277

Osuch, Mary, 387
Osuch, Michael, 387, 434n
Owoc, Victor, 278

Pachucki, Adolf, 188, 382
Paczynski, Thomas, 363, 398
Paderewska, Helena, 112, 246, 317, 440n
Paderewski, Ignacy, 4, 30, 90, 104, 106-11,
    114-16, 120, 159, 238, 268, 314, 317, 320,
    372, 395, 397, 438n, 440n, 444n, 448n,
    458n
Page, William, 273
Pankhurst, Emmeline, 452n
Parafinczuk, Bogdan, 199, 336, 448n
Parcinski, Henry, 272, 276, 278, 458n
Parot, Joseph, 425n, 428n, 430m, 433n
Paszkowski, Basil, 453n
Paul VI, 293
Pawlowski, Jerome, 231
Percy, Charles, 288, 449n
Pershing, Gen. John, 369, 440n
Petlura, S., 113
Piasecki, Frank, 277
*Piatkiewicz, Karol, xvi, 50, 154, 177, 188,
    210, 214, 216-7, 219, 362, 387*, 434n,
    456n
Piatkiewicz, Stanley, 272
Piatkowska, D., 456n
*Piatkowski, Romuald, xviii, 266, 268, 276,
    388*, 438n, 458n
Piekarski, Frank, 365
Pienkos, Angela, xii, 425n, 426n, 427n, 428n
Pienkos, Donald, 297n, 328, 426n, 432n,
    440n, 445n, 446n, 451n, 460n
Pierzga, Michael, 199, 336, 448n
Pietkiewicz, Stanislaw, 454n
Pietkiewicz, Victoria, 199
Pigon, Stanislaw, 5, 428n, 432n
Pilch, Stanley, 337
Pilsudski, Gen. Jozef, 19, 30, 39, 46, 84-5, 95,
    98, 101, 104, 106, 108, 113-5, 120, 128-9,
    142, 144, 160, 215, 234, 316-20, 370-1,
    379, 391, 393, 396, 400, 438n
Pinderski, Louis, 363
Piotrowicz, Felix, 228
Piszek, Edward, 277
Pitass, Rev. John, 10
Piwowarczyk, Anthony, xviii, 189, 449n

Piwowarczyk, Prof. Anthony, 458n
Piwowarczyk, Gregory, 232, 442n
Placzek, Floyd, 293
Plater, Wladyslaw, 54, 62, 394, 438n
Pliezga, Matthew, 273
Plusdrak, Edward, 179, 182, 365
Pobog, Iza, 452n
Podkomorska, Gladys, xviii, 182, 336
Polomski, Josephine, 337
Poniatowski, Gen. Jozef, 79
Poniatowski, King Stanislaw August, 37, 310
Popiel, Antoni, 89, 438n
Popiel, Stanislas, 276
Popielinski, John, 53, 55, 57-8, 389, 434n
Poranski, Walter, 277
Powers, William, 276
*Prochot, Frank, 182, 188-9, 220, 238, 373,
    389*
Prokesz, Helen, 442n
Prosniewski, Walter, 363
Przybylo, Thaddeus, 209
Przybylski, Marian, 336
Przybyszewski, Val, 61-2, 76, 133, 364, 389,
    434n
Przyluski, Jerzy, 459n
Przypkowski, Alexander, 363
Przyprawa, John, 135, 210, 216, 362
Pstrachowski, Henry, 57
Puchalski, Henry, 199
Pucinski, Roman, 175, 182, 278, 449n, 460n
Pula, James, 435n, 445n
Pulaski, Kazimierz, xii, 4, 28, 88-90, 264, 310,
    435n, 438n

Rabiega, Hedy, 336
Raczka, John, 442n
Radosz, Thaddeus, 199, 336, 448n
Radzialowski, Thaddeus, 455n
Radzyminski, John, 182, 199, 336, 448n
Rakoczy, Adolf, 104, 139, 379, 439n
Ramza, John, 199, 336, 448n
Rawski, Czeslaw, 363
Reagan, Ronald, 205, 288, 290-1, 293-4,
    325-6, 420ff, 458n
Rej, Mikolaj, 308
Renkiewicz, Frank, xx, 429n, 430n, 432n,
    433n, 452n
Rewerski, Joseph, 434n